www.wadsworth.com

www.wadsworth.com is the World Wide Web site for Wadsworth and is your direct source to dozens of online resources.

At *www.wadsworth.com* you can find out about supplements, demonstration software, and student resources. You can also send e-mail to many of our authors and preview new publications and exciting new technologies.

www.wadsworth.com
Changing the way the world learns®

Public Administration

Clashing Values
in the Administration
of Public Policy

Second Edition

Michael C. LeMay
California State University, San Bernardino

THOMSON
™
WADSWORTH

Australia • Brazil • Canada • Mexico • Singapore
Spain • United Kingdom • United States

Public Administration: Clashing Values in the Administration of Public Policy, Second Edition
Michael C. LeMay

Publisher: *Clark Baxter*
Executive Editor: *David Tatom*
Development Editor: *Drake Bush*
Associate Development Editor: *Rebecca Green*
Editorial Assistant: *Eva Dickerson*
Senior Marketing Manager: *Janise Fry*
Marketing Assistant: *Teresa Jessen*
Marketing Communications Manager: *Kelley McAllister*
Project Manager, Editorial Production: *Marti Paul*
Creative Director: *Rob Hugel*
Art Director: *Maria Epes*
Print Buyer: *Doreen Suruki*

Permissions Editor: *Stephanie Lee*
Production Service: *G & S Book Services*
Text Designer: *G & S Book Services*
Art Editor: *G & S Book Services*
Photo Researcher: *Sue Howard*
Copy Editor: *Elliot Simon*
Illustrator: *Integra*
Cover Designer: *Sue Hart*
Cover Image: *© Rick Rappaport/CORBIS*
Cover Printer: *Coral Graphic Services, Inc.*
Compositor: *Integra*
Printer: *Courier Corporation/Stoughton*

Library of Congress Control Number: 2005923994

Student Edition: ISBN 0-534-60137-5

Thomson Higher Education
10 Davis Drive
Belmont, CA 94002-3098
USA

For more information about our products, contact us at:
Thomson Learning Academic Resource Center
1-800-423-0563

For permission to use material from this text or product, submit a request online at **http://www.thomsonrights.com.** Any additional questions about permissions can be submitted by e-mail to **thomsonrights@thomson.com.**

To Lynda R. LeMay,

for her understanding and patience

during the writing of this book,

and whose love and support

make it all worthwhile.

Brief Contents

Contents

Chapter 3   The Anatomy of Public Organization: Bureaucratic Power and Politics   *53*

Chapter 4   Administration in the Federal System: Intergovernmental Relations
and Constitutional Sources of Values   *83*

Chapter 5   Alternative Theories of Organizational Behavior: Classic Models
and Ideological Sources of Values   *113*

Chapter 11   Communication Flows in Administration: The Fuzzing of Values   *273*

Chapter 12   Financial Management: Taxing, Budgeting, and Spending   *301*

Chapter 13   Administrative Law and the Control of Public Agencies   *335*

Chapter 14   Clientele Pressure and Government Policy: Interest Groups as Sources of Values   *363*

List of Boxes, Cartoons, Figures, Photos, and Tables

Photos

Tables

Preface

The reader, and certainly the instructor as potential adopter of this textbook, might well ask, Why another textbook on public administration? It is a fair question. Having taught the subject for thirty years, I have used most of the many books now available on the market. So why would I undertake the arduous task of writing yet another book on the topic? This book is not a scholar's textbook on public administration; it is a teacher's textbook. It is written as an introductory volume for undergraduate courses in public administration. The sources used in writing each chapter are listed at the end of the book, as are chapter endnotes, which were kept to a minimum to keep the text user-friendly to most readers. I have striven to write in a clear, succinct, and straightforward style to make it a text that is easy to read and to study.

Three Distinguishing Features

Among the more distinctive elements of this text are three distinguishing features.

First, its thematic approach is different. Far from being value-neutral, this text explores the theme that values and the clash of values are at the heart of public administration. Values are considered here as things thought to be desirable and esteemed for their own sake as intrinsically worthy. Values connote principles, goals, or standards held by an individual, a class, an organization, or a society. Students are led to consider how often and in what ways bureaucrats deal with values and how they must draw a line between competing values as they implement public policy. This theme, moreover, is not just some device to loosely organize the book—it infuses every chapter. The clash of values in the administration of public policy is an inherently interesting concept, one that should make this textbook more readable.

Another area of exploration is the many roles that public administrators play throughout the policy process. Bureaucrats are not seen as mere implementers of policy adopted by the legislative branch or imposed from above by elected executives. Instead, bureaucrats are seen as affecting every stage of the policy process—from perceiving a problem to placing it on the agenda of government, to structuring and constraining the alternatives that elected officials use to make decisions, to sharing in the adoption of policy, to implementing public policy through programs and procedures largely determined by bureaucrats, and to evaluating that policy's success or failure.

The book's second distinguishing feature is its consistent focus on bureaucrats at all levels of government, especially at the state and local levels. Frankly, it is puzzling why most textbooks about public administration pay little attention to state and local government bureaucracies—even though they are at least three times larger than national-level bureaucracies, whether measured by the number of programs, the numbers of employees, or the total amount of funding. A few textbooks have a single chapter on state and local government at the end of the book or touch on these levels briefly in a chapter that deals with federalism and intergovernmental relations; otherwise, these books use examples exclusively from national agencies to illustrate their main topics. Such a focus ignores the fact that, especially with devolution, state and local governments and their bureaucracies are where the action is in the administration of public policy. They tend to be more innovative, so this textbook draws from many examples of state- and local-level bureaucracies. As with the theme of the clash of values, a focus on state and local administration constitutes a significant portion of most chapters of this book.

The third distinguishing feature of this text is its use of pedagogical devices throughout: boxed material, readings, cartoons, tables, figures, glossaries, and InfoTrac® College Edition references. Almost every chapter illustrates key points or concepts with boxed materials from current and practical experiences of administrators at all levels of government. Readings at the ends of chapters obviate the need to assign a separate reader along with the text. These selections are lively, current, and add interest to the text. Of course, if the instructor prefers to use a reader of longer, scholarly journal articles, many excellent ones are available with classic articles collected in a single volume. Insightful cartoons are also included to enliven the text for the student—and to make thought-provoking points.

Most public administration textbooks rely heavily on tables of data to make their points. This textbook recognizes that the learning styles of today's students are more visual. Instead of relying solely on tables of data, we use graphs and figures throughout to present key data by adding visual "punch." Hopefully, these graphics make the textbook more readable and easier to study.

Public administration is a subject that also uses jargon and a considerable number of acronyms. This textbook employs an extensive glossary of key terms in each chapter to make it easier for the students to study and review.

We also integrate InfoTrac articles throughout the discussion. An online system, InfoTrac enables students to access a library of more than 5,000 journals, magazines, and other periodicals. These publications offer current material that helps illustrate the key points being made; the items range from longer scholarly articles in key journals to shorter op-ed pieces in newspapers and magazines of opinion. This online guide is a twenty-four-hour-a-day reference resource. Each chapter cites five to ten current InfoTrac articles.

Many professors require students to undertake a research project. Users of this volume are fortunate to have an excellent search system on the Internet for questions and topics relating to public administration and U.S. politics. When appropriate, the special icon appears next to the text to indicate to the student that InfoTrac will provide an especially helpful and relevant article. InfoTrac lets students ask specific questions, and the system takes students where they need to go to find relevant information, including full-text articles that the students may print or have sent to their e-mail addresses. It will hopefully start students on the road to becoming scholars of the subject.

Important journals that are available on InfoTrac include: *Administration and Society, American Political Science Review, International Migration Review, Journal of American Planning Association, Journal of Human Resources, Journal of Public Policy and Marketing, Journal of Social Issues, Journal of Systems Management, National Review, Policy Studies Journal, Political Science Quarterly, Public Innovator, Public Interest, Public Relations Review, Science, Social Policy, State Legislatures, Washington Monthly, Washington Quarterly, World Policy Journal*, and *Yale Law Journal*.

In addition, the following journals, most of which can be found in most university libraries, are especially appropriate for this course: *Academy of Management Review, Administrative Law Journal, Administrative Law Review, Administrative Science Quarterly,*

American Journal of Political Science, American Review of Public Administration, Civil Service Journal, Congressional Quarterly Weekly Reports, Governing, Harvard Business Review, Intergovernmental Perspectives, Journal of Policy Analysis and Management, Management Science, Midwest Review of Public Administration, National Law Journal, Public Administration Quarterly, Public Administration Review, Public Personnel Management, Public Policy, Publius, State and Local Government Review, State Government, and *Transaction.*

The text also uses photographs to illustrate key points and enliven the book. These are captioned with leading questions to integrate them into the text and to challenge students to think further about the point being made.

Each chapter's summary recapitulates the main points and presents review questions for the student to consider. One of these questions focuses the student back to the end of chapter reading to consider more fully the points being made or illustrated throughout.

Finally, each chapter ends with a collection of valuable Web sites that the student can consult on the chapter's subject matter that cover various levels and aspects of government and administration.

The pedagogical concerns emphasized throughout the textbook are more extensive than most other available textbooks. I believe they make this book more readable, more user-friendly, and easier to study and review for examinations and quizzes. An accompanying instructor's manual suggests additional essay questions, a multiple-choice test bank, further InfoTrac citations, various Internet and other study assignments, and suggested classroom activities.

Organization

For the convenience of the instructor in organizing the course especially for examination purposes, the book is divided into three broad parts. Chapters 1 through 5 discuss the sources of values and value conflicts. Chapter 1 serves as a general introduction, providing an overview of the art and science of balancing values in the administration of public policy. Chapter 2 covers the social, political, economic, and environmental context of public administration—how the political system provides both values and social change. Chapter 3 presents an anatomy of public organization, discussing bureaucratic power and internal sources of values in administration. Chapter 4 examines the federal system and intergovernmental relations with an emphasis on the constitutional framework of federalism as a source of values. Chapter 5 discusses the alternative theories of organizational behavior and how these models of organization become sources of predominant values in administration.

Chapters 6 through 11 look at internal operations of bureaucracy and how they shape or are affected by values and value conflict. Chapter 6 concerns decision making in the administration of public policy, and how decision-making processes deal with the problem of goals and values. Chapter 7 deals with the management of bureaucratic organizations and the strategic use of values in policy making and administration. Chapter 8 examines the evaluation of public policy implementation and the special role bureaucracy plays in that evaluation. It views evaluation as the swinging of the pendulum of administrative politics between and among competing values. Chapter 9 covers personnel issues and unionism in public administration with an emphasis on unions as a source of value conflict. Chapter 10 concerns leadership, the relationship of the chief executive and bureaucracy, and the political values associated with the search for accountability. Chapter 11 discusses communication flows in administration and what one might well call the "fuzzing" of values.

Chapters 12 through 14 look broadly at the use of values to control and evaluate public policy processes and administration. Chapter 12 examines financial management—taxing, budgeting, and spending processes—and the productivity challenge of the budget process. It illustrates budgetary politics and financial management as placing monetary values on the priorities of any given administration. Chapter 13 looks at administrative law and the use of courts and the law to control public agencies. It stresses law and ethics as important sources of values and value conflict in public administration. Chapter 14 covers clientele pressures and governmental regulatory administration. It examines interest groups as sources of values and the use of regulatory politics for governmental attempts to determine societal values.

Values as Themes

Consistent throughout the text and integrated in each chapter are the following values: freedom, equality, order, responsiveness, efficiency, neutrality, tolerance, societal versus individual rights, limited government, popular sovereignty, separation of powers and checks and balances, judicial review, judicial activism or restraint, federalism, freedom of expression, the right to assemble, functional administration, chain of command, standard operating procedures, national versus local standards, accountability, comparable worth, affirmative action, reverse discrimination, entitlement, rationality, and maximum participation.

I have attempted to write a textbook that will be readable and easier for students to review. This book also reflects the contributions of many others who gave advice during its various revisions. I especially wish to thank two editors—content editor Abigail Baxter and copy editor Elliot Simon—for their many suggested improvements to the manuscript. Clark Baxter, who first urged me to write this book, has been a continual source of encouragement and optimism from the first rough draft to this final version.

In addition, my department secretary, Debbi Fox, assisted in the formatting of the instructor's manual and test bank volume that accompanies this textbook. The department's student assistant, Laura Flores, helped look up many InfoTrac citations for both the textbook and the instructor's manual. David Bellis, a colleague at CSUSB, offered many useful suggestions and much encouragement.

Finally, I wish to acknowledge the many valuable suggestions made by the following reviewers who critically read and evaluated earlier drafts of the manuscript: David L. Aronson, University of South Dakota; Don Barber, California State University, Long Beach; Kay Hofer, Southwest Texas University; Christopher Larimer, University of Nebraska at Lincoln; Nancy Lind, Illinois State University; and Dr. Buck Miller, Christopher Newport University.

Michael C. LeMay
California State University, San Bernardino
August 2005

Chapter 1

It is the object of administrative study to discover, first, what government can properly and successfully do, and secondly, how it can do these proper things with the utmost possible efficiency and at the least possible cost either of money or of energy. . . . The object of administrative study is to rescue executive methods from the confusion and costliness of empirical experiment and set them upon the firm foundations laid deep in stable prinoiplo. . . . The province of administration . . . lies outside the proper sphere of politics. Administrative questions are not political questions. . . . Politics sets the tasks for administration, [but] it should not . . . manipulate its offices.

Woodrow Wilson
The study of administration,
Political Science Quarterly, 2 (June 1887).

Balancing Values in the Administration of Public Policy

Introduction

In 1887, Woodrow Wilson, then president of Princeton University, advocated a normative ideal. He articulated the view that legitimate authority to make public policy should be limited to elected officials, courts, and political appointees—not to civil servants. This is the central point of the dichotomy of politics and administration. Implicit in this view is the value of political neutrality. This value holds that civil servants, when implementing public policy, should be neutral in terms of partisan politics—neither Democratic nor Republican. Abundant empirical evidence, however, suggests that in the real world, as opposed to the normative ideal, such neutrality is seldom attained. Simply put, a **value** is something thought of as being desirable or useful, a thing esteemed for its own sake as being intrinsically worthy. Values, as used here, are social principles, goals, or standards held by or accepted by an individual, class, organization, or society. The essential politics of **public administration** lies in determining which and whose values will predominate. Central to the study of public administration are concerns with how those values arise, where they come from, and how they infuse the implementation of public policy.

Consider, for example, regulation of the nursing home industry in California. A study by the United States General Accounting Office (GAO) found that nearly 40 percent of California nursing homes were deficient in "providing care that enhances human dignity," compared with a national rate of 13 percent. Nearly

The nursing home industry in California can truthfully brag that they have the best legislators money can buy.

Pat McGinnis of California Advocates for Nursing Home Reform

PHOTO 1.2
California's Nursing Home Industry
Can you think of an interest group active in U.S. politics that could well serve as an advocate of the clients of nursing homes to counter the influence of corporate owners of nursing homes?
Source: *The National Voter*, League of Women Voters.

one-third of all nursing homes in the state were cited for serious or potentially life-threatening problems in the administration of care. Behind these statistics are real people with real families who simply want a safe and caring environment for their loved ones. The study cited one nursing home in which a resident was found naked in bed, dehydrated, and severely malnourished. That resident died the next day. Examiners found eight other residents lying in urine-soaked sheets. Two residents in yet another nursing home were hospitalized, one of whom died after being given an excessive dose of insulin. At a third home, an 84-year-old resident was found naked with her hands tied to her bed while her "caregiver" had gone to lunch.

Despite being under fire for years for providing substandard care, nursing homes in California changed little, in part because the state's political leaders have consistently thwarted measures to tighten industry oversight and enforce industry regulations. Why did the governor and legislature look the other way while California's nursing home residents were at risk? Partisan politics unquestionably played a role in the regulation—or lack thereof. The nursing home industry bestows hundreds of thousands of dollars annually in political contributions to elected lawmakers. The California Association of Health Facilities (CAHF), which represents approximately 1,500 nursing homes, contributed more than $500,000 to California lawmakers in 1996 and spent $200,000 more on lobbying activities in Sacramento, the state capital, that year. Both Democrats and Republicans have enjoyed the nursing industry's largess. As one advocate for nursing care put it, "The nursing home industry in California can truthfully brag that [it has] the best legislators money can buy."[1] Through its lobbying efforts, the industry's views on issues often dominate policy debate, whereas nursing home residents and public health advocates have to fight hard just to be heard.

Reform efforts are hindered by the state's campaign-financing rules. Proposition 208, a statewide initiative passed by Californians in November 1996, sought to impose tough limits on political contributions and spending, but it was held up by the courts. Currently, nearly anyone can give any amount to any candidate at any time. Californians for Political Reform, a coalition supporting Proposition 208, found that more than half of the 3,000 bills introduced into the state legislature in 1995 were carefully crafted to benefit only a narrow special interest, often providing special exemptions from regulations.

A counterbalancing influence to the nursing home industry has scored some success since 2000. Organized labor in the state won a higher minimum wage and stiffer rules to enforce California's overtime law. These provisions are being used by the California Labor Federation, and particularly by the Service Employees International Trade Union, to help organize employees in the health care industry. Four large trade groups, representing nearly 19,000 California companies, sued to throw out the new law. But the largest health care union in the nation has made organizing the nursing home industry in California its top priority. Union focus on the industry comes at a time when it is vulnerable due to bad pay and tough duty, causing severe staff shortages in nursing homes. The California Association of Health Facilities, a trade group, estimated in 2001 that there were more than 1,000 job vacancies in Sacramento alone (the state's capitol). Nursing homes are woefully underfunded and underregulated; there is a need for reform of the industry and its rate structure. By 2001, a third of the nursing homes in the state were organized.

INFOTRAC
COLLEGE EDITION

Pro-union laws will continue taking effect in 2001.

These examples show that the concern for the place of values in the administration of public policy remains as viable today as it was in 1887. The study of public administration no longer advocates the strict dichotomy of politics and administration, but the issue of the origins and the role of values in administration remains of perennial concern. It is simply impossible to have a value-free or value-neutral public administration. The very attempt to develop a value-free or politically neutral administration imposes a value—that of neutrality—on the system of public administration. This textbook will illustrate the contrary idea— that values are at the heart of public administration. Indeed, its underlying theme is that the public administration of policy in U.S. politics can well be understood at all levels of government as a sort of pendulum that moves between or among competing values that are pursued by the political system even as they infuse public administration. Sometimes these competing values clash. At other times they reinforce one another. But the values are ever present. In many respects, *whose* values are being imposed at any given time is what public administration is all about.

Consider briefly a few such value-conflict issues and how they infuse public administration:

- efficiency versus responsiveness,
- public versus private structures to administer public programs,
- neutrality versus tolerance,
- uniformity versus diversity,
- national standards versus local or regional peculiarities,
- the rights of society to pursue economic capitalism versus individual rights, and
- limited government versus popular sovereignty.

Later chapters will focus on these and other value conflicts to show how they help us understand public administration in various activities that are traditionally associated with public policy implementation: the structures of

- government,
- personnel,
- budgeting,
- management,
- decision making,
- communication,
- control of agencies by the legislature and the courts,
- relations with clientele groups and regulatory administration, and
- the evaluation of public policy.

Value conflict in public administration will be shown at the state, local, and intergovernmental levels as well as within national agencies and bureaucracies.

We begin by examining some key concepts and special terms used in the study of public administration. We discuss various approaches to studying public administration as a separate field or discipline of analysis. We examine how the impact of the Internet affects state and local governments in the area of education and the development of home schooling, illustrating anew that Woodrow Wilson's concern of a century ago remains viable today. Some suggested useful websites are provided for further information on topics central to this discussion, as are InfoTrac® College Edition article citations that exemplify key points or concepts. Suggestions for additional readings close the chapter.

The Clash of Values in the Administration of Public Policy

Efficiency versus Responsiveness

Among the most central values our political system pursues is **responsiveness**. The nation was founded in large measure to ensure a government that was responsive to the will of the people. After establishing their independence from Great Britain, the United States of America wrote a federal constitution that established a commonwealth and agencies of government that would react readily to suggestions or appeal from citizens. To do so, the founders established government as a democratic republic. They said little, however, about the organization of government agencies. They mentioned an army and navy but left most of the work of establishing specific bureaus to the national legislature, or Congress.

To promote the value of responsiveness in government, Congress created structures—agencies, bureaus, and departments—to ensure that citizens were guaranteed their rights of "Life, Liberty and the pursuit of Happiness." At any level of government, the legislature had to establish structures of policy implementation that responded to citizens' demands. Government was to be open to and use common citizens to conduct its business. If citizens needed and desired safety and security (core values of society), then the government would need to establish an army, a navy, a war department, and a state department to ensure national security.

If citizens wanted to pursue commerce, then they would need to communicate across state boundaries, so the legislature would have to establish a postal service. To exchange goods and services, citizens needed a means to measure the comparative worth of those goods and services. The government would have to create a currency and mint coins and print paper money to stabilize commercial enterprise, so Congress established a treasury department.

Making government responsive to the will of the people is dangerous, however: It could quickly become *too* responsive. Citizens might want their government to provide so many goods and services that it would be too costly. In establishing a responsive government run by and for the common citizen, then, it might be better run by officials who were incapable of effectively providing such goods and services—and of venally seeking their own benefit rather than the common good. In short, to prevent a government from excessive responsiveness, government also had to reflect a competing value, that of **efficiency**; or the ability to produce the desired good, service, or effect with a minimum of effort, expense, or waste.

To run efficiently, government would sometimes have to refuse to produce some good or service that some, even many, citizens were demanding. To be efficient, government might have to employ citizens in its service who had special skills, training, or expertise rather than the common man. In short, to be efficient, government had to be *less responsive*.

Public versus Private

Values closely allied to those of efficiency and responsiveness are public versus private ownership of the means to produce essential goods and services demanded by citizens. Some activities are viewed as being best conducted by a public agent. The army, navy, and post office were seen to be essentially public enterprises. In contrast, raising cash food crops and selling them to others at a fair market price were viewed as private enterprises. Government agencies, however, at times might have to regulate or control private commerce lest the private pursuit of commerce create publicly harmful results. An individual has every right to purchase beef cattle or pigs at market, slaughter them, and pack them in tin cans to sell to the public as cheap and convenient sources of canned meat. If diseased or contaminated meat is packed in the process, however, the government may have to step in to regulate the meatpacking industry to ensure public health and safety.

Sometimes, too, the private ownership and provision of an essential good or service simply fails. Then government might need to step in and acquire ownership of a previously private enterprise deemed essential to the common good. If private rail passenger service proved so unprofitable that railroad companies would abandon the service, then the common good might require the government to continue the provision of such transportation. The government might establish a publicly owned rail service, such as Amtrak.

Public safety may require that individuals found guilty of crimes and who pose a danger be locked up and kept away from society. The arrest, trial, and sentencing of individuals to prison are essential *public* functions. The management of the prisons used to incarcerate convicted felons, however, may be handled by a private business corporation. In other words, the running of a state's prisons may be privatized.

Amtrak has paid millions for others' fatal accidents.

Neutrality versus Tolerance

The Bill of Rights to the Constitution of the United States of America guarantees certain rights to all citizens, and government is charged with maintaining such rights. We expect government agencies to deal with all individuals, certainly all citizens, equally and with **neutrality**. Government should not play favorites and grant to some citizens benefits or services that it denies to other citizens or groups of individuals based on their race, creed, or political affiliation. We demand that government be neutral in the provision of goods and services. Yet we also expect government to uphold the value of **tolerance** toward individuals who may be perceived by some as different. To ensure tolerance in society, government might have to intervene and protect the rights of some individuals or groups against the actions of other citizens, quite often the majority of citizens. To secure and maintain tolerance, the government may have to define certain individuals or groups as "protected classes" who are treated not neutrally, but preferentially. In short, upholding tolerance may necessarily limit neutrality.

Uniformity versus Diversity

The nation was founded in no small measure on the principle that all men are created equal and should be treated equally before the law. Citizens demand equality of treatment by government — *uniformity*. Most state constitutions require, for example, uniformity of tax rates on property. The United States Supreme Court ruled, in *Roe v. Wade* (1971), that legal access to a medically safe abortion should be the same in Alabama as in California. But the political culture of regions of the country also support the value of *diversity*. What is considered pornographic material subject to criminal jurisdiction may not be defined in the law the same way in Alabama as in California. Local community standards imbue the law and its implementation far differently across the country. Likewise, how university admissions committees develop and administer admissions programs will differ from state to state, just as their needs for and the value placed on such diversity in enrollment will vary across the country. The need for preferential treatment programs to achieve more diversity in ethnic, gender, and racial backgrounds in university-level students may differ in Michigan and California.

Economic Capitalism versus Individual Rights

The United States was established, in part, to promote economic **capitalism**, that is, to develop and promote an economic system in which all or most of the means of production and distribution—land, factories, railroads, extractive mines, and industries exploiting the abundant natural resources—are privately owned and operated for profit under fully competitive conditions. The economic system was controlled by the operation of a free, private marketplace. Government's role was to promote and protect the free operation of the private marketplace. Unfettered capitalism, however, can easily harm **individual rights**. Government had to regulate the system of capitalism to guard the rights of individuals from excessive manipulation by capitalist economic forces pursuing unbridled profit. Thus, government may regulate the conditions under which laborers work to ensure their health and safety. It might regulate the manner in which advertisements and trade is conducted, to protect children from harmful exploitation. Government might even prohibit the provision of certain goods and services deemed harmful or dangerous, pulling certain products from the market and prohibiting their manufacture and sale. Some

local government city councils or zoning boards have refused permits or rezoning to establish superbox retail stores (such as Wal-Mart Supercenters) in order to protect or maintain their downtown shopping areas.

Limited Government versus Popular Sovereignty

The government of the United States and the more than 87,500 subgovernments are expected to maintain **popular sovereignty**, or to reflect the will of the majority while protecting the rights of individuals. That requires another value to be sought: **limited government**. The value of limited government is reflected in the truism "That government is best which governs least." Cartoon 1.1 gently spoofs the partisan political machine for corruption of popular sovereignty by selling appointed offices like commodities on the private stock market or at auction. As discussed later, the Progressive Party advocated changes to limit the corrupting influence of the political machine. Each value just described is desirable as "good" in itself. Each is a value we expect our government to protect or promote. Yet each value—and many more that will be discussed later—cannot be maximized without impinging on some other value. The administration of public policy involves constantly drawing and redrawing a line between competing values.

The Study of Public Administration

Key Concepts in the Study of Public Administration

The study of any field of human endeavor requires us to grasp certain key terms or concepts that are central to understanding that area or discipline of knowledge. The study of public administration is no exception. It is replete with key terms—the jargon of the field. These key terms or concepts have special definitions or connotations that you must be familiar with if you are to fully understand the field of study. Several key terms will be developed here, and others will be covered in succeeding chapters.

Administration and Red Tape   One such term is *administration*, which concerns the management of the affairs of government and its primary institutions. Central to the term's meaning are the execution and implementation of public policy. Administration connotes all of the rules, regulations, and procedures developed to manage the affairs of government. A negative connotation associated with administration is the concept of **red tape**, or the excessive use of rules and regulations and the insistence on cumbersome and often self-serving procedures. These rules and regulations sometimes seem to be developed by and for the convenience of administrators more than for the public.

Many in the progressive political reform movement and many early scholars of the discipline of political science called for a new field of study to be developed, a "science of administration." The opening to this chapter quoted Woodrow Wilson's essay on the subject of administration. Early textbooks (e.g., Leonard White, 1926) advocated that administration is a unitary process that can therefore be studied at all levels of government; that it is more art than science but that its transformation to a body of knowledge was feasible and worth pursuing; and that administration was at the very heart of the problem of modern, large-scale government.

Bureaucracy   A key concept of public administration is **bureaucracy**. Bureaucracy is defined as the administration of large-scale organization through departments and their agencies (in government such subdivisions are often called *bureaus*) that are managed by a set of appointed officials who follow established routines or "standard operating procedures" (SOPs). Bureaucracy concentrates government authority into a complex structure of administrative bureaus. As with the term *administration*, bureaucracy has such negative connotations as inefficient organization, excessive red tape, and structural arrangements that impede as much as or more than they serve the implementation of public policy. The term may even denote the dehumanizing effects of formal organizational structures that were originally designed to promote "neutrality" but that can develop into pathological elements. *Excessive* bureaucracy becomes dysfunctional and inefficient. It then socializes agency employees to follow rules and regulations to the point that they become ends rather than means to a public policy goal.

Public Policy   **Public policy** refers to the decisions made by government, to a purposive course of action taken by governmental actors in pursuing solutions to perceived problems. In many respects, it is public administration's very reason for being. Administrative structures are directed by governmental leaders, that is, elected officials or politicians who "set" policy. These actors use policy—conscious action or inaction—to cope with problems. Public administration becomes a tool by which policy is implemented. Public policy, then, frequently requires the creation of governmental organizations—agencies, bureaus, or departments—to carry out policy decisions or directives. These bureaus or agencies, in turn, create more policy to guide their employees, the bureaucrats, through a complex policy process to attain overall public policy goals.

Like the structures created to implement it, public policy is hierarchical. Wide-ranging policy of the broadest scope is made at the top of government. As it flows down the levels of the bureaucratic organization, policy becomes increasingly narrow

INFOTRAC
COLLEGE EDITION

The Endangered Species Act: Who's saving what?

INFOTRAC
COLLEGE EDITION

Red tape foils firearms for felons.

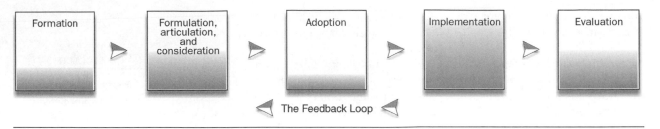

FIGURE 1.1
Stages in the Policy-Making Process: Relative Contribution of Public Administrative Agencies
From Frederick S. Lane, *Current issues in public administration* (5th ed.). © 1994. Reprinted with permission of Nelson, a division of Thomson Learning, Inc.

or focused. The United States Supreme Court may proclaim a policy—for instance, its *Miranda* v. *Arizona* (384 U.S. 436, 1966) decision that people accused of a crime have certain rights—to ensure the protection of due process when dealing with people. In this case, the police officer on the beat—literally, a street-level bureaucrat—has less discretion as a result and carries a card in his or her wallet so that the person being arrested can be read his or her rights, or be "Mirandized." When fear of excessive crime rates became pervasive in society, however, the need for "law and order" led to considerable "relaxation" in how police administered U.S. Supreme Court–mandated provisions on search and seizure rules and even on Miranda rights.

The Policy Process   Public policy can best be viewed as a process, a set or series of stages through which policy is established and implemented. The **policy process** consists of a succession of analytical stages. The first stage involves the identification of a problem and the development of a consensus that this is a problem with which government should be concerned. This is known as the *agenda-setting stage*.

When a specific agency, such as the Centers for Disease Control, plays a central role in establishing the existence of a problem (AIDS, for example), that agency is typically given a central role in formulating policy solutions to cope with it. Public policy next passes through a *formulation stage*. Here various alternative methods to deal with the problem are discussed and refined. This stage involves determination of which level of government and often which department, agency, or even branch of government best or most appropriately should decide from among the alternatives that have been identified. This formation stage further entails assessing the costs and benefits associated with each alternative solution. The *policy enactment stage* is when an authoritative agency of government—a legislature, a president or governor, or a court, for example—makes a specific and discrete decision to "adopt" a policy alternative. The next stage involves *implementation*. Generally, this entails the authorization and funding of a specific government program and the decision about which particular government agency will deal with the problem. This stage is followed by a *policy analysis* or *program evaluation stage*. Evaluation assesses how well the policy is addressing, solving, or at least mitigating the problem. The final stage in the public policy process is *feedback*. The policy adopters weigh information about whether to continue, revise, or terminate the policy.

Figure 1.1 summarizes and graphically portrays the public policy process. Cartoon 1.2 spoofs the complexity of the public policy process that often allows a proposal to change dramatically as it moves through the various stages of becoming public policy.

As legislator introduced the bill

As committee reported it

As House amended it

As Senate amended it

As passed into law

As state agency implemented it

What the budget allowed

What the taxpayer really wanted

CARTOON 1.2
What the taxpayer really wanted
What does this cartoon reveal about the nature of the policy process?
Source: Anonymous.

Public administration, then, refers to what government agencies do to develop and implement public policy. This is a deceptively simple definition, however. In reality, public administration is a complex concept, and this entire volume elaborates on the rich complexity of the term in some important respects. Suffice it to say here that public administration is about the political process. Political decisions and processes are precisely what distinguishes public administration from private administration, or what is often called business administration. It is about what governments do, focusing on the bureaucrats within the structure of government to act or consciously refrain from acting on some problem that the political decision-making process has defined as worthy of public attention. Administration is about the allocation of limited or scarce resources. It concerns those structures of government and their interaction with one another and with other political actors within and without government who constitute the political system.

Public administration involves the bureaucratic agents of government in all stages of the public policy process. These agents are often the actors who alert society to a problem. They help shape perceptions about the nature of the problem when brought to the agenda of government by outside forces such as political parties, interest groups, the media, and other political actors (for example, elected officials at the same or another level of government). They often play a critically important role in placing a problem on the agenda of government.

Public administrators can and frequently do play a crucial role in defining the alternative solutions to a problem. Administrators typically assess or at least are heavily involved in assessing the relative costs and benefits associated with each proposal to public policy. Whereas elected officials enact policy decisions, they do so only after a considerable involvement of public administrators who shape the parameters of their decision. Once a policy is officially adopted or enacted, it is generally turned over to public administrators to develop specific program options to implement the policy. Public administrative bureaucrats often play a central role in assessing or evaluating the impact of a public policy. They frequently provide feedback to policy

Box 1.1

The Policy Process

Definition: The policy process is a sequential pattern of action that involves many functional categories of activity that can be analytically distinguished.

Subconcepts

Policy: A purposive course of action followed by an actor or set of actors in dealing with a problem

Public policy: Policies developed by governmental bodies or officials

Policy demands: Requests of government officials by other actors in the political system for action or inaction on some perceived problem

Policy decision: Discrete acts by public officials that authorize or direct public policy such as enacting statutes, executive orders, administrative rules, judicial decisions, and the like

Policy statement: Formal expression of public policy in written or oral form

Policy output: Tangible manifestations of public policy; what government actually does or refuses to do rather than what it says it will or will not do

Policy outcomes: The consequences for society, intended and unintended, that flow from the action or decided inaction of government

Categories of Action in the Policy Process

- *Policy formation* addresses such questions as: What is the policy problem? What makes it a public problem? How does it get on the agenda of government?
- *Policy formulation* addresses such questions as: Who participates in policy formulation? How are alternatives to deal with the problem developed?
- *Policy adoption* addresses such questions as: How is the policy adopted or enacted? What requirements must be met? Who adopts the policy?
- *Policy implementation* addresses such questions as: What is done or not done to carry out a policy? What effect does this have on policy content?
- *Policy evaluation* addresses such questions as: How is the effectiveness of policy measured? Who evaluates the policy? What are the consequences of the policy evaluation? Are there demands for revision or repeal?

The public policy process is inherently political.

- It involves conflict and struggle among individuals and groups who have conflicting desires on issues of public concern.
- Because it is a process—that is, a sequence of actions—it has no definite beginning or end. To some extent, the time frame is arbitrarily imposed by the analyst.

decision makers to continue, modify, or revise a policy. Occasionally, they are subjects of decisions by others to terminate a particular public policy program.

Line versus Staff Agencies

The next section briefly describes the principle structures that constitute public administration. These structures can be distinguished in several ways, depending on the perspective from which we view them. All agencies, for example, can be categorized as either a **line agency** or a **staff agency**. Line agencies meet directly with and provide a particular good or service to the public. The U.S. Department of Agriculture, for instance, assists farmers. It exemplifies a line agency of the national level of government. Police or fire departments are line agencies at the local level, and state highway or health departments are line agencies at the state level. Staff agencies serve executives. The staff concept emerged during the 19th century out of the military, where aides-de-camp served modern generals in leading huge and complex military forces. The staff concept developed as a structural device to overcome the inherent limitations of a single mind (the leader) to cope with complex problems and manage large governmental entities. A centralized personnel office, budget office, and purchasing office each exemplify a staff agency. They serve an executive and interact with other line agencies rather than with the general public.

The Structures of Government in the Executive Branch

Government in the United States is a truly vast enterprise. More than 87,500 government entities have independent powers to raise revenue, levy taxes and fees, and determine how to expend those revenues. Table 1.1 presents the number of governments in the United States by level and type as of the 2002 Census of Governments. Collectively, these governments employed about 20 million persons. The respective size of their bureaucracies were 3 million at the federal level, 5 million at the state level, and 12 million at the local level.

One way in which values affect public administration, then, is through the shape of a governmental structure. For example, if we desire government to be more responsive, then it is logical to set up a department of government in which the top management is appointed and serves at the pleasure of the elected executive. Making the department's budget subject to the control of the elected officials, both executive and legislative, enhances responsiveness.

If we desire a more "neutrally competent" administration, then it is more logical to establish an independent agency with many top managers who are appointed for specific and staggered terms and with a significant portion of its budget not subject to legislative manipulation. If, however, we desire government to be more businesslike, then a government corporation structure is the arrangement of choice.

The next section briefly describes the major structural arrangements of the U.S. federal government. Similar structures are found at the state and local levels, and examples will be discussed more fully in later chapters. The executive branch of the U.S. government is headed by an elected president and comprises several structures designed to implement national policy as established by the Constitution or through legislative means. Five such structural arrangements will be briefly discussed here: (1) the executive office agencies, (2) the executive or cabinet-level departments, (3) independent public agencies, (4) government corporations, and (5) intergovernmental bodies.

The Executive Office of the President

When George Washington was elected president, it was literally to a one-person office. He hired and was assisted by a few close personal aides, a mere handful of people. Over the decades, the role of the presidency expanded and the size and complexity of the entire executive branch grew. As the United States emerged as a world power, the need for greater efficiency in the office led to the establishment of the **Executive Office of the President (EOP)**, a sort of umbrella office made up of 10 top presidential staff agencies.

INFOTRAC
COLLEGE EDITION

Merit, management, and neutral competence

INFOTRAC
COLLEGE EDITION

The Bush staff and cabinet system

TABLE 1.1

Numbers and Type of Governments in the United States

| | U.S. (Federal) | State | Local | | | | | Totals |
			County	Municipal	Towns	School Districts	Special Districts	
Number of governments	1	50	3,034	19,429	16,504	13,506	35,052	87,576

The EOP was established during the administration of President Franklin Delano Roosevelt, who appointed a special group, the Brownlow Committee, to advise him on administrative management so that he might better cope with the enormous strain on the federal government as it grew to cope with the Great Depression. This advisory committee recommended a sweeping reorganization of the executive branch. The United States Congress did not approve the major reorganization, but it did authorize the president to create the EOP to provide staff assistance to the chief executive and to assist the president in managing the ever-enlarging national bureaucracy. The size of the staff agencies grew as well. The White House staff created by Roosevelt had 45 people. President George W. Bush's staff numbers over 630.

Roosevelt established the EOP by executive order under the Reorganization Act of 1939. Today it comprises 10 staff agencies employing over 1,600 people. Not all staff agencies within the EOP are of equal importance. The dominant agencies are the White House Office, the Office of Management and Budget, the Council of Economic Advisors, and the National Security Council. These "inner" staff agencies of the EOP have greater and more frequent contact with the president, more media coverage and prestige, and more sweeping political clout within virtually any presidential administration.

The Office of Presidential Personnel oversees the appointment and related personnel tasks of over 5,000 individuals. These include presidential appointments requiring Senate confirmation, such as cabinet secretaries and agency heads, deputy secretaries and undersecretaries, members of regulatory commissions, ambassadors, district attorneys, federal marshals, and various appointments in international organizations. In 2000 these numbered 1,125. Additionally, a typical presidential administration appoints about 200 federal judges. There are over 2,000 nonpresidential, noncareer positions appointed by agency heads, but only with the approval of the White House Office of Presidential Personnel. There are more than 2,300 part-time presidential appointee positions established by statute—such as members of advisory boards and commissions. The total noncareer universe of positions that can be filled by the White House during a typical presidential term is about 6,500.

The Bush Administration continued the established pattern of using the "cabinet council" structure to integrate and supervise diverse policy issues. The council itself comprises the heads of relevant departments and agencies. It and its staff were intended to oversee policy planning and implementation in major policy areas while coordinating with the specialized White House policy bodies dedicated to drug control, AIDS policy, and faith-based initiatives. From the outset, the domestic policy staff was charged with translating President Bush's "compassionate conservative" policy agenda, including education and health care reform, into legislation.

Cabinet-Level Departments

By far the largest and most important structures of the national bureaucracy are the 15 line agencies that make up the **executive departments**. These departments are directly accountable to the president and are responsible for performing specific government functions, such as printing money, conducting research on energy sources, training military forces, and securing the nation from terrorism. These departments have been created by Congress over the last 200 years. A president may request a new department to be established or an old one abolished or changed, but that can only happen with the approval of Congress. Collectively, these departments make up the president's cabinet and are therefore referred to as cabinet-level departments.

PHOTO 1.3
President Franklin Delano Roosevelt (1882–1945)
What was happening in the United States during the period of Franklin Roosevelt's New Deal that made his proposal to restructure the executive branch so logical for the time?
Source: Courtesy of the Library of Congress.

In June 2002, President Bush, reacting to political pressures brought about by the attacks of September 11, 2001, and by survivors and families of the victims of those attacks, general public pressure, and Democratic congressional proposals, switched from opposition to support for a law to establish a Department of Homeland Security (DHS). The newly established department was given direct supervisory and budgetary control over 22 agencies under its own secretary, Tom Ridge. The behemoth known as the DHS represented the most extensive government reorganization of the federal bureaucracy since World War II and the establishment of the Department of Defense. As will be discussed more fully in subsequent chapters, however, instead of streamlining our domestic preparedness strategy, the DHS became simply another agency added to the mix, equal but not primary to the counterterrorism activities of the Department of Defense, the Justice Department (particularly its FBI), and the CIA. Chapter 4 discusses further the changes in intergovernmental relations (with state and local governments especially) accompanying the newly established DHS. Chapter 6 focuses on the decision-making process involved in its creation. Chapter 8 refers to its impact on personnel administration and the struggles in its establishment centering on federal unions. Chapter 10 highlights some communication issues arising out of its creation.

As with the EOP, not all cabinet-level departments are equal in influence. All cabinet secretaries are equal in rank and salary. Four departments, however, are considered the **inner cabinet**—State, Defense, Treasury, and Justice—and are more

prominent and influential in every presidential administration than the rest of the cabinet (the **outer cabinet**). The secretaries of these four departments enjoy greater prestige, more access to the president, and enhanced public visibility through greater media attention. These are discussed more fully in Chapter 2.

Independent Agencies

Several agencies are known as *independent agencies:* independent executive agencies and independent regulatory agencies. **Independent executive agencies** are bureaucratic structures not located within a department. They report directly to the president, who appoints their chief officials. They are headed by multiple people rather than a single secretary. Whenever a new federal agency is established—for example, the National Aeronautics and Space Administration (NASA)—Congress decides where to locate the program or agency within the federal bureaucracy. Since World War II, presidents have often asked that a new agency be kept separate or independent from an existing department, especially if it has what is considered a single or special function. Agencies can be created only through the joint cooperation of the president and the Congress.

Independent regulatory agencies are established separately from all three branches of government. Congress creates them to handle complex and technical regulatory functions. These agencies are set up as commissions, with multiple heads appointed for fixed and staggered terms. They involve functions of all branches—executive, legislative, and judicial. They legislate specific rules, implement those rules, and then adjudicate any disputes that arise from the rules.

Government Corporations

The **government corporation** structural form is the newest among federal bureaucracies. It is essentially a business that is owned and operated by the U.S. government. These corporations are similar to businesses, in that they provide a good or service for which they charge a fee, although often a lesser one than what the consumer would pay for substantially similar services provided by a privately owned corporation because taxpayers subsidize any deficits. Generally, they are similar to independent regulatory agencies in some of their structural arrangements. They are headed by multimember boards with fixed and staggered terms, produce their own revenues, are therefore less subject to budgetary control by Congress, and have greater flexibility than most standard departmental government agencies. Sometimes Congress selects this form when a private-sector corporation had been providing an unprofitable service and went out of business. If the service is one that government feels is essential, then Congress may choose to establish a government corporation to continue providing the service. Amtrak is one of the best-known examples.

Sometimes the government uses this format when it promises to be "more businesslike," as when Congress changed the United States Postal Service from a regular department to a government corporation. Sometimes Congress selects this form when no private business corporation can afford to start up such a business, as in the case of COMSAT, the communication satellite corporation. Sometimes Congress uses this form to provide a necessary business service associated with government agencies who have covert operations needs (witness protection in the justice department, the CIA's need for air transport business, and the like). In such cases, the value of secrecy is every bit as important as efficiency. These various forms and structures are summarized in Figure 1.2, which presents an organizational chart of the government of the United States.

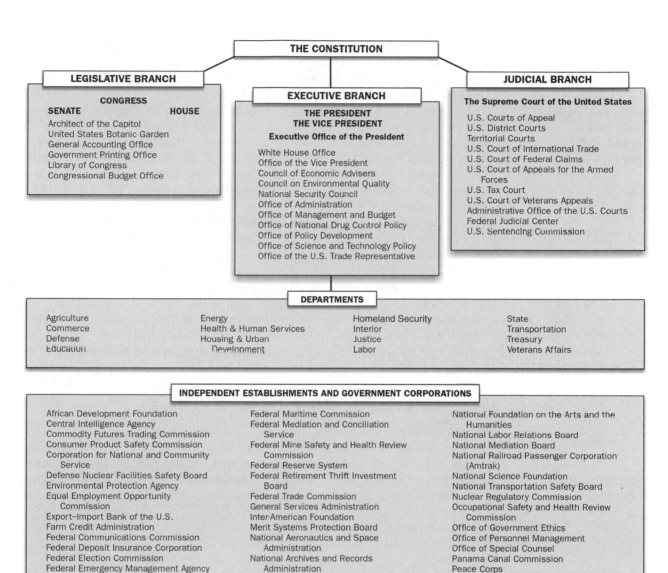

FIGURE 1.2

Organizational Chart of the Government of the United States

Source: U.S. Government, *United States government manual, 2001–2002* (Washington, DC: Author, 2003): 22.

Intergovernmental Agencies

Over the years, various regional governmental organizations have been established that span national–state, state–local, and even interlocal boundary lines. They manage bureaucratic organizations inherently intergovernmental in structure and financing. Interstate compacts have been adopted to cover a broad range of policy issue areas: conservation, transportation, law enforcement, health, education, parks, and water use and control. The Interstate Compact on the Placement of Children, for example, helps regulate the placement of children across state lines. Such compacts peaked in

the 1950s and 1960s. They are increasing in number, as are the number of multistate compacts. The Delaware River Basin Commission, for instance, is an interstate compact among four states—Delaware, New Jersey, New York, and Pennsylvania—and the national government. It was created to manage conflict over the use of water from the rivers of the Delaware River basin region and to help control flooding on a regional basis.

Some of those compacts were created primarily for economic-development purposes. The Appalachian Regional Commission, established in 1965, consists of a federal chairperson and a state cochairperson from each of the 11 states in the Appalachian region. It lobbies for federal benefits for the region and works to foster economic growth in the area.

Many interstate compacts and even multilocal special-district governments manage huge capital-investment enterprises to provide special functions. Some manage the exploitation of natural resources best handled via a multistate approach, as in the case of the Interstate Oil and Gas Compact created in 1935. Others may provide mass transit on a regional basis. These intergovernmental enterprises can become huge, multibillion dollar special districts, such as the Port Authority of New York and New Jersey, the Los Angeles County Metropolitan Transportation District, the Washington Metro Transit District, and the Bay Area Rapid Transit Authority. Indeed, 103 state, county, city, and special-district governments are now in the billion dollar club.[2]

Evolving Approaches to the Study of Public Administration

Over the nation's more than 200 years, governments in the United States evolved as structural arrangements reflected changing values. As government developed, so did the study of public administration. We distinguish here several phases or periods of that history, each of which can be characterized by the predominant value emphasized during that era.

The Era of Representativeness

The entire 19th century can be looked on as the era of representativeness. Making a government that was truly representative was a bold experiment that concerned society generally and politics particularly throughout the century. The value of representativeness was structured into government by establishing strong legislatures and comparatively weak executives. At the local level, the latter half of the century witnessed the development of the urban political machine and its political "boss," who ruled over fragmented local government structures. During this century, the nation's political party system developed and became institutionalized to reflect a means for citizen influence in policy making. As the economy industrialized and the nation absorbed tens of millions of immigrants, it developed many and varied interest groups with powerful lobby organizations to ensure that government would be *responsive* to their needs.

Neutral Competence and the Period of Reform

During the 19th century, the study of government and politics, and particularly of public administration, was undeveloped at best. It was mostly an area of concern within the study of law. As awareness of the boss system and resulting political corruption grew, and as the excessive power of special interest groups became ever more obvious, a call for reform arose that developed into a social and then a political movement. By the end of the century, a growing academic movement developed as well, pushing for reform and advocating the value of "neutral competence." The period of **neutral competence** began roughly in the first decade of the 20th century and ended with World War II. In politics, it was manifested in the Progressive movement. In government, it was seen in three areas: (1) the establishment and spread of the civil service system, (2) the dichotomy of administration and politics, and (3) the development of structural arrangements such as state-level independent regulatory commissions and boards and local-level structures such as the commission and council-manager forms of city government. The study of public administration went through some stages.

For roughly the first two decades of the century, the study of public administration reflected concern for the dichotomy of administration and politics. More important than Woodrow Wilson's essay, which was briefly cited in the chapter opening, were two books: Frank J. Goodnow's *Politics and Administration* (1900) and Leonard White's *Introduction to the Study of Public Administration* (1926). Goodnow's work stressed that government was characterized by two distinct functions: (1) politics, or the expression of the state will, and (2) administration, or the execution of policy.

A movement within political science emerged at the same time. The American Political Science Association formed a Committee on Instruction in Government that called for training for citizenship, professional preparation in law and journalism, and training "professional experts to be specialists for government positions." A Committee on the Practical Training for Public Service was established by the association in 1912.

In state and local government, Progressive practitioners launched a similar movement. The New York Bureau of Municipal Research was founded in 1906. The nation's first school of public administration, the Training School for Public Administration, began in 1911. The study of public administration as a discipline gained academic legitimacy in the 1920s, exemplified by the publication of Leonard White's aforementioned book, the first true public administration textbook.

The Principles of Administration

A second phase, roughly between 1910 and 1937,[3] emphasized the "principles of administration." In many respects, this period represents the zenith of the reputation of public administration. The period began with the publication of W. F. Willoughby's *Principles of Public Administration* (1927) and developed through the works of several notable scholars: Mary Parker Follett, Henri Fayol, James Mooney, Alan Reiley, and, most famously, Frederick W. Taylor in his *The Principles of Scientific Management* (1911). Both government and business sought to hire students of the field, and its leading scholars often served as "consultants." The American Society for Public Administration began in 1939, publishing the field's leading journal, *Public Administration Review*. The development of a separate subfield of public administration within political science was symbolized in the 1937 publication of a landmark book, Luther Gulick and Lyndall Urwick's *Papers on the Science of Administration*. Many of the ideas and principles of this movement are discussed more fully in Chapter 5. They are one of the major sources of values that infuse public administration in both theory and practice.

By the 1940s, however, the dichotomy of politics and administration began to be challenged. Works by Chester Bernard (1938) and then Herbert Simon critiqued the assumption of the dichotomy advocates. Fritz Morstein Marx edited an important book, *Elements of Public Administration* (1946), that directly questioned the dichotomy and argued that what purported to be value-free administration was really value-laden politics. Moreover, scholars such as Robert Dahl (1947), Dwight Waldo (1948), and Herbert Simon with his book *Administrative Behavior* (1947) directly challenged the whole array of "principles of administration." By mid-century, the dichotomy and principles of administration had been essentially abandoned by the field.

The Executive Leadership Era
Post–World War II developments launched a third major phase, an era of executive leadership. The highly fragmented nature of government structures, coupled with increasingly complex societal problems, led many theorists to question a "bureaucracy run amok." Various study commissions to reform and restructure government proposed strengthening the executive's ability to control the bureaucracy. These commissions served as yet another major source of competing values.

The Systems Framework and the Ecology of Public Administration
In the study of political science, the systems model posited by David Easton in his book *The Political System* (1953) became influential. The study of public administration within the discipline was reestablished as an "emphasis" or subfield. Comparative public administration received greater attention. Public administration as a field of study reflected a value shift that was emerging from the broader discipline of political science: Bureaucracy should serve democracy. By the 1960s, a focus on management emerged, marrying an emphasis and values derived from business administration with those from organizational theory. One such effect of the stress on management within the study of public administration was a renewed concern over public versus private differences and similarities in the management of large-scale bureaucratic organizations.

The system's model and broader societal concern over the environment emerging in the 1980s combined in a focus on the "ecology" of public administration. The direct and indirect effects of various types of environmental influences on public administration was explored. The study of public administration examined how public policy making was affected by differing types of ecology. Physical ecology reflected how climate and terrain influence policies such as the administration of highway construction and maintenance. Technology noted the effects of computers on behavior in government, politics, and the bureaucracy. The ecology of demographics studied changes in population and how they modify demands, as in the administration of public schools, for example. Cultural ecology noted the shift in values as youth emerged into the adult world or as new cultural minorities entered into society. Economic ecology studied how economic development affects budgets, demands, and supports. Finally, structural ecology focused on the effects of government structures on decision making, such as how the changing nature of the federal system affects bureaucracy.

The Public Choice Model and Public Administration
Another perspective that has more recently played a dominant role in the study of public administration is the *public choice model*, which is discussed more fully in Chapter 6. Public choice theory is based on the fundamental proposition or view

that people behave in the political arena as they do in the economic market arena. The model assumes that the same rational, self-interest-seeking motives inspiring human behavior in the economic marketplace apply to decision making in the public sector. The model assumes that all persons, in or out of government, pursue their self-interest. Just as consumers seek to maximize their utility in purchasing goods and services and just as firms seek to maximize their profits, so too public policy makers seek to maximize their welfare.

In the public choice model, government actors produce laws and regulations; interest groups and individual voters are consumers of such laws and regulations. Lawmakers seek to maximize their self-interest by acting to promote their long-term retention in office or to increase their electability or promotion to higher office and generally to increase their overall influence. Bureaucrats act to aggrandize their power and influence. Consumers of laws and regulations respond to maximize their self-interest by voting, donating, and influencing those producers of laws and regulations who best serve them and their needs. Generally speaking, smaller groups of more intensely affected parties will be more able to influence such "public decision-making markets" than broader or more diffuse interest groups or coalitions, whose information and organization costs may prohibitively exceed gains they may expect to make from lobbying.

Reading 1.1, "The Net and School Choice," illustrates environmental influences and value conflicts that bureaucrats face each day. It demonstrates how development of the net impacts "responsiveness" in school choice and school reform. Later chapters examine and more explicitly detail the threads of those value shifts and concepts as the study of public administration changed over time.

Reading 1.1

The Net and School Choice

Political activism is highly dynamic in character. When individuals and interest groups seeking to influence public policy or its implementation are too rigid in their tactics they invite failure. Even once-powerful tactics grow stale over time. The use of demonstration politics—protest marches, sit-ins, and so on, were effective in the 1950s and 1960s, but by the 1990s went out of fashion as the tactic's novelty wore off and the indispensable media publicity waned. Today, funding sympathetic think-tank research or establishing "independent" political advocacy groups exempt from campaign finance laws are now better bets as vehicles of influence. Since savvy activists realize that countergroups may develop effective counter-strategies, success demands freshness in their tactical approaches. Once-formidable though tedious letter-writing campaigns on the eve of legislative debate can now be virtually instantly trumped by a countercampaign of e-mail. As political rules shift, old standbys become impractical or even illegal.

It is scarcely an exaggeration to say that "school politics" involves one of the nation's great and enduring political conflicts. School politics engage such issues as racial integration, instruction of morality, varying philosophic approaches to pedagogy and school discipline, the equality of school funding and per-pupil expenditure rates, and so on. Until the 1990s, parents who were very dissatisfied with their public school system had few direct alternatives short of moving elsewhere, requesting approval of intradistrict school transfers, or opting out of the public realm and sending their children to private schools. These options often entailed heavy burdens with often only marginal improvements, given the paucity of choices. Job-related needs, housing costs, community ties, and limited economic resources further constrained such "escape" from the monopoly of the public education provider. Likewise, useful information as to student performance and per-pupil spending levels was typically controlled by the bureaucratic monopoly. These facts often intimidated parents in their quest for accountability. Thus, school battles tended to be large-scale conflicts seeking systemwide policy changes. Filtered information went from government to school bureaucracies and only then to parents. School teacher unions, educational professionals, and a host of

education-related interest groups each had their own specialized agendas. Religious lobby groups advocated the use of school prayer. Civil rights organizations pushed affirmative action hiring policy, and so on. Parents seeking change had little alternative but to enlist as foot soldiers for interest groups possessing sufficient resources to make an impact on bureaucracies mired in inertia.

With the development of the Internet, vital information about student academic performance, school programs, and similar vital details even on a district-by-district basis became increasingly available on the net. Such data can be instantly forwarded by e-mail to potential allies suspicious of official assessments. Dissatisfied parents can now find educational alternatives previously nearly invisible. Finding specialized private schools, once a task requiring tedious and uncertain library-like research can now be accessed with a click of the mouse to specialized websites.

For example, if parents are seeking more military-style discipline, one site lists 26 U.S. high school military academies offering coed and same-sex education. Another site details multiple therapeutic schools for the emotionally disturbed or children with learning disabilities. For the sports-minded or theatrically inclined, websites provide easy access to appropriate schools. Simply entering in "Christian schools" into search programs like Google.com or Yahoo.com brings up hundreds of major Christian school organizations from which one can instantly and electronically tour hundreds of possibilities. Similar two- or three-click searches will uncover places catering to Jewish and Catholic parents, or even academies for more esoteric interests, such as Afrocentric instruction.

Arguably the greatest beneficiaries of net-supplied information are parents seeking home-schooling solutions. A few clicks generate immense assistance in navigating state statutory requirements, tips on dealing with bureaucratic paperwork, and ways to circumvent legal challenges. The net, moreover, is an easy gateway to numerous state-based home-school organizations. Once home schooling is in place, the net has ready for purchase practically every teaching aid and book, school items like class rings, and materials for subjects like driver education, that reflect almost every pedagogical or ideological perspective.

The net has contributed to the explosion in home schooling. According to estimates by the National Home Education Research Institute, the number of home schoolers rose from an estimated 345,000 in 1994 to an estimated 2 million today. In addition, the impact of the trend is magnified by the development of newly emerging "cyber schools." Such schools owe their existence to state laws permitting schooling outside a pupil's immediate neighborhood and are often hybrids, drawing funds from both public and private, for-profit schools.

These developments allow dissatisfied parents alternatives to the traditional, cumbersome educational politics. Instead of battling entrenched school boards or teachers unions over curriculum reform, for example, that aim can be addressed and accomplished far faster and easier by going online to find more acceptable teaching materials and other options.

Source: Data and information excerpted from Robert Weissberg, Technology evolution and citizen activism: The net and rebirth of limited government, *Policy Studies Journal*, *31*(3) (August 2003): 385–396. Reprinted with permission of Blackwell Publishing.

Net Assignment

Using local websites that describe your town or city government, find and describe those government services that local citizens want to be responsive and others that they more notably want to be efficient.

Summary

Rather than justifying a dichotomy between politics and administration, values lie at the very heart of policy implementation. As we see when we look at major eras in U.S. political history, values—in their unity or conflict—have been dominant, have influenced governments' structural arrangements, and have affected the developing field of the study of public administration. Those values that tend to conflict with one another are efficiency versus responsiveness, the public good versus private good, neutrality versus tolerance, national standards and uniformity versus regional or local diversity, economic capitalism versus individual rights, and limited government versus popular sovereignty.

The major structural arrangements within the government of the United States include the Executive Office of the President and its 15 cabinet-level departments, independent boards and commissions, and government corporations. Intergovernmental structures, which are exemplified by interstate compacts and regional special-district government entities, also play significant roles.

Key Concepts—administration, bureaucracy, public policy, and the role that administrative agencies play in the policy process—plus the specialized terms that make up the jargon of the field of public administration introduce you to the study of public administration.

Glossary of Key Terms

administration   The management of the affairs of government and of its primary institutions. The execution and implementation of public policy.

bureaucracy   The administration of government through departments and agencies managed by a set of appointed officials who follow an inflexible routine.

capitalism   An economic system in which all or most of the means of production and distribution are privately owned and operated for profit under fully competitive conditions.

efficiency   The ability to produce a desired good, service, or effect with a minimum of effort, expense, or waste.

executive departments   The 15 primary line agencies of the United States that together make up most of the president's cabinet.

Executive Office of the President (EOP)   An umbrella term referring to the 10 top staff agencies that serve the president.

government corporation   A business owned and operated by the government to provide a good or service for which it charges a fee.

independent executive agencies   Bureaucratic structures not located in regular departments; they report directly to the executive and perform a single task.

independent regulatory agencies   Commissions to regulate a specific industry or area; they have executive, legislative, and judicial functions.

individual rights   Rights guaranteed to individuals by the Bill of Rights and other laws that serve to limit government.

inner cabinet   The Departments of State, Defense, Treasury, and Justice; the most influential of the cabinet-level departments.

limited government   The national political value that holds "That government is best which governs least."

line agency   A governmental unit that meets directly with and provides a particular good or service to the public.

neutrality   Dealing with all citizens equally before the law and not playing favorites by granting some citizens benefits or services but denying them to others because of race, creed, national origin, or political affiliation.

neutral competence   The application of technical skills to jobs without regard to political affiliation or issues.

outer cabinet   The 11 "lesser" cabinet-level departments: Interior, Agriculture, Commerce, Labor, Housing and Urban Development, Transportation, Energy, Health and Human Services, Education, Veterans Affairs, and Homeland Security.

policy process   A set or series of stages through which policy is established and implemented.

popular sovereignty   Governmental actions that reflect the will of the population.

public administration   Whatever governments do to develop and implement public policy.

public policy   Decisions made by government to pursue a purposive course of action taken by governmental actors to cope with a perceived problem.

red tape   Excessive use of rules, regulations, and procedures to the point they become ends in themselves rather than means to an end.

responsiveness   The extent to which government reacts readily to suggestions or appeals from its citizens as individuals or groups or through institutions.

staff agency   A governmental unit that serves an executive; it deals with line agencies to supply, assist, or help control them.

tolerance   The value of protecting the rights of individuals and groups who are perceived to be different.

value Something thought of as being desirable or useful; a thing esteemed for its own sake as being intrinsically worthy; the principles, goals, or standards held by or accepted by an individual, class, organization, or society.

Review Questions

1. With much fanfare, the Bush administration announced its plan to "increase home-land security," by establishing the new DHS. Why does government tend to grow so large and why does it tend toward centralization? Do you think the creation of the new DHS substantially increases the nation's security?

2. Can you compare and contrast the structural arrangements of the department, the independent agency, and the government corporation forms? What are some advantages or disadvantages of each? What factors relate to why certain policy issues tend to be assigned to each of these types of organization? What value is enhanced by each type?

3. In this chapter, we dealt with six sets of policy value conflicts. What are some other values in U.S. politics? What are some sets of values that reinforce one another rather than conflict?

4. Can you relate the stages of the policy process and describe how the bureaucracy is involved at each stage in that process?

5. Reading 1.1 on the Net and School politics illustrates the values clash of adminis-trative competence versus parental responsiveness. What other values are stressed or arise from the development of the Net? What are some other public policy areas in which the Net is making a similar impact?

Surfing the Net

The Internet provides a wealth of useful Web sites to which the reader can go for further information. A few are highlighted here, and others will appear in subse-quent chapters.

The Library of Congress site (**http://cweb.locgov/global/executive/fed.html**) provides links to virtually every federal government branch and agency.

Policy.Com (**http://www.policy.com**) supplies daily policy briefings and a wide array of policy-related resources.

The comprehensive University of Michigan website on political science (**http://www.lib.umich.edu/libhome/Documents.center/polisci html**) offers a host of governmental publications and innumerable government links.

The site of the federal government's human resource agency, the Office of Personnel Management (**http://www.opm.gov**), lists federal employment information.

Every federal agency has its own website. Federal World (**http://www.fedworld.gov**) is a government site that links to numerous federal agencies and government information.

Similarly, the Federal Web Locator (**http://www.law.vill.edu/Fed-Agency/fedwebloc .html**) enables you to search for any agency name and link to information about that bureaucracy.

The most recent edition of *The U.S. Government Manual* (**http://www.gpoaccessgov/ gmanual/index.html**) is cited several times in this chapter and contains basic information on the functions, organizations, and administrators of every federal department.

The Council of State Governments site (**http://www.csg.org**) is loaded with state government news, issues related to federalism, policy alerts, and reports, and links to all 50 state websites.

Every state government has a home page. A few of the largest websites are those of California (**http://www.state.ca.us**), New York (**http://www.state.ny.us**), and Texas (**http://www.texas.gov**).

The Bureau of the Census site (**http://www.census.gov**) is most useful for accessing information about federal agencies and a host of statistical data on U.S. society and politics.

Similarly, the *Federal Register* (**http://www.access.gpo/nara/fedreg/fedreg.html**) provides information on all U.S. laws and regulations.

The National Home Education Research Institute's website is (**http://www.nheri.org**).

In addition to the InfoTrac® College Edition articles cited in this chapter, you may use InfoTrac College Edition to access the following journals that are especially useful to consult for related articles.

INFOTRAC
COLLEGE EDITION

Academy of Management Review

Administration and Society

Administration Law Journal

Administrative Law Review

American Journal of Political Science

American Review of Public Administration

Civil Service Journal

Congressional Quarterly Weekly Reports

Governing

Harvard Business Review

Intergovernmental Perspectives

Journal of Policy Analysis and Management

Journal of Public Administration Research and Theory

Law journals (any of the major journals online—*Harvard Law Review, Cornell Law Review*, and so on)

Midwest Review of Public Administration

National Law Journal

Political Science Quarterly

Public Administration Review

Public Personnel Management

Public Innovator

Publius

State and Local Government Review

State Government

Transaction

Chapter 2

In June 2003, a sharply divided United States Supreme Court upheld a law school's affirmative action admissions program. Many Fortune 500 corporations filed amicus curiae briefs supporting the law school's admission plan, as did the United States Armed Forces. Corporations across the country actively pursue diversity through a variety of programs. . . . In its decision, *Grutter v. Bollinger, et al.*, the Supreme Court addressed only affirmative action by the state in an educational context. In splitting its vote five to four, the Supreme Court upheld the University of Michigan's Law School program, while in a related case, *Gratz and Hammacher v. Bollinger, et al.*, the Court struck down the program at the college by a vote of six to three. In *Grutter*, the Court held that the "Law School has a compelling interest in attaining a diverse student body."

The Social, Political, Economic, and Environmental Context of Administration

Lisa E. Chang
Grutter v. Bollinger, et al.,
Employee Relations Law Journal, 30(1) (Summer 2004), 3–19.

Introduction

The Political System, Values, and Social Change

The opening citation illustrates how a university's bureaucracy can become embroiled in a controversy when the values in its social environment change. Michigan's admissions staff was being buffeted by conflicting demands. Minority students wanted no change in the existing policies and procedures that had been developed at the university to attract more minority students. Many corporations and the U.S. military agreed. University officials, from the chancellor down to admissions office personnel, on the other hand, were responding to political pressures demanding changes in admissions policies to reflect growing societal pressure to end **affirmative action**. The racial preferences used by the university's admissions staff to recruit representative numbers of minority students had come to be viewed in the general public as **reverse discrimination**, as a racial preference rather than the elimination of bias. Admission office personnel were caught in a value conflict. Whereas they believed in affirmative action's efforts to recruit minorities and advance the diversity of the university's student body, they were aware of the increasing number of state laws—led by California's enactment of Proposition 209, which the state's voters had approved by a wide margin of over 60 percent—that explicitly forbid affirmative action procedures.

This controversy illustrates a common development that puts bureaucrats in a dilemma as they are pressured to pursue conflicting values. To better understand how such pressures develop, we will discuss a **systems model**, or systems framework, and place public administration within the context of a broader political system. It is these environments—the political, social, economic, and physical—within which public administrators must operate and that create the primary sources of value conflicts with which bureaucrats must often daily cope.

We will introduce and explain the political system model and apply that conceptual framework to public administration as well as discuss various environmental influences at work on public administrators as they implement public policy. We will also explore the political, social, economic, and physical environments as sources of policy concerns—and thus of values and value conflicts—within public administration.

The Concept of Administrative Agencies in the Political System

The concept of a system emerged in the social sciences after World War II.[1] The idea of a system reflects the understanding that anything from a car or a computer to the entire universe may be viewed as more than a collection of parts. The car is not just individual pieces of steel, plastic, rubber, wires, and glass, but an assembly that interacts in specific ways to move people from place to place. The computer is more than a plastic case, screen, wires, processor, disk drives, keyboard, and mouse. It is a system of communication, data storage, and data manipulation that processes information at tremendous speed. It can connect with the information flow of a World Wide Web. It is a system that shrinks the globe.

Of equal importance, one system can be viewed as related to other, higher-order systems. The car may be seen as part of a transportation system or as part of the ecosystem because of its role in producing air pollution. The computer affects our business, education, mass media, and governmental systems. Each system is profoundly affected by the development of the computer. In short, every system may be perceived of as being part of a larger system as a subsystem or as part of an encompassing supersystem.

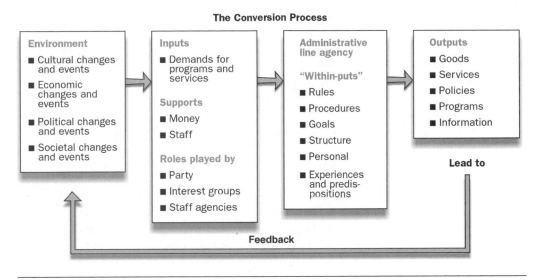

The Conversion Process

Environment	Inputs	Administrative line agency	Outputs
■ Cultural changes and events	■ Demands for programs and services	**"Within-puts"**	■ Goods
■ Economic changes and events	**Supports**	■ Rules	■ Services
■ Political changes and events	■ Money	■ Procedures	■ Policies
■ Societal changes and events	■ Staff	■ Goals	■ Programs
	Roles played by	■ Structure	■ Information
	■ Party	■ Personal	
	■ Interest groups	■ Experiences and predispositions	**Lead to**
	■ Staff agencies		

Feedback

FIGURE 2.1
Administrative Agencies within the Political System

Figure 2.1 presents a conceptual framework that sees public administration taking the central role or stage in a broader political system (the conversion process in the systems model). The model emphasizes the interrelated nature of the parts and how change in an external environment (cultural, economic, political, social) causes change in the structures and internal processes of public administration. These changes, in turn, influence the outputs of the bureaucracy, that is, what goods, services, policy programs, rules, and regulations are implemented by bureaucracy. As in any system, a feedback loop develops in which the outputs affect the environment, which causes further change and often new demands from the environment to continue, increase or decrease, modify, or occasionally even cease a public policy or program.

The Systems Model, Public Administration, and Transportation Policy

To better understand how the systems model views public administration, consider how the model might apply to a specific line agency. Imagine trying to understand a major metropolitan area's streets department during the 1960s and 1970s. Why did the department build an expansive metropolitan expressway system of highways? This is an enormously costly enterprise. Why did city governments build four-, five-, and six-lane divided highways right through the heart of an already developed city? Why did they tear down existing buildings used for housing and commercial enterprise and replace them with ribbons of concrete and asphalt to move millions of people over dozens of miles right in the midst of a huge urban complex?

The systems model explains the behavior of the city highway bureaucracy by looking first at changes in the agency's environment, such as shifts in the population to the suburbs after World War II that led to a tremendous growth in metropolitan areas. A cultural shift in journey-to-work patterns emerged after the war, when many more people could suddenly own private automobiles. Fuel was readily available and cheap. Postwar changes in the economy led to a shift in industry from heavy to light. In turn, transportation modes shifted goods from railroad to truck.

Politicians responded to the demand for better roads and faster ways to travel from the suburbs to the central city. Politicians love something "concrete" to point out as an accomplishment of their administration, and these ribbons of superhighways fit the bill nicely. Support for urban expressways came in various ways. Tax money from state and national government sources were **earmarked**; that is, law required that money raised from gasoline taxes be spent on road construction or maintenance. Society's attitudes shifted as well. Bigness was seen as progress. The expanding economy generated both money to build the expansive road system as well as the need for roads to transport people and goods. Downtown business associations experienced a postwar downturn and saw the expressway as a means to bring shoppers to the downtown area. Businesses saw expressways as major means to promote expansion, enabling them to move their goods or bring the supplies their factories needed to manufacture new consumer-oriented products. The postwar economy was booming, and there was pent-up demand for consumer goods after years of postponement during World War II and the Korean War. Finally, the American "dream home" became a place in the suburbs, a profound cultural shift. To afford it, though, both parents often had to work. Equally as often, they lived in the suburbs but wanted to travel to and from their city jobs quickly on expressways.

The national postwar government also experienced a change in values. National defense policy emphasized nuclear deterrence through intercontinental ballistic missiles, which were best transported by trucks. Their huge size, however, demanded wider roads, so the interstate highway system was expanded. Before the 1950s, the federal government's rules limited states' use of highway grants to intercity (that is, from city to city) highways. These rules were changed, and this allowed funds to be used to build intracity highways (as metropolitan expressways or beltways). The grants, moreover, became even more attractive to public administrators because they supported expressways with a new funding formula. Before the National Defense Highway Act of 1957 (enacted during the Eisenhower administration), the ratio of federal aid to state aid for the interstate highway construction was 50:50; the new law changed the formula to 90:10—that is, the federal government now picked up 90 percent of the tab. State and local governments together split the remaining 10 percent. City highway departments could now build hugely expensive intraurban metropolitan expressways and someone else would pick up 95 percent of the cost.

With such a funding system, major cities across the nation began to construct their own urban expressways. Highway departments worked with their respective states' departments of roads to link their new urban expressways and beltways to the federal interstate highway system. This meant, however, changing internal procedures in street design and maintenance to conform with the accompanying federal rules and regulations that governed the interstate highway system. That was a small price for having the state and federal governments pick up 95 percent of the extremely expensive construction and maintenance costs.

Developing Value Conflicts

As more and more cities poured more and more concrete and developed bridges, tunnels, overpasses, and loops to control the flow of traffic, and as more motorists used the expressways, they soon became outdated. Increasing traffic flows soon became gridlock. The loss of housing, historic buildings, and green space to ever-expanding roads fueled a new political movement to limit and even oppose such road building. Existing groups also changed their attitudes. Citizen groups directly affected by proposed highway routes began to fight urban highways and fed a new phenomenon—Not in my backyard! (**NIMBY**)—that shifted from opposing new roads in specific locations or routes to opposing such roads altogether. Other people began to promote mass transit instead of superhighways as the best way to move millions of people in and out of the nation's cities. Conservation groups opposed roads to save green space. Citizen tax groups opposed the tremendous expense. Downtown business groups also weighed in against such projects after discovering that expressways promoted flight to the suburbs and to suburban shopping malls as much as they brought customers downtown.

Intergovernmental rivalries developed as well. Local engineers and highway departments resented the rules and regulations imposed from above. Professional ethics also shifted as planners began to see the highway as something other than a ribbon of concrete to move cars from place to place. The loss of green space, the depressing effects of miles of concrete slabs, increases in air and noise pollution along expressway routes—all of these led to changes in the planning goals of local highway departments.

The rules of highway right-of-way acquisition also changed as the locations of businesses along the expressways drastically altered local land values. States changed their policies to require that the route of planned highways be publicly announced and that public hearings be held. Other agencies and the courts entered the fray. The federal Environmental Protection Agency, for example, demanded environmental impact studies. State courts upheld county parks and recreation departments in suits against state highway department plans to use park lands to build roads.

The building of an expressway changed people's living and travel patterns so quickly that almost as soon as a highway was built there were demands to widen or improve it or build some parallel route to ease the resulting gridlock. By the 1980s, demands arose for metropolitan governments to stop building such roads or to replace planned developments with mass transit systems.

In the early 1970s, as member nations of the Organization of Petroleum-Exporting Countries (OPEC) began to escalate the price of gasoline by more than 300 percent in just a few years, support for road building also weakened. Federal laws changed the funding formula of the earmarked gasoline tax, for the first time allowing money from the Highway Trust Fund to support mass transit projects as well as highway construction. The consequences of past highway construction and unanticipated consequences of policy implemented during the highway-boom decades of the 1970s and 1980s led to new demands.

The speed with which change rippled through society, affecting more and more "parts," enhanced the likelihood of unanticipated consequences. Policy planners came to recognize that some unanticipated consequences were implicit in the policy process. Cartoon 2.1 gently notes how the huge bureaucracy of the nation's local school system is slow to keep up with technological change.

CARTOON 2.1

Keeping up with the system

As this cartoon illustrates, the rapid speed of techno-logical change is one reason why school district admin-istrators may fall behind the times. What other system influences account for the gap between the rates of change in our schools and society as a whole?

Source: *Phi Delta Kappan* (October 1990): 123. Reprinted by permission of Harley L. Schwadron.

"I DON'T GET IT. THEY MAKE US LEARN READING, WRITING AND ARITHMETIC to PREPARE US FOR A WORLD OF VIDEOTAPES, COMPUTER TERMINALS AND CALCULATORS."

Figure 2.2 shows the external forces that influence public administrators. Environmental influences affect administrative agencies that develop and implement public policy. Social changes such as the public dissatisfaction with highways generate value conflicts within the bureaucracy as public administrators try to keep up with such social change.

Social Change and Value Conflict in Administration

Social values regularly undergo change. As values shift in society at large, they present value-conflict problems for public administrators. Two additional major shifts in social values—over abortion and affirmative action—are now presented to illustrate the point more fully.

Abortion

Reflecting decisions by the U.S. Supreme Court, American society in the late 1960s and early 1970s dramatically altered its view of the legality of abortion. In two critical cases, the Court tried to strike a balance between two central values: the right to privacy and the right of society to control the medical practice of abortion to protect the life of an unborn fetus. In *Griswold* v. *Connecticut* (381 U.S. 479, 1965) the Court found a constitutionally protected right to privacy with respect to family planning practices (for example, access to birth control pills or devices). Then in *Roe* v. *Wade* (410 U.S. 113, 1973), the Court held that a woman's right to privacy extends to a constitutionally protected right to abortion during the first trimester of pregnancy. By the mid- to late 1970s, the number of abortions had risen dramatically. Many state laws required county health agencies to provide abortion services for certain population groups—those incarcerated in penal facilities and those deemed incompetent to make their own medical decisions.

By the late 1980s and early 1990s, abortions were so pervasive that the feedback process galvanized the right-to-life social movement to new action. This movement advocated increasingly restrictive measures on abortions to protect the life of the

INFOTRAC
COLLEGE EDITION

Economics of prevention

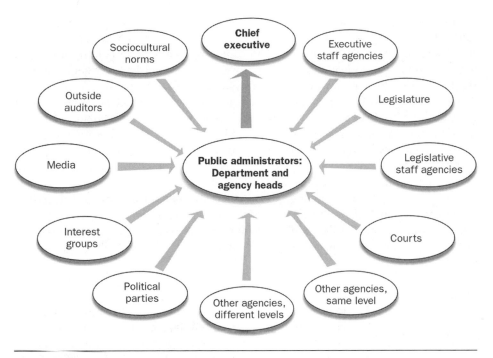

FIGURE 2.2
External Influences on Public Administrators

fetus. Its members pressed moral and ethical issues that put physicians into a fundamental dilemma. Public hospitals' ethics committees had to deal most directly with this dilemma. On the one hand, for instance, doctors were county employees sworn to uphold the law and legally obligated to provide state-mandated abortion services. On the other hand, states began passing so-called **conscientious objection** laws that allowed doctors to refuse to perform procedures to which they had fundamental moral objections. This raised problems for public hospital administrators who could no longer find adequate numbers of physicians willing to cover elective abortions. In some counties, even those qualified to perform unassisted second-trimester abortions were not willing to do so. Entire obstetrics and gynecology departments approached their hospitals' ethics committees asking to be relieved of the burden of providing abortions. Public hospitals could no longer fulfill their legal duty to provide state-mandated abortion services. County hospitals in rural areas with state prisons often had no other option than to transport pregnant inmates to hospitals in major metropolitan areas. That option could be prohibitively expensive when the need for such transportation included prison guards as well as medical personnel. Such a dilemma put county hospitals and county governments squarely between a rock and a hard place. In the 1990s, the demand for abortion remained fairly constant, but fewer and fewer physicians were willing to perform them. One study found that 83 percent of U.S. counties had no abortion providers.[2]

The abortion service dilemma illustrates the conflict between individual rights and community needs. There is an inherent conflict between the right of the individual doctor to avoid participating in an activity he or she finds morally objectionable or personally dangerous, on the one hand, and the right of the community to have a legal medical service made available on the other. Similar dilemmas exist with respect to such issues as the right to die and living-will statutes, the provision of care to Medicaid patients with highly dangerous contagious diseases such as AIDS, and the use of physicians to provide lethal injections in capital punishment, although these latter issues involve less explicit and direct conflicts between physicians' rights, patients' rights, and socially mandated needs and physicians' obligations.

Some members of the right-to-life movement used radical tactics, moreover, that increased the threat to physicians' personal safety and led to harassment and intimidation, including anonymous calls and mailings and picketing at work and home. Several doctors were murdered in sniper attacks, and several abortion clinics were bombed. These developments raised the stakes and increased greatly the number of doctors who simply refused to perform abortions.

The abortion dilemma is sharpened when the late-term abortion procedure known as a **partial-birth abortion** is considered. Dr. C. Everett Koop, former U.S. Surgeon General, raised the conflicting moral value issues at stake in the partial-birth controversy when he publicly advocated that partial-birth abortions should not be legal.[3]

Affirmative Action

As was alluded to in the opening section of this chapter, value conflicts in public administration are likewise evident in programs associated with affirmative action. Implementation procedures for affirmative action programs gradually led to their being viewed as "quota" programs and thus as reverse discrimination.

Defending diversity

The battle over affirmative action can be traced as far back as 1941, when then-President Franklin Roosevelt issued an executive order that barred discrimination based on race or national origin in all industries that had federal contracts. The principal architect of affirmative action, however, was President Lyndon Johnson, who pushed through Congress the sweeping Civil Rights Act of 1964, which prohibits all forms of discrimination in public- and private-sector hiring. The law expanded coverage from Roosevelt's executive order to include African Americans, Asian Americans, Hispanic Americans, and native Americans. In 1965, President Johnson also issued Executive Order 11246, directing all companies with federal contracts to take "affirmative action" to provide equal opportunity in employment (both hiring and promotion). The order covered several hundred thousand government contractors who collectively employed some 26 million workers, roughly one-fourth of the nation's labor force.[4] Women were extended coverage in 1967. Congress followed President Johnson's executive order with the Age Discrimination and Employment Act and, in 1972, with the Equal Employment Opportunity Act. By it, Congress provided a statutory basis for affirmative action programs, prohibiting discrimination based on race, religion, sex, or national origin. The resulting legislation covers more than 2 million federal employees and roughly 15 million state and local employees. Congress established the Equal Employment Opportunity Commission to implement the law and oversee compliance.

Disregarding intent

Congress amended the Age Discrimination and Employment Act in 1974, 1978, and 1986. Congress began minority **set-aside programs** that required federal, state, and local governments to reserve a percentage of their business contracts for minority-owned businesses when it amended the Public Works Employment Act in 1977. The law was upheld as constitutional in *Fullilove* v. *Klutznick* (1979). Set-aside programs are implemented by the Small Business Administration.

PHOTO 2.1
Former Supreme Court Justice Thurgood Marshall
A giant of the civil rights movement, Thurgood Marshall rose from the lawyer arguing Brown v. Board of Education, *1954 before the Court to become a justice of the Court. Do you agree with affirmative action approaches, or do you believe they involve reverse discrimination? In terms of administering policy, how do judges like Marshall promote their position? Who does the change in policy hurt? What value is diminished as a result?*
Source: Courtesy of the Library of Congress.

In 1990, Congress passed the Americans with Disabilities Act, which included provisions that prohibit discrimination against the disabled in employment and accommodations. Its broad definition of those who are disabled covers some 36 million Americans, making it one of the most sweeping antidiscrimination laws since the 1964 Civil Rights Act. These equal opportunity employment laws were administered with some success. Federal, state, and local governments hired many more minorities, as did the private sector, although to a lesser degree. Table 2.1 presents changes in employment by race and national origin from 1990 to 2002.

Affirmative action program successes, however, did not come without consequences. An increasingly diverse workforce meant increased tensions in the workplace. Such tensions, not only between black and white workers but also among women and men, Asians, Hispanics, and gays, are partly the result of affirmative action programs' increasing ethnic diversity in the workplace.

The very success of affirmative action programs, often exaggerated in the general society's perceptions, led to a backlash against such programs and the accusation that they constituted reverse discrimination. These feedback effects are seen in various ways. Several notable Supreme Court decisions narrowed and increasingly attacked the use of quotas.[5] Popular public opinion against affirmative action increased and resulted in a political movement to end such programs via the initiative process; the most notable action was California's aforementioned passage of Proposition 209 in 1996.

TABLE 2.1

Employees by Gender and Race, 1990–2002

		Total Workforce		Federal Employees	
		1990	**2002**	**1990**	**2002**
Gender	Male (%)	56.5	53.4	57	55
	Female (%)	43.7	46.5	43	45
Race	White (%)	72.7	67.0	72.7	69.2
	Minority (%)	28	33.6	28	30.8

Source: Table by author. Data from *Statistical abstract of the United States, 2003*, Tables 501, 591.

INFOTRAC
COLLEGE EDITION

Electoral connections

The Development of the Political Party System

Political party organizations have long played an important role in American politics and are an important source of values in public administration. A **political party** may be defined as any group of politically active persons outside of government who organize to capture government by nominating and electing officials who thereby control the operations of government and determine its policies. As such, parties are **linkage institutions**—that is, agencies that forge links between citizens and policy makers.[6] They operate at all levels of government and perform multiple functions.

1. They recruit, support, and help elect candidates to office.
2. They organize and help run elections.
3. They articulate alternative policies.
4. They help organize, move, or affect the agenda of government.
5. They are responsible for the operation of government.
6. They serve as the loyal opposition to the government in power.

The political **party in government** comprises all persons from the party who won election and hold public office—presidents, governors, and other statewide-elected executive officials, members of Congress and the state legislatures, and many judges at the state and local levels who are elected by partisan ballot. The party helps organize the government's agenda by convincing its own members to support and vote for the policy alternatives it advocates. For the political party to transform its promises into policy, the party in government needs to do its job. The **party platform** is a document drawn up by the party at its state or national conventions that proposes the party's policies and positions (*planks* in the platform) on current public problems or policy issues.

The party in government becomes a major method for coordinating policy making among the various branches and levels of government. The party serves as the major institution through which the executive and legislative branches cooperate with each other. The parties also play an important role in accomplishing the peaceful transfer of power from one government to the next. Their struggle for power becomes a means through which value conflict enters government and the policy implementation process. They are instrumental in setting the agenda of government that develops into the policy and programs to be implemented by the bureaucracy.

No longer used as often as earlier in our history, political parties nonetheless employ **patronage**, or the system of rewarding party faithful with appointment to government jobs or awarding government contracts. Patronage was used most extensively by urban political machines to run city governments from the 1860s to the turn of the 20th century. Widespread political corruption, however, including the sale of public offices and contracts and raids on city treasuries, was associated with the machines and led to Progressive demands for political reform. In recent years, the Supreme Court has grappled with the appropriate role of patronage in the political system.[7]

The major political parties became dominant by forging broad-based coalitions of groups and social programs. They espoused a political **ideology**, a set of comprehensive and logically ordered set of beliefs about human nature and the role of government and how its institutions should be organized and managed. Political reform movements that advocate a major change in societal values and the agenda of government and how it should be managed often come about through the advocacy of minor-party, or so-called third-party, movements.

The Role of Third Parties as Value Sources

Third parties are often barometers of change in the nation's political mood. They offer a voice to voters frustrated with and alienated from the positions of the major parties.[8] Third parties (which are simply minor parties and may actually be a fourth, fifth, or sixth party) have emerged historically by advocating some major shift in political values. They serve as something like a safety valve for political dissent. Their goal is to form a dominant party. The Republican Party emerged in 1860, displacing the Whig Party as one of the two major parties. It arose because of its position on the issue of slavery and the national political union. The party went on to emphasize economic development and modernization, becoming the dominant political party and capturing all but four presidential elections between 1860 and 1932.

Minor parties that have endured for any length of time have been founded on strong ideological bases that are at odds with the majority society. Notable minor parties in U.S. history include Socialist Labor (founded in 1877), Socialist (1901), Communist (1919), Socialist Workers (1938), Libertarian (1972), and Reform (1996). Among ideological minor parties, the Socialist was the most important for its impact on public administration. Led by Eugene Debs from 1901 through the 1930s, the Socialist Party was antiwar and strongly opposed U.S. entry into World War I. It was militantly pro-union, advocating what were then considered radical ideas such as the 40-hour work week, the 8-hour day, child and women's labor laws, and increased regulation of business.

Another type of minor, or third, party is the splinter party, or **spin-off party**. The most important such spin-off party in U.S. history was the Progressive Party (early 1900s to 1930s) because of its effects on bureaucracy and the organization of public administration. The Progressive Party developed from a major schism in the Republican Party between loyalists and Bull Moose Progressives in 1912. It advocated extensive electoral reforms, including the short ballot, the primary election, expanded voter registration, and split-ticket voting. The Progressive Party movement stressed government efficiency and "neutrally competent" public administration. It advocated replacing the patronage system with a **merit system**, in which public employees are selected, retained, and promoted on the basis of competitive examinations or formal educational credentials. One of its most important public administration reforms was the establishment of the *civil service system*, in which public employees are selected and managed through the merit system. Among the most significant Progressive Party reforms were controls on monopoly, regulation of many businesses in a variety of ways, the use of the sealed bids in the awarding of government contracts, and the development of the independent regulatory agency structure.

Today's minor, or third, parties tend to be ideological, often coalescing around a single issue, candidate (e.g., H. Ross Perot, Ralph Nader), or value. They usually advocate a more "pure" ideological stance than does either of the major parties. In the 2004 presidential election, for example, a dozen such political parties ran presidential campaigns and fielded candidates for the presidency and for many state and local offices.[9]

Minor parties often do not expect to win office. They run to influence the electorate and bring about a shift in attitudes and opinions, even in society's major core values. Ralph Nader's Green Party, for example, emphasizes policy issues concerning environmental regulation. He also opposed the war in Iraq and advocated an immediate pullout. Ross Perot and his Reform Party followers created so much concern over the federal budget deficit that a "balanced budget" became a central position for both the Democratic and Republican parties throughout the 1990s. Minor political parties affect bureaucracy indirectly by shifting public opinion about attitudes and values or by popularizing structural reforms that influence the way administrative agencies operate. They also influence the agenda of government through their role in highlighting certain problems as worthy of public policy attention. They sometimes participate in developing the policy alternatives seriously considered for adoption. Third parties influence public administration in much the same manner as do organized interest groups, the topic to which we next turn our attention.

INFOTRAC
COLLEGE EDITION

Who wins? Campaigns and the third-party vote

Interest Groups and Values in Public Administration

The United States is extraordinarily diverse, a pluralistic society that has long recognized the need for and significance of interest group affiliations. We are truly a nation of joiners. Thousands of groups seek to influence the administration of public policy and do so in a variety of ways. Interest groups can be categorized by the reasons why they form: economics, ethnicity, ideology, and so on. Interest groups affect the policy process at all stages. They advocate issues to get them on the agenda of government; lobby the executive and legislatures to get preferred policy options adopted or to stop those alternatives they oppose; influence bureaucratic agency implementation; and help to determine the evaluation of policy.

As public administrators increased their role in policy making, interest group lobbying became more common in the executive branch. Today, government administrators interact with literally thousands of interest group representatives. Administrative agencies often formalize their relationship with such groups by establishing "advisory committees." Federal departments and agencies have more than 1,000 advisory committees with more than 22,000 members. Annually they hold nearly 4,000 meetings and issue almost 1,000 reports.[10] The Federal Advisory Committee Act of 1972 made legal interest group lobbying for their own policy alternatives. Bureaucratic agencies work with interest groups not only through such committees, but also by often going to them to seek advice, data, and reaction to proposed laws, rules, regulations, and procedures. The agencies often craft standards based heavily on relevant interest group comment and advice. Interest groups also interact with administrators outside of formal committees. They work with legislatures by revising draft policy proposals, and they influence appointments to key political executive positions in administrative agencies.

The study of interest groups and public administration has been influenced by three group theorists: Arthur Bentley, David Truman, and Earl Latham. Bentley's *The Process of Government* (1908) advocated a shift in political analysis away from the forms of government to the actions of groups, which he maintained are the critical action mechanisms that enable large numbers of people to achieve their political, economic, and social goals. David Truman wrote *The Governmental Process* in 1951 and defined interest groups in an analytical way, noting how group pressure developed lines of access and influence and how the administrative process provides many points of access. He emphasized how groups interact, function, and affect the entire political system. Earl Latham's *The Group Basis of Politics* (1952) conceptualizes government as a reflection of the various private groups that attempt to influence it. Government becomes a sort of referee of group conflict, and public policy becomes the "score" of that competition. Latham also analyzes what makes group coalitions successful. He views regulatory agencies especially as being deluged by interest group coalitions who seek to change rules, regulations, and procedures. He develops a typology of groups based on their phase of development: incipient, conscious, and organized groups.

Relationships between Regulators and the Regulated

Often the interactions between and among interest groups, the legislative body that makes policy, and the specialized agencies that implement that policy area can form such close and long-term working relations that they develop into a kind of subgovernment known as an **iron triangle**. This triangle is formed by the three angles of the policy process for a particular policy area: (1) the bureaucrats who implement a policy, (2) the lawmakers and their staff members who craft and adopt a policy, and (3) the lobbyists from a vested or "clientele" coalition of interest groups, all of them working formally and informally on specific policy issues.

Figure 2.3 presents examples of the iron triangle concept with a specific **clientele agency**—that is, a bureaucratic agency that serves, protects, or promotes the interests of those it was established to oversee, often at the expense of the public interest rather than the organized special interest groups' interests. Figure 2.3 shows such iron triangle formations at the national, state, and local levels.

When interest groups are regulated by an agency, they often seek to *capture* the agency, or gain direct or indirect influence over a specific agency's personnel and decision makers. **Captive agencies** become clientele agencies, often serving more to promote than to regulate the industry they were created to oversee.

Even when the ongoing influence of interest groups is less developed and not formalized into an iron triangle type of arrangement, interest groups may be involved in **issue networks**. These temporary collections of lobbyists, lawmakers,

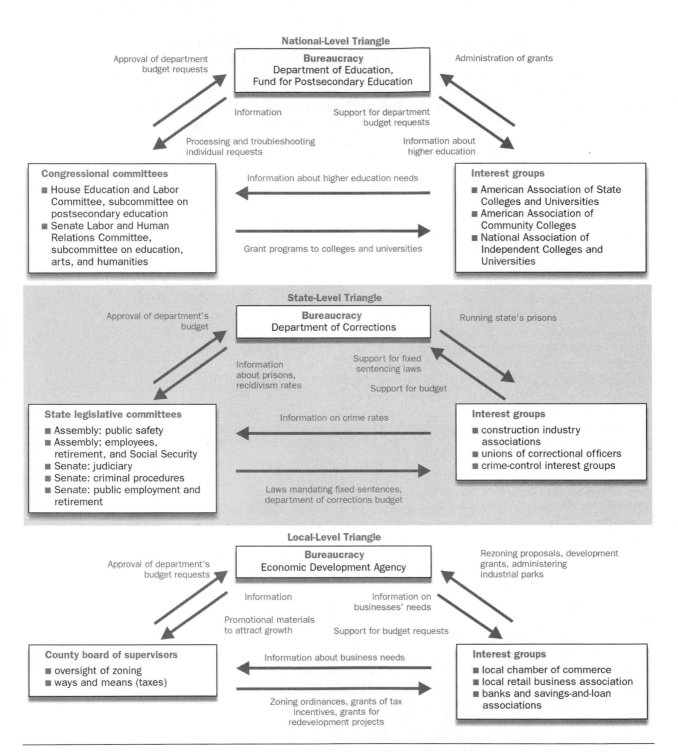

FIGURE 2.3
Iron Triangles and Clientele Agencies

bureaucrats, and experts work together to shape a particular policy. Interest groups further influence the policy-making process by forming political action committees (PACs). These networks serve as electioneering arms of interest groups and channel enormous amounts of campaign funds into executive and legislative races in order to curry influence with policy makers, ensure access to them, and thereby insert the interest groups' values into policy administration.

Interest groups can sometimes develop veto-like power over executive agency appointments. The leadership of such agencies, especially independent regulatory agencies, often comes from the industry being regulated or served, and such appointees and career civil servants often return to employment in those industries after their time in governmental service. These patterns have raised political concern that bureaucrats become unduly influenced by the very industries they were established to oversee. Such individuals have the necessary expertise to understand and better control decision making for a policy area, but they may become biased toward or collude with the industry. Federal laws have attempted to close this "revolving door" between federal administrative appointees and corporate executives.

Interest groups also conduct **grassroots lobbying** of their own members and the general public by using mass mailings, phone banks, faxes, e-mail campaigns, talk radio call-in campaigns, and the like to marshal public opinion toward their position on a policy issue. The National Rifle Association, the AARP, and the Moral Majority and similar religious right groups have been especially active and successful in using grassroots lobbying techniques. (See Reading 2.1 at the end of this chapter regarding the tobacco industry's efforts to counter ordinances prohibiting smoking in bars.)

Interest groups also influence public administration through court actions. They support test cases to challenge laws and administrative rules and procedures. They file *amicus curiae* (friend of the court) briefs in cases about which they have an interest. Recent court decisions involving environmental protection, abortion, affirmative action, and physical disability rights have been notably influenced by interest groups.

Interest groups become important players as well in shaping economic policy. It is to the economic context of public administration that we now turn.

INFOTRAC
COLLEGE EDITION

Grassroots gusto

The Economic Context of Public Administration

The economy affects the administration of public policy in myriad ways. It generates problems that policy needs to address, determines the level of financial resources potentially available to public administrators, shapes the demands placed on government for the goods and services provided, and often sets the parameters of what possible solutions will be adopted to meet those demands. In times of economic expansion, the economy offers top-level administrators the ideal opportunity to expand their operations and services. During recession, it compels governmental agencies to defend their agencies against strong demands for deep cutbacks in personnel, programs, and services.

Changes in the nature of the economy in which a bureaucratic agency operates may immediately affect it. Consider two examples. In the 1950s, the sleepy southern town of Orlando, Florida, was basically a small urban center serving a largely rural, agricultural economy. Then the Disney Corporation bought land and developed Disney World, which went on to become the leading tourist attraction in the world.

Suddenly, great demands were placed on Orlando's city government. It had to greatly expand its police, fire, health, and inspection efforts. The inspection of restaurants, for example, grew dramatically as the area experienced a virtual explosion in the number of hotels, motels, and restaurants of all types. Financing changed as the local entertainment tax grew to exceed property taxes as a source of revenue. Road construction and maintenance changed drastically as millions of tourists poured into the region. Solid-waste collection, removal, and recycling were revolutionized in size, scope, and nature of operation. Police, fire, and education bureaucracies ballooned in size and changed how their service delivery responded to the explosion in the population being served. The airport expanded in both size and the scope of its services. Indeed, the entire local government structure evolved considerably in response to Disney World.

Conversely, an industry leaving an area can devastate a local government and its bureaucracy. Numerous New England towns, for example, many with local economies based on a single large industrial concern (so-called one-company towns), virtually died when the entire milled fabric and textile industry moved to the South. Every government operation was drastically cut back as a result. Currently, the globalization of the U.S. economy and the recent trend of "outsourcing" jobs to countries, such as Korea, China, and India, where labor is much cheaper has led to the economic "death throes" of many smaller communities that were also essentially "one-company towns." When the local economy is overly dependent on a single source as employer and that company moves or closes down, then every agency of the local bureaucracy suffers as well.

Industrialization and Changing Economic Values

Governmental bureaucracy changed markedly with industrialization. There was little regulation of business before industrialization. The development and rapid expansion of industry, however, created air and water pollution that soon required national, state, and local agencies to protect the environment. Industry also needed to be regulated to protect the health and safety of its employees as well as the safety of consumers from industries' products. The development of huge national and even international industrial complexes led to the development of a vast array of national independent regulatory agencies to control these industries when their power and scope exceeded state governments' abilities to regulate them through their laws of incorporation.

As national industries shifted from heavy to light, demands also shifted from government programs that subsidized railroads through benefits such as land grants to programs that supported the growing trucking and airline industries. This trend necessitated new agencies and new rules, regulations, and procedures by existing agencies. The industries themselves also changed in response to the competition, including that from government corporations. Amtrak, for example, has had to respond to change in values as passengers increasingly use airlines and autos rather than railroads. To compete, Amtrak has stressed service. In June 1999, for example, Amtrak officials announced a service pledge that would give dissatisfied customers refund vouchers good for future travel. Amtrak has also initiated a variety of service improvements, including training and incentives for its 24,000 employees, enhanced food-service options, and improved onboard amenities. In 1998, more than 21 million passengers used Amtrak, and the government corporation posted its best on-time performance in 13 years.[11]

Governmental agencies are often instrumental in developing policy that revitalizes and uses older industrial facilities as a local economy changes. Consider, for example, Pennsylvania's land-recycling program, which addresses a problem common to many aging factory towns. Thousands of commercial sites sit vacant because developers know the sites were polluted by their former occupants. Investors and bankers build new facilities in the suburbs rather than run the risk that regulators will force them to cover the cost of removing all traces of contamination. In 1995, Pennsylvania sought to bring such sites into productive use. Three related land-recycling laws lifted a prior state requirement that every site be restored to pristine condition. Now developers could choose from among three options: (1) restoring their properties to pristine levels, (2) meeting statewide standards for acceptable chemical concentrations, or (3) substituting criteria developed for a specific site based on its future use. By using one of these three standards, landowners and lenders are released from future liability for further cleanup action. In the first two years of the land-recycling program, more than 100 sites were recovered and the cleanup process for another 150 sites was begun.[12]

Economic shifts often dramatically alter the level and degree of support of government bureaucracies. As property taxes skyrocketed in California during its economic boom period of the 1970s when its population soared, a taxpayer revolt followed. In June 1978, California voters enacted Proposition 13, which set a cap on property taxes. A host of local government agencies, from cities to school boards, were draconian in cutting back on personnel and services when property tax revenues plummeted. The tax revolt's effects have altered local governmental finances ever since.

The U.S. economy is the largest and most robust in the world. The nation, however, has a highly porous 2,000-mile border with Mexico, among the poorest of the world's developing countries. That economic fact of life contributes to the enormous attraction of the U.S. economy, and it annually attracts more than 1 million legal and undocumented immigrants. These immigrants produce profound shifts in government operations. This ongoing population shift helps to promote **multiculturalism**, or the belief that the many cultures that make up the U.S. population—more than 160 national origin groups, each with more than 10,000 members, for example—ought to be maintained as distinct cultures and that laws should protect and even encourage their distinctiveness. This trend toward cultural diversity has generated demands for bilingual education programs, for example, which itself has engendered a backlash, the "English-only" social movement. These conflicting value issues have significant effects on local bureaucratic agencies across the spectrum of services—from education to health to police and prisons to welfare agencies.

The cyclical expansion and contraction of the economy results in corresponding problems of inflation and recession or depression. These lead to demands that government cope with these economic trends. In times of excessive, say, double-digit inflation, citizens might call on government to control or reduce the inflation rate. In response, government imposes various fiscal or monetary policies, from reducing government spending (thereby increasing unemployment levels and "cooling off" the economy) to raising taxes (to lower overall demand), raising interest rates, and encouraging savings by offering higher returns on government bonds. During periods of recession, the government is expected to "prime the pump." It may lower taxes, lower interest rates, use deficit spending to boost employment, or use variations

INFOTRAC
COLLEGE EDITION

Schoolyard revolutions

on any or all of these strategies. Today, citizens expect the national government to manage the economy and to lower inflationary hills and flatten out and shorten the duration of recessionary valleys.

Value Shifts and Technology Changes in the Postindustrial Era

Technological development is a major source of change in the economy, resulting in changes in societal values and value conflict in public administration. Changes in technology, from the computer to telecommunications, for instance, have had profound ripple effects. The 1980s marked the development of the United States as a postindustrial economy, or one based more on information and communication than manufacturing.

The notion that the federal government could "manage" an economy as vast and complex as is that of the United States could only have been considered seriously after the development of the computer. The War Department during World War II was central to development of the computer. Private-sector research and development, of course, proved essential to expanding the computer and its myriad applications, especially the development of hardware and software to enable popular use of the personal computer (PC). Development of the PC has had revolutionary effects on the behavior of governmental bureaucracies. It changed dramatically the nature of the government's workforce at all levels. Virtually every agency at every level of government now employs people who understand and use PCs on a daily basis.

Data manipulation by government also changed profoundly. Suddenly, an agency could acquire and manipulate vast amounts of information. Through such agencies as the Bureau of the Census in the Department of Commerce, business developed an insatiable need for government-produced and -analyzed data. The enormous volumes of data required faster and more complex data processing. National databases were developed and used for a variety of policy areas, from government promotion of business, to police control of crime and welfare agencies tracking down "deadbeat dads," to the vast interlinkings of the nation's rail, airline, telephone, and electric power systems. Sometimes, however, such expectations outstripped the government's capability to manage the new technology. California's efforts to create a statewide automated child support system finally crashed after several years of effort and nearly $50 million in costs.

The corresponding development of the telecommunication system, with satellite-based technology that only the national government of the United States could have developed, transformed the United States from an industrial economy to a postindustrial, global information economy. Government policy was essential to develop the global Internet. But development of the Internet changed not only the way business did business, but also how government did business, and it birthed a host of unanticipated consequences. Soon, for example, access to pornography on the Internet led to demands that governmental agencies police the World Wide Web. Sometimes the development of technology outpaces society's ability to manage it well. Proposals to fix technology problems by means of technology itself can be frustrated by a generational gap in knowledge and understanding. The proposal to police the web by using blocking software might be frustrated by societal culture and generation gaps—by parents depending on their children to install the new technology on the home computer. Simple

INFOTRAC
COLLEGE EDITION

**Value orientations:
A study of black college
students**

PHOTO 2.2
Chairman Alan Greenspan of the Federal Reserve Board
Greenspan exercises enormous influence over the economy and the stock market. What political difficulties does his influence pose for a presidential administration? When the Fed raises interest rates to cool off an economy or to ward off anticipated inflationary pressures, who in society most benefits? Who is most hurt by this change in value priority?
Source: AP/Wide World Photos.

solutions—parents unplugging a TV set to block objectionable programs—might be better for some societal problems than some elaborate set of government standards to censor the nation's airwaves.

The Ecological and Environmental Context

Another important source of values and value conflict that influences public administration in the United States comes from the physical environment: the forces that drive the natural world. **Ecology**, that subfield of biology that studies the relationship of people and all living things to their natural environment, has in recent years emphasized the concept of the **ecosystem**, which may be rather simply defined as any group of plants, animals, and nonliving things interacting within their environment.[13]

In 1971, Barry Commoner identified these four laws of ecology:

1. Everything is connected to everything else. This means it is exceedingly difficult to change one aspect of any ecosystem without unintentionally affecting some other aspect of it.

2. Everything must go somewhere. Earth is a closed unit, like a spaceship. Things we burn come back to our rivers and lakes as acid rain or contribute to the greenhouse effect as global warming.

3. Nature knows best. When humans tinker with natural systems, it almost always proves detrimental to those systems.

4. There is no such thing as a free lunch. Any interaction with nature carries some cost.[14]

Environmental Concerns and Value Conflicts in Public Administration

Environmental problems and public policies that are designed to address them are influenced by the dominant **political culture**—the cluster of attitudes, beliefs, ideologies, and values that shape our thinking about society, government, and the role of individuals within them. The dominant political culture includes many beliefs and values, but for our purposes here it emphasizes acceptance of laissez-faire capitalism in the economic system, individualism, the belief in growth as progress, and a strong faith in science and technology. The dominant political culture shaped the development of environmental policy, the public's attitudes toward the environment, and the use of governmental regulation to "manage" the environment.

Environmental policy making has evolved through seven stages: (1) a period of dominance, (2) early awakening, (3) early conservationist, (4) later conservationist, (5) a reawakening, (6) complacency, and (7) the little Reagan revolution.[15]

By the late 1960s, concern over environmental issues caught the national attention of both the public and policy makers. In 1969, a sailor threw a cigarette into the Cuyahoga River in Cleveland, and the river burst into flames! That year a huge oil spill off the coast of central California also heightened public awareness. Policy makers soon turned their attention to environmental issues, and economists began to consider the costs of **externalities**—that is, the positive or negative effects that entail costs. When humans burn fossil fuels in an unregulated manufacturing process, it produces air and water pollution. These pollutions involve real costs to society by contributing to respiratory illness and damage to fish, wildlife, and even crops through acid rain. A flaw in the economic market system is that all too often the costs of negative externalities are not borne by their producers but are passed on to society to deal with.

Concern over the environment leveled off somewhat in the late 1970s and early 1980s. The little Reagan revolution ushered in a decade in which the administration promised to "get regulators off our backs." Within a year of his election, however, concern over a perceived antienvironmentalism ethic led to something of a public backlash. After a slight rollback in standards, enforcement, and spending, a new environmentalism developed.[16] Federal spending on environmental matters rose again in the mid-1980s and throughout the 1990s.

Starting in the mid-1980s, then, many environmental issues emerged or were taken up again on the agendas of national, state, and local governments: air and water pollution, the negative environmental externalities of energy policy, the problems of dealing with toxic and hazardous waste, and environmentally sensitive land-management issues emerged in national decision making. The 1990s also witnessed a growing movement to approach the problems of the environment globally as a sense of international crisis deepened and became more pervasive. Global overpopulation and worldwide food production and distribution issues were linked to concern over environmental policy. Much of the so-called developing world faces growing populations, deteriorating resource bases, and profoundly unhealthy environments. The World Resources Institute estimated that $20 billion to $50 billion per

INFOTRAC
COLLEGE EDITION

**Superfund: The
ascendancy of enabling
myths**

year will be needed to save the environment in the developing world—but the budget of the United Nations' environment program is less than $30 million a year. What is lacking is the will, the incentive, and an institutional framework to develop and implement environmental policy making on a global scale.[17]

This chapter closes with Reading 2.1, "Bar Wars." In the 1990s a campaign to ban smoking in public places developed that gradually used local ordinances and local public health bureaucracies increasingly to achieve its aim. Reading 2.1 describes a somewhat different sort of "iron triangle," this one of a coalition of interests attempting to thwart or get around the consequences of the "smoking-ban" policy efforts. It shows how political actors in the environment of public bureaucracies can rapidly change their tactics in response to public policy and do so in ways that such local officials, in this case health officials, are often slow to respond to in coping with a changing environment.

Reading 2.1

Bar Wars

Since the mid-1990s there has been an increasing level of public support for restrictions on smoking in public venues. Yet exceptions are often made for bars. The usual arguments against smoking bans—for instance, fears of decreased profits, the rights of business owners to choose whether to permit smoking, the rights of individuals to smoke—apply equally to bars as to restaurants. Yet bars are often exempt where restaurants, for example, are not.

Various research studies have shown that the tobacco industry has increased its use of bars and clubs as promotional venues. Smoking bans in bars deprive cigarette makers of critical marketing tools at a time when they are legally blocked from using most forms of mass marketing. There are economic incentives for bars and nightclubs, but not restaurants, to continue this relationship.

The tobacco industry often works with the alternative press to reach young adults who frequent these establishments. Smoking restrictions encourage people to quit or at least to reduce their consumption. As such, local public health ordinances are viewed as a serious threat to the profit margins of tobacco companies, drinking establishments, and alternative publications.

Documents that had been secret from RJ Reynolds describe the industry's strategy to use alternative publications to manipulate the preferences and behavior of American youth. This involves a new marketing ploy referred to as *trend influence marketing* (TIM). TIM abandons standard advertising campaigns and jumps directly into the arena of trying to "become the trend maker." This new strategy speaks directly to the continued deception associated with the tobacco industry. By the early 1990s tobacco industry executives came under intense pressure from antismoking advocacy groups. Education efforts increased awareness among consumers about the dangers of smoking and about the illusions in traditional tobacco product advertising. Faced with declining sales, the industry searched for a new approach. The key element in TIM is to conduct an aggressive promotion covertly. To succeed, the marketing company will appear almost invisible.

In RJR internal papers, executives emphasized that to reach the "cool trend setters," they must "dress their dress and walk their walk." The original RJR strategy was entitled "Camel Club." Its marketing company recruited field marketing staff from the "inside": people who worked in and around the nightclub/bar business and trendy community.

TIM efforts were reinforced by savvy, localized alternative media campaigns. These media vehicles were a critical part of the network to help spread trends. They used free periodicals distributed at most trendy nightclubs and in the stores and coffeehouses that the club crowd frequented. Aligning Camel with certain publications by way of advertising in this "free media" lent immediate hip credibility to the brand.

Most U.S. cities have such alternative publications. These tabloid-type newspapers are generally free to the public and published on a weekly basis. Many young people under 18 read the weekly editions, available at restaurants, grocery stores, college campuses, select retailers, and various downtown locations. Typically, coverage in them includes politics, humor, film, opinion, music, art and entertainment.

There are frequently numerous TIM advertisements per issue. The alternative publications have become the home base for modern tobacco marketing. Although the health community bureaucracy has succeeded in blocking Big Tobacco's encroachment into traditional markets, they are falling behind the collaborative efforts between the tobacco industry, bar and nightclub owners, and the alternative press.

TIM promotion represents an aggressive form of tobacco marketing. The "iron triangle" formed by the tobacco industry, the bar and nightclub lobby, and the alternative press forms a powerful political alliance. So far, TIM has largely escaped the attention of and regulation by local public health officials promoting an antismoking policy.

Source: Based on excerpts from Scott Goold, USA: The battle for the bars, *Tobacco Control*, *12*(3) (March 2003): 6–8. Reprinted with permission.

Net Assignment

Using InfoTrac, Internet search engines, and some of the sites listed at the end of this chapter, find information about other public-supported institutions in your local area—hospitals, police forces, and so on. Describe how they are handling, or not handling, the goal of diversity.

Summary

By viewing a conceptual framework of the political system, we can understand the sources of values—and their conflicts—inherent in the administration of public policy. Conflicts between and among values are inevitable within public administration, especially in the midst of social change.

Values and their conflicts arise out of three main sources in society:

1. The political context of political parties and interest groups and their timely representation of society's conflicting viewpoints provide vital links between society and public policy.

2. The economy—specifically the shift from an agricultural to an industrial to a postindustrial society—has affected policy making. Now in a global information age, the development of the personal computer and the World Wide Web triggers conflict over which values best determine how society will manage telecommunication technology.

3. The ecological or physical environment reveals the conflict implicit in managing the economy as well as an interrelated and increasingly global ecosystem.

Glossary of Key Terms

affirmative action The removal of artificial barriers to employment of women and minority groups; compensatory plans for previously disadvantaged groups, as in specific programs to recruit, hire, and promote qualified members of designated disadvantaged groups so as to eliminate the continuing effects of prior discrimination.

captive agency An agency whose personnel and decision makers are directly or indirectly influenced by outside interest groups from the very industry the agency is required to regulate or serve.

clientele agency A bureaucratic agency that serves, protects, or promotes the interests of those it was established to oversee, often at the expense of the general public rather than organized special interest groups.

conscientious objection State laws that allow doctors to refuse to perform a procedure to which they have fundamental moral objection (e.g., abortions).

earmarked Funds or tax revenues from a given source that legally must be spent for a given program or service. For example, gasoline taxes must be spent on highway construction or maintenance.

ecology The study of the relationship of living things to their natural environment.

ecosystem Any collection of plants, animals, and nonliving things that interact with one another within their environment.

externalities Positive or negative effects of one thing that entail costs to another.

grassroots lobbying A type or method of lobbying in which an interest group uses its own rank-and-file membership to send mass mailings, work phone banks, send mass e-mails, phone talk-radio shows, and walk the halls of the legislature to marshal public opinion and government policy toward its position on an issue.

ideology   A comprehensive and logical set of beliefs about human nature and the role of government and how its institutions should be organized and managed.

iron triangle   A type of subgovernment; refers to the three angles of the policy process for a particular policy area—(1) the bureaucrats who implement a policy, (2) the lawmakers and staff members who adopt a policy, and (3) the lobbyists from "clientele" interest groups—all of them working both formally and informally on specific policy issues.

issue networks   A temporary collection of lobbyists, lawmakers, staff members, bureaucrats, and experts who collaborate to shape a particular policy.

linkage institutions   Agencies, such as political parties, interest groups, and the media, that forge links between citizens and public policy makers.

merit system   The selection, retention, and promotion of public employees based on competitive examinations or formal educational qualifications.

multiculturalism   The belief that the many cultures that make up American society ought to be maintained as distinct and that laws should be used to protect and even encourage them; the value of appreciating the richness of cultural diversity.

NIMBY   The acronym for *not in my backyard*; denotes opposition to certain government programs or facilities deemed undesirable but that are or could be located in one's neighborhood or area; typical examples are sewage-treatment plants, solid-waste recycling plants, and prisons.

partial-birth abortion   A medical procedure to terminate pregnancy during the last trimester in which doctors crush the cranium of the fetus and then induce delivery.

party in government   All the people from a party who hold public office.

party platform   A document drawn up by a political party at its state or national convention that establishes the party's policies and positions on current public issues.

patronage   The practice of awarding government jobs and contracts to faithful members of the political party in power.

political culture   The cluster of attitudes, beliefs, ideology, and values that shape our thinking about society and government and the role of the individual within both of them; the part of the overall societal culture that determines societal attitudes toward the quality, style, and strength of its political and governmental processes.

political party   A group of politically active individuals who organize for the purpose of capturing government by controlling the nomination and election of officials and thereby control the operation of government and determine public policy.

Proposition 209   An initiative passed in California that ended affirmative action programs by banning the use of preferences in state hiring and contracting and in admissions to public colleges and universities.

reverse discrimination   The perception that social programs to promote integration are racial preferences that promote the interests of minorities at the expense of members of the majority (usually considered to be white and male).

set-aside programs   A type of affirmative action program that includes the use of quotas (set-aside percentages) to award government contracts to minority businesses.

spin-off party   A minor, or third, party that begins as a faction within a major party, such as the Bull Moose Republicans or the Dixiecrats.

systems model   The concept that things are viewed as more than the sum of a collection of parts; an entity in which everything relates to everything else.

Review Questions	**1.** How does viewing politics as a system influence our perception of public administrators and their role in policy making? Given the great diversity of U.S. society, is value conflict inevitable? How can value conflict in administration be viewed as beneficial to the "system"?

1. How does viewing politics as a system influence our perception of public administrators and their role in policy making? Given the great diversity of U.S. society, is value conflict inevitable? How can value conflict in administration be viewed as beneficial to the "system"?

2. In what ways does a political party perform the linkage role? How do parties facilitate changes in values? How do parties help coordinate governmental policy making and implement policy toward a given goal?

3. How do interest groups help articulate values? How do they influence which values dominate public administration at any given time? Describe their role in forging a dominant political culture.

4. In what ways does government manage the economy? Why do economic forces contribute to so many value conflicts? Can the economy be better managed through technological development? How does technology complicate value conflict in the political system? in public administration?

5. How often do you read the sorts of "alternative publications" discussed in the reading, "Bar Wars"? Do you see evidence of TIM advertisements for tobacco and other products? How might local public health officials counter the TIM ploy to promote smoking and undermine the efforts of their antismoking policies?

Surfing the Net

The following are useful websites for the issues covered in this chapter.

For national policy making, go to the Electronic Policy Network (**http://www.epn/org**).

For political parties, check the web pages for the Democratic Party (**http://www.democrats.org**), the Republican Party (**http://www.rnc.org**), the Libertarian Party (**http://www.lp.org**), and the Reform Party (**http://www.reformparty.org**).

Interest groups can be found at many sites. You may want to consult the following:

Policy.com (**http://www.policy.com/community/pytopic**) provides links to various interest groups categorized by issues such as agriculture, civil rights, energy, and welfare.

Public Interest Research Group (**http://www.lgc.apc.org/pirg**)

American Civil Liberties Union (ACLU) (**http://www.aclu.org**)

AARP (**http://www.aarp.org**)

American Conservative Union (**http://www.townhall.com/conservative/acu.html**)

National Association for the Advancement of Colored People (NAACP) (**http://www.naacp.org**)

National Rifle Association (**http://www.nra.org**)

For economic policy issues and concerns go to any of the following sites:

Economic policy (**http://epn.org/idea/economy/html**)

Department of Commerce (**http://www.doc.gov**)

Congressional Budget Office (**http://www.cbo.gov**)

National Economic Council (**http://www.whitehouse.gov/WH/EOP/nec/html**)

Department of the Treasury (**http://www.ustreas.gov**)

Office of Management and Budget (**http://www.whitehouse.gov/OMB**)

Council of Economic Advisors (**http://www.whitehouse.gov/WH/EOP/CEA/html**)

Federal Reserve Bank (**http://woodrow.mpls.frb.us/info/policy**)

For technology policy, browse the following sites:

Center for Democracy and Technology (**http://www.cdt.org**)

Office of Science and Technology (**http://www.whitehouse.gov/WH/EOP/OSTP/html**)

Also consult the sites of these so-called think tanks:

Rand Corporation (**http://www.rand.org**)

The Urban Institute (**http://www.urban.org**)

For environmental policy and issues, check these sites:

U.S. Department of Energy (**http://www.doe.gov**)

Department of the Interior (**http://www.doi.gov**)

Code of Federal Regulations (**http://www.house.gov**)

Chapter 3

Keon S. Chi, Kelly Arnold, and Heather Perkins
Privatization in state governments: Trends and issues,
Spectrum, *76*(4) (Fall 2003): 12.

The topic of privatization—outsourcing of contracting—has reemerged recently as a controversial management issue for state policy makers facing tough budgetary times. The rationale for privatization was articulated well by former Michigan governor John Engle: "It is my belief that the private sector is often better at getting the job done than government. First, the competition promotes operating costs effectively, and the greater accountability helps ensure quality products and services. The private sector also excels at using innovative technology to solve problems, while government agencies do not always have the same latitude to innovate or take risks. Finally, the private sector has vast resources in computer technology, high-volume processing equipment, and specialized personnel, plus the flexibility to assign them wherever they are most needed."

On the other hand, opposition to privatization has been persistent over the years. Gerald McEntee, president of the American Federation of State, County, and Municipal Employees (AFSCME), articulated well the perspective against it: "For public employees and the people we serve, the price of privatization is high—and getting higher. For workers, privatization threatens job security, pay and benefits, working conditions, and career opportunities. For the public, it means less quality, less access, and less accountability. For local economies, because privatization is often nonunion, it means fewer good jobs and a reduced tax base."

The Anatomy of Public Organization: Bureaucratic Power and Politics

Introduction

Internal Sources of Values

The chapter-opening quotes illustrate the effect of values on a bureaucratic organization and the often-critical role played by the higher levels of management, elected politicians who serve as policy makers, and the unions representing public employees who comprise the bureaucracy of the organization in setting or changing critical values for the organization.

In this chapter we examine the critically important concepts of organizational culture and bureaucratic ideology. An organization's culture profoundly affects the cognitive processes and value systems of its members. The use of specialized language within an organization socializes its members into its culture and specific bureaucratic ideology.

We also discuss the foundations of bureaucratic power. Bureaucracy often projects an aura of expertise. The presumed or acknowledged expertise of members of an organization enables them to powerfully influence the development and implementation of public policy. Political leaders, in fact, often defer to such bureaucratic expertise. The organization's culture and ideology are used to cultivate and maintain political support.

Power becomes institutionalized when it infuses an organization's structure. Bureaucratic managers use the culture of the organization as actors in the public policy process and to influence the broader political process.

Bureaucratic organizations are about problem solving or, at least, about problem coping. Values shape the organization's approach to problem solving or coping and are derived from various sources. The internal sources of values espoused by an organization are what we emphasize here. Values arise from budgetary needs and constraints as well as from the standards promoted by powerful unions of public employees who make up the agency. For many public agencies, codes of ethics adopted by professional associations who share members with that bureaucracy are yet another important source of values.

An organization's reason for being leads certain units to be seen as critical units that are central to the core of the organization's mission. Such critical units make demands on the organization, and values implicit in those demands become part of the agency's ideology. The need to be efficiently productive is another internal source of values and sometimes of value conflict. The morale of members of an organization also shapes its value system, and the level of morale can sometimes trigger attempts to redefine the mission or reorganize an agency or to privatize the delivery of the agency's service, as evidenced in the opening quotes.

The perspective on the world implicit in an organization's culture shapes the organization, links it to its external environment, and offers insight into the nature of bureaucratic behavior. Organizational culture can help us understand the "why" of sometimes-puzzling bureaucratic behavior, perhaps providing a rationale for what otherwise seem to be irrational behaviors.

The chapter ends with a reading that illustrates an all-too-common problem arising out of organizational ideology—groupthink, in this case focusing on how the groupthink issue affected the failure of our national intelligence community to prevent the terrorist attacks of September 11, 2001, and to discover the truth about Iraqi weapons of mass destruction. Like every other chapter, we end with a glossary of key terms, review questions, and a list of useful websites.

INFOTRAC
COLLEGE EDITION

Governing the globalization of public health

The Concepts of Organizational Culture and Bureaucratic Ideology

Organizational culture may be defined as the way an organization views its role within the broader society. It is something that provides a worldview. Organizational culture is a complex interlinking of assumptions, attitudes, beliefs, norms, and values that collectively guide an organization.

When individual members become part of an organization, they are socialized into it. They gradually acquire its attitudes, beliefs, norms, and values. When such socialization is complete, the members share the organization's basic assumptions. These then serve as "presumptions," shaping their view of the external world. Values are applied by the members who cope with policy problems that are central to the agency's goals and mission. Norms of bureaucratic behavior common to the agency are acquired by members and guide their routines in dealing with problems. In a sense, then, bureaucrats are made, not born.

The Organizational Culture

To function well in the broader culture of the society it serves, an organization must share many of the culture's core values. Organizational values cannot differ greatly from societal values, although the organization may stress some more than others. An organization may define and symbolize core values in specialized ways, but bureaucrats reflect the values of the society from which they come or for which the organization was established to implement public policy. Organizations produce specific goods or services that are viewed as necessary by the broader culture. In American society, liberty, equality, the sanctity of private property, and freedom of religion are among its core values, each largely defined and delineated in terms of individualism.[1]

An organization's culture, then, serves many useful purposes. Through its unique perspective, the culture provides members with a way to understand and make sense of uncertainty, events, and symbols. It becomes the members' primary source of guiding beliefs. The organizational culture pervades their socialization process, determining what they see as right and wrong and how they should deal with certain circumstances and problems. Its norms provide them with routines with which to handle problems.

Organizational culture reduces the need for authority, rules, and controls. When internalized by an organization's members, the culture becomes a powerful mechanism that guides their actions by approving or prohibiting varied patterns of behavior. Organizational culture uses norms and mores, ideologies, and internalized systems of incentives and disincentives (rewards, sanctions, and taboos) to pervasively guide the behavior of members toward commonly held goals. The culture of an organization, in fact, comes to shape the members' cognitive processes and becomes the underlying and largely unquestioned reason for "the way we do things here."

The following summarizes the principal aspects of organizational culture.

1. Each organizational culture is relatively unique.
2. Each is a socially constructed concept.
3. Each provides its members with a way of understanding and making sense of events and symbols.
4. Each is a powerful tool for guiding organizations.[2]

Organizational culture is not solely beneficial in its effects. It also can have negative effects. The process of emphasizing assumptions can become like blinders to members of an organization. They may simply stop asking important questions. Unquestioned acceptance of historically based premises can develop into excessive organizational inflexibility. As a result, the organization can become so rigid in its decision making that it becomes ill adapted to adjust to changes in its external environment. Of particular danger to an organization is the tendency to develop symptoms of what has been called *groupthink*, a situation in which agency or public policy decision makers subordinate the making of calculated, carefully considered decisions to a concurrence among group members.

Groupthink

Groupthink is a mode of thinking within a cohesive group that is engaged in by people who so strongly seek consensus that there is no realistic appraisal of alternative courses of action. A drive for consensus at all costs completely suppresses dissent. Symptoms of groupthink that lead to bad decision making include:

1. an illusion of invulnerability;
2. collective rationalizations that lead group members to ignore warnings or other types of negative feedback;
3. unquestioned belief in the moral correctness of the in-group;
4. strong, negative, and often stereotyped views about the leaders of out-groups;
5. quick application of pressure to conform that is applied to any group member who expresses even momentary doubts about whatever the group shares;
6. careful, conscious, and individual avoidance of any deviation from the group consensus;
7. shared illusions of unanimity of opinion; and
8. establishment of mind guards—that is, people who act to protect the group members from adverse information that might disrupt or disturb their sense of the effectiveness and morality of past decisions.[3]

Groupthink can emerge at any level of government and concern virtually any area of public policy making, but it is especially dangerous in crisis-management situations. Groupthink is more likely to occur when the amount of useful information is severely constrained such that viable policy alternatives cannot be generated (Kowert, 2002). A classic example of groupthink was the Bay of Pigs invasion of Cuba during the first few days of John F. Kennedy's administration in 1961.[4] The Kennedy administration inherited a plan for a CIA-backed invasion by Cuban exiles. The new administration team accepted the plan without any critical examination of other options. Cuba's dictator, Fidel Castro, had agents who had infiltrated the Cuban exile organization and knew of the invasion's plans. As a result, the Cuban exile force was met and destroyed; members who were not killed were captured. The result was a foreign policy fiasco that led to the Kennedy administration's cautious approach in later foreign policy crises, particularly the Cuban missile crisis. Another, more recent, but just as deadly example of groupthink decision making was NASA's failure to react to news of defective O-rings. In that case, groupthink led to the loss of the space shuttle *Challenger* and all its crew.

Groupthink can develop at any level of government. The state of Florida, for example, tried two programs intended to reform workers' compensation by helping previously injured employees to return to work: the obligation-to-rehire program and the preferred worker-program. The failure of these return-to-work programs are in part the result of "groupthink" issues (Jewett, 2001).

Another example at the local level is provided by the decision to build a 7.5-kilometer highway through the Red Hill Valley area in Ontario, Canada. The Red Hill Expressway project is opposed by the provincial government and a by a federal environmental assessment. Despite these influences, the region still plans to build the expressway. Groupthink is affecting the region's decision-making process, preventing local politicians from seeing the importance of the new external influences. Three components of groupthink behavior are evident in the case: antecedent conditions promoting rigidity of the local decision makers, symptoms of groupthink behavior by local governing boards, and symptoms of defective decision making (McKay, 2001).

In times of war, the federal government has always attempted to manipulate the discourse of patriotism to rally political support and to limit dissent, and it has been no different in response to the attacks of September 11, 2001. In the aftermath of the attacks, the Bush White House revived and expanded the national security state with unprecedented speed and minimal debate. After but two days of debate and in an atmosphere that clearly reflected something like national hysteria, Congress enacted the Uniting and Strengthening America by Providing Appropriate Tools Required to Intercept and Obstruct Terrorism Act (USA Patriot Act), and President Bush signed it into law in November 2001. Among its many provisions, it reduces constraints on the government's ability to conduct searches, deport suspects, eavesdrop on Internet communications, monitor financial transactions, and crack down on immigrant violations. It defines a new crime, "domestic terrorism," so vaguely that it can easily be applied to acts of civil disobedience. Many state legislatures are following the lead of the federal government by passing antiterrorism laws that similarly blur the distinction between terrorism and political protest, granting broad powers of surveillance to state and local police. Cartoon 3.1 shows Attorney General John Ashcroft exhibiting groupthink behavior by not allowing questions of his decision making.

One year after enactment of the Patriot Act, the Congress approved establishment of the Department of Homeland Security. The Senate approved this action by a vote of 90 to 9. As mentioned previously, it represents the most significant change in the federal bureaucracy since President Harry S. Truman in 1947 created the Department of Defense to fight the Cold War.

The post-9/11 atmosphere clearly stifles dissent. A cautionary note as to the danger of that atmosphere was raised recently:

> For a nation to be, in the truest sense, patriotic, its citizens must love their land with a knowing, intelligent, sustaining, and protective love. . . . And they must not allow their patriotism to be degraded to a mere loyalty to symbols or any present set of officials. (Wendell Barry, cited in "Patriot Acts," *Social Justice* (Spring 2003): 5)

Box 3.1, "Terrorized Decision Making: The Creation of the TSA," illustrates this problem in the establishment of the Transportation Security Administration, clearly a "rush to judgment."

INFOTRAC
COLLEGE EDITION

Groupthink and the Gulf crisis

CARTOON 3.1

Don't ask me that.

Attorney General Ashcroft is spoofed for the manner in which he implements aspects of laws such as the USA Patriot Act. What are some ways the USA Patriot Act and the Department of Homeland Security Act influence first responders at the local (police and fire) level?

Source: Cartoon by Kevin Kallaugher. Copyright 2004, *The Baltimore Sun.* Image courtesy of the Library of Congress.

Functions of Organizational Culture

Bureaucratic organizations serve society in some manner, and organizational cultures generally have compatible values. The narrower needs of the organization and its emphasis on values perceived to be central to its core mission may lead to value conflicts with the external societal culture. Table 3.1 suggests some value conflicts, comparing values from the political environment with those in administration, particularly power, efficiency, interest, and accountability.[5]

An organization uses its culture to recruit certain types of individuals: people who are likely to hold similar values. The culture influences new-member socialization and helps clarify diffuse or unclear outcomes. And when new technologies are imposed on an organization, its culture is useful for coping with uncertain technologies.

An important function of an agency's organizational culture is to deal better with multiple or even conflicting goals imposed by a legislature. These conflicting goals typically reflect the compromises made to get certain bills passed into law. Legislative coalitions, for example, may include conflicting goals. Purposely

Box 3.1

Terrorized Decision Making: The Creation of the TSA

Emergencies all too often cry out for drastic and expensive changes in public policy that later, upon more careful reflection, seem ill advised. Consistent with this pattern, U.S. policy makers reacted to the terrorist suicide hijackings of September 11, 2001, with the largest expansion in federal powers and the most free-handed spending of new federal dollars seen in decades. Congress and the Bush Administration expanded the powers of federal law enforcement to detect and detain terrorists or suspected terrorists, increased dramatically investments in counterterrorism intelligence, placed thousands of National Guard troops at airports for months, and expanded the use of armed air marshals on domestic flights. Similarly, among their most ambitious reforms was the creation of a huge new federal agency, the Transportation Security Administration (TSA), to perform security screening at U.S. commercial airports.

The airlines previously operated the screening system under Federal Aviation Administration (FAA) regulation. The FAA required each airline to screen passengers at each gate before boarding its planes. Most airlines simply contracted out that task to private security firms, such as Argenbright Security, International Total Services, and Globe Aviation Services.

On November 16, 2001, Congress nationalized the nation's 28,000 airport screeners by establishing the new agency that by itself had more personnel than the Department of Labor and the Department of Housing and Urban Development combined. Soon after TSA was launched, however, a Department of Transportation (DOT) spokesman estimated the agency would need more than 70,000 passenger and luggage screeners. Congress soon approved funding for 45,000 screeners, while TSA officials insisted they needed at least 20,000 more. If Congress funds that request, the TSA will rival or surpass in personnel strength the behemoth Social Security Administration, at 65,000, and will dwarf the personnel of the legislative and judicial branches of the U.S. government combined. Even at its current size, the TSA is the largest new federal agency established by the Congress since the 1930s.

Creation of the TSA resulted from an environment of rare bipartisanship. Such a climate, however, is uniquely hostile to rational policy making. It was handled mostly outside normal committee processes. Scholars of group dynamics have long noted that in circumstances of extreme crisis, "group contagion gives rise to collective panic, violent acts of scapegoating, and other forms of what could be called "group madness" (Janis, 1982: 3). Policymaking in crisis situations can take on moblike characteristics exemplified by mindless conformity and collective misjudgment of risk.

The steep panic curve of Congressional action in the wake of 9/11 is simply illustrated by the vote on the screener-takeover legislation. On October 11, one month after the destruction of the World Trade Center and the attack on the Pentagon, the U.S. Senate voted 100 to 0 to federalize screening.

As proponents of the Aviation and Transportation Security Act insisted, much went wrong in airport security on 9/11/01. Nineteen men with short-bladed "box-cutter" knives, several of them wanted by law enforcement officials for months, boarded four transcontinental flights. The suicide terrorists had apparently selected the four hijacked flights carefully, scouting dozens of flights. According to the FBI, they were well financed and had practiced for the attacks for months by repeatedly riding the flights they later hijacked, learning of the flight crews' patterns, counting passenger loads, and testing airline security. They had scouted other flights but eliminated them, perhaps because they regularly carried too many passengers.

Viewed from the most practical perspective, the 9/11 hijackings were caused not by the failure of screeners on the ground but by failures of airline personnel in the air, who were inadequately equipped to defend their cockpits. Passage of the Aviation and Security Act exemplifies policy making at its worst: frenzied, panicked, and overreactionary.

The term *moral panic* might be used to describe what happened to Congress in November 2001. A moral panic is a response to a condition, episode, person, or group of persons that society defines as a threat to societal values and interests. A moral panic is predicated on an exaggerated fear, taking alarm without conducting a careful and sober assessment of the evidence. The group dynamic generated at such moments of social unity often yields startlingly extreme results.

Source: This article is reprinted with permission of the publisher from *The Independent Review: A Journal of Political Economy,* 7(4) (Spring 2003): 503–518. Copyright © 2003, The Independent Institute, 100 Swan Way, Oakland, CA 94621–1428 USA; info@independent.org; www.independent.org.

TABLE 3.1

Value Conflicts in Organizations: Pluralism versus Administrative Efficiency

Pluralist (Political System)	Administrative Efficiency
Power is dispersed, divided, and decentralized.	Power is concentrated and centralized.
Executive power is regarded with suspicion.	Power is centralized in the hands of the chief executive for greater accountability.
Power is given to politicians and interest groups.	Power is given to experts.
Political bargaining and accommodation are at the heart of the democratic process.	Efficiency dictates that politics be kept out of administration.
Individual assesses his or her own interests.	Stress is on scientific or technical rationality.

obscure language is frequently used, leaving it to the bureaucracy to clarify intent as it implements policy. A good example of this was enactment of a highly complex immigration law by the United States Congress in 1986.

The Immigration Reform and Control Act (IRCA) imposed on the Immigration and Naturalization Service (INS) a new approach to immigration policy: employer sanctions. But IRCA embodies more than immigration policy. It involves policy on employment, agricultural labor, civil rights, welfare, and federal reimbursement to states.[6] It is a highly complex law that emerged from a contentious legislative process. It implicitly pursues a complicated legislative strategy. Its primary purpose was to reduce illegal immigration through employer sanctions. To get that approach passed, its sponsors included a generous amnesty program as a humanitarian provision. The law thereby involved the INS in simultaneously trying to ferret out undocumented aliens to more swiftly deport them, beefing up the Border Patrol to do so, and reaching out to undocumented aliens who met its amnesty conditions to entice them to come forward to be "legalized." Congress simply assumed that the INS would administer the legalization program in a liberal manner. It assumed the INS could conduct sufficient outreach to inform those eligible about the program's opportunities and requirements and that the INS had the capacity to do so within a highly designated time frame. Congress simply assumed there would be widespread voluntary employer compliance with its sanctions provisions. The organizational culture of the INS matched the employer sanctions approach well, but it was ill matched to the goals of the amnesty program. IRCA failed to stem the flow of undocumented aliens into the United States, in no small measure because its policy goals were too multifaceted and contradictory.

The Use of Symbols

Organizational culture functions by the use of symbols. Cultural values are communicated through symbols to members of the organization as well as to relevant actors in the organization's external environment. These may be specialized words, phrases, and even anthems. The symbols also may be gestures, such as a salute, or an open or closed door. The symbols are used and can be projected through the organizational structure. They are imbedded in stories about organizational heroes.

Organizations are not solely rational, goal-driven structures. Myths, rituals, ceremonies, stories, and sagas help members and nonmembers deal with complexities, allowing people to reduce uncertainty by creating new and comforting realities.[7]

The Bureaucratic Ideology

An important subset of organizational culture concerns the concept of **ideology**, which has been usefully defined as a verbal image of the good society and a chief means of constructing such a society. Uncertainty in society makes ideology more useful because it is relatively stable and coherent, helping bureaucracy cope with uncertainty by providing shortcuts to calculating which policies, procedures, and programs will be most acceptable to its external society.[8]

A bureau is a large organization whose members are full-time workers who depend on it for most if not all of their income. They are hired, retained, and promoted based on how they perform organizational roles. Anthony Downs defines a **bureaucratic ideology** as "a verbal image of that portion of the good society with which a particular bureau is concerned, plus the chief means of constructing that portion."[9]

A bureaucratic ideology flows downward from the organization's higher levels of formal authority and infuses its communication systems, both formal and informal. Top-level officials develop the ideology to provide an efficient means of communicating with both the external environment and bureau insiders. Higher management faces pressing needs to communicate to people who might not be disposed to listen carefully and well, especially when a crisis develops or an environment rapidly changes. The bureau ideology states agency goals in terms of the organization's ultimate policy objectives in serving the broader society. The verbal images of the bureau's ideology enable others—legislators, voters, officials with other relevant agencies, related interest group members, and even lower-level bureau members—to use the ideology in decision making without paying excessively high information costs.[10]

INFOTRAC
COLLEGE EDITION

Pathologies of decision making

Bureaucratic Symbols

Managers of government agencies have well-developed ideas of what government "ought to do." These ideas are sharply defined to each agency's narrow area of expertise. Agency ideology may be *soft* or *hard*.[11] The soft version of an agency ideology is that the existing program of the agency constitutes a set of ideas favored by the bureaucracy out of familiarity if for no other reason. Political executives appointed to oversee and control bureaucratic structures frequently report on both overt and covert resistance by the organization's bureaucratic members. They generally see the "department's view" about policy as limiting the effectiveness of any political leader. In his first term, President Ronald Reagan appointed a secretary of education with the intention of essentially disbanding the department. The secretary quickly became an advocate of the department, in no small measure because he came to adopt its ideology.

The hard version of an agency ideology holds that the bureaucracy must be interested not only in preserving its existing policies, but also in imposing a new set of policies. Civil servants often remain in place longer than do politicians or their political appointees and so have a greater chance over time to alter policies in ways they see fit.

The views of civil servants themselves tend to change over time. Civil servants are often members of a professional association and subject to professional qualification and training. Their policy perspective may change over time to correspond to what is deemed the "best practice" in their profession. Professionals in an agency thus become the source of new policy, having both expert knowledge and a goal to expand their agency's influence.

Symbolic Management

So far we have explained why upper-level bureaucrats develop bureaucratic symbols to form a cohesive ideology and why it is useful to manage these symbolic images to communicate internally and externally. But why do the consumers of bureaucratic ideology use them? Anthony Downs answers that question by categorizing the types of potential consumers and showing why bureaucratic imagery is useful to them.[12]

Downs distinguishes what he calls *active external consumers*, agents whose functions require them to explicitly consider the bureau in making their own decisions. They might be members of a similar or related agency at another level of government or members of a clientele or vested interest group. On the other hand, *passive external consumers* are those external agents whose functions are only remotely affected by an agency's behavior but whose own actions can strongly affect the agency. *Active internal consumers* are those members of the bureau who must use its ideology in their dealings with external agents. Finally, *passive internal consumers* are those members of an agency whose functions do not require them to use its ideology. Active consumers, whether internal or external, are motivated by their social functions to use the bureau ideology. Because they need to make decisions that affect the bureau's actions, they find its ideology useful. When developing or changing a bureau ideology, then, it is in the managers' interest to manipulate the agency's symbolic imagery so that it provides ideological information relatively cost free to its consumers. Bureau managers use free information streams—newspapers, wire services, radio and television broadcasts, and popular magazines—to transmit information about the agency and its ideology. This manipulation of media allows them to get the attention of many people who might otherwise simply not find out anything about the bureau.

Another method to overcome consumer apathy is to make the consuming of information itself a source of benefit. Some agencies, such as NASA, the Centers for Disease Control and Prevention, the Bureau of the Census, and state government economic-development agencies produce data that are markedly superior to those produced by many other agencies. All government agencies produce ideological imagery. They present their data with a coating of novelty or entertainment to make consuming them seem easier. Press releases by government agencies are designed to create the impression that they are performing important services—and doing so efficiently.

Bureau ideology serves several functions: It emphasizes the positive benefits of agency policy and deemphasizes the costs of achieving those benefits. It justifies expanding agency activities rather than contracting them. It emphasizes the benefits the agency provides society as a whole rather than those provided to its special or vested interests. It emphasizes the desirability of its efficiency and centralized coordination, which are widely accepted values in society, making the bureau seem worthy of support. It promotes achievements and future capabilities rather than past failures or current inabilities.[13]

The process of building and promoting agency ideology involves the investment of time and effort to build external support and internal cohesion. This contributes to ideological inertia and to time lags in major images within an ideology. When events demonstrate that an ideology is somewhat outmoded (the *Challenger* disaster for NASA, for example), bureau managers can choose one of three alternatives: They can (1) retain the obsolete ideology and keep their behavior consistent with it, (2) retain the obsolete ideology but modify their behavior to be consistent with the true interests of their beneficiaries, even when the interests are inconsistent with the stated ideology, or (3) advance a new ideology that is more consistent with the true interests of their beneficiaries and behave in a manner consistent with the new ideology.

Because a bureau's constituency—its vested interest group supporters or clientele—is a major source of external support, including direct beneficiaries and suppliers, it is likely to be well informed about the bureau and less likely to develop ideological lags. This makes bureaucratic ideologies more flexible than political party ideologies in response to changes in the environment. It also means that agencies with a strong external support system of special interest groups (an iron-triangle type of relationship) can operate for extended periods of time counter to the interests of a preponderant majority in society that is largely unaware of the bureau or its ideology.

Organizational Effects on Cognitive Processes and Value Systems

One important way in which managers manipulate symbols and develop the imagery inherent in a bureau ideology is through **jargon**—the specialized vocabulary and idioms of those in the same type of work or profession. Value content is often implicit in the use of jargon. The specialized meaning given to the use of more common words as well as the creation of new words carry certain value connotations. The language of the ideology becomes in part the prism through which the ideology influences the cognitive processes of the bureaucracy's members.

Special Uses of Jargon

Government in general and bureau administrators in particular are replete with the use of **acronyms**, or words that are formed by using the first letter or first few letters of a series of words. Acronyms are shortcuts that provide meaning to those familiar with them; but to those who do not know them, they can seem incoherent, incomprehensible, and occasionally outlandish. In these ways, jargon becomes the specialized language of experts. Figure 3.1 offers a list of some typical government acronyms, and Figure 3.2 lists some specialized jargon commonly used in government.

ACIR	Advisory Commission on Intergovernmental Relations	**NASA**	National Aeronautics and Space Administration
BOB	Bureau of the Budget	**OSHA**	Occupational Safety and Health Administration
CSCA	Conference of State Court Administrators	**PACE**	Professional and Administrative Career Examination
DOD	Department of Defense	**QDE**	qualified designated entity
EPA	Environmental Protection Agency	**RIF**	reduction in force
FDIC	Federal Deposit Insurance Corporation	**SEC**	Securities and Exchange Commission
GIS	geographic information system	**TQM**	total quality management
HHS	Department of Health and Human Services	**USDA**	United States Department of Agriculture
ICC	Interstate Commerce Commission	**VAP**	Victims Alert Project
JAG	Judge Advocate General's Office	**WDNR**	Wisconsin Department of Natural Resources
KDA	Kansas Department of Agriculture	**X GEN**	Generation X
LIB	line item budget	**YNP**	Yellowstone National Park
MSPB	Merit Systems Protection Board	**ZBB**	zero-based budgeting

FIGURE 3.1
From A to Z, Acronyms Used in Public Administration

arbitrary deprivation of life   U.S. Department of State's term for murders committed by governments friendly to the United States.

bureaupathic behavior   Adherence to rules and regulations to the point of losing common sense.

contributions   President Clinton's term for taxes.

decruiting   Firing government workers.

event   Term to describe the meltdown of the Three Mile Island nuclear reactor in 1977.

failure to maintain ground clearance   National Transportation Safety Board's term for a plane crash.

global positioning satellite   Satellites placed in permanent orbit allowing for precise location of ships, airplanes, and even people on the ground.

human resource investment   Euphemism for poverty programs.

investment   Clinton administration's term for taxes.

job action   Government unions' term for an illegal strike.

knowledge deprivation   Agency's state of having insufficient data to make a decision.

learning organization   Term for agencies in which new patterns of thinking are nurtured.

managerialism   Approach to public management that stresses a policy entrepreneurial style and reinvigorated scientific management techniques.

neutralize   Pentagon's term for inflicting combat casualties.

organic biomass   Better known as sewage.

POSDCORB   Mnemonic device referring to fundamental elements of a chief executive's work.

qualified designated entities   Immigration and Naturalization Service's term from the Immigration Reform and Control Act; nongovernmental organizations authorized to assist the INS in processing applications for the legalization program.

riffing   Meaning "to fire"; derived from reduction in force.

streamlining   Another governmental term for firing staff.

think tank   Nongovernmental organization, such as the Rand Corporation or the Brookings Institute, that studies governmental policy.

ultralocalism   Presence of a large number of local governments, often overlapping in authority and jurisdiction, in a metropolitan area.

venture capital   Money given by an organization or a government to encourage investment in business, often to start a new area or service or to bring jobs to economically depressed areas.

whistle-blower   Person who believes the public interest overrides the agency's interest and exposes corrupt, illegal, fraudulent, or harmful behavior by the agency or its executives.

xenophobia   Fear of the unknown or the foreign.

Y2K   Year 2000 problem with computer technology; also known as the millennium bug.

zero-based budgeting   Approach to budgeting that requires an agency to justify its entire budget submission.

FIGURE 3.2
From A to Z, Jargon Used in Public Administration

Sometimes the requirements of law and governmental policy necessitate the precise definitions of words. How government defines a concept such as *pornography* has great legal significance. Someone who says, "I know pornography when I see it," may be speaking a personal truth, but the law requires a more precise definition of the concept before a bureaucratic agency such as a local police department or local court system can apply and enforce an antipornography statute. Box 3.2 illustrates the point by discussing municipal ordinances regarding legal definitions of "junk," as in "junk cars," as part of a neighborhood cleanup campaign.

Legislatures often pass general laws using words that have a meaning in common language but must be more precisely defined in bureaucratic rules, regulations, or standards before the agency can apply them or implement the program. If certain welfare benefits are to be given to "the poor," then an agency has to define precisely what constitutes *poverty*. Who exactly is entitled to a given benefit or service? An agency can neither ban nor enforce antidiscrimination statutes against the disabled unless it precisely defines who is or is not disabled.

Box 3.2

Definitions in the Law

As with pornography, most people would maintain they would know a "junk car" when they see one. But municipal ordinances concerning abandoned automobiles, typically banned in conjunction with neighborhood cleanup campaigns, have been challenged in court for being "too vague." Like one person's "terrorist" is another person's "freedom fighter," one person's obvious "junked car" can be someone else's "spare parts" or "my second car, just waiting for me to drop an engine in it." Municipal ordinances have had to be rewritten to avoid such legal challenges and to distinguish the true junk car from those that are raced at local racetracks (which may lack fenders, windshields, and so on).

Typically, such revised local laws ban rusting vehicles from being parked in someone's front yard and in open

view (there being no renewal problems if the vehicle is enclosed in a garage or in a fenced-in backyard) by defining the "junk car" as one that is unlicensed and unregistered, and when said vehicle is missing two or more operationally necessary features, such as glass windshields and side and back windows, two wheels or tires, central body panels or bumpers, and components essential to operation, such as an engine, operable brakes, and a front driver's or passenger seat. Other municipalities may add further descriptive detail, such as the vehicle is placed on cement blocks, has vegetation growing in or around it, or is kept in such manner as to allow insects, vermin, or birds to occupy or nest in it.

Source: By author. For a description of one such local law, see Christopher Swope, *Governing*, *12*(6) (1999): 14.

Using jargon is but one method by which bureaucrats assert their expertise, one of the basic elements of bureaucratic power. The obscurity of their specialized language makes it more difficult for others to challenge them.

INFOTRAC
COLLEGE EDITION

The struggle for the soul of Medicare

The Foundations of Bureaucratic Power

As society became more complex and organizations grew larger, organizations (both private and public) increased their division of labor into more and smaller specialized units. Larger institutions began to defer to the judgments of these units, which shows that a major foundation of bureaucratic power is expertise, or specialized knowledge. As society became more complex and specialized, decision makers relied on expert advice. Some bureaucratic agencies, then, developed a near monopoly on the technical data or criteria used to decide policy.

Depending on the type of policy they implement, agencies have discretionary power, either more or less. Agencies that implement distributive policy tend to have less discretion than those that implement redistributive policy—and these have less discretion than those that implement regulatory policy. Agencies that implement self-regulatory policy have the widest discretion from the legislature's policy making. How vigorously or casually to implement policy, for instance, is the question the agency with jurisdiction must answer. Bureaucrats, moreover, often define the decisional alternatives not only for higher-level political appointees but also even for elected officials.

The foundations of bureaucratic power, then, are the following: the level and acceptance of bureaucratic expertise and the level of political support an agency can develop within the legislature and the executive branch, among clientele or other vested interest groups, and among the general public. The formal

Box 3.3

How Specs Supposedly Live Forever

Question: What value does this untrue but often-cited testament to bureaucracy really reflect?

The U.S. standard railroad gauge (distance between the rails) is 4 feet, 8.5 inches. That's an exceedingly odd number. Why was that gauge used? Because that's the way they built them in England, and the U.S. railroads were built by English expatriates. Why did the English people build them like that? Because the first rail lines were built by the same people who built the prerailroad tramways, and that's the gauge they used.

Why did "they" use that gauge then? Because the people who built the tramways used the same jigs and tools that they used for building wagons, which used that wheel spacing.

Okay! Why did the wagons use that odd wheel spacing?

Well, if they tried to use any other spacing the wagons would break on some of the old, long-distance roads, because that's the spacing of the old wheel ruts.

So who built these old rutted roads? The first long-distance roads in Europe were built by Imperial Rome for the benefit of its legions. The roads have been used ever since.

And the ruts? The initial ruts, which everyone else had to match for fear of destroying their wagons, were first made by Roman war chariots. Since the chariots were made for and by Imperial Rome, they were all alike in the matter of wheel spacing.

Thus, we have the answer to the original questions. The United States standard railroad gauge of 4 feet, 8.5 inches derives from the original specifications for an Imperial Roman army war chariot.

Specs and bureaucracies live forever. So the next time you are handed a specification and wonder what horse's end came up with it, you may be exactly right. Because the Imperial Roman chariots were made to be just wide enough to accommodate the back ends of two war horses.

Source: Anonymous, but see http://www.railway.org/railroadgauge.htm.

---

organizational structure—how centralized or decentralized the agency is and what jurisdiction it has in certain policy areas—is another base of bureaucratic power. Finally, such power rests also on the political capability of the bureaucrats themselves.[14]

Expertise is a source of power because specialized knowledge contributes to bureaucrats' staying power. While politically elected executives and their high-level appointees come and go, civil service bureaucrats stay on and on. The rules and regulations they develop to implement policy may remain in place for a long time as well. This staying power of bureaucrats is illustrated humorously in Box 3.3, "How Specs Live Forever," which is apocryphal but nonetheless shows how some standards might be perpetuated over time.

Bureaucratic power also rests on the level of support within the political environment. At its apex, an agency's level of support takes on the strength of steel when it achieves the status of an iron triangle, as described earlier.

Even when the coalition of interest groups that support an agency is less fixed than an iron triangle arrangement, a bureaucratic organization can garner political support by expanding the coalition of groups who view it as an ally. "Shared knowledge" groups can develop into issue networks—less permanent alliances of groups formed around a particular issue or established to resolve a particular policy problem.[15] Such loose coalitions of groups with shared beliefs are willing to support an agency, even if only temporarily. They are less well defined than a subsystem or iron triangle coalition, but the power of issue networks can expand as the number of groups aligned with them increases.

Organizational Structure

Public administrative agencies tend to be structured along one or more of four bases of organization: purpose, process, place, and clientele. Modern governmental organizations that tend to be large are typically organized in a pyramid structure or hierarchy. An example of an organization based on purpose would be a state park agency. An agency based on process would be a regulatory organization, such as a state environmental protection agency. Another such type of agency is one that primarily dispenses grants—for example, a state agency that assists local governments. Many agencies are based largely on geographic place, for instance, regional agencies to control pests or to regulate or develop a particular water resource, such as the Colorado River. Agencies based on clientele, for example, would include state departments of agriculture and labor as well as a small business administration. The base on which an agency is structured shapes the values it espouses.

The hierarchical structures of public agencies influence their acceptance of many values and bureaucratic norms, such as the principle of unity of command, chain of command, and a narrow span of control.[16] We previously distinguished line and staff agencies. This aspect of organizational structure also affects values. A line agency structured on a clientele base will likely value responsiveness. A staff agency organized on process—centralized purchasing, budgeting, personnel, and so on—will emphasize accountability or efficiency.

The values accepted and advocated by bureaucrats are transmitted through the socialization process and enforced and reinforced by both group norms and the agency's system of incentives and disincentives—its reward and control processes.

A critically important aspect of organizational structure is the degree to which an agency is centralized or decentralized. These aspects of administrative decision making affect the agency's delivery of service to its clientele as well as its ability to mobilize resources to perpetuate itself and its values.

The more decentralized an agency, the more difficult it is for managers to impose or change the values of organization members. Decisions cannot be imposed from the top down unless the members at the lower levels of the agency accept both the values and the methods that have been selected to implement policy and provide its services. How members view problems and, more important, alternative solutions to those problems is partly determined by where in the organizational structure each member is located. This observation of bureaucratic behavior has been expressed by "Miles Law," which states, "Where you stand [on an issue] depends on where you sit [your place in the organization or in the decision-making process]."[17]

The structure of an organization often reflects the political power of an agency and its support system. When President Jimmy Carter established the Department of Education in 1977, it reflected the growing importance the administration placed on education and the power of educational interests such as the National Education Association (NEA) and the American Federation of Teachers (AFT) within the Democratic party. Similarly, when President George H. Bush supported congressional establishment of the Department of Veterans Affairs through the Veteran Affairs Act of 1988, it reflected and symbolized the political clout of veterans groups.

Such organization or reorganization also can signify a group's declining power. State governments, for example, have merged separate programs into larger "super"

INFOTRAC
COLLEGE EDITION

Framing pragmatic aspirations

departments to save money or streamline administration, as Wisconsin did when it established a Department of Natural Resources and merged previously separate departments such as fisheries and game, parks and recreation, and water resources. These constituent agencies lost power and visibility with the merger. The consolidation of local school districts into larger school districts is another example. Such changes are often opposed by parents, PTA groups, and the like, who favor maintaining their access and influence over local neighborhood schools. In such mergers, the efficiency offered by economies of scale are valued over the responsiveness afforded by neighborhood schools.

Many communities struggle with the destabilizing forces resulting from the globalization of the U.S. economy. Local governments grapple with the effects these forces have on their local economies. The quest for community economic stability, which can be described as possessing sufficient job opportunities and a general level of economic activity to secure a decent standard of living for their populations over a sustained period of time, preoccupies the hearts and minds of local policy makers across the nation. One such policy strategy for enhancing community economic stability in face of the global economy seeks to facilitate the creation and expansion of economic enterprises—both public and private and combinations thereof—that are owned in ways that potentially anchor or root the enterprise in place. It is referred to as **place-based ownership models of economic enterprises** (Imbroscio, Williamson, and Alperovitz, 2003: 31). In place-based ownership models, enterprises are owned and controlled in a more collective or community-oriented fashion, an attribute that gives such enterprises their rootedness in place and, by inference, their potential to act as a buffer against hyper capital mobility of economic globalization and/or the outsourcing of jobs to other nations. Six such models are briefly described and illustrated here.

1. *Community-owned corporations.* These are similar to traditional corporations, save in one crucial factor—they are owned primarily by citizens living in or strongly connected to the local community. The most celebrated example of such is Wisconsin's National Football League franchise, the Green Bay Packers. They are owned by about 110,000 shareholders, more than half of whom live in the state. Its corporate bylaws prevent any one individual from owning more than 20 shares, guaranteeing broad-based ownership and making it almost impossible for the team to be sold and moved to another city because it is a nonprofit corporation and shareholders would receive no capital gains upon resale; the bylaws require all proceeds from such a sale to be donated to the local chapter of the American Legion.

2. *Nonprofit corporations.* Traditional nonprofit corporations comprise a broader category of organizations that have the ability to stabilize jobs and economic activity in communities. Nonprofits account for over 6 percent of the nation's economy and over 7 percent of total employment. They are sometimes called the "third sector" because they are the third major economic structure in the United States after private firms and government entities. Nonprofits are fairly rooted geographically, enhancing community stability. A celebrated example of nonprofit enterprise is Pioneer Human Services (PHS) in Seattle, Washington. Begun in 1962, PHS assists addicts, homeless people, parolees, and others on society's margins to attain economic and social betterment by providing housing, job training, and rehabilitation services. It is a $55 million

operation serving more than 6,000 clients annually and employing 1,000 people in its programs.

3. *Municipal enterprise.* Perhaps the most direct way for local governments to contribute to community economic stability is to enter the market for themselves. Locally scaled public ownership anchors economic endeavors and the jobs they generate to specific places. They have a long and noteworthy history in the United States, where governments have traditionally owned and operated utility enterprises in such areas as electricity, water, sewer, solid-waste collection, and nonutility businesses such as airports, seaports, civic centers, parking facilities, recreational facilities, public transportation systems, hospitals, and emergency services. One industry with an abundance of such public enterprise is telecommunications. City governments, most often municipal electric utilities, are increasingly seeing the Internet, cable television, fiber-optic networks, telephone service and other telecommunications provision as a way to survive in a deregulated electricity market. As of 2000, about 100 local governments across the nation had either constructed their own publicly owned telecommunications network or were doing feasibility studies to build one.

4. *Consumer cooperatives.* Another model of place-based ownership enterprise is the consumer cooperative, found mainly in housing, health care, the retail grocery industry, and rural electricity distribution. They are self-help economic structures that provide quality goods and services to their members at reasonable cost. They are rooted strongly in local communities, in that each coop member is entitled to only a single vote in the affairs of the business. Coop members typically elect representatives to serve on the coop's governing board and participate in coop-wide referenda or other democratic decision-making activities. Such democratic control enhances community economic stability. For example, according to the National Rural Electric Cooperative Association (NRECA), 865 electricity distribution coops serve 35 million people, 12 percent of the country's population, in 46 states.

5. *Employee ownership.* Employee ownership of firms is perhaps the most discussed and best-developed modification of the traditional corporate ownership structure in the United States. Such enterprises fall into two broad categories: cooperatives and employee stock ownership. Today there are 200 wholly owned worker cooperatives in the United States. Employee stock ownership is an even more common vehicle for worker ownership.

6. *Community development corporations.* Community development corporations (CDCs) are nonprofit enterprises dedicated to bringing about community economic stabilization in a clearly defined geographic area—typically an urban neighborhood scarred by decades of disinvestments or the concentration of poverty or an underdeveloped rural area. Run by boards of directors made up mostly of local residents, most CDCs engage in some form of economic development and job generation in their service areas. The original flagship CDC is the Bedford Stuyvesant Restoration Corporation (BSRC) in Brooklyn, New York. It owns two-thirds of the Restoration Supermarket Corporation, which provides 126 part-time and 46 full-time jobs and earns profits of roughly $300,000–400,000 annually. Its revenues exceeded $28 million in 2000.

Bureaucrats as Politicians

How well an agency is protected from such influence-sapping mergers or benefits from its elevation in status from a bureau or division in one agency to its own cabinet-level status (with its attendant expansion) depends in no small measure on how well the organizational leadership plays the game of bureaucratic politics. Far from being apolitical, above politics, or politically neutral in the sense described by Woodrow Wilson or advocated by Frederick Taylor in his principles of scientific management, high-level bureaucratic leaders must perform as bureaucratic politicians to protect the status and importance of their agency and its programs.

This perspective on bureaucratic behavior and the norms and values implied by it has been refined into a model of bureaucratic politics by Graham Allison (1971), who explains governmental behavior as the outcomes of bargaining among individuals and groups within government. Policy is made not by rational choice but by the pulling and hauling of internal politics. Bargaining takes place over issues because individuals in government share power and see different sides of the same issue. In Allison's model, senior players are the President, his most senior advisors in the executive office, and the various heads of departments or agencies involved in the policy decision. Junior players are members of Congress, spokespeople for interest groups, and members of the news media. Issues determine who plays, how much power or bargaining advantage that clusters of groups or individuals have in the decision-making process, and how much bargaining actually takes place. The longer a policy issue is debated, the more groups and individuals will become involved in the bargaining process.

Issues that fall within the clear responsibility of a particular group or individual enhance that agency's or group's bargaining power and minimize the overall bargaining that will take place. When issues do not fall clearly within a particular agency's or individual's responsibility, then the bargaining power is not concentrated, which increases the total amount of bargaining over the issues.

Each player's stand on the issues is determined by his or her position within government, the interests of the agency or organization, domestic political interests, personal interests, and the basic beliefs held throughout government. These factors determine which "face" of an issue participants will see and thus the position they will take on the issue and how its resolution will affect their concerns. These individual calculations define their stakes in the issue. The higher the stakes, the more involved the individual or agency will become in the bargaining game.

As noted, issues that clearly fall within an agency's jurisdiction increase its bargaining power and decrease the total bargaining over the issue. This also reflects the group's or agency's monopoly of information on the issue and control over the implementation of any decision made. Other players in the game hesitate to bargain and fight with an agency when the issue falls within its domain because they see little chance of success in effecting changes they want. They may have little hope of gathering support for their viewpoints, given their lack of direct information on an issue or their ability to police the implementation of any decision. Other factors that lead to bargaining advantages are (1) persuasiveness with other players, (2) the ability to affect other player's objectives in other decision games, and (3) other players' perceptions of the bargaining advantages and ability of the agency leader and his or her willingness to use them.

INFOTRAC
COLLEGE EDITION

Using multiple informants in public administration

Bargaining takes place on an issue because players who share power see different sides of an issue. But some individuals are more powerful than others—so why can't such players simply command? The answer lies in the very structure of government, Allison maintains.

Once decisions are assigned to specific organizations—which are, of course, players in the game of bureaucratic politics—those agencies are in charge of implementation. Agencies have great freedom in implementing decisions handed to them. Allison's model postulates the following about how decisions are carried out.

1. The less an organization is involved in a decision, the less it will be inclined to implement it, especially when the decision is harmful to the organization's interests. Key decision makers thus must bargain and argue to bring lesser players around to their point of view. Central or senior players must convince subordinates that a particular decision not only is good for the country but also is in their own best interests. If these players fail in that persuasion, then subordinates will often maneuver to restrict implementation or even disobey the decision made.

2. Consequently, agencies and subordinates have great influence over the type of decisions that will actually be made. Central or senior players in the game will not make an important decision without seriously considering their subordinates' views.

3. Other factors motivate senior players to get their subordinates on board, thus compromising the formers' own opinions and wishes on a given issue. These include the lack of information or distorted information to gain advantage in the bargaining (subordinates may leak this information to destroy a policy they do not want implemented), threatened resignation, with its attendant political fallout, and subordinates' willingness to complain to organizational committees, Congress, and news media.

One must remember, also, that problems or issues rarely arise as single issues and that decisions are not made one at a time. Rather, issues tend to emerge piecemeal over time, one lump in one context, a second in another. Also, many issues compete for the players' attention every day, and players are often forced to focus on the "issue of the day" before facing a new and different issue the next day. One more nuclear submarine, one more nuclear reactor to India, another later to Egypt—these individual decisions in sum beget nuclear proliferation. Governmental decision makers do not decide to proliferate nuclear weapons or power, it just happens as the sum of many discrete and well-reasoned decisions that still may lead to an unintended consequence, such as proliferation. The bureaucratic politics model explains such occurrences quite well. Big decisions rarely form official policy. Instead, public policy is derived from many small decisions made every day, sometimes dealing with what is considered a crisis, that add up to shape the overall policy of the nation, state, or locality.

Bureaucratic leaders must manage their alliances with supporting clientele groups, legislative committees and subcommittees with whom they regularly interact, and other staff or line agencies at their own and different levels of government. They seek to influence their own reputation or that of their agencies for expertise and knowledge to strengthen these sources of bureaucratic power. Whether loosely knit into issue networks or more permanently fixed in an iron triangle, the bureaucratic leader politically operates to establish a policy **subsystem**—a political alliance comprising the agency, related or vested interest groups, and legislative committees or subcommittees with which the agency shares values and preferences in the particular area of policy making.[18]

Internal Sources of Values

Any number of internal sources of values and value conflict can be found in public agencies. An obvious one arises from the constraints of budgeting. The budget process imposes strict time limits on decision making, and although an ideal process to reach rational decisions may stipulate searching for all possible solutions to a problem to arrive at the best one, the practical time constraints of budgeting allow no such luxury. Time limits force compromises in values and how well they are accepted.

Some solutions are too expensive to be adopted. Value conflicts may arise, for example, when the public demands certain solutions and then balks at the cost when the bills for the resulting policies come due. Consider, for instance, mandatory sentencing. Citizens in many states called for tough stances on crime during the 1990s, and dozens of states passed "three-strikes-and-you're-out" laws. The public, however, has frequently objected to the high costs that such laws impose on the judicial system and on the administration of state correctional facilities. The need to fund those program areas has often cut into funding for other equally popular programs, such as education and health delivery services.

Budget constraints involve administrators in value conflicts when one branch or level of government imposes mandates or rulings on another without considering the effects of the costs involved. When a federal judge rules that a state's prison system is unconstitutional because excessive overcrowding violates the Eighth Amendment's prohibition on "cruel and unusual punishment," the judge does not consider how the state will pay to reduce prison density. But prison officials must. Do they seek to build more prisons to lower density? Will the public and the central administration accept such an expensive way to respond to the federal ruling? Or should they reduce density by releasing some prisoners early? This last solution may be the most cost effective, but it arouses public ire for "turning felons loose on our streets."

Among the most critical and important decisions made by a correctional facility's supervisor is the hiring of the right people. Two innovative approaches to hiring "the best and the brightest" are exemplified by California's and Ohio's experiences. The California Board of Corrections (CBOC), which has responsibility for oversight of local correctional facilities and jails, has researched the question of who makes the best and brightest staff in corrections. Its psychologists combined various job analysis and interview data to develop a comprehensive list of basic abilities and added two more procedures to collect information related to personnel requirements of corrections work: the collection of critical incidents and measuring personality variables using the Personality-Related Position Requirement Form (PPRF). The CBOC then used and refined the PPRF. Similarly, the Ohio Department of Rehabilitation and Correction (DRC), in 1994 established an Ohio Correction Assessment Center (OCAC) to improve, centralize, and streamline the correctional officer selection process. The DRC operates 32 institutions; having 32 different hiring authorities was unrealistic. The rapid growth in inmate population since the 1990s led to a near-exponential growth in prison staff. Ohio, like California and many other states, had a situation in which correctional facilities and staff made corrections a "growth industry." Dedicating a centralized location to specialize in staff hiring allowed for a more professional human resources process. Implementation of the OCAC streamlined the hiring process for correctional officers.

Another, related internal source of values—and often of clashing values—are public employee unions. Unions impose standards within their negotiated contracts, and these often entail values that differ from what the management of the bureau or agency considers wise or even appropriate policy. Management may want merit pay increases, whereas the union wants salary increments to be standardized step increases across the board or based on seniority considerations rather than on what administrators evaluate as merit. Generally, unions work hard to protect the rights of employees. Union standards, however, may run counter to what administrators believe is required for efficiency or to weed out unproductive employees. Unions insist on procedural safeguards when employees are disciplined, demoted, or fired, yet administrators may view such procedures as inordinately time consuming and costly. Unions make it difficult to institute change into an older bureaucracy whose members are set in their ways of doing things.

Increasing numbers of public employees also belong to professional associations. Literally hundreds of professional associations have members who work for public agencies. Most, if not all, professional associations develop codes of ethics to govern the conduct of their members. The American Society for Public Administration and the International City–County Management Association, for example, have both adopted elaborate codes of ethics. These are internalized by those bureaucrats who are members of such associations as the "proper" values they should observe. But what happens when public policy directives clash with those codes of ethical standards? Does a hospital administrator obey a mandate from the state governor's office (his or her ultimate boss) not to provide a health benefit or service to someone suspected of being an undocumented alien? Or does the administrator follow a professional code of ethics that demands that health service be provided to the sick?

Sometimes values and value conflict arise from the demands of critical units in a larger organization. High-level administrators may be caught in a dilemma. Do they respond to the policy directives imposed by a political appointee—say, the Secretary of Health and Human Services, who may be pushing for fast approval of drug therapies for AIDS treatment—or do they go slow to satisfy the standards of health experts in a critical research unit who demand a slower and more rigorous scientific approach that is more costly in time and money? Such organizational goals and formal rules of authority restrain organizational members' personal preferences. But long-term organizational goals may be perceived by individual members or subunits of an organization as naive or unrealistic. For these reasons, internal value conflict is inevitable.

Power is specific to a context and to a relationship. Organizational conflicts among people from different professional backgrounds and organizational affiliations often involve efforts to protect status or turf rather than disputes over goals.

Upper-level administrators must maintain members' morale, which greatly limits the top-down issuance of "orders." If lower-level employees refuse to change certain policy or procedures, then it is exceedingly difficult to impose them from above. What people outside an agency view as red tape, members of agencies may see as

INFOTRAC
COLLEGE EDITION

The middle-aging of new public management

INFOTRAC
COLLEGE EDITION

"The politics and administration of privatization."

essential or simply as "the way we do things here." Elected officials promote a new reform to cut red tape, only to flounder on the resistance of civil servants. This is why repeated efforts to streamline government have met with limited success. Such efforts have ranged from the Brownlow Committee to **reinventing government** efforts in the 1990s. In 1936, for example, President Roosevelt established the Brownlow Committee to study the staffing needs of the executive office and make recommendations to reorganize the executive branch; modest revisions resulted, including the creation of the Executive Office of the President. The post–World War II Hoover Commission, led by former President Herbert Hoover, similarly sought to reorganize the federal government, but with only moderate success. More recent efforts have been President Ronald Reagan's appointment of the Grace Commission to have business leaders study and reform the federal government and the Clinton Administration's attempt to reinvent government, headed by Vice President Al Gore. This latest manifestation of the trend emphasizes **political** or **administrative decentralization**, or allocating power down to states and localities, and **privatization**, or the process of turning over government property or functions to the private sector.

Pragmatic local government managers use markets in a dynamic way: They contract out and they bring unsuccessful contracts back "in-house" for direct public provision, and they mix public provisions and private contracts for the same service. Even with careful attention to monitoring, local government experience with contracting has not always been positive, despite a strong trend since the 1980s to use the "market approach" to government service delivery.

Among the newest of paradigms in reforming public management is the trend emerging since the 1990s of government entities coming together for integrated informational technology (IT). They have achieved cost savings through the sharing of electronic resources to advance their own unique public policy needs and strategies by involving state and federal levels of government working together within a forum called "Government Without Boundaries." Some local governments, for instance, Palo Alto, California, have become contractors and consultants for other cities. States are contracting with each other to supplement services they lack instead of buying an entire IT system for themselves. It would have cost the government of Hawaii $40 million on the commercial market for what it purchased for $11 million from the government of Arizona. These types of intergovernmental entrepreneurial relationships, known as government service providers, or **GSPs**, are become more common. Rather than contracting with a private company, cities find it easier to contract with GSPs who can better understand their governmental constraints and challenges (Coates, 2004: 25).

The nationwide budget crisis faced by nearly every state has led to changes in the fundamental approach some are using in budgeting. The state of Washington exemplifies well the approach referred to as **results-based budgeting**. When state elected and agency leaders demonstrate that the tough decisions they have made are designed to deliver the results that are most important to citizens, citizens respond. A *Seattle Times* editorial of November 17, 2002, noted:

> The usual, political way to handle a projected deficit is to take last year's budget and cut. It is like taking last year's family car and reducing its weight with a blowtorch and shears. But cutting $2 billion from this vehicle does not make it a compact; it makes it a wreck. What is wanted is a budget designed from the ground up.

Nearly every state is facing the most dire fiscal situation since the end of World War II. In fiscal 2002, state revenues actually declined for the first time since they began keeping records. The dire fiscal situation results from four converging factors: an explosion of health care costs, a collapse of capital gains tax revenues, slow economic growth, and outdated revenue systems that tax less and less of the new economy (for example, a retail sales tax that does not capture tax revenues from the growing e-market approach to purchasing). Many states have exhausted budget cuts and have drawn down or even totally expended rainy-day funds. As of February, 2003, states faced deficits of $30 billion, and fiscal 2004 state budgets were projected to fall short by $82 billion.

This process frustrated Washington Governor Gary Locke (D) and his staff. Instead of imposing across-the-board cuts, they asked: What should state government do, and what should it stop doing? Facing nearly $3 billion in deficits, Governor Locke and his chief of staff asked the Public Strategies Group, Inc. (PSG) for help. Instead of a 15 percent across-the-board cut, PSG shifted the focus from spending cuts to helping them to buy the best possible results for citizens with the resources they had. PSG helped the governor and his budget staff turn the budget process on its head by designing a process to answer four key questions: (1) How much are citizens willing to spend? (2) What results form the core of what must be done and done well to serve the citizens of Washington? (3) How much will the state spend to produce each of these priority outcomes? (4) How best can that money be spent to achieve each of these outcome's core results? The four questions evolved into a four-part plan of action for the budget. The governor's staff of senior people from the Office of Financial Management assisted a "guidance team" that developed a top-10 list called the "Priorities of Government." The staff team then put

PHOTO 3.2
Governor Gary Locke (D-Washington)

PHOTO 3.2
Governor Gary Locke (D-Washington)
Governor Gary Locke was elected Washington State's 21st governor in 1996, the first Chinese American governor in U.S. history. He was reelected in 2000 and 2004. Why is it important for a performance-budgeting reform initiative to have the support of the governor?
Source: Courtesy of Governor Locke's office.

together 10 "results teams," one for each outcome, chaired by a senior staff member from the Office of Financial Management. The results team members were charged by Governor Locke to forget the loyalties to the agencies they represented, and instead to "be like citizens," telling them where to put the money to get the best results. Governor Locke warned everyone that the budget would be painful, and it was. It eliminated health insurance for nearly 60,000 of the working poor, dental, hearing, and optometric coverage for poor adults on Medicaid, and 2,500 state jobs. It suspended cost-of-living increases for state employees, eliminated teacher pay increases, and suspended a $221 million class-size reduction effort mandated by citizen initiative. It raised university tuition by 9 percent a year for two years, projected early release of 1,200 low-risk felons, and involved the shutdown of a series of smaller programs. Editorial commentary was surprisingly favorable to the brutal state spending plan, endorsing the process by which the staff had arrived at the hard choices about the core priorities of state government. Even his Republican opponent for the governor's office in 2000 referred to it as a work of bold and impressive statecraft, praising the governor's willingness to face down the most powerful interest groups in his own party.

In late January 2004, a survey of voters agreed. Sixty-four percent endorsed the following statement: "Whether or not I agree with all of the Governor's budget recommendations, I respect his leadership and vision to solve the current problem and get the state's economy back on track" (Opitz, Nelson, and Osborne, 2004).

PHOTO 3.3
President Bush Signs the USA Patriot Act in the East Room, October 26, 2001
Despite many questions being raised, after its passage, about the sweeping powers the Patriot Act gives the federal government that concern issues of citizens' civil rights, the bill passed Congress by an almost unanimous vote and with extensive bipartisan support. What factors account for its speedy and nearly unopposed enactment?

Source: White House photo by Eric Draper. Courtesy of the White House Photo Office.

We conclude this chapter with Reading 3.1, "The Groupthink Failure," which describes how two bureaucratic dysfunctional behaviors, termed *groupthink* and *stovepipe*, contributed to the intelligence failures to prevent the attacks of September 11, 2001, and to discover the truth about Iraqi weapons of mass destruction. The reading demonstrates the interagency clash of values and a variety of forces affecting their value system. It raises questions as to what really must be done to enhance our national security.

Reading 3.1

The Groupthink Failure: A Centralized Bureaucracy Won't Improve Intelligence

When it comes to the failure of our intelligence community to prevent 9/11 and to discover the truth about weapons of mass destruction, there are two words you need to know—stovepipes and groupthink.

Stovepipes is Beltway talk for the inability to two different intelligence agencies to share information. The intelligence flows up and down a single pipe—within the FBI or the CIA, for example—but not between them.

Groupthink describes the failure to challenge assumptions, the pressure to interpret ambiguous evidence to back the collective wisdom and to ignore or minimize information that challenges it.

Stovepipe and groupthink figure prominently in two devastating reports issued in July. The 9/11 Commission report documents how stovepiping made it almost impossible to connect the dots of intelligence that could have painted a picture of al-Qaeda and its plot. A Senate intelligence committee report details how biased groupthink led to false conclusions about the existence of Iraqi WMD.

These two reports have prompted a rush in Congress to create a centralized intelligence bureaucracy. In its most radical form, a new national intelligence director would have total control over the 15 intelligence agencies, now spread between different departments. It follows the model of the Department of Homeland Security, which grouped existing agencies from different departments.

Putting all the little boxes into one big box looks good on paper—in theory it ought to yield more coordinated and better intelligence. But centralization actually only worsens the problems of stovepipes and groupthink.

"The whole thing would just be recreated inside that box," said one former senior defense and intelligence official, who served both Democratic and Republican administrations.

"Reorganizing organizations rarely fixes the problem that caused the organization to fail," says former Defense Secretary Bill Perry. "New leadership can, new processes can, and new resources can."

Perry also brings to this subject his experience as a Stanford University engineering professor and his work as a venture capitalist in Silicon Valley.

The stovepiping of information can better be tackled by finding new systems to connect disparate information in different organizations, Perry told me. Technology can do this. "We need a Google-like process to solve the problem," he said. "We don't need a new organization to do it."

Beneath the proposals to reorganize the intelligence bureaucracy, the 9/11 Commission also recommends creating a searchable, linked database available to all agencies, something that, remarkably, does not exist.

Even more troubling, centralization is certain to reduce the competition of analytical views. Agencies that tried to challenge the CIA's groupthink on Iraq—such as the State Department's Bureau of Intelligence and Research or the Department of Energy's nuclear experts—would have even less chance of being heard.

"Decision makers need to be presented with multiple alternatives," Perry said. But if political leaders don't want to hear conflicting ideas, even a powerful new intelligence director is not likely to change that.

"Presidents want intelligence that agrees with what they're doing," said Donald Gregg, a former CIA official who served as national security adviser to the first President Bush. When they hear contrary intelligence, "they resist it like mad."

Good leaders—and Gregg puts the first Bush in this category—ask tough questions and listen to the answers. But in this Bush administration, the groupthink in Iraq began at the top. The intelligence agencies "knew exactly what the White House wanted to hear," Gregg told me.

The reorganizational steamroller now revving up in Congress is just groupthink in another form. If the aim is to improve our national security, not to deflect public ire, then Congress should take the time to engage in real deliberation.

Source: Daniel Sneider, *San Jose Mercury News*, September 10, 2004. Reprinted with permission of the *San Jose Mercury News*.

Net Assignment

Using the Internet, explore how your local bureaucracy works. Is it responsive? What values does it represent? Is it successful in its representation? What is its culture? Its institutional memory? Is change needed? Who are the people running the bureaucracy, and who, if anyone, is advocating reform and change?

Summary

Organizational culture helps develop and maintain an agency's political support. By linking assumptions, attitudes, beliefs, and norms, the culture becomes a primary source of both values and value conflict in its worldview. A process of socialization spreads an organization's culture among its membership and allows the culture to shape members' cognitive processes and guide their actions while helping them cope with uncertainty, events, and symbols. Organizational culture also provides shortcuts to thinking about decisions. These can lead to such negative or dysfunctional behaviors as groupthink. Leaders themselves promote an agency's culture by using it to shape recruitment and socialize new members. The culture's own imagery provides language and symbols to deal with the organization's external and internal environments. By infusing the communication process of the organization, the culture adds jargon to enhance a sense of expertise.

A bureaucratic ideology —the verbal image of the good society that is relevant to the function of a particular bureaucracy—emerges from a pressing need for cost-effective images to aid decision making. The ideology flows from the top down, infuses the formal and informal communication systems, and helps an agency garner support or limit attacks from outsiders. It helps define the goals of an organization and enhances the self-esteem of its members by providing a socially acceptable rationale for its goals and policies.

Bureaucratic agencies depend on several bases of power: expertise and specialized knowledge, a near monopoly on technical data, and discretion in making decisions about alternatives in policy and implementation. Expertise is closely associated with staying power, which, along with procedures, rules, regulations, and standards, tends to remain operative in an agency for long periods of time.

Agencies also develop issue networks and triangle arrangements to ensure political support from vested interest groups and a favorable relationship with legislative committees.

Glossary of Key Terms

acronyms   Words formed from the first (or first few) letters of a series of words.

administrative decentralization   The delegation of authority to subordinate levels within a department or agency.

bureaucratic ideology   A verbal image of that portion of the good society that is relevant to the functions of a particular bureau as well as the chief means of constructing that portion.

groupthink   A mode of thinking within a cohesive group; a practice engaged in by people whose agreement seeking overrides a realistic appraisal of alternative courses of action. The drive for consensus at any costs suppresses dissent.

GSPs   government service providers; entrepreneurial electronic communications ventures wherein one government sells its IT services to another.

ideology   A verbal image of the good society and a chief means of constructing such a society.

jargon   The specialized vocabulary and idioms of those who are in the same type of work or profession.

organizational culture   How an organization views its role in broader society; a complex of assumptions, attitudes, beliefs, norms, and values that guide an organization.

place-based ownership models of economic enterprises   A variety of models or approaches used by local governments to promote economic development which are based on the local geographic locale of the enterprise.

political decentralization   The allocation of powers among territories or areas governed by subunits (in the United States by states, counties, cities, school districts, special districts, and intergovernmental agencies).

privatization   The process of returning to the private sector certain property or functions previously owned or performed by government.

reinventing government   The latest manifestation of the progressive tradition of continually improving government by tinkering with its operations—in this case, by emphasizing privatization.

results-based budgeting   Approach to the budgeting process that eschews incrementalism and across-the-board cuts and instead asks fundamental questions about the priorities in governmental services.

stovepipes   Beltway jargon for the inability of different agencies to share information.

subsystem   A political alliance of an agency, related interest groups, and legislative committees that shares values and preferences in a particular area of public policy making.

Review Questions

1. Compare and contrast internal versus external foundations of bureaucratic power. How does the nature of an organization's structure influence its reliance on internal versus external sources of power?

2. What role does bureaucratic ideology play in an organization's culture? How is a bureau's ideology used to influence the external environment of an agency? How is it used to support internal cohesion?

3. How do acronyms and jargon enhance bureaucratic expertise and power? How do they contribute to the problem of stovepiping?

4. Compare and contrast an agency's internal and external sources of values. Is value conflict the result of different values coming from internal versus external sources? Can value conflicts emerge within both internal and external sources?

5. What competing values are illustrated in the "The Groupthink Failure" reading? How did a value such as agency loyalty contribute to the stovepiping problem? Do you agree with the author that the "groupthink" problem in the case of Iraqi WMD and the failure to prevent the attacks of 9/11 can be first laid at the feet of President Bush? Is groupthink mostly a top-down organizational dysfunction problem?

Surfing the Net

Useful websites for the material discussed in this chapter include the following:

U.S. Department of Agriculture (**http://usda.gov**)

U.S. Department of Labor (**http://dol.gov**)

U.S. Department of Veterans Affairs (**http://www.va.gov**)

For professional associations and their codes of ethics, consult the following sites:

American Society for Public Administration (**http://www.aspanet.org**)

Government Accounting Standards Board (**http://www.rutgers.edu/accounting/raw/gasb**)

International Personnel Management Association (**http://www.ipma-hr.org**)

International City Managers Association (**http://www.icma.org**)

For public employees unions and their standards and codes of ethics, see the following sites:

Association of Government Accountants (**http://www.rutgers.edu/accounting/raw/aga**)

National Education Association (**http://www.nea.org**)

IPL Associations on the net (**http://www.ipl.org/ref/AON**) has links to more than 700 professional and trade association sites.

For more general approaches to the topic of standards and codes of ethics in government, see the following sites:

Center for Responsive Politics (**http://www.crp.org**)

John C. Stennis Center for Public Service (**http://www.stennis.gov**)

Chapter 4

When George W. Bush was sworn in on January 20, 2001, as the 43rd president of the United States, he became only the third president in the nation's history to be elected by the electoral college despite having received fewer popular votes than his election rival.* Bush's election was singularly unique in U.S. history, however: It was the first time the nation's highest court decided the outcome of a presidential election.

Bush won the presidency by the barest margins possible—a 5–4 U.S. Supreme Court vote, a 271–262 electoral college vote, and an official but disputed Florida total of fewer than 600 votes out of nearly 6 million popular votes cast on election day in the state.

Administration in the Federal System: Intergovernmental Relations and Constitutional Sources of Values

The 2000 presidential election vividly exemplifies the clashing values in an issue that is the central focus of this chapter: the complex intergovernmental relationships that result from our federal system. At issue in this instance is the relationship between the national government and the states as well as the relationships among the three branches of government at the state level.

---

*The others were Rutherford B. Hayes over Samuel Tilden in 1876 and Benjamin Harrison over Grover Cleveland in 1888.

Box 4.1

Election 2000: The Dimpled Chads War

The presidential election of 2000 was unique in U.S. history. For the first time, rather than the ballot, the electoral college, or Congress deciding a contested election, the nation's highest court settled it. George W. Bush won the presidency by the narrowest of margins: a 5–4 vote in the U.S. Supreme Court; the smallest possible margin in the electoral college, 271 for Bush to 262 for Gore; and, in an official but disputed count by Florida's secretary of state, fewer than 600 out of nearly 6 million popular votes cast on election day in Florida. Following are the highlights of what might fairly be called the "dimpled chads war."

- *November 8:* The television networks initially declare Vice President Al Gore the winner in Florida, then withdraw that projection, then give the state to Bush, and then finally place the state in the too-close-to-call column. Gore almost concedes to Bush but reconsiders when his advisers tell him the vote is too close to call. Florida's 25 electoral college votes remain up for grabs and will determine the winner of the electoral college majority. Bush leads in the state's popular vote by 1,784 votes.
- *November 9:* Gore has 262 electoral college votes in 19 states and the District of Columbia. Bush has 246 electoral college votes in 29 states. Gore leads in the popular vote by an estimated 300,000 votes and demands a recount of Florida's votes.
- *November 11:* After a machine recount, Florida Secretary of State Katherine Harris—the state's top election official and a Republican who campaigned for Bush—puts Bush's winning vote margin at 960 votes (2,910,074 to Gore's 2,909,114). Gore initiates the protest provisions of Florida's election law and requests manual recounts in four predominantly Democratic Florida counties: Palm Beach (with 425,000 ballots to be recounted), Broward, Miami–Dade, and Volusia.
- *November 14:* Partial manual recounts cut Bush's lead to 388 votes as Secretary Harris determines to end the recount at 5 p.m. Governor Bush files suit in the U.S. District Courts to block manual recounts and places former Secretary of State James Baker III in charge of the legal effort to seek an injunction to stop the count. Gore presses the case for manual recounts.
- *November 19:* Bush's narrow margin climbs to 930 after the final tally of overseas absentee ballots. James Baker argues that Gore is twisting Florida law to change the rules after the election and strongly objects to counting so-called dimpled chads, or the indented but not punched-through

Introduction

For five weeks after the election on November 7, 2000, the candidates and the nation waited to learn who would be the next president while battles raged on in Florida's counties and courts. Box 4.1 offers the highlights of that election and the postelection campaign in what might fairly be called the "dimpled chads war."

Of significant issue in this chapter is the relationship between the national government and the states. The election was for the national office of the presidency, but, as is true for every state, state laws governed how Florida conducted the election. As is true in most states, Florida's legislature had passed implementation of the election along to the local level—specifically, 67 county governments reporting to Florida's secretary of state in the executive branch. Boards of elections in those counties—and across the country—have adopted and implemented a wide variety of ballot-casting devices, ranging from paper ballots and so-called butterfly ballots to punch-card ballots and an equally wide variety of machines to count cast ballots. When disputed or contested, the county election officials of Florida were legally empowered to determine the execution pieces of paper in punch-card ballots. It is the issue of chads that becomes a predominant concern for both candidates.

- *November 21:* In the Florida Supreme Court, after 13 days of legal maneuvering, Gore lead attorney David Boies argues for the state supreme court to order manual recounts. The court agrees and rules in Gore's favor. He picks up 166 more votes.

- *November 27:* Florida Secretary of State Harris officially certifies Bush the winner with a 537-vote margin. She disallows partial recounts of 180 votes for Gore in Palm Beach County. The election moves into what is called the contest phase, a legally sanctioned period under Florida law when a candidate or party can contest the results.

- *November 30:* Time was running out before Florida's electors were to be certified by the state legislature before they could meet with other states' electors in the electoral college. Florida Circuit Court Judge N. Sanders Sauls orders 1.1 million disputed ballots to be brought to Tallahassee in a Ryder rental truck from Palm Beach and Miami–Dade counties. The trucks transporting the ballots arrive to protest signs declaring Tallahassee a "no chads zone."

- *December 1:* In the contested phase with cases in the two highest courts—Florida's Supreme Court in a case brought by Gore and the U.S. Supreme Court in a case brought by Bush—Gore fights on.

- *December 8:* The Florida Supreme Court orders manual recounts across the state of more than 45,000 "undercounted" votes (neither candidate has been clearly chosen on these

ballots), gives more partial recount votes to Gore than Bush, and cuts Bush's official lead to 537 votes.

- *December 9:* With the threat of a recounted popular vote going to Gore and thus a Democratic slate of electors, the Republican-led Florida legislature prepares to fight by calling a special session to select state electors committed to Bush. An unofficial Associated Press tally puts Bush's lead at 177 votes. His lawyers argue before the U.S. Supreme Court that the manual recounts "must be stopped because the 2000 presidential election is spinning out of control." The U.S. Supreme Court suspends the manual recounts pending oral arguments by both sides' attorneys. The Florida House of Representatives passes a resolution, 79–41, to select electors for Bush.

- *December 11:* Governor Bush files before the U.S. Supreme Court, and oral arguments are heard on whether the Florida Supreme Court has violated the federal Constitution by superseding the authority vested in the Florida legislature to set election law.

- *December 13:* The U.S. Supreme Court rules 5–4 to reverse the Florida Supreme Court's decision on manual recounts. The majority justices declare there is no time for an "equitable" manual recount and fault the Florida Supreme Court for not setting a "uniform standard" for the various county election officials who were conducting the manual recounts.

- *December 14:* Vice President Gore concedes the election to Bush, calls for unity, and pledges to lend his support to the president-elect. Governor Bush vows to "mend divisions." The chad wars cease.

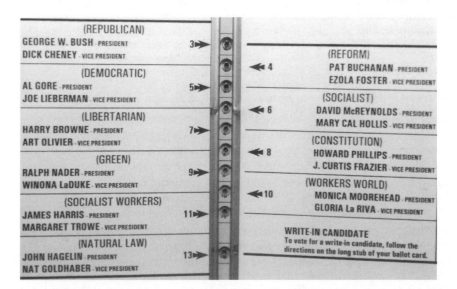

PHOTO 4.1

The Infamous Butterfly Ballot

The Florida election raised questions that most voters had never heard before: When should a dimpled chad count? Should undervotes (that is, the ballots that had no presidential candidate selected) be counted? If so, on what standard would the "clear intent of the voter" be determined? Do you think there should be a uniform national ballot for all nationally elected offices?

Source: AP/Wide World Photos.

PHOTO 4.2
Looking for Hanging Chads
By the 2004 presidential election, many county election districts across the country went from the "punch-card" voting machine to electronic voting devices. Do you agree with the election policy of using touch-screen voting devices that lack a "printed-trail" option? Are "recounts" in such cases really "recounts"?

Source: © Lannis Waters/*The Palm Beach Post.*

of their manual recounts. Would one-, two-, or three-cornered "hanging" chads count? Would a "dimpled" chad count? In the words of Florida state law's vague standard, which ballots reflected "the clear intent of the voter"?

The Florida election case further illustrates the checks and balances in federalism by pitting the judicial and legislative branches against one another and both of them against the executive branch's secretary of state office and the 67 county election offices. The case also involved the power of judicial review, with both the Florida Supreme Court and U.S. Circuit and Supreme Courts overruling lower courts, various state election officials, and the state legislature—and, in the final case, the U.S. Supreme Court overruling the Florida high court.

The Backdrop of Federalism

The presidential election of 2004 went off without many such administrative hitches. Congressionally mandated reforms between 2000 and 2004 required states to allow for "provisional ballots." Many states, with some assistance from the U.S. government in the form of grants to county election districts, changed from the punch-card machines to electronic "touch-screen" voting. Increased numbers of voter watchers and poll assistances prevented the 2000-like alleged voter intimidations. There were no significant "overcounted" or "undercounted" ballots. And to the surprise of most political pollsters, politicos, and pundits, a powerful new force in American elections was evidenced—the *values voter*. Whereas the campaigns stressed the issues of the economy, terrorism, and the war in Iraq, election-day exit polling indicated that a whopping 80 percent of President Bush's supporters, a bloc that included an overwhelming majority of the most frequent churchgoers and who provided the president with his margin of victory, ranked moral values at the top of their reasons for voting. Such moral-value policy issues as the ban on partial-birth abortions and the question of gay marriage strongly motivated the tens of millions of such voters, many of whom were voting for the first time.

Another major source of values in public administration is the U.S. Constitution and the federal system of governance it establishes. The final document and the convention that led to its creation reflected the advantages of centralism as seen by the Founders in reaction to perceived problems under the Articles of Confederation that had governed the union of states from 1776 until 1789.

Federalism permeates every aspect of U.S. politics, including the administration of policy. **Federalism** is commonly defined as a system of government in which an overarching government operates at the national level and shares its sovereign power and authority with various subnational governments. Federalism is a political arrangement as well as a governmental structure arrangement.

A federal system of government may be contrasted with two other approaches or categories of government: the unitary and confederal forms. A **unitary system** of government has all authority centralized within it. Each state within the United States is a unitary form with respect to its local governments. The unitary government may decide to decentralize some authority by delegating responsibility to smaller administrative units, but in doing so it freely grants the authority and may limit or even rescind it without the consent of the lower level. Such administrative subdivisions are "creatures of the state" in a unitary system.

In a **confederal system**, power and authority reside in subnational or state governments that collectively establish an overarching government to which they delegate some powers. They retain veto power over the national entity. Examples of confederal-type systems would be the original 13 states that fought a war of independence from Great Britain, the European Union (formerly the European Economic Community), the United Arab Emirates, the Commonwealth of Independent States (some countries of the former USSR, which was itself a federal system), the 11 states of the Deep South that seceded in 1860 and 1861 to form the Confederate States of America, and some regional councils of government at the local level within the United States.

The federal system created by the U.S. Constitution has layers, or levels, of government: the national and state levels. States, in turn, created their own local levels of government. Each level was assigned certain duties and responsibilities.

Some of the Founders considered their proposed new form of government to offer distinct advantages, which they advocated in a set of essays collectively known as the Federalist Papers. The advantages of federalism are linked to certain values promoted by this formal arrangement of power that became more apparent as the nation grew in size, complexity, and diversity. These values now include:

1. greater scope for diversity;
2. a greater ability to experiment and create innovative policy approaches to public problems;
3. a capacity to represent and reflect the vast array of different ethnic groups, religious, and cultural minorities in the population;
4. governmental policy making that is decentralized and often "closer to the people";

Box 4.2

Core Values in the Constitution and U.S. Society

Principles built into the federal Constitution set core values about how government and politics will operate in the United States. We can summarize them as follows.

1. *Supremacy:* National laws take precedence over state and regional laws.
2. *Representation:* Voters' will is expressed by elected officials, who are (a) elected to the House of Representatives based on state population and (b) elected to a uniform number of two seats per state in the Senate.
3. *Separation of powers:* Three branches of government—the legislative, the executive, and the judicial—each have distinct responsibilities and powers.
4. *Checks and balances:* Each branch of government exercises a check on the others.
5. *Electoral college:* A separate representative body meets every four years following a presidential election to elect the president and vice president, their votes largely predetermined by the results of the election.
6. *Amendments:* A complex process of amending the Constitution has two steps, one federal and one state, that each require supermajorities.
7. *Bill of Rights:* A basic guarantee of rights for individuals as well as the limits of government are spelled out with some but not complete specificity.

We can summarize American society's core values as follows:

1. *Achievement:* We value individual effort and believe that education and hard work will pay off.
2. *American exceptionalism:* We believe in the special moral status and mission of the United States and the American culture.

3. *Caring beyond self:* We place a high value on concern for others, such as members of our families and ethnic groups, as well as on neighborliness and caring for the community.
4. *Democracy:* We value the belief that the judgment of the majority should be the basis of all sovereignty and governmental power.
5. *Equality:* We place a high value on the same rules of law for everyone—rich and poor, black and white, male and female, and so on.
6. *Equality of opportunity:* We value the freedom of individuals in the marketplace, which helps resolve tensions between the values of freedom and equality.
7. *Fairness:* We believe in people getting what they deserve as the consequence of their individual efforts and actions.
8. *Freedom:* We value political liberty, free speech, freedom of assembly and of movement, freedom of religious belief and practice, and the freedom to pursue happiness.
9. *Luck:* We believe that an individual's good fortunes and circumstances are not permanent and that good fortune can happen to anyone at any time.
10. *Patriotism:* We value loyalty to the government, society, and its symbols and dedication to the way of life it represents.
11. *Religion:* We hold reverence for a meaning that transcends the realm of the secular and the practical.
12. *Supremacy of deeds:* We believe that each individual should be judged by what he or she does or accomplishes, not by the station in life to which he or she may be born.

Source: Adapted from Daniel Yankelovich, How changes in the economy are reshaping American values, in Henry J. Aron, Thomas E. Mann, and Timothy Taylor (Eds.), *Values and public policy* (Washington, DC: Brookings Institution, 1994): 23–24.

5. a greater ability to protect the needs and interests of minority population groups; and
6. a sharing of power that limits the power of government and better avoids autocracy or tyranny.

Federalism entails core principles written into the Constitution that serve as fundamental values of American society. These values become part of the "rules of the game" by which politics is played, affecting the behavior of all participants and most particularly that of the bureaucracy. These values are presented in Box 4.2.

The division of power and authority into three layers and the sharing of concurrent power mean that the relationships between and among the bureaucracies established at each level become two-way streets. Power, funding, ideas, and interactions flow up and down the system of governmental structures. **Vertical federalism** refers to the relationship between government at different levels: national-to-state, state-to-local, and national-to-local. **Horizontal federalism** concerns the relationships among governments at the same level: state-to-state, county-to-county, and city-to-city.

A federal system of government reflects and attempts to balance such values as equality, responsiveness, tolerance, limited government, popular sovereignty, separation of powers, checks and balances, diversity, and localism. The U.S. federal system was unique when it was established in 1789. As this model of federalism has evolved and developed over the years, our perceptions of it also have changed.

Models of U.S. Federalism

Models or conceptual explanations of government can help us describe the various relationships among the various levels and bodies of government.

The Layer-Cake Model

The first model to be developed became known as the *layer-cake model*, and it was used to characterize relations within the federal system during the republic's early years. It emphasized the division between powers at the national and state levels, a dual-federalism period that will be discussed more fully later.[1] It portrays a functional division of authority between the levels of government, which are like layers in a cake, attributing certain programmatic authority to each level and emphasizing their distinctiveness. The national-level bureaucracies implement national defense, mint or print money, provide postal services, and regulate interstate commerce. The state-level bureaucracies provide public education, build and maintain roads, and provide health services. City-level bureaucrats provide such basic services as fire and police protection, waste removal, and sewage treatment. In this model, there is little interaction among bureaucrats at the different levels.

INFOTRAC
COLLEGE EDITION

Horizontal federalism in the new judicial federalism

The Marble-Cake Model

With the New Deal programs of President Franklin D. Roosevelt in the 1930s, a period of **Cooperative Federalism** developed. It was characterized as a *marble-cake model*.[2] In this model, intergovernmental cooperation and the sharing of functions blurred the distinguishing lines between the levels, making it difficult to clearly say where the national government ended and the state and local levels began. It emphasized a separation of government structures—that is, who paid the salaries of bureaucrats—rather than of programmatic functions. In the marble-cake model the national, state, and local bureaucrats are all involved in providing educational services, police protection, building and maintaining roads and highways, and staffing health service agencies.

The Picket-Fence Model

By the 1960s, Cooperative Federalism developed in which increasingly close fiscal relationships among the various levels of government led to a national government that was financially better off and could provide various grants-in-aid to states and localities that were presumably less well financed. The federal government is considered to

FIGURE 4.1
The Picket-Fence Model of Federalism

Source: Adapted with permission from Deil S. Wright, *Understanding intergovernmental relations* (3rd ed.). Copyright © 1988 by Brooks/Cole.

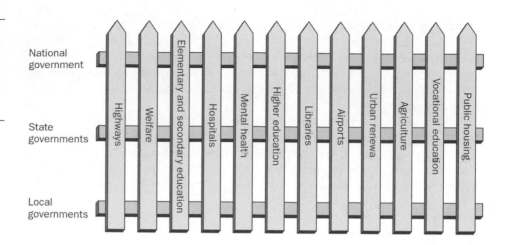

be far better at raising revenue because it has corporate and personal income taxes as its primary tax base; these taxes generate the greatest amount of revenue. Grants of financial aid set more stringent or less stringent standards, rules, or procedures for their use, emphasizing those values the granting government wishes to promote. The interactions among all levels of government over a policy area that is being promoted through a grant program develop into a complex pattern of interaction. Political scientists refer to this pattern as the *picket-fence model* of federalism. It features program specialist bureaucrats at all three levels of government who develop fiscal and other working relationships with each other that are independent of the different legislatures, chief executives, and courts. In this model, the bureaucrats at different levels of government share a common policy or programmatic concern, and they interact more often with each other than with others at their same level of government but who are involved in other functional areas. This approach to federalism promotes a type of "functional fiefdom" among bureaucrats who are involved in a particular public policy area. A model of picket-fence federalism is shown in Figure 4.1.

Grant-in-aid programs have grown extensively since the 1960s. The U.S. Advisory Commission on Intergovernmental Relations (ACIR) estimates that such grants grew from 45 in 1961 to more than 400 by the end of President Richard Nixon's administration in 1974 and to 540 at the start of President Ronald Reagan's first term in 1981. The number dropped to 400 by the end of that term but gradually increased again to more than 600 by the late 1990s.[3]

Varying approaches to federalism denote distinctive periods in the nation's political development. Each period of federalism exhibited specific developments regarding bureaucratic structures, emphasized different values, and showed variations in the manner of intergovernmental relations, especially regarding government financing and intergovernmental transfers of funds (grants-in-aid). The periods in total demonstrate the highly dynamic nature of U.S. federalism.

INFOTRAC
COLLEGE EDITION

Multilevel governance and metropolitan regionalism in the United States of America

Approaches to Federalism

United States political structures are amazingly fragmented. An independent unit of state or local government, such as a city, county, school district, special district, state, or town government, is one that has its own power to raise revenues through

CARTOON 4.1
Localism versus federalism
What difference does it make whether power is centralized or decentralized in U.S. politics? Do you think any programs now administered from Washington, D.C., should be moved to the state or local level? Are there things that state and local government do that you think would be better done at the national level?

Source: Jack Ohman, Tribune Media Services. Reprinted with permission.

taxation and to determine how to spend those revenues. There are more than 87,500 such units of government in the United States (see Table 1.1). How they interact with one another characterizes the various eras of federal relations.

Dual Federalism

The first period of U.S. federalism has been called **Dual Federalism**. It marked the beginnings of our federal system and dominated intergovernmental relations among governments in the system from the early 1800s until 1930. Dual Federalism reflects a 19th-century view of government that saw the national and state levels as distinct and separate from each other in terms of functions. Each level could and largely did ignore the other. Each had its own jurisdiction, and authorities rarely crossed jurisdictional lines.

The national level was relatively small during this period. Few if any grants-in-aid were granted from national to state or local levels, and few were provided by the states to their localities. Patronage was the preferred method of staffing the agencies of the small bureaucracies that operated at all levels of government, and the public viewed government as appropriately staffed by the "common man." Services were simple. The departmental structural form was almost exclusively used. Not until the late 1800s, toward the last years of the era, did the national and even the state level develop the independent regulatory form of structure for agencies. By the turn of the century, however, problems controlling the excesses of industrialization necessitated governmental regulation.

The era of Dual Federalism emphasized the value of responsiveness. Most regulatory agencies were state or local. In the nation's economic life, freedom of the individual was emphasized, and government reflected that value by practicing the principle of **laissez-faire** (almost literally, "Let the people do as they choose") economics. Limited government and individual rights meant that states' rights and the primacy of localism were the prevailing values. Governments at the various levels tended not to cooperate with each other, often viewing one another with suspicion and as competitors more than partners in service. Cartoon 4.1 illustrates

**Unidimensional
federalism**

the ideal of the value of localism that was so broadly accepted during the era of Dual Federalism.

The external environment changed after World War I, however, as the nation moved onto the world scene as a major international power. The economic boom of the 1920s ballooned until the economy burst in 1929 with the crash of the stock market and the start of the Great Depression. These external developments led to massive changes in attitudes about government and politics as well as changing values in the federal system. A new era of **Cooperative Federalism** emerged that lasted from the 1930s through the 1950s. This phase emphasized that national, state, and local governments were cooperating agents who interacted with each other, jointly facing and solving common problems rather than viewing one another as hostile competitors pursuing conflicting goals. The magnitude of unemployment and poverty manifested in the Great Depression were clearly problems that stretched beyond jurisdictional lines. Poverty spilled over from city to city and state to state. It was a problem well beyond the capacity of any one state or local government to address. Only the national government, with the cooperation of states, had the financial resources to cope with the Depression.

As the Great Depression waned and the national economy recovered during the enormous national effort of World War II, the New Deal programs of the Roosevelt administration called for greater cooperation among state, federal, and local authorities. The effects of World War II—with its civilian-defense organizations of citizens at the local level and the need for rationing of gasoline and other resources that were critical to the war effort at the national level—led naturally to greater cooperation. The public gladly accepted an intrusion of government, especially of national government agencies and bureaucrats, into their lives as part of the war effort that would never have been tolerated during peace time.

Cooperative Federalism

Cooperative Federalism witnessed a new prevailing theory of economic management by the national government. The need for total economic reconstruction justified what became known as *pump priming*. Government spending programs were designed to spur demand, increase employment, and generally stimulate the economy out of the Depression. The influence of British economist John Maynard Keynes was significant. He advocated deficit spending by the national government to stimulate the economy during a recession or depression by borrowing money to spend on public works, defense, and welfare. This new Keynesian approach replaced the prior economic theory, which had assumed the need for the gold standard (that is, all money was ultimately redeemable in gold at a fixed price) and a balanced federal budget.

Cooperative Federalism enhanced horizontal federalism. The era witnessed a growth of interstate compacts and commissions to deal with specific governmental programs that crossed state jurisdictional lines. These dealt with such policy problems as river-basin management—in part led by the successful federal example of the Tennessee Valley Authority (TVA) in the 1930s—as well as transportation, wildlife and natural resource conservation, and criminal extradition. At the local level, the era of Progressive reforms culminated in interlocal agreements such as the Lakewood Plan, in which the Southern California city of Lakewood contracted for certain services, such as police and fire protection, with Los Angeles County. Soon many and varied interlocal agreements were established.

At the national level, the growth of industrial and other types of corporations that grew beyond the capacity of states to control led to the creation of independent regulatory agencies. The federal government expanded its areas of policy concern and programming. It developed new agencies and structures to deal with national domestic issues and to respond to its emergence as a world superpower and world leader. This era of federalism saw the establishment of several federal independent regulatory agencies—for instance, the Federal Communications Commission (FCC) and the Securities and Exchange Commission (SEC) in 1934 and the National Labor Relations Board (NLRB) in 1935. It also saw considerable expansion of older agencies, such as the Interstate Commerce Commission (ICC), the Federal Reserve Board (the Fed), and the Federal Trade Commission (FTC). New federal agencies and the restructuring of the Executive Office of the President (EOP) were exemplified by the creation of such agencies as the Central Intelligence Agency (CIA) in 1947, the General Services Administration (GSA) (which became the federal government's centralized purchasing staff agency) in 1949, the National Science Foundation in 1950, the Small Business Administration in 1953, and the National Aeronautics and Space Administration (NASA) in 1958.

Creative Federalism

Combined developments—a revived postwar economy, the United States as a world superpower, the Cold War in international relations, and the civil rights movement in domestic politics—finally culminated in a new era of federalism that has been called **Creative Federalism**. This period, which marked the 1960s, reflected the enormous influence of the administration of President Lyndon Johnson and his efforts to create a "Great Society" and conduct a domestic "War on Poverty." These federal efforts led to a truly massive expansion of grants-in-aid programs—literally, from just dozens to 300 such programs.

This era of federalism was characterized by joint planning and decision making at all levels of government, including partnerships with business and nonprofit social organizations. Great Society programs emphasized the value of *maximum feasible participation* in their antipoverty welfare efforts and advocacy programs in national civil rights efforts. They led to a great expansion in national welfare programs and the development of *entitlements*. New federal programs included Head Start, and two new cabinet-level departments also were created: Housing and Urban Development in 1965 and Transportation in 1967. A new independent commission, the Equal Employment Opportunity Commission (EEOC), was established in 1964 to promote a new value—affirmative action. The Department of Health, Education, and Welfare changed dramatically as it moved from pushing desegregation to massive efforts to promote integration. In the EOP, two new staff agencies were established: the Office of U.S. Trade Representative in 1963 and the Council on Environmental Quality in 1969. The Bureau of the Budget (since renamed the Office of Management and Budget, or OMB) developed a new approach to management, first in the Department of Defense and later in other federal agencies, known as the Program Planning Budgeting System (PPBS).

The era of Creative Federalism witnessed enormous expansion of federal governmental programs, activities, and bureaucracies and in financial aid from the national level to the state and local levels. Different values were emphasized from

those of the preceding era: national standards over local standards, comparable worth, affirmative action, entitlements, maximum feasible participation, and the protection and even promotion of diversity.

New Federalism

A reaction to the efforts of the Great Society set in, partly from disillusionment with the national government because of the Vietnam War. This ushered in a new period, known as **New Federalism**, from 1968 to 1980. This era was an attempt to return more autonomy to the states. First articulated by President Richard Nixon, it maintained a significant level of federal funding but modified grants-in-aid from categorical (or **project grants**) to **block grants**. These had fewer strings attached, and states increasingly used formula grants to aid their own localities. Even the national government adopted the formula grant approach exemplified by general revenue sharing established in 1972. New Federalism saw the reorganization of the budget office in the EOP into the OMB, the creation of the Office of Science and Technology Policy in 1976, and the establishment of the Office of Administration in 1977. A new cabinet-level Department of Energy also was created in 1977. Several independent agencies were established or revamped from older ones: the Federal Elections Commission (FEC) and the reformed Nuclear Regulatory Commission (NRC), both in 1974. Values characteristic of the period helped establish two new federal government corporations in 1970: the United States Postal Service (replacing the cabinet department with a more business-like government corporation) and Amtrak (to take over and manage railroad passenger transportation, which had been given up by the private sector).

New Federalism promoted decentralization by devolving some programs from the national government back to the states and by decentralizing some federal management, exemplified by the creation of 10 coterminous regions, each with a regional center. It attempted to return both power and funding to the states. Several values thus became characteristic of New Federalism: localism, technology, efficiency of government, a business-like approach to government management, economic capitalism, and judicial restraint in the federal judiciary.

Renewed Federalism

These values were expanded upon during the 1980s in what might be called **Renewed Federalism**, the Reagan administration's version of New Federalism. Reagan's approach differed from that begun by President Nixon by promoting *supply-side economics*, which relied on massive, across-the-board tax cuts that were supposed to expand the economy enough to raise federal tax revenues and thus recover the costs of the tax cuts. In addition, Reagan strengthened national defense by significantly increasing defense spending and new technology development efforts, such as the antimissile system that became labeled as "Star Wars."

The federal government's deficit in the eight years of the Reagan presidency, however, tripled the federal debt that had accumulated over the preceding 200 years. One result of the enormous deficit increase was the administration's ending of the general-revenue-sharing program in 1986. This period saw cuts in the number of categorical or project grants and an even greater shift toward block grant funding. Joint partnerships with business were emphasized. Job Corps, a program created by the Joint Partnership Training Act, replaced the Johnson-era Comprehensive Employment Training Act (CETA). Reagan promised to "get government off our backs" in his campaign for the office, and his administration led an effort to deregulate various aspects of government and industry.

The efforts to boost national pride and strengthen defense that began in Reagan's first term and continued in his second and then in President George H. Bush's administration resulted in the establishment of a new cabinet-level department, the Department of Veterans Affairs, in 1988. The following year, the war on drugs effort also saw the creation of a new staff agency within the EOP, the Office of National Drug Control Policy.

Renewed Federalism emphasized several primary values:

- order in society (as seen in the war on drugs and the war on crime);
- economic capitalism;
- individual rights;
- limited government;
- rationality in government decision making, with new efforts at assessing cost–benefit analyses of federal programs, especially those of a regulatory nature; and
- the value of deregulation and **devolution** of responsibilities from Washington, D.C., down to the states and localities.

These values and efforts continued during the administration of President Bill Clinton in such approaches as the reinventing government program led by Vice President Al Gore. President George W. Bush added another approach by promoting nongovernmental organizational involvement with his "faith-based initiative" program.

INFOTRAC
COLLEGE EDITION

Bush's faith-based legacy

Fiscal Federalism

Intergovernmental relations within the federal system are driven by the transfer of funds from one level to another or by the sharing of financing between or among governments at the same level. Transferring or sharing funding requires considerable interaction as money is requested, agreements to share financing are hammered out, and granted funds are monitored and evaluated. Fiscal Federalism simply refers to the financial relationships that exist between or among independent units of government in a federal system.[4] Fiscal Federalism, or the multiunit financing of a government service, addresses how best to design governments in a federal system. In theory, Fiscal Federalism must answer three fundamental economic questions:

1. How do we attain the most equitable distribution of income?
2. How do we maintain high employment while avoiding excessive inflation?
3. How do we distribute resources efficiently?

The national government is viewed as more efficient in raising revenues, whereas state and local governments are seen as closer to the people and thereby better at spending revenues in ways that are more responsive and accountable to the taxpayers. Higher levels of government, however, may approach problems and be able to finance programs that benefit from economies of scale. Buying a fleet of 500 automobiles enables the government to negotiate a lower per-unit cost price than if several lower-level units each purchased 50 units from the provider. Federalism copes with fundamental economic problems well because it is more flexible. The national level is better able to provide answers to the first two questions, whereas subnational (state or local) units are theoretically better at answering the third question.

Grants-in-aid programs enable higher-level governments, whose resources are stronger and more resilient to economic upswings and downswings, to assist lower-level governments in stimulating spending to support national policy goals. Such programs also help set nationwide standards for uniform or minimal service purposes, or to compensate for problems of **externalities**, or the costs or benefits from one thing affecting another, or the costs and benefits not accounted for by the free-market exchange. Costs or benefits accrue to someone other than the buyer or seller. With externalities, government services cross jurisdictional boundary lines, particularly in program areas such as clean water and air-pollution control, health, education, and public safety. Such services are most often provided by local government agencies, frequently in compliance with policy standards set at the state level.

Intergovernmental programs that provide goods and services may separate responsibility from accountability for policy decision making. Governments may spend monies not collected directly from taxpayers in their jurisdiction. In any federal system, two or more governments may have legal jurisdiction over the same geographic area. This may raise problems with voters, who fail to see the need to pay taxes to two or more authorities, and it may not persuade taxpayers of the fairness of taxing them for some benefit that largely assists some other jurisdiction.

State and local governments are not all equal in their capability to raise revenue, in part because they rely on different sources of revenue and in part because other levels of government may be able to legally constrain the type or level of revenue the lower level might acquire. Higher-level governments may be able to impose policy program requirements (mandates) that they may not fully or even partially fund. They may impose a burden without concern for how the lower-level government will provide funds to meet that burden.[5] Grants-in-aid programs were developed as one method to address these thorny issues of Fiscal Federalism.

Types of Governmental Grants-in-Aid

A grant is any intergovernmental transfer of funds or other assets. The national level provides grants to both states and local governments, and states provide grants to local governments. Since the 1930s, federal grants have increased enormously in number, scope, and the relative proportion for state and local projects. When a grant-in-aid is provided, the granting government or agency prescribes certain standards or requirements and then actively monitors the grantee's spending of those funds to ensure compliance with the grant's intended purpose. This reflects the adage "He who pays the piper, calls the tune." All grants-in-aid vary in type by how many "strings," or guidelines or conditions, are attached to the grant. Federal grantees must comply with federal standards that may go beyond the immediate policy problem for which the program provides a good or service. Compliance is also required with federal regulations about equal employment opportunity in selecting personnel or awarding of contracts. Federal grants in aid have grown consistently since the late 1960s and have done so under every presidential administration, no matter the public policy orientation of the respective presidents.

Categorical grants are those limited to highly specific, narrowly defined activities—for example, for a community to create small green spaces or vest-pocket parks in an urban redevelopment area. Categorical grants may include and also be called *project grants*. This type of grant is given from a higher- to a lower-level government and must be applied for with respect to an individual project. These are the most common type of grant. They are generally less well funded and often require the grantee to spend matching funds. Categorical grants grew rapidly from the 1930s through the 1970s, expanding in number to some 500 such grants distributed by virtually every department of the U.S. government.

Compared with other types of grants, receiving governments dislike categorical or project grants because they have more strings attached, are distributed less equally (governments that hire full-time grant writers receive more grants), and are more burdensome to implement and evaluate.

Ever since the Nixon administration, Congress has moved toward block grants; the trend accelerated in the mid-1990s when the Republicans gained control of Congress. These grants are distributed based on a statutory formula. They may be used in various ways within a broad policy area, such as criminal justice or mental health programs. The Personal Responsibility and Work Opportunity Act (PRWOA) of 1996 (PL 104-193)*—widely known as the Welfare Reform Act—used the block grant approach for welfare reform. It replaced the Aid to Families with Dependent Children program (AFDC) with the Temporary Assistance to Needy Families (TANF) program. Although it gives state and local governments greater latitude to set standards and regulations for welfare assistance, it also funds the program less generously, shifting the financial burden to the administrative-level governments (administered by county governments with policy guidelines set at the state level).

---

*PL is an abbreviation for Public Law.

CARTOON 4.2
A thousand points
How much does the federal system of U.S. politics allow each level of government to blame the other? What period of federalism does this cartoon best
illustrate?

Source: Dennis Renault, *Sacramento Bee*.

INFOTRAC
COLLEGE EDITION

**Changing safety net
of last resort**

It also tightened eligibility requirements for Food Stamp and Supplemental Security
Income (SSI) recipients. This approach enhances the value of flexibility but at a cost
of accountability. This so-called workfare approach to welfare reform exemplifies
federalism in which state-level governments (Wisconsin, for example) innovate
a policy approach that is ultimately adopted at the national level and spreads
thereafter to the other states and localities.

Flexible spending implicitly means a lessening of control over how the money is
spent. Block grants may be spent less wisely than if more strings were attached. Local
bureaucracies may be induced to enter program areas and spend money they otherwise would not if the decision were solely up to local elective officials. Block grants
implicitly involve devolution, or the transfer of power from a central authority to
a more local authority. Grants-in-aid programs confuse voters about who is responsible for a program. Each government involved may point the finger at another one
for any perceived policy failure, a point humorously made in Cartoon 4.2.

In passing TANF, welfare reform moved from a categorical grant to a block grant
approach. PRWOA states that the purposes of the TANF program are to assist needy
families, to fight "welfare dependency" by promoting work and marriage, to reduce
nonmarital births, and to encourage the formation and maintenance of two-parent
(i.e., "traditional") families The transition to block grant funding emphasized performance indicators by the states—a central one being a decline in caseload. Prior to
the reform, states, counties, and the federal government shared the costs of welfare
according to a fixed formula in which the federal government bore 50 percent of all
costs. Since the reform, block grants have been in fixed amounts based roughly on

the size of the caseload in 1994, regardless of the current caseload size. In turn, most states delegated implementation responsibility to counties and applied mechanisms to monitor the performance measures to which PRWOA made each state accountable. State flexibility allows states to choose whom they will assist, what requirements they will impose on those who receive aid, and what supports, other than cash, those families will receive. States have also made different decisions about which of these choices should be made at the local level.

Generally, proponents of TANF have trumpeted its success based on the declining caseloads and on the increased employment among poor single mothers. They maintain that this focus is the primary goal of welfare reform and should remain the primary policy focus. TANF was proclaimed a success only a few years after its enactment and implementation and before one of its harshest provisions, the 5-year limit, took effect. Supporters hailed the nearly 40 percent decease in the number of welfare recipients, from 13.6 million in 1995, the year before passage of TANF, to the 8.9 million recipients in 1998. However, merely counting the number who have left welfare provides only a partial picture. Some still question whether TANF *caused* the decrease and, even if so, whether or not the former recipients actually achieved the program's stated goal of self-sufficiency (Lens, 2002).

Critics note that the enactment of TANF coincided with a period of unusual prosperity and growth in the U.S. economy. Welfare rolls have always declined during times of economic expansion, since, in times when more jobs are available more opportunities exist for poor women to work. In 1997, a report by the Council of Economic Advisors attributed as much as 31–45 percent of the decline in the welfare rolls to economic expansion. Critics of TANF argue, moreover, that although welfare caseloads have fallen and employment has increased, the TANF reforms have not fundamentally improved the living standards of many of the families it has affected.

Most states have adopted a "work-first" approach to moving welfare recipients into the labor market, which emphasizes the rapid placement of recipients into jobs for which they are currently qualified (rather than further education or job training to enable them to qualify for higher-paying jobs). Thus, those who left the welfare rolls generally have low earnings, face higher levels of job instability, have little upward mobility, and receive few benefits (Ridzi, 2004; Weil and Finegold, 2002). Nearly 80 percent of TANF recipients face one or more of six commonly identified "barriers" to work: poor mental or physical health, limited English proficiency, a disabled child at home, a child at home under the age of 1, less than a high school degree in formal education, and the lack of recent work experience. The more barriers a recipient faces, the less likely she is to work and the more likely she is to hit TANF time limits.

TANF has been aptly characterized as a "fair-weather ship"—the strong economy of the mid- to late 1990s contributed significantly to what are widely seen as its most positive outcomes (the falling caseloads and increased employment rates among single mothers). That stronger economy of the 1990s means that welfare reform has not yet been fully tested. Clearly, the strong economy played a significant, though largely unmeasured, role in the encouraging data on work, earnings and poverty. Welfare recipients in most states have only recently begun facing the 5-year limit on benefits. Some of the more important of the long-term outcomes of welfare reform may not be observable for a decade, some even for a generation.

Critical assessments done by 2002, often in conjunction with the TANF program's reauthorization, showed that contrary to popular opinion, the goal of self-sufficiency remains elusive for many and that many poor women and their families are being hurt rather than helped by TANF (Lens, 2002). The failure of TANF to adequately address obstacles to self-sufficiency in the workplace threatens to create an even worse welfare problem in the future.

TANF and other federal policies of "devolution" have also contributed to the fiscal crisis faced by 47 of the 50 American states in 2002–2004. State costs are being driven up by health care inflation, rising caseloads, increasing prescription-drug costs, and higher premiums for private health insurance, which has further increased the number of uninsured Americans. The federal government shares some responsibility for the states' fiscal crisis, in that it has loaded costs onto states by policy changes and conditions of aid for programs such as Medicaid and No Child Left Behind, where it has failed to fund its mandates, declined to appropriate fair shares of funds for new policy initiatives, and preempted or curtailed the states' authority to adjust their tax systems to current economic realities (Kincaid, 2003). As one critic noted, most state officials saw the federal government as being partly, or even substantially, to blame for the states' fiscal crisis, for several reasons:

> First, they viewed unfounded federal promises and mandates in health (especially Medicaid), education, welfare, homeland security, and election reform as significant strains of state budgets. For example, the federal government had not provided the $3.8 billion promised to help train and equip state and local police, firefighters, and rescue personnel for terrorism. The U.S. Conference of Mayors reported that cities were spending $2.6 billion of their own money on homeland security. Similarly, the No Child Left Behind Act of 2001 imposes an estimated $35 billion in annual costs on the states for student testing, data collection, and higher education and curriculum standards for public schools; yet the promised $28 billion for student testing and teacher training did not come through from the federal government. The Help America Vote Act of 2002 requires states, among other things, to supply voting equipment guaranteeing minimum errors, maintain voter-registration rolls, establish voter-identification rules, assure voting access for persons with disabilities, and create procedures to resolve voter complaints; however, Congress appropriated only $1.5 billion of its promised $3.8 billion. (Kincaid, 2003: 6)

Using **formula grants**, a higher level of government (national or a state) provides a lower-level government funds for stipulated purposes, which are distributed according to a set formula. The grants often have not even been applied for but are offered to a local government, seemingly out of the blue. At the national level, general-revenue sharing exemplified a formula grant approach. This program began in 1972 with the New Federalism approach of the Nixon administration and ended in 1986 when the rising federal budget deficits convinced the Reagan administration and Congress to end this approach. Its formula was heavily weighted by population. All governments received some general-revenue–sharing funds, whether they asked for them or not, with larger amounts going to more populous jurisdictions but with overall funds being broadly distributed so that every governmental unit got some piece of the pie. This approach was more popular with Republican Party–controlled jurisdictions, such as suburban cities, small towns, and rural counties.

States use the formula grant approach more than the national government does—for example, to aid local school districts. These formula are often weighted to equalize funding (that is, poorer school districts receive more than richer school districts in an effort to equalize per-pupil spending). Sometimes the formula is weighted to reward local effort—giving greater amounts to those jurisdictions that tax themselves more heavily.

One critical aspect of the increased use of federal grant programs, especially those related to health and welfare programs that have been established as entitlements, affects the level of mandatory spending. An **entitlement** is a governmental benefit required by law for eligible individuals, groups, or other governments. Medicare, Medicaid, Social Security retirement benefits, and unemployment benefits all exemplify entitlement programs. Mandatory spending rose from slightly more than 22.7 percent of the federal budget in 1963 to more than 47 percent by 1993 and topped 58 percent of the federal budget by 2003.[6]

A good example of an entitlement program fraught with many unintended consequences affecting federal–state and even state–local relations is the Individuals with Disabilities Education Act (IDEA) of 1990 (PL 101-476, 20 U.S. Code [subsections] 1401–87.) The Education for all Handicapped Children Act (EAHCA) was passed in 1975. The predecessor to IDEA (1990, amended in 1997), it provided all disabled children the right to "free, appropriate public education" in "the least restrictive environment." When EAHCA was reauthorized in 1990, it became IDEA. It established very specific procedural requirements in order to protect the rights of children with disabilities and to ensure that they could not be unfairly removed or excluded from school. The procedures were updated in the 1997 reauthorization of IDEA and by the Assistance to States for the Education of Children with Disabilities Act (1999).

When federal oversight is limited and when ambiguities exist in the law and when elected politicians are either silent or intentionally ambiguous on issues, then judges and courts have become especially influential players in the creation and recreation of the law. This is particularly the case with IDEA, for which federal compliance monitoring finds that 90 percent of states fail to ensure proper oversight of their local education agencies, resulting in the filing of suits by individuals who believe their children are not being appropriately protected by the law. Court decisions resulting from such suits directly affect policy (Palley, 2003: 605).

Just one provision of IDEA, that concerning early-intervention programs, illustrates the issue. In excess of 200,000 children are identified as having a disability or being at risk for one before 36 months of age and being enrolled in early-intervention programs under Part C of IDEA. The law mandates 16 components of early intervention and provides an accompanying set of regulations to guide program implementation. As with other block grant programs, however, wide variability exists across states in the nature and extent of services provided. Congress left substantial ambiguities in each version of IDEA. Although some of these have been clarified by federal and even state regulations, many have been clarified by federal courts. Indeed, Congress has relied on court decisions when drafting the law and allowed room for courts as well as federal, state, and local administrative agencies to define some aspects of the law. It left many substantive provisions vague. Courts at all levels have made decisions that helped to define IDEA and subsequently to interpret its many provisions. As a result, the courts have been extremely influential in the development of policy related to it (Palley, 2003).

One political result of the increase in mandatory federal spending is that Congress is induced to find ways to spread the costs downward, increasing the share of the burden to be covered by lower levels of government. This trend has led to what some refer to as "coercive federalism" through the use of **unfunded mandates**.

Coercive Federalism and the Use of Unfunded Mandates

Mandating describes the situation where a higher level of government obliges a lower-level government to offer or provide some program as a matter of law or as a prerequisite to full or partial funding for either that program or some other, unrelated program. Unfunded mandates involve federal or state laws that impose programs or policy on lower-level governments without granting them any funds for their implementation.

Mandates may seek to do various things. Some mandates simply constrain lower levels of government and their bureaucracies. In *Mapp* v. *Ohio* (1961), for example, the U.S. Supreme Court constrained local police officers from performing searches without judicially sanctioned warrants. Other mandates issue direct orders that often can be costly, such as federal court orders for state prisons to reduce their density. The Americans with Disabilities Act (1990) compels state and local governments (as well as federal agencies) to provide access for the physically handicapped to all public buildings. The Family and Medical Leave Act (1993) specifies how time off should be provided for a woman to deliver a baby. Such acts impose financial burdens on lower-level governments. Other mandates are best described as conditional.

If the lower level of government accepts financial aid through some grant program, then it is obliged to meet certain standards and procedures. As mentioned earlier, these often require the expenditure of matching funds by the grantee governmental agency.[7] Nobody knows the exact number of mandates, but surely there must be hundreds of thousands nationwide. In New York State, then-Governor Mario Cuomo established an Office of Mandate Relief. The office conducted a study in 1992 that found 1,700 state and federal mandates were affecting governments within the state.[8] A study by the U.S. Conference of Mayors found that, on average, 12 percent of all city budgets are devoted to meeting the costs associated with mandates.

A good example of some of the intricacies of unfunded or underfunded mandates is the previously mentioned No Child Left Behind Act (NCLB) of 2001 (PL 107-110), which requires states to set academic goals for all students and for separate groups of students characterized by race, ethnicity, poverty, disability, and limited English proficiency. It mandates annual testing of all students in grades 3 through 8 and testing at least once in grades 10 through 12. It requires schools to make annual progress in meeting state-determined student performance goals. By 2013–14, NCLB mandates that 100 percent of students in each subgroup perform at a proficient level as determined by test standards established by each state. Schools that fail to meet their adequate yearly progress goals will be subject to sanctions. To help states meet requirements imposed by NCLB, Congress increased federal funding over 2 years for elementary and secondary education by over 40 percent.

NCLB has been extremely controversial, figuring prominently in both the Bush and Kerry presidential campaigns of 2004, for instance. Some critics object to such frequent student testing, on philosophical and pedagogical grounds. State and local officials, however, have focused on the very high costs of implementing the law and of meeting the accountability standards. In states that had not previously conducted frequent and uniform standardized testing, the financial burden of establishing such student accountability has been especially burdensome. Other states have voiced concerns about the high costs of ensuring that all students are able to satisfy the new academic performance standards. Debate over the effectiveness of NCLB will continue. But one fact is clear: State and local governments have to fund the new responsibilities while balancing tight budgets and facing ever-greater demands for education services.

The budget crisis facing virtually every state imposes a further obstacle to improving and funding public education. The National Conference of State Legislatures reported that collectively state budget deficits in fiscal year 2003 ranged from $22 billion to $30 billion. It projected that in 2004 those deficits would range between $54 billion and $78 billion. Such financial pressures at the state level are equaled by similar pressures at the local level, forcing local officials across the country to make drastic cuts in school district expenditures. For example, several school districts in California are projecting cuts ranging from $23 million to $25 million for FY 2005, and many Minnesota school districts are facing cuts in the range of $10 million to $20 million (Dodson and Garrett, 2004: 270).

In 2004, several state legislatures, for example, Maine and Wisconsin, have concluded that increased federal funding is insufficient to cover the costs imposed by NCLB. A fair number of state legislatures have passed resolutions urging Congress to change the law. Other state legislatures are actively considering foregoing federal funding and opting out of the provisions of NCLB. One scholarly study of the impact of NCLB on 10 of the states found that the additional costs of meeting the accountability standards mandated by the law were substantially greater than the money the federal government allocated to elementary and secondary schools (Mathis, 2004). The National Conference of State Legislatures (2004) published a Mandate Monitor in which they concluded that in fiscal 2005 the gap between the cost of NCLB and the available federal money would be at least $10 billion.

NCLB is viewed by its critics as especially problematic with respect to students of racial or ethnic minorities. The sole remedy NCLB presents for dealing with the problem of pervasive and deep-seated racism (which, for example, often manifests itself in the form of inequitable rates of per-pupil funding expenditures and widespread neglect of urban schools) is to increase accountability through mandatory testing. The prospect that real reform can occur in the near future, especially regarding racial and ethnic minorities, is debatable, indeed even bleak, when the costs of military defense and the war on terrorism is leaving little money for domestic priorities. Black youngsters are overrepresented in each category of special education services and in every U.S. state. Moreover, states with a history of de jure segregation account for five of the seven states with the highest overrepresentation of African Americans labeled as mentally retarded (Mississippi, South Carolina, North Carolina, Florida, and Alabama). Latino children, on the other hand, are overidentified in some states and underidentified in others (Paul, 2004; Dodson and Garrett, 2004).

The effects, intended and unintended, of NCLB are gently yet insightfully spoofed in Box 4.3, "No Cow Left Behind," written by Ken Remsen, the principal at Underhill I.D. school in Jericho, Vermont.

States have complained bitterly about the burdens imposed on them by unfunded mandates from Washington, D.C., but they, in turn, impose many unfunded mandates on local governments and their bureaucracies. The political movement against the use of unfunded mandates reached sufficient force that Congress enacted the Unfunded Mandates Act (PL 104-4) in 1995. This law makes it more difficult for Congress to impose new laws, regulations, rules, or standards that add any significant costs to local government. The Congressional Budget Office is responsible for estimating the costs of all future mandates. The law exempts all previous mandates but still allows unfunded mandates in an emergency—which Congress, of course, defines.

Box 4.3

No Cow Left Behind

As a principal facing the task of figuring out all the complexities of the No Child Left Behind legislation and its impact on education, I have decided that there is a strong belief that testing students is the answer to bringing about improvements in student performance.

Since testing seems to be a cornerstone to improving performance, I don't understand why this principle isn't applied to other businesses that are not performing up to expectations. I was thinking about the problem of falling milk prices and wondering why testing cows wouldn't be effective in bringing up prices since testing students is going to bring up test scores.

The federal government should mandate testing all cows every year starting at age 2. Now, I know that it will take time out of the farmers' necessary work to do this testing every year and that it may be necessary to spend inordinate amounts of money on testing equipment, but that should not distract us from what must be done.

I'm sure there are plenty of statistics to show what good milk-producing performance looks like and the characteristics of cows who achieve this level of performance. It should, therefore, be easy to figure out the characteristics necessary to meet this standard.

We will begin our testing by finding out which cows now meet the standard, which almost meet the standard, which meet the standard with honors, and which show little evidence of achievement.

Points will be assigned in each category, and it will be necessary to achieve a certain average score. If this score is not achieved, the Department of Agriculture will send in experts to give advice for improvement. If improvements do not occur over a couple of years, the state will take over your farm or even force you to sell.

Now, I'm sure farms have a mix of cows in the barn, but it is important to remember that every cow can meet the standard. There should be no exceptions and no excuses.

I don't want to hear about the cows that just came to the barn from the farm down the road that didn't provide the proper nutrition or a proper living environment.

All cows need to meet the standard.

Another key factor will be the placement of a highly qualified farmer in each barn. I know many of you have been farming for many years, but it will be necessary for all farmers to become certified. This will mean some more paperwork and testing on your knowledge of cows, but in the end this will lead to the benefit of all.

It will also be necessary to allow barn choice for the cows. If cows are not meeting the standard in certain farms, they will be allowed to go to the barn of their choice. Transportation may become an issue, but it is critical that cows be allowed to leave their low-performing barns. This will force low-performing barns to meet the standard or else they will simply go out of business.

Some small farms will probably go out of business as a result of this new legislation. Simply put, the cost per cow is too high. As taxpayers, we cannot be expected to foot the bill to subsidize farms with dairy compacts.

Even though no one really knows what the ideal cost is to keep cows content, the legislature will set a cost per cow. Expenditures too far above this cost will be penalized. Since everyone knows that there are economies of scale, small farms will probably be forced to close and those cows will merge into larger farms.

Some farmers may be upset that I proclaim to know what is best for these cows, but I certainly consider myself capable of making these recommendations. I grew up next to a farm and I drink milk. I hope you will consider this advice in the spirit it is given, and I hope you will agree that the No Cow Left Behind legislation may not be best for a small state like Vermont.

Source: Reprinted with permission of Ken Remsen, No cow left behind, originally published in the *Burlington Free Press*, July 25, 2003.

In many respects, the Welfare Reform Act reflected this trend to reduce the burden on state and local governments. Initial indications are that the act has indeed led to significant reductions in administrative burdens and reporting requirements—along with funding. The financial burden on local governments may increase in the future, particularly in times of recession.

The effects on public administration from intergovernmental relations goes far beyond the financial effects, which are, of course, significant. Policy and administrative effects of intergovernmental relations unrelated to financial aid or burdens shape values and value conflict and daily affect public administration in the United States. Intergovernmental relationships reflect, and sometimes structurally establish, certain values in administrative politics.

Intergovernmental Relations and Public Administration

Although sometimes used as synonyms, *federalism* and *intergovernmental relations* are not equivalent. **Intergovernmental relations** refers to a complex of interrelationships among federal, state, and local governments that involve political, fiscal, programmatic, and administrative processes in which higher-level governments share revenues with lower-level governments but with special conditions that the lower units must meet to receive the financial aid. The term also refers to the interactions among governments that entail both vertical and horizontal federalism. The concept of intergovernmental relations encompasses all of the permutations and combinations of relations among the more than 87,500 units of government in the United States. Congress acted to cope with the maze of intergovernmental relations when it established the ACIR in 1959. It was designed to monitor relations among the levels of government and to make recommendations to Congress for improving such relations. It was governed by a bipartisan group of 26 members serving 2-year terms. In recent years, many state governments have established their own such commissions to study state and local developments within their states.[9]

Just as federalism evolved through various phases or periods, so have intergovernmental relations in the United States since the 1800s. Deil S. Wright, one of the foremost scholars of intergovernmental relations, has characterized these several phases; they are shown in Table 4.1.

One aspect of intergovernmental relations that flows from the devolution revolution and from the complexity of Fiscal Federalism is the expansion of intergovernmental units and regional governments. Interstate compacts, interlocal agreements, councils of government (COGs), and more than 300 special-district governments, especially those found within the nation's metropolitan areas, have all increased in number and importance in response to changing values inherent in the system of intergovernmental relations. **Substate regionalism** refers to the multijurisdictional cooperative arrangements between or among local government entities, such as metropolitan special districts or councils of government. These structures provide regionwide views or approaches to dealing with local problems that spill over local jurisdictional boundaries. They are most often used for planning, economic or physical development, transportation, and environmental policy problems that affect a whole region.

Many regional governments administer regulatory policy that has been mandated through national air- and water-pollution-control laws. Regional bodies are often the best way to cope with pollution problems that literally blow or flow across jurisdictional lines. Many regional entities are advisory in nature, but some have fairly strong regulatory powers. COGs, however, are mostly advisory in nature. Various city, county, and some special-district governments located within a metropolitan area may join a COG to discuss mutual problems and coordinate approaches to those problems—on a strictly voluntary basis. COGs frequently ease the way to receiving federal grants.

They also can make recommendations, but member units may ignore such recommendations if they choose. Some COGs are quite complex. In California, for

INFOTRAC
COLLEGE EDITION

Matching rates and mandates

INFOTRAC
COLLEGE EDITION

Breaking the welfare cycle

TABLE 4.1

Phases of Intergovernmental Relations (IGR)

Phase Descriptor	Main Problems	Participants' Perceptions	IGR Mechanisms	Federalism Metaphor	Approximate Climax Period
Conflict	Defining boundaries Proper spheres	Antagonistic Adversary Exclusiveness	Statutes Courts Regulations	Layer-cake federalism	19th century–1930s
Cooperative	Economic distress International threat	Collaboration Complementary Mutuality Supportive	National planning Formula grants Tax credits	Marble-cake federalism	1930s–1950s
Concentrated	Service needs Physical development	Professionalism Objectivity Neutrality Functionalism	Categorical grants Service standards	Water taps (focused or channeled)	1940s–1960s
Creative	Urban-metropolitan Disadvantaged clients Grantsmanship	National goals Great Society Participation	Program planning Project grants	Flowering (proliferated and fused)	1950s–1960s
Competitive	Coordination Program effectiveness Delivery systems Citizen access	Disagreement Tension Rivalry	Grant consolidation Revenue sharing Reorganization	Picket-fence (fragmented) federalism	1960s–1970s
Calculative	Accountability Bankruptcy Constraints Dependency Federal role Public confidence	Gamesmanship Fungibility Overload	General aid— entitlements Bypassing Loans Crosscutting regulations	Façade federalism (confrontational)	1970s–1980s
Contractive	Borrowing and budget balancing Federal aid cuts and changes Juridical decision making Managing mandates	Aggressiveness Contentiousness Defensiveness Litigiousness	Congressional statutes Court decisions Information sources Negotiated dispute settlement	De facto federalism Telescope(d) federalism Whiplash federalism	1980s–1990s

Source: Adapted with permission from Deil S. Wright, *Understanding intergovernmental relations* (3rd ed.). Copyright © 1988 by Brooks/Cole.

example, the San Francisco Bay Area has the Association of Bay Area Governments (ABAG), made up of eight counties and 89 cities. In Southern California, the Southern California Association of Governments (SCAG) comprises six counties and 175 cities. The San Diego Association of Governments (SANDAG) involves 14 cities, and the Sacramento Area Council of Governments (SACOG) has four counties and 14 cities joined together.[10]

Increasingly, regional governments are formed for regulatory purposes. Again, California provides good examples. The Bay Conservation and Development Commission (BCDC) approves all waterfront development in the San Francisco Bay Area. The California Coastal Commission (CCC) grants permits for development within the coastal zone, approximately 1,000 yards from the shoreline. In New York City, the

New York–New Jersey Port Authority is a multibillion-dollar regional special district that runs the port facilities that span the neighbor states of New York and New Jersey. Regional governments also are used for transportation (for instance, the Bay Area Rapid Transit Authority, or BART), whether rail, highway, or air.

Regional governments also may regulate the use of river flows across state lines. The Colorado River, for example, supplies water to seven states—Arizona, California, Colorado, Nevada, New Mexico, Utah, and Wyoming. Other regulatory governments regulate the extraction of oil reserves in the Gulf of Mexico and regulate the crabbing industry in the Chesapeake Bay region.

Interstate agreements may be used in more informal but reciprocal arrangements, often called a *consortium*, to share educational specialties and allow students from one state to study in another without paying out-of-state tuition fees. State governments may exchange personnel with expertise. Florida, for example, might send a professor of marine biology to Wisconsin to assist the state in dealing with the problems facing its freshwater-fishing industry by the introduction of lampreys into Lake Michigan through the St. Lawrence Seaway.

When cities, counties, and special-district governments receive major funding from the national level through various grant programs, they acquire a corresponding degree of autonomy from their state government, even as they come under greater influence by the federal government. As depicted by the picket-fence model of federalism, these relationships encourage the creation of informal **vertical functional autocracies**—largely self-governing professional guilds comprising members of bureaucratic agencies from all three levels of government who are able to function as autocracies, running narrow policy areas as functional fiefdoms mostly independent of other agencies or branches of government.

Intergovernmental relations involve not only the transfer of funding from one level to another (along with corresponding strings), but also the informal exchange of ideas and approaches. Innovation in policy is greatly enhanced. Before a state enacts a new law, it frequently contacts nearby states, often sharing regional cultural, economic, and political characteristics so as to learn from their experience with a problem or model program. Not only do directives flow downward from the national level to the state or local level, but also ideas flow upward. Many times the national standards that are imposed are developed and proven on the basis of the experiences of state and local bureaucracies in coping with a particular policy problem.

The rich complexity of intergovernmental relations in the United States is illustrated in Reading 4.1, "No Child Left Behind Act." It discusses how appropriate or not it is to apply the values of business and the market economy to the reform of education. It highlights how various states have been impacted by the NCLB act.

Reading 4.1

No Child Left Behind Act: What Will It Cost States?

Whether education is or is not a market commodity, business model education reforms are ascendant. The theory is that an emphasis on efficiency, outcomes, the bottom line, and tough-minded business management will result in more effective schools. However, when we give the federal No Child Left Behind (NCLB) Act business-like scrutiny, we find it to be a bad piece of business.

- Your accountants tell you that you will be entering into a contract with the federal government that will require expenditures about 10 times higher than your revenues.
- You will be required to produce a product to very precise and narrow specifications at 100 percent accuracy with little control over the inputs or the production process. That is, you cannot control family, community, and personal factors that influence school success.
- Your research, planning, and development departments (fussy and unimaginative folks that they are) bring you studies that show that no one knows how to accomplish this task, and professors from the nation's most prestigious universities say that if it can be done, than far greater social and family investments are needed.
- Your legal department has advised you (with much wringing of hands) that your company will be legally liable for producing the absolutely perfect results and warn that your legal and financial exposure will be huge.
- Of course, any wise and responsible corporate CEO, accountable to the shareholders, who takes this contract should be immediately fired. As 45 of the 50 states struggle with red ink, this is the highly regulated business prospectus the federal NCLB act mandates on state and local governments.

Every child must be given high-quality educational opportunities. This is a moral imperative. However, it is such a national tragedy that property-wealthy districts spend 23 percent more than less wealthy school districts that the Organization for Economic Cooperation and Development (OECD) rates the United States as being one of the most inequitable of the industrialized nations. . . .

When the Gallup Poll asked citizens specific questions about the elements of the NCLB law, the federal reform proved highly unpopular. . . .

- "Sixty-six percent believe a single test cannot provide a fair picture of whether a school is in need of improvement. NCLB bases this judgment on a state test administered annually in grades 3 through 8."

"Eighty-four percent believe that the job a school is doing should be measured on the basis of improvements shown by students. NCLB requires that a specified percentage of students—in the school as a whole and in each subgroup—must pass a state test and improvement is not a factor."

Furthermore, a large number of independent scholars have demonstrated that it is not possible to have 100 percent of students achieve a high standard. (By definition, a high standard is high because few can pass it.) . . .

In my May 2003 review of 10 states who had recently calculated the costs of bringing all children up to state academic standards as required by NCLB, seven of the 10 states showed total education cost increases greater than 24 percent. Of these, 6 percent saw cost increases between 30 percent and 46 percent. Two were in the 15 percent range and one estimated only added administrative costs—not the added costs for the extra teaching of children. (The states included in the study were Indiana, Maryland, Montana, Nebraska, New Hampshire, New York, South Carolina, Texas, Vermont, and Wisconsin.)

What is amazing about this set of independent studies is that they use a wide variety of outside experts, different research methodologies, different standards, different geographic regions, and a range of sponsors, from legislative mandated research to vested interest groups. Nevertheless, they uniformly find that massive new investments are needed.

The largest single reason for the added costs is that the cost of helping at-risk children has been woefully underestimated. The average state provides 17 percent additional money for these students, but the costing studies found the effective figure to be double (or 100 percent) the base amount. . . .

[Since his study, he notes other states have found highly increased costs as well: Alabama, Arkansas, Illinois, Kansas, Kentucky, Missouri, North Dakota, and Washington.]

These results are completely consistent with the previous estimates of the set of 10 other states noted above. Again, these studies were conducted using a wide variety of methods, state government review panels, different authors, and different sponsors. Nevertheless, all 18 studies, taken together, show massive increases necessary to meet the requirements of No Child Left Behind. . . .

The federal government has repeatedly claimed that the law is fully funded. President Bush said, "And we've committed the resources to help the students achieve these standards," on January 8, 2003. More recently, Secretary [of Education] Paige wrote an opinion article for the *Wall Street Journal* (October 29, 2003) responding to the claims that NCLB is underfunded. "Nothing could be further from the truth," he said. Unfortunately, the federal government has not conducted a cost analysis of NCLB along the lines of those done by the 18 states referenced here. . . .

The repeated rationale given for "adequate federal funding" is best illustrated in Secretary Paige's opinion article: "President Bush has increased K–12 education spending by 40 percent since he took office. . . . In raw terms, this president has increased education spending by $11 billion. As a nation, we now spend $470 billion a year on K–12 education locally and federally—more than on national defense."

These statements are true enough. However, metaphorically, they overlook the fact that a 40 per-cent increase in nothing is still nothing. In apples-to-apples comparisons, the federal Title I allocation under the NCLB law is under 3 percent of total education revenues, while the cost of the programs adds 27.7 percent to state and local budgets.

Most of the overall federal appropriations are earmarked for higher education, special education, technical education, vouchers, and other purposes. Seven of the $11 billion in new money is directed to non NCLB programs. Further, while new money was added, the federal share of education spending has slipped from 10 percent to 7 percent.

Secretary Paige compares education spending to national defense to imply that education spending is too high. To say one costs more than the other says nothing about the value of either. A new television may cost more than a bicycle, but that doesn't tell us whether they are good value for the money. Further, national defense is a federal government expenditure, while state and local districts pay 93 percent of public education expenses. . . .

From an economic perspective, NCLB will cost states about 10 times as much as they receive from the federal government. The rules are so prescriptive that, in time, virtually all public schools and districts in the states will be declared as failing, regardless of their achievement pattern. Districts and advocates will take political actions to repeal the unpopular aspects of the law, and court actions will be filed asking the states to provide the dollars.

Source: William J. Mathis, *Spectrum*, *77*(2) (Spring 2004): 8–12. Reprinted with permission of William J. Mathis.

Net Assignment

Using InfoTrac, the websites listed at the end of the chapter, and Internet search engines, find discussions of the Florida Supreme Court's and the U.S. Supreme Court's decisions in the 2000 U.S. presidential race. Discuss the implications of those decisions for election process reforms that the various state governments could or should consider in light of this flawed election. What are some long-term implications of the U.S. Supreme Court's intervention in the conduct of a state election? Should there be a uniform national ballot for the presidential race?

Summary

The federal system in the United States rests on the fundamental core values that infuse the Constitution and American society. Picket fences, marble cakes, and layer cakes serve as models for our federal system's structure, which involves several levels of government—vertical and horizontal components—and operates like a two-way street. Throughout our history, varying approaches to federalism have characterized distinct periods: Dual, Cooperative, Creative, New, and Renewed.

Fiscal Federalism describes the theoretical considerations behind various types of intergovernmental transfers: grants-in-aid, including project and categorical grants, block grants, formula grants, and general-revenue sharing. Mandates, especially unfunded mandates, characterize coercive federalism.

Intergovernmental relations among the various units of government in the United States affect public administration—particularly as seen in the devolution revolution that shapes regional governments. National-to-local relations affect state-to-local control and encourage the development of functional fiefdoms. Interstate compacts and consortia, councils, special districts as regional governments, and other relationships not related to financial aid also influence public administration and policy.

Glossary of Key Terms

block grants   Grants from higher-level governments to lower-level governments that are distributed on the basis of a statutory formula. They may be used in various ways within a broad policy area, with considerable discretion left to the recipient governments.

categorical grants   Grants-in-aid that are limited to specific and narrowly defined activities—for example, creating small green spaces, or "parklets," in an urban development project area.

confederal system   A system of organizing government whereby power and authority reside in subnational or state governments that collectively establish an overarching government to which they delegate some powers while retaining veto power over the national entity.

Cooperative Federalism   An era of U.S. federalism from the 1930s to the 1950s that emphasized national, state, and local governments as cooperating agents who interacted with each other to jointly face and solve common problems.

Creative Federalism   An era of U.S. federalism in the 1960s characterized by joint planning and decision making at all levels of government, including partnerships with businesses and nonprofit social organizations.

devolution   The transfer of power from a central authority to a local government.

Dual Federalism   An era in which each level of government was viewed as supreme within its areas of responsibility, with relatively distinctive functional divisions of authority and independent operations by bureaucratic agencies. Limited intergovernmental funding.

entitlement   A government benefit required by law provided to eligible individuals, groups, or other governments, such as Medicare, Medicaid, and Social Security retirement benefits.

externalities   The costs or benefits from one thing affecting another or those not accounted for in free-market exchanges; those costs or benefits then accrue to someone other than the buyer or seller.

federalism   A system of government in which an overarching national government shares power with subnational governments.

formula grants   A type of grant-in-aid in which a higher level of government (national or state) provides funds to a lower level for stipulated purposes and distributes them according to a set formula that treats all applicants uniformly.

horizontal federalism   Concerns the relationships among governmental units at the same level: state-to-state, county-to-county, and city-to-city.

intergovernmental relations   A complex set of interrelationships among federal, state, and local governments that involve political, fiscal, programmatic, and administrative processes in which higher-level governments share revenues with lower-level governments, with special conditions attached that the lower-level unit must meet to receive the financial aid.

laissez-faire   A term for the economic principle that government should "let the people do as they choose" or generally keep its hands off regulating the private sector's economic life.

mandating   A higher level of government obliging a lower level to offer or provide some good or program as a matter of law or as a prerequisite to full or partial funding for either that program or some other, related program.

New Federalism   An era of U.S. federalism from 1968 to 1980, attributed to President Richard Nixon, that returned more autonomy to the states and emphasized block grants rather than project or categorical grants.

project grants   A type of grant-in-aid given from a higher to a lower level of government that must be applied for, with an individual project as its focus. Many strings are attached. Project grants are more numerous than formula grants, generally offer fewer funds, and often require matching funds from the recipient government.

Renewed Federalism   An era of federalism in the 1980s promoted by President Ronald Reagan that emphasized economic capitalism; individual rights; limited government; rationality in government decision making by assessing costs and benefits of federal programs, especially regulatory ones; and devolved authority and funding down to the state and local levels.

substate regionalism   A multijurisdictional cooperative arrangement between or among local government entities, such as metropolitan special districts or councils of government, that provide a regionwide view or approach to a local problem. Most often used for planning, development, transportation, and environmental policy problems that affect a whole region.

unfunded mandates   Federal or state laws that impose on lower-level governments a program that requires expenditures but no implementing funds.

unitary system   A form of government in which authority is centralized but some responsibilities may be delegated to smaller administrative units; in doing so, the upper level freely grants authority but may limit or even rescind it without the consent of the lower level. Each state within the United States is a unitary system with respect to its local governments.

vertical federalism   The upper–lower relationships between governments at different levels: national-to-state, state-to-local, and national-to-local.

vertical functional autocracies   Largely self-governing professional guilds of members of bureaucracies at the federal, state, or local levels who are able to function as autocracies, running a policy area as a functional fiefdom mostly independent of other agencies or branches of government. Associated with the picket-fence model of federalism.

Review Questions

1. This chapter refers to three types of government systems—confederal, federal, and unitary. Explain where each form can be found in the United States.

2. Discuss the ways in which the U.S. Constitution and our political norm of constitutionalism provide for both horizontal and vertical federalism.

3. Who were the winners and losers when the growing centralization of power shifted from the states to the national level of government?

4. Describe the various types of grants-in-aid. Why do state and local governments prefer block, formula, and general-revenue-sharing grants while the national level prefers project or categorical grants?

5. Identify the horizontal and vertical federalism relationships described in Reading 4.1 about the No Child Left Behind Act. What fiscal and nonfiscal aspects of federalism are illustrated in the reading?

Surfing the Net

The following are useful websites to visit for more information about the topics covered in this chapter.

U.S. government agency directories (**http://www.lib.lsu.edu/gov/fedgov/html**)

U.S. Constitution and Federalist Papers (**http://www.law.cornell.edu/syllabi? constitutional+unconstitutional**)

FindLaw state constitutions (**http://www.Findlaw.com**)

National Constitutional Center (**http://www.constitutioncenter.org**)

Council of State Governments (**http://www.csg.org**)

National Association of Counties (**http://naco.org**)

National League of Cities (**http://www.nlc.org**)

Another useful site for various state and local government-related issues is State and Local Government on the Net (**http://www.piperinfo.com/state/index.cfm**).

Consult the Urban Institute's excellent Assessing the New Federalism project (**http://newfederalism.urban.org**).

Each state government has a web page; a few are cited here for convenience.

California (**http://www.state.ca.us**)

New York (**http://www.state.ny.us**)

Texas (**http://www.texas.gov**)

Wisconsin (**http://www.wisconsin.gov/state/home**)

Also see this U.S. Supreme Court–related site, Northwestern University's The Oyez Project (**http://oyez.nwu.edu/oyez.html**).

FindLaw also covers general district court decisions (**http://guide.lp.findlaw.com/ casecode**).

Not all state court decisions are on the web, but WashLaw (**http://www.washlaw.edu**) is a good site for state court issues.

Chapter 5

[With] the rise of reinvention and the crystallization of a New Public Management in the 1990s . . . what was once called "contemporary" or "modern" public administration might now be thought of as "conventional" administration. . . .

The first National Performance Review report attempts to resuscitate the politics–administration dichotomy as a basis for reform: "This performance review is not about politics. . . . We want to make improving the way government does business a permanent part of how government works, regardless of which party is in power (Gore, 1993: iv). It calls for thoroughly "liberating agencies from congressional micromanagement. . . . It claims to embrace "the traditional values that underlie democratic governance—values such as equal opportunity, justice, diversity, and democracy" and to "seek to transform bureaucracies precisely because they have failed to nurture those values (Gore, 1993: 8). But it fails to recognize that the "red tape and regulation so suffocating that they stifle every ounce of [administrative] creativity" (Gore, 1993: 2) were put in place in the 1940s and later, largely to protect these values.

Alternative Theories of Organizational Behavior: Classic Models and Ideological Sources of Values

David H. Rosenbloom
History lessons for reinventors, *Public Administration Review,*
61(2) (March 2001): 162.

Introduction

Common to many organizations is this question: What is the best mix of full-time and part-time employees in an organization? Using part-time employees has several advantages. Using more of them keeps fixed costs down, saving both salary and accompanying fringe benefits. Lower fixed costs allow an organization to be more flexible. The constant influx of new blood when adding new part-time employees can also enhance employee flexibility. Part-timers come in with new ideas about ways of doing certain tasks. With a smaller percentage of the budget locked in by fixed salaries, the managers of the organization have more freedom to revise and amend the budget to meet changing demands from the environment. On the other hand, part-time employees lack the loyalty, stability, and continuity that full-time employees bring to an organization. The overreliance on part-time workers, moreover, reduces employee morale; this, in turn, can affect productivity levels of the organization. What is the best mix between these two ways of organizing staff? How does an agency best blend the values associated with each approach? Organization theory addresses these questions.

An **organization** is a group of individuals working together to achieve common goals and structured into a division of labor to better pursue those goals. **Organization theory** is a set of "laws" or propositions about organization that are used to explain how people and groups behave within varied structures. A major component of any theory of organization is a focus on **organizational development**, an approach to organizational management that analyzes organizational problems and their solutions.

The relationship between administrators of public organizations on the one hand and the elected leaders and the public on the other is at the very heart of the practice of public administration. Public administrators have to reconcile the tensions among the aims of complying with the directions of elected officials, maintaining their own professional integrity, and serving the "public," be that the general public or special "clientele groups" who so often comprise the "relevant public" of an agency (Svara, 2001: 176).

Since the turn of the 20th century, social scientists have been examining organizations to explain how and why they behave as they do as well as to suggest ways to improve their performance. Large-scale organizations are mostly a recent phenomenon, and organizational theory has emerged from studying large-scale military and economic organizations (that is, industrial corporations). These groups became the foci of scholarly attention. As a body of knowledge with a set of accepted assumptions, however, organizational theory began with the study of the factory system in Europe.[1]

Schools of Organizational Theory

Many scholars have emphasized similar tenets or principles about organizations, so it is useful in thinking about these issues and controversies and we can conveniently classify them as different schools of thought (Dobel, 2001: 166). This chapter discusses five such schools of thought: **classical theory, humanist theory, neoclassical theory, systems theory**, and **new public management theory**. Several scholars from each school will be briefly covered, and their major tenets or principles of organization will be examined. Each school emphasizes certain values in organization that help to characterize that school of thought.

Scholars who make up a school of thought accept certain values and shared assumptions about organization. As conditions in society varied over time, organizations in society shifted, developed, and evolved in their values and in certain structural arrangements. These shifts in the nature of organizations resulted in a change in theories about organization. Theorists shifted their attention and the value assumptions that were preeminent in their thinking as organizations evolved. All such school of thoughts, then, dealt with values and the clash of competing values. Often they varied not so much as to which values they addressed, but in the relative importance or emphasis they gave to some values over others or simply about what values they assumed with little or no question. Traditional thought of the classical school exhibited more respect for law, citizens, and values than did the "customer-oriented" managerialism of the new public management school (Lynn, 2001: 144). Some developments in organizational theory reflect reactions toward preceding theories.

Variations in theory also reflect how scholars have analyzed the natural tension that exists between democracy and bureaucracy. Where democracy promotes the values of freedom, individual rights, and responsiveness, bureaucracy emphasizes order, **group cohesion** toward a common purpose, and efficiency. These conflicting basic values must be balanced. The various schools of organizational theory differ in how they balance them. Natural tension also exists between public and private organizations. Organizational theorists have differing ideas on the best way to structure or manage public and private organizations. They develop different ideas on which is the "best" organization. Their differences partly reflect whether they have been examining more public or more private organizations as they built their theoretical constructs. Kaufman (1956) sees administrative institutions as having been organized and operated for the pursuit, successively, of three values: representativeness, neutral competence, and executive leadership. He attributes the shift from one to another as occurring as a consequence of the difficulties encountered in the period preceding the change (p. 1057).

The Classical School of Organizational Theorists

The traditional, or classical, school of organization theorists was the first to develop. Its scholars laid the foundation on which later scholars built their own work. Classical theorists examined military organizations and the initial structures of the Industrial Revolution. These sources shaped the values, tenets, and imagery of the classical school. Concepts and metaphors from mechanical engineering, industrial engineering, and economics abound in the writings of classical theorists.[2]

Classical theorists stress the structural arrangements of organization and often depict organizations as machine-like. For these theorists, an organization's cardinal value is **efficiency**—that is, accomplishing production-related and other economic goals in the most expeditious manner and at the least cost. Classical theorists assume there is a single best way to structure an organization to maximize productivity that can be discerned by systematically examining the way organizations behave. These theorists also emphasize the need for a division of labor, assuming that individuals and organizations of people behave in ways that allow rational economic decision making. Classical theory, then, is the original construct of organizational development and how it closely resembles military organizations and emphasizes such characteristics as the hierarchical structure, chains of command with formal systems of authority, and bureaucratic behavior. Classical theorists were more often concerned with explaining how modern organizations developed. If they dealt with an issue like "reform" of an organization, they would more likely advocate tinkering with the structural forms. David Rosenbloom (2001), among others, has labeled the group of ideas common to the traditional school an "orthodoxy." He identifies four major principles or tenets as being characteristic of the scholars of the classical school.

1. A separation should exist between partisan politics on the one hand and the organization and staffing of the civil service on the other. This broader dichotomy is often attributed to Frank Goodnow (1900), who provided a sort of bridge between reformers and Progressives by showing how political reforms for improving the expression of the people's will (the "representativeness" or "responsiveness" values) were connected to administrative reforms ("efficiency" or "effectiveness" values) for executing it.

2. Much of what government does is "business" and should be insulated from control by elected officials.

3. Public administration could be a design science. Though this idea was raised by Woodrow Wilson (1887), it gained prominence with Frederick Taylor's *Principles of Scientific Management* (1911). By 1923 "science" was claimed as the basis for a fundamental administrative technology—that of position classification.

4. Public administration should be based on the principle of "unity of command," which would organizationally control specialization. Politically, it would make public administration "executive centered" (as opposed to legislative) and advocate a reduced role and involvement of the legislature in administrative decision making. For example, the President's Committee on Administrative Management (PCAM, 1937), more commonly known as the Brownlow Committee, to enhance "efficiency" called for the "systematic organization of all activities in the hands of qualified personnel under the direction of the chief executive" (Rosenbloom, 2001: 161–162).

Adam Smith   It was in the milieu of the factory system on the British Isles that the first classical theorist studied organization. Scottish economist Adam Smith published his major work, *An Inquiry into the Nature and Causes of the Wealth of Nations*, in 1776.[3] Largely because of this work, Smith has been considered the founder of economics and the intellectual base for laissez-faire capitalism. *Wealth of Nations* revolutionized fundamental thinking about economics and economic organization, emphasizing the value of centralizing equipment and workers into factories, specialized labor, and managerial contributions to specialization. He demonstrated the economic advantages of the factory system and the economic value of the industrial organization. Modern organizations, he noted, are *force multipliers*: They allow for the labor of individual parts to be combined in such a way that the sum of their efforts is greater than those of their parts. Modern military organizations are good examples, because they make each soldier more effective on the battlefield. In fact, good organization and the proper use of technology together are as powerful a force multiplier as any machine. Like the machine, this combination allows for efficiency of productivity.

INFOTRAC
COLLEGE EDITION

Exploring organizational citizenship behavior

Frederick Taylor   The machine-like efficiency of the modern economic organization became a central concern of the second major theorist of the classical school, the acknowledged founder of the scientific-management movement—Frederick Winslow Taylor.[4]

Taylor's theory of **scientific management** formed the bases of the managerial tradition within organization theory. He emphasized a method—time-and-motion studies—to assist private-sector management in adapting production methods to the needs of the emerging industrial economy of the United States. Before Taylor's study, there was little systematic organization of work within private industry. He focused on the need for and prescribed a "science" of management that stipulated specific steps and procedures of implementation.

Scientific management emphasized formal structure and rules, largely ignored customers and the workers themselves, and equated the control needs of upper management with the needs of the entire organization.

Scientific management assumes four fundamental values. First, *efficiency* in production involved obtaining the maximum gain in productivity from the minimum investment of resources. The second value was *rationality* in work procedures, or the most direct relationship of work to the organization's objectives. *Productivity* was the third value; the ultimate goal of any organization was to maintain the highest possible level of productivity. The fourth value of Taylorism was *profit*—the ultimate objective of any economic organization in a capitalistic system.

Scientific management makes several critical assumptions. First, it assumes that **authority**—the rightful power to make decisions in legally defined limits with the expectation of widespread compliance—is best when highly centralized at the top levels of management. Taylor assumed that a hierarchy of low to middle levels of management would pass orders from above to the workers below. Second, it assumes there is one best way to perform any task, the ideal method for performing any given task.[5] Scientific research was a method to discern and apply that one best way. Third, management's job was to select workers for their capabilities in performing tasks, organize work arrangements to best perform tasks, and train workers in the most rational way to achieve the organization's overall objectives.

Standardized procedures enable workers to perform tasks routinely and efficiently. Top management was solely responsible for implementing this "scientific management" approach, and for establishing logical division of work and responsibility between workers and management.[6]

Like any theory or model, the scientific management model had shortcomings when applied first to industrial and later to governmental organizations. Critics noted that the model viewed workers as mere cogs in an industrial machine, motivated solely by financial incentives and with no other needs on or off the job that were worthy of inclusion in the theory. These shortcomings will be discussed more fully later as they were articulated by the human relations theorists.

Perhaps the most lasting contribution of Taylorism and the scientific management approach was its emphasis on the principles approach to management in public administration. It embodied **administrative doctrine**—the rules and standard operating procedures of an organization that form its basic values and core tenets. While Taylorism was not oblivious to the values of democracy and responsiveness, its emphasis on efficiency influenced the public administration reformers of the 1930s. For example, when applied to local government, the "dichotomy" idea as a means to greater efficiency is evident in the call for strict confinement of the city manager to administration that was the established view of the International City Management Association (ICMA) and embodied in its 1938 code of ethics (Stillman, 1974: 43–53). There was support for giving the lead role in planning to the executive and administrators, with city legislators acting as reviewers of plans (Gulick, 1933).

INFOTRAC
COLLEGE EDITION

Roadblocks in reforming corrupt agencies

Harrington Emerson   The term *scientific management* was coined by attorney Louis Brandeis in a 1910 case involving railroads that were seeking permission from the ICC to raise rates for hauling freight. Brandeis called in Harrington Emerson, a consultant "expert" who had systematized the Santa Fe Railroad. Emerson testified that the eastern railroads did not need to raise rates because they supposedly could save millions of dollars a day by incorporating scientific-management methods. Emerson became known as the "high priest of efficiency" and one of the first management consultants in the United States.[7] The scientific-management movement became widely popular in the early 20th century and enshrined efficiency as the principle value of classical organization theory.

Henri Fayol   A French executive engineer, Henri Fayol (1841–1925) developed the first comprehensive theory of management. His major work, *Administration Industrielle et Generale*, published in France in 1916, articulated six **principles of management**— fundamental "truths" or working hypotheses that shape management thinking and action and that can be applied to any organization.[8] Fayol's primary emphasis was on his sixth principle, the managerial, which concerned the coordination, control, organization, planning, and command of people. Fayol's work emphasized such variables as the division of work, authority and responsibility, discipline, unity of command, unity of direction, subordination of individual interest to that of the general interest of the organization, remuneration of personnel, and centralization. His primary values included order, stability of personnel, initiative, and **esprit de corps**. These variables and values are themes of central importance to most if not to all classical organization theory.

Max Weber   The most notable classical theorist who dealt with the bureaucratic or hierarchical structure of organization was German sociologist Max Weber (1864–1920).[9] Bureaucracy and democracy are the two pillars of public and private organizations in modern U.S. society and are somewhat at cross-purposes. Bureaucracy has largely authoritarian tenets and is vertical in its implementation. Democracy, however, seeks to be egalitarian and leveling in its application.

Bureaucracy may be seen as the totality of all government offices or all government employees. It is also applied as a derogatory term to inefficient organizations that are plagued by red tape or are calcified and inflexible. Weber, however, viewed bureaucracy as an impersonal system of organization run on the basis of "calculable rules" and staffed by full-time professional employees rather than political appointees. In his perspective, bureaucracy presupposes a hierarchy based not on social status or some other extraneous consideration, but on organizational rank.[10] Weber postulated an *ideal type* of bureaucracy, the fundamental characteristics of which can be found in any organization.[11]

Although Weber's observations, first published in 1922, are based on his study of German military and industrial organizations at the turn of the 20th century, he postulated that the ideal type is the best means to ensure rationality at the institutional level. The applicability of his model to U.S. society and current organizational structures is limited in important respects. The model's strength lies in its description of bureaucracy as a structure of social organization, as a means of promoting hierarchical control over any organization, and as a foundation for theory, explanation, and prescription regarding any large and complex organization, public or private.[12]

Weber suggests that a stable system of authority rests on a belief in the legitimacy of a system of authority; this is the source of command in the organization. He characterized three types of authority: traditional, charismatic, and legal–rational. **Traditional authority** is based on the widely held belief that the organization's immemorial traditions are sacred, as is the resulting personal loyalty to the individual who attained leadership in the traditional way. Weber defined **charismatic authority** as resting on the personal devotion to an individual based on his or her exceptional or exemplary sanctity, heroism, or character. These types of authority allow legitimacy to be exercised arbitrarily, so they may lack rationality. Weber characterized **legal–rational authority** as resting on "legally established impersonal order"—the rule of law, not of humans. Obedience is due the person who exercises the authority of office by virtue of the legal system and only within the scope of authority of the office. For Weber, such rationality implies efficiency.[13] Implicit in the emphasis on the rule of law is support for applying professional knowledge—broadly defined to include substantive, public-service, and technical values—in an impartial, nonpartisan way to address public problems.

Leonard White In 1926, Leonard White argued that organizational management can be studied scientifically to determine the best method of operation. As did other scholars of public administration in the United States then, he advocated a dichotomy—a separation of politics from administration.[14] Public administration reformers, influenced by the classical theorists, emphasized the values of economy and efficiency and the notion that the study of public administration ought to be "value-free" science. For these reformers, the scientific study of management practices was at the core, the founding theory, of public administration (Sayre, 1958). The principles of administration emerged in the writings of the neoclassical school, which is discussed later. New approaches in psychology and sociology brought attention to the people who were the workforce of an organization. Reformers were critical of the mechanistic emphasis of classical organization theory.

The Human Relations School of Organizational Theorists

The classical school offers a formal, abstract, and mechanistic view of organization as one composed ideally of clearly defined units and subdivisions arranged in a pyramidal or hierarchic structure of authority. The *human relations*, or *humanist*, school of theorists developed largely in reaction to that image. They saw the classical model as overly authoritarian, believing that it suppressed creativity and lacked a focus on the human beings who worked in the bureaucratic organization. While they also were interested in the basic values of efficiency and productivity, they saw a different way to achieve those ends. Human relations theorists also emphasized a need to recognize informal aspects of organization.

Where the classical school theorists assumed that workers were rational and economically motivated, the human relations theorists viewed workers as having numerous noneconomic needs and as being partly motivated by such noneconomic needs. They sought to understand what noneconomic factors affected organizations, their workers, and their performance.

Sociologist Robert Merton (1936) provided a basis for such concern with his idea of *unintended consequences*, the basic idea of which goes back in Western social science at least as far as David Hume and Adam Smith. Merton made the unintended effects of social action a central element of sociological analysis. For Merton, common sources of unanticipated consequences included limited information, various forms of erroneous assumptions or tunnel vision, and self-defeating prophecies. Moore and Tumin (1949) morphed Merton's observation into an "iron law" of human organization, claiming "there is no exception to the rule that every time a culture works out an empirically valid answer to a problem, it thereby generates a host of derivative problems" (794–795, as cited in Hood and Peters, 2004: 268).

We review here the work of six scholars generally associated with the human relations tradition.

Mary Parker Follett   Mary Parker Follett (1868–1933) was a transitional scholar between the two schools. Writing in the early 1920s, in many respects she was an early prophet of human relations thinking, predating the major theorists of the school by a decade.[15] She was among the first social psychologists who anticipated many of the conclusions reached through the **Hawthorne experiments** in the 1930s as well as the post–World War II behavioral movement. Follett emphasized the psychological factors that affect people in organizations. In two books, *The New State Group Organization* (1918) and *Creative Experience* (1924), and various papers and articles, she signaled the development of the human relations tradition.

Follett viewed administration as reconciling the agendas and needs of both individuals and social groups. In her view, the principal tasks of an organization were (1) to determine what it wanted its employees to do and (2) to guide and control their conduct to get them to do it. Follett emphasized that the organization needed to stop trying to suppress differences within it. She advocated that the organization integrate those differences to help its growth and development. Where the classical theorists stressed the law of authority (chain of command), Follett espoused a "law of the situation." She admonished organizations to exercise "power with," rather than "power over," their employees.[16] Follett died before the results of the Hawthorne experiments were published. In many ways, these results were what launched the human relations movement in organizational theory and within the study of public administration.

Chester Bernard   Another transitional scholar between the classical and human relations schools was Chester Bernard (1886–1961).[17] As president of the New Jersey Bell Telephone Company, Bernard was influenced by the Hawthorne experiments. His theory of organization emphasized a view of the organization as a system. He examined the informal as well as the formal aspects of organization, particularly the role of the executive.

In his book *The Functions of the Executive* (1938), Bernard distinguished between the purposes of the organization and the motivation of individual members. Rather than a formal structure, he saw organizations as a collection of actions toward a goal. To sustain itself, an organization must attain a degree of equilibrium between its goals and the motivation of its members. The effectiveness of leadership in organization depends on the willingness of followers to accept and respond to leadership. The organization benefits from the energy and productivity of its members.

The employees, in turn, receive compensation, benefits, and meaning from their work for the organization. In 1938, Bernard introduced the distinction between formal and informal organization as a means to study organizational behavior. He maintained that workers had a social-psychological zone of acceptance, referring to their relative willingness to obey the leader's directives. In his terms, *formal organization* refers to the consciously coordinated activities of people, whereas *informal organization* refers to the unconscious group feelings, emotions, and activities of individuals. Formal and informal organization are essential to one another. Bernard stressed that because of informal organization, not all the activity of an organization is capable of being structured within a chain of command.

Bernard focused particularly on an organization's *executive functions*, which he characterized as maintaining its communication, securing essential services and resources, and formulating its purposes and objectives. He described coercive leadership as relying on negative incentives such as punishment and wage reductions. These, he held, were less effective than supportive leadership through positive incentives. Bernard thought the carrot was more effective than the stick.

Elton Mayo   The human relations school of thought was launched by a series of studies conducted at Western Electric's Hawthorne Works plant in Hawthorne, Illinois (near Chicago), between 1927 and 1932 by Elton Mayo (1880–1949) and associates from the Harvard Business School. Their five-year study was published as *The Human Problems of an Industrial Civilization* (1933).[18]

Mayo and his team began their studies in the tradition of the classical school. Organizational consultants would take up their positions in an organization and study its workers to suggest means to improve productivity. They began measuring the effect that worker fatigue had on productivity, but the study soon evolved into the study of various job-related factors not linked to economic reward. Their study soon focused on how workers reacted to the actions of management, how variations in physical working conditions affected output, and how the various social interactions among workers shaped their job performance. Mayo had not intended to look at those variables, but the team's investigation shifted to them when early results did not turn out as anticipated or as predicted by classical theory expectations (specifically, by the expectations of Taylorism).

Essentially, Mayo and his team discovered that many worker/management–related problems were not the result of insufficient task specification or inadequate wages, but reflections of social and psychological factors. The studies were the first systematic research into the human factor in work situations, and they became a turning point in the history of administrative theory and practice. As a direct result of these experiments, management began to perceive an organization as fundamentally a type of social institution.[19] The productivity of women workers, for example, rose after changes in working conditions (e.g., better lighting, more frequent work breaks) were seemingly made—regardless of whether or not conditions actually had been improved. Women workers were responding to the attention given them as subjects of an experiment, a reaction now known as the *Hawthorne effect*.

Elton Mayo and his associates concluded that the informal structures of groups and teams influenced the behavior and motivation of workers. In-group pressures to produce at the group's production level were more influential than those tied to management.[20] Among both men and women workers, there was pressure to regard oneself as a team member and to react to management as such rather than as an individual. Mayo's research revealed for the first time in a systematic way that noneconomic incentives and motivations on the job were as real and as influential as the rational-economic assumptions postulated by the classical theorists. Their study showed there simply was no one best way to motivate employees to be more productive. The authoritarian way of running an organization thus was viewed as

PHOTO 5.1

Abraham Maslow (1908–1970), Human Relations Motivation Theorist

As humankind enters the 21st century, do you think Maslow's hierarchy of needs should be modified? How might Maslow describe the activities that would constitute self-actualization today?

Source: Courtesy of the Archives of the History of American Psychology, University of Akron, Akron, Ohio.

INFOTRAC
COLLEGE EDITION

**Leadership for
community building**

just one of several options. Scientific management was no longer accepted as gospel; the human relations movement was launched.[21]

Abraham Maslow   Among the more important work in the movement was that conducted by psychologist Abraham H. Maslow, who advanced the basic findings of Elton Mayo when he proposed his famous **needs hierarchy** in a 1943 article, "A Theory of Human Motivation," and his 1954 book, *Motivation and Personality.*[22]

Maslow asserted that humans have five sets of goals or needs. He arranged these in a hierarchy of strength of need (see Figure 5.1). Once the lower needs are met, they cease to be motivators of human behavior. The higher needs, however, will not serve as motivators until the lower needs are met. A person will risk danger to get food, water, or shelter. Only after the body is sustained will thoughts turn to safety and then to other higher needs. According to Maslow, "while it is true that man lives by bread alone," it is only the case when there is no bread. When there is plenty of bread, higher needs emerge—and these needs, rather than simple physiological hungers, dominate the human organism. As these needs are met, higher needs emerge, and so on to the top of the hierarchy.

Another set of scholars within the humanist school tradition developed what has been termed *organizational humanism.*[23] These social psychologists brought to their research and theory certain assumptions about human motivation and work. First, they assumed that work itself could have intrinsic interest that would motivate workers to perform well. Second, they assumed that individuals work to satisfy needs both on and off the job. This assumption means that individuals sought satisfaction of needs in their work separate from other motivations for working. A third assumption was that a person's work life was central to his or

FIGURE 5.1
Maslow's Hierarchy of Needs

Source: Adapted from Abraham Maslow, *Motivation and personality* (2nd ed.) (New York: Harper & Brothers, 1970): 35–58.

her overall life, not merely something to be endured for the sake of extrinsic and largely monetary rewards. Fourth, they assumed that management should promote positive motivation, an assumption based on their own research findings. Based on these assumptions, they developed a set of managerial philosophies.

Douglas McGregor The most noted proponent of organizational humanism was Douglas McGregor, who pioneered the notion that workers could be self-motivated from their own interest in and inclination to perform their work. In his book *The Human Side of Enterprise* (1960),[24] McGregor posited two contending constructs of managerial philosophy that he coined the **Theory X** and **Theory Y** sets of assumptions.

McGregor postulated that a manager's assumptions about human behavior determine his administrative style. He offered a set of assumptions of managers for both the Theory X and the Theory Y approaches as well as an alternative set—which came to be called **Theory Z**—that was developed after the influence of systems theory. Theory X refers to the set of assumptions about human nature that guide managers who believe that (1) most people dislike work and will seek to avoid it and (2) mangers must threaten them to get them to work. Managers who operate under Theory X assumptions maintain that individuals prefer to be directed and will avoid taking responsibility. In contrast, Theory Y assumptions hold that work is natural, that workers can be self-directed, and that imagination, ingenuity, and creativity are common.

Theory Z refers to the patterns of organization and managerial operations from contemporary Japanese corporations. Managers who use this style assume that productivity is largely a function of social and managerial organization that has been

enhanced by greater communication, feedback, and the involvement of workers in the decision-making process. In this perspective, **motivation** refers to all of the factors of the working environment that have any positive or negative effects on an individual's work.

McGregor created his Theory X and Theory Y constructs after examining differing types of organization: Theory X from military organizations, Theory Y from professional organizations. Different managerial philosophies and approaches to management are appropriate to different organizational environments. What works for a military or paramilitary agency (such as a police, fire, or correctional department) would be less appropriate to a university setting, health delivery agency, or medical research bureau. Much of the humor of the movie *MASH* and the long-running television series of the same name hinged on the juxtaposition of highly educated and professional medical personnel in an army field hospital setting and their resistance to the managerial style of career military officers. Cartoon 5.1 spoofs the point of clashing management styles by depicting a manager who exhibits some aspects of both Theory X and Theory Y styles of management. What in the cartoon would be appropriate to each style?

The goals and missions of public organizations are often vaguely specified and may not actually be the true goals and missions. A correctional facility's stated goal may be rehabilitation, but its actual mission may be simply maintaining public order by warehousing those who are perceived to be dangerous or career criminals.

Chris Argyris   Another important organizational humanist was Chris Argyris.[25] This social psychologist sees work as a central life interest. He notes the need of workers to identify with their work as a critically important source of motivation to perform it well. **Bureaucratic dysfunction**—the pathological aspects of bureaucracies that make them inefficient—often emerges when workers feel no intrinsic interest in their work and are being motivated and controlled through a Theory X management style. The unthinking adherence to rules as ends in themselves, rather than as means, is a source of much of what has been called *red tape*.

Rensis Likert   Organizational humanist Rensis Likert identified four systems that positively or negatively influence the conjunction of individuals and the organizations at which they work.[26] The first he labels *punitive authoritarian*. It closely resembles Theory X, in that managers have no confidence or trust in subordinates. The second he labels *benevolent authoritarian*. In this system, the manager is more generous and humanitarian toward employees but rewards them only as prescribed directives are followed. Managers in this system tend to be condescending toward their subordinates. Likert called a third system a *consultative system*. This system allows more participation by employees, with organizational leaders more often democratic in style, allowing free discussion of policy but assuming final responsibility for all decisions. Managers in the third system demonstrate substantial but not complete trust and confidence in their subordinates. Likert's fourth system is called a *participative group model*. It closely resembles McGregor's Theory Y. In this system, upper management promotes confidence and trust in employees, who are involved in and work in coordination for problem solving. They are motivated through positive incentives. According to Likert, the fourth system's administrative leaders achieve the greatest degree of productivity. System-four organizations have higher employee satisfaction, better employee health, less absenteeism, less turnover, higher quality control, and better customer satisfaction than do managers using any of the other three systems.[27]

Partners in discord only

The human relations theorists criticized classical theorists for too heavily emphasizing formal structure and rational economic incentives, but critics of the human relations approach fault those theorists for ignoring work-related conflict as a real problem with which any comprehensive theory of organization must deal. Critics argue that the human relations theorists paid too little attention to organizational structures, monetary incentives, and wage or salary differentials that affect the degree of conflict and tension between labor and management.[28]

Such critics of the humanist tradition fault its theorists for not paying enough attention to the type and complexity of technologies used in an organization. These critics contend that these factors may be more important in shaping informal social structures and human interaction than the factors that Mayo, Maslow, and others considered to be pivotal.[29]

The Neoclassical School of Organizational Theorists

Just as the human relations approach arose in reaction to classical theory, the neoclassical school emerged by reacting to perceived inadequacies of both its predecessors. The neoclassical theorists sought to save classical theory by introducing modifications based on empirical findings drawn from the behavioral sciences. The neoclassical approach is represented in the works of Luther Gulick and Herbert Simon and later scholars such as Philip Selznick, Dwight Waldo, and Catheryn Seckler-Hudson. Scholars in this tradition emphasize decision making as the heart and soul of administration. Like the classical theorists whose work they refine and elaborate on, administrative capacity is measured by the cardinal value of efficiency. Neoclassical theories emphasize organizational roles over individual roles, especially as they relate to decision making. For these theorists, the center of operation of an organization is instrumental rationality.[30] On the issue of reform, for example, they would put more emphasis on changes in decision-making rules and less on changes in the structure of organization.

The incoherent emperor

Luther Gulick   Luther Gulick and his colleague Lyndall Urwick edited the *Papers on the Science of Administration* (1937). In his highly influential essay "Notes on the Theory of Organization," Gulick introduced the acronym **POSDCORB**—shorthand for *planning, organizing, staffing, directing, coordinating, and budgeting*—for the essential work of the chief executive in a series of tasks. This essay has influenced the field of public administration ever since. Gulick subscribes to the Wilsonian concept of separation of administration from politics (see Chapter 1).

Herbert Simon   With the publication of his essay "The Proverbs of Administration" (1946), Herbert Simon became the most influential neoclassical theorist.[31] He challenged the principles of management approach popularized by Taylor, Fayol, Gulick, and others by asserting that such principles were more like proverbs. He elaborated on this theme more fully in his later (1997) work *Administrative Behavior*. Simon viewed decision making as the central act of administration and proposed that the individual decision maker is rational only within the environmental context of the particular organization. It is the organizational environment that encompasses the purposes of rational behavior.

Simon distinguished between value premises and actual premises. In his view, administrators validate value judgment. The facts of any circumstance are validated by the given set of values in which those facts or actions occur. Administrators weigh means and ends as well as assess the consequences of acting. Decisions, in Simon's view, may be "objectively rational," "subjectively rational," "deliberatively rational," "organizationally rational," or "personally rational."[32]

To be rational means the administrator considers those choices presented within a prescribed set of values. The organizational environment articulates the values that incorporate the determination of rational behavior. Values, however, are arbitrary. Human decree, sanction, or authority validates a given set of organizationally accepted values. Policy-making actors (elected officials, legislators, and judges, for example) decide by fiat that a set of values—enacted into law and implemented by bureaucrats—are held to be of importance to the organization and society as a whole. Public organizations respond to rules, regulations, and boundaries imposed on them by these accepted and often-unquestioned values.

Herbert Simon stressed that the "principles" acted simply like "proverbs" and were of little value to practical administration because of the problem of *ambiguity*. He argues: "A fact about proverbs that greatly enhance their quotabilty is that they almost always occur in mutually contradictory pairs. 'Look before you leap'—but 'He who hesitates is lost'" (Simon, 1946; 53). His point is that such pairs provide no useful advice but can be used to justify whatever action one prefers. In examining Gulick's principles of administration, he shows that the key information needed is how to decide which bit of advice one is to follow, and this is the information missing in early 20th-century administrative "science." Thus, such principles fulfill the same role as proverbs. We will elaborate more fully on this ambiguity aspect of the principles-as-proverbs issue later in this chapter when discussing the new public management school.

Organizational decisions, in Herbert Simon's terms, only satisfy and suffice—that is, they "satisfice." This "satisficing" nature of organizational decision making recognizes that rationality—human reasoning—is bounded by its administrative context. Simon concluded that bureaucrats' reasoning options are limited by unconscious habits and skills, by values, by organizational and personal purposes, and by their degree of information and knowledge.[33]

Simon was the first organizational theorist to distinguish "programmed" from "unprogrammed" decisions. Rather than some sort of structural reform, he emphasized the importance of management information systems, and he pioneered improved organizational decision making through quantitative methods such as operations research and computer technology. He led the way in studying the processes by which administrative organizations make decisions.[34]

INFOTRAC
COLLEGE EDITION

**Managerial allocation
of time and effort**

Philip Selznick   One neoclassical theorist whose work presaged the systems school was Philip Selznick (1948). His article "Foundations of the Theory of Organization" posits the view that organization will never completely be able to cope with the nonrational aspects of organizational behavior (what he termed *bureaupathic* behavior). He emphasized that the individual within an organization has personal goals that often clash with the organization's formal goals. Like Simon, Selznick opened the field of organization theory by drawing on interdisciplinary sources of insight— sociology, anthropology, political science, and economics—as well as borrowing from the traditional public administration field.[35]

Dwight Waldo   In his 1948 book, *The Administrative State*, Dwight Waldo discussed how the societal values of democracy and bureaucracy are at once antithetical and complementary.[36] There are two problems in reconciling them. The first problem involves defining an administrative unit. The functions of a bureaucratic agency are determined by the manner in which it interacts with its clientele. Waldo's second concern is with the status and weight given to nondemocratic values—national security, personal safety, productivity, and efficiency. Unit heads in bureaucracies often give precedence to these values over democratic values. Bureaucracy itself, Waldo asserted, is neither good nor bad. It exists for accomplishing tasks. An excessive concern over formalism, rules and standard operating procedures, impersonality, expertise, record keeping, efficiency, and effectiveness work to make bureaucrats less democratic and more bureaucratic in their values and in the manner in which they deal with the public. Such value-laden behavior gives rise to the pejorative interpretation of the terms *bureaucrat* and *bureaucracy*. Waldo called for a future society in which bureaucracy in the Weberian sense is replaced by a more democratic, flexible, although more complex form. He called such a society *postbureaucratic*.[37]

Catheryn Seckler-Hudson   A final example from the neoclassical tradition comes from the work of Catheryn Seckler-Hudson (1902–1963). In the tradition of Luther Gulick, she published her own 12 principles of management in 1955. She cautioned, however, that her principles should be viewed as working hypotheses, not as immutable laws.[38]

Box 5.1 offers a brief synopsis of a case study concerning roadblocks in reforming corrupt agencies focusing on the New York City school custodians. It illustrates well how difficult reform of an organization can be.

The Systems School of Organizational Theorists

The fourth school examined here—**systems theory**—emerged after World War II. Systems theory emphasizes an interactive and interrelated set of elements: an environment, **inputs** (resources such as equipment, supplies, the energy of employees), processes, **outputs** (the products or services of the system), and feedback (the positive or negative effects of the outputs of a system on its environment). A **system** refers simply to "any organized collection of parts united by prescribed interactions and designed for the accomplishment of a specific goal or purpose."[39]

Box 5.1

Roadblocks in Reforming Corrupt Agencies

Reformers have traditionally assumed that agencies can combat corruption through controls such as tight oversight, increased regulation, internal audits, reorganizations, and performance accountability mechanisms. But this case study of the New York City school custodial system shows how a corrupt agency can derail these devices. New York City's $500 million custodial system, responsible for maintaining its 1,200 schools, has been unleashing scandals since the 1920s despite decades of regulations, multiple reorganizations, and layers of oversight. Its history shows that a deviant culture—a management "captured" by special interests—and an infrastructure enmeshed in abusive policies will resist controls, no matter how well crafted. True reform requires tackling institutionalized corruption through strategies like overhauling management, eradicating special interests, and aggressively punishing misconduct. . . .

But corruption may not result merely because an organization's internal accountability mechanisms are not tight or numerous enough. The history of the New York City custodial system, the subdivision of the city's board of education (BOE) that is responsible for cleaning and maintaining its 1,200 schools, shows that the assumptions underlying traditional corruption controls do not allow for organizations whose cultures are so deviant and whose missions have been so twisted that managers can barely recognize conduct that is deviant and employees regard wrongdoing as their right. . . .

Repeated scandals put pressure on top officials of the BOE and the Division of School Facilities (DSF), the BOE subdivision responsible for overseeing the system's 1,000 custodians, to try traditional corruption controls, including stripping custodians of discretion, tightening central oversight, and auditing custodian's financial records. . . . But most of these initiatives turned to dust in the custodial system's daily operation as managers failed to enforce them, custodians and their supervisors refused to follow the rules, and incentives for corruption remained embedded in the agency infrastructure.

In 1993, in the wake of a highly publicized investigation, the state passed a law changing custodians' incentives. It stripped them of some of their civil service protections and tried to make them accountable for performance to principals. But scandals persisted because the law did not change the culture or fix the broken DSF bureaucracy that was supposed to oversee custodians.

The case of the New York custodians challenges the commonly held assumption that when an agency repeatedly proves unable to police itself, external agents (such as prosecutors) will clean it up. The custodial system shows how a corrupt agency can escape such control by, among other things, sanitizing wrongdoing through collective bargaining.

The custodial system's ability to elude internal and external controls is intriguing in light of how destructive corruption has been to the agency's core mission. Unlike some forms of corruption such as police perjury, which arguably further the agency's mission, custodial misconduct directly undercuts its central purpose: to maintain a clean, safe learning environment. As custodians diverted resources, children sat in filthy classrooms surrounded by peeling paint, falling plaster, and broken windows. . . . Water dripped on their desks from holes in the ceilings; rodents sometimes ran over their feet. . . . Nails stuck out of doors; wires hung from walls. . . . As one commission put it, schools were "more suitable to prisoners than academics" (Levy, 1995: 5). Sometimes these conditions even became dangerous: A toppling cinderblock killed one girl, leaky furnaces sickened dozens of pupils (Kolbert, 1998).

The reform pitfalls highlighted in this case study are not unique. Many agencies, from hospitals to police departments, and many of the country's large public school custodial systems, from Chicago to Detroit to Los Angeles, face patterns of ingrained wrongdoing that have not responded to traditional corruption redress devices. As experts in these agencies grapple with how to reduce fraud, they should consider the lessons of the New York custodians case. This article examines the types of controls tried in the custodial system, the reasons they failed, and the broader implications for corruption reform around the nation.

Source: Lydia Segal, Roadblocks in reforming corrupt agencies, *Public Administration Review*, *62*(4) (July/August 2002): 445–446. Reprinted with permission of Blackwell Publishing.

Where classical theory was simplistic and unidimensional (its top-down hierarchy, for example), systems theory is multidimensional and more complex in its assumptions about organizational relationships. Where classical theory sees organization as formal and static, systems theory sees organizations as dynamically seeking shifting states of equilibrium, adapting to and integral parts of their environment. As a school of thought, it proponents are more likely to favor reform efforts; indeed, they would consider them as nearly inevitable results of the feedback processes of the system. They would favor organizational structures that are less hierarchical and rigid, for *flexibility* is a core value of systems theory. To survive, organizations must constantly adapt to ever-changing conditions; their actions affect the environment, bringing about new change.

> Within organization theory, M. Cohen, March, and Olsen's (1972) famous *garbage can model* of organization, which produces bizarre and unpredictable decisions as a result of fluid participation and shifting agendas, might be considered as a mixture or a complex system and culture clash approach to understanding how surprise and paradox develop [within organizations]. (Hood and Peters, 2004: 272)

In the systems approach, then, the dichotomy of politics and bureaucracy is completely rejected. From this perspective, policy and administration cannot be separated because the systems theory or model would not see any significant difference between policy making and administrative decisions. Charles Lindblom's work (1959)on *incremental* changes in policy, informed through experience and in his view superior to policy making dependent on the policy maker's theoretical understanding, demonstrated two defects in the "dichotomy" perspective. First, he argues that theory-bound rational analysis, the special contribution of the policy side of the dichotomy, is frequently unreliable. Second, the practical element of experience involved in incrementalism requires close linkage between policy making and administration (see the discussion in D. Williams, 2000).

Norbert Weiner   The model of organization as an adaptive system was presented by Norbert Weiner in his 1948 groundbreaking book *Cybernetics*.[40] The term, which is Greek for "steersman," was used by Weiner to refer to the multidisciplinary study of the structures and functions of control and information-processing systems in animals and machines. Central to cybernetics is the concept of self-regulation. Biological, social, or technological systems can identify problems, react to them, do something about them, and receive feedback from their actions to adjust themselves automatically. Weiner developed his model while working on antiaircraft systems during World War II. Variations of Weiner's model have been used by systems theorists since he first published it. The systems model can be applied to anything that works as a system: an automobile, a computer, a community hospital, the Department of Labor, General Motors, or the United Nations. (See Figure 2.1.)

INFOTRAC
COLLEGE EDITION

**Methodologies
in conflict**

A system may be either open or closed. A **closed system** views an organization as a physical system or machine whose operation is unaffected by its environment. A closed-system view emphasizes the values of physical planning and controlling, stability, and predictability within an organization. An **open system** sees an organization as a biological entity that lives in and exchanges inputs and outputs with its environment. An open system is viewed as a highly complex organization, interdependent both internally and externally. Change is valued, as are spontaneity and self-stabilization.[41]

David Easton   Among the most notable of systems theorists to apply the cybernetic or systems model to political analysis was political scientist David Easton.[42] His

model of the political system, as with any social entity, assumes the existence of inputs, some means of responding to those inputs, outputs, and feedback from the environment in response to the system's outputs. Feedback results in further inputs into the system.

Daniel Katz and Robert Kahn An open system views organizations as more than formal structures depicted in an organization chart, more than interpersonal relations among its members, more than a worker's involvement in and productivity on the job. An open-system approach sees bureaucratic organizations as whole beings, complex and constantly interacting with their environment. This perspective is exemplified in the 1978 work of Daniel Katz and Robert Kahn, who describe the self-regulating aspect of an organization as adaptive to its environment.[43]

In the systems school, the central value of an organization is *change* rather than a static task productivity or interpersonal relationships among members. Organizational change emphasizes those aspects of an organization that either promote or retard change in response to changing demands from the external environment. The systems school focuses on the dynamic aspect of organization, particularly on **group dynamics**—a subfield of organizational behavior that stresses how groups develop and behave internally and externally. Important, too, is organizational development.

The systems theorists' dynamic view of organization leads them to favor management by task, which allows for variation in structural form according to task rather than from following a single structure from top to bottom. This allows for considerable diversity in the arrangement of subunits in a large and complex organization as each unit shapes itself somewhat differently structurally, socially, and technologically in response to how its task is best accomplished given environmental constraints and inputs.[44]

William Ouchi and Clyde McKee   The systems theory of organization and the value placed on dynamic change leads to the management style described earlier as Theory Z. Proponents such as William Ouchi and Clyde McKee[45] assume that productivity is determined by social and managerial organization and improved by greater communication, feedback, and greater worker involvement in self-managed work teams. Some public agencies have employed this management approach and adopted the Japanese practice of using quality circles and total quality management (TQM). **Quality circles** are small groups of from 3 to 15 workers who meet regularly to discuss, analyze, and solve problems they experience on the job. These concepts are discussed more fully in Chapter 7.

Peter Senge   Peter Senge incorporates these concepts in his book *The Fifth Discipline* (1994).[46] He notes that an organization, whether public or private, is a **learning organization**—his term for organizations that nurture new patterns of thinking so that its members learn together to improve both the organization and their personal lives. *TQM, process reengineering, organization learning,* and *continuous learning theory* have emerged as the key concepts in the discipline of organizational behavior.[47] Peter Senge and other scholars of the systems school of theorists suggest that bureaucratic organizations, indeed all organizations, are capable of learning and growing, as do individuals, from their interactions with their environments. Change is task related. Organizations committed to learning develop opportunities, policies, and resources that support individual growth of members in the organization. In turn, the behavior of the organization can be transformed from this process. Creating a continuous learning environment is especially appropriate for service bureaucracies, both public and private.[48]

INFOTRAC
COLLEGE EDITION

Environmental scanning: radar for success

The New Public Management School of Organizational Theorists

The final school of organizational theory examined here emerged as a significant force in the field in the 1990s. The new public management (NPM) is integral to the "reinventing government movement," particularly as manifested in the national performance review (NPR) (Gore, 1993). It advocates a shift from administrative bureaucracy to entrepreneurial organization. Incorporating much of the decision-making perspective of the *public choice model*, its sees policy decisions as being market driven. The NPM school of theorists are reform driven as well. The NPM movement's emphasis on bureaucratic reform focused especially on exploring the dynamics of the executive–bureaucratic relationships (Arnold, 1986; Gore, 1993; Lowery, 2000). Critics of the movement see a political objective of the NPR as changing the balance of power, control, and authority over the federal bureaucracy. One such critic noted: "In treating government as a Wal-Mart, the NPR ignores the fact that many operational assumptions based on customer service have implications for broader system values such as the rule of law, representative government, separated and shared power, and individual liberty" (Carrol, 1995: 310). This brief discussion will highlight several notable scholars whose works exemplify the school of thought.

TABLE 5.1

Principles of Reinvention Management

1. There should be a clear separation of the responsibilities of ministers and department chief executives (CEs): Ministers should be responsible for selecting the outcomes they wish to achieve and purchasing their desired outputs; CEs should be responsible for selecting staff required to produce the desired outputs with the minimum practicable interference.

2. The government should only be involved in those activities that cannot be efficiently or effectively carried out by nongovernmental bodies.

3. Any commercial enterprises retained within the public sector should be structured along the lines of private-sector companies.

4. Potentially conflicting responsibilities should, wherever possible, be placed in separate institutions.

5. The goals of governments, departments, Crown agencies, and individual pubic services should be stated as precisely and clearly as possible.

6. Wherever possible, publicly funded services should be made contestable and subject to competitive tendering. The quality, quantity, and cost of publicly funded services should be determined by the purchaser's (i.e., minister's) requirements rather than the producer's preferences.

7. Institutional arrangements should be designed to minimize provider capture.

8. Preferences should be given to governance structures that minimize agency costs and transaction costs.

9. In the interests of administrative efficiency and consumer responsiveness, decision-making powers should be located as close as possible to the place of implementation.

Source: Boston et al., 1996, 4–5, as summarized in Daniel Williams, Reinventing the proverbs of government, *Public Administration Review, 62*(6) (2000): 522–534. Reprinted with permission of Blackwell Publishing.

Jonathan Boston et al. The intellectual foundations of this school are evidenced in the *New Zealand model* of the new public management (Jonathan Boston, John Martin, June Pallot, and Pat Walsh, 1996). Like the neoclassicists, they proposed a series of "principles of reinvention management," summarized in Table 5.1. Although these ideas and principles are promoted as "new management," others note that none of the techniques are new (C. Miller, 1998: 168); instead, they are popularizations of ideas that have been around for half a century or longer (Goodsell, 1992; D. Williams, 2000). Table 5.2 presents seven "innovations" stressed by the reinventing government reform movement that are decidedly not new.

Barzelay, Osborne, Gaebler, and Plastrik By far the scholars most noted for popularizing the new public management school of thought and the "reinventing government" movement are Michael Barzelay (1992, 2000), David Osborne and Ted Gaebler (1992), and Peter Plastrik (Osborne and Plastrik, 1997). They claim to establish a new governmental paradigm based on liberating employees and citizens to do their best and by using "new" management methods, to get the most out of what government does. They emphasize particularly five ideas as values: competition, privatization, decentralization, innovation, and empowerment. They produce a series of specific "reform recommendations" for "reinventing government" for each of those values.

Like Herbert Simon's critique of the "proverbs of administration," however, critics of NPM and NPR charge they produce inconsistent recommendations that are uninformed by history and cannot be applied because of the problems of inconsistency and ambiguity (D. Williams, 2000). A few such contradictory recommendations and inconsistencies will be noted here. For each of the five topics (competition, privatization, decentralization, innovation, and empowerment), they offer specific advice

TABLE 5.2

Innovations That Are Not New

Innovation	Origins of Idea/Innovation
Performance measurement	1910
Performance budgeting	1950
Privatization	1600s
Not-for-profits	Early 1800s
Long-range budgeting	1960s
Management by objectives	1960s
Recognition of rule dysfunction	1942

Source: Adapted from Daniel Williams, Reinventing the proverbs of government, *Public Administration Review, 62*(6) (2000): 522–534. Reprinted with permission of Blackwell Publishing.

that contradicts or at the minimum is intensely difficult to reconcile with other advice they provide. This sort of ambiguity renders their advice fundamentally inapplicable. For example:

- They want competition but oppose duplication. As a result, the reinventor is given no useful direction for action. Should she allow government units and programs to compete with one another in order to provide the best services? Or should governmental units be rationalized to eliminate duplication? How much duplication is too much? What considerations should lead to streamlining and which to competition?
- [They] also recommend that the public sector turn its attention to governmental profit making and investment, . . . which are activities ordinarily found in the private sector. . . . Where a policy objective can be met, government can intervene in the private sector up to and including acquiring businesses. However, as the objection to socialist business ownership indicates, not all policy objectives are allowed. . . . [Thus] the reinventor is left without clear guidance as to when the government is permitted to participate in the private sector and when not, unless she has some insight into the rationale permitting some interventions while rejecting others. (D. Williams, 2000)

This lack of policy neutrality produces several problems for the reinventor:

- He must either know or guess the political agenda in order to apply the principles correctly;
- He must work in an environment that is not hostile to the political agenda to apply these principles;
- As the political agenda develops over time, correct applications of the reinventing government principles may retrospectively become incorrect.

Likewise, their decentralization recommendations are often incompatible with the rationalizing of government decisions. Rational decision-making techniques rely on strong centralized authority structures that require them to be used, ensure that the outcomes of rational analysis lead to decisions, and prevent bureaucrats from subverting rational decisions while implementing policies. Yet they recommend use of flat budgets to force financial reform, which is an irrational but effective use of raw political power.

Decentralization is at odds with another important recommendation they make. They urge fragmented city governments to merge into regional governments. While such regionalization may be a reasonable response to the problems arising from excessive fragmentation of governments, it is a movement toward centralization, not decentralization. Thus, their apparent message is: "If things are not going well with centralized government, decentralize; however, if fragmented government seems problematic, centralize."

Closely linked to decentralization and competitive government is the recommendation to empower employees to innovate. If empowerment is to work, employees must know that their ideas are valued; thus, if follows that failure be tolerated and penalties for poor performance be avoided, since such penalties suppress innovation. But elsewhere it is recommended that governments pay only for results and that there should be "real consequences for failure." They propose to improve efficiency and effectiveness by sharing power with employees. Yet empowerment conflicts with the use of rational decision-making techniques and with recommendations to establish real consequences for failure.

Concerning structural reform, organizations should be broken into smaller, more functionally homogeneous bureaucracies. Such advice is problematic. It is a throwback to the idea of organization by purpose, process, clientele, or place. But these factors are too ambiguous to be useful. Is the purpose of the Farmers Home Administration farming, housing, or banking? Medicare and Medicaid in combination are a classic case of the unavoidable ambiguity arising from programs organized by purpose, process, clientele, or place. Medicare and Medicaid provide similar services to different people—providing health care financing for clientele of differing descriptions, thus organized by clientele (those over 65 or those below the poverty line, respectively). However, some people meet the descriptions for receipt of services from both, as in poor people at least partially insured by Medicare. People like these, whose receipt of benefits depends on the highest level of cooperation among organizations, are most at risk. Social Security says, "We don't run these programs. They're run by the Health Care Financing Administration." HCFA says, "We have oversight, but they're administered by the states."

> In summary, the reinventing government movement [is] . . . yet another overreaching effort to solve our society's ills through an overly simplistic panacea promoted by charismatic advocates. . . . Indeed, the contradictory nature of the advice contained therein prevents the reader from obtaining real advice concerning how to go about performing the real work of government. As with beauty and biblical interpretation, the advice . . . is in the eye of the beholder. (D. Williams, 2000: 530)

This chapter closes with Reading 5.1, "The Budget-Minimizing Bureaucrat?" It describes a study of whether or not there is empirical evidence from the *Senior Executive Service (SES)* to assess how well the top ranks of the federal government represent the demands of the citizenry. It examines the extent to which two conflicting values, bureaucratic self-interest and public representativeness, are evident in spending priorities of the SES.

Reading 5.1

The Budget-Minimizing Bureaucrat? Empirical Evidence from the Senior Executive Service

In a representative democracy, we assume the populace exerts some control over the actions and outputs of governmental officials, ensuring they comport with public preferences. However, the growth of the fourth branch of government has created a paradox: Unelected bureaucrats now have the power to affect governmental decisions (Meier, 1993; Rourke, 1984; Aberbach, Putnam, and Rockman, 1981).

In this article . . . I assess whether Senior Executive Service (SES) members mirror the attitudes of the populace or are likely to inflate budgets for their own personal gain. Contrary to the popular portrayal of the budget-maximizing bureaucrat (Niskanen, 1971), I find these federal administrators prefer less spending than the public on most broad spending categories, even on issues that fall within their own departments' jurisdiction. As such, it may be time to revise our theories about bureaucratic self-interest and spending priorities. . . .

Concern over bureaucratic behavior stems from the increasingly important role that public administrators play in American governance. If they neutrally executed policy decisions made by their political superiors without personal involvement, their attitudes and values would be of marginal concern, as we would not expect them to affect the decision-making calculus. However, it is widely recognized that bureaucrats, especially those in executive positions, do engage in policy making (Aberbach, Putnam, and Rockman, 1981; Meier, 1993; Rourke, 1984). Because these individuals hold unelected positions protected by civil service personnel regulations, how can the public be certain their decisions will comport with the public interest? Can substantial bureaucratic involvement in governance be reconciled with democratic ideals?

Focusing specifically on budgetary preferences, this article addresses how well the top ranks of the federal civil service represent the demands and preferences of the American citizenry. I empirically assess the competing claims of representative-bureaucracy and budget-maximization theories by focusing on members of the Senior Executive Service, those employed within the top career ranks of the federal government. Because SES members are career civil servants who are intimately involved in policy making, focusing on how well their attitudes reflect public sentiments provides important information about the representative nature of the top ranks of the fourth branch of government. . . .

Competing theories in the bureaucratic politics literature lead us to different expectations about whether public administrators can be expected to heed public demands on budgetary matters. . . . However, very little existing research focuses specifically on budgetary behavior and whether bureaucrats heed public preferences for government spending. A notable exception is Lewis' (1990) work, which focuses specifically on budget preferences. Using General Social Survey data from 1982 to 1988, he compares spending attitudes among federal, state, and local public administrators with those of the general public and finds remarkably few differences between the two groups. As such he concludes that "government employees are no more likely than the average citizen to favor bigger government budgets" (p. 222) and thus are relatively in sync with the public's demands for government spending. As such, elite administrators can be trusted to accurately represent public demands for government spending. . . .

[I]n his seminal book *Bureaucracy and Representative Government* (1971), William Niskanen claims that bureaucrats are primarily self-interested individuals attempting to maximize their own utility through larger budgets, or larger discretionary budgets, as he later argues (Niskanen, 1975). As such, they cannot be expected to legitimately represent public demands for government spending. Anthony Downs (1967) similarly reasons that bureaucrats are driven primarily by self-interest, and he is skeptical that the bureaucracy performs as a broadly representative institution. Referring to the behavior of bureaucratic officials, he argues, "The pressures on them to seek representative goals is much weaker than the pressure of their own personal goals or those of their bureaus" (p. 233).

A number of studies have empirically verified that bureaucrats attempt, directly or indirectly, to maximize their budgets. . . . [For example,] Aberbach, Putnam, and Rockman (1981) also confirm greater leftist leanings among federal executives compared to the public.

Strong attitudinal and behavioral evidence demonstrates that public administrators are out of sync with public preferences for government spending, preferring greater spending than the median voter.

One reason such previous studies have reached such contradictory conclusions is that they have examined public officials employed in different positions and arenas of government . . . These studies rely on a combination of local, state, and federal employees, but the survey questions inquire only about federal-spending priorities, calling into question the validity of using state and local employees' expressed attitudes to predict their behavior within their own governments. . . .

Expectations and Hypotheses

If the budget-maximizing theory is correct, public administrators should prefer greater spending than the public on issues that are likely to affect or come under their agency's jurisdiction. Attempting to secure larger budgets for their own organizations may not affect their preferences for spending issues outside their department's jurisdiction, however. Perhaps government employment is correlated with higher preferences for government spending across the board. If budgeting across the federal government is perceived as a zero-sum game where one agency's losses are another's gains, administrators should favor relatively greater spending on their own policies and programs while showing less support for spending on other government programs. But if administrators represent the policy attitudes of the public, they will not prefer greater spending than the average citizen. These conflicting theories lead to three testable hypotheses:

- *Budget-maximizing hypothesis:* Compared to the public, public administrators prefer greater spending in areas that are likely to come under their organization's jurisdiction.
- *Zero-sum game hypothesis:* Compared to the public, public administrators prefer less spending in areas that do not fall within their organization's jurisdiction.
- *Representative-bureaucracy hypothesis:* Compared to the public, public administrators prefer similar levels of government spending.

These hypotheses allow me to assess how well senior executives represent the spending priorities of the general public while accounting for the possible affects of self-interest. . . .

Findings

Overall, there is some evidence of attitude congruence between the general public and senior executives, lending tentative support to the representative-bureaucracy hypothesis. Examining the percentage of senior executives and the general public who agree that spending should be increased . . . shows that the two groups largely resemble one another in their priorities for government spending. Public schools, crime, and the environment are policy areas ranked highly by each group, while food stamps, welfare, and defense spending are accorded relatively low priority.

Closer examination reveals that public administrators are more frugal and less inclined to favor increased government spending than the general public, lending tentative support to the zero-sum hypothesis. . . . Contrary to the popular portrayal of the budget-maximizing bureaucrat (Niskanen, 1971), these federal bureaucrats actually prefer less spending than the public on almost all broad spending categories. . . .

These findings question the assumption that bureaucrats uniformly prefer larger budgets. On the contrary, they are more likely to advocate decreased government spending. Even on issues where they are likely to benefit most from increased spending, SES members are seldom more likely than the public to advocate increased spending. . . .

Conclusion

This article compares public executives' demands for public spending with those of the general public to determine whether the public can trust elite bureaucrats to make decisions that reflect their demands for government services. In contrast to previous attempts to assess the budget-maximizing behavior of public administrators, this research improves upon earlier attempts in a number of ways. First, Senior Executive Service employees make more appropriate units of analysis than do lower-ranking administrators, because they hold discretionary positions and are intimately involved in federal-budget matters. Second, by focusing specifically on items that are likely to be relevant to these government officials, that is, federal spending priorities, there is greater likelihood that responses are applicable to their work experiences. Further, accounting for potential self-interest in one's own program area by focusing on departmental spending issues ensures greater validity of findings. . . .

Taken together, these findings do not support any of the originally specified hypotheses. Federal employment does indeed exert some influence on senior executives' federal-spending priorities, but in the opposite direction than is usually assumed. Senior executives are less likely than the general public to favor increased spending on the vast majority of government programs, contrary to assumptions about self-interested bureaucratic behavior. Further, there is little evidence that administrators act in a zero-sum fashion, inflating spending in their own programs while decreasing funds for competing programs. In both the Defense and Health and Human Services departments, senior civil servants advocate less spending on their own programs than does the public, and they rank other programs as being more deserving of increased funding. The representative-bureaucracy hypothesis is not supported either. While senior executives and the public generally prefer increased or decreased spending for the same type of programs, senior administrators clearly prefer less spending than the public. To be consistent with representative-bureaucracy theory, federal bureaucrats would actually need to inflate their own preferences to truly represent public demands for federal spending. . . .

In sum, the budget-minimizing tendencies of federal administrators reported here suggest that self-interest is not as powerful a motivator as previously believed, and they suggest we should revise our theories about self-interested bureaucracies inflating government budgets for their own gain.

Source: Julie Dolan, The budget-minimizing bureaucrat? Empirical evidence from the senior executive service, *Public Administration Review, 62* (1) (January/February 2002): 42–51. Reprinted with permission of Blackwell Publishing.

Net Assignment

Using InfoTrac College Edition, Internet search engines, and some of the websites listed at the end of this chapter, enter the key words *Theory Z* or *total quality management* to search for other government programs that have emphasized cooperation over competition. Describe the goals and results of any programs found.

Summary

Organizational theory influences the values, structures, and operations of agencies throughout the United States. Over the last century, five schools of organizational theorists have distinguished themselves as they reacted to and built on previous theories.

The first school, classical theory, places a central value on efficiency. Its theorists emphasize a formal and hierarchical structure, division of labor, chain of command, narrow span of authority, and management control of employees through fixed, rational-economic motivation. They view the organization as a closed system, stressing impersonal, professional behavior in an attempt to separate politics from administration and achieve stability and predictability.

The human relations school shares with the classicists the closed-system view of organization and efficiency at its core. Humanists, however, disagree with classical assumptions on how best to achieve efficiency. Because humanists assume that motivation is as important to the individual as his or her economic needs, humanist theory emphasizes an informal organization devoted to a fundamental goal or task. Productivity, communication (both formal and informal), and the intrinsic value of work affect efficiency and make the role and style of managerial leadership important.

The neoclassical school of organizational theorists also focuses on efficiency as the core value. But because they believe that decision making lies at the heart of administration and can observe nonrational aspects of organizational behavior, they see the route to efficiency lying not in the individual but in organization roles. Neoclassical scholars prefer instrumental rationality and refer to principles or proverbs as guides to good management. Because neoclassical theorists especially value the purpose or mission of an organization, decision making must be "satisfying"—that is, the decision may not objectively be the best way to achieve maximum efficiency, but it will satisfy and suffice, or "satisfice."

The systems school of organization theorists differs from all three preceding schools. To systems theorists, the cardinal value of organization is not efficiency but change. In systems theory, organizations are open, complex, and multidimensional systems. Organizations are akin to biological entities, self-regulated by constant interaction with their environments and intrinsically dynamic. Systems theorists emphasize communication and feedback and prize such values as spontaneity and adaptability, integration and coordination, cooperation over competition, and differentiation and elaboration. Government agencies, therefore, along with all organizations, strive toward an equilibrium with their environments and do so by constantly adapting to change.

The new management theorists emphasize a public choice or market-based approach to organization. These scholars stress such values as competition, privatization, decentralization, innovation, and government-employee empowerment. They often propose guidelines and make recommendations that critics fault as being "proverb-like," that is, vague, inconsistent, or contradictory. They favor smaller and functionally homogeneous bureaucracy.

Glossary of Key Terms

administrative doctrine   The rules and standard operating procedures of an organization that embody its basic values and tenets.

authority   The rightful power to make decisions within legally defined limits, with the expectation of widespread compliance.

bureaucracy   The totality of government offices or all government employees; also used as a derogatory term to refer to an inefficient organization plagued by red tape or calcified into an inflexible structure.

bureaucratic dysfunction   Pathological aspects of bureaucracies that make them inefficient; unthinking adherence to rules as ends rather than as means; a source of red tape.

charismatic authority   Authority that rests on personal devotion to individuals because of their sanctity, heroism, or exemplary character.

classical theory   The original theory about organizations that closely relates them to military organizations and emphasizes hierarchical structure, chain of command, division of labor, formal authority systems, and bureaucratic behavior.

closed system   An organization made analogous to a physical system, such as a machine, whose operation is unaffected by its environment.

efficiency   Accomplishing production-related economic goals in the most expeditious manner and at the least cost.

esprit de corps   Group spirit; a sense of team shared by those in the same group or undertaking.

feedback   The positive or negative effects of the outputs of a system on its environment.

group cohesion   Shared assumptions, beliefs, and values that help organizational members operate as a team.

group dynamics   A subfield of organizational behavior that stresses how groups develop and behave internally and externally.

Hawthorne experiments   A set of management studies conducted by Elton Mayo and associates from the Harvard Business School in the late 1920s and early 1930s at the Hawthorne Works of the Western Electric Company near Chicago; instrumental in developing the human relations school of organization theory.

humanist theory   A reaction to the overly authoritarian perceptions of classical organizational theory; approach emphasizes the creativity of human behavior and views efficiency and productivity as strongly influenced by informal aspects of organization; humanists stress noneconomic needs as motivating workers' performance.

inputs   Resources such as equipment, supplies, and the energy of employees used by an organization.

learning organization   Peter Senge's term for an organization that nurtures new patterns of thinking so that its members learn together to improve both the organization and their personal lives.

legal–rational authority   Based on a legally established impersonal order—the rule of law.

motivation   All of the factors of the working environment that either positively or negatively affect on an individual's work.

needs hierarchy   A set of five goals or basic needs arranged in a hierarchical order; associated with Abraham Maslow and the human relations school of organization theory.

neoclassical theory   A perspective that revises and expands on classical organization theory.

new public management theory   A school of organization that advocates a shift from administrative bureaucracy to entrepreneurial organization and the use of the public choice model of decision making that views decisions as market driven.

open system   An organization made analogous to a biological entity that lives in and exchanges inputs and outputs with its environment.

organization   A group of people structured into a division of labor and working together to achieve common goals.

organizational development   An approach to organizational management that focuses on analyzing organizational problems and finding solutions.

organization theory   A set of laws or propositions that explain how people and groups behave in various organizational structures.

outputs   Products or services of a system that affect its environment and create feedback.

POSDCORB   An acronym for *planning, organizing, staffing, directing, coordinating, and budgeting*; the term was coined by Luther Gulick in 1937 to stress the essential elements of the work of a chief executive.

principles of management   Fundamental "truths" or working hypotheses that shape management thinking and action.

quality circles   Small groups of 3 to 15 workers who meet regularly to discuss, analyze, and solve problems they experience on the job.

scientific management   An approach to managing people in an organization that believes there is "one best way" to do any task; it is the fastest and most efficient method to do so and is discovered through a scientific process of observation.

system   Any organized collection of parts united by prescribed interactions and designed for the accomplishment of a specific goal or task.

systems theory   A theory of organization that emphasizes an interactive and interrelated set of elements—an environment, inputs, processes, outputs, and feedback.

Theory X   A term coined by Douglas McGregor that describes a set of assumptions about human nature that guide an individual on how to manage people; it emphasizes that people dislike work, must be threatened to perform, prefer to be directed, and avoid responsibility.

Theory Y   A term coined by Douglas McGregor that describes a set of assumptions about human nature that guides management of workers; it holds that work is natural, workers can be self-directed, and imagination, ingenuity, and creativity are common.

Theory Z   Patterns of organization and operations of contemporary Japanese corporations that assume productivity is a function of social or managerial organization and can be greatly enhanced by communication, feedback, and worker involvement.

total quality management (TQM)   A new phase for quality control in its most expanded sense of a total and continuing concern for quality and the production of goods and services; seeks organizational performance at an optimal level.

traditional authority   Authority that rests on a belief in the sacredness of immemorial traditions; obligation of personal loyalty to chiefs selected in the traditional way.

Review Questions

1. Compare and contrast classical theory and human relations theory. Identify the major assumptions or tenets accepted or advocated by exemplary scholars of each tradition. How do their basic images of bureaucracy differ?

2. Compare and contrast the neoclassical and systems schools. Discuss three scholars who exemplify each school. What values do they have in common? What differing values does each school or tradition emphasize? How does each tradition envision bureaucracy?

3. Compare and contrast Theories X, Y, and Z as alternative styles of management. Which organizational theory is most associated with each management style? For each style, suggest what types of governmental organizations it would most appropriately manage.

4. This chapter dealt with values associated with bureaucracy and democracy. Which organizational approach is more appropriate to the value systems stressed by bureaucracy? by democracy? How can theories of organizational behavior help to achieve a balance between democratic and bureaucratic values?

5. Reading 5.1 concerned the budget attitudes among SES members. How would the "reinventing government movement" view the SES structure? Using InfoTrac, find articles that concern the equivalent form of the SES as used by the state level of government.

Surfing the Net

The following are useful websites for the topics discussed in this chapter.

To access a variety of associations located on the Internet, go to Associations on the Net (**http://www.ipl.org/ref/AON**).

American Psychological Association (**http://www.apa.org**)

American Society for Public Administration (**http://www.aspanet.org**)

American Sociological Association (**http://www.asanet.org**)

Public Administration Institute at Fairleigh Dickinson University (**http://www.fdu.edu/centers/pai.html**)

National Partnership for Reinventing Government (**http://www.npr.gov**)

Chapter 6

What one "knows" is relative to and affected by one's values, assumptions, and perspectives; in addition, learning and teaching occur in a social and cultural context. These tenets underpin the idea of rational or contextual knowledge, and challenge the conventional view of "received knowledge," which involves deference to authority and reliance on "expertise," a belief in knowledge (especially science) as a set of truths, and a view of education as authoritative explanation of these truths. . . .

Decision Making in the Administration of Public Policy

Citizen participation, community involvement, local knowledge, collaboration, and shared decision-making processes are now prominent themes in both public and academic discussion, part of the democratization of hitherto authoritarian processes. . . . Increased participation is upheld as democracy in action, a goal in and of itself. In addition, participation is seen to play a role in producing more effective, responsive, and informed policy on a variety of matters and has been "applied" across a variety of realms, ranging from the creation of social policy, to community and economic development, to sustainability, environmental and resource planning, management and problem solving. It is therefore seen as a means to substantive ends. Finally, participation is deemed to play an important psychological and educational role in the development of individuals and community.

Susan Dakin
Challenging old models of knowledge and learning,
Environments, 31(1) (August 2003): 93.

Introduction

The chapter-opening quotation refers to and illustrates potential problems in making decisions. Rationality in decision making in strict cost–benefit terms may be difficult to achieve when one level or branch of government has the power to impose mandates on another level without regard to the costs involved for the lower-level government or whether citizen demands for service outstrip a local government's ability and resources to provide such. Planning experts using their expertise may recommend on policy option to the elected decision maker, who ignores such "best-laid plans" in response to citizen input and pressures. Mandates from court decisions have huge impacts on the budgets of local school districts, local and state correctional agencies, and so on. This chapter is about making decisions—a process that is at the heart of bureaucracy and public administration. As will become clear, it is a complicated and sometimes messy process. It is also inherently value laden. A definition of **decision making** is deceptively simple: It is the process of choosing one course of action from among the choices available.

Making decisions is what administrators do. Administrative organizations make decisions to establish goals, set priorities, develop procedures, run programs, and mount responses to what are determined to be public problems. In organizations, decisions are complex and collective, involving many actors, both inside and outside the organization. They are often made in pursuit of differing, competing, reinforcing, or often even conflicting goals.

Who makes decisions within agencies? How do they go about making them? What standards are they using? To what ends, by what costs, and for whose benefit are these decisions made? These are central questions about the policy-making process. Understanding the process means figuring out who has influence over authoritative decision making, how accessible they are to special- and general-interest advocates, the effects of their decisions, the standards and values that are being applied, and their subsequent accountability.

The goals for which decisions are being made can be a problem for administrators, in that the goals themselves may be complex and even contradictory. To get a bill through the legislature and passed into law, for example, its goals are sometimes kept purposely vague. But bureaucrats cannot administer vague laws. To administer a program authorized by a vague law, they must clarify and determine specific programmatic details. They inevitably must choose how to clarify vagueness, a process that involves making value judgments. More of this problem is discussed later.

When making decisions, bureaucrats must rely on information; quite often, it is the information that they themselves must gather and analyze. But bureaucracy often deals with problems for which clear information is unavailable. How to interpret and analyze data is always a problem. Even with the best of intentions, bureaucrats make mistakes in gathering, assessing, and applying information.

Decision makers who participate in the process may be formally or informally involved. Formal decision makers are those who hold supervisory positions in a hierarchy and whose positions give them the legal authority and responsibility to make decisions. They sit at desks on which "The Buck Stops Here" sign might well be placed. Informal decision makers are typically functional specialists or administrative assistants, secretaries, other employees, and even the "kitchen cabinet," or involved parties who advise elected or high-level appointed decision makers in reaching authoritative decisions.

The participants involved may make programmed or unprogrammed decisions. Programmed decisions are familiar. They have become routinized in the bureaucracy, often determined by budget or legal mandates incorporated in a program's authorizing legislation. These decisions deal with anticipated problems and events. Unprogrammed decisions are, by definition, the nonroutine type. They deal with problems or events that have not been anticipated and often take on the aura of a crisis decision. They are the decisions most likely to engender unanticipated policy consequences. They often create the most notable "feedback."[1]

In making decisions, administrators must choose to draw a line—to create a balance—between or among competing and often-conflicting values. Even the decision not to act has value-selection implications. Moral and ethical considerations are often the heart of the choice involving bureaucratic program implementation. When life and death matters are decided, the luxury of making mistakes extracts a terrible toll indeed. Such results make administrators feel the weight of their decisions. The study of decision making has become central to public administration—a constant search to develop a model of decision making to "get it right."

Models of Decision Making in Administration

The traditional approach to management in public administration reflects the classical theorists' view of organization and heavily emphasizes how bureaucratic structures and their managers can efficiently function. This approach is perhaps best exemplified by Luther Gulick's prescribed "principles for administrators" to use in organizations. This view emphasizes what became known as the rational-comprehensive model of decision making. Decision making pervades an organization from top to bottom. In administering policy, administrators determine what the policy is and what their role will be in implementing it, in giving it life. As such, decision making is the "quintessential administrative act."[2]

Rational-Comprehensive Model

The **rational-comprehensive decision-making model** emerged from the classical school and is derived from economic models of decision making. In this model, decision makers consciously order their behavior so that it is "reasonably directed toward the achievement of conscious goals."[3] This is intended to "maximize outputs for a given input, or to minimize input for a given output."[4] Decision makers, acting as rational people, move toward their goals in ways that, to the best of their knowledge, use the least input of scarce resources per unit of valued output.[5] The model holds efficiency as the highest value. The rational-comprehensive model of decision making[6] distinguishes five basic steps administrators take in any decision:

1. Identify the problem and verify that it is a public problem.
2. Clarify the goals and determine the objectives of public policy.
3. Identify alternatives by considering the means or alternative ways to reach the goals.
4. Calculate the consequences of public policy by measuring the benefits and costs of each alternative considered and by rank ordering the alternatives on that basis.
5. Select the alternative that has the greatest likely benefit for the least discernible cost.

In Anthony Down's view, a rational person can always make a decision when given a set of alternatives when

1. he knows the probable consequences of choosing each alternative,
2. he ranks each alternative in order of preference,
3. he always chooses the highest-ranked option, and
4. he always makes the same decision each time the same alternatives are available.

The decision maker distinguishes ends from means, concentrates on one or a few primary goals, seeks to gather all possible data pertaining to each alternative available, objectively weighs the alternative options, and selects the best one. The analysis and methodology must be comprehensive, employ precise evaluation procedures, and quantify the costs and benefits while weighing the relative values.[7]

The model assumes a single actor is making a rational decision. It assumes, in the interest of efficiency, that a cost–benefit analysis can be made and that a cost–benefit ratio for each alternative can be quantified and used to rank the alternatives and thereby distinguish clearly among the values involved. In theory, this enables the decision maker to determine the best or optimal ratio of costs to benefits and thereby allow the best possible choice (sometimes referred to as the *mini-max* solution) to be made.

The rational-comprehensive model is prescribed by political economists to avoid, or at least reduce, the problem of **externality**, wherein the costs generated by one person or organization are borne by another. A **negative externality** is the effect of decision making that imposes social costs on the community; air and water pollution are prime examples. Business decisions that entail negative externalities are a major reason for governmental regulation.

The rational-comprehensive model assumes that the administrative decision-making process is value neutral—without reference to whether goals are also rational. The ultimate test of the rationality of a good decision is that it can be seen as the most efficient and appropriate means to reach the desired end.[8]

Critics of the rational-comprehensive model question it for several reasons, all of them based on the view that it is simply not possible to construct a purely rational, value-neutral decision-making process for any but the simplest and lowest-level decisions.[9] Critiques of the model point out that its assumptions are virtually impossible to meet in the real world. They note how difficult it is to distinguish facts from values and to analytically separate ends from means, as well as the improbability of getting agreement among multiple decision makers who, in the real world, are normally involved in decisions on predetermined goals.

In the real world, decision makers are pressured by time and cannot explore all options or handle more than a limited amount of information about all options at any one time. Other problems with the model include the difficulty decision makers face in giving their undivided attention to a single problem or decision, the high costs (in both time and money) involved in acquiring the information, defects in the communication process among the many individuals and levels of government commonly involved in solving vexing social policy problems, and the inability to project accurately the consequences of a given choice. This enhances the inevitable unanticipated consequences during and after the decision process.[10]

INFOTRAC
COLLEGE EDITION

**Economies of prevention:
the public health
research agenda**

PHOTO 6.1
Who Pays the Costs?
The problem of externalities arises when regulatory agencies become "captive" of the very industries they are designed to oversee. Who will prevent the industry from passing on social costs to the general taxpayer? What can be done to interrupt the tendency for regulatory agencies to become clientele agencies?
Source: AP/Wide World Photos.

The rational-comprehensive model involves some aspect of the following six problems.

1. There are individual barriers. Decision making typically involves many actors, not just a single actor. For various reasons, individuals put up barriers to solutions, values, ends, means, and alternatives that are suggested by others.

2. There are organizational barriers. In the real world, decisions almost always involve more than one subunit of an organization or agency, usually more than one agency, and often more than one level of government. The multiplicity of agency actors involved means there will be "turf" considerations that serve as barriers to several of the model's assumptions.

3. The effect of inputs from outside the organization can be significant. Nonorganizational actors in the process are nearly always involved in its decisions. Their influences and comments complicate the decision in all of the ways suggested in the second point and normally carry with them resources and political clout that present even greater barriers to realization of the model.

4. Time frame problems can limit decision making. Real-world decisions are driven by various time considerations in the budget cycle, legislative calendars, personnel procedures built into employee contracts, mandates issued by higher-level governments, and so on. These time constraints simply preclude all possible alternatives from being considered, carefully rank ordered, and analyzed for maximum cost–benefit ratios.

5. The civil service system also imposes values and limits that frequently serve as barriers to meeting the model's assumptions.

6. There are problems in securing and processing the information needed. In the real world, decision makers often lack data and sometimes cannot even achieve a consensus as to what data are needed and relevant. The bureaucracy also often cannot properly process and analyze the information, at least within a timely and cost-effective manner.

The clash or disagreement among actors about values and ends, as well as the means to those ends, limits permissibility in decision making. In other words, the most cost-effective option may not be politically or ethically permissible. To deal with AIDS, for example, an absolute quarantine of all persons who test positive for HIV might be the optimal way to prevent the spread of the deadly disease, but such a massive quarantine would simply be unacceptable for a wide range of civil rights and civil liberties reasons.

The rational model of decision making is also subject to limitations set by previous commitments. **Sunk costs** (or the costs involved in previous, related decisions), the careers and reputations of career civil servants and political appointees, and the historical reputations of elected officials may all dictate continuing down one policy path once it has been taken—even when it later proves to be less than optimal, if not a tragic mistake. The pressures of prior commitments on the actors involved may seem inevitable. These problems were discernible in perhaps the most conscious attempt to employ the rational-comprehensive model in decision making at the federal level: the case of the Planning Programming Budget System (PPBS) introduced by Secretary of Defense Robert McNamara to the Pentagon in 1961. President Lyndon Johnson was so impressed with its initial results that he extended it in 1965 to most federal departments and agencies. The unforeseen results were enormous. PPBS produced such a mountain of paperwork that by June 1971 OMB ceased requiring agencies to submit PPB documents with their budget requests. The system was considered a failure, an ill-tailored program for the organizational environment in which it had to work.[11]

The near impossibility of fulfilling the rational-comprehensive model of decision making's assumptions led to alternative models. One variation has been referred to as the *bargaining model*, or as an incremental approach to decision making.

INFOTRAC
COLLEGE EDITION

Spending time versus spending money

Bargaining Model

The more pluralist approach to administration implicit in both the human relations and systems theories of organization (especially the latter) suggests that decisions by organizations and their bureaucratic actors involve conflict, negotiation, persuasion, and individuals with varying stakes in the outcomes of policy decisions. These concepts lead to a decidedly different view of rationality and to a **bargaining**, or incremental, approach to decision making. Among the first and foremost advocates of this decision-making model is Charles Lindblom, who argues that it is paradoxically most rational to conduct limited analysis and then bargain out a decision that can attract sufficient political support to become acceptable.[12]

Lindblom first articulated the model in 1959, arguing that decision makers need not seek prior consensus on goals to make rational decisions, because so many actors and agencies involved may make goal consensus impossible, and to insist on such consensus might make decision making even more difficult. He referred to the process of decision making as "muddling through," noting that the means–ends type of analysis called for by the rational-comprehensive model is not possible where means and ends are confused—which is often the case in the real world. Public opinion is so highly ambiguous and diverse that identifiable goals either do not exist or are not sufficiently clear to serve as a guide to administrators. Lindblom noted that many worthy public policy goals are so broad they often conflict with one another.

Incremental Model

Lindblom proposed an **incremental approach** to decision making: making a series of limited, successive comparisons—"continuing incremental adjustments"— among a narrow range of alternatives rather than comparing all possible options. *Incrementalism* uses the status quo in place of some abstract goal as the key reference points in decisions and focuses on short-term effects. The incremental model looks at the most crucial consequences of action instead of all possible consequences, and it uses considerably less formal ways to measure benefits and costs.[13]

The model emerges from the political approach to public administration and stresses the need for administrators to be responsive to their political community, representative of the groups It comprises, and more accountable to elected officials. These values—responsiveness, representativeness, and accountability—are weighted as more important than efficiency and emphasize the need for public participation and administration based on political coalitions and consensus rather than on "expertise."[14]

The incremental model specifies two general steps for administrative decision making.

1. *Redefining ends and means.* In the bargaining or incremental model, ends and means are not treated as analytically distinct. Objectives may be too vague to serve as ends in any programmatic sense. Public policy may be defined by the means available to the agency within the confines of some broad policy direction. The model recognizes that it is often politically impractical to reform a policy in one fell swoop. Rather, minor adjustments to policy are more attainable and allow for the gradual accretion of small incremental reforms over time.

2. *Arriving at consensus.* In the incremental model, the key test of a "good" decision is agreement or consensus in favor of the policy and its prescribed method of implementation. Means and ends are viewed as packages that are more or less acceptable to the relevant interests involved. The combination of means and ends that can achieve the greatest consensus is considered to be best. In this model, representativeness and responsiveness outweigh the values of efficiency, economy, and even effectiveness. These more traditional managerial values are not ignored, but they are not treated as preeminent. By the standards of this model, a program that does less and costs more may be more acceptable than one that is economic and efficient.

The incremental model also implies other points of view. A good policy may be largely symbolic yet considered successful. The test of a good policy may be the support it generates rather than its measurable effect on some target in society. Such procedures for evaluating administrative decisions make both policy evaluation and performance appraisal (of administrators or of agencies) more difficult. But the administrative actors involved in the policy process may prefer that to be the case.

In the bargaining process of decision making, the rationalist's attempts to "minimax" all phases of decision making is replaced by attempts to simply **satisfice** (in Herbert Simon's terms; see Chapter 5), or to reach a decision that is satisfactory and yields benefits that suffice to meet situational needs of the decision maker. Administrators can accept "good enough" rather than despair at finding "the best" answer to a policy problem. Incrementalists acknowledge that this permits subjective values to influence decisions, but they argue that subjectivity can never be eliminated entirely and that it is better to openly include sound subjective judgment than to vainly attempt to exclude all traces of subjectivity.[15]

Graham Allison examined the Cuban missile crisis of October 1962 using three different analytical models of decision making.[16] Model I used the rational-human approach. Model II was based on administrative process. He called Model III the **bureaucratic politics model**. In the third model, decisions are understood as the results of various bargaining games among the players in the national government. Analysis of the policy decision depends on understanding "the perceptions, motivations, positions, power, and maneuvers of the key players."[17] In the missile crisis, the policy alternative of using a naval blockade (rather than a surgical air strike or simply strong diplomatic language through the United Nations) emerged as the result of a bargaining process among the key players who made up the Executive Committee of the National Security Council (**ExComm**) who handled the missile crisis.

In Allison's words, players followed Miles Law: "Where you stand depends on where you sit." In this assessment, who wins the bargaining game depends on who has the strongest hand and who bargains the most effectively.[18]

The bargaining model has generated some related procedures. Among the more notable is what has been coined the *garbage-can* approach. In this imagery, participants dump problems and solutions into a garbage can. Decisions are not so much made as occur in response to many ambiguous values and objectives.[19] These types of decisions occur under conditions of **pervasive ambiguity** that involve so much uncertainty that the assumptions of the rational-comprehensive model simply do not apply. The garbage-can model refers to almost random streams of people, problems, and solutions as being so interdependent of each other that the choice of the appropriate solution to any such problem is more a product of chance than of "objective rationality."[20]

The incremental approach of the various bargaining models has also been criticized.[21] Critics focus on the values inherent in the approach, contending that incrementalists value the status quo too highly. Innovation and bolder change are discouraged. Small-scale incremental change, moreover, favors short-term needs and may overlook larger needs and demands. Policy making is more likely to miss the mark. This approach, critics maintain, favors the bureaucratic decision maker who behaves as a "conserver," in Anthony Downs's words. Such bureaucrats are interested in maintaining their own and their agency's power, prestige,

INFOTRAC
COLLEGE EDITION

Collaborative ecosystem planning processes in the United States: evolution and change

and income (or budget). They tend to be overly cautious, taking a low-risk approach to decision making.[22]

These criticisms were expanded on by Amitai Etzioni, who suggested a modification to both the bargaining and incremental models that he called **mixed scanning**.[23] Etzioni emphasizes the failure of the incremental model to distinguish between fundamental and nonfundamental decisions. He explains his perspective using an analogy of a high-altitude weather satellite. It has two cameras onboard: a wide-angle lens that scans large areas and a narrow-angle lens that can zoom in on specific turbulence. Each camera needs the other. The wide-angle lens discovers the large systems of turbulent weather. The zoom lens enables detailed analysis of storm centers and related weather phenomena. Each camera supplies useful information, but maximum advantage comes from using them in combination. Fundamental decisions explore main alternatives as viewed by decision actors in terms of broad goals, but the more incremental-like adjustments of nonfundamental decisions contribute to continuous mutual adjustments. Etzioni argues that this mixed scanning will reduce the effect of the shortcomings of the other two models. Its incremental features reduce the unrealistic aspects of rationalism by limiting the details required in fundamental decisions, and its rational-comprehensive aspects overcome the conservative bent of incrementalism by exploring long-term alternatives.[24]

Participative Model

Another model that has been suggested to understand and portray decision making is the **participative model**. It assumes at the most general level the participation of those who will be affected by the decision, ensures their participation in the process, and maintains that the rationality of the decision depends on their inclusion.[25]

Participation often involves consultation. Those who have authoritative decision-making power seek the input of those who are affected by the decision. Elected executive and legislative officials and high-level managers of agencies choose to share decision-making power. This may be as basic as adopting policy through a referendum—for example, voters determine whether or not a policy put on a ballot by legislative action or by voter initiative is adopted into law or rejected.

Claims as to who should be allowed to participate generally are made by employees of organizations, by persons the agency serves or regulates (its clientele or vested interest groups), and taxpayers who fund the program that the decision will enact. The participative model emphasizes the value of representativeness. Decisions thus made may be decidedly less rational from the view of the traditional decision-making model. Voters may reject necessary but unpopular programs from being located in their neighborhoods, evidencing the NIMBY syndrome (see Chapter 2). One example is a state legislature, which may seek the participation of nongovernmental groups in producing regulation. The regulation of most professions at the state level and of many occupations at the local level is typically "self-regulatory": a nongovernmental professional group (a state bar association, for example) essentially writes the standards that are imposed in the policy.

Congress, too, sometimes establishes professional advisory boards to advise on health care finance. The Federal Housing Authority, for example, mandated boards in which representatives of the residents of public housing projects were included. During World War II, the War Production Board had literally thousands of advisory groups at the regional and national levels to form joint industry–labor–government boards to settle labor disputes.

Many federal agencies establish advising boards or commissions that regularly seek to routinize input from clientele groups. National advisory boards influence the awarding of research projects and contracts to individual scientists, universities, or so-called think-tank research institutes. The National Science Foundation (NSF), the National Institutes of Health (NIH), and the National Foundation for the Arts (NFA) exemplify this type of structured participative decision making.

The federal government uses local committees whose part-time members represent communities or neighborhoods. The Selective Service Board administered the draft in this manner. The Department of Agriculture has long used farmer groups on advisory committees at the county level. Urban renewal programs involve local committees that oversee some projects. The Equal Employment Opportunity Act required citizen advisory committees for various programs in the War on Poverty to administer "with maximum feasible participation" the areas and members of the target group being served. The Department of Housing and Urban Development used a similar approach with its Model Cities Act and the 1974 Housing and Community Development Act.[26]

Perhaps a classic example at the state and local levels of participative decision making is the jury system, wherein a jury of one's peers actually makes the decision of guilt or innocence as well as the sentencing in some criminal cases and the amounts of fines or damage awards to plaintiffs in some civil cases.

An obvious advantage of the participative approach to decision making is the wealth of information it can provide. A disadvantage is the flip side: Sometimes, advisory boards provide too much information in an undifferentiated mass that can overwhelm the official decision-making body or simply stack the deck so that only one alternative can be selected. Too much information can be as bad as too little.[27] This is one way in which clientele interest groups capture their agency. Their values become the agency's values, their goals, the agency's goals.

The participative model raises several value issues. Too narrow a clientele group of advisors promotes policy geared to narrow special interests. Too broad a group can result in mixed clientele who lack keen interest or real insight into the problem. If an advisory board gets to be too large, it may not be an effective voice in representing the clientele to the appointed or elected committees, councils, or boards that are officially assumed to be representative. Part-time board members may simply and uncritically rubber-stamp staff recommendations, lending an aura of democracy to decision making that is really done by the experts or bureaucrats with little substantive influence from the token board. Finding the proper balance between general interest and vested interests is the dilemma of this approach.

Linking participative budgeting to organizational performance

Public Choice Model

Another model of decision making that involves a variation of the rational-comprehensive approach is the **public choice decision-making model**. Various *microeconomists* (those who develop economic theory to explain the behavior of individuals or organizations) have used the most basic of economic assumptions—

that human beings are rational and seek to maximize their self-interest—to elaborate a model of decision making.[28] This model assumes that the most rational thing is to promote one's self-interest. Public choice theory is fundamentally a theory about nonmarket failure. Under ideal conditions, markets both provide *consumer* sovereignty and are justified by it. Public officials, like all other individuals, are motivated by self-interest. From that assumption, the public choice model portrays bureaucrats as people involved in decision making whose self-interest dictates that they avoid risks and promote the growth of their agencies' programs and budgets and thereby produce bigger but usually less efficient government.

To avoid this, proponents of the public choice model advocate that whenever possible government policy should be turned over to the private sector. The public choice perspective sees public agencies as an efficient means for allocating decision-making capabilities in order to provide public goods and services responsive to the preferences of individuals (E. Ostrom and V. Ostrom, 1971). This might be accomplished by **contracting out** for services or by **privatization** (the selling of services produced by government to the private sector). Contracting out for services, its proponents argue, simulates private-sector competition and dilutes the influence of bureaucrats.[29] At the local level, using charter schools and voucher systems are, in the model's perspective, the best vehicles for school reform. Or, for example, we might ask, are prisons overcrowded warehouses of the criminal element? If so, then the solution is simple—privatize them.

The public choice model values efficiency above all else, and it presumes that the free-market mechanism for making decisions—responding to the inherent rationality of economic self-interest—will be superior to decisions made by government bureaucracies. The model assumes that information is available for free-market conditions to prevail. Market-based mechanisms such as contracts are assumed to maximize efficiency. Decision makers are viewed as aggressively seeking the right information because failure to do so allows others to outcompete them. The power of the model rests on its assumption that bureaucrats, as rational human beings, will single-mindedly value and pursue their own self-interests: power, security, and personal income. The model's weakness lies in the fact that its assumptions do not always pertain. Many top-level bureaucrats could double or triple their salaries in the private sector, yet they continue in public service. For some, at least, a devotion to the public good seems to be a motivating factor beyond economic self-interest.

The delivery of public goods and services by local governments has been profoundly changed since the 1980s by substituting "quasi-markets" for the traditional institutions of government: by using vouchers, contracting-out-for-service, and the Tiebout model (1956) instead of centralized bureaucratic production within metropolitan governments as the preferred mechanism for goods and services. The success of these approaches is based on their claim to bring market-like forces to bear on the production of goods and services, either directly by separating provision and production so that production is generated by the market, as in the cases of vouchers and contracting, or indirectly by arranging public production institutions so that they are subject to market-like constraint of residents who can simply "vote with their feet," as in the case of the Tiebout model (Lowery, 1998: 138).

INFOTRAC
COLLEGE EDITION

Differences in social and public risk perceptions and conflicting impacts

The public choice model is particularly popular now because its explanation of government problems matches the conservative economic mood that has prevailed in U.S. politics since the early 1980s. The model offers simple and neat solutions: privatize and deregulate. Its very simplicity is also a weakness.

The model pursues the value of efficiency at the expense of equality. Some government services, moreover, at their core are public interests that cannot be privatized. The self-regulating effect of the market does not always work well, and contracts do not administer themselves. Government administrators still must exercise considerable discretion in managing contracts. The use of contracts may simply replace one set of values with another, and the responsibility to manage cannot be contracted away.

Various critics have noted the limitations of the public choice model and its assumptions as to the value of the marketplace approach to public decision making, a few of which will be highlighted here (see, for example, Boston, 1994; Lowery, 1998, 1999; Lowery and Lyons, 1989; C. Miller, 1998).

1. Monopoly strikes at the heart of consumer sovereignty by eliminating competition. Lacking competition, no incentive exists to be efficient. In the case of local government, legal barrier to entry can preclude efforts to establish Tiebout-like quasi-markets. One of the core recommendations of the advocates of Tiebout quasi-markets is the elimination of such legal barriers by such devices as consolidated governments and permissive annexation laws. The public choice advocates castigate public officials when discussing nonmarket failures (Savas, 1987) but simply assume that bureaucrats are somehow transformed into responsive public servants once contracting is adopted. But the Tiebout model itself raises issues of monopoly. For example, how many independent communities are needed in order for the benefits of quasi-market competition to succeed? Satisfying heterogeneous tastes in such a way as to encourage productive efficiency may require a large number of municipal jurisdictions. Legal barriers to "quasi-market" formation allow the cornering of vital resources.

2. Another major issue involves lack of information. Indeed, markets, non-markets, and quasi-markets can fail if "consumers" lack sufficient information to make choices that reflect their true preferences. They all involve debates about what constitutes "informed preferences." And what about cases where a host of services, rather than a single service, are at issue? When consumers "purchase school services" in a Tiebout quasi-market by moving to a new city, they also purchase police, fire, sanitation, and street-lighting and street maintenance services. To be informed consumers, citizens must know about each of these goods and services in order for the "efficient distribution of goods and services" aspects of the Tiebout quasi-market mechanism to pertain in voucher transactions or even most market transactions. And in contracting out, if government does not specify what it wants from suppliers or does not evaluate well what it has received, it cannot expect to get what it needs. City governments, like citizens, can fail to be adequately informed consumers. And while many municipal services are readily definable and easy to measure and evaluate, many others are not, especially human services. Yet sufficiently complete

specification of requirements of contracts presupposes a rational process that can deal with this complexity by clarifying means-and-ends relationships, identifying valid and reliable measures of performance, and often doing so in the context of inadequate theory and limited experience.

3. Besides not knowing or sufficiently understanding consumer preferences, we also have the issue of preference manipulation. A number of studies of contracting out have raised questions about the power of vendors to manipulate the preferences of local governments.

4. Another source of preference error concerns externalities, that is, interdependencies between the consumption by individuals not captured by prices. For example, technological externalities occur when somebody physically affects you or your good directly without considering the impact when doing so. A study of 64 metropolitan areas regarding externalities in police services provided by one jurisdiction to residents of another and diversions of criminal activity across jurisdictions, for example, found that negative externalities dominated the results: Greater density of jurisdiction leads to higher-than-optimal spending on policing as each city tries to divert crime into neighboring jurisdictions (E. Ostrom, Parks, and Whitaker, 1978). Such externalities are not only possible within quasi-markets, they may be quite common.

5. Pecuniary externalities arise when the choices on one actor influence the exchange value of another actor's goods or services. These are especially likely in cases of contracting.

6. Preference substitution can also be a failure in quasi-markets. Lowery gives an interesting hypothetical example. Suppose Texas provides secondary education vouchers (as they do). Assume the Texas legislature fully intended to provide quality education as commonly understood in terms of reading, writing, and arithmetic. But assume also that parents select schools with their vouchers based on the quality of the school's football teams. In such a case of preference substitution, Texas schools would efficiently provide very high-quality football teams. School choice would then likely have no effect on the quality of education, since selection would operate on an entirely different set of traits. Likewise, in a Tiebout quasi-market situation, preferences for *segregation*, rather than about tax and service packages, may govern choices in metropolitan settings. In such cases, we should expect the quasi-market to provide segregation in an efficient manner, since that is the trait upon which selection is based.

As Lowery sums it up:

Public choice scholars have contributed much to critical thought about the public sector by pointing out that market failure does not imply nonmarket success. Proponents of progressive reform institutional arrangements now carry a heavier burden of proof by having to demonstrate that they will indeed do what they are purported to do. By the same token, nonmarket failure does not imply quasi-market success. Therefore, advocates of quasi-market institutional arrangements should be asked to shoulder a comparably more rigorous burden of proof. This

Box 6.1

The Effects of Public Policies and Prices on Youth Smoking

Government regulation of the tobacco industry can be justified in several ways. Smoking, for example, is clearly associated with market failures, such as negative externalities and imperfect information among market participants (i.e., smokers), and these failures provide one reason for government intervention in the form of regulation (mostly by state and/or local bureaucracies). Another is the huge health care costs associated with the health consequences of smoking. The cost of medical treatment for smokers and for secondhand smokers inflates health care premiums for everyone, regardless of smoking participation, and many of these expenses are paid from public funds.

The declining trend in smoking prevalence among youth was triggered, in part at least, by a new financial liability of tobacco companies toward 46 states under the Master Settlement Agreement of November 1998, which amounted to a $206 billion financial burden for the industry over the following 25 years. The increasing smoking prevalence among youth and young adults during the early 1990s prior to that agreement and its decreasing trend toward the end of the decade suggest that this age group is highly sensitive to cigarette price incentives.

Public officials, particularly health officials, alarmed at the rising youth cigarette consumption in the early to mid-1990s, designed, promoted, and adopted numerous antismoking policies and state tobacco control programs. Cigarette market interventions currently cover a wide range of areas: tobacco excise taxes, smoke-free indoor-air laws, ordinances restricting access of minors to tobacco, including retail tobacco licensing, restrictions on advertising and promoting tobacco products, requirements for placing warning labels on tobacco products, requirements for product ingredient disclosure, and the like.

Not all states were equally aggressive, however, when it came to the taxing of tobacco and to antismoking policies. The largest gap evident is between tobacco-producing and -nonproducing states. As of the end of 2002, state excise taxes ranged from 2.5 cents a pack in the state of Virginia to $1.51 a pack in Massachusetts. Tax differences at the state and municipal levels, however, create incentives for the interstate smuggling of tobacco products. Certain states are especially noteworthy for their antismoking polices, the most outstanding being Arizona, California, and Massachusetts. By voter amendment in 2004, Colorado increased the tax on cigarettes by 64 cents per pack, and the tax on other tobacco products will rise from 20 percent to 40 percent of the manufacturers' list prices.

Beginning in the early 1990s, the federal government took the initiative in the area of enforcement and inspection. In July 1992, for instance, Congress passed the Synar amendment requiring states to enact and enforce laws that prohibit tobacco sales to minors (defined as consumers under the age of 18). The amendment requires states to actively inspect and enforce the laws. They are obligated to demonstrate that the age limits are being enforced by annually conducting random and unannounced compliance checks of retailers selling tobacco products. If states fail to comply, they are subject to reductions in their substance abuse block grants funds. A General Accounting Office (GAO) study in 2001, however, expressed some doubts with respect to the methods and accuracy of the enforcement data because states had an incentive to underestimate violation rates.

Source: Based on Hanna Ross and Frank Chaloupka, The effect of public policies and prices on youth smoking, *Southern Economic Journal*, 70(4) (April 2004): 796–816.

entails demonstrating that quasi-markets are competitive and provide equal access to all, that choice is based on informed and unbiased preferences, and that the preferences exercised by production consumers fall within the bounds set by provision consumers. (Lowery, 1998: 155)

INFOTRAC
COLLEGE EDITION

**Research ethics
and misguided moral
intuition**

The complexity and limits of decision making in a case where there is intentional market-preference manipulation are illustrated in Box 6.1, "The Effects of Public Policies and Prices on Youth Smoking."

Table 6.1 compares five organizational decision-making models with the five schools of thought discussed in Chapter 5. In comparing their differing ideological bases, the table lists some of the values emphasized by each model. The values

TABLE 6.1

Overview of Five Organizational Decision-Making Models and the Five Schools of Thought on Organization Theory

School of Organizational Theory	Model of the Decision-Making Process
Classical	Rational-comprehensive
	Centralized, orderly, with emphasis on values of efficiency and effectiveness
Humanist	Participative
	Very decentralized, ad hoc with emphasis such values as flexibility, loose coupling, randomness, responsiveness, participation
Neoclassical	Bureaucratic
	Less centralized, with greater reliance on rules, procedural rationality embodied in programs, standard operating procedures, and emphasis on such values as incrementalism, stability, fairness, and predictability
Systems	Political power or bargaining
	Consistent with social actors, pluralistic within the organization; emphasis on values such as participation, incrementalism, the interplay among interests, struggle, conflict, and winners and losers
New management	Public choice
	Free play of market forces and the strategic management of information; emphasis on the value of efficiency above all else; cost/benefits to maximize self-interest

noted as implicit to each model highlight the inherent ethical dimension to all decision making. This dimension may be institutional or personal, but it is always present in the decision-making process.

The Ethical Dimensions of Decision Making

When making decisions, public administrators inevitably pursue certain goals, whether personal, organizational, or some mixture of both. The pursuit of goals involves strategies and tactical choices to achieve them (means and ends). Such decisions raise questions about the propriety of the tactics used in implementing a course of action to deal with a vexing public problem. This raises the issue of the ethical standards used to assess the tactics.[30]

Any discussion of the ethical issue in decision making raises the obvious point of needing to define ethical behavior. This is no simple task because the ethics of a decision may involve institutional as well as personal behavior.

Institutional Ethics

When an institution of government pursues organizational goals and sets on a course of action toward reaching those goals, the end itself may be seen as so

PHOTO 6.2

Hiroshima Then and Now

Fifty years after the bombing of Hiroshima, Japan, the city appears fully restored, but the U.S. decision to use atomic weapons remains controversial. What institutional ethics justified the dropping of the first atomic bomb in 1945?

Source: AP/Wide World Photos.

compelling as seemingly to justify any means. Murder is justified in the name of national security. People's reputations and lives may be ruined and justified as necessary to save a bureaucratic organization's reputation. A nation at war, for example, in pursuing an end to that war may develop and use weapons of mass destruction. World War II presents perhaps the only modern example. Was the United States ethically justified in dropping atomic bombs on Hiroshima and Nagasaki in 1945? They certainly ended the war more quickly and thereby saved the lives of perhaps tens of thousands of American soldiers. But was it justified in doing so at the cost of hundreds of thousands of Japanese citizens, most of whom were noncombatants? The ethical dimensions of that decision are still vigorously debated all these years later.

Less apocalyptic but still ethically problematic decisions can still be found in U.S. society. Consider, for example, medical policy such as AIDS research. To scientifically test a new drug to treat a deadly disease such as AIDS, for example, the National Institutes of Health conducts blind studies, in which some subjects are given the drug being developed to treat the illness and some subjects in a control group are given a placebo. Is it ethical to deny the patients given the placebo treatment a drug that is quickly seen to be effective? Does the greater interest of a controlled study in the name of science justify denying effective medicine to many individuals who will surely die if their diseases are not treated?

Organizations have often striven to clarify such dilemmas in decision making by articulating codes of ethics to guide the behavior of their members. Box 6.2 offers one such code, that of the American Society for Public Administration. It is like many such general codes of ethical behavior developed by professional associations, agencies of government, and even the government itself (Congress has established a code of ethics for its members, for instance).

Personal Ethics

Often at issue in decision making are personal ethics as well. Bureaucrats oversee huge budgets—often in the hundreds of millions of dollars and even in the billions of dollars. The temptation to divert some of those funds to personal use can be great and the risk of exposure often small. In addition to awarding contracts worth millions, government decisions routinely affect business in ways that also can create or cost millions of dollars. Lobbyists may try to buy favorable decisions by bribing administrators. The temptation to sell one's political influence over policy is great. Insider access to information can be worth a fortune, and individuals can and do offer considerable sums to bureaucrats for just that sort of information.

Ideological considerations can also color personal ethics. The director of a county government's economic development agency, for example, may easily justify giving special tax breaks to attract a business because her ideological view that creating "jobs" in the local economy is a primary value to be pursued. The attracted firm, however, might not hire local workers. Or if it is a manufacturing concern that pollutes the county's air or water, then is the decision to grant tax concessions morally justified? Will the agency director accept gifts of free golf trips or Hawaiian vacations because the decision is in the county's best interests by increasing employment, raising property tax values, and thereby adding revenues to county government?

The problem of corruption is endemic to politics and to government simply because government decisions involve so much power and wealth. It becomes commonplace at all levels of government—in the ways contracts are awarded, jobs are created and filled, people are hired, offices are sold, favored political friends are rewarded, power is exerted, and the needs or plight of others are ignored. Corruption, however, can involve sins of omission as well as those of commission. Corruption is a form of privilege indulged in by those in power. It is inherently unethical and clearly undemocratic because it concentrates power in the hands of a few who can make decisions based not on the good of the whole but on the interests of the few. Corruption is an offense against the value of equality. Bureaucratic experts often enjoy concentrated power, and the danger of corruption is correspondingly high. Despite being a cliché, it is nonetheless true: Power corrupts, and absolute power corrupts absolutely.

The Limits of Decision Making

No one model or approach to administrative decision making can guarantee a correct, rational, best, or even sound decision. All approaches share problems common to the very process of decision making. Time, uncertainty, the distortion of information, and the crisis nature of much decision making are highlighted here.[31]

Time

Real-world decisions are always constrained by time. A model may call for acquiring information about all possible alternatives, considering all options, involving all possible participants, or making the partnership between business and government

Colorado's term limits: consequences, yes, but were they intended?

Box 6.2

Code of Ethics of the American Society for Public Administration

The American Society for Public Administration (ASPA) exists to advance the science, processes, and art of public administration. The Society affirms its responsibility to develop the spirit of professionalism within its membership and to increase the public awareness of ethical principles in public service by its example. To this end, we, the members of the Society, commit ourselves to the following principles:

I. Serve the Public Interest

Serve the public, beyond serving oneself.

ASPA members are committed to:

1. Exercise discretionary authority to promote the public interest.
2. Oppose all forms of discrimination and harassment, and promote affirmative action.
3. Recognize and support the public's right to know the public's business.
4. Involve citizens in policy decision making.
5. Exercise compassion, benevolence, fairness, and optimism.
6. Respond to the public in ways that are complete, clear, and easy to understand.
7. Assist citizens in their dealings with government.
8. Be prepared to make decisions that may not be popular.

II. Respect the Constitution and the Law

Respect, support, and study government constitutions and laws that define responsibilities of public agencies, employees, and all citizens.

ASPA members are committed to:

1. Understand and apply legislation and regulations relevant to their professional role.
2. Work to improve and change laws and policies that are counterproductive or obsolete.
3. Eliminate unlawful discrimination.
4. Prevent all forms of mismanagement of public funds by establishing and maintaining strong fiscal and management controls and by supporting audits and investigative activities.
5. Respect and protect privileged information.
6. Encourage and facilitate legitimate dissent activities in government and protect the whistle-blowing rights of public employees.
7. Promote constitutional principles of equality, fairness, representativeness, responsiveness, and due process in protecting citizens' rights.

III. Demonstrate Personal Integrity

Demonstrate the highest standards in all activities to inspire public confidence and trust in public service.

responsive to free-market forces, but no decision maker has the luxury of sufficient time to research all possible solutions, assess all costs and benefits, involve all relevant participants, or form partnerships or privatize a program. Time limits and constraints can be found throughout the decision-making process and with various parties. Budget cycles impose them, as do the calendars of legislative bodies and other branches or levels of government that must be consulted or involved. Some governments also can impose mandates that set specific time limits on others. Union contracts that govern the treatment of staff members—retention, promotion, and disciplinary actions—also have time requirements about notification. Enabling legislation that authorizes programs may have time limits. Sunset laws also require decisions by a certain time, or a program dies for lack of reauthorization. Grants from one level to another have to be sought, applied for, implemented, and evaluated according to time frames specified in the grant. Public policy may be viewed as a dynamic, never-ending process, but it progresses in definite stages, each with its own time constraints.

ASPA members are committed to:

1. Maintain truthfulness and honesty and not to compromise them for advancement, honor, or personal gain.
2. Ensure that others receive credit for their work and contributions.
3. Zealously guard against conflict of interest or its appearance: e.g., nepotism, improper outside employment, misuse of public resources, or the acceptance of gifts.
4. Respect superiors, subordinates, colleagues, and the public.
5. Take responsibility for their own errors.
6. Conduct official acts without partisanship.

IV. Promote Ethical Organizations

Strengthen organizational capabilities to apply ethics, efficiency, and effectiveness in serving the public.

ASPA members are committed to:

1. Enhance organizational capacity for open communication, creativity, and dedication.
2. Subordinate institutional loyalties to the public good.
3. Establish procedures that promote ethical behavior and hold individuals and organizations accountable for their conduct.
4. Provide organization members with an administrative means for dissent, assurance of due process, and safeguards against reprisal.
5. Promote merit principles that protect against arbitrary and capricious actions.

6. Promote organizational accountability through appropriate controls and procedures.
7. Encourage organizations to adopt, distribute, and periodically review a code of ethics as a living document.

V. Strive for Professional Excellence

Strengthen individual capabilities and encourage the professional development of others.

ASPA members are committed to:

1. Provide support and encouragement to upgrade competence.
2. Accept as a personal duty the responsibility to keep up to date on emerging issues and potential problems.
3. Encourage others, throughout their careers, to participate in professional activities and associations.
4. Allocate time to meet with students and provide a bridge between classroom studies and the realities of public service.

Enforcement of the Code of Ethics shall be conducted in accordance with Article I, Section 4 of ASPA's Bylaws. In 1981 the American Society for Public Administration's National Council adopted a set of moral principles. Three years later, in 1984, the Council approved a Code of Ethics for ASPA members. In 1994 it was revised.

Uncertainty

A degree of uncertainty is also nearly ever-present in decision-making situations. Economic forecasts project the expected behavior of markets, individuals, businesses, and the actions of other governments, both domestic and foreign, but such projections are never more than good "guesstimates" and inherently involve some degree of uncertainty.

Distortion of Information

Good information, especially data that are quantifiable and usable in vigorous statistical analysis, is often hard to come by. A governor's budget office, a county health agency's advisory board, a mayor's urban renewal board, or a county's land use planning commission all share the problem of getting reliable data. They make decisions on data that are months to years old and must project trends months to years into the future. This makes for a high level of uncertainty at best, and political wishful thinking often trumps hard analysis.

The complexity of society raises similar problems of uncertainty. Science often does not know how to deal with a problem (a cure for AIDS, for instance). Catastrophic

events—earthquakes, floods, tornados, fires, a 300 percent increase over a year in the cost of crude oil, for example—that are unforeseen when earlier decisions were made also increase the uncertainty of policy effects. Policy makers who have to decide in periods of uncertainty often try to shift burdens (and blame) to other agencies or levels of government.

An issue about which there is a great deal of uncertainty becomes a political hot potato to be passed to someone else. This tendency to avoid making difficult decisions with great uncertainty is spoofed in Cartoon 6.1. The variety of state solutions to the abortion issue may satisfy federal courts' interest in coping with the uncertainties involved ("Let local community standards prevail"), but it means no national standard on the question is attainable. What is legal in one state is a crime in another. An equity issue is raised by a lack of consistent and uniform law. A wealthy woman who has the means to travel can get a legal abortion; a poor woman must resort to "criminal" behavior if she seeks the same solution to an unwanted pregnancy.

Information is also distorted as it moves up and down the hierarchical levels of a bureaucracy.[32] Information that may reflect unfavorably on lower-level bureaucrats or simply be information higher-level managers do not like to hear may travel up communication channels slowly. Reports going upward also may have to be condensed, and information is distorted this way, too. The *Challenger* disaster in 1986 exemplified the sometimes-fatal nature of such communication pathologies. Midlevel managers rejected the advice of an engineer for one of NASA's contractors, refused to pass along his concerns over cold-weather effects on critical O-rings, and disaster struck.[33]

The Bush Administration has struggled with a thorny ethical issue: how to prevent the misuse of powerful gene-engineering technologies without hobbling beneficial studies. They opted to "balance the ethical issues" by adopting an incremental approach. It was supportive of the "self-regulation approach" in creating flexible mechanisms that can respond to changing risks. It essentially relies on expanding an existing self-governance system that evolved out of earlier battles over the risks of recombinant DNA research. Under this approach, institutional biosafety committees at some 400 U.S. institutions review gene-engineering experiments and can toss controversial cases to a national Recombinant DNA Advisory Committee (RAC) housed at the National Institutes of Health (NIH) (Malakoff and Enserink, 2003).

Crisis

Crisis situations often require immediate decisions. Catastrophic events, political upheavals, natural disasters, acts of terrorism, and international conflicts can move to the top of the agenda of government problems that must be dealt with immediately. The crisis nature of such decisions enhances the problems of time and uncertainty and may change the psychology of the participants as well. A national security crisis may be limited to a handful of experts and top political executives. The danger of groupthink mentality increases in a crisis situation, because all involved feel greater pressure to achieve consensus as how to best deal with the crisis. By their very nature, crises upset the normal order of decision making. Routine solutions do not apply. Past experience may be nonexistent or of limited relevance. Sometimes the nature of the crisis—if serious enough—will demand broad consensus and a bipartisan agreement about how to deal with it.

At a state level, should an employer such as a major automobile-manufacturing corporation be bailed out with an emergency loan or through special tax credits to save thousands of jobs that are extremely valuable to the state's economy? Locally, when a military base closes or the business in a one-company town decides to locate elsewhere, an economic crisis may confront the local economy and thus impact the city or county government's coffers. What is politically acceptable in a crisis may be the second choice or the least ill among options rather than the best solution. Obviously, crisis decisions pose incredibly high risks for the decision makers involved.

Reading 6.1, "Comprehensive Administrative Reform Implementation," discusses a Florida State effort to comprehensively reform the state bureaucracy. It illustrates the complexity of ambitious (and ambiguous) reform efforts and how such policy implementation involves many veto points that can influence the success or failure of the reform effort. It also shows the inherently conflicted nature of the values involved.

INFOTRAC
COLLEGE EDITION

Crisis management, crisis response

Reading 6.1

Comprehensive Administrative Reform Implementation

Comprehensive administrative reforms have emerged episodically in state governments. Such episodes vary in form and cut across methods, but typically they are justified as means to greater efficiency, effectiveness, and responsiveness (Conant, 1986). Other scholars note that such comprehensive reforms generally have little to at most modest success since policy implementation in such cases involve a large number of veto points and complexities related to inducements and capabilities of those who are involved in the implementation. The policy reforms are subject to the hazards of "shaky coalitions," policy ambiguity, media influence, and executive turnover. Incrementalism (Lindblom, 1959), mixed-scanning (Etzioni, 1967, 1986), and more recently "goal groping" (Behn, 1995) have all been offered as descriptive of both typical change patterns and normative statements of how change should occur. It is little wonder that comprehensive reforms are infrequently attempted.

A comprehensive reform effort was begun by then–Florida Governor Lawton Chiles in 1990. It had been more than 25 years since the last major overhaul of the state's administrative and constitutional system. Governor Chile's package of reforms included total quality management (TQM), organizational restructuring, decentralization, deregulation, downsizing, strategic planning, civil service reform, innovation and productivity incentives, and performance-based budgeting (Berry, Chackerian, and Wechsler, 1999).

[Our study shows that] the extent of reform success is importantly influenced by interactions (namely, synergies, tradeoffs, and avoidance) between reform components and that these interactions are constrained by the institutional environment. . . . While immediate impetus for comprehensive reform might come from fashionable rhetoric, . . . such as reinventing government, . . . or from broad-based changes in the social and economic environment, we suggest that the reforms implemented also will depend on interactions among the reforms.

The reform of public administration literature emphasizes the difficulties of implementation, the importance of political influences, the technical constraints, and the serendipitous outcomes.

Kingdon (1984) believes that subgovernment politics affect original objectives at the implementation stage due to tradeoffs and compromises that have to be struck by network participants interested in the policy. Kingdon's work depends conceptually on the garbage-can model of administrative decisions, which is of theoretical importance to multifaceted reform that can be characterized as having inconsistent and ill-defined preferences, unclear technology, and fluid participation in organized anarchies (Cohen, March, and Olsen, 1972).

Matland (1995) provided a valuable synthesis stressing the critical resources necessary for success under varying conditions of policy ambiguity and conflict. He suggests that different types of implementation (administrative, political, experimental, and symbolic) are appropriate, depending upon the mix of policy characteristics. Implementation success of each type is hypothesized to be disproportionately influenced by whether or not required resources are available. Matland's is a contingency perspective on how successful implementation works (see Exhibit 6.1).

[A] limitation of the Matland model is that it does not directly address institutional conditions. Policy makers and organizations operate in an institutional environment, which imposes important constraints on decision processes. Institutions shape standards for what must be done, how it should be done, and what is generally acceptable. . . .

In the Florida case, the civil service received the greatest attention in the early years of the reform movement. . . . The hopes for change were rather conventionally defined as reducing waste, increasing productivity, employee empowerment through training and participation, and performance evaluation linked to rewards. Managers would be given more discretion in employee selection and retention; the number of classifications and pay systems would be reduced.

Such proposals generally followed prescriptions for good practice found in professional journals and widely accepted among experts. One reason the reforms attracted such wide attention nationally was

EXHIBIT 6.1

Policy Conflict, Ambiguity, Implementation Type, and Required Resources

Policy Ambiguity Low	Policy Conflict Low Implementation Type	Policy Conflict High Implementation Type
	Administrative, top-down Required resources: Administrative	Political, top-down Required resources: Power
High	Implementation Type	Implementation Type
	Experimental, bottom-up Required resources: Local actor resources	Symbolic, bottom up Required resources: Local coalitions

that they reflected widely held institutional views of how government should be "reinvented." . . .

Civil Service

The extent of civil service implementation success is subject to varying interpretations. . . . The Chiles administration strongly supported the reforms and was credited with a legislative victory when they successfully lobbied a legislative measure that provided a sunset of the civil service law. . . . Despite this reform receiving the appropriate type and level of support from the governor early in the process, the support diminished later when the Department of Administration secretary, Mr. Pieno, was removed from his position in the midst of the reorganization. . . .

Early in the reform process there was talk of linking budgets to agency performance. One reward for high performance would be flexibility in the use of budget resources. Such authority was provided initially only to a demonstration project in the Department of Revenue. It did not help budget flexibility implementation when the legislature revoked the flexibility given to the Department of Revenue, even though the demonstration appeared to be successful. Without budget flexibility, and with declining general revenues, the civil service reforms required tradeoff in personnel decisions from lower-level budget decision makers, which they were not willing to make. As the reform matured, the availability of critical top-level political support diminished, and the reform legislation was left as a hollow shell.

Restructuring

Reorganization, some have suggested, is frequent because it is a reform that is well understood and likely to be adopted. . . . In Florida, reorganization implementation guidelines did not have to be invented. Additionally, staffs in the Executive Office of the Governor and in the legislature were experienced in the use of reorganization rules and procedures.

Given the political agreement that was created by term limits and the low incremental implementation costs, it is not surprising that structural reorganizations were widespread and quickly implemented. A longer-term view of costs and tradeoffs, however, gives a somewhat different picture. As was the case with civil service reform, as implementation moved toward a micro level, the marginal costs and tradeoffs increased. Morale was hit hard in consolidated agencies (i.e., Management Services, Business and Professional Regulation). In Environmental Protection, professionals accused the leadership of focusing so narrowly on expediting the permitting process that it jeopardized the enforcement of environmental statutes. . . . A similar outcome is seen in the merger of the cabinet agency, General Services, with the governor's Department of Administration, which created the Department of Management Services.

The merger of two regulatory agencies into a single Department of Business and Professional Regulation represents a different set of costs, . . . and there is no evidence of savings associated with the change. Furthermore, the merger did not diminish the ability of clientele groups to resist the merger of critical functions and related licensing boards that perform the regulatory functions.

The tradeoff effects of the reorganizations also are very clear in relation to total quality management. There is not a single agency that has been reorganized that has any semblance of a TQM program; . . . respondents to a survey reported that it was impossible to devote sufficient attention to TQM when the uncertainties of position and authority associated with reorganization prevailed.

TQM

Early in 1990, the first year of the Chiles administration, John Pieno, director of the Department of Administration, announced that the department would bring TQM to state government. It was hoped that TQM would be forced into place by the 1990 legislation that eliminated the existing civil service law one year after the sunset statute's adoption. . . . [But] John Pieno, the major supporter of TQM in the Chiles administration, was replaced by someone who was not committed to it. TQM developed in the private sector, and unlike budgeting practice, there are no standardized ways of understanding and practicing TQM in the public sector. Developing training packages requires more than deciding on the pedagogy; it requires translating private-sector logic to public-sector conditions, a difficult, complex, and costly process. . . . Few agencies received basic TQM training. After these agencies were given the discretion to pursue TQM or forget it, most never went beyond basic training and fragmented implementation. . . . TQM could not be implemented unless developing synergy with other reform efforts reduced the implementation costs. The deregulation

initiative, unfortunately, began with the second Chiles term, and by that time TQM was virtually dead.

Strategic Planning

Like TQM, although the technology for strategic planning is well known, . . . it was not widely known in Florida State government, and little money was available for training or for hiring new personnel with this expertise. . . . Under these conditions, the strategy of the Governor's Office of Planning and Budgeting was sensible; . . . their budgeting personnel would learn how to link strategic planning to budgeting. OPB required the agencies to submit budget information consistent with this format if they were to be rewarded by greater discretion over budget expenditures.

An evaluation of strategic planning and management in the Department of Corrections . . . found a high proportion of senior managers (94 percent) to be committed to the strategic planning process, with positive assessments of many outcomes, including less-centralized control of department decision making and a view that planning and budgeting were finally becoming linked.

The costs of the strategic planning reform were minimized by linking it to the budgeting reforms and by implementing it incrementally. Local budget personnel are increasingly involved in the process, contributing their competence, learning from their involvement, and providing support. The process survived the transition to the new Governor Jeb Bush administration.

Source: Richard Chackerian and Paul Mavima, *Journal of Public Administration Research and Theory, 11*(3) (July 2001): 353–365. Reading plus Exhibit 6.1 reprinted with permission of Oxford University Press.

Net Assignment

Using InfoTrac College Edition, Internet search engines, or some of the websites listed at the end of this chapter, enter the key search words *performance budgeting*. Find other state or local bureaucracies that use this technology. Describe who they are and how and why they use it.

Summary

Goals, information, and values feed the complex process of decision making. Five models—rational-comprehensive, bargaining, participative, public choice, and new management—offer conceptual frameworks. Each decision-making model rests on basic assumptions and emphasizes specific values. (Table 6.1 visually breaks down the five models.) Ethical dimensions affect decision making in public administration—institutional ethics, personal ethics, and the pervasive problem of corruption. The factors that tend to limit decision making are time, uncertainty, the distortion of information, and the effects of crises.

Glossary of Key Terms

bargaining   An approach to decision making and a model articulated by Charles Lindblom; involves incrementalism to analyze policy decisions.

bureaucratic politics model   A model suggested by Graham Allison; views policy decisions as the result of a game and the push–pull of bureaucratic actors.

contracting out   Refers to having work performed outside an agency's own permanent staff of employees; a major means of privatization and an attempt to reduce the size of the public sector.

decision making   The process of choosing one course of action from among the choices available.

ExComm   The National Security Council Executive Committee, which managed the Cuban Missile Crisis of 1962 during the Kennedy Administration.

externality   The costs generated by one person or organization that are passed on to another or to society at large.

incremental approach   Decision-making model in which a series of limited, successive comparisons among a narrow range of options through continual incremental adjustments determine the outcome of the decision.

mixed scanning   A model of decision making suggested by Amitai Etzioni; sees decisions as the result of fundamental and nonfundamental choices that embody aspects of the rational model and the bargaining model of decision making.

negative externality   An effect on decision making that imposes social costs on the community, such as air and water pollution by private-sector industry.

participative model   A decision-making model that assumes participation by all who will be affected by it, thereby ensuring their participation in the process; the rationality of the decision depends on their inclusion.

pervasive ambiguity   A decision situation with so much uncertainty that the assumptions of the rational model do not apply; an assumption of the garbage-can model of decision making.

privatization   The sale of government services and operations to the private sector.

public choice decision-making model   A view of decisions that assumes that (1) the self-interest of government officials causes inefficient programs and (2) the simple solution is to turn over as many public programs as possible to the private sector.

rational-comprehensive decision-making model   Model emerging from the classical tradition; assumes an economic model of decision making involving five steps to rationality: (1) identify the problem, (2) clarify goals, (3) identify alternatives, (4) calculate cost–benefit ratio for each alternative, and (5) choose the alternative with the best cost–benefit ratio.

satisfice   Herbert Simon's distinctive term for an organizational decision that does not maximize, but only *satisfies*, or *suffices*, or (combined) *satisfices*.

sunk costs   Certain irrecoverable costs associated with prior commitments of resources to pursue a policy; they raise the stakes in decision making.

Review Questions

1. Compare and contrast the basic assumptions and major ideas about decisions associated with the rational-comprehensive and bargaining models of decision making. Who were the major proponents of each model? What values are empha-sized by each approach?

2. What are some similarities and differences between the participative and the public choice models? The participative model might be exemplified by California's use of the initiative to enact criminal-sentencing policy. The public choice model reflects the trend to privatize prisons and even schools. What values shape the ideological assumptions of each model? What political considerations contributed to their popularity?

3. Charles Lindblom maintains that decision making not only is at the very heart of administration, but also is an inherently value-laden process. Do you agree? Why or why not?

4. Discuss how the limits of decision making (time, uncertainty, distortion, and crisis) exacerbate ethical problems.

5. Comprehensive administrative reform, as discussed in Reading 6.1, forces govern-ment decision making to go "outside the box." Why does such change obviate some existing routines for decision making? Can you think of another agent or type of change that can similarly affect state and local decision making?

Surfing the Net

The following are useful websites to visit for topics discussed in this chapter.

General Accounting Office (**http://www.gao.gov**)

Congressional Budget Office (**http://www.cbo.gov**)

National Security Council (**http://www.whitehouse.gov/WH/EOP/NSC/index.html**)

Pick your decision-making policy topic at Policy.com (**http://www.policy.com/community/pytopic**).

Several think tanks are good sources on policy and decision-making issues. See, for instance, the following websites:

Rand Corporation (**http://www.rand.org**)

Hoover Institution (**http://hoover.org**)

Cato Institute (**http://www.cato.org**)

Brookings Institution (**http://www.brookings.org**)

Also visit the Roper Center for Public Opinion Research (**http://www.ropercenter.uconn.edu**) for public opinion statistics on a host of government issues and decisions.

Chapter 7

Management of Bureaucratic Organizations: The Strategic Use of Values in Policy Making and Administration

The most important change in budgeting utilizing Missions and Measures, Alaska's performance-based budgeting method, was moving from the concept of "How much are agencies spending?" to "What are Alaskans getting for their investment?" It seemed like a simple change, but it has caused a revolution in the budgeting process and the discussion between the legislature and state agencies."

An interesting dynamic occurs when the questions changed from "How well did you do your job?" to "What did Alaskans get for the money they invested?" Legislators began to focus on the worth of an activity and how it contributed to the overall mission.

Changing the debate from "how we spend" to "what policy outcome is desired" allows legislators to set policy and holds the administration accountable for results. This change in debate allows both the majority and the minority to focus on policy discussions. . . .

The articulation of policy in the context of Missions and Measures results in accountability. Legislators begin to have the tools to measure if the outcome is being achieved; if it is not, they ask, "Why not?" . . .

A clear, simple mission with a few objective measures accomplishes more than a hyperbole-laden mission and dozens of measures. . . .

The ultimate success is not in the first or second year. It is in the fourth or fifth year.

Training focused on Mission and Measures is imperative. Alaska has spent time training its legislative members and its staff. The staff of the House Finance Committee has a two-day work session. . . . We discuss how we did last year and how we can improve the product in the next budget cycle.

Eldon Mulder, Co-Chair, Alaska Finance Committee
Performance-based budgeting in Alaska,
Spectrum (Spring 2002): 14.

Introduction

The chapter-opening vignette illustrates a problem and value central to the role of management—accountability. Central concerns of management are to discern problems in the agency's environment; articulate and plan methods and programs to deal with those problems; develop mission statements, goals, and objectives of the agency to address those problems; organize the resources needed to achieve those goals and objectives as effectively and efficiently as possible; and evaluate the agency's efforts to do so. This chapter deals with the management of public agencies. It discusses how managers empower employees to work toward specific goals and looks at some of the values and value conflicts inherent in the management process.

Various approaches to management also are compared, and examples of the methods and values emphasized by each are presented. Strategic management and planning are discussed, as are the capabilities and constraints of managing. Several strategic factors involved in managing and several important challenges to strategic management also are identified.

Management and Managerialism

Management refers to the process of running an organization and the use of resources to accomplish its goals. The term also refers to those individuals formally authorized to run the organization. **Managerialism** refers to an entrepreneurial approach to public management, one that emphasizes the rights of managers to run the organization and the application of reinvigorated scientific management techniques.[1]

How to better manage large organizations has long been an important focus of public administration. The national government has gone through periodic efforts to reform management. Table 7.1 summarizes the most important efforts. Many state and local governments have had similar efforts to reform their respective management structures and methods.

Recall that the traditional approach to management, perhaps best exemplified by neoclassical theorist Luther Gulick, embodied the principles approach to management, as summarized in his acronym POSDCORB (planning, organizing, staffing, directing, coordinating, reporting, and budgeting). This approach emerged from the

TABLE 7.1

Major Attempts to Reform the Federal Government

Name and Date of Reform	Presidential Administration	Head	Reform
Brownlow Committee (1936)	Franklin D. Roosevelt	Louis Brownlow	Increased president's control over the bureaucracy.
First Hoover Commission (1947–49)	Harry S. Truman	Herbert Hoover	Created EOP and strengthened agency management.
Second Hoover Commission (1953–55)	Dwight D. Eisenhower	Herbert Hoover	Minor revisions made to executive branch.
Program planning budgeting system (PPBS) (1965–68)	Lyndon B. Johnson	Robert McNamara (Secretary of Defense)	Instituted PPBS in Department of Defense; attempted in other departments.
Ash Council (1971)	Richard M. Nixon	Roy Ash	Ended PPBS. Created Office of Management and Budget (OMB). Used management by objectives (MBO). Launched New Federalism.
Zero-based budgeting (ZBB) (1977–78)	Jimmy Carter	Peter Pyhrr	Failed attempt to use ZBB in federal budget process. Created Office of Personnel Management (OPM). Merit System Protection Board and Federal Labor Relations Authority replace the Civil Service Commission.
Grace Commission (1982)	Ronald Reagan	J. Peter Grace	Private-Sector Survey on Cost Control led to a few minor adjustments. Devolved government, deregulated the private sector, and established Renewed Federalism.
National Performance Review (1993)	William J. Clinton	Vice President Albert Gore Jr.	Government Performance Results Act launches Reinventing Government efforts.

report of the Brownlow Committee, on which Gulick and colleague Lyndall Urwick served. Gulick's views were highly influential and came to represent an orthodox view of management. As we learned earlier, as government swelled in size, complexity, and variety of functions and structures at all levels, the bureaucracy became increasingly difficult to manage. The view of managers as neutral, competent officials who could and should run the government using the principles approach to management fell into disrepute.

The orthodox approach to management deals with change in a purposely gradual, evolutionary, and incremental manner. It values formal changes in the administrative structures or prescribed procedures of government. Periodic reorganization plans typically involved agency or department consolidation, the expansion of the executive office and its support (and control) staff, or modifications in personnel administration. Traditional management values incremental change that is primarily designed (1) to promote bureaucratic responsiveness to centralized control by executive staff agencies and (2) to professionalize administrative practices and personnel.

Rapid change in the environment of public administration, however, and the growing complexity of society and the private economy led some government reformers to advocate a more radical approach. These reformers advocated taking organization beyond the traditional focus by completely rethinking how to manage programs and policy by using new technology, particularly the computer. They emphasized that mere "tinkering with reorganization" produces confusion, inefficiency, and demoralization of personnel. They called for replacing traditional incremental reorganization with a **reengineering** approach[2] that uses three basic steps: process mapping, customer assessment, and process "visioning."

Process mapping replaces the traditional organizational chart with a flowchart that depicts how government delivers its services; the flowchart focuses on process rather than the organization's formal and highly fixed structure. Values of flexibility and innovativeness are emphasized over uniformity and predictability.

With *customer assessments*, a government agency evaluates its clientele using focus groups, surveys, and informal meetings to assess current and future needs. The **focus group** is a relatively small number of individuals (say, a dozen or less) who share a common characteristic and who are brought together in a neutral setting to discuss an agency's service under the leadership of a trained observer. Such assessments are a major tool for discovering the motivations of clients using the government service. The value of responsiveness is emphasized over efficiency.

Process visioning involves a thorough rethinking of how the government's processes and procedures ought to be done by using the latest technology available. "Newness" is valued over tried-and-true standard operating procedures.

The reengineering approach emphasizes new techniques of management to solve productivity problems by blending the orthodox to create new forms of employee involvement and participation in management (a Theory Z approach, for example). New perspectives promote organizational flexibility and participatory decision making. Tall and fixed hierarchy is replaced by flat hierarchy and the empowerment of work groups or self-directed teams.[3] A significant value shift is involved. In place of formal hierarchy with multiple levels of supervisors to coordinate, control, and monitor the agency to achieve maximum efficiency, the team approach assumes that group members seek personal and professional growth, self-expression, and greater job satisfaction.

Self-directed teams differ from the traditional work group in five distinct ways.

1. There are fewer job categories (one or two in place of a dozen).

2. Authority is diffused, with first-level supervisory staff changing their role to that of facilitators.

3. The reward system of the agency is modified to provide incentives that promote flexibility.

4. Employees are compensated for mastering a range of skills.

5. Top-level executives concentrate on strategic planning and mid-level managers act as coaches, encouraging innovation and client satisfaction.

Approaches to Management

Several management techniques have become popular since the 1960s, some of them perhaps only being fads.

Management by Objectives

Management by objectives (MBO) is an approach to program or policy management that defines short- and long-term objectives and keeps a record of actual program results to determine effectiveness. The government supervisor and the subordinate mutually agree on objectives, setting measurable goals to be met by the individual, team, or unit over a set period of time. This approach was popularized by Peter Drucker in 1954 with the publication of *The Practice of Management*.[4] It has been widely adopted by both public- and private-sector organizations worldwide. It distinguishes between functions and objectives. Given the rapidity of change in the environment of organizations, it emphasizes that organizational objectives also change rapidly. Government managers must be flexible and innovative instead of rigid and predictable. An **objective** is a short-term goal; something that must be achieved on the way to a larger, overall mission. Objectives are stated or expressed in a way that can be empirically measured over time.

Organizational Development

Organizational development (OD) is a process for increasing an organization's effectiveness by integrating an individual's desire for personal growth with the organization's goals. A leading proponent of the theory is Chris Argyris.[5] Managers use intervention strategies to bring about deep, long-term, and organization-wide change by using outsiders (referred to as *change agents*). Organizational development employs organizational diagnosis, consultation, team building, action research, data feedback, job enrichment and enlargement, and conflict-management techniques.

INFOTRAC
COLLEGE EDITION

Process performance management system: a tool to support process-based organization

Operations Research

Operations research (OR)[6] is a technique that emphasizes efficiency by maximizing some payoff in the goals the agency is trying to accomplish. Managers use OR after value choices are made. The method relies on such means as probability theory, queuing techniques, and mathematical model building. These are used to allocate and maximize resource use in a particular agency subsystem. Operations research began in England during World War II to help develop radar and then to study and analyze bombing runs and submarine warfare. Allied command groups used OR extensively; through that experience, the approach's value was recognized and thus it came to be applied in the United States to problems such as bus scheduling, mail delivery, waste management, land use and urban planning, highway safety, education reform, agriculture-improvement experiments, and even birth control programs. Its use burgeoned even more when computer technology increased data-processing capabilities. Operations research was popularized by C. P. Snow. Its proponents view it as a value-free approach that can be applied to any purpose. Its use in the military during the Vietnam War produced estimates of "kill ratios," "body counts," and "overkill." It is often used with overlapping management techniques, such as PERT, or the critical path method (see next section).

Program Evaluation and Review Technique

The **program evaluation and review technique (PERT)** is an analytical management tool that maps out a series of steps to carry out a program. It is sometimes referred to as the **critical path method (CPM)**.[7] It seeks the path with the smallest margins of extra resources with which to complete all assigned program activities. PERT, or CPM, was developed in the 1950s by a team working on the Polaris missile project. To ensure that the highly complex task of constructing the new missile and nuclear submarines from which they are launched would finish on schedule, PERT was designed to monitor their construction processes. PERT enabled the project to be completed nearly two years ahead of schedule. Since then, it has been used by various government research and development agencies for systems analysis and scheduling purposes. It has been used by all of the U.S. military services, NASA, the Federal Aviation Administration (FAA), by the Nuclear Regulatory Commission, and the OMB. Many large states now use PERT, and some large paramilitary agencies of local government, such as the New York City Police Department, use CPM.

A critical path analysis concerned with coordination of decisions is called a *decision tree*. PERT and CPM are useful tools for clarifying interagency dependencies in a program, system, or process and can aid the allocation of resources accordingly. Ultimately, their utility depends on the accuracy of estimates made by the manager about how much time it might take to complete a task or phase and how much it might cost to complete an activity. If managers know what they are doing, their estimates can be highly accurate. If they do not, then the process is no more valuable than the traditional "guesstimates."

Quality Circles

A **quality circle (QC)**[8] is a small group of employees who work in the same unit and meet regularly to identify, discuss, and solve problems that directly affect their work. Quality circles are associated with the Theory Z management style. This technique, popularized by W. Edward Deming and others, is part of a broader technique known as *total quality management*. The technique highly values participation, innovation, and flexibility.

Total Quality Management

Total quality management (TQM)[9] involves a new phase in management techniques for quality control. In its most expanded sense, it involves a total and continuing concern for quality in the production of goods and services. TQM seeks organizational performance at an optimal level. First popularized by Deming, its reemergence in the 1990s in the United States followed its highly successful usage by private-sector organizations in Japan. Governments at all levels have applied it, borrowing the technique from the private sector.

INFOTRAC
COLLEGE EDITION

Getting going together

Entrepreneurialism

These techniques of management reflect variations on a theme: the approach to management that has been called *entrepreneurialism*.[10] Emerging from the private sector, this approach advocates that managers become change agents who transform their organization's culture by infusing it with a new vision. To be effective, the new vision must permeate an entire government organization, not just its upper-level management. The technique assumes (1) that competitiveness can be infused into the public sector, (2) that practices from private-sector organizations can be transferred to the public sector, and (3) that government organizations can be managed in a more business-like way. One of entrepreneurialism's major proponents, Christopher Pollitt, refers to it as "a label under which private-sector disciplines can be introduced into the public services, political control can be strengthened, budgets trimmed, professional autonomy reduced, public service

unions weakened, and a quasi-competitive framework erected to flush out the 'natural' inefficiencies of bureaucracy."[11]

Reform movements like the voucher system in public education reflect this philosophical view of government and public administration. It is assumed that making agencies competitive with other agencies or with the private sector will force them to compete and thereby improve their efficiency. This view of government management has become increasingly mainstream in U.S. politics. Some of the value conflicts inherent in this movement are addressed in Box 7.1.

Among the most effective proponents of this new entrepreneurial approach to public management are David Osborne and Ted Gaebler, whose 1992 book *Reinventing Government* became a best seller.[12] In the tradition of the neoclassicists, they proposed "10 principles" for reinventing government that reflect "client-driven," "mission-driven," and "results-oriented" values. They advocate that government managers meet the needs of the client, not the bureaucracy. Managers should steer rather than row. Enterprising government should focus on earning rather than spending. "New" managers promote a decentralized government instead of a tall hierarchy. Participation and teamwork are valued, as is a market-oriented approach to government wherein forces of the competitive market are used to bring about organizational change. Partnerships with business replaces government regulation of business.

Indeed, the field of American public administration and its literature are filled with debates, arguments, and discussions of the pros and cons of the reinventing government paradigm; even to the extent of whether it is a paradigm or not. One scholar (Frederickson, 1996) compared the reinventing government movement to the new public administration along six dimensions. He notes:

> A strongly felt need to change bureaucracy informed each movement, although each would change bureaucracy differently. Both movements seek relevance and responsiveness, but in different ways. Issues of rationality, methodology, and epistemology are more important in the new public administration than in the reinventing government movement. Both movements conceptualize organization similarly. The reinventing government movement has a stronger commitment to market approaches for the provision of public services and to mechanisms for individual choice. Reinventing government is popular electoral politics for executives (presidents, governors, mayors) and is more radical than new public administration. The new public administration prompted subtle, incremental shifts toward democratic management practices and social equity. The results of reinventing government, so far, are short-run increases in efficiency purchased at a likely long-run cost in administrative capacity and social equity. (p. 263)

He observes that while change is a phenomenon central to reinventing government, the details of the idea of change are not central. Change is articulated in dichotomous couplets, such as: "steering rather than rowing," "empowering rather than serving," "replacing bureaucratic processes with market processes," "meeting the needs of customers, not the bureaucracy," "earning rather than spending," "preventing rather than curing," and "moving from hierarchy to participating and teamwork." Frederickson notes that the conceptual and theoretical nuances of the new public administration literature are significantly different from the "success stories" of the reinventing government movement, perhaps explained by the fact that the new public administration was largely developed by scholars, theorists, and researchers, whereas reinventing

Box 7.1

The New Managerialism

Half a century ago, a now-forgotten American book, James Burnham's *The Managerial Revolution*, was much discussed. Its argument was that power in industrial enterprises had shifted from the shareholders to the managers.

I have seen much less comment on another managerial revolution that we have been witnessing over the past 20 years. Readers of this journal, whether they are members of planning committees or teachers, architects or planners, engineers or foresters, hydrologists or geographers, will confirm that in the fields in which they work the most influential and best-paid jobs go to people who are described as Masters of Business Administration, who, when appointed, impose a regime of squeezing out the more expensive employees—for example, very experienced teachers at the upper end of the salary scale—and the more expensive bits of the curriculum—for example, the wasteful use of space in drawing studios in architecture schools (so much more extravagant than cramming everyone into lecture rooms).

Plenty of readers in further and higher education will have stories to tell about the increasing use of part-timers or graduate students to take classes, as they are a useful way of evading the conditions of employment for full-time staff. Sooner or later, the students will realize that at the very time when they are obliged to incur a mountain of future debt to pay for their education, they are being offered a penny-pinching product.

These impressions were confirmed for me by Christmas greetings and readings. One friend was leaving a celebrated planning school, after observing "the turmoil and distress caused to a dedicated staff by managerial actions like the forced mergers of departments and the compression of two-year courses into one year," while another, who had brought glory and awards to his institution, talked about his gradual withdrawal.

And the book I read over Christmas was the autobiography of the celebrated sociologist A. H. Halsey, *No Discouragement* (Macmillan, 1996): He remarked that the consequences of the amount of form-filling for teaching and research evaluation are "tragic," and he added that "A great deal is at stake here. One often hears with sadness that a new management is needed to promote efficiency and cut out waste. . . . I don't believe it.

Management speak is management speak. Parkinson's law works for pasts independently of the character of their incumbents."

Another friend, with immense knowledge and experience, was driven ill by the grotesque paperwork demanded of him in his busy life as a conservation officer for a local authority. He left because he couldn't stand the hypocrisy and fantasy of mission statements and output targets demanded of him, finding this make-believe humiliating. Anyone with a friend or spouse who is a teacher will have learned about the incredible amount of pointless form-filling that is now imposed on people in that profession.

I see this as tragic in its implications, because all my experience leads me to support the conclusion, frequently reported by industrial psychologists, that satisfaction in work is directly related to the "span of autonomy" it offers, meaning the amount of the working day or week in which the workers are free to make their own decisions. At the beginning of my working life, my span of autonomy was minimal. But it had become virtually total by the time I ceased to be employed.

This natural progression is contradicted by the introduction of expensive external consultants peddling this year's managerial wisdom, which, as experience will tell us, will be seen as obsolete next year. Think of the history of the National Health Service, which hired one expensive management consultancy after another, to dispense its sloganized wisdom, now regarded as disastrous in terms of the hard-working people who actually keep the Health Service operating.

For many years industrial psychologists have been showing us that what "keeps the show on the road" through shortages and overloads is not the diagrammatic chain of command and decision making: It is the unofficial networks that have built up through friendly cooperation and accommodation. And it is these informal relationships, closely studied over 30 years ago by the American sociologist Seymour Melman in his book *Decision-Making and Productivity* (Oxford, 1968) that are most at risk from the new managerialism.

Source: Colin Ward, The new managerialism, *Town and Country Planning*, 73(2) (February 2004): 44. Reprinted with permission of Town and Country Planning Association.

government is largely the work of commentator-journalist-government specialist David Osborne and former city manager, now lecturer-trainer, Ted Gaebler.

Proponents of the reinventing government movement (i.e., Barzelay, 1992; Boyne, 1998; Calista, 2002; Delulio, Garvey, and Kettl, 1993; Ingraham and Romzek, 1994; Knott, 1998; Nicholson-Crotty, 2004; Peters, 1996; Winograd, 1998) collectively argue it does constitute a fundamental shift. Advocates of reinventing government assert it offers an administratively sound model for reforming the civil service (Knott, 1998: 665); that competitive pressures of the market can increase efficiency, reduce costs, and improve service quality (Boyne, 1998; Ferris and Graddy, 1991; Kettl, 1993). They argue that NPR is promoting interagency cooperation in such areas as drug control, food safety, and providing recreation in public lands; that NPR designated 32 federal agencies as high-impact agencies—that is, those that account for about 90 percent of American's interaction with the federal government. It outlined 260 specific recommendations that, if carried out, its proponents argue, would transform how Americans view their government (Winograd, 1998). It would constitute a full-fledged reform tide, a shift as fundamental as the development of the administrative management approach of the early 20th century (Barzelay, 1992; Ingraham and Romzek, 1994; Peters, 1996).

Critics of the reinventing government movement (see, for example, Brudney and Wright, 2002; Carroll, 1995; Gilmour and Jensen, 1998; Goodsell, 1993; Moe, 1993, 2000; D. Morgan et al., 1996; Nathan, 1995; Nowland-Foreman, 1998; Rosenbloom, 1994; L. Williams and Leak, 1996) assess it far differently. In their view, the movement is a response to political factors, such as conservative opposition to "big government," as much as to economic factors, such as the need to cut costs or increase efficiency. The decision to "contract out," for example, particularly at the state level, is often a two-stage process, whereby elected officials create a favorable statutory environment before administrators of public agencies consider proposals from private vendors (Nicholson-Crotty, 2004; U.S. General Accounting Office, 1997).

Moe (2000) notes that in the new government management model, "four key principles" of reinvention should guide behavior: (1) cast aside red tape, (2) satisfy customers, (3) decentralize authority, and (4) work better, cost less. He argues that rather than a set of principles cast in a theoretical context, subject to proof and disproof, these are rather a listing of aphorisms, calls to right behavior.

Other critics note that privatization is more than an answer to inefficient government administration. Rather, it involves the transfer of government authority to "private third parties" implicated in a wholesale loss of government accountability (Gilmour and Jensen, 1998). Others observe that the reduction of middle-level managers, often recommended for local government by the reinventing government movement, raises questions:

> Can we afford to eliminate middle managers in local government? . . . Middle managers play distinctive roles as "keepers of two functions" essential to the health of our democratic polity: helping to define "acceptable service," and making the delivery of public services accountable. . . . Efforts to eliminate layers of middle management through contracting out for services, privatizing, reinventing government, and other mechanisms to reshape the role of democratic governance need to be carefully informed and guided by a full understanding of the essential functions that middle managers play in maintaining a healthy functioning of our democratic order. . . . That is, [the] stewardship role will become increasingly more important as national and state governments continue to decentralize the locus of responsibility for regulation and service delivery. (D. Morgan et al., 1996: 359)

The use of private, nonprofit agencies for contracting, also prevalent in the recommendations of the reinventing government movement, can raise issues as well. The use of voluntary organizations, both in privatizing previous government-provided services and in reigning in more autonomous voluntary-sector services previously supported by grants-in-aid, raises questions about their impact on civil society. Whereas voluntary organizations are frequently idealized as producing civic "golden eggs" of community resource mobilization and more appropriate and accessible services as well as providing avenues for citizen participation and involvement (all laudable goals and values), the risk is that the tightening control of government funding contracts may end up "killing the goose that is laying these golden eggs" (Nowland-Foreman, 1998: 108).

One critical study of privatization is offered here as an example of the view of critics of reinventing government movement's overrated claims to efficiency.

> The case of Baltimore's Tesseract schools clearly illustrates the pitfalls of school privatization. The city was the first to carry out large-scale contracting out of instructional services to a private company. It selected Education Alternatives Inc. (EAI) to provide instructional management to nine public schools. However, the results of the Comprehensive Test of Basic Skills of the students of the nine Tesseract schools indicated that EAI did not make any difference to school achievement. It was also found that the cost of education in the Tesseract schools was 7 percent higher than in the comparison elementary schools. The Tesseract program was cancelled after four years. (L. Williams and Leak, 1996: 56)

Performance Management

When managers lead organizations rather than control them, performance management becomes their primary responsibility. **Performance management** is defined as the systematic integration of an organization's efforts to achieve its objectives.[13] It entails the comprehensive control, audit, and evaluation of all aspects of an organization's performance.

To do so, managers must do the following:

Assigned to patrol

1. Specify clear and measurable objectives.

2. Develop and systematically use performance indicators to assess outputs.

3. Apply performance appraisal to individual employees, harmonizing their efforts toward organizational goals and objectives.

4. Use merit or performance pay as incentives to reward exceptional personal efforts toward organizational goals.

5. Link human and financial resource allocation toward an annual budget cycle.

6. Review on a regular basis and in staged planning cycles the extent to which goals have been achieved, and assess why performance has been better or worse than planned. These reviews serve as system feedback to start a new cycle.

The rank-and-file employees of an organization often fear and resist such a performance-management approach. They typically fear that managers will use performance-based budgeting to play favorites with programs or individual employees.

Performance management is politically popular, but its use depends on implementing new management information and control systems. Clients of a public organization's services are viewed as **stakeholders**, or as people affected directly or indirectly by the organization's activities. Performance management is associated with another recent trend in public administration: contracting out for service.

Contracting Out

Contracting out refers to sending work to be done outside of the agency's own permanent staff of employees. Linked to the privatization movement, it seeks to reduce the size of the public sector. It assumes the validity of the premise that private-sector organizations are more efficient than public-sector agencies.[14] Using formal or informal contracts, an agency head employs outside people to perform certain functions or provide services that the public agency has previously done. Contracts specify the delivery of such services to agreed-upon levels of performance.

Contracting affects a bureaucratic organization internally when it engages in **productivity bargaining**, the process whereby public managers attempt to use private-sector approaches to contract negotiation and link employee wage increases to various cost-cutting efforts, including increasing on-the-job productivity.

Exploring Total Quality Management

The new approach to management is perhaps best exemplified by TQM techniques. Certainly the high value that performance management places on increases in productivity is notable in the TQM movement. TQM has many proponents, but Deming can justifiably be called its founder. He was a professor of management who distilled his approach of emphasizing customer service and quality control while working at the Hawthorne plant in the 1920s and 1930s. He was first "discovered" in Japan when he visited there in 1950. Japanese executives revered him and adopted his philosophy to overcome the image of a "Made in Japan" label as a reference to cheap and shoddy goods. Deming was followed by Joseph Juran, who went to Japan in 1954. Juran's work focused on management aspects of the quality control movement.[15] Japanese industry adopted the TQM approach wholeheartedly, and by the 1970s Japan was recognized as a world leader in both quality and productivity.[16] Japanese industry became so competitive, especially in electronics and automobiles, that U.S. industries finally took notice, and TQM became an administrative fad in the United States.

TQM turns the orthodox approach to management on its head. Where the more traditional approach emphasizes the role of upper-level management and a top-down flow of ideas and control over the organization and its productivity, TQM emphasizes a bottom-up flow, with quality circles of workers sharing in the management process to identify problems and advance solutions. Although developed in the private sector, TQM has been applied to government. One federal program, the National Institute of Standards and Technology Quality Program, promotes the TQM approach in government at all levels. Figure 7.1 graphically contrasts TQM and the traditional management approach.

Between 1975 and 1995, nearly two dozen volumes and more than 500 articles were published on TQM.[17] It has been widely used at all levels of government.[18] The Department of Defense used it extensively in the 1980s. The National Institute of Standards and Technology Quality Program, exemplary of the national government's overall commitment to the approach, developed its own seven-point guide to TQM. Figure 7.2 compares three different TQM prescriptive formulations.

TQM has been characterized as both a philosophy and a set of guiding principles for any organization, public or private, that seeks to adapt and continuously improve. More than 500 local government programs have employed it since the 1980s.[19] There are estimates that more than 25 percent of all cities with populations

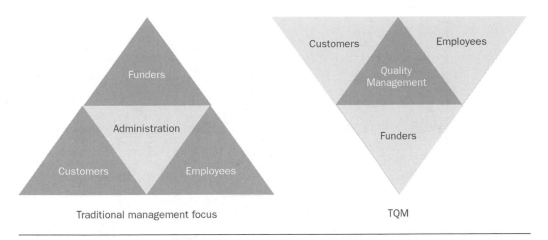

Traditional management focus   TQM

FIGURE 7.1

TQM Compared with the Traditional Management Focus

Source: Marc Holzer, Productivity and quality management, in Jack Rabin, Thomas Vocino, W. Bartley Hildreth, and Gerald J. Miller (Eds.), *Handbook of public personnel administration and labor relations*, Chapter 25. Copyright 1995 by CRC Press LLC. Reprinted with permission of CRC Press LLC.

National Institute of Standards and Technology Quality Program

1. Top management leadership and support
2. Customer focus
3. Long-term strategic quality planning
4. Employee training and recognition
5. Employee empowerment and teamwork
6. Measurement and analysis of products and processes
7. Quality assurance

Swiss (1992) has an alternate seven-point formulation:

1. The customer is the arbiter of quality.
2. Quality should be built into the product or service rather than weeding out failures through inspection.
3. Quality calls for consistency.
4. Group or team performance is emphasized rather than individual performance.
5. TQM is a continuous process.
6. Success is dependent on the participation of the workers.
7. TQM requires the total commitment of the organization.

The GAO surveyed high-scoring Baldrige Award applicants* and concluded that six features were important:

1. Corporate attention is focused on meeting customer quality requirements.
2. Management leads the way in disseminating TQM values throughout the organization.
3. Employees are asked and empowered to continuously improve all key business processes.
4. Management nurtures a flexible and responsive corporate culture.
5. Management systems support fact-based decision making.
6. Partnerships with suppliers improve product or service delivery.

*The Baldrige Award is a national competition administered by the Department of Commerce primarily for the private sector.

FIGURE 7.2

A Comparison of Three TQM Prescriptions

Source: Adapted from Marc Holzer, Productivity and quality management, in Jack Rabin, Thomas Vocino, W. Bartley Hildreth, and Gerald J. Miller (Eds.), *Handbook of public personnel administration and labor relations*, Chapter 25. Copyright 1995 by CRC Press LLC. Reprinted with permission of CRC Press LLC.

CARTOON 7.1
Dilbert on strategic planning
What problems in making strategic plans does Dilbert spoof in this cynical view of managers as strategic planners?

Source: DILBERT: © Scott Adams/Dist. by United Feature Syndicate, Inc. Reprinted with permission.

of 25,000 or more are using it in at least one functional area. The most common areas are police, parks and recreation, personnel management, and budgeting.[20]

TQM values internal regulation and worker self-direction, often referred to as *empowerment*. It encourages strategies that reduce internal competition, foster team-work, improve decision-making processes, and reduce costs. The OMB has led a joint public- and private-sector quality improvement effort to adopt TQM as the official management improvement system for all federal agencies.[21] The General Accounting Office (GAO) has even published its own six features (its version of a principles list) of TQM prescriptions (see Figure 7.2). To be effective, TQM most be integrated into an agency's strategic management process.

Strategic Management

In strategic management, an agency plans where it wants to be at some future date. Such planning involves six stages:

1. Identify the objectives to be achieved.
2. Adopt a time frame (often referred to as a *planning horizon* along which these objectives are to be reached).
3. Apply systematic analysis of current circumstances of the organization, especially of capabilities.
4. Assess the environment, both current and into the planning horizon.
5. Select a strategy to achieve the objectives within the time frame.
6. Integrate all organizational efforts around the strategy.[22]

Strategic management is a philosophical approach to management that links strategic planning with day-to-day operations and decision making by agency managers. An objective, or a short-term goal, requires the application of specific **tactics**: short-term, immediate decisions that in their totality lead to the achievement of strategic goals. Tactics are incorporated into a **strategy**, or the overall conduct of a major undertaking to achieve long-term goals, the pattern of which is found in a series of agency decisions. These are linked through **strategic planning**: a set of processes used by an agency to assess the strategic situation and develop strategy and tactics for the future. Of course, managers vary greatly in their capability and abilities to do strategic planning in pursuit of strategic management. This point is spoofed in Cartoon 7.1. Not all managers are adept at discerning the planning horizon.

Capabilities and Environmental Constraints

When problems in the environment are discerned within the planning horizon, managers apply agency resources to reach objectives that are planned to confront those problems. When the organization's capability (all of its resources of funding, supplies, procedures, and personnel) fails to match environmental constraints, the entrepreneurial manager takes action to match staff resources to emerging environmental conditions. This may involve hiring new staff members with needed skills or changing the attitudes or the training of existing personnel to better meet the demands of the new environment. Managers may seek increased funding levels or reallocate existing funds to better match those needs. Managers may develop or adopt new technologies or procedures and integrate them into the agency to meet such needs. The development of the fixed-satellite technology to create the global positioning system (GPS), for example, led to the development of global information systems (GIS), which have revolutionized strategic planning efforts within a host of governmental agencies at all levels.

SWOT Analysis

Agency managers employ a technique known as **SWOT analysis**: analysis of strengths, weaknesses, opportunities, and threats. Consultants or senior managers typically use SWOT analysis during interactive, brainstorming sessions among senior management groups. Ideally, these sessions identify major organizational strengths and weaknesses and focus attention on capability issues. Such analysis is designed to identify opportunities on the horizon as well as threats to the organization to better ensure agency survival.

SWOT analysis may focus on the development of a government's infrastructure or extrapolate new programs or investments for growth. It assesses organizational investment as to **opportunity costs**—the value that resources would have when used in the best possible or simply another specified alternative way.

Strategic Factors in Management

Strategic management is increasingly used at all levels of government and in virtually every functional area. Four factors have been identified as particularly important to its use in the public sector: (1) resolution of the public–private paradox, (2) the centrality of power in bureaucracy, (3) the language and culture of an organization, and (4) place.[23]

Public administration sustains a basic paradox. On the one hand, it holds that business and government are fundamentally different. On the other hand, it recognizes that business administration and public administration have much in common. Government and its managers have a mandate of political legitimacy. Government policy is enacted into law and may be implemented by force. Government is responsible to all and to values that are equitable to all. Government decision making must involve accommodation, compromise, and incremental change. Government managers cannot use the bottom line of profit as a measure of success. Business, however, pursues profit and does so for the benefit of its shareholders, not that of society as a whole. Business measures its success by the bottom line. Business managers reflect feedback from the private, competitive marketplace. Yet both private and public organizations can be usefully considered complex systems. Both are large bureaucracies led by a small leadership (management). Both recruit from the same pool of the population for their employees. The organizational cultures of the private and public sectors interact with one another.

All large organizations have central management structures. Power in organization is structured. Strategic management and planning is conducted by centralized staff, whereas policy is mostly implemented by rank-and-file members. In recent years, many government agencies have used not-for-profit organizations in place of state or local government agencies as primary program deliverers. This trend makes strategic management difficult in the public sector. Agency managers share power with many other important actors. Bureau functions are decided politically, not rationally. Political decision makers often lack concurrence on how to measure performance. Government managers have far less overall autonomy than do private-sector managers. This makes it more difficult to coordinate and implement action plans. As a result, strategic management is more complex and difficult in public-sector than in private-sector environments.

Strategic-management studies have highlighted the importance of organizational culture and the specialized language and style with which an organization approaches its tasks. Strategic management has its own culture and is more likely to be successfully adopted in an agency that emphasizes and values change and innovation.

An important factor that affects the use of public-sector strategic management is location. The closer an organization is to the center of decision making, the more difficult it is to sustain a strategic-management effort. The failed attempt of the Clinton administration to fundamentally reform health care illustrates the case. In health care reform, the problem was so large and the competing interests so powerful and yet so diverse that compromise was paralyzed amid the "horse trading" that characterizes decision making in Washington, D.C.

In geographic terms, a government agency will more readily adopt strategic management when

1. it is further removed from the heart of political leadership at the national, state, or local level;
2. it is more self-contained and autonomous with respect to funding, personnel, and overall destiny;
3. it is smaller;
4. its results are more consistently measured; and
5. its funding comes more from user fees than from general tax revenues.[24]

Table 7.2 summarizes the reported use of selected public management techniques by U.S. municipalities over two decades. It demonstrates the somewhat faddish nature of various techniques but also the growing popularity of TQM at the local level and the comparatively sustained effort to improve local management and productivity through these methods of management.

Challenges to Strategic Management

Public-sector managers today commonly face six challenges: (1) mandates, (2) efficiency, (3) competitiveness, (4) boundaries, (5) public versus private interests, and (6) service.[25]

TABLE 7.2

Reported Use of Selected Public Management Techniques by U.S. Municipalities, Selected Years 1976–1993

	Percentage Reporting Use			
Technique	1976 N = 404	1982 N = 460	1987 N = 451	1993 N = 520
Techniques for resource and expenditure control				
Program or zero-base budgeting	50	77	75	69
Financial trend monitoring	—	—	70	75
Revenue and expense forecasting	—	—	68	75
Techniques for achieving broad-based goals and objectives				
Management by objectives	41	59	62	47
Strategic planning	—	—	60	63
Techniques for raising the level of efficiency and effectiveness				
Productivity improvement programs	43	67	54	53
Program evaluation	64	—	80	75
Total quality management	—	—	—	39
Techniques designed to assure individual and group performance				
Employee incentive programs	16	48	64	58
Productivity bargaining*	10	22	16	13
Quality circles	—	—	32	33

*Pertains only to cities with unionized employees.

Sources: Nicholas Henry, *Public administration and public affairs* (7th ed.), p. 164. © 1999. Reprinted by permission of Pearson Education, Inc., Upper Saddle River, NJ. Data for 1976 are derived from Rackham S. Fukuhara, Productivity improvement in cities, *The municipal year book, 1977* (Washington, DC: International City Management Association, 1977): 193–200; 1982 data are derived from Theodore H. Poister and Robert P. McGowan, The use of management tools in municipal government: A national survey, *Public Administration Review, 44* (May–June 1984): 218; 1987 data are from Theodore H. Poister and Gregory Streib, Management tools in municipal government: Trends over the past decade, *Public Administration Review, 49* (May–June 1989): 240–248; 1993 data are from Theodore H. Poister and Gregory Streib, Municipal management tools from 1976 to 1993: An overview and update, *Public Productivity and Management Review, 18* (Winter 1994): 115–125.

Mandates

Strategic management requires managers to assess an agency's central roles, missions, and objectives. They must struggle with the question of mandate: Why should this government or this level carry out this function? Sometimes, government agencies have or are given a monopoly to provide a service—for example, provide electricity or public transportation. Economies of scale or simply society's interest in avoiding inefficient duplication of expensive facilities may call for a governmental monopoly to provide a good or service. National defense, for example, is viewed as a natural monopoly of the national level of government. An agency may serve a special community or clientele group (a state-run school for the blind, for instance). Sometimes, only government can serve as a sort of umpire to regulate competition in the private-sector marketplace.

Government typically is the organization charged with producing "public goods"—safe streets, clean air and water, fire protection. Some centralized functions of government are unsuitable for privatization—budgeting and centralized administration, for example.

There are natural mandates for a government organization to provide a given good or service. And sometimes, as we have already seen, a higher level of government may simply mandate (often without funding) that a lower level of government provide a good or a service. Mandates also sometimes assist in strategic management by making the objectives and mission of an agency clear. Often they entail considerable burdens and constraints on effectively using strategic management. They may impose seemingly impossible burdens on the agency that are beyond the capacity of the managers to effectively address.

Efficiency

Public-sector management faces a challenge common to all organizations: efficiency. But for public-sector agencies, this may be especially difficult to measure. Without a bottom-line indicator, how do managers determine how efficiently their agency is operating? How does one measure efficiency when a government corporation such as Amtrak is tasked with providing a service that private-sector ventures abandoned because it was unprofitable? How does one compare the efficiency of the U.S. Postal Service, with mandated delivery requirements that are inherently unprofitable, with that of a private-sector provider such as FedEx or UPS? Competition is often an important precondition to efficient operation, yet a specific government agency commonly has a mandated monopoly over a service and therefore lacks competition against which to measure its efficiency.

Competitiveness

A central challenge to public-sector strategic management is that of competitiveness. A private-sector concept such as competition is embraced by public-sector managers because they recognize that competition drives strategic thinking. Private-sector organizations are often direct competitors to public agencies, particularly those established as government corporations (e.g., the U.S. Postal Service, Amtrak, TVA, COMSAT). Agency managers must be innovative to deal with the threat of competition from the private sector.

Privatization is a growing political movement that encroaches on many governmental functions previously considered natural government functions. Competition and privatization in public education have become popular concepts, and many services performed at the state and local levels have been privatized. Charter schools, magnet schools, and voucher programs are public education reforms that are all based on the competition concept. They pit public schools against one another and against private schools.

The concepts of *consumer sovereignty* and government clients as customers have, as we have seen, infused the culture of many public agencies, so even agencies that do not privatize may be run by their managers with a more business-like approach. Such managers assume the values prevalent in the private sector.

Boundaries

Public agencies are limited by their jurisdictional boundaries (for example, a given geographic area or to a specific function). Private-sector competitors may acquire specific advantages in competition with public agencies when they are not limited by such boundaries. Governments today push traditional boundary limits: State bodies may operate in interstate markets, and local governments may run international airports. Technology increasingly blurs the logic of and need for some boundary lines.

CARTOON 7.2
Man was not born to crawl?
What constraints on strategic planning are illustrated by this cynical view of highway planning? How does this illustrate that governmental outputs can lead to unanticipated consequences?

Source: Copyright 1966, Los Angeles Times. Reprinted by permission.

Problems may spill over jurisdictional lines and require new approaches to solve them. Local police agencies, for example, rely on FBI crime labs and fingerprinting identification services. Interlocal agreements and interstate compacts are entered into so that governments may enjoy economies of scale or simply plan and coordinate programs to cope with problems that cross traditional legal boundary lines.

Public versus Private Interests

Managers of public agencies are further and consistently challenged by the public–private interest dilemma. Public interests in such social programs as free education for children may be challenged when private interests—say, public teachers' unions or professional educators' associations—capture a school district. They may adopt policy that is designed to meet more the narrow interests of these special groups than the broader interests of the general public. Regulatory agencies are often viewed as captives of the special interests organized in the industry the agencies were created to oversee. Where an agency manager draws the line is a common dilemma: Should it always be between a given program or service that is in the interests of the general public as opposed to the interests of special-interest groups? That may be difficult when the managers are indebted to interest groups for vital political support. Obviously, the problem of drawing a line between public and private interests is a source of constant challenge to public-sector managers who attempt to use strategic management techniques.

INFOTRAC
COLLEGE EDITION

How should the HR department of 2004 be structured?

Service

The actual provision of a good or service can bring about vast changes in public demand that quickly outstrip the public agency's capability to meet. Cartoon 7.2 illustrates this dilemma. Highway planners often design expressways that are nearly immediately outmoded because the existence of the new road changes demand. Consumers change their driving habits and routes and often even relocate their housing in response to a new superhighway, and thus soon help it become outmoded.

Reading 7.1, "Performance-Based Budgeting in a Performance-Based Budget-Cutting Environment," discusses the values and value conflict inherent in the performance-based budgeting reform approach to performance management. It exemplifies the use of this method at the local government level. It illustrates values pursued by both state and local governments as well as the value conflicts that arise when the political environment dictates deep budget cuts.

Reading 7.1

Performance-Based Budgeting in a Performance-Based Budget-Cutting Environment

Times are tough for budgeters. State budget shortfalls of approximately $40 billion are expected in the current fiscal year. . . . Thirty-nine states had a reduction of their fiscal year (FY) 2002 enacted budgets by $15 billion after they were passed—20 more states than in FY 2001. . . . A national recession has swept in and stymied politicians and public officials. The stock market is at an all-time low. Okay, maybe times are not that drastic, but the current fiscal environment for state and local jurisdictions is tougher now than it has been in the past decade.

Rosy Times for Performance Measurement

Times are rosy for performance managers. The measurement of government performance—department performance measures, balanced scorecards, individual performance contracts, managing for results, and performance-based budgeting—is at an all-time high. In a recent Government Accounting Standards Board (GASB) survey of city and county officials, 70 percent of those responding indicated that a majority of their departments were using input and output measures, while nearly 50 percent noted the use of outcome measures. . . . On the state level, at least 47 states have performance-based budgeting requirements. . . .

Officials at all levels of government are beginning to not simply collect and report performance information, they are using this information to manage how elected officials direct the public's money and how policy makers manage programs once policies are in place. Performance management has never had a greater penetration into how government works than it does now—and that penetration continues to grow.

It is indeed the best of times, the worst of times. But what happens when these two worlds collide, when the momentum of performance gathering runs smack into the realities of budget reductions? Are jurisdictions able to leverage the information that is available through performance-based budgeting (PBB) and performance management to make thoughtful budgetary decisions in an era of fiscal constraints?

The Theory

Performance measurement is not a new concept. Harry Hatry, in *Performance Measurement: Getting*

Results, details performance measurement back as far back as the 1950s and 1960s, and performance-based budgeting back to the Department of Defense in the late 1960s. More serious discussion on the subject took root with Osborne and Gaebler's Reinventing Government and the passage of the Government Performance and Results Act (GPRA) in the early 1990s. Since then, there has been a national debate on the various uses of performance data. The most basic rationale is that departments can begin to measure the outcomes of the services they provide, which gives citizenry some accounting of their return on investment for their tax payments. But the seed of this basic performance idea has given way to a veritable tree of knowledge: Performance measurement data has been set up to be used all across governments to prepare program budgets, in program evaluation, for individual performance evaluations, and to develop performance-based budgets. This rationale for measuring outcomes of service delivery serves as the theory behind PBB—funding decisions regarding programs can be made depending on what level of service delivery policy makers desire.

Revenue Shortfalls

In a time of plenty, few governments—if any—had to worry about running out of money to fund new programs. Indeed, as budgets across the land doubled and tripled over the decade of the 1990s, throwing budget money towards new programs and systems was easy. As an example, even in the District of Columbia, as we faced additional expenditure pressures on the budget, revenue growth kept up to provide the income necessary to cover all expenditures without forcing it to think about its spending priorities. During the past 12 months, public budgets at all levels have changed. Revenue shortfalls across the country are forcing states and localities to reduce budgets for the current year and their projections for the future. In another example, the Commonwealth of Virginia has announced that it will cut an additional $1.6 billion out of this year's budget, after it had already cut $3.8 billion several months ago.

Fortunately, PBB is a tool that can be used to not just set program priorities, but to determine the return on investment by defining and measuring performance. In this regard, PBB can be used to determine not just increased funding, but also decreased funding for programs that are of lesser priority or simply not performing. In fact, one can argue that PBB is intended exactly for times like these to help decision makers make informed judgments about how to spend limited resources to accomplish desired policy goals. The question becomes, are those jurisdictions operating in a PBB environment using it to make not just incremental decisions on spending, but also decremental ones?

The Practice

When we examine how PBB is being used in an era of scarce resources, we can look at three groups of PBB system users: those who have utilized performance initiatives more than five years and who have, mostly, moved into the use of performance management systems; those who are relatively new to the process of measuring performance but have jumped wholeheartedly into the process during the past five years and have committed to it; and those who are just beginning to institute performance measurement programs.

Group 1: The Pioneers: Austin, Texas, as a Model

The first group is well established in the use of performance measurement and has used its years of experience to fully implement a management system. The money has been spent, the time has been given, and true performance data is starting to be realized—a commitment has been made to management based on performance. There is no turning back. Nor should there be. The hard part has been done. If we are to find PBB being used to make budget reductions, it is in this group that we look to first. If it abandons PBB when making budget reduction decisions, we are not likely to see it in the second or third group.

The City of Austin serves as a good model here. It has been operating in a PBB environment for a number of years and it has taken root. Budget officials from the city met with their city council in May to discuss the budget reductions that would happen both for the current year and in the budget process upon which they are embarking. They asked the council to pass a formal declaration to use performance data in budget reductions (Austin Budgetary Guideline #9, FY 2002–2003). The City Manager should utilize the

Managing for Results program and data as a key information in making budgetary decisions where they do not result in a conflict with policy.

Did the budget gap disappear once the council approved the use of performance data as a tool in budget reductions? No. The city still faced difficult financial decisions. In fact, in the 16-page budget transmittal letter from the city manager to the city council you will find only a couple of sentences devoted to strategic reductions in programs rather than across-the-board cuts. However, what makes this significant is the recognition that performance data can be used in concert with other traditional budget reduction tools in decision making.

Once performance data collection mechanisms are in place and being used to their potential, program and activity funding decisions can be made based on the effects funding will have on service. If an activity is performing well, that does not mean it will not be cut. But at least decision makers will have the tools necessary to know which services are performing well and the effect of service-level cuts. The lesson gained is that managers should not turn away from performance when times are tough. They must believe in their performance management system and believe in the data it can provide. But that is not all. They must help use the data to make tough decisions.

Group 2: The Emulators: District of Columbia as an Example

The second group of governments with performance management systems has been implementing its work for less than five years and is just on the verge of seeing results. This group has the most to lose if it abandons performance initiatives, simply because it typically has invested financially in the initiative and has seen little results to date. As with the first group of agencies, it must affirm its commitment to the process and stay the course, even in tough budgetary times. There are several ways to do this:

- A strong advocate must take the lead. Key decision makers have made the initial commitment and have decided to travel down the performance road. If no one continues to champion the use of performance management, it will surely go away.
- Press the issue. Stakeholders must continually be reminded that performance management is a long-term process, but it is a process that can produce

valid results. Keep the issue in the forefront of the debate.

- Require the use of performance nomenclature during the debate. When discussion begins on budget reduction, performance terms are likely to be forgotten. A program/activity/service structure is not the same as a control center/responsibility center structure. Force the use of performance terminology during debates, no matter how evolved it is in your government.
- Make reductions based on priorities. This may sound simple, but it is true. Priorities have been identified through the performance initiatives that have been started. These priorities should be maintained. Traditional budget-cutting mechanisms pay little or no heed to priorities that have been established. The easiest way to give credence to established priorities is to make budget reductions based on them.
- Agency-wide performance goals must be elastic. Because the system has not been fully developed and the results rarely have been seen, there may be a need for adjustment of original goals. Make no mistake—decision makers will make budget cuts based on their priorities. Once funding decisions have been made it might be necessary to revisit the government-wide performance goals that have been established to ensure validity in the face of budget cuts.

The District of Columbia is a good example of this case. Two years into its PBB initiative, District managers find themselves having to reduce FY 2002 expenditures by $75 million because of revenue shortfalls. FY 2003 will most likely see even more significant revenue shortfalls resulting in budget reductions.

The opportunity exists to use the tools above to make program reductions to balance departmental budgets. Because several departments have PBB structures in place, reductions can be made within those structures rather than by using traditional methods

alone. However, for performance management to survive in tough financial times, a leader must emerge to keep the process valid. The most common problem is not that performance becomes invalid in these debates, only that it is disregarded. Decision makers must continually be reminded of prior decisions.

Group 3: The Nonstarters

The final group of performance users is the broadest. It has heard the buzz over the past few years. It may or may not have given resources to the cause. The trouble is that in a budget-cutting environment, performance management, especially a system that is not yet in place or funded, is one of the last considerations. In fact, it would not be a surprise if funding for PBB initiatives fell victim to the ax as a cost-reduction measure. When governments are just getting started with performance initiatives, they are most likely to resort to traditional methods of budget cutting since they do not have the performance information with which to make reliable budget decisions. But performance initiatives are no less valid for these governments. Even if funding for PBB is reduced or eliminated, a plan of action should be established on how best to stay the course in instituting PBB.

Conclusion

This is a critical time for performance-based budgeting. It can serve to inform decision makers not just on how much to cut, but also on what the program consequences of these cuts are for service delivery. The approach of Austin and the opportunity for the District of Columbia show how valuable a tool PBB can be in informing financial and program management decisions. But as with all tools, it is only as good as the hand that wields it.

Source: John Craig, Performance-based budgeting in a performance-based budget-cutting environment, *The Public Manager, 31*(3) (Fall 2002): 57–60. Reprinted with permission of The Bureaucrat, Inc.

Net Assignment

Using InfoTrac College Edition, Internet search engines, and some of the websites listed at the end of this chapter, find two local government reform proposals. What values lie behind each recommendation? What are the pros and cons of each proposal? What conflicts do you foresee in the implementation of each proposal?

Summary

Managerialism describes the management of large, public organizations. The reengineering approach and its array of management techniques that promote a reengineering focus—MBO, OD, OR, PERT, CPM, and TQM—reflect developments in management theory. Performance management, contracting out, and total quality management have become prominent tools. Each method of management incorporates and promotes particular values. Strategic management and strategic planning are integral to the new approaches. Various factors influence and challenge the effective use of strategic management.

Glossary of Key Terms

critical path method (CPM)   An analytical management technique that seeks the path with the smallest margin of extra resources with which to complete all assigned program activities.

focus group   A small number of individuals (generally a dozen or fewer) who share a common characteristic and are brought together to discuss a product or service under the leadership of a trained observer.

management   The process of running an organization; the use of resources to accomplish goals; the individuals who are formally authorized to run an organization.

managerialism   An entrepreneurial approach to public management that emphasizes a set of beliefs that better management (that is, a reinvigorated scientific management) will solve a wide range of economic and social ills.

management by objectives (MBO)   An approach to program or policy management that defines short- and long-term objectives and keeps a record of actual program results to determine effectiveness.

objective   A short-term goal; it must be met on the way to a larger overall achievement.

operations research (OR)   A management technique that stresses efficiency by maximizing some "payoff" function clearly within the goals being sought; comes into play only after value choices have been made; relies on the use of probability theory, queuing techniques, and mathematical model building to allocate and use resources within a designated subsystem.

opportunity costs   The value resources would have when used in the best possible way or simply another specified alternative way.

organizational development (OD)   A process for increasing an organization's effectiveness by stressing that maximum effectiveness is achieved by integrating an individual's desire for personal growth with organizational goals.

performance management   The systematic integration of an organization's efforts to achieve its objectives.

productivity bargaining   Method applied by public managers to use private-sector approaches to contract negotiation; links employee wage increases to various cost-cutting efforts, including increasing on-the-job productivity.

program evaluation and review technique (PERT)   A management analytical tool that maps out a series of steps that will carry out a program.

quality circle (QC)   Small group of 3 to 15 workers who meet regularly to discuss, analyze, and solve problems they experience on the job.

reengineering   A fundamental rethinking and redesign of organizational processes to bring about significant improvements in costs or quality of services.

stakeholders   People affected directly or indirectly by an organization's activities.

strategic management   A philosophy of management that links strategic planning to an organization's day-to-day operations and decisions.

strategic planning   A set of processes used by an organization to assess a strategic situation and develop strategy for the future.

strategy   The overall conduct of a major enterprise to achieve long-term goals; the pattern found in a series of organizational decisions.

SWOT analysis   A review of an agency's strengths, weaknesses, opportunities, and threats.

tactics   The short-term, immediate decisions that, in their totality, lead to the achievement of strategic goals.

total quality management (TQM)   A new term for quality control in its most expanded sense of a total and continuing concern for quality and the production of goods and services; seeks organizational performance at an optimal level.

Review Questions

1. Discuss how the *reengineering* approach differs from the orthodox management approach.

2. List the scholars and tenets most associated with each of the following approaches to management: MBO, OD, OR, entrepreneurial management, and reinventing government.

3. What are the principles of management advocated by the TQM approach? Identify two scholars most notably associated with the TQM movement.

4. Briefly discuss the stages involved in strategic management. Why are local governments more able or likely to use strategic management than is the national government?

5. Performance-based budgeting is just one approach to public administration management reform. Using InfoTrac College Edition, Internet search engines, and some of the websites listed at the end of this chapter, find two other reform proposals. What values lie behind each recommendation? What are the pros and cons of each proposal? What conflicts do you foresee in the implementation of each proposal?

Surfing the Net

The following are useful websites for the material covered in this chapter.

Alliance for Redesigning (**http://www.alliance.napawash.org/alliance/index.html**), a National Academy of Public Administration site, promotes reinventing government initiatives and publishes *The Innovator*.

American Management Association (**http://www.amanet.org/usindex.htm**)

American Planning Association (**http://www.planning.org**)

American Society for Public Administration (**http://www.aspannet.org**)

The Council for Excellence in Government (**http://www.excelgov.org**)—750 leaders in the private sector who previously served in government—is dedicated to improving government performance.

National Institute of Standards and Technology Quality Program (**http://www .quality.nist.gov**)

International Personnel Management Association (**http://ipma-hr.org**)

National Academy of Public Administration (**http://www.napawash.org/napa/ index.html**)

National Center for Public Productivity (**http://www.andromeda.rutgers.edu/ ∼ncpp/ncpp.html**)

Chapter 8

Evaluation of Public Policy: Swinging the Pendulum of Administrative Politics

I was recently given a demonstration of a sophisticated, automated pharmaceutical-dispensing system. In addition to speeding up the mechanical and sorting functions of the process, the developers were keen to point out that with the incorporation of such technology as automated bar-code-labeling and -reading systems, multiple automated inspection and verification steps, as well as a parallel paper trail following the process from order to delivery, the system virtually "eliminated" the possibility of dispensing errors.

I was asked to participate in the demonstration by fabricating and writing down an order that the operator then read aloud and input into the system. We then followed my order all the way through the process until it was ultimately delivered to me in a neat little package along with a printed receipt. I must say it was all quite impressive.

Unfortunately, it was also wrong. Although the operator had accurately announced my order, he had input the quantity incorrectly. Now, there is no earth-shattering new lesson to be learned from this. It's the same old *garbage-in, garbage-out* principle we're all familiar with. But, what should be of concern is that somehow this simple truism was obscured in the haze of technological sophistication. Certainly, the automated system followed the appropriate SOPs (standard operating procedures) to the letter, in so much as it could. However, no SOPs (at least for demonstration purposes) called for a check of the final (out of automation) deliverable against the original (before automation) order. And only an operator, properly trained to conduct such a final SOP, would be able to close this particular loop.

John Haystead, Editor-in-Chief
Pharmaceutical Technology (February 2003): 130.

Introduction

The chapter-opening vignette illustrates an all-too-common situation: the apparent failure of a "best-laid plan," a program, due to an all-too-common aspect of human behavior—user error.

This chapter discusses the evaluation stage of the administration of public policy. It emphasizes how the evaluation of public policy acts to move policy, like the swinging of a pendulum, between or among competing values. In the real world of policy analysis, evaluation is never value neutral. It inherently concerns applying standards—which are implicitly value laden—to assess a program's effectiveness. Value conflict in program evaluation often reflects the differing perspectives of the political versus the administrative process. According to James Fesler and Donald Kettl, "Advocacy and compromise are the hallmarks of the political process. Administration, in contrast, aspires to efficiency."[1]

The evaluation of programs typically involves multiple and sometimes conflicting goals in the process itself. Evaluation may be designed to shed light on how well or poorly a program is being implemented, but it also may be intended to develop political pressure on a bureaucracy to get the agency to change. "Program analysis," write Fesler and Kettl, "such as those done by the GAO, are intended to bring heat, as well as light, to bear on agencies that are ineffective."[2]

Results-oriented management and its effects on program assessment emphasize the significant role that bureaucracies play in the policy-making process. In playing their special role in determining policy, bureaucratic administrators interject their values. These may conflict with the values advocated or sought by citizens, consumers of government's goods and services, organized interest groups who have vested **stakes** in the policy outcomes, elected political officials who enact or oversee policy implementation, and even bureaucratic actors themselves.

As we review the stages in the policy process, we will (1) highlight program implementation and evaluation and (2) describe the critical role that administrators play in the policy process with respect to measuring policy results and the major techniques used to assess or measure policy results. We also will distinguish between program and policy evaluation and see experiences and problems with performance and performance measurement at the national, state, and local levels of government administration. We close with a reading that examines organizational values and a systems-of-care approach for children with severe emotional disturbances, illustrating the need for aligning core system goals (the values of effectiveness, efficiency, and equity) at the practice, program, and system levels, with the state of Vermont serving as a case study example.

Values and the Public Policy Process

Values are inherent throughout the public policy process. Specific values infuse the standards or tests by which policy is evaluated, because a program's success or failure is largely measured by how well it achieves its goals. How values imbue the evaluation of programs is offered in an examination of social programs designed to strengthen families and help rebuild community and neighborhoods, such as Head Start.

The Example of Head Start

Head Start is a federally funded preschool program that began in the early 1960s and targeted 3- and 4-year-old children who were predominantly from low-income families. Head Start's stated goals are to improve participating children's health,

---

1. Successful program are comprehensive, flexible, responsive, and persevering.

2. Successful programs see children in the context of their families.

3. Successful program deal with families as parts of neighborhoods and communities.

4. Successful programs have a long-term preventive orientation and a clear mission, and they continue to evolve over time.

5. Successful programs are well managed by competent and committed individuals who have clearly identifiable skills.

6. Successful programs are staffed with individuals who are trained and supported to provide high-quality, responsive services.

7. Successful programs operate in settings that encourage practitioners to build strong relationships based on mutual trust and respect.

FIGURE 8.1
Attributes of Successful Programs in Community Building

---

nutrition, social skills, and academic readiness to assist their parents in contacting needed societal resources. Head Start expanded during the 1990s to become a full-day program, reflecting the need for complete day care. It was extended to children from birth to age 3, reflecting the growing perception that these early years in child development are critically important. Figure 8.1 shows analyst Lisabeth Schorr's list of attributes of effective government community-building programs such as Head Start. A mixture of various core values are associated with each attribute of a successful program.[3]

At issue in program evaluation are the core values associated with measures of success or failure—and *whose* values will predominate in public policy. One noted policy scholar, Thomas Dye, argues that elites and their value biases predominate in the U.S. public policy process. He argues that elites run the United States. Figure 8.2 presents his model of the elitist policy-making process. It portrays wealthy individuals and corporations as having the resources necessary to shape the nature of solutions to policy problems.

The Role of Elites

Figure 8.2 portrays elites dominating the policy process through grants to foundations and universities and using interlocking directorates to so affect the policy-planning groups that they are able not only to determine decision making but also to shape opinion so that society's lawmaking structures reflect the elite's views and accept its policy recommendations.

Cartoon 8.1, for example, spoofs Congress's inability to see the need to regulate cigarettes because lawmakers are strongly influenced by the powerful tobacco lobby. The tobacco lobby elite dictates how our representatives view the problem, blinding them to the need to seriously regulate tobacco.

Core values involved in the policy process vie for attention and influence. Core values include agency competence, merit, political responsiveness, social equity, and, of course, the rights and well-being of program administrators and bureaucrats. As one scholar notes:

> Often, the pursuit of certain core values involves tradeoffs with others. This means that civil service systems perennially run the risk of being damned if they do and damned if they don't. It emanates from difficulties in forging consensus on the

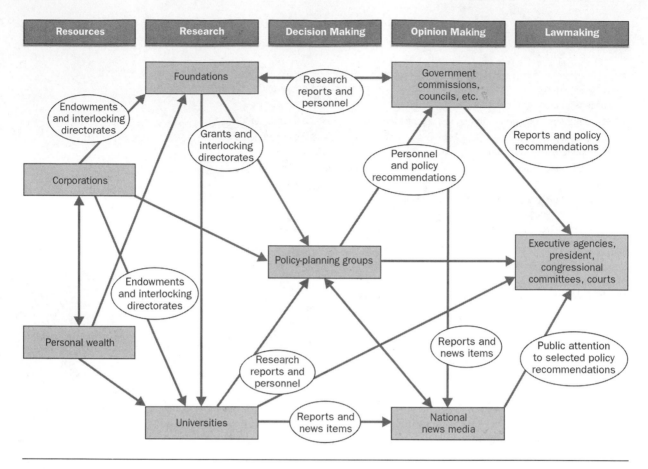

| Resources | Research | Decision Making | Opinion Making | Lawmaking |

FIGURE 8.2

The Elitist Model of the Public Policy Process

Source: Thomas R. Dye, *Who's running America? The Bush restoration* (7th ed.), p. 173. © 2002. Reprinted by permission of Pearson Education, Inc., Upper Saddle River, NJ.

CARTOON 8.1

Selective vision

Why is Congress so blinded by the tobacco lobby? What value does a Congress member see more strongly than the public interest?

Source: Kevin Stiers, *The Charlotte Observer*. With permission from *The Charlotte Observer*.

appropriate weight to be assigned particular core values—in defining the optimal mix of achievement. This inability to reach agreement means that reform movements often sow the seeds of new discontent and assume a cyclical pattern. When reform succeeds in promoting certain core values (e.g., more political responsiveness), it prompts others to pursue change on behalf of the core values that have become less dominant (such as merit or agency competence).[4]

Both policy analysis and the evaluation of how specific programs are implemented are intended to be useful not only to the elected politicians who make policy but also to the public administrators who manage the programs designed to implement policy. In the ideal world, policy analysis and program evaluation improve the way programs are run—at least in the short term. Such research, however, does not always work so well in the real world. There are barriers to its effective use. Bureaucracies are often poorly designed to digest such **evaluation research**. Besides, *evaluation* and *bureaucratic organization* can be somewhat contradictory terms. According to Aaron Wildavsky, "Organizational structures imply stability, while the process of evaluation suggests change. Organization generates commitment, while evaluation inculcates skepticism. Evaluation speaks to the relationship between action and objectives, while organization relates its activities to programs and clientele."[5]

Results-Oriented and Process-Oriented Management

Government managers may differ in their approaches to management in ways that shape their use of evaluation research. Joseph Wholey (1983) describes two contrasting views of government management: (1) **results-oriented** (or outcome-oriented) **management** and (2) **process-oriented management**.

Figure 8.3 presents the structure of resource expenditures, program activities, program outcomes, information flows, and uses of information that characterize results-oriented management. Managers set realistic, measurable, and outcome-oriented program objectives that they assess and report to higher policy-making levels (that is, to chief executives or legislative bodies). Figure 8.4 shows the structure that characterizes the process-oriented management, which is often more typical of government. Here program objectives are limited to comment, feedback, and process objectives. Reports to policy levels are based on comment and process data.

Administrative organizations differ in how they interpret evaluation studies, many of which are inconclusive at best. Analysis that fails to find clearly significant outcomes or measurable results may suffer from some combination of the following factors:

1. the policy itself,
2. its implementation,
3. the design and methodology of the evaluation study, or
4. errors in carrying out the research.

Failure to find a policy "impact" may lead supporters to press for more resources or expanded authority to make the policy work. Opponents may assert that the policy itself is flawed or that its implementation is unworkable. Both sides can, and often do, speculate on the likelihood that the policy will work better in the long run.

Policy evaluation studies frequently do not resolve political debates over public policy.[6]

INFOTRAC
COLLEGE EDITION

Misperceptions, the media, and the Iraq war

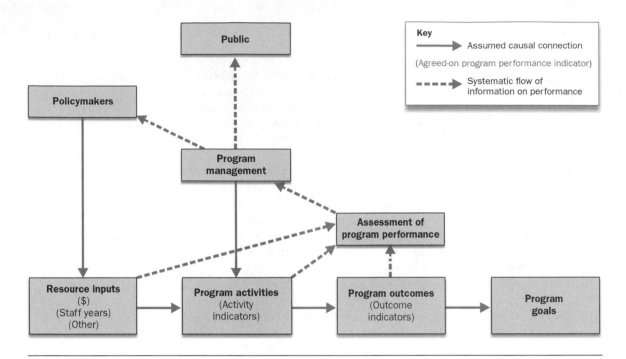

FIGURE 8.3
Results-Oriented Management

Source: Joseph Wholey, *Evaluation and effective public management* (Boston: Little, Brown, 1983): 6. Reprinted with permission of Joseph Wholey.

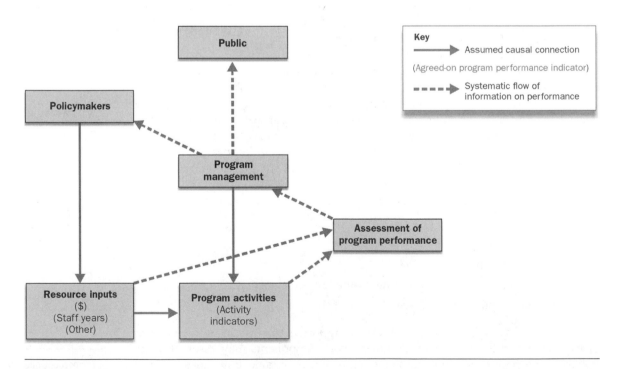

FIGURE 8.4
Process-Oriented Management

Source: Adapted from Joseph Wholey, *Evaluation and effective public management* (Boston: Little, Brown, 1983): 7. Reprinted with permission of Joseph Wholey.

Box 8.1

The Unintended Consequences of School Lunch Programs

As elementary and secondary schools across the nation grapple with budget cutbacks resulting from state and local revenue shortfalls, many school systems have contracted out to vendors to enhance their revenue flow. The increased availability of vendor-dispensed and fast-food franchises in our elementary, secondary, and even higher education schools has resulted in unintended consequences, as noted in one 2003 program evaluation. Children in middle schools with a la carte dining eat fewer fruits and vegetables and more fat than children in schools that do not offer that option, based on research reported in the *American Journal of Public Health* (93 (2003): 1161–1168). The researchers obtained infor-

mation on the lunch options and eating habits of 7th-grade students (age about 12–13 years) at 16 schools in the St. Paul–Minneapolis area. The study found that for every snack-vending machine present in the schools, students' average daily consumption of fruit dropped by 11 percent. The study's authors also investigated the nutritional value of the food sold through these venues, separating them into high-fat and lower-fat groups. In the 13 a la carte programs, 84 percent of the foods offered and 93 percent of the foods actually sold were items that fell into the high-fat category.

Source: Based on data in School lunches bad for nutrition, *The Lancet* (July 5, 2003): 51.

Results-oriented management is not found solely among private-sector organizations; similarly, process-oriented management is not used just by government organizations. Box 8.1 presents an example of the failure of results-oriented management within the public school system. It shows how specific and significant "revenue-enhancing" incentives can lead elementary and secondary public school systems to adopt school lunch programs that result in unintended consequences.

The Policy-Making Process

The importance of perspective and orientation is not limited to program managers. All actors in the policy-making process come to it with a given perspective that shapes how they view a problem and how they would develop and implement policy to deal with the problem. Their perspectives also influence how they develop evaluation procedures and the type of evaluation data they seek, collect, analyze, and interpret. Bureaucratic participants in the policy process affect it at every stage. One useful model to explain the policy process is called the *bureaucratic politics model*, which reflects its emphasis on the role of bureaucracies in policy making.[7]

The Bureaucratic Politics Model

The bureaucratic politics model explains government behavior as the outcomes of bargaining among individuals and groups within government. It merges the views of group-theory and game-theory models of policy making. The groups on which it focuses are those within government (and their allies outside of government). Policy is seen as being made not by rational choice but by the pulling and hauling of internal governmental—*bureaucratic*—politics. Bargaining takes place over issues because the actors in government must share power; and given their positions in government, they see different sides of the same issue.

The bureaucratic politics model sees policy making as a sort of internal government game. The senior players in this game are such actors as the President (or chief executive at the state or local level), senior political advisers to the chief executive, cabinet officers, and agency heads. The junior players in this game, according to this model, are members of the legislature (Congress or a state legislature), spokespeople for vested interest groups, and lower-level members of agencies and departments.

The issues determine who plays and how much power or bargaining advantage in the policy-making process any group of players or individual actors actually have, as well as how much bargaining takes place. The longer a policy issue is debated, the more groups and individuals are likely to become involved in the process. When an issue clearly falls within the legally recognized responsibility of a particular agency, then that agency's group of players will have increased power in the bargaining process and less total bargaining will take place. When an issue (or policy problem) does not clearly fall within a particular agency area of responsibility, then bargaining is not concentrated and the total amount of bargaining will increase. Competing agencies and their respective actors intrude themselves or are asked by the political actors to become involved.

A player's stand on an issue in the decision-making process may be determined or influenced by any of six factors:

1. position in government,
2. domestic political interests,
3. organizational interests,
4. personal interests,
5. basic beliefs that are widely held throughout government, and
6. the individual's personal background.

The combination of these factors determines the "face of the issue" that participants each see and shapes their positions on the issue. Given the face of the issue seen, each participant in the bargaining process calculates how the resolution of the issue will affect his or her concerns. This calculation determines the player's stake in the issue at hand—how and how much the individual or the agency stands to gain or lose, depending on the outcome of the policy bargaining game. The higher the stakes (which are defined in terms of the agency's power and interests, in personal political interests, and so on), the more involved the individual or the agency will become in the bargaining game.

Several factors can lead to bargaining advantages. When an issue clearly falls within the responsibility of a given agency or person within government, then that player will have an increase in bargaining power and less total bargaining will take place because:

- the player or agency has a relative monopoly over information pertaining to the issue, and
- the agency can control the implementation of any policy decision.

Other players in the bargaining game will hesitate to bargain and to compete with an agency when the issue clearly falls within its domain. This hesitancy results from the fact that other agencies within government and outside groups see little chance of success under such circumstances. Other players realize that they would have little hope of gathering support for their viewpoint, given their lack of information on the issue or their inability to control the implementation of any decision made. Their stakes may not be high enough to justify a significant fight over the issue.

INFOTRAC
COLLEGE EDITION

Political culture, economic structure and policy

Additional factors that lead to bargaining advantages include:

- the persuasiveness of the player with other players;
- the ability to affect other player's objectives in other games, especially domestic political policy games; and
- the other player's perceptions of the agency and its actors' bargaining advantages and ability and willingness to use those advantages.

One might ask, though, why bargaining takes place at all? Why don't people who are clearly more powerful simply give orders or simply command a solution? The answer lies within the very structure of government. Bargaining takes place partly because people who share power see different sides of the same issue. Once decisions are made, they are assigned to specific agencies to be implemented. The specifics on the way the policy is to be implemented are usually not included. Agencies have considerable freedom in implementing decisions handed down to them by policy makers. This fact means that policy decisions tend to be carried out according to the following:

- The less an organization is involved in the decision, the less it will strive to implement that decision. This is particularly true if the decision is harmful (or at least seen to be harmful) to its interests.
- Central decision makers have to bargain to bring lesser players around to their point of view. Central and senior players must convince subordinates that a particular decision is not only good for the country but also in their or their agency's best interests. If they do not, then subordinates will often maneuver to resist the spirit of the decision and restrict the implementation to the letter of the decision, delay implementation, or even disobey the decision.

Consequently, agencies and subordinate players have considerable influence over the type of decisions that will actually be made. Central or senior players cannot or will not make an important decision without seriously considering the wishes of their subordinates—and also without compromising their opinions to meet the wishes of subordinate players.

Other factors that motivate senior players to include their subordinates by compromising and bargaining include:

- leaking information or distorting of information to gain advantage in the bargaining process, often by subordinates, who leak information to damage or prevent a policy that they do not want to see implemented;
- threatening resignation, with all its consequent political fallout; and
- complaining by subordinates to congressional or state legislative committees or to other relevant outside interest groups, thus expanding the bargaining over an issue.

Program evaluation: looking in the mirror

Stages in the Policy Process

The Feedback Effect

Implicit in the concept of the feedback effect in the policy process is the notion that administrative managers learn by doing, by reacting to positive or negative responses to their actions. Figure 8.5 illustrates the feedback effect of the political

---

1960s   Disturbance: Increasing "drug use" culture and rapidly rising crime rates fan public fears of a "crime epidemic."

1970s   Corrective action: Incarcerations increase because of various "get tough on crime" laws enacted by Californians.

1980s   Corrective action: Federal court orders the state to reduce its prison density because it constituted "cruel and unusual" punishment.

Mid-1980s   Corrective action: Some prisons employ early-release programs, and local courts explore alternative sentencing strategies for nonviolent offenders.

Early 1990s   Reaction to corrective action: Recession and continuing rise in crime rates fuels demands for mandatory sentencing and "three strikes and you're out" laws.

Mid-1990s   Corrective action: California's prison construction booms, and the Department of Corrections becomes the state's major growth industry.

Late 1990s   Effects of corrective action: New "disturbance" as state cuts funding for higher education to finance prison boom; court costs rise and court delays increase.

2000   Corrective action: A revived economy produces budget surpluses, and dropping crime rates fuel demands to build more schools and reduce classroom size.

FIGURE 8.5
California's Crime Control Dilemma: How Feedback Affects the Policy Process

---

system in the case of California, which attempted to control crime through incarceration—that is, through a policy that was designed to "warehouse" career criminals.

The feedback effect on policy making is complicated also by the fact that perceptions often change more slowly than does reality. Throughout the 1990s, for example, public opinion polls indicated that people felt the nation was making little progress on or was even losing ground in controlling crime. City streets were considered to be unsafe for anyone walking alone at night. This public perception persisted despite the fact that, beginning in 1991, the violent crime rate dropped steadily throughout the decade and the overall crime rate also consistently fell.

PHOTO 8.1
Overcrowding Afflicts California's Prisons
When federal courts order state prisons to lower their density rates, what value conflicts are inevitably involved?

Source: AP/Wide World Photos.

The Influence of Administrators

Administrators' values enter the policy process during the planning-and-analysis stage. Their view of the nature of the problem to be dealt with and its more likely solutions shapes the broad approach to be enacted in policy. Administrators are often able to define the problem and thereby determine criteria to be used to analyze the policy or program they will ultimately manage. The value that administrators place on cost effectiveness and procedural due process may outweigh the value of public satisfaction desired by the "consumers" of the program or the value of political accountability stressed by elected executive or legislative policy makers. Administrators often have nearly a monopoly on knowledge or specific data about complex public policy issues, which gives them a decided edge in policy design. Agency managers favor approaches that maximize the agency and the empowerment of its personnel in dealing with a problem. Program recipients and elected officials tend to favor approaches that more strictly limit the discretion of program administrators.[8]

Values and Implementation

Public policy involves more than a plan of action. Policy must be implemented. Values enter the process again at the implementation stage. A goal of most government programs is to motivate public employees to work hard and efficiently implement services. State and local governments increasingly attempt to achieve that goal through merit pay or incentive programs. More and more state and local governments, for example, are exploring pay-for-performance programs to motivate their employees, replacing or enhancing pay systems based on longevity, for example. As Box 8.2 demonstrates, the struggle to recruit or retain qualified employees at the federal level highlights the need for program evaluation of their "human capital" to enhance personnel management. It illustrates the use of workforce analysis by the U.S. Census Bureau.

Assessing whether or not a program is working or even if measurable improvements or increased problems can be attributed to a particular program also can prove to be quite tricky. Program assessment, whether internal or external, is another stage at which often-conflicting value perspectives enter the policy process.

Box 8.2

Measuring and Managing Human Capital Intelligence

One of the greatest ironies of the Internet age is that, far from replacing people, as some feared it would, widespread use of advanced technology has confirmed that human talent is truly an organization's greatest asset. Organizations can gain a real advantage by applying Internet technology to the measurement and management of its talent needs—the human capital of the organization.

Government organizations are no exception. Reforms such as the Government Performance and Results Act . . . have taken government to new levels of efficiency and accountability. The President's Management Agenda (PMA) has laid out five government-wide initiatives, . . . including the strategic management of human capital. General Accounting Office (GAO) reports estimate that 31 percent of the federal workforce will be eligible to retire in 2006; . . . [this] represents a major challenge for federal workforce planning.

Over the past 12 months, the Office of Management and Budget (OMB) has ordered every major agency to conduct a workforce analysis. As part of the PMA, OMB and the Office of Personnel Management (OPM) issued a scorecard to rate agencies in their strategic management of human capital. OPM also ordered agencies to develop human resources (HR) accountability systems to track the effectiveness of HR offices and developed a survey to measure employees' satisfaction with workforce management at their agency. . . .

Case Study: US Census Bureau

Since the first population count in 1790, the US Census Bureau has been charged with providing the best mix of timeliness, relevance, quality, and cost of all the data it collects and the services it provides. With responsibilities of this magnitude, Census employees understand the ability to leverage their own internal data; much like the data they collect on citizens, it is highly valuable and important to achieving organizational goals.

Internally, the Census Bureau has volumes of data on each of its 10,000 employees. In the past, when a manager needed personnel information to analyze his or her staff or to make a business decision, the manager called the HR division for a specific report or analysis. The Census HR division discovered that it could not address a large amount of additional reporting needs and keep track of all the reports with its legacy system. The division was overloaded fielding numerous inquiries and manually writing reports. . . .

Using SAS Human Capital Management—a solution that allows organizations to measure and manage HR information in an accurate, integrated way—the bureau began the process of alleviating its data burden. Accessing the bureau's database with SAS Human Capital Management has given these HR analysts the ability to do ad hoc queries and create reports from their desktops—reducing manual reporting. Now they are able to analyze their personnel data at both a summarized and a detailed level, giving them a more accurate picture of the workforce. . . .

Census is making great strides toward meeting and exceeding workforce initiatives and the President's Management Agenda. In fact, in September 2002 Secretary of Commerce Don Evans presented the Census HR division with a gold medal for "exceptional and creative contribution to the automation of HR programs." The medals are the highest awards granted by the Department of Commerce. They recognize leadership, personal and professional excellence, scientific/engineering administrative/technical support, and heroism.

HR professionals need a clear picture of how human capital management initiatives support and add value to the organization's mission. To successfully serve the country, the government needs to focus on activities that add the greatest value to the recruitment and retention of qualified employees. That requires the ability to easily explore, analyze, and present integrated information specific to HR while incorporating information from outside the HR function. HR departments need the technology to make rapid business decisions supported by quantifiable, accurate information. They need the ability to supply the information whenever and wherever it is needed—without relying on the IT department. By recognizing the value of human assets and empowering HR to manage it effectively and efficiently, government can come one step closer to fulfilling its mandate to be citizen-centric and results-oriented.

Source: Nicole Hardee and Betty Silver, Managing human capital, *The Public Manager*, *31*(4) (Winter 2003): 33–36. Reprinted with permission of The Bureaucrat, Inc.

PHOTO 8.2
NASA's Pathfinder—An "Out of This World" Success
How much and what public relations value does an undisputed success such as the Pathfinder program have for NASA? What are the risks to the agency when it has an equally spectacular failure?
Source: AP/Wide World Photos.

The Bald Eagle Protection Act and the Pathfinder Program Examples

Sometimes a program's failure or success is clear to one and all. The program's nature may enable clear-cut assessment. The American bald eagle, once near extinction, has made such a powerful comeback that it is being removed from federal protection. Wildlife experts estimate there were as many as 75,000 nesting bald eagles when it was designated the national bird in 1782. During the 20th century, however, large numbers of the birds were killed by ranchers and farmers who believed them to be predators of their chickens and domestic livestock. The biggest source of their near-extinction, however, became the pesticide DDT, which accumulated in fish, one of these birds' favorite meals. In 1940 Congress enacted the Bald Eagle Protection Act, making it illegal to kill, harass, possess, or sell the bird. By the 1960s, however, due largely to the ravages of DDT, fewer than 450 eagle pairs were believed to exist in the lower 48 states. In 1967 the eagle was declared an endangered species, and in 1972 DDT was banned. Since then, the bird has rebounded dramatically, with more than an estimated 5,000 nesting pairs of bald eagles roaming the countryside.

Space exploration programs provide another good example. When NASA launches a satellite and it is destroyed at launch or is lost in space, the failure cannot be denied or explained away as something other than agency mistakes in implementation. Likewise, when NASA put men on the moon and safely returned them to earth, its success could not be questioned. When the agency's Pathfinder vehicle landed on Mars and beamed back photographs and a wealth of scientific data, its program managers could justly talk of it as an out-of-this-world success.

The Welfare Reform Example

More often, success or failure cannot be so easily attributed to a program. The movement to reform welfare into workfare, for example, began at the state level and culminated in the 1996 national welfare reform law that replaced the AFDC program with the **Temporary Assistance to Needy Families (TANF)** program.[9] President Clinton's administration, as well as Republican congressional advocates of welfare reform, quickly proclaimed it a huge success. In the first year, national welfare rolls dropped by 2 million recipients and to a total below 10 million, the lowest number since 1970; the decade ended with the smallest percentage of the population on welfare since the War on Poverty began. Today, virtually every state has some sort of workfare program. Several states initiated their own welfare reform programs before the 1996 law, using waivers from the AFDC program's regulations.

How clearly the drop off in welfare rolls can be attributed to this new workfare approach is a matter quite different from the Pathfinder program's accepted success. Welfare rolls were declining for nearly two years before Congress enacted TANF. Some states posted declines without ever enacting such reforms. How much the drops are the result of welfare reforms and how much they simply resulted from a robust national economy is a major and still-unanswered question. Almost everyone agrees that the main goal of welfare reform is to get people off welfare rolls and onto payrolls, yet that goal faces difficult structural obstacles. Approximately 30 percent of welfare recipients have long-term physical handicaps, suffer chronic illnesses, or have learning disabilities, alcohol or drug addiction problems, and the like that essentially render them unable to hold full-time jobs. Nearly as many current welfare recipients have no prior work experience, and two-thirds of them lack high school diplomas. Nearly half the recipients have more than two children, making day-care arrangements difficult. In short, a hard core of welfare recipients are unlikely to be helped by counseling, job training, or job placement programs. They may never be able to get and maintain jobs that would keep them above the poverty lines. Economic analysts disagree about whether 5 million jobs are actually available to unskilled mothers. Others argue that even if that many jobs were generated by the economy, most would be so low-paying that they would not lift these workers above the poverty line.[10] If the success of TANF is measured by getting people off welfare rolls and onto payrolls, then the program is doomed to a degree of failure, in that perhaps one-half of recipients will never make it to a viable payroll.

Sometimes, the critics of an agency or program assess it to be such a failure that reform is not possible. Agency critics may propose disbanding the agency altogether or otherwise radically altering the agency beyond a point that might be reasonably seen as reforming it.

Modest and inconsistent results of program evaluation is also common. Box 8.3 presents some reflections of the challenge of program evaluation as they pertain to the evaluation of programs directed to serve families with children who are especially at risk.

Administrators and Measuring Policy Results

Values are inherently involved in any attempt to measure program results. Administrators play a central role in determining such values by typically determining a program's goals and articulating standards of and measures for accomplishing

Box 8.3

Reflections on the Challenges of Program Evaluation

Current evaluation results of the Parents as Teachers (PAT) program revealed that the effects on low-income parents and children were both modest and inconsistent, similar to findings from other evaluations of two-generation programs, especially home-visiting programs. . . .

Policy directives have called for evaluations of programs designed to serve families parenting children who are especially at risk (e.g., PAT; Gomby, Culross, and Behrman, 1999). There is little doubt that this and similar evaluations in the past have provided valuable information regarding the potential effects, as well as the limitations, of a variety of programs. Unfortunately, what many of these large-scale evaluations fail to adequately provide is the kind of information needed to help practitioners and researchers understand the intricacies of the programs and the participants or their interactions with each other. . . .

If we are to meet the challenge of enhancing developmental outcomes and educational achievement . . . for all young children, program evaluation work must move beyond simply measuring intervention outcomes to the equally important task of helping us understand the complex interactions between family and child characteristics, intervention goals addressed, processes employed by the programs, and outcomes. Questions that need systematic attention include the following:

1. What intervention goals are established for specific programs and/or for individual participants?
2. What intervention should be delivered to those goals?
3. How can the interventions be delivered more effectively?

The challenge of supporting the optimal development of all children is huge; we need to capitalize on the effectiveness of all available intervention strategies and programs. Designers, implementers, and evaluators of all intervention programs should think more carefully about the specific theory of change guiding the program, operationalizing that theory of change by developing effective intervention strategies to target identified goals, delivering the intervention with fidelity, and doing careful analyses of what actually occurred during the intervention process. Only then will evaluation yield results that can effectively guide implementation efforts, clarify research directions, and inform policy on behalf of children and families.

Source: Excerpted from Carla A. Peterson, *Topics in Early Childhood Special Education* (Summer 2002): 82–86.

them. Even when outside evaluators assess a government's program, administrators supply much if not all of the data used in the assessment. For example, 35 of the nation's largest city governments (as measured by total revenue) were assessed by *Governing* magazine. The researchers based their conclusions on criteria used to assess five enterprises deemed essential for municipal governance: (1) financial management, (2) human resource management, (3) information technology, (4) capital management, and (5) managing for results. The cities responded to the lengthy surveys and sent piles of supporting documents. Public administration experts at the Maxwell School at Syracuse University joined *Governing* magazine's expert staff in reaching conclusions about the data as well as in conducting interviews with many others both in and out of state and city government. The special role that the leadership of an organization plays in this process is illustrated in Box 8.4, "Organizational Values and Leadership." It focuses on the fact that all too often leaders of organizations begin strategic planning processes without deliberating on certain fundamental questions related to organizational beliefs and core values.

Box 8.4

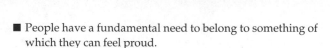

Organizational Values and Leadership

We live in a time when more than ever our values, our core beliefs, are being challenged and questioned. Our governmental, economic, philanthropic, and religious institutions are facing harsh and often-justified scrutiny for fraudulent and abusive behaviors resulting in tremendous psychological and financial losses for thousands of innocent people. As leaders try to chart the direction for their organizations, they cannot help but face these underlying concerns about their enterprise.

Unfortunately, organizational leaders too often plunge into a long-term strategic planning process without first deliberating on certain fundamental questions related to organizational beliefs and values. These questions include: Who are we (core ideology)? Why do we exist (core purpose)? What do we believe in (core values)? What inspires us (envisioned future)? Where are we going (vision statement)? What will we look like when we get there (vivid description)?

Reaching a common understanding about the inherent beliefs in the organization provides a platform for further explorations of the norms of behavior that help define the organization's culture. This exploration, especially if facilitated by a skilled practitioner, also can help reveal the impact that the organization's structure (the system) has on behaviors. By the nature of systems, structure includes how people make decisions—the operating values whereby we translate perceptions, goals, rules, and norms into actions. People often focus on their own decisions and ignore how their decisions affect others. Frequently when an organization is faced with moderate threat or opportunity, people begin to replace old behavior patterns with new ways of thinking and behaving. . . .

Aligning Core and Operating Values

Core values and core purposes in enduring great organizations remain stable, while their operating values—practices, strategies, tactics, processes, structures, and methods—change continually. If vision is the picture we want to create and if mission is the reason why the organization exists, then core values answer the question: "How do we act–what are the norms of behavior that define our culture?" Inevitably, one of the factors that makes significant change difficult is discontinuity between core and operating values and norms.

Core values possess the following characteristics essential to the healthy growth of an organization:

■ Shared core values and purposes ultimately define every individual's membership in the organization.
■ Core values define the desired goal or end state of the culture of the organization.

■ People have a fundamental need to belong to something of which they can feel proud.
■ Shared core values fulfill the deepest needs of every person and create a committed workforce.
■ Core values cannot be determined; they must be an authentic extension of your personal values.
■ Core values are instilled in an organization not by what you say but by what you do!

Unlike core values, operating values are the principles that govern the actual decision-making process in an organization. But because these principles are usually unknown, even denied, they are resistant to change. The paradox of operating values is that while they are resistant to change, they provide the most leverage for creating significant change in an organization. In fact, the ability to align operating values with core values determines the overall health and success of any organization. This alignment creates a high level of trust within the organization. . . .

Leadership and Aligning Values

If one of the keys to every healthy organization is the rigorous alignment between core values and operating values, principles and practices, what is the primary task of the leader today? Today, leadership means influencing the community to face its problems. Leadership means addressing the conflicts in the values people hold—the willingness to expose the internal contradictions within individuals and the organization.

If the leaders of an organization can determine their decision-making principles, and if they can align their decision-making principles with their core values, they can focus the organization, increase performance and productivity, and develop a committed workforce.

One of the major barriers that keeps chief executives and executive directors from having the impact they want to have on their organization is the lack of understanding about the power of aligning core and operating values in creating positive change and high performance. Without this understanding, the focus becomes directed toward changing everyone and everything else rather than focusing on leader behavior and decision making as the real mechanism for forging culture and creating desired changes. Every leader must know the difference between what is sacred and what is not, what should never change and what should always be open to change, and finally between "what we stand for" and "how we do business."

Source: Mark Tannenbaum, Organizational values and leadership, *The Public Manager* (Summer 2003): 19–21. Reprinted with permission of The Bureaucrat, Inc.

The combined research group measured the cities, on the criterion of capital management, by how well each city managed or performed the following:

1. thoroughly analyzed future needs, including
   a. formal capital plans that coordinated and prioritized capital activities,
   b. multiyear linkages between operating and capital budgeting,
   c. multiyear linkages between strategic planning and capital budgeting, and
   d. sufficient data to support analyses;
2. monitored and evaluated projects throughout their implementation; and
3. appropriately maintained capital assets (notably streets and facilities), including generating sufficient data to plan and fund maintenance at adequate levels.[11]

Program Evaluation and Policy Development

We can analytically distinguish policy analysis from program evaluation, although the terms are often used as if they were interchangeable. **Policy analysis** is best viewed as a study to assess the probable effects of a policy. **Program evaluation**, on the other hand, is the systematic examination of all activity undertaken by government to determine both long- and short-term effects of a program already in effect.[12]

Policy analysis generally involves using systematic research models and techniques developed by the social sciences to assess the formulation, execution, and evaluation of policy to establish a more rational policy administrative system. Program evaluation is a type of analysis that focuses on an after-the-fact examination of a policy; it is typically conducted by researchers who are independent from those who actually implement the program.

Since the 1960s, program evaluation has become increasingly prominent and more regularly institutionalized. Sometimes, policy evaluation is undertaken for political purposes—to postpone action, evade responsibility, manipulate public opinion by putting a certain "spin" on a program (often during budget allocation times), or simply fulfill grant requirements.[13] When vested-interest groups are strong enough to form part of an iron triangle and thereby determine policy for a given area, they use program evaluation to promote their favored programs.

Congress established the GAO as its principal agency to conduct program evaluation. Several state governments (notably Hawaii, Wisconsin, and Michigan) have organized similar agencies. Some states (New Jersey, New York, Illinois, and Virginia) have used the legislative commission form to conduct program evaluation. Still other states (Connecticut and North Carolina) have discrete legislative committees that are linked to their appropriate committees and staffed to perform evaluations.[14]

Preauditing program evaluations may require formalized studies to assess likely program effects (financial or environmental, for instance). Most do postaudit studies after a program has been implemented. These postaudits emphasize particular values: authority compliance, equity, efficiency of process, duplication of efforts, and sometimes culpability. Directly political studies emphasize values such as representation and accountability. The purpose of the evaluation shapes the type of evaluation to be conducted and often the type of supporting data to be used, how open it will be to public hearings, whether internal sources or external consultants will be used, and so on. The legislature may require a program review to support an agenda

Box 8.5

Chaos in California: The Perils of Partial Deregulation

January 2001 may have begun the new millennium, but in California it also ushered in an energy crisis. Many observers considered the crisis a classic example of the failure of deregulation. Others saw it as the unanticipated consequences of a policy of partial deregulation.

The basic problem arose in the early 1990s when a coalition of traditional manufacturing firms, led by California's cement and steel industries, both of which use enormous amounts of electricity, were seeking relief from high energy costs. Republican Governor Pete Wilson, who then harbored presidential aspirations, became the driving force behind a historic change in California's energy policy. He seized on deregulation of the state's power utilities as the policy initiative needed to improve the state's economic climate, which was then plagued by a severe recession, and thereby revive his electoral prospects in 1994.

The state's utilities were split on the issue, but Southern California Edison, one of the state's two largest power utilities, and leading businesses in the state joined the fight for the Wilson plan. In August 1996, after a series of marathon hearings chaired by Democratic State Senator Steve Peace, California legislators, in a rare unanimous vote, ratified a deregulation law that was packed with special provisions designed to pacify potential foes.

State regulators who were implementing the new law pushed the utilities to sell many of their generating plants and thus foster competition. The 1996 law required investor-owned utilities to sell power-generating plants to independent (and often out-of-state) generator companies. But economic growth, an enormous expansion in the state's population (approximately 2 million through the decade of the 1990s), water shortages in northern California, and the failure to bring new generating plants online all led to vastly increased demands to which the utilities could not adequately respond.

The law froze retail electric rates until March 2002 or until certain utility costs (largely associated with the closing of nuclear power-generating plants) were paid off. In response to competition, policy makers had expected wholesale costs to drop, allowing the utilities to recover the costs of noneconomical assets such as unused nuclear plants and compete better in the open market. In the summer of 2000, however, wholesale prices soared while retail rates remained frozen, drowning the utilities in red ink: $12 billion worth.

A power exchange opened to set prices each hour based on bids from buyers and sellers. It was opened to a multitude of suppliers and customers to encourage competition. Investor-owned utilities were battered by price spikes on the spot market and were forbidden by law to enter long-term contracts that would stabilize prices. To guarantee open access to electricity buyers and sellers, an independent systems operator (ISO) in Folsom, California, took control of the state's electricity transmission lines from private utilities.

INFOTRAC
COLLEGE EDITION

The integration of tax and spending programs

that legislators have to continue, terminate, or transform a program. Differing functions of government programs lend themselves more or less readily able to collect so-called hard data to be used in the analysis.

Program Evaluation Standards

Program evaluations typically assess the program against the agreed-upon standards of (1) compliance, (2) efficiency, and (3) effectiveness.

Compliance standards rely on auditing: Are the program transactions in accordance with the law? Do they follow prescribed and accepted accounting practices? Are the records accurate and free of fraud? Efficiency analyses examine the productivity of the program versus resources expended: Are tasks clearly defined and properly delegated? Are employees qualified to do the tasks? Is waste avoided? Effectiveness emphasizes whether or not the use of government resources achieves the program's stated purposes or goals: Have problem rates or levels been reduced? Are target groups better off than if the program had not been implemented? Have duplications of effort been avoided?

In the plan, the ISO was expected to balance supply and demand by purchasing an anticipated 5 percent of the state's power, which would be just enough to ensure the system's reliability.

In reality, the ISO became the power purchaser of last resort when a statewide electricity shortage developed. The ISO paid extremely high prices to supply as much as 40 percent of the electricity requirements of investor-owned utilities. Prices soared from less than 7 cents per kilowatt-hour to 13 cents per kilowatt-hour, far more than what it had been costing the utilities to generate their own power. Residential customers had not been motivated to conserve power because their rates were frozen. Wholesale power marketers, mostly out-of-state-owned companies, discovering that they could not make enough profit in the residential market, pulled out. By winter, rates rose to 16 cents per kilowatt-hour on the spot market.

Southern California Edison and Pacific Gas & Electric contend that the $12 billion in losses they incurred since May 2000 pushed them to the brink of bankruptcy. California's Public Utilities Commission (PUC) granted the companies temporary emergency rate hikes of 9 percent for homes and 7–15 percent for businesses. A full-blown case of energy chaos—rolling blackouts and Silicon Valley businesses losing millions of dollars per hour—quickly escalated into a political crisis.

Governor Gray Davis, a Democrat himself harboring presidential ambitions, faced widespread political fallout from the crisis. A poll indicated that nearly two-thirds of California voters believed he had performed poorly in the crisis. Davis hoped the federal government would come to his rescue by placing price caps on wholesale rates.

The Federal Energy Regulatory Commission, however, refused to do so. The incoming administration of George W. Bush was even less friendly to California and Governor Gray Davis's request than the outgoing Clinton Administration. One of the biggest beneficiaries of the California power crisis, in fact, was a Texas energy conglomerate that more than any other single company bankrolled Bush's political career. Enron Corporation of Houston, Texas, was among a handful of a new generation of independent electric power brokers and producers who have reaped giant revenue increases not only from California's power shortages but also from higher natural gas prices nationwide.

Another state politician hurt by the crisis was Loretta Lynch, PUC president. Critics described the PUC's record on utility regulation as "sorry" and believed that the commission's decrees had caused many of the problems. Critics stopped just short of accusing Lynch of lying about the crisis; the legislature's chief auditor, however, was ready to sue her to obtain information on the PUC's role in the crisis.

Likewise, Bill Campbell, the state assembly's newly installed Republican leader, was unable to gain from Davis's troubles because he and senate Republican minority leader, Jim Brulte, had been among the chief architects of the 1996 utility legislation that led to the current mess.

One politician stood to gain from the crisis, however: California state assembly speaker Bob Hertzberg. The Democrat was widely credited by legislators of both parties with moving rapidly and comprehensively on the crisis. Likewise, State Treasurer Phil Angelides—an aspiring Democratic gubernatorial candidate—gained politically by publicly advocating the establishment of a public power authority.

Sometimes, government programs run services that are considered essential and that the private sector has been unable to provide at a reasonable profit. In such cases, government programs may be inherently less efficient but still viewed as nonexpendable; the programs are seen as necessarily being subsidized from general revenues. Amtrak, the national rail passenger service, exemplifies such a program.

At other times, the government may privatize or deregulate a service it has been providing. If not carefully designed and implemented, such deregulation can lead to unintended and dire consequences. Box 8.5 presents the situation in which California found itself after the state government deregulated the electric power industry in 1996. By 2001, prices had skyrocketed, two of the state's major power utilities were facing bankruptcy, and rolling brownouts and blackouts and power shortages swept the state. Many critics called for re-regulating the state's power industry. The state struggled with the crisis and offered to buy electric power lines and was spending billions of dollars on the spot market buying power from out-of-state producers in a chaotic crisis that everyone agreed was an unmitigated political and economic mess.

INFOTRAC
COLLEGE EDITION

Serving children of low-income families

PHOTO 8.3
California Governor Gray Davis Addresses the State's Power Crisis

When California enacted its deregulation plan, then-Governor Pete Wilson and every state legislator anticipated great benefits. What they got was an unprecedented power crisis and fiasco that could cost consumers $10 billion to $20 billion. What were some unanticipated and contributing events in this crisis?

Source: AP/Wide World Photos.

Likewise, local governments have generally had to subsidize mass transit systems. The social benefits of such programs (for the environment, for example) may outweigh the extra costs of subsidizing essential programs from general revenues.

The chapter closes with Reading 8.1, "Deconstructing Research on Systems of Care for Youth with EBD." It explores how the goals of effectiveness, efficiency, and equity can collide and produce contradictory information, exemplified in the state of Vermont's System-of-Care policy framework.

Reading 8.1

Deconstructing Research on Systems of Care for Youth with EBD

Integrated service systems of care for children with severe emotional disturbance based on the systems-of-care framework have historically been viewed and studied as programmatic and clinical interventions. Consequently, researchers have most commonly applied program evaluation methods to study their effectiveness. These methods rely largely on quasi-experimental designs with repeated-outcome measures. Systems of care can also be understood, however, as a set of systems-level policies and principles designed to alter the delivery of services provided to youth and their families. From this perspective, researchers can apply analytical and methodological tools traditionally used in health policy analysis to study the multiple levels of systems-of-care impacts. This article examines how these and other methods for policy analysis can be utilized to measure the impact of the systems-of-care evaluation studies approach. . . .

At its core, the systems-of-care approach is a systemic, policy-oriented change in the structure and delivery of services. . . . The systems-of-care approach is an extraordinarily popular form of service delivery in the United States. CMHS has provided grants to 67 states, communities, and tribal nations for the implementation of systems of care (Holden and Brannan, 2002), and states from California to Vermont have implemented the reforms statewide in their public mental health systems. . . .

The systems level refers to the structure, organization, and financing of services. There are many examples of systemic reform in health services. For example, managed care is predominantly a reform that occurs at the systems level where fiscal changes (such as capitation) and structural changes (such as utilization reviews) are put in place to provide more efficient service delivery. . . . The systems-of-care model emphasizes many systems-level alterations, including developing linkages among child-serving agencies (e.g. mental health, juvenile justice, child welfare, and education), using community-based care in lieu of restrictive placements, developing a continuum of services, restructuring service financing (i.e., blended funding pools), and creating interagency policy and treatment teams for coordinated care. . . .

The knowledge typically generated by health services research regarding the impacts of systemic, programmatic, or clinical service-level reforms can be grouped into three broad categories: effectiveness, efficiency, and equity. . . .

To date, effectiveness research on systems of care has been widely discussed and has focused on a clinical perspective. . . . For example, evidence exists to indicate that a systems-of-care approach can affect county-level placement rates for all youth residing in a county, not just those receiving mental health services. . . .

The second research domain, efficiency, has two key dimensions: productive efficiency (producing services at the lowest cost) and allocative efficiency (maximizing health given constrained resources). . . . The drive for efficiency is a powerful force in the creation of public policy and a key factor in the adoption of efficacious treatments in children's mental health. . . .

Finally, equity relates to health disparities and the fairness and effectiveness of procedures for addressing these inequities. At the most fundamental level, equity has to do with fair access to appropriate and effective services. . . .

The goals of effectiveness, efficiency, and equity can collide and produce contradictory information. A service system may be highly efficient yet ineffective and inequitable. . . . Many of the treatments with the most convincing data regarding efficacy are clearly resource intensive, requiring extensive training and low caseloads when compared to standard outpatient care. . . . Similarly, some efficacious treatments may create serious problems with regard to equity. . . .

Developing the knowledge base for a policy analysis of systems of care is complicated and multifaceted because the systems exist across multiple levels, have multiple goals, are mutable by design, and can be judged by a wide range of criteria. Table 8.1 provides a preliminary framework for this research, including the three core elements of health services research (effectiveness, efficiency, and equity) with the three levels of

TABLE 8.1

A Framework for Understanding and Conducting Services Research on Systems of Care and Sample Research/Evaluation Topics

System Goal	Practice Level	Program Level	System Level
Effectiveness	The effect of a clinical intervention on outcomes	The effect of program philosophy/culture on outcomes	The effect of standards of care, service provision, and/or funding on outcomes
Efficiency	The effect of provider productivity on costs	The effects of staffing choices, provider mix, and/or work hours on costs	The effect of fiscal incentives and service system integration on costs
Equity	The effect of provider choice and decision making on disparities	The effect of program location and accessibility on disparties	The effect of program mix and/or fiscal incentives on disparities

the human service delivery system (practice, program, and system). Table 8.1 also provides examples of potential areas of focus for research and evaluation efforts when the three levels of service delivery are examined within the three primary domains of health services research.

Taken as a whole, the systems-of-care approach may have overall impacts on the effectiveness, efficiency, and equity of a service delivery system; however, not all systems-of-care values or principles are necessarily closely related to these goals. For example, the principle that youth should have access to a comprehensive array of services may well address equity goals more than effectiveness or efficiency goals. Perhaps more directly, the goal of providing services without regard to race, religion, or other distinguishing characteristics of the child or family is clearly tied to equity and intended to reduce disparities in service delivery. On the other hand, family-focused services may link directly to effectiveness, given the research indicating that family involvement relates to positive outcomes; however, its link with efficiency or equity is relatively weaker. . . .

Vermont System-of-Care Policy Framework

In the early 1990s, state policy executives, families, and community partners in Vermont began to work together to agree upon, collect data on, and achieve common state outcomes to improve the well-being of children, families, and communities. . . . The resulting 10 outcomes not only evaluated community efforts, but they are also the basis for state funding and were codified in state law, compelling people to act and contribute to the common goals. . . . The state's Agency of Human Services requires that all departments submit budget requests with justifications showing how their agency will work to achieve the 10 indicators, and as an incentive, the state of Vermont has been willing to negotiate fiscal arrangements with communities. For example, if they can demonstrate achievement of an outcome (e.g., reduction of child abuse or children's out-of-area placements), then communities can keep a percentage of the system's savings to invest in preventive services in their area.

Table 8.2 presents Vermont's system of care with respect to the level of impacts on the three service systems goals and across the three levels of service delivery.

Source: A. Rosenblatt and M. W. Woodbridge, *Journal of Emotional and Behavioral Disorders*, *11*(1) (Spring 2003): 27–38. Copyright 2003 by PRO-ED, Inc. Excerpt and Tables 8.1 and 8.2 reprinted with permission.

TABLE 8.2

The Vermont System of Care: Sample Research Studies by Systems-Level Focus and Impacts on Service System Goals

	Practice	Program	System
	Impact of system respite care	Effect of wrap-around care	Comparison of systems functioning to philosophy and values
Goal			
Effectiveness	High	High	Low
Efficiency	Low	Medium	High
Equity	Low	Low	High

Net Assignment

Using InfoTrac College Edition and Internet search engines, find an analysis of a government program—preferably on the state or local level—and write a précis. Be sure to include a summary of the project itself, the criticisms, the praise, the underlying values that come into conflict, and, if necessary, your recommendation for a solution.

Summary

Conflicting values enter the policy process at various stages. The elitist and bureaucratic politics models of the policy process provide useful conceptualizations. An understanding of policy actors and their varying stakes in policy reveals how different values invariably become involved in the policy process.

Policy analysis is not the same as program evaluation. The latter rests on results-oriented management and process-oriented management styles, each with its own set of value assumptions. Even when evaluators use standards to assess several policy programs at the national, state, and city levels of government, program evaluation remains complex.

Glossary of Key Terms

evaluation research An attempt to assess specific policy options by conducting experiments, assessing their outcomes, and recommending whether or not an experimental policy option should be more broadly implemented.

policy analysis Study to assess the probable effects of a policy.

process-oriented management Style of management that focuses on objectives limited to feedback and process objectives.

program evaluation The systematic analysis of any activity or group of activities conducted by a government to assess short- and long-term effects, both anticipated and unanticipated.

results-oriented management Style of management that stresses realistic, measurable, and outcomes-oriented program objectives.

stakes   How much an individual or an agency stands to gain or lose, depending on the outcome of policy bargaining.

Temporary Assistance to Needy Families (TANF)   Welfare-to-workfare approach enacted in the 1996 federal welfare reform law.

Review Questions

1. Discuss the various values that are evident in the Head Start program.

2. Compare and contrast the elitist model with the bureaucratic politics model of the policy process. How does each model view what determines public policy? How do they differ in the relative roles played by bureaucrats in policy making?

3. Can you discuss the concept of feedback in the policy process? How do modifications in policy result? In what ways are values used to make corrective actions to perceived policy problems?

4. Compare NASA's Pathfinder program with welfare reform and how the success of a program is measured.

5. What values are evident in the case of the effort to reform by integrating Vermont's health care system for children with severe emotional disturbances? How did applied program evaluations assess their effectiveness? What are some of the evaluation roles played by the bureaucracies of the multiple levels of the system of-care delivery for those children? What contradictions in values can you see evident in this reading?

Surfing the Net

The following are useful websites for information on policy evaluation at the national, state, and local levels of government evaluation.

The American Evaluation Association (**http://www.eval.org**) has a wealth of information.

For a variety of financial and audit links, go to FinanceNet (**http://www.financenet .gov**), especially its Accounting site (**http://www.financenet.gov/financenet/start/ topic/accnt.htm#govt**).

The Government Accounting Standards Board (**http://accounting.rutgers.edu/ raw/gasb/index.html**) is a helpful site associated with Rutgers University.

For U.S. government agency evaluations, among the most useful sites is the GAO (**http://www.gao.gov**).

Useful evaluations of state and local governments are found at each state's website, of course, but may also be linked at *Governing* magazine's site (**http://www .governing.com**).

The Government Performance Project (**http://www.maxwell.syr.edu/gpp**) rates states and various localities and cities. The Pew Charitable Trust (**http://www .pewtrusts.com**) funds the project.

Learn about the California power crisis at the Public Utilities Commission (PUC) website (**http://wwwcpuc.ca.gov**).

Much of California's power is generated by hydroelectric plants in the Pacific Northwest. Check the website for the California Water Resources Control Board (**http://www.swcb.ca.gov**).

Chapter 9

Personnel Administration and Unionism in Public Administration

In a case of first impressions, a federal judge has held that the Hatch Act, which bars federal employees from running for office, does not violate the U.S. Constitution's Qualifications Clause.

Roger Merle, a postal worker and the Green Party candidate for Congress in the Second District, sought an emergent declaration that the Hatch Act unlawfully added to the constitutional qualifications, arguing that he would lose his mail-carrier job if he tried to campaign.

This law "does not prevent . . . participation as a candidate . . . but instead constitutes a valid attempt on the part of Congress to insulate public employees from partisan political influence," U.S. District Judge Joseph Irenas wrote in *Merle* v. *United States,* Civ. 02-3469.

Irenas likened the Hatch Act, 5 U.S.C. 7323, to other "resign-to-run" laws that have been upheld as constitutional. The statute has withstood many challenges since it was enacted in 1939, including a First Amendment challenge in 1973.

Mary Gallagher
Judge upholds Hatch Act prohibition . . .,
New Jersey Law Journal, 169(12) (September 16, 2002): 7.

Introduction

The opening vignette reveals a value conflict that has perennially plagued personnel administration in government: how to balance partisan political neutrality with the freedom of individuals who happen to be public employees and their protected rights as employees. It illustrates problems common to managing personnel at all levels.

This chapter discusses personnel management and the clash of values involved in that most basic of public administration activities. **Public personnel administration** can be defined as the totality of government organization, policies, procedures, and processes used to match the needs of public agencies with the people who staff those agencies.[1] This chapter examines who local, state, and federal government agencies employ and how the agencies go about selecting them. The chapter also traces the major developments in personnel administration, from the period of patronage and the spoils system to the development and spread of the civil service and merit systems and to efforts to reform or revise the civil service. We also assess the influence of public employee unionism and how it has accentuated the clash of values in personnel management.

Personnel refers both to the employees of an organization and to the function and administrative unit responsible for hiring. Personnel management involves position classification, recruitment and selection, collective bargaining, performance appraisal, training and development, and labor relations functions. Historically, personnel administration shifted from emphasizing the value of responsiveness to emphasizing politically neutral competence among public employees. A notable development was the establishment and spread of the **civil service** system, which refers to all non-military employees of government and is sometimes considered a **merit system** (an approach to staffing based on formal qualifications for selecting, retaining, and promoting employees) as opposed to both the **spoils system** and the **patronage system**, which select employees and award government contracts on the basis of party affiliation or loyalty.

In recent years, personnel managers have struggled with how best to balance the need for neutral competence with the value of democratic representativeness. They also have struggled with the value and issue of diversity within the workforce: How can public service agencies draw employees who more nearly represent the general social groupings in the population? Finally, an emphasis on neutral competence and professionalism intensified debate over the issue of accountability.

Public-sector personnel administration and management differs somewhat from that of the private sector. Democratic political institutions and values implicitly constrain public personnel management in various ways. The public realm must acknowledge and reflect the wishes and needs of an agency's clientele groups, professional associations of employee unions, interest groups, political parties, and the mass media. Personnel processes also help determine who makes and implements public policy. These processes must balance demands that inherently involve conflict—improve productivity, protect employee rights, promote affirmative action hiring and promotion practices—yet reflect the traditional merit system reforms. Personnel hiring and training practices often clash with values from partisan political debate and conflict that, in turn, affect public agencies through elected political executives and legislators as well as the principles and values promoted by public employee unions (seniority as an overarching basis for promotion, for example, or standardized across-the-board pay increases rather than merit-based pay schemes).

The rapidly changing environments within which public agencies operate—the political, social, cultural, and economic—increases demands for flexibility, adaptability, and the need to hire or train staff to keep up with rapid technological development. Yet those demands are placed on a hierarchical structure with long established and frequently entrenched standard operating procedures that are often highly resistant to change.

Public personnel management also developed historically in ways that reflected broader social and political trends. Scholars, in fact, have distinguished the following six phases in public personnel administration:[2]

1. From 1789 to 1829, government by "gentlemen" emphasized nepotism and limited entry into government service to just the landed gentry of U.S. society.

2. From 1829 to 1837, government by the "common man" emphasized the spoils system, political party patronage (hiring based on *who* one knew), and strong political executives.

3. From 1883 to 1906, government by the "good" was marked by a self-conscious egalitarianism and intensive idealism, reforms to create the civil service system, a strong desire to replace patronage with a merit system at all levels of government, and, above all else, government efficiency.

4. From 1906 to 1937, government by the "efficient" promoted scientific management and the values of merit, morality, neutrality, and science. The civil service merit system (hiring based on *what* one knows) was expanded to cover some 80 percent of the government workforce.

5. From 1937 to 1955, government by "administrators" spearheaded the growing professionalization of employees and reforms of administrative structures in response to Franklin Roosevelt's vigorous New Deal leadership.

6. From 1955 to the present, government by "professionals" has been characterized by the use of service entrance exams, expansion of the civil service system, extension of professionalism in public service, and the increasing power of professional associations of employees who have been incorporated into administrative processes.

Merit management and neutral competence

Public-sector employment has grown dramatically in recent decades, particularly as the United States has emerged as the world's superpower. Collectively, local governments employ more than 13.2 million workers. State governments employ nearly 5 million, and the national level employs nearly 3 million (*Statistical Abstract of the United States, 2003,* Table 500). At all levels, public employee unionism has increased dramatically. Among all government civilian employees, of whom about 87 percent are employed at the state and local levels and 13 percent at the federal level, about 50 percent are unionized (Tables 656 and 658).

Affirmative Action and Reverse Discrimination

The struggle to ensure that government employees better reflect the increasingly diverse U.S. population has been long and contentious. A major policy effort to ensure diversity involved what are now known as **affirmative action** programs—policies and programs intended to bring into public service or to promote minority citizens who previously had been excluded: women, African Americans, Hispanic Americans, and

Native Americans. Affirmative action programs (discussed more fully later) have affected all levels of government as agencies attempted to add people of more diverse racial, ethnic, and gender backgrounds to their staffs. The administrative processes implemented to do so used "targets" that frequently came to be viewed as "quotas." In fact, the use of fixed quotas by government agencies for hiring and promoting as well as for awarding government contracts to private-sector businesses, was ruled to be **reverse discrimination**—that is, compensation for past discrimination that discriminates against members of the majority (mostly white males).

The Functions of Personnel Administration

The personnel function is often structured so that it is performed by a separate staff agency that serves line management. This function and the separate unit that performs it are often called **human resource development (HRD)**, and that agency is responsible for administering and making policy for people and positions in the public sector. The term better connotes the multiplicity of functions associated with personnel management. More than 90 percent of all executive branch employees are covered by some sort of civil service system. At the national level, the system is administered by the **Office of Personnel Management (OPM)**. Most state governments and most larger city and county local governments have similarly centralized offices. Personnel functions commonly conducted by a human resource development agency include

- position classification,
- recruiting and selecting employees,
- negotiating with collective bargaining units (i.e., labor relations with unions),
- doing performance appraisals of current employees, and
- conducting training and professional development events.

Each function is described more fully next.

Position Classification and the General Schedule System

Position classification organizes jobs under a civil service system into classes based on job descriptions that denote similarities of duties and responsibilities, delineate authority, establish chains of command, and detail pay scales. The number of positions covered under the competitive merit system grew steadily from approximately 10 percent when the federal system began with the Pendleton Act in 1883 to more than 85 percent after World War II—and more than 90 percent by the mid-1970s[3]; currently it is at 93 percent. After Congress enacted the Intergovernmental Personnel Act of 1970, federal grant requirements helped spread the merit system to state and local levels.

Position classification is central to personnel administration. At the federal level, jobs are classified into various levels, or grades, in the **General Schedule (GS)** system, the pay scale and job classification system that has rating levels 1 through 15. Grades GS 1 to GS 4 are lower-level positions, typically secretarial and clerical. Grades GS 5 to 11, middle-level positions, are divided into two subschedules. The first subschedule covers technical, skilled craft, and senior clerical positions (GS 6, 8, and 10). The second covers professional career grades (GS 5, 7, 9, and 11). GS 5 and 7 career grades are typically the entry-level positions for college graduates. Grades GS 12 through 15 are upper-level positions. Table 9.1 presents data on the federal GS

TABLE 9.1

Federal Employment by Salary Level, Race, Hispanic Origin, 2002

GS Level	Salary Level ($)	Total Number	Black (%)	Hispanic (%)
GS-01–GS-04	13,870–24,833	55,005	43.3	15.1
GS-05–GS-08	21,370–38,108	237,807	40.3	0.4
GS-09–GS-12	29,577–61,040	405,583	21.3	8.4
GS-13–GS-15	55,837–100,897	275,562	12.9	5.2
Total, executives, senior level		15,428	7.8	3.8

Note: Amounts in 2002 dollars. Pay schedules effective January 2002.

Source: Based on data from *Statistical abstract of the United States, 2003*, Table 502.

system, listing by these grade-level groupings, the salary level (as of 2002), the number of positions, and the percentage of workers at each grade level who are African American and Hispanic American.

Senior Executive Service

Above the GS system is the **Senior Executive Service (SES)**, which was established in 1978 by the Civil Service Reform Act. It is intended to promote professional growth, mobility, and versatility among upper-grade career officers and some political appointees, or what are referred to as the *supergrades*. Salaries begin at $100,000 per year, and officers in the SES are eligible for performance bonuses within their pay grades.

In the typical civil service system, employees with greater seniority (measured as years of service) have privileges over those with lesser seniority, allowing them to transfer to different departments and agencies without losing pension benefits or grade levels. Such interagency mobility benefits both the employee who searches for new opportunity and challenge and the employer agency that looks for staff members with skills and experience. State merit systems show higher mobility, and employees move up those ladders more rapidly than in the federal system.

Basically all civil service classification systems operate under the same five principles:[4]

1. Positions, not individuals, should be classified.

2. Duties and responsibilities characterize and distinguish a position or mark its similarity to other positions.

3. Qualifications—in education, knowledge, experience, and measurable skills—are identified as necessary for certain duties based on the nature of those duties; these are important ingredients in determining how the position is classified.

4. Individual characteristics of an incumbent employee should not bear on how the position is classified.

5. People holding positions in the same class should be viewed as equally qualified for any other position in that class.

INFOTRAC
COLLEGE EDITION

The Senior Executive Service: gender, attitudes and representative bureaucracy

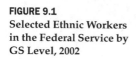

FIGURE 9.1
Selected Ethnic Workers in the Federal Service by GS Level, 2002

Source: Based on data from *Statistical abstract of the United States, 2003*, Table 502.

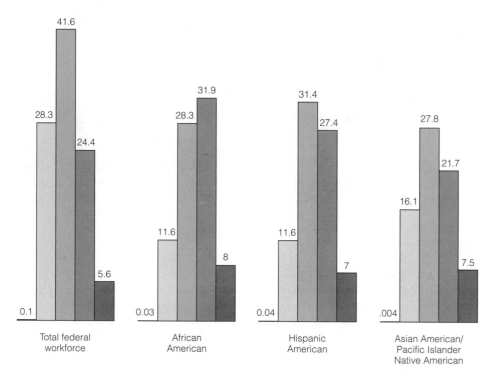

The increasingly diverse U.S. population has brought greater diversity to the government workforce, although those of minority background are still concentrated at the lower GS levels. Figure 9.1 presents data for selected ethnic workers in the federal service as of 2002.

Recruitment

Once positions have been described and classified, they need to be filled, a process that involves recruitment and selection. **Recruitment** is the process of advertising job openings and soliciting candidates to apply for them. It attempts to secure adequate numbers of qualified candidates for an agency from which managers can choose. How easy or difficult that task is varies greatly, depending on the level of the position, general socioeconomic conditions, the level of government, the type of agency seeking staff members, and how rigorous and organized is the competition from private-sector employers. Many positions, especially at the entry level and for local governments, require that individuals be employed within the jurisdiction. Outsiders may not be admitted to take promotional exams; for example, police officers who apply for a lieutenant's examination must be currently employed police sergeants, and only currently employed police officers are eligible to take the sergeant's examination.

Some occupational fields may have special recruiting needs or problems. A recent article, for example, noted such for the corrections field:

> Corrections is like a mosaic—a conglomeration of various parts, pieces, shapes, colors, and patterns that come together to form a work of art. In corrections, the conglomeration of components is assembled to create a viable organization. Corrections must attract people of varied interests who represent the diversity that is necessary to successfully respond to the complex needs of the organization. As in assembling a mosaic, corrections' job is to attract and select all the right components in seeking to build its workforce.
>
> Each correctional entity has unique features, each with very distinct characteristics that are influenced by geographic location, political inclinations, culture, etc. These characteristics, when combined, influence the organization by shaping its mission, vision, objectives, and operations. However, despite the individual uniqueness of corrections settings, there are some common goals—public safety and a desire to return offenders to their communities as more responsible citizens. A common challenge is the selection and retention of the right staff to meet those objectives. However, each entity has its own set of challenges that come into play when attempting to hire the right staff who will be responsible for making the organization work effectively. (Clark and Layman, 2004: 80)

Similarly, some fields evidence chronic, if cyclical, crises in being able to recruit and retain an adequate staff level. Nursing is a prime example. One nursing executive recently noted that situation:

INFOTRAC
COLLEGE EDITION

The nursing shortage: strategies for recruitment and retention

> According to an old joke, a nurse dies and stands before St. Peter. She is given a choice of going to heaven or the "other place." She is allowed to spend 3 days in each place before making a final decision. She goes to hell first, which she is surprised to find is a really wonderful place, nothing like what she's been told. She then goes to heaven, which is also nice but not nearly as great as hell was, so despite the rather unorthodox decision, she chooses to go to hell. However, when she arrives to take up residence she finds it is now the exact opposite of what it was 3 short days ago. The environment is toxic, the people are in agony, and it is absolutely horrific. When she asks the devil what has happened, the devil replies, "Nothing has happened. It's just that yesterday you were being recruited, today you are staff."
>
> Unfortunately, many nursing educational institutions and nursing practice environments have collectively set up nurses for exactly the same type of experience. Students newly admitted to our nursing school say the same thing. They are there because they want to care for patients. Yet, when they get out and begin their practice, they inevitably tell me that they cannot take adequate, proper, and in some cases even safe care of their patients in the present practice environment. This sense of frustration and disillusionment eventually drives many of them out of medical-surgical nursing and into something else or, worse, out of nursing entirely.
>
> Very little research reveals what can be done within the existing health system to recruit and retain nurses, or if what has been done is making any difference in the attitudes and satisfaction of nurses in the long run. It seems that every few years we see a nursing shortage and throw money at the problem through recruitment

bonuses, government scholarships, and media advertisements. These seem to work in the short run. Then the nurses recruited enter the same environment as their predecessors, and it isn't very long before another nursing shortage is looming on the horizon. (E. West, 2004: 346–347)

Examinations test skills used in varying agencies, yet they must be specific enough to test for the skills and competencies needed for a given agency and position. Increasingly, governments use multiple exams: one to test general skills levels and then more specialized tests, interviews, and written work that are submitted by each applicant. General exams tend to be written and standardized, although some incorporate oral portions. For middle- and upper-level positions, a combination of written and oral examinations, personal interviews, background education, experience, and written statements is employed to evaluate applicants.

Courts have examined the validity of exams—that is, how well they actually test for the required skills and job-related factors. Built-in bias in tests has come under increasing court scrutiny. The Professional and Administrative Career Exam (PACE), for example, became the focus of lawsuits brought against OPM by Hispanic Americans and African Americans in 1979; they alleged that the exam was culturally biased and tested for aspects of knowledge not required for the 118 job categories for which it was used to screen applicants. The Reagan Administration abolished PACE in 1982.[5] Under the Bush Administration, in May 1990 OPM instituted a new exam: the Administrative Careers with America (ACWA).

Typically, when an agency has a position open or a new position approved, it notifies the centralized personnel office, which recruits applicants and often administers a qualifying examination. The names of qualified applicants are placed on a register that indicates they are officially under consideration for appropriate positions as they become available within the bureaucracy. The centralized personnel office sends to the agency the names of those it found qualified for the described position, typically following the so-called rule of three: sending three names at a time to the agency with a position to fill. A veteran's preference is another frequently used guideline. All veterans who pass the general exam with a certain minimum score receive bonus points. Veteran bonuses have been criticized for their discriminatory effect against women. They also illustrate the clash of values inherent in the selection process: affirmative action and merit versus a veterans preference.[6]

How well the federal government has done in recruiting minority-background employees into the federal service also is shown in Figure 9.1, which presents data for selected ethnic workers in the federal service as of 2002. Figure 9.2 compares the success of the private sector and the federal government in recruiting and selecting minority applicants by presenting data on selected racial and ethnic groups.

Collective Bargaining

A related function of personnel administration deals with employees after they are recruited and selected, **collective bargaining**—that is, bargaining by a **union** on behalf of a group of employees as opposed to an individual worker representing him- or herself. The centralized personnel agency is formally charged with representing management in the collective bargaining process with public employee unions. State and local governments often mandate collective bargaining.

In recent years, public employee unions have grown in number, size, and militancy. For example, the four largest public employee unions nationally are the

INFOTRAC
COLLEGE EDITION

Minority recruitment for the 21st century

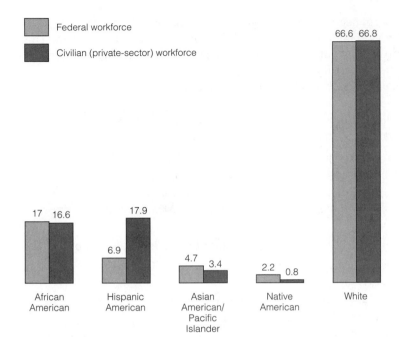

☐ Federal workforce

☐ Civilian (private-sector) workforce

FIGURE 9.2
**Selected Racial and Ethnic Groups in Federal
Civil Service Compared with the National
Workforce, 2002**
Source: Based on data from *Statistical abstract of the United States,
2003*, Tables 500, 587, 589.

National Education Association, the American Federation of State, County, and Municipal Employees, the Service Employees International Union, and the American Federation of Teachers. Their combined growth exceeded 22 percent, and their membership now totals over 6 million. These unions are affiliated with the American Federation of Labor–Congress of Industrial Organizations (AFL-CIO) the nation's largest "umbrella" union organization.

Many personnel issues and procedures that in past years were strictly determined by management are now partly shaped by employee union–won provisions in negotiated labor contracts. Employee contracts determine the distribution of responsibility on the job as well as pay rates for work performed, a host of provisions that govern the presentation and resolution of grievances, and general workplace conditions. Unions now share with management a voice in directing an agency, and public management of labor often involves multilayer bargaining. Unions of public employees can have a strong voice in policy where their workers have a virtual monopoly on providing an essential service, such as police and fire protection, solid waste disposal, and sanitation. A strike (or, where illegal, a "blue flu" or work slowdown) can be nearly devastating to a local community. A garbage collectors' strike in a city such as New York can quickly reach crisis proportions.

Professional organizations of public employees are increasingly involved in collective bargaining. Huge public employee unions, such as the American Federation of State, County, and Municipal Employees (AFSCME), the National Education Association (NEA), and the American Federation of Teachers (AFT), have become more involved and more militant.[7] Labor relations today typically involve top management, personnel offices, employee supervisors, community special-interest groups, and employee unions, all of them involved in complex bargaining. States such as California and New York have **sunshine bargaining laws** requiring in areas such as education that proposals be publicly discussed before governing bodies such

INFOTRAC
COLLEGE EDITION

**Fact-finding in state and
local government**

as school boards begin negotiations with teachers' unions. Such laws are designed to guarantee a voice by the public in setting the parameters of the negotiations. This step ensures formal roles for organized public groups such as parent–teacher associations and taxpayers' associations.

A typical bargaining cycle involves the following 10 steps:[8]

1. An organizing effort is followed by a particular union's seeking recognition as the bargaining agent for a group of employees.

2. A bargaining team is jointly selected by management (typically the OPM or HRD agency or office) and employees.

3. The scope of bargaining is determined—that is, what will or will not be covered in the contract and what elements are constrained by legislative or executive limits.

4. Proposals and counterproposals are set forth by management and union negotiators.

5. A tentative agreement is reached.

6. The tentative agreement is submitted for a ratification vote by employees and approval by senior management.

7. If agreement cannot be reached or if the tentative agreement is rejected, then an attempt is made to resolve the impasse. An **impasse resolution** process occurs when, during labor negotiations, either labor or management concludes that no further progress can be made toward a settlement. Typically, the resolution process leads to one or more impasse procedures: mediation, fact-finding, arbitration, or referendum.

8. A potential strike is discussed.

9. Once a contract is signed, its provisions are implemented (referred to as *contract administration*; it involves both management staff and union representatives).

10. The process or sequence begins again, starting at the second step.

Box 9.1, "Screening on the Cheap," illustrates some problems for federal employees, in this case airport security screeners, when they are not allowed to unionize and engage in collective bargaining.

Performance Appraisal

Another major function of personnel management is evaluation of current employees. **Performance appraisal**, the formal method of assessing an employee's work performance, is used for decisions about retention and promotion as well as to document any disciplinary action taken with respect to an employee. Appraisal is an essential but often-difficult task for supervisors. Writing useful and objective performance reports is challenging, so personnel offices frequently attempt to improve the process by developing "objective" evaluation forms. This counters the strong tendency of supervisors to make appraisals that are subjective, impressionistic, or cannot be compared with ratings done by other evaluators.

Box 9.1

Screening on the Cheap

It's risky up there, on the front lines of the war against terrorism. You work long hours under constant pressure not to make a single mistake, not to let a single weapon or potential weapon escape your notice, not to permit a single shady character slip by while at the same time not discriminating against any class of travelers. In return, at least, you get the thanks of a grateful nation—if not plaudits and parades, at least decent pay and respect on the job.

Or not. George W. Bush's administration wants its Americans to feel safe in the air, but that doesn't mean it wants American workers to feel too safe in their jobs. On January 9 [2003], Adm. James Loy, the undersecretary of transportation and security, denied the nation's 56,000 airport-security screeners the right to join a union and bargain collectively for higher pay and better working conditions. "Mandatory collective bargaining is not compatible with the flexibility required to wage war against terrorism," Loy said.

If the airport-security screeners feel they've been arbitrarily discriminated against, they're right. City police officers form unions and bargain collectively. So do the transit police at airports and train and bus stations. So do baggage handlers, pilots, and flight attendants. So do the civilian employees of the Pentagon.

And it's not as if the baggage screeners have no reason to organize. Employees have long complained of working shifts so long that their ability to detect signs of danger has diminished. Not surprisingly, the American Federation of Government Employees had embarked on a nationwide organizing campaign of screeners. But it was to keep this very thing from happening that the administration went to the wall in the fight over the homeland-security bill. For the White House, the issue was a twofer: It stuck it to unions and to Democrats, who, by opposing the bill that stripped workers of their rights, rendered themselves vulnerable to security demagogy in the November elections.

Source: *The American Prospect*, *14*(2) (February 2003): 6.

Performance appraisal is designed to meet several purposes and to promote certain values. It is intended to change improper, inefficient, and dysfunctional work behavior. Appraisals share management's views about the quantity or quality of an individual's work performance as well as his or her future potential. Performance appraisal guides decisions about employee training and recommendations for possible promotion. It may assess whether the current duties of a position have the appropriate compensation level. It documents disciplinary actions and any decision to separate or fire an employee.

Common Performance Appraisals

There are five common types of performance appraisal:[9] supervisor ratings, self-ratings, peer ratings, subordinate ratings, and group ratings.

- *Supervisor ratings.* This is the most common type of appraisal and may or may not involve a standardized appraisal form. The employee's immediate supervisor rates the employee's job performance.

- *Self-ratings.* An employee rates him- or herself using a standardized form, often with a narrative report on his or her own work or submitting work products to substantiate performance.

- *Peer ratings.* Each individual rates every other employee in his or her own work unit.

- *Subordinate ratings.* Subordinates rate a supervisor's performance.

TABLE 9.2

A Comparison of Various Performance-Appraisal Methods

Performance-Appraisal Objectives	Forced Distribution Rankings	Personal Trait Scales	Checklists	BARS	Management by Objectives
Validation of selection technique	Poor	Poor	Good to very good	Good to excellent	Fair to good
Rationale for personnel decisions	Fair to good	Poor to fair	Fair to very good	Good	Good to fair
Measuring performance accurately	Poor to fair	Poor to fair	Good to very good	Good	Good to excellent
Feedback and development	Poor	Poor to fair	Good to very good	Very good	Fair to good
Assessing training needs	Poor	Poor to fair	Good to very good	Very good	Fair to good
Allocation of rewards	Good to very good	Fair	Very good to excellent	Very good to excellent	Good to excellent

Source: Adapted from Richard W. Beatty and Craig E. Schneier, *Personnel administration: Experiential skill-building approach*, 2nd ed., pp. 106–107. © 1981. Adapted by permission of Pearson Education, Inc., Upper Saddle River, NJ.

INFOTRAC
COLLEGE EDITION

High tech and high performance: managing appraisal in the information age

■ *Group ratings.* An independent person—often an outsider recognized as a qualified expert—rates the performance of an entire work unit based on selected interviews or on-the-job visits; the visits are often for periodic program review purposes (for example, once every five years).[10]

Table 9.2 compares various performance-appraisal methods and assesses them from poor to excellent according to how well each method achieves certain objectives: validation, rationale for personnel decision making, accuracy of performance measure, usefulness for employee feedback and development, usefulness for assessing training needs, and usefulness for allocating rewards (incentives).

Training and Development

Training employees is a responsibility common to HRD agencies and offices, although it is most often the first and sometimes the most deeply cut responsibility during cutbacks. In public agencies, an emphasis on the training function developed long after it had become common in the private sector. Congress passed the first law on the issue, the Government Employees Training Act, in 1958, but the U.S. Civil Service Commission did not establish a management training facility until 1968, when it chartered the Federal Executive Institute at Charlottesville, Virginia. Federal funds were not allocated to grants to state and local governments to assist training programs until the Intergovernmental Personnel Act in 1970. These grants ended during the cutbacks of the mid-1980s.

To be effective, training programs must be evaluated and then incorporated into broader employee-development goals. Public-sector training programs are often superficially evaluated, if at all, and commonly contracted out to private providers. Sometimes a provision for training is included in government contracts (for equipment, software, and so on), with the private-sector provider of equipment or technology agreeing to train employees in its use.[11]

Public Employee Strikes and Job Actions

The threat or actual use of a strike is the ultimate tool workers have when bargaining with management. A strike is an agreement among workers to temporarily stop work; it is designed to obtain or resist some change in working conditions or pay level. Unions consider the strike an essential tool of collective bargaining, and public employee unions have used it in the past, although less frequently since the 1980s. Union activism in the 1960s and 1970s was often engaged in obtaining the legal right to collective bargaining or to strike.[12]

Especially where strikes are illegal, unions sometimes use alternative "job actions." Firefighters come down with a "red rash," police officers with a "blue flu," teachers with "chalk-dust fever" or "sick-ins," and sanitation workers with "slowdowns." Another ploy is for police officers to exercise their powers to write traffic tickets and make arrests to the full extent and strict letter of the law. These job actions are designed to engender public opinion pressures on legislatures or agency management during periods of contract negotiations. During the past couple of decades, many states have passed comprehensive public employee relations laws. As a result of such laws and the economic downturn or recession of the early to mid-1990s, labor strife generally declined. States that permit at least some public employee strikes include Alaska, California, Hawaii, Idaho, Illinois, Minnesota, Montana, Ohio, Oregon, Pennsylvania, Vermont, and Wisconsin.[13]

Rights of Employees

Job actions, strikes, and public employees' labor union activism are intended to guarantee the rights of public employees beyond wages and working condition issues within contract negotiations and agreements. These rights may deal with processes and procedures concerning a **reduction in force (RIF)**, or public employee layoffs. They often concern issues of what type of work can be contracted out to the private sector—that is, through privatization. They involve such values as employee rights to privacy and the rights of employees to participate voluntarily in political activities.

Through legislation and court rulings, public employees have established many legal rights and protections, the more notable of which are summarized here.[14]

1. Employees have a *right to join a union*, although there is no constitutional right to collective bargaining.[15] The National Labor Relations Act of 1935 (known as the Wagner Act) protects both public- and private-sector workers' exercise of the full freedom of association, self-organization, and their right to designate representatives of their own choosing for purposes of negotiating terms and conditions of their employment as well as for other mutual aid or protection.

2. The Supreme Court has ruled that the constitutionally protected *freedom of association* prohibits "union shops" that require all employees to join a union.[16]

3. The Court also has ruled that unions can collect *agency fees* (union dues withheld from a paycheck) but only with an adequate explanation as to the

basis of the fees, with a member having the prompt opportunity to challenge the amount of the fee before an impartial decision maker, and with an escrow account for any amounts in dispute while such challenges are pending.[17]

4. Public employees do have the right to express themselves and their views in matters of public policy in public forums.[18] This decision by the Supreme Court limited prior restrictions placed on the voluntary political activities by public employees by the Hatch Acts of 1939 and 1940.

5. In 1996, the OPM revised its rules on privatization. These rules now require employee involvement in decisions on whether to contract out a function or produce it in-house.[19]

6. The Civil Service Reform Act of 1978 stipulates several principles to govern federal employee relations that protect the following rights:

   a. Fair and equitable treatment in personnel management matters without regard to race, color, religion, national origin, sex, marital status, age, or physically handicapping condition and with proper regard for the individual's privacy and constitutional rights

   b. Equal pay for equal work

   c. Retention of employees who perform well

   d. Protection against arbitrary action, personal favoritism, and political coercion

   e. Protection of employees against reprisal for lawful disclosure of information (a whistle-blower provision).

INFOTRAC
COLLEGE EDITION

Georgia state merit system

Box 9.2, "Bush Invokes Rare Process," highlights the recent use of a recess appointment by the Bush Administration to appoint to an official civil rights enforcement position an individual with the values and perspectives desired by the administration but vehemently opposed to by the NAACP.

The Historical Development of Personnel Administration

The power of political parties to determine who worked for government that predominated during the era of the spoils system (1829–1883) led to corrupt excesses in which public service often involved bribes and graft. These excesses gave rise to a reform movement that had a primary goal of ridding government service of those bureaucrats who owed their positions solely to party loyalty—so-called party hacks. From the end of the Civil War until 1883, reformers struggled to incorporate into government service the concept of merit—the heart of the civil service reform movement.[20] The assassination of President James Garfield by a disgruntled office seeker was the incident that propelled legislation through Congress.

The Pendleton Act

In 1883, Congress enacted the Civil Service Act, better known as the Pendleton Act, after the name of its sponsor. It was signed into law by President Chester A. Arthur on January 16, 1883. It created a bipartisan civil service commission responsible to the president to fill government posts by a process of open competitive exams, probationary periods, and protection against political pressure. Its primary focus was to eliminate the use of patronage.

Box 9.2

Bush Invokes Rare Process

In 2002, Gerald Reynolds was the White House choice to fill the vacant slot of assistant education secretary responsible for the department's Office for Civil Rights. Reynolds, an African American, served as president and legal counsel for the Center for New Black Leadership, a conservative group. He also served as legal analyst for another conservative organization, the Center for Equal Opportunity. His private-sector experience includes senior counsel at Kansas City Power and Light.

But Reynolds' past statements on civil rights enforcement drew harsh criticism from many left-leaning organizations. People for the American Way, a Washington-based organization, urged groups to oppose the nomination, and the NAACP also was against his selection.

"Reynolds has consistently called for the elimination of a variety of programs that have helped racial and ethnic minorities, as well as women, the elderly, and disabled Americans," said Kweisi Mfume, NAACP's president and chief executive officer. "It is inconceivable that a person with such strong convictions should be charged with implementing and protecting the laws for which he has shown such contempt."

Critics of affirmative action criticized President Bush for installing a new civil rights chief at the U.S. Department of Education without Senate confirmation. Bush invoked the rarely used recess appointment process to bring Gerald Reynolds into the administration as assistant education secretary in charge of the Office of Civil Rights. Reynolds had been nominated for the job in June 2002 but faced strong opposition from many liberal organizations for his views on affirmative action and civil rights. It was unclear that the Senate would approve the nomination.

Because of that uncertainty, Bush appointed Reynolds to the job without Senate endorsement through a process known as a recess appointment. Such appointments can be made when Congress is out of session, and lawmakers were away for the Easter and Passover holidays.

Source: Based on excerpts from *Black Issues in Higher Education, 19*(3 & 5) (March 28 and April 25, 2002): 10 & 8, respectively.

The Pendleton Act was hardly sweeping in nature. Initially, it covered approximately 10 percent of federal positions. Over the years, Congress gradually expanded its coverage and established other, similar merit systems to cover other agencies, such as the TVA and the foreign service, or diplomatic corps. By the end of World War I, coverage had risen to approximately 70 percent. Today 94 percent of federal positions are covered. The Pendleton Act became the basis for a detailed system of classification that developed later with practical entrance exams keyed to specific positions. The act allowed for an open civil service by specifically enabling lateral entry for all positions. The U.S. civil service system avoided ties such as those found in the British civil service system between public service and specific universities. Likewise, it did not set up a special administrative class of permanent undersecretaries. Top-level positions were to be responsive and occupied by political executives. The primary value of the Pendleton Act was to promote government efficiency by ending political corruption. It emphasized values of ethics and egalitarianism and only incidentally addressed managerial effectiveness.

Expansion of civil service systems at the state and local levels, as in the federal system, was gradual. By 1935, only 12 states had established formal systems. After World War II, the trend accelerated, and today nearly all states have some general merit system and 36 states have comprehensive coverage. At the local level, only a few cities had merit systems by 1900. By the 1930s, several hundred cities had such a system, and today only some 10 percent of cities with populations in excess of 25,000 lack merit systems. Now approximately 95 percent of municipal employees are covered. Counties use civil service systems less extensively. Nineteen states require their counties to have a merit system, but only 10 percent or so of all county employees are so covered.[21]

A central thrust of the civil service reform movement, especially as manifested in the scientific-management approach, was to separate personnel management from general management. The reformers' emphasis on the values of ethics and morality in public service generated internal tension in personnel administrative agencies. On the one hand, a personnel agency was to assume neutrally competent service. On the other, such an office had the role of being the agency's police. Tension between these two goals is a central dilemma of public administration today.

Values in the public shifted by the late 1970s, when both the public and legislatures viewed the civil service as a maze of bureaucracy that was too unresponsive and too tolerant of poor performance and that abused legitimate employee rights and mired personnel policy in excessive red tape, delay, and outright confusion. In 1978, President Jimmy Carter supported a reform bill designed primarily by Alan Campbell, then chair of the U.S. Civil Service Commission and its most effective advocate before Congress. Public employee unions opposed the bill as excessively favoring management, but Congress enacted the measure, in no small part because of Campbell's efforts.

Civil Service Reform Act of 1978

The Civil Service Reform Act of 1978 (CSRA) replaced the old Civil Service Commission with two agencies: the Office of Personnel Management (whose first director was Alan Campbell), to serve as the personnel arm of the president, and an independent Merit System Protection Board (MSPB), charged with handling employee grievances. The law further established the Federal Labor Relations Authority (FLRA), to manage federal labor relations policies. The law delegated such personnel management activities as performance appraisal to the individual federal agencies and bureaus. The act streamlined the process to terminate employees and strengthened procedures to protect whistle-blowers. It also created a framework for labor–management relations. The law further established the Senior Executive Service and revised the merit pay system for midlevel managers by basing the system on performance rather than longevity. The act required the development of objective, job-relevant, and measurable performance evaluations, and it established a set of merit principles and prohibited personnel practices.[22]

As had the Pendleton Act before it, the CSRA had considerable effects on other governments, sometimes with even greater impact than in the federal system. A comparable CSRA measure was enacted by the governments of 24 states and 14 other countries.[23] As Box 9.3 demonstrates, however, the existence of a state or local civil service system does not in and of itself prevent partisan political tampering (political patronage) or simply avoidance of the intent, spirit, and even some of the rules and regulations involved in such a system.

Affirmative Action and Comparable Worth

Efforts to establish affirmative action programs and ensure equity in pay and comparable worth constituted a trend that is perhaps equal in importance and effect on personnel management and has profoundly affected government personnel management.[24] Affirmative action was a product of the civil rights era of the mid- to late-1960s that emphasized values of representativeness and equity. The movement had

Box 9.3

Spoils for the Vanquished

In war, the spoils go to the victor; in politics, they sometimes go to the vanquished. New Jersey, as a result of the November 6, 2001, general election, is about to experience a sea change in government, a shift of control from the Republicans to the Democrats. Although the election made that shift a certainty, it is a shift that will not occur until tomorrow.

During the two months since the election, the vanquished reaped their spoils, increasing salaries, bonuses, and pensions; making partisan appointments; directing the construction of facilities for favored municipalities; and adopting rules and laws that benefit their own constituencies. . . .

The victors, relegated to the sidelines, were powerless to prevent the plunder. They sat idly by, watching the thoughtless distribution of largess to the Republican faithful, fruitlessly lamenting its unfortunate effect on a state economy moving rapidly into the red.

We do not suggest that the spoils system would be addressed any differently if the Democrats were the vanquished party. Nor do we suggest that the spoils system operates only at the state level. It is ready for use whenever the control of a county or a municipality shifts from one political party to another, and we suspect that it is used much too often.

We do suggest that something should be done about it. Perhaps the current victors will be sufficiently bruised during the exchange of government control to respond with public-spirited legislation. They have that obligation.

What would be required is an amendment to the [New Jersey] Constitution. It should either prohibit outright certain appointments and appropriations during the post-election lame-duck interval, or, to allow genuine emergencies to be addressed, it should require a two-thirds majority for such actions.

Source: Editorial, *New Jersey Law Journal, 167*(1) (January 7, 2002): 22.

---

as its goal the hiring and promotion of minorities who were previously excluded or decidedly underrepresented in government service.

Three issues involved in the federal government's attempt to end discrimination in employment are of special relevance to women: (1) bona fide occupation qualifications, (2) comparable worth, and (3) sexual harassment. The bona fide qualification issue involved revising work-entry requirements and exam standards to eliminate gender bias.[25] The issue of equity in pay was addressed in two laws: the **Equity Pay Act of 1963**, a federal law that stipulates equal pay for equal work, especially for women workers, and the closely related provision in Title VII of the Civil Rights Act of 1964.

Comparable worth is of more recent concern within affirmative action efforts. It means to compensate at the same rate of pay work that is judged to be comparable in value to the employer or to society. This principle is advocated to redress past pay inequities, particularly with respect to women. Jobs roughly on the same level of importance, knowledge, stress, skill levels, and responsibilities, even though the tasks themselves may be quite different, are to be paid at the same rate. Practically speaking, the principle is used to pressure employers to pay women the same amount as men. On average, women earn one-fourth less than men, although the differential is less pronounced in the public sector. The principle has been making headway among state and local governments. Thirty states have established commissions on the issue; a handful have adopted comparable worth plans, as have approximately 10 percent of all cities and counties.[26]

Salaries hold significant meaning in this society, where the value and worth of a profession and its professionals are measured, in part, in monetary terms. The importance of wage levels to recruitment into such occupations has just been stated.

INFOTRAC
COLLEGE EDITION

So how far have we come? Pestilent and persistent gender gap in pay

It is a matter of livelihood. As noted, salary levels affect recruitment and retention of workers and indicate the status afforded work by the larger society.

National Performance Review

The most recent trend in public administration to affect personnel management has been the *reinventing government* movement. A primary emphasis of the 1993 National Performance Review (NPR) report is civil service reform.[27] The NPR calls for an overhaul of the entire personnel system—recruiting, hiring, classification, promotion, pay, and incentives. Its central focus is decentralization. The movement emphasizes downsizing (doing more for less), privatization, and a continuation of the "devolution revolution" of the Reagan administration. The NPR itself had five achievements:

1. It deregulated personnel policy.
2. It decentralized authority, allowing agencies to conduct their own recruiting and exams and abolishing all central registers and standard application forms.
3. It greatly simplified the current classification system, allowing for greater flexibility in classification and pay.
4. It allowed agencies to develop their own performance management and reward systems.
5. It sought to cut in half the time required to terminate federal managers and employees for cause.

INFOTRAC
COLLEGE EDITION

High tech and high performance: managing appraisal in the information age

The Ebb and Flow of Union Strength

Union strength and involvement in government collective bargaining have ebbed and flowed over recent decades, influenced in part by the state of the economy, in part by the attitudes of different administrations, and in part by the ability of public employees to organize and assert their voices.[28]

Currently, over 13 percent of all workers in the United States, or about 17 million—are organized; and just over 14 percent are represented by unions. Of those, approximately 37.5 percent, nearly 7 million workers, are employed in the public sector, and labor unions represent almost 50 percent of all government workers in their collective bargaining. At the national level, roughly 59 percent of all federal employees are represented by some 125 unions in approximately 2,200 bargaining units. The four most dominant public employees unions are

1. the American Federation of Government Employees, which has nearly 153,000 members but represents more than 600,000 federal workers in bargaining;
2. the National Treasury Employees Union, with more than 74,000 workers and representing some 150,000 employees;
3. the Postal Workers Union, with more than 220,000 members; and
4. the National Association of Letter Carriers, with 210,000 members representing some 845,000 postal service employees.

Box 9.4

Camden to Pay $1.1 Million to Settle Suits by Passed-Over In-House Lawyers

Camden's city council agreed last Thursday to a $1.1 million settlement of federal suits by six attorneys and a secretary who alleged political influence in the city's law department.

The city agreed to the settlement on condition that the secretary, Rachel Thomas, and two attorneys still on the payroll, Golden Sunkett and Lisa Roberts, tender their resignations. The four other plaintiffs, Calvin Fisher, Lloyd Henderson, Theo Primas, and Carolyn Clark, previously resigned or were dismissed.

The settlement was reached in a conference June 19 that was arranged by state Department of Community Affairs Commissioner Susan Bass Levin. She arranged the meeting out of frustration over the continuing legal costs from the employees suits, says Community Affairs spokesman E. J. Miranda.

Tony Evans, a spokesman for Mayor Gwendolyn Faison, confirmed the settlement and said the city's legal bills from

the case recently reached over $1 million. "We're just glad to get beyond this point," he said.

Filed in 1999, the suits claimed that the seven were harassed and passed over for promotions based on political favoritism. The plaintiffs, all black, asserted that Mayor Milton Milan and City Attorney John Misci tried to force out longstanding black employees from the city attorney's office in favor of whites.

The plaintiffs had also lodged racial discrimination counts, but U.S. District Judge Stephen Orlofsky dismissed those claims in January.

Milan has since been convicted of fraud and conspiracy to solicit bribes and is serving a 7-year jail sentence. Misci resigned in August of 2000.

The city council will pay $500,000 of the award. The remainder will come from a city insurance policy.

Source: Charles Toutant, *New Jersey Law Journal*, *169*(6) (August 5, 2002): 7.

More white-collar workers are represented by federal unions than are blue-collar workers, although more blue-collar employees than white-collar employees are unionized (91 versus 53 percent).[29]

At the state and local levels, nearly 40 percent of all full-time employees are members of a union: 31 percent of state and 42 percent of local workers. The largest of these are firefighters, teachers, and police. Significant unions at the local level are the National Education Association (NEA), with nearly 1.7 million members; the American Federation of State, County, and Municipal Employees (AFSCME), with nearly 1.2 million members; the American Federation of Teachers (AFT), with over 600,000 members; the Fraternal Order of Police, at more than 150,000 members; and the International Association of Firefighters, with over 151,000 members.

Box 9.4 discusses a case, in Camden, New Jersey, involving city employees who successfully sued the city for passing over employees or forcing them out based on partisan politics.

The Evolution of Collective Bargaining

The right to collective bargaining has developed largely since the 1960s. Currently, 42 states have labor relations policy, 37 use collective bargaining as their primary method of dealing with unions, 32 have laws that authorize their cities to enter into collective bargaining with unions, and 28 authorize their counties to do so as well. Eighty-eight percent of all cities use collective bargaining with their employees.

At the federal level, collective bargaining began in 1962 with Executive Order 10988. President Nixon faced the major postal union strike in 1970, and he amended previous executive orders with some substantial improvements for

INFOTRAC
COLLEGE EDITION

**Constitutional and
practical pitfalls of
a federally mandated
public-sector collective
bargaining system**

labor. The Reagan Administration broke the Professional Air Traffic Controllers (PATCO) union over its 1981 strike. Hard economic times in the late 1980s and early 1990s led to diminished public employee union organizing strength and militancy. A decade of hiatus ended with the NPR report in 1993.

As the economy revived, President Bill Clinton issued Executive Order 12871. It required agencies to negotiate with unions to downsize the numbers, types, and grades of employees assigned to the various organized subdivisions as well as to bargain with unions over such topics as equipment and technology impacts. The NPR expansion of federal bargaining was desired more by union representatives than by managers.

President Clinton's executive order further established a new National Partnership Council composed of high-level officials of the Department of Labor, the Office of Management and Budget, the Office of Personnel Management, and the Federal Labor Relations Board plus four union representatives. The council has sought to foster a new sense of partnership between labor and management. By 1995, more than half of the 1.3 million unionized federal workers were represented through partnership councils.

Public unions have become highly skilled in bargaining and in financial research to advocate their positions. They have made significant salary and wage gains since the 1970s, although public-sector pay still lags behind that of the private sector, and gains made earlier have declined in recent years.

Public employee unions have played a significant role in raising salaries, gaining health and pension benefits, and, of course, adding to the costs of public budgets. Nonwage issues have included the regulation of work hours, caseload limits, assignment and transfer provisions, promotions, RIFs, and professional development provisions.

In recent years, the downturn in the number of employee strikes and other work stoppages reflects not only tighter economic times and public dissatisfaction with unions, but also the trend toward cooperation rather than conflict between public administrative managers and public unions.

Reading 9.1, "Merit, Management, and Neutral Competence," examines linkages between institutions and outcomes in implementation of merit system protections. It shows that the fate of merit principles depends on two influences that compete with neutral competence—partisan responsiveness by counterbureaucracies and the interest of managerial prerogatives at the agency level. It focuses on an analysis of the U.S. Merit System Protection Board (MSPB) processes, caseloads, and decisions between fiscal years 1988 and 1997.

Reading 9.1 —————————————————————————

Merit, Management, and Neutral Competence

Merit principles have helped to define the character of bureaucracy in the United States for more than a century. Indeed, civil service protections of employee rights have affected American government in ways that extend far beyond the boundaries of public administration. Moreover, as current reformers offer prescriptions for reinventing public personnel systems at all levels of government today, a central matter of concern has become how best to protect the merit principles in an era of fundamental change (Barzelay, 1992; Kettl, Ingraham, Sanders, and Horner, 1996; Condrey, 1998).

Notwithstanding the importance of merit principles, scholars have practically ignored the linkages between institutions and outcomes of merit system protections. As a result, we have little understanding of how objectively and consistently merit is implemented. To be sure, scholars have described the negative impact of complex, confusing, and often-contradictory merit procedures on public service recruitment, on managerial flexibility, and on agency efficiency and effectiveness.... Thoroughly documented as well are the obstacles to applying merit pay in the public sector.... Nevertheless, our understanding of the performance of the "counterbureaucracies" (Rourke, 1984; W. T. Gormley, 1993) charged with protecting employee rights and of the efforts by public agencies to balance managerial flexibility with merit principles rests largely on insightful but impressionistic evidence....

The passing of the 20th anniversary of the U.S. Civil Service Reform Act (CSRA) of 1978 provides an appropriate occasion for addressing this neglect as it applies to federal agencies. Partly to combat the partisan abuses of the merit system that occurred during the Nixon Administration (Nathan, 1975), the CSRA reassigned the old Civil Service Commission's management and merit protection responsibilities to the Office of Personnel Management and the MSPB, respectively. The MSPB was created as an independent agency in order to ensure that the line between employee rights and the prerogatives of agency managers would be drawn objectively, consistently, and in a nonpartisan fashion....

At a minimum, the protection of merit principles at any level of government can be influenced by two variables. The first is the extent of partisan responsiveness to political appointees by **counterbureaucracies** (like MSPB) that are charged with holding other agencies accountable to merit principles. The second influence is the balance maintained within line agencies between managerial prerogatives and fair treatment of employees. Thus, any analysis of merit principles in the federal government profits from knowing two things: (1) if the implementation of merit principles by the MSPB has been a function of the political appointment process, and (2) if variation exists across agencies in the enforcement of merit....

We find that the MSPB is largely the objective counterbureaucracy that Congress intended it to be. Although presidential appointment of the Board's members yields predictable, partisan differences in philosophy, such longitudinal variation in its policy orientation occurs within a narrow range of discretion circumscribed by statutory law and norms of judicial professionalism. Yet our analysis also reveals that federal agencies vary in the extent to which the MSPB reverses, remands, or mitigates their personnel actions. As a brief consideration of the Justice Department illustrates, these differences raise more serious issues than the subtle and arguably benign responsiveness that results from presidential appointment of Board members. They are especially germane to reinventing government reforms that delegate personnel management to agencies or to line operators within agencies....

Philosophical Differences between Republicans and Democrats

Several prominent scholars have concluded that the behavior of other independent boards and commissions have been a function of turnover among the elected "principals" who appoint their top executives and who allocate money and authority through the legislative process (T. Moe, 1982; Weingast and Moran, 1983). Although the MSPB hardly operates within the kind of politically charged environment of agencies such as the Federal Trade Commission, the tension between the needs of management and the rights of employees is still one of a handful of core issues that differentiate the Republican and Democratic parties. . . .

Cross-Agency Variation

As we noted, the integrity of the merit system is not solely a function of what the MSPB does. It is contingent to an equal or greater extent on how faithfully agency managers initially implement civil service laws in the context of countless personnel decisions. Our case data and interviews suggest that unevenness in the application of merit principles across the bureaucracy ultimately poses more important and difficult institutional policy issues than the subtle political responsiveness described above. . . .

That conventional personnel systems pose formidable problems for management is well documented and justifiably lamented. . . . However, we feel that our analysis should give pause to those touting radical reform of personnel systems, questioning the utility of tenure, or advocating the decentralization of personnel functions to federal, state, or local agencies (such as Maranto, 1998). Caution is especially appropriate in an era when downsizing and reengineering heighten the relevance of merit-related issues (as our data on the impact of RIFs indicate). Merit principles may be stretched to their limit—and beyond—under these trying circumstances.

Consider the warning flags hoisted by our findings. When settlement, reversal, and mitigation rates are combined across agencies, a sizable proportion of managerial personnel decisions are changed on the basis of compromised or ignored merit principles and procedures. . . . Equally troublesome are the differences we note in agency conformance with merit system protections. Under these circumstances, and without understanding the sources of these violations, indiscriminately delegating the protection of merit principles to agencies or to line operators within agencies is worrisome. . . .

But whether personnel reforms are involved or not, our analysis indicates that it may at times be fanciful to rely exclusively or predominantly on agency managers to strike the right balance between protecting their employees' rights and wielding their managerial prerogatives to accomplish agency missions. At other times (for example, when agency goals or functional needs suffer egregiously from uniform and inflexible merit protections), preserving managerial prerogatives is mandatory. Yet we cannot know how best to pursue this balance until researchers begin determining the sources of behavioral variations in the agencies when it comes to merit appeals, how to sort out needed variations from the venal or pernicious, and how to mitigate them in ways that balance agency needs and merit principles.

Our analysis of MSPB decisions suggests that variations in the factors of production facing managers (for example, RIFs), in agency cultures, and in legitimate functional needs may distort the balance between agency goals and merit protections in favor of the former. Certainly, cultures exist that are unsympathetic to merit, reinforced by decentralized authority structures, and unjustified by agency goals or legitimate functional needs. Such cultures must be consistently and aggressively challenged, and ways must be found to offset those that delimit managerial discretion.

In sum, a balance must be sought between the flexibility needed to accomplish agency purposes and fair treatment of employees by managers. Our analysis indicates that thousands of federal employees, in some agencies more than in others, were supported by the MSPB in their claims that this balance tilted against them. But only by knowing the substance of the rules violated, what the sources of the variation are, and/or who within agencies tend to be chronic offenders (by occupational or professional type or specific persons) can we ensure that merit procedures and principles truly advance the public interest. Discerning under what conditions this balance between flexibility and fairness is best realized, as well an understanding how best to strike it, should challenge the acumen of practitioners and researchers for years to come.

Source: William West and Robert F. Durant, *Public Administration Review, 60*(2) (March 2000): 111–121. Reprinted with permission of Blackwell Publishing Ltd.

Net Assignment

Using InfoTrac College Edition, Internet search engines, and some of the websites listed at the end of this chapter, find three similar job titles—one each in engineering, social services, and information technology (computers)—in both the state government job bank and private businesses in your state. Create a table that compares the qualifications, duties, and salary range for each job.

Summary

A clash of values between unions and management is inherent in personnel management. Over time, changing values have influenced government's approach to personnel matters, especially as the public employee workforces at the local, state, and federal levels have grown in size and diversity.

The primary functions of personnel management are:

- position classification,
- recruitment and selection,
- collective bargaining,
- performance appraisal,
- training and development, and
- labor relations.

Major trends in personnel administration have evolved from the Pendleton Act of 1883, the Civil Service Reform Act of 1978, the affirmative action and comparable worth movements, and the National Performance Review of 1993. Organized labor has played a role in these trends as public employee union strength has ebbed and flowed at all three levels of government.

Glossary of Key Terms

affirmative action   A policy or program intended to hire into public service or to promote to higher levels citizens from minority backgrounds who previously were excluded or underrepresented in the workforce, including women, African Americans, Hispanic Americans, and Native Americans.

civil service   Term for all nonmilitary employees of government; sometimes refers to a merit system as opposed to a patronage system.

collective bargaining   Union bargaining on behalf of a group of employees as opposed to an individual worker representing him- or herself.

comparable worth   A principle of equal compensation—that is, the same rate of pay for work judged to be comparable in value to the employer or to society; used to redress past pay inequities, particularly with respect to women.

counterbureaucracies   Agencies, such as merit system protection boards at federal, state, or local levels, charged with protecting employee rights and the efforts of public agencies to balance managerial flexibility with merit principles.

Equity Pay Act of 1963   Federal law to have equal pay for equal work, especially for women workers.

General Schedule (GS)   The pay scale and job classification system for the federal government; has ratings 1 through 15.

human resource development (HRD) The process of (and the unit or agency responsible for) administering and making policy for people and positions within the public sector.

impasse resolution A process occurring when either labor or management concludes that no further progress can be made toward a settlement during labor negotiations; typically leads to one or more impasse procedures—mediation, fact-finding, arbitration, or referendum.

merit system Approach to staffing based on formal qualifications for selection, promotion, and retention of employees rather than party affiliation.

Office of Personnel Management The federal agency responsible for managing the national government's personnel system.

patronage system The system of selecting employees or awarding contracts on the basis of political party loyalty or affiliation.

performance appraisal Formal method of evaluating an employee's work performance; used for promotion and retention and to document disciplinary action.

personnel The employees of an organization; also refers to the personnel function and the administrative unit responsible for it.

position classification A system of job description used to organize jobs under a civil service merit system into classes or categories based on the duties and responsibilities; the purpose is to delineate authority, establish chains of command, and denote pay scales.

public personnel administration The totality of government organization, policies, procedures, and processes to match the specific needs of public agencies and the people who staff them.

recruitment The process of advertising job openings for qualified candidates for an agency from which managers can choose.

reduction in force (RIF) Laying off public personnel.

reverse discrimination Compensation for past discrimination against racial, ethnic, or gender minorities that has the effect of discriminating against the majority members of society (mostly white males); typically involves the use of fixed quotas to ensure minority hiring or promotion.

Senior Executive Service (SES) Established in 1978 by the Civil Service Reform Act, the SES promotes professional growth, mobility, and versatility among upper-grade career officers and some political appointees.

spoils system Practice of hiring for jobs or awarding contracts on the basis of party loyalty and connections rather than on merit.

sunshine bargaining laws Laws that require open proceedings among state and local governments concerning negotiations with public employee unions.

union Group of employees who establish a formal organization to represent them when negotiating with management over wage and working conditions or in cases of disciplinary action.

Review Questions

1. Discuss how the trend toward greater diversity in the workforce has affected government personnel management as practiced at the local, state, and federal levels.

2. Compare and contrast the values implicit in the GS system versus the SES system of position classification at the federal level.

3. Discuss the advantages and disadvantages associated with various methods of employee performance appraisal.

4. Discuss similarities and differences in the values stressed by the 1883 Civil Service Act with those of the 1993 National Performance Review approach.

5. What values associated with public service employment make it attractive to potential employees? Can these values be protected by counterbureaucracies, such as discussed in Reading 9.1?

Surfing the Net

The following useful websites cover the topics discussed in this chapter.

American Federation of State, County, and Municipal Employees (AFSCME) (**http://www.afscme.org**)

National Education Association (NEA) (**http://www.nea.org**)

Service Employees International Union (SEIU) (**http://www.seiu.org**)

American Federation of Teachers (AFT) (**http://www.aft.org**)

American Federation of Labor–Congress of Industrial Organizations (AFL-CIO) (**http://www.aflcio.org/home.htm**)

Office of Administration (**http://www.whitehouse.gov/oa/index.html**)

Office of Management and Budget (**http://www.whitehouse.gov/OMB**)

U.S. Office of Personnel Management (**http://www.opm.gov**)

International City/County Management Association (**http://www.icma.org**)

National Performance Review (**http://www.npr.gov**)

Association of Government Accountants (**http://www.agacgfm.org**)

Conference of Minority Public Administrators (**http://www.compa.org**)

International Personnel Management Association (**http://www.ipma-hr.org**)

National Association of State Personnel Executives (**http://naspe.net**)

National Public Employer Labor Relations Association (**http://www.npelra.org**)

U.S. Department of Justice, Civil Rights Division (**http://www.usdoj.gov/crt**)

Federal Personnel Guide (**http://www.fedguide.com**)

Chapter 10

One element of the debate over New Public Management concerns public-sector entrepreneurship. Critics see entrepreneurs as people prone to rule breaking, self-promotion, and unwarranted risk taking, while proponents view them as exercising leadership and taking astute initiatives . . . Innovators are creatively solving public-sector problems and are usually proactive in that they deal with problems before they escalate into crises. They use appropriate organizational channels to build support for their ideas. They take their opponents seriously and attempt to win support for their ideas through persuasion or accommodation.

Leadership: The Chief Executive, the Bureaucracy, and the Search for Accountability

Sanford Borins
Loose cannons and rule breakers, or enterprising leaders?
Some evidence about innovative public managers,
Public Administration Review, *60*(6) (November 2000): 498.

Introduction

The chapter-opening quotation focuses on a characteristic often associated with effective leadership—the ability to envision a future, to innovate, and the capability to make that vision happen, to implement that innovation.

This chapter, in fact, concerns leadership. It defines and describes such concepts as authority and leadership. It discusses what happens when a leader exhibits too much or too little leadership. And it explores the power of moral leadership. The chapter also discusses variations in approaches to and styles of leadership. If leaders have specific functions—and they do—are there characteristic leadership traits that make some people natural leaders? Research indicates such traits are not natural. Rather, the chapter emphasizes the concepts of transactional and transformational leadership. It describes such leadership styles as director, motivator, coordinator, catalyst, spokesperson, crisis manager, and facilitator.

Effective executives are accountable leaders. We elaborate here on the interaction of the legislature with the executive by discussing how the value of accountability infuses the oversight function performed by legislative bodies. Exploring the theme of values in administration, the chapter discusses political values in relation to organizational goals. There are inherent value conflicts between political and organizational goals and values. Leaders, as managers of organizations, attempt to overcome value conflict and achieve consensus.

Effective organizational accountability is best achieved when internalized by members of the organization. Reading 10.1, "Aspects of Leadership," discusses leadership as affected by personal characteristics, organizational factors, situational contexts, and how all those may interrelate and reinforce one another, thus determining truly effective leadership, or fail to do so, resulting in perceived weak or ineffectual leadership.

Defining Authority and Leadership

Authority is the legal basis by which a leader has the right to use an organization's powers and resources. **Leadership** is simply the exercise of authority in directing the work of others. Leadership may be formal or informal. When exercising authority, leadership consists of getting people to do something the leader wants them to do in pursuit of an organization's goals. The methods by which leaders or managers get members of an agency to do something collectively to achieve their goals has been used to develop a typology of leadership based on leadership style.

Political scientists John Harrigan and David Lawrence, for example, characterize the leadership of chief executives—be they state governors, county executives, mayors, or presidents—as one of four distinctive styles: demagogue, caretaker, policy entrepreneur, and frustrated warrior.[1]

Demagogues   A **demagogue** rallies support by appealing to emotions and prejudice. An example would be Governor Pete Wilson of California, who used a campaign against undocumented aliens to win reelection in 1994. His demagoguery on the issue came back to hurt the Republican Party in the state in 1998.

Caretakers   A **caretaker** is a politically conservative leader who sees him- or herself as a custodian of the status quo. Caretakers are often lieutenant governors

who became governors but who lacked the vision or skill to be strong leaders. A California governor regarded as a caretaker was George Deukmejian (1982–1990).

Policy Entrepreneurs A **policy entrepreneur** is a progressive, highly activist executive who not only proposes new programs but also funds them. Former New York City Mayor Rudy Giuliani was an example, as was Bill Clinton when he served as governor of Arkansas. California also saw this gubernatorial style in former Governor Earl Warren.

Frustrated Warriors A **frustrated warrior** is an unsuccessful policy entrepreneur who is unable to achieve his or her vision and whose term ends in frustration. In fact, this is how David Lawrence characterizes Governor Wilson's final term. Governors who use this style frequently lead the executive branch when the legislative branch is controlled by the opposition party. In his final term, Bill Clinton illustrated the frustrated warrior type as a presidential leader.

Another scholar (Conner, 1998) argues that what is needed today to manage torrential change is a menu of "change-leadership" styles. He distinguishes six distinct leadership styles related to change: antichange, rational, panacea, bolt-on, integrated, and continuous. Each leadership style, he posits, "represents a unique set of perceptions, attitudes, and behaviors regarding how organizational disruption should be addressed" (p. 148). According to Conner, each style provides a pivotal lesson about leadership and change:

> The key lesson for the antichange leader is how to avoid as many fluctuations as possible. The rational leader is focused on how to contain change with logic and linear execution. For the panacea leader, the solution to disruption problems is found within such things as communication and motivational training. The bolt-on leader is trying to learn how to regain a sense of control by attaching change management techniques to projects on a discretionary basis. The Integrated leader is searching for

ways to use the structure and discipline of human due diligence as individual change projects are addressed. Finally, the continuous leader is attempting to leverage ability into a strategic asset to increase adaptation capacity and reduce unnecessary implementation demands. (p. 186)

In an examination of the role of president as leader in domestic policy, Lammers and Genovese (2000) argue persuasively that leadership performance in domestic policy is an expression of both the styles and the strategies that presidents employ in their efforts to govern. They formulate, effect, and implement domestic policy through four tasks or dimensions: decision making, administrative work, public leadership, and relations with Congress.

Personality Types

Presidents, as leaders, also have been characterized by their personality types.[2] Political scientist James Barber, for example, classifies presidents as one of these four types:

- **Active-positive** presidents are those who desire to achieve results above all else; good examples are Franklin Roosevelt, Harry Truman, John Kennedy, Gerald Ford, Jimmy Carter, and George Bush.

- **Active-negative** presidential personalities have a driving need to get and keep power—a personality exemplified by Woodrow Wilson, Herbert Hoover, Lyndon Johnson, and Richard Nixon.

- **Passive-positive** presidents seek to be loved and revered; William Taft, Warren Harding, and Ronald Reagan are good examples.

- **Passive-negative** presidents stress civic virtue—classically exemplified by George Washington, Calvin Coolidge, and Dwight Eisenhower.

Micromanagement

Leaders of organizations may try to lead too much. Such managers supervise too closely: They micromanage. The problem with excessive management is that it discourages subordinates from exercising real authority or responsibility and inhibits their development into effective managers. When leaders micromanage, they tend to become so busy with it that they fail to develop longer-term strategy and overall vision. President Jimmy Carter was criticized as a leader for this characteristic. When the leader goes beyond articulating a broad vision and instead attempts to define all the details to also bring it about, he or she is probably overmanaging. President Clinton's attempt to reform health care during his first term provides an example of a failed attempt that was due, in part, to such overmanagement.

Too little leadership or management, however, is also problematic. A lack of sufficient management can contribute to corruption—as in the case of the bankruptcy of Orange County, California, in the late 1990s when billions of dollars were being lost as investments in high-risk stocks—or to the abuse of power by subordinates, a criticism leveled at the Los Angeles police chief in the 1980s as well as against Presidents Reagan and Nixon.

The essence of leadership is often considered to be the ability to move people in new directions, to lead them to places they did not know they wanted or needed to go. Such leaders exercise moral leadership.[3] They use their stature to effect moral leadership and their position as a "bully pulpit," as President Theodore Roosevelt expressed it. Uncommon leaders have the ability to inspire an agency to accept their vision and then work collectively to bring it to fruition. Governor Mike Leavitt of Utah is a good example. In 1999, he was selected as a "public official of the year" by *Governing* magazine on the basis of his leadership in inspiring his state.

In sharp contrast, when a leader such as a president loses moral leadership, the ability to inspire followers with a vision of the future suffers greatly. President Clinton spoke well and projected a vision of leading the nation across a "bridge to the 21st century," but his lapse in moral judgment undermined his ability to inspire the nation to build that bridge or cross it under his leadership.

Box 10.1 presents yet another view of effective leadership. It presents a model of mayoral leadership especially appropriate to the council-manager form of city government—the facilitative model.

Approaches to Leadership

Leadership in administrative organizations is exercised by agency or department managers. Leadership is thus exercised within a particular organizational setting or situation. The organizational context affects the leadership style and approach as does the leader's personality or background. This organizational context affects the leader's legitimacy. How well the leader's characteristics and abilities affect the achievement of organizational goals contributes to or detracts from the sense of legitimacy accorded the manager.

In managing an agency, the **functions of leadership** are

- to define an agency's mission and goals,
- to be viewed as the institutional embodiment of its purpose,
- to defend its integrity, and
- to bring order to internal conflict.

Leadership viewed in a government agency context involves three distinct levels of responsibility and control:

1. technical,
2. managerial, and
3. institutional.[4]

At the technical level, the agency leader deals with problems concerning the effective performance of the technical function: seeing that "the trains run on time." Leadership at the managerial level involves mediating between the lower levels of the agency and those who use its services and acquiring the resources needed to carry out its central functions, such as purchasing, hiring, and general operations. At the institutional level, leadership is concerned with developing long-term policy and providing upper-level support to achieve the agency's goals.

Elected chief executives often rely on sizable staffs to assist in leading large-scale organizations. The U.S. president, for example, relies on the various staff agencies of the EOP and the White House staff to run the executive branch. The institutional presidency thus comprises many hundreds of staff members. In recent years, for example, the White House staff has totaled far more than 500 members (over

INFOTRAC
COLLEGE EDITION

The new public service: serving rather than steering

INFOTRAC
COLLEGE EDITION

Do public neighborhood centers have the capacity to be instruments of change in human services?

Box 10.1

Effective Mayoral Leadership in Council-Manager Cities: Reassessing the Facilitative Model

To understand the kind of leadership that the chief elected official in a council-manager government can provide requires rethinking standard assumptions and models. Americans are accustomed to looking for strong executives in Washington and state capitols, who put their own stamp on government; many presume that mayors are supposed to do the same thing. This approach is common in scholarly thinking as well. The common presumption in the political science literature is that mayoral leadership is dependent on the acquisition of power and its skillful use. The innovator or entrepreneur, as the prototypical type of mayoral leadership is labeled in this model, is adept at pyramiding power to overcome the checks on the mayor's authority in a governmental form based on separation of powers.

These standard assumptions overlook a fundamental characteristic of the council-manager form of government: It does not have separation of powers. It is based on a unitary model of government organization: All authority is lodged in the legislative body that delegates authority to a city manager selected by and accountable to the city council. There are two important features of council-manager government that have an impact on mayoral leadership. First, the mayor and council are "constitutionally" checking and balancing each other; they are part of a governing body. Second, the mayor does not execute or directly promote the accomplishment of tasks. Thus the mayor can and should exert a different kind of leadership. The mayor leads by empowering others— in particular, the council and the manager—rather than seeking power for himself or herself, and the mayor accomplishes objectives through enhancing the performance of others. The characteristics of council-manager government both permit and require another kind of leadership on the part of the chief elected official who is not the executive officer in the government. Power is not a precondition to effective leadership in this setting.

The council-manager form supports a model of mayoral leadership that stands in contrast to the standard power-based model. The alternative found in these governments is a *facilitative* model of leadership. The ideal mayor in council-manager cities is a facilitator who promotes positive interaction and a high level of communication among officials in city government and with the public, and who offers guidance in goal setting and policy making. This type of leadership is well suited to the conditions of the council-manager city for two reasons. First, cooperative relationships among officials are common; the mayor is not primarily a leader who overcomes resistance and exchanges favors for support. Second, the city manager provides professional leadership in city government, and the manager supports the elected officials in accomplishing their goals. The city manager is accountable to the council rather than being a bureaucratic force whose resistance must be overcome. These characteristics do not mean that city managers are passive or unsubstantial figures in city government; rather, they reflect the fact that managers accept the ethical obligation to use their leadership in the service of elected officials and the citizens of the community. Elected officials recognize the important leadership contributions that city managers make and give them high marks for helping the council fulfill its responsibilities.

In this setting, the mayor does not have to confront a council that is defending its own powers, or seeking to establish control over a city's administrative apparatus. The mayor can work on improving the sense of purpose and the interaction between the council and a city manager who wants to work with elected officials. Describing the context for leadership in this way is not intended to ignore that there can be divisions within the council—indeed, they may be growing—or conflicts in the community that may have to be overcome for the city to develop coherent approaches. Still, effective leadership by the mayor can improve working relationships among officials, make the form of government function more smoothly, and increase the focus of elected officials in setting goals and policy.

It is possible to conceive of leadership in government as collaborative and focused on the accomplishment of common goals. . . . The facilitative model presumes that the relationships among officials are essentially cooperative—a condition commonly produced by the integrated authority of the council-manager form.

Source: James H. Svara, Mayors in the unity of powers context: Effective leadership in council-manager governments, *The future of local government administration.* Copyright 2002. Reprinted with permission of the International City/County Management Association, 777 North Capitol Street, NE, Suite 500, Washington, DC 20002. All rights reserved.

600 during the administration of Presidents George H. Bush and George W. Bush, and just over 500 under President Clinton), and the EOP has exceeded 1,600 staff members. Large states similarly have comparable staff and executive branch support for their governors' offices. California's executive branch, for example, totals more than 276,000 employees covered by its civil service, and the governor appoints more than 2,500 of those to various posts.[5] California's executive branch (see Figure 10.1) has a branch structure that is typical of most states. The office of governor in California, however, also illustrates the strong-governor form, and its place in the bureaucratic hierarchy provides it with a considerable structural basis that can help a strong leader.

Leadership and Management

Two scholars of leadership, Robert Tannenbaum and Warren Schmidt, have developed a continuum of leadership behavior that links the role or style of leadership to the manager's behavior.[6] Figure 10.2 presents their continuum of manager–nonmanager behavior. Leadership is more effective, they argue, when the manager has a vision and adopts a style of leadership appropriate to the agency being managed.

A good case in point is that of Shelby County (Tennessee) Mayor Jim Rout, who has served as an elected county official for more than 20 years. In 1998, Rout became embroiled in a dispute over annexations and incorporations. The controversy led him to realize how important it was to adopt a regional view. The mayor had been a county commissioner for 16 years after a successful career in business when he was elected Shelby County mayor in 1994. Running for reelection in 1998, Rout made regional leadership the centerpiece of his campaign. Winning by a wide margin, he followed through by hosting a "Crossing the Line" conference and enlisting the assistance of the governors of Tennessee, Arkansas, and Mississippi to create the Governors' Alliance for Regional Excellence.

Rout's shift in perspective came after the Tennessee legislature enacted a law that made it easier for existing towns to incorporate as new cities. A flood of complaints, especially in the Memphis area, followed from existing cities that had hoped to annex new territory but were thwarted in their desires to expand. Rout came to realize the area had to look beyond traditional city limits, county boundaries, and even state borders to cope with the issue.[7]

Groupthink (see Chapter 3) is a particular problem associated with chief executives and the managerial staff agencies or units that serve them, especially when they are collectively involved in crisis-management or decision-making situations. The strong desire or need for consensus in how to manage a crisis tends to lead staff members to tell the agency leader only what they think the leader wants to hear. Groupthink often leads to disaster in policy making because the leader cannot effectively lead an agency when the information about a problem is incomplete or, in the worse case, distorted—especially during crises when a chief executive sees no dissent and hears no opposition and the staff speaks no alternatives other than the consensus.

Effective agency leaders bring all organization members together and move them in a consistent and coherent new direction toward the organization's goals and objectives. As we have seen, the New Public Management movement has championed a vision of public managers as the entrepreneurs of a new, leaner, and increasingly privatized government incorporating the practices and values of business.

INFOTRAC
COLLEGE EDITION

The leadership styles of men and women

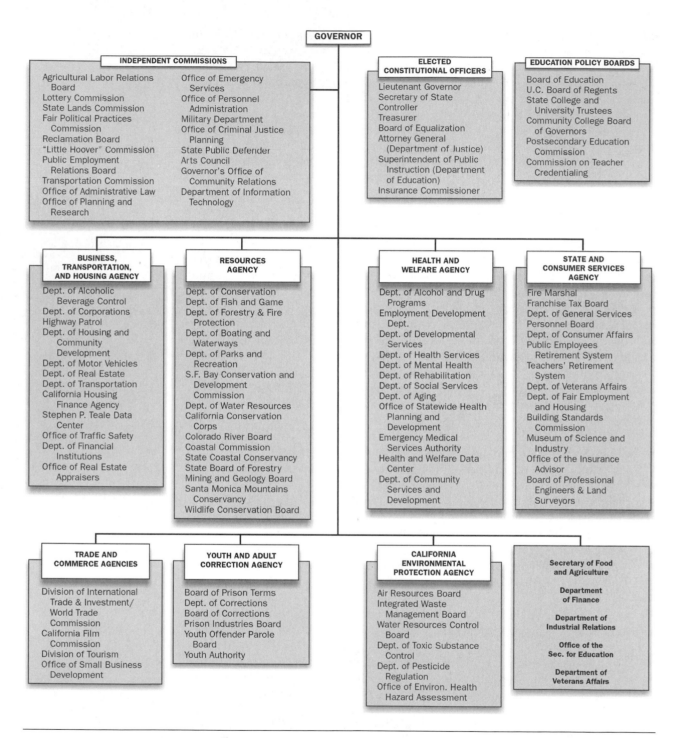

GOVERNOR

INDEPENDENT COMMISSIONS

Agricultural Labor Relations Board
Lottery Commission
State Lands Commission
Fair Political Practices Commission
Reclamation Board
"Little Hoover" Commission
Public Employment Relations Board
Transportation Commission
Office of Administrative Law
Office of Planning and Research

Office of Emergency Services
Office of Personnel Administration
Military Department
Office of Criminal Justice Planning
State Public Defender
Arts Council
Governor's Office of Community Relations
Department of Information Technology

ELECTED CONSTITUTIONAL OFFICERS

Lieutenant Governor
Secretary of State
Controller
Treasurer
Board of Equalization
Attorney General (Department of Justice)
Superintendent of Public Instruction (Department of Education)
Insurance Commissioner

EDUCATION POLICY BOARDS

Board of Education
U.C. Board of Regents
State College and University Trustees
Community College Board of Governors
Postsecondary Education Commission
Commission on Teacher Credentialing

BUSINESS, TRANSPORTATION, AND HOUSING AGENCY

Dept. of Alcoholic Beverage Control
Dept. of Corporations
Highway Patrol
Dept. of Housing and Community Development
Dept. of Motor Vehicles
Dept. of Real Estate
Dept. of Transportation
California Housing Finance Agency
Stephen P. Teale Data Center
Office of Traffic Safety
Dept. of Financial Institutions
Office of Real Estate Appraisers

RESOURCES AGENCY

Dept. of Conservation
Dept. of Fish and Game
Dept. of Forestry & Fire Protection
Dept. of Boating and Waterways
Dept. of Parks and Recreation
S.F. Bay Conservation and Development Commission
Dept. of Water Resources
California Conservation Corps
Colorado River Board
Coastal Commission
State Coastal Conservancy
State Board of Forestry
Mining and Geology Board
Santa Monica Mountains Conservancy
Wildlife Conservation Board

HEALTH AND WELFARE AGENCY

Dept. of Alcohol and Drug Programs
Employment Development Dept.
Dept. of Developmental Services
Dept. of Health Services
Dept. of Mental Health
Dept. of Rehabilitation
Dept. of Social Services
Dept. of Aging
Office of Statewide Health Planning and Development
Emergency Medical Services Authority
Health and Welfare Data Center
Dept. of Community Services and Development

STATE AND CONSUMER SERVICES AGENCY

Fire Marshal
Franchise Tax Board
Dept. of General Services
Personnel Board
Dept. of Consumer Affairs
Public Employees Retirement System
Teachers' Retirement System
Dept. of Veterans Affairs
Dept. of Fair Employment and Housing
Building Standards Commission
Museum of Science and Industry
Office of the Insurance Advisor
Board of Professional Engineers & Land Surveyors

TRADE AND COMMERCE AGENCIES

Division of International Trade & Investment/ World Trade Commission
California Film Commission
Division of Tourism
Office of Small Business Development

YOUTH AND ADULT CORRECTION AGENCY

Board of Prison Terms
Dept. of Corrections
Board of Corrections
Prison Industries Board
Youth Offender Parole Board
Youth Authority

CALIFORNIA ENVIRONMENTAL PROTECTION AGENCY

Air Resources Board
Integrated Waste Management Board
Water Resources Control Board
Dept. of Toxic Substance Control
Dept. of Pesticide Regulation
Office of Environ. Health Hazard Assessment

Secretary of Food and Agriculture

Department of Finance

Department of Industrial Relations

Office of the Sec. for Education

Department of Veterans Affairs

FIGURE 10.1

The Executive Branch of California

Which agencies are staff agencies helping the governor manage California's executive branch?

Source: California Department of General Services, *State of California directory* (Sacramento: Author, 2000).

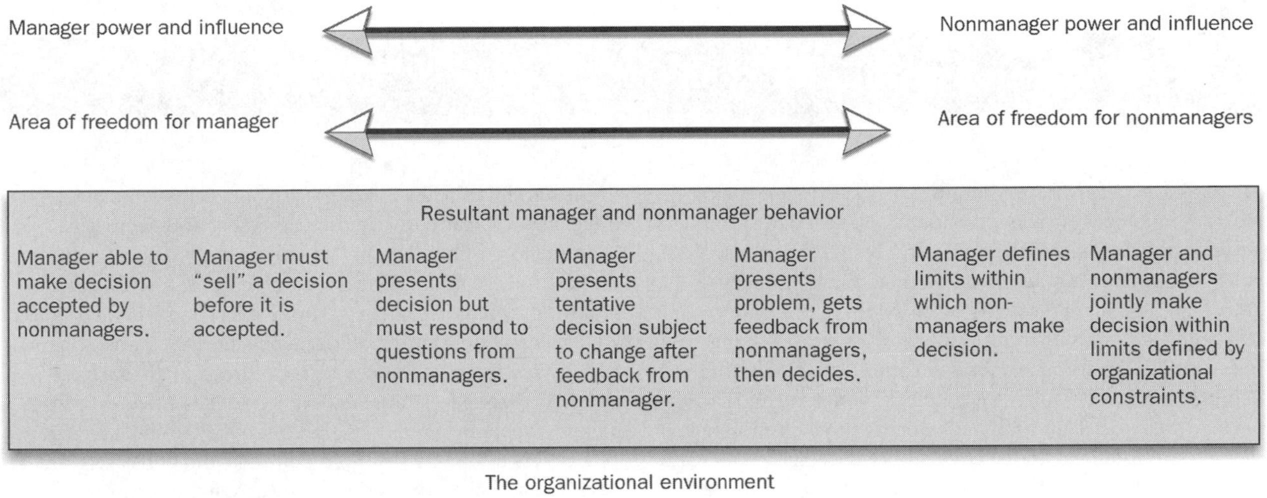

Manager power and influence ⟷ Nonmanager power and influence

Area of freedom for manager ⟷ Area of freedom for nonmanagers

Resultant manager and nonmanager behavior						
Manager able to make decision accepted by nonmanagers.	Manager must "sell" a decision before it is accepted.	Manager presents decision but must respond to questions from nonmanagers.	Manager presents tentative decision subject to change after feedback from nonmanager.	Manager presents problem, gets feedback from nonmanagers, then decides.	Manager defines limits within which non-managers make decision.	Manager and nonmanagers jointly make decision within limits defined by organizational constraints.

The organizational environment

FIGURE 10.2

A Continuum of Manager–Nonmanager Behavior

Source: Robert Tannenbaum and Warren Schmidt, How to choose a leadership pattern, *Harvard Business Review* (May–June 1973): 167.

Public management has undergone a revolution. Rather than focusing on controlling bureaucracies and delivering services, public administrators are responding to admonishments to "steer rather than row," and . . . as a result, a number of highly positive changes have been implemented in the public sector. . . . But as the field of public administration has increasingly abandoned the idea of rowing and has accepted responsibility for steering, has it simply traded one "adminicentric" view for another? Osborne and Gaebler write, "Those who steer the boat have far more power over its destination than those who row it" (1992: 32). If that is the case, the shift from rowing to steering not only may have left administrators in charge of the boat—choosing its goals and directions and charting a path to achieve them—it may have given them more power to do so. (Denhardt and Denhardt, 2000: 549)

Box 10.2, "Agency Managers as Political Leaders," discusses the difficulties agency managers often face when they have to juggle many competing values to lead their agency.

The Search for Leadership Traits

To be truly effective, the leaders of large-scale bureaucracies must bring coherence to a multitude of activities within an agency. For many scholars, the key to leadership lies in the characteristics or traits the leader brings to this task, and several scholars subscribed to what came to be called **trait theory**: the belief or assumption that leadership is based on unique characteristics, qualities, or traits that leaders possess that enable them to assume responsibility. The belief in trait theory assumes there is a quality of "born leadership," an assumption that has given rise to a search for leadership traits and to something of a tradition within

Box 10.2

Agency Managers as Political Leaders

The public administration literature on local government management has long argued that the supposed dichotomy between policy and management simply no longer describes well what managers actually do. Although city managers are engaged to an increasingly large extent in policy decisions, they are often uncomfortable with acknowledging their expanded role since they were often educated with the dichotomy between policy and politics in mind. This discomfort level becomes especially noteworthy when their policy role becomes political. Indeed, few experienced city managers and many agency managers would deliberately act in ways seen as overtly political. They avoid taking the limelight at the expense of elected officials. They avoid making unrequested or politically controversial recommendations on policy when the mayor and/or city council are struggling to develop their own consensus.

Most city and agency managers avoid acting with motives hidden from the city governing body on important matters of policy, particularly so when the council body is divided. Considerable research has demonstrated that managers protect their neutrality. They do so by keeping the council informed, by working unobtrusively behind the scenes to maintain a community focus on the elected officials. They do so by acting in relationship to the council, either following its lead or filling in a gap in leadership and defining their work as "problem solving, not politics." But what happens when managers simply cannot avoid being thrust into a leadership role that they see as jeopardizing their political neutrality? What happens when a city manager or a state or federal agency secretary has to juggle a variety of competing values, responsibilities, and constituencies, all within the context of very diverse, often highly professionalized, and frequently relatively autonomous programs, agencies, and divisions within the city bureaucracy or in a large state or federal department of government?

As Beryl Radin (2002) notes, up to a point they have to travel in nonlinear paths; in directions that are seemingly contradictory rather than highly consistent. Needed flexibility is often built on not making irrevocable decisions. To put it bluntly, they have to waffle, assuring everyone that their voices will be heard, but putting off decisions until the smoke clears, thereby keeping a necessary degree of freedom. In such circumstances, making decisions explicit makes enemies, and making too many enemies is a sure-fire way to end a career.

Leaders often fear being preempted from choices, from having insufficient discretion in the absence of central control. That fear, rather than having some fixed-preference commitment to specific operational goals, is why agency leaders frequently want to centralize resources and monitoring capabilities. That is often hard to do, however, when the agency is a sprawling and highly diverse or highly professionalized one, such as the federal department of Health and Human Services or a typical large state university.

The shopping list of recommendations made by reinventing government are much like the proverbs of administration noted by Herbert Simon: They are something like a laundry list of leadership lessons, at once altogether sensible yet mostly contradictory. An agency or city manager is recommended to put together a loyal team yet look for allies in unexpected places. How can loyalty be accommodated to flexibility of this sort? Must the loyalty be to the leader as a person rather than to the leader's policy plans? And if so, is that not acting as a political leader?

City and agency managers often cannot learn such leadership lessons from a list; they have to be instinctive or learned from experience.

Source: Adapted from John Nalbandian, The manager as political leader, *National Civil Review, 90*(1) (Spring 2001): 63–68; and Beryl Radin, *The accountable juggler: The art of leadership in a federal agency* (Washington, DC: Congressional Quarterly Press, 2002).

---

public administration. Subscribers to this theory attempt to discern and describe the essential traits of all good leaders.

For some time, mostly before World War II, public administration scholars who were interested in leadership aspects of those who managed large-scale bureaucracy assumed that leaders possessed traits or qualities that set them aside from followers. They believed leaders were born. Leaders had **charisma**, and their leadership was based on their personalities rather than on their formal positions of leadership or on any rational or legal authority. Many traits or qualities have been suggested, including these 12:[8]

1. achievement
2. charisma
3. creativity
4. decisiveness
5. dependability
6. energy

7. enterprise
8. intelligence
9. judgment
10. optimism
11. technical proficiency
12. verbal ability

INFOTRAC
COLLEGE EDITION

Cultural variation of leadership prototypes across 22 European countries

No agreement about precisely which such traits were essential to leadership was ever reached. All such traits clearly are useful to a leader, but no set traits could be theoretically demonstrated as essential.

Since the 1960s, the emphasis on traits has increasingly been viewed as outmoded. Other variables were seen to be at least as or even more important than any personal qualities of the leader. Some of the qualities just suggested as essential could be seen as counterproductive in some contexts. Take, for example, technical proficiency. Government has long valued technical competency among those selected for leadership positions in administrative agencies. Educators, public health administrators, aeronautics and space engineers, city planners, public accountants, and so on were viewed as needing a certain technical expertise to lead an agency. Supervisors of such agencies needed a degree of technical expertise to gain the respect of subordinates in a way that no nontechnician could. Other scholars viewed such qualities as sometimes dysfunctional. Large-scale organizations were often ineffectively led by supervisors who exhibited a "specialist syndrome." As the 1970s bestseller *The Peter Principle* noted, the "best" teacher does not necessarily make a good principal. The best accountant, precise and meticulous in detail, may make a poor manager of other accountants. The brilliant medical researcher may be a poor manager of a health research agency.[9] The specialist syndrome might lead the supervisor to overvalue some activities and listen to some people more than others. Such a supervisor might lack the overall objective perspective a generalist administrator needs. This view accepts the administrative adage that the expert should be "on tap" but not "on top."[10]

Decisiveness is also often suggested as a quality that marks effective leaders. Yet many notable leaders in government and private enterprise said that if there is any doubt about what should be done, the wise manager does nothing. And, although charisma may be positive in many ways, it clearly can block out important advice and challenges from subordinates and enhance the danger of groupthink.[11]

More recently, leadership has been seen as relational, as an interaction between individuals. Douglas McGregor emphasizes that leadership is a relationship involving four major variables:

1. the characteristics of the leader;
2. the followers' attitudes, needs, and other personal characteristics;
3. the organization's characteristics, such as its purpose, structure, and the nature of the tasks performed; and
4. the social, economic, and political milieu within which the organization operates.

In McGregor's words: "This is an important research finding. It means that leadership is not a property of the individual, but a complex relationship among these variables.[12]

To the extent that McGregor's perspective is valid, there often may be an association between types of organization and leadership style. Large, strongly hierarchical (such as military or paramilitary organizations) might favor the care-taker style, for example. New agencies and those that are highly diverse and often professionalized (such as NASA, a university, and a health department) may attract the policy entrepreneur type. Old and well-established agencies (say, the Department of Agriculture) may often be led by frustrated warriors, and so on.

Transactional Leadership

INFOTRAC
COLLEGE EDITION

The role of transforma-tional and transaction leadership in creating, sharing, and exploiting organizational knowledge

Another view of leadership emphasizes not the leader's personal qualities or traits but the central question of how such leadership was established. The *trans-actional leadership* approach is concerned with how the leader gains **credibility**: the recognition by an organization that a leader is competent to use its powers and command its resources. Under this theory, leaders are classified as one of three types: authoritarian, democratic, or laissez-faire.[13] Authoritarian leaders are task oriented and attempt to determine all policies, set all work assignments, and criticize subordinates personally. Authoritarian-led groups were more aggressive in behavior and the least satisfied but also highly productive. McGregor found that agencies headed by democratic leaders were more satisfied and productive. Groups led by laissez-faire leaders showed lower satisfaction and production.

This approach assumes that leaders could be trained to act in particular ways that are more appropriate to the agency, a belief that has sometimes proven to be no more than wishful thinking. Leaders who attended leadership-training seminars often exhibited little behavior change. In fact, an entire agency must adopt to change, not just certain employees. In the real world, leaders apply different styles, depending on differing circumstances and situational contexts.

Organizations, like individuals, can be viewed as having life cycles, of going through various phases and stages. What leadership style is appropriate to the organi-zation may be influenced not only by the general nature of the organization (more or less hierarchical, more or less comprising professional employees, more or less techni-cal or general in its services and tasks), but also by the phase and stage within the organization's life cycle.[14] Figure 10.3 graphically portrays the organizational life cycle.

How open or closed a leader is to the influence of advisors reflects not only the leader's personality and traits, but also the institutional constraints and aspects of organizational structure. The presidency of the United States, for instance, is now thoroughly institutionalized. Power and influence within the presidency reflect its institutionalized nature. Who has access and influence is determined in part by where the individual is positioned within the institutional structure.

Transformational Leadership

Another perspective or approach to leadership has been called **transformational leadership**. The term refers to leaders who strive to change an agency's culture and goals. This approach emphasizes that an organization reflects the leader's ability to develop a *values-based* vision for it and to convert that vision into reality and sus-tain it over time. Where transactional leadership stresses incremental change,

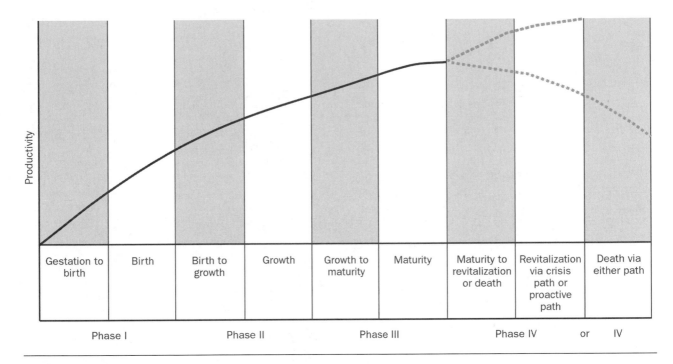

FIGURE 10.3
Organizational Life Cycle

Source: James G. Hunt et al. (Eds.), *Emerging leadership vistas* (Lexington, MA: Heath, 1988): 132.

transformational leadership emphasizes radical organizational change. To implement such change, the leader must develop and sell a new strategic vision to the agency's rank and file and key players.

Transformational leadership emphasizes almost a "great man" aspect of leadership by focusing once again on the influence the individual leader has on the organization. Such a leader is more likely to adopt a demagogue or policy entrepreneur style and more likely to be an active-positive personality type. Figure 10.4 illustrates transformational leadership, which focuses on the behavior of both the leader and followers in the organization for the leader to successfully "transform" it. The reinventing government movement discussed in Chapters 5 and 9 includes much of the transformational leadership approach.[15]

These approaches to leadership recognize that leaders manage organizations with a variety of styles, especially when they seek to transform their organizations. We next examine alternative styles of leadership: the leader as director, motivator, coordinator or facilitator, catalyst, spokesperson, and crisis manager.

Styles of Leadership

The focus on how the leader relates to the agency he or she leads raises the question of what style of leadership is appropriate for any particular organization.[16] What works well with a paramilitary organization—a police or fire department, for example—may be far less suitable for an education or health agency. Leaders of

INFOTRAC
COLLEGE EDITION

Social work perceptions of transformational and transactional leadership in health care

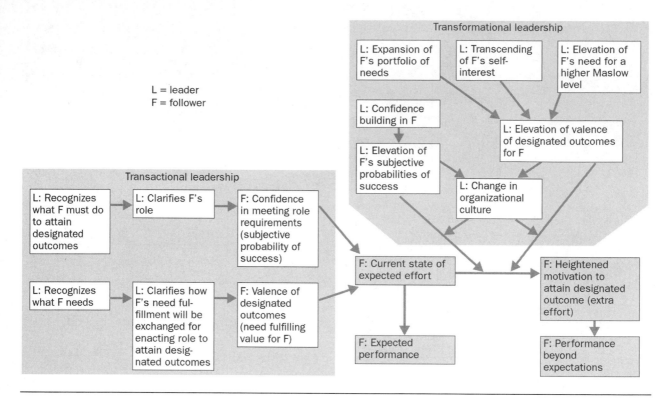

FIGURE 10.4
Transformational Leadership: Add-on Effect
Source: James G. Hunt et al. (Eds.), *Emerging leadership vistas* (Lexington, MA: Heath, 1988): 31.

highly decentralized agencies may have to differ in style from those that are more centralized in organization. Newer agencies and older agencies may require different styles. When an agency is undergoing reform, and whether such reform pressure is largely generated externally or internally, will likely require a different style than a well-established agency not being viewed as needing extensive reform.

The Director

One style of leadership is that of *director.* This style emphasizes the function of leadership in bringing coherence to the many activities typically performed by a large, complex department. The leader as director seeks to reconcile personal goals of organizational members or subunit goals with overall organizational goals. He or she uses both direct and indirect persuasion to reduce or mitigate conflicts and spends considerable time, energy, and resources winning support for the overall agency goals. Such leaders need to have a clear vision of and dedication to those goals, which are seen to outweigh any personal objectives. The leader as director seeks widespread consensus of intent among organizational members and issues executive orders to articulate clearly that consensus on overall goals and objectives.

The Motivator

Another style is the leader as *motivator*. Leaders as motivators are concerned about the quality of face-to-face supervision, tangible benefits and incentives, and using the intrinsic interest of tasks to motivate employees.[17]

Douglas McGregor describes the assumptions of the Theory Y approach to management (see Chapter 5), which clearly involves a motivational style of leadership:[18]

1. The expenditure of physical and mental effort in work is as natural as play or rest. The average human being does not inherently dislike work. Depending on controllable conditions, work may be a source of satisfaction (and will be voluntarily performed) or a source of punishment (and will be avoided if possible).

2. External control and the threat of punishment are not the only means for bringing about effort toward organizational objectives. Humans will exercise self-direction and self-control in the service of objectives to which they are committed.

3. Commitment to objectives is a function of the rewards associated with their achievement. The most significant rewards—for example, the satisfaction of ego and self-actualization needs—can be direct products of human efforts directed toward the achievement of organizational goals.

4. The average human being learns, under proper conditions, not only to accept but also to seek responsibility. Avoidance of responsibility, lack of ambition, and emphasis on security are generally consequences of experience and are not inherent human characteristics.

5. The capacity to exercise a relatively high degree of imagination, ingenuity, and creativity to solve organizational problems is widely, not narrowly, distributed in the population.

6. Under the conditions of modern industrial life, the average human's intellectual potential is only partially used.

These ideas assume that the limits of human collaboration in organizations do not result from human nature but from a manager's ingenuity—or lack of it—to realize the potential in the agency's human resources. If employees are lazy, indifferent, unwilling to take responsibility, intransigent, uncreative, and uncooperative, then Theory Y places the cause squarely on the manager's methods of organization and control.

Box 10.3 discusses how successful urban renewal efforts depend on a motivational leader at the city level. Such mayors lead a city revival by espousing a clear vision of what the city could become and by engaging a diverse group of interests to accept that vision and work cooperatively to achieve it. It requires managing a remarkable degree of civic reengagement, including downtown revival around a centrally focused area—a harbor, riverfront, and so on. Such mayors exemplify the transformational leadership model described in Figure 10.4.

INFOTRAC
COLLEGE EDITION

The law, presidential memoranda, and executive orders: of patchwork quilts, trump cards, and shell games

Box 10.3

Visions of Renewal

A number of U.S. cities have undergone impressive renewal efforts that have significantly reshaped them. Baltimore, Maryland; Pittsburgh, Pennsylvania; Rochester, New York; San Antonio, Texas; and San Bernardino, California. These are some of the cities that have experienced major renewal efforts led by strong mayors who politically sold their "vision" of a renewed city. These city renewal efforts exhibit some common features. They focus on a core area of the renewal project. Baltimore's Harbor Place, San Antonio's Riverwalk, Rochester's Riverfront Renewal, and San Bernardino's City Lakes are all focused on a particular section of the city seen as sparking renewal that will revitalize the entire city.

These cities are typically ones in which past boom eras went bust, where their manufacturing centers declined. They are cities whose renewal efforts share having a mayor able to manage diverse forces and channel those forces in a coordinated effort. Their mayors sold a massive urban renewal project to the federal government. They encouraged and developed partnerships with private enterprise to heavily invest funds that matched or exceeded public sources at the federal, state, and local levels.

These mayors involved a variety of city and county agencies, particularly economic development, urban planning and renewal, and zoning. They coordinated disparate groups: business coalitions, such as local chambers of commerce and building trade associations; and both public and private local labor unions heavily engaged in such projects, such as electrician and plumbing unions. They built bipartisan political coalitions.

Such mayors as managers of renewal have to ensure the inclusion of ethnic and minority groups, linking neighborhood and downtown commercial interests with those concerned about safe streets or the high cost of doing business in the nation's urban centers. They have to sell a vision that "urban renewal" will not be merely seen as "ethnic removal." This requires a mayor who is an exceptional motivational leader, one who espouses a clear vision of what the revitalized city could be and who involves a wide variety of diverse interests to agree with that vision and to work together to achieve it. No small task! Such mayoral leadership is sufficiently rare that these successful examples stand out clearly in the public eye.

Revitalization of large urban centers, especially in the nation's "rust-belt" region, required pushing an economic redevelopment scheme that made the city less reliant on a single economic enterprise or sector. Various economic interests had to be convinced that the renewal project could revitalize the local economy so that all experienced a "win-win" situation. To avoid the all-too-common NIMBY syndrome, neighborhood interests had to be formally involved in the planning and development. City reengagement requires concrete evidence of progress, such as major food stores and commercial complexes being located in previously run-down and undesirable neighborhoods, along with the associated economic development focused on the central part of the renewal effort—for example, the city harbor, riverfront, or central-city lakes area.

The "renewal mayor" must shape forces outside his or her direct control but ones that can directly affect a city's future—city school boards, neighboring city councils, county planning and development agencies, and any nearby regional associations of government. Getting internal and external forces working toward a common goal truly requires a vision and a mayor who is a "transformational leader."

Source: By author. For a detailed example of one such effort, read about the transformation of Rochester, New York, in William A. Johnson, Jr. (1999), *Governing* (November 1999): 24.

The Coordinator or Facilitator

Another style is the leader as coordinator. This style recognizes that the role of leadership of a complex organization is to coordinate and integrate the varied functions and tasks of the increasingly specialized subunit staff members—to get the organization to mesh like the gears of a complex machine. Leaders of large and complex organizations typically are generalists and must rely on the competence of specialized experts while striving to organize the efforts of the various staffs and subunits into a coherent whole. The city manager as facilitator, discussed in Box 10.2, illustrates well this style of leadership.

Individual members and specialized subunits have a tendency to develop tunnel vision, seeing their own work and tasks as worthy but failing to appreciate fully the other aspects of the department's or agency's activities. Leaders typically encounter resistance to change, because agency members believe their procedures and outputs are already adequate for their units' purposes. The leader's frame of reference, however, is the organization as a whole; the subunits and specialized staffs' frames of reference are those of the subunits.

The leader as coordinator generates ideas for changing an organization and support for those ideas by using surveys, newsletters, suggestion boxes, question-and-answer sessions, and advance notice of proposed actions to the organization's members. Regularly scheduled brainstorming sessions in the manner of the Theory Z approach to management involves members in decision making and makes any final decision more palatable to larger numbers of people in the agency. Leaders as coordinators attempt to mesh department personnel, materials, financial resources, and services to clientele in a way that integrates all aspects into its ongoing activities. Advance planning thereby becomes a key leadership function with this style. The leader seeks to keep departmental subunits from working at cross-purposes, making sure all units share the same vision or understanding of the organization's overall mission and goals.

The Catalyst

The leader can also be the "spark plug"—the catalyst or innovator—who makes things happen. The catalyst stimulates group action and is most effective when the group is well structured and ready to be directed. Staff members expect to be told what needs to be done, and the leader activates the group toward short-term, clearly defined goals and objectives. Even in cases where agency goals are more routine and time consuming, the leader using the catalyst style can promote the objective, relating individual and subunit goals to overall goals. The catalyst leader brings innovation to the agency's routine operations. The challenge to the leader who uses this style is to show organization members how the proposed change is necessary to those larger goals.

The Spokesperson

The leader also may function as the external spokesperson for the organization, representing its views and interests to the external environment. The leader as spokesperson is an advocacy role that secures additional resources for the agency or protects its resources during times of external cuts. The most common setting for this role of leadership is in budgetary decision making; the leader attempts to decisively influence budgetary decisions for the next fiscal year. The leader's task, however, is ongoing: standing up for the agency and its members when there are complaints about it, anticipating and preparing for external environmental changes that can adversely affect the agency, and maintaining the agency's values, work, and well-being. The leader as spokesperson affects group morale by visibly defending the group's welfare. Members view the leader as part of the organization rather than as standing apart from it, as aloof and controlling. The leader as spokesperson is an agency cheerleader, bestowing praise publicly and collectively. Defense or advocacy on behalf of an agency inherently involves collective praise.

The Crisis Manager

Leaders can also be crisis managers, directing organizational responses to critical challenges of various kinds: cultural, economic, military, natural disaster, and political. Leaders as crisis managers cope with resource scarcity. The ability to lead calmly during a time of crisis is a powerful influence on an agency and is often viewed as a mark of greatness in a leader. Three U.S. presidents who are consistently rated as the greatest led the nation during times of war and crises of national survival: George Washington at the nation's founding after the Revolutionary War, Abraham Lincoln during the Civil War, and Franklin D. Roosevelt during World War II. Former New York City mayor Rudy Giuliani, who led the city so effectively in the aftermath of 9/11, is a good example at the local level.

When a leader rises to the occasion and successfully copes with a crisis, then he or she is marked as great. When a leader fails to meet the crisis effectively, then he or she is marked as a failure. Among presidents, the contrast between Herbert Hoover's failure to cope with the Great Depression and FDR's success in doing so distinguishes the former as a failure and suggests why many historians believe FDR to have been among the three greatest presidents of all time and clearly the greatest of the 20th century.

To play the various roles expected of a president requires that leader to use several of these styles, mixing them as required by each given situation. As presidential scholars have noted:

> In the typical rendering of the American presidency, chief executives encounter formidable barriers to decisive leadership: a far-flung, entrenched bureaucracy; a largely independent and often-recalcitrant Congress; an array of news media operating under distinctive incentive structures; and a sporadically attentive and increasingly cynical public. . . . Richard Neustadt's (1990) description of presidential power as "the power to persuade" captures the conventional scholarly wisdom of a constrained executive office. . . . Presidents clearly labor under the dual burdens of high expectations and contested power, a challenge apparent to many occupants of the White House. In a typically forthright moment, President Truman suggested a man would be crazy to want the office if he knew what it required (McCullough, 1992). Decades earlier, President Grover Cleveland offered a young Franklin Roosevelt one wish as they shook hands: that the boy not grow up to be president of the United States. Only a handful of postwar presidents—Eisenhower, Reagan, and Clinton—have left office with public approval ratings substantially above the low point of their respective administrations.
>
> Notwithstanding the conventional view of the impossible presidency, political scientists have rediscovered arguments that chief executives enjoy meaningful unilateral authority even in a system of separated institutions sharing power. Amassing a rich body of descriptive data about unilateral presidential action, this literature has elaborated a theoretical framework to fit the pieces together and advance our understanding of presidential power (T. Moe and Howell, 1999; Howell, 2000). (Mayer and Price, 2002: 367)

Some of the difficulties of managing a huge departmental bureaucracy, especially in an atmosphere of "national crisis," are highlighted in Box 10.4, "Heading a Behemoth." It raises a number of issues about the difficulties faced by Secretary Tom Ridge as he oversees the creation and management of the new Department of Homeland Security and some of the conflicting values involved in doing so.

Accountability in Public Administration

Leaders influence agency values through their leadership in determining missions, goals, and objectives. Leaders are subject to constraint by a value highly prized in U.S. politics: accountability.[20] **Accountability** is the degree to which a person must answer to some higher authority for actions in the larger society or in the agency. Elected public officials are accountable to voters. Public agency managers are accountable to elected executives and legislatures. Agency leaders are held accountable to the political culture of society, which holds general values and ideas of democracy and public morality. Leaders are also answerable to special legislative mandates.

Accountability is determined both externally (by codes of ethics, legal mandates contained in a constitution and authorization laws, and professional codes or standards) and internally (by agency rules and regulations or personally internalized norms of behavior and moral ethics). There is a persistent and natural tension between internal and external controls to maintain accountability. Democracy requires a system of accountability: checks and balances on government structures, the scrutiny of regular audits, and the inquisitive eye of community and media watchdogs.

Constitutional and Legal Constraints

At the federal level, the U.S. Constitution and various laws legally constrain government and set broad parameters within which public administrators must operate. The Constitution specifies both executive and legislative accountability by its system of checks and balances.

Executive Accountability   **Executive accountability** resides in the federal Constitution's specified chief executive role, which charges the president with enforcing laws and federal court decisions as well as executing treaties ratified by the United States. The visibility of the chief executive's office results in the president's being given both the credit and the blame for how government seems to be operating.

Legislative Accountability   **Legislative accountability** refers to the legislative branch's responsibility to answer for how government is run. **Congressional oversight** is a primary legislative function. It involves monitoring by the U.S. Congress of all activities and actions of executive branch agencies and assessment to see whether laws are properly implemented. The Constitution's checks and balances were designed to enable Congress to ensure that the president faithfully executes the laws it enacts.

The General Accounting Office and Other Oversights   A major staff agency of the Congress charged with this oversight function is the General Accounting Office (GAO), which audits all federal agencies to prevent theft and wasteful practices. Legislative oversight is also achieved through legislative hearings of various types: budget hearings, confirmation hearings on major executive branch appointments, and investigative hearings. Congressional committees also investigate scandals (for example, Watergate, Iran-Contra, Whitewater, and the Clinton/Lewinsky affair). Congress acts somewhat like a permanent sitting grand jury, waiting to hear about and investigate improper acts by members of the executive branch.

INFOTRAC
COLLEGE EDITION

Mr. Justice Brandeis and the creation of the *Federal Register*

Box 10.4

Heading a Behemoth

An effective national preparedness policy requires three things: first, a coordinating agency with authority to set comprehensive federal policy; second, an agency willing to use that authority to establish clear and effective strategies; and, finally, a recognition that a domestic-preparedness policy must not only prepare for and prevent terrorist attacks, but also ensure that such efforts don't threaten a free society. . . .

At first blush, it might seem like the administration has in place an effective coordinating agency. When President Bush switched gears in June 2002 and accepted Democratic congressional proposals to establish a Department of Homeland Security (DHS), he conceded the need for a permanent, centralized agency with budget authority over the domestic-preparedness mission. That change reflected a grudging recognition by that the White House Office of Homeland Security, set up right after the terrorist attacks of September 11, was simply too weak. To rectify that, the new department was give direct supervisory and budgetary control over 22 agencies, plus its very own [cabinet-level] secretary, Tom Ridge.

Behind the headlines, however, the behemoth known as the DHS is less than what it seems. Guided by advisors from the Defense and Justice departments and the CIA, the administration ensured that the DHS has quite limited authority. So, now, while the DHS oversees a number of areas—everything from federal airline safety to federal responses to hurricanes and floods—it has no authority to oversee the counterterrorism activity and priorities of other agencies. These include the Defense Department, the Justice Department, and the CIA, the very agencies that are crucial for homeland defense. Instead of streamlining our domestic preparedness strategy, the DHS has simply become another agency added to the mix, equal but not primary.

Now, it may be true that vesting all counterterrorism and domestic-preparedness powers in the DHS would be unwise, and doing so could make the agency too unwieldy and even Orwellian. . . . But it remains deeply problematic that the administration left the Pentagon, the Justice Department, and the CIA untouched. As a consequence, the DHS has no legal power to monitor much of the spending for domestic preparedness. . . . Without that authority, the DHS has bowed to the agendas of distinct, rival, and often-warring agencies. And, of course, by virtue of its limited jurisdiction, the DHS has no real power to do anything about what Congress identified as perhaps the most glaring hole in our counterterrorism effort: the absence of an effective system for intelligence gathering.

Surely the administration can do better. In other areas, it has used executive orders to achieve centralized oversight. Indeed, when it comes to environmental or health and safety regulations of numerous departments, including the Environmental Protection Agency and the Department of Health and Human Services, the White House has seized direct coordination of policy making. Yet there seems to be no similar attention from Pennsylvania Avenue when it comes to the antiterrorism efforts of the Pentagon, CIA, and Justice Department. In fact, those agencies responsible for fighting the war on terrorism are in some ways the ones freest from direct control by the commander-in-chief.

But the problem isn't only that the administration has failed to give the DHS sufficient power. . . . The department set out its agenda in its National Strategy for Homeland Security only a month after the most massive restructuring of government in more than 50 years. Not surprisingly, the strategy was a catalog of conventional wisdom, suggesting such evident steps as "Secure Our Borders," and "Protect

---

Impeachment hearings exemplify the ultimate oversight of an elected official by the legislative branch. Because of his involvement with White House intern Monica Lewinsky, President Bill Clinton was only the second president in history to have been impeached (neither was convicted by the Senate). The only state governor to be impeached and removed from office was Governor Evan Meacham of Arizona, largely because of his bizarre behavior and outlandish statements that attacked virtually every minority group in his state.

Casework

Legislatures also use **casework**—services performed by legislators and their staffs in response to requests by constituents and on their behalf—to oversee the bureaucracy.

Cyberspace." Indeed, when asked before its release what the nation could expect, [Secretary] Ridge replied that the strategy would contain "no surprises." He was right. The 90-page report detailing 80 agenda items is all things to all people.

Worse, about a year after he took office, Ridge seems no closer to crafting clear, specific guidance. During that time, there has been an outpouring of suggestions from think tanks and universities on how to prioritize domestic-preparedness programs. But Ridge is still talking in generalities. As he speaks to governors, first responders, chambers of commerce, police and fire officials, citizen groups, think tanks, and public health managers about beefing up their systems, there is little sense of the critical priorities that must be satisfied, let alone how and with what money. It cannot be, however, that supporting a citizen corps is as equally compelling, or necessary, as enhancing money and equipment for first responders. A reader of DHS statements would be justified in concluding that the current strategy is "try anything and everything." . . .

Furthermore, the DHS has, to date, done little to integrate the private sector in domestic-preparedness planning. As any lawyer in the Washington area will tell you, while federal government employees were being evacuated on 9/11, the law firms surrounding much of downtown D.C. received no similar guidance. During the subsequent anthrax attacks, the administration remained silent on what private institutions—many of them with their own mail and delivery services—should be doing. While the DHS has provided its much-maligned list of must-haves for those at home, including the notorious duct tape, the truth is that the institutions—some as large as mini-cities—where most working people spend a good portion of the day have received virtually no guidance on terrorism preparedness.

Finally, the DHS' most notable attempt to guide the country in terrorism response was with its color-coded threat scheme, where colors change as the perceived threat of terrorism increases or decreases. But that scheme is now understood to be unworkable, forcing jurisdictions to respond to vague threats, pay police overtime, and wait it out. So the DHS has revamped it to make it harder for the threat level to change. But that doesn't help with the big question: What should jurisdictions do in response to fluctuating terrorism threats? . . .

As currently configured, the DHS is poorly suited to the task of ensuring that a homeland security strategy, whatever it might be, properly assesses the competing interests of security and liberty. That's not an accident. The administration fought proposals to establish an Office of Civil Rights and Liberties within the DHS, one that would monitor the department's compliance with constitutional norms as it conducted the war on terrorism. Such offices exist in other agencies, such as the Department of Education, where an independent review of government actions is deemed necessary. And certainly there are few agencies as likely to have as significant an impact on civil rights and liberties as the DHS. After all, the department may have a good justification for violating Americans' civil rights: It's just trying to prevent the worst from happening. All the more reason for an internal oversight body.

In addition to offices within DHS focused on the personal rights of citizens, it is also critical that a department with as massive a mission as the DHS has to be relatively transparent to the public and generally open to self-criticism. To that end, the legislation establishing the DHS created an Office of the Inspector General (OIG) to "prevent and detect fraud, abuse, mismanagement, and waste" in DHS programs. Hereto, however, due to Republican congressional efforts, the OIG has less power than it needs. Democratic proposals to create a more aggressive office were rejected during the debates leading up to the creation of DHS, and the law now permits the DHS secretary to prohibit the OIG from continuing any investigation that might disclose sensitive national security information.

Source: Excerpted from Juliett N. Kayyem, The Homeland Security muddle a year later: Tom Ridge's department still lacks a coherent strategy or adequate authority, *The American Prospect*, *14*(10) (November 2003): 46–48.

Agency administrators, responding to the legislature's power of the purse over them and to specific agency authorizations, are held accountable through casework activity. Patterns of casework alert administrative agency managers to administration problems that need to be addressed and fixed before they grow to crisis proportions. The value of accountability, in large measure, determines how successful an agency leader is perceived to be by the general public.

Administrative accountability is achieved through a balance between the elected executive, the legislature, mass media playing their watchdog role over government, and the public in expressing its approval or disapproval in both public opinion polls and voting booths.

Political Values versus Organizational Goals

While many values remain stable over time in society and form the general framework for government and constrain how it behaves, some values change and shift in response to cultural, economic, political, and social events. Changing values in administrative agencies often lag behind changing value orientations in society at large. These differences result in a degree of inherent conflict between the public's expressed political values at any given point in time and those values espoused and articulated by administrative agencies pursuing longer-term organizational goals. Elected executives tend to respond more quickly to changing political values than does a permanent and somewhat insulated civil service. Such inherent value conflicts result in clashes between executives and administrative agencies over what specific values are being promoted and emphasized at any point in time. Political leaders who do anything at all inevitably please some portion of the public and anger others because of what the governmental bureaucracy is seen as doing or not doing.

Both political leaders and agency leaders must manage conflict in values. Leaders seek to achieve a consensus of values between the agency and society at large as well as among the agency's many members and subunits. Successful leadership balances both internally conflicting values and external and internal forces to meet the demands of accountability. Ultimately, accountability works best when the predominant norms and values of both society and a particular agency are consistent and internalized by a majority of the organization's members. Leadership is an often lonely position. Accepting responsibility involves a heavy burden and can demand a heavy price.

We close with Reading 10.1, essentially an essay on all the complex aspects of leadership. It illustrates the complex interactions of these aspects and the special role the leader plays in organizational authority. As you read this discussion of leadership, think about which style of leadership might best fit which type of organizational structure. What values do leaders tend to promote? What are some consequences that result from leadership style and its compatibility, or lack thereof, to organizational purpose or structure? Can good organization survive poor leadership? Can great leadership transform outmoded organization?

Reading 10.1

Aspects of Leadership

Leadership in a public bureaucracy is a complex role. To be a truly effective leader of an agency requires balancing many aspects which will be discussed here. Effective leaders bring to bear personal traits and characteristics. They employ a leadership style appropriate to their agency, fitting its organization and mission. They are inspiring, with a vision for the future of the agency, and project that vision to others. They play bureaucratic politics well, securing support, financial and otherwise, for their agency and protecting it in times of budgetary cutbacks. They infuse the agency with mission-appropriate values. They articulate its goals both to their internal membership and to external stakeholders. Effective leadership is situational and contextual.

As this chapter has shown, leaders are not born. Simply put, there is no set array of traits that leaders have or must possess. But effective leaders do have personal characteristics they can, and do, bring to their leadership roles. Not every bureaucratic agency leader is charismatic or comes to head the agency with a fulsome vita of prior achievements in that agency or its field of endeavor. Not all leaders are exceptionally creative or intelligent or enterprising. Not all are notable for their technical proficiency or verbal acuity. Not all are decisive decision makers or exhibit Solomon-like wisdom of judgment. But effective leaders have some of these traits and inspire others because of them. Agency leaders exhibit different such traits, but they need to lead, and having several of the traits among the dozen or so discussed in this chapter is exceedingly helpful in doing so.

A central argument of transformation leadership theory (Bass, 1985) is that such leadership goes beyond transactional behaviors. Transformational leadership involves four conceptually distinct factors: (1) charisma, (2) intellectual stimulation, (3) individual consideration, and (4) inspirational motivation. Charisma is the leader's ability to arouse devotion and articulate a vision through personal dynamics. Charismatic leaders exude self-confidence and use emotional appeal with which subordinates identify. The leader develops higher-order goals that instill respect and loyalty. By developing intellectually stimulating goals, he or she is able to understand and

solve problems in novel ways that break with the past. Transformational leaders treat each subordinate with care and concern, inspiring and motivating subordinates toward action, building confidence, and inspiring belief in a cause. Followers are inspired to put aside their own interests for a collective purpose. Transformational leaders generate increased levels of subordinates' efforts and performance, and enhance positive attitudes and behaviors among their followers (Gellis, 2001: 25).

Transformational leaders are described as being proactive. They are willing to take risks, promote innovation, and accept and incorporate change. Their vision of the future for the organization transcends the status quo. Their followers are described as thereby performing beyond expected levels as a consequence of the leader's influence. The followers' extra levels of effort result from their commitment to the leader; their intrinsic work ethic, which is better motivated by the leader; their level of development; or their sense of purpose, which drives them to excel beyond ordinary limits. Transformational leaders help their agencies maximize performance through shared values. Thus, agencies more open to innovation and risk taking may be more conducive to transformational leadership and transformational behaviors can be learned in organizations (Bass, 1985).

Transactional leaders tend to be reactive. They are depicted as maintaining the status quo and avoiding risk and change. Leader-to-follower relationships are based on a series of exchanges between them. In cases of passive transactional leadership, leaders interact with followers by focusing on mistakes, delaying decisions, or avoiding situations until problems arise (Bass, 1985).

The purpose or mission of an agency and its organizational structure can render these two types of leadership more or less appropriate. Older, larger, and more hierarchically structured public agencies, for example, paramilitary departments such as big-city police or fire departments, tend to attract and work well under transactional leaders. Human service organizations staffed with many professionals, for example, large county health departments, public universities, or even smaller professionally staffed agencies such as planning or economic development, respond better to interactive leadership (that is, a more transformational approach) that emphasizes the pattern of personal interaction between the manager and other staff in the organization, using the problem-solving approach within participatory groups (Gellis, 2001: 18).

Transformational leadership has been shown to play an important role in many outcomes of particular interest to organizational researchers. Several studies have shown that ratings of leadership effectiveness relate positively and significantly to transformational leadership factors and negatively to management by exception (that is, the more transactional approach). Transformational leadership has been described as having a greater effect on a follower's performance in organizations experiencing change and unstable work environments. A study of social workers reported more satisfaction with the style and method of transformational leaders. Social workers rated their leaders as more effective in meeting their job-related needs, representing them to higher-level administrators, and contributing to organizational effectiveness. Such findings corroborate recent studies in which transformational leadership was, on average, strongly and positively correlated with the three outcome measures of extra effort, satisfaction with the leader, and leadership effectiveness, when compared to transactional factors (Bass and Avolio, 1997; Gellis, 2001).

Transformational leadership may be more desirable, even necessary, with agencies in their mature stage when dealing with an environment of rapid change. In such cases, it may take a transformational leader to overcome calcification in the standard operating procedures of the agency, to avoid excessive rigidity in how it does business, or simply to better anticipate problems on the horizon and deal with them before they develop into a crisis situation.

In short, effectiveness in leadership is contextual in the sense that the leader must employ an appropriate style of leadership to the type or structure of the organization, to its mission, and to that stage in the life cycle of the organization at which he or she leads it. A motivator style, for example, is more appropriate to a newer agency not yet so set in its standard operating procedures and so developed an organizational culture. The director style better fits an agency in the growth to maturity or mature

phase. The catalyst style might be best to lead during a revitalization phase. Large, complex agencies with multiple tasks and goals and a widely dispersed geographic operation typically need a coordinator style of leadership. The crisis manager, cool under pressure and inspiring of others, best rises to the occasion when the agency faces the inevitable crisis. Mayor Rudy Giuliani's leadership of New York in the post-9/11 period brought him justifiable acclaim in his handling of that crisis, and resuscitated his image as an effective mayor of that city. Or consider the case of then Secretary of State Colin Powell as an articulate, persuasive, and thereby effective leader of that federal department in selling the nation on the need to go to war in Iraq. The catalyst, one who innovates and sparks an agency to life or renewed life, is often the best leadership style for an agency needing rebuilding after a traumatic scandal or during a severe recessionary period. Governor Gary Locke of Alaska, discussed in Chapter 3, comes to mind. A transformational leader is not always appropriate to an agency, but when needed, a transformational leader cannot be effective without the traits of charisma, optimism, energy, and verbal ability.

An effective leader is accountable and relates well to the legislature, the elected executive under whom he or she serves, and the judiciary. Such a leader projects accountability to the general public as well. In the mid-1990s, Orange County, California, faced bankruptcy following a $1.6 billion dollar investment loss. Janice Mittermeir was selected as its chief executive officer (CEO). She had previously served as the county's chief auditor, and for a five-year period immediately prior to her appointment, she had served as director of the John Wayne Airport. As the former chief auditor, she was steeped in knowledge of the ins and outs of how Orange County agencies worked. She seized the opportunity to modernize the management structure of the county, instituted performance measurements, and improved long-range planning for county decisions. She put Orange County's financial house in order and was widely hailed for that accomplishment [see Lemov, *Governing*, 12 (November 1998): 23]. Her leadership exemplifies well the importance of the contextual situation to effective management style and the possession of appropriate personal characteristics. The county executive, the county commissioners, the county judiciary, and the general public all believed in her integrity and accountability.

On the other hand, critics of the new public management movement point out that the entrepreneurial and innovative style of leadership can result in such agency leaders taking unwarranted risks, becoming prone to rule breaking and undue self-promotion and bureaucratic power politics. Public-sector entrepreneurs can exhibit such traits as single-mindedness, tenacity, and a willingness to break rules to the point of being agency leaders who are difficult to control. They can become "loose cannons" [see Terry, 1998; deLeon and Denhardt, 2000].

A study published in 2000, however, found that agency heads, middle managers, and even front-line staff are frequently innovators, and that getting autonomous agencies to work together requires commitment to the effectiveness of the partnership that tends to downplay egotism and the desire for individual dominance. *Effective* policy innovators cannot be loose cannons [Borins, *Public Administration Review*, *60*(6) (November 2000): 498].

Public agency innovators must develop support for their ideas from many sources, both inside and outside the public sector. Local agency heads need state support, including the governor and the legislature, as well as support from appropriate lobbies and the general public, or their innovations will fail. Innovations often encounter opposition from professional groups when they require professions normally having little contact to work together, or when professionals must do something not traditionally viewed as being within the scope of their professional work, and when such programs involve the use of volunteers, community workers, or paraprofessionals. Far from being loose cannons, public sector innovators who achieved beneficial results, such as enhanced client well-being, improved service, and lower cost, did so with integrity (Borins, 1998: 67, 288).

Source: By author. This discussion drew especially from the following: B. M. Bass, *Leadership and performance beyond expectations* (New York: Free Press, 1985); B. M. Bass and B. J. Avolio, *Improving organizational effectiveness through transformational leadership* (Thousand Oaks, CA: Sage, 1994); B. M. Bass and B. J. Avolio, *Full range of leadership* (Palo Alto, CA: Mind Garden, 1997); Sanford Borins, *Innovating with integrity* (Washington, DC: Georgetown University Press, 1998); Linda deLeon and Robert Denhardt, The political theory of reinvention, *Public Administration Review*, *60*(2) (2000): 89–97; Zui D. Gellis, Social work perceptions of transformational and transactional leadership in health care, *Social Work Research*, *25*(1) (March 2001): 17–31.

Net Assignment

Using InfoTrac College Edition and other Internet sources, search for three biographies of contemporary governors in your region of the country, including your state's governor. Describe and support—by specific accomplishments and public statements—each governor's leadership style.

Summary

A leader tailors his or her leadership style to the type of agency being led and the situational context of the task at hand. Furthermore, these factors define the limits and degree of accountability inherent in any leadership role. The concepts of transactional and transformational leadership illustrate the vision of leadership as a relationship rather than as a single authority. Leaders typify various styles— most notably, director, motivator, coordinator or facilitator, catalyst, spokesperson, and crisis manager. Finally, a leader plays a prominent role in balancing the clash of values and developing a consensus between society's general political values and the values that an organization has designed to meet its own goals.

Glossary of Key Terms

accountability Degree to which a person must answer to some higher authority for actions in the larger society or within an agency or organization.

active-negative Type of presidential personality wherein the president has a driving need to achieve and maintain power; Woodrow Wilson, Herbert Hoover, Lyndon Johnson, and Richard Nixon are good examples.

active-positive   Type of presidential personality in which the president desires to achieve results above all else; Franklin Roosevelt, Harry Truman, John Kennedy, and Jimmy Carter are examples.

authority   Legal basis by which one has rights to use an organization's power and resources.

caretaker   Style of leadership in which the executive is a political conservative seeing him- or herself as a custodian of the status quo.

casework   Services performed by legislators and their staffs on request from and on behalf of constituents.

charisma   Leadership based on the personality of the leader rather than on a formal position.

congressional oversight   Monitoring by U.S. Congress of executive branch agencies' activities and actions to assess if laws are being properly implemented.

credibility   Recognition by an organization that a leader is competent to use the organization's powers and command its resources.

demagogue   Style of leadership that rallies support among followers by appeals to emotions and prejudice.

executive accountability   Constitutionally specified role of the president as chief executive and responsible for enforcing laws, court decisions, and treaties.

frustrated warrior   Style of leadership in which an unsuccessful policy entrepreneur ends up simply frustrated in his or her attempts to lead, usually because of legislative branch opposition.

functions of leadership   To define an organization's missions and role, the institutional embodiment of purpose, defending an institution's integrity, and ordering internal conflict.

leadership   Exercise of authority in directing the work of others; may be formal or informal.

legislative accountability   Legislative branch's responsibility to answer for how government is run.

passive-negative   Type of presidential personality in which the president emphasizes civic virtue; George Washington, Calvin Coolidge, and Dwight Eisenhower are good examples.

passive-positive   Type of presidential personality in which the president seeks to be loved and revered; William Taft, Warren Harding, and Ronald Reagan are examples.

policy entrepreneur   Style of leadership involving a progressive and highly activist executive who proposes and funds new programs.

trait theory   Belief or assumption that leadership is based on traits that leaders possess that impart unique characteristics and qualities that enable them to assume responsibility. A belief in "born" leadership.

transformational leadership   Leadership that strives to change an organization's culture and goals, reflecting the leader's ability to develop a values-based vision for the organization and to convert the vision into reality and sustain it over time.

Review Questions	**1.** Discuss the functions of leadership. How do trait theory, transactional theory, and transformational theory vary in their respective emphases on the functions of leadership?

2. Compare and contrast two leaders portrayed in the chapter's boxed materials. Are there any consistent traits apparent with each leader? What situational contexts contributed to the leaders' reputations or their perceived shortcomings as leaders?

3. Discuss the styles of leadership. What organizational or situational contexts lead an agency manager to adopt a particular style of leadership?

4. Compare and contrast executive and legislative accountability. How does accountability affect the perception of a president's success or failure as a leader?

5. Using the aspects of leadership from Reading 10.1, discuss how well Tom Ridge performed as secretary of the Department of Homeland Security. Which approach did he exemplify: transactional or transformational? What style did he project: demagogue, caretaker, policy entrepreneur, or frustrated warrior? Was he more a director, motivator, coordinator, catalyst, spokesperson, or crisis manager?

Surfing the Net

The following are useful websites for the topics discussed in this chapter:

General Accounting Office (GAO) (**http://www.gao.gov**)

Executive Office of the President (**http://www.whitehouse.gov**)

For general documents and academic sources concerning the presidency and presidential leadership, see Texas A&M's White House Archives (**http://www .tamu.edu/whitehouse**).

Every state government also has its own state home page. Here are a few:

California (**http://www.ca.gov/state/portal/myca_homepage.jsp**). The governor's website links to the state home page.

Georgia (**http://www.state.ga.us**)

Utah (**http://www.state.ut.us**)

Most if not every county government also has a home page. Here are a few:

Orange County, California (**http://www.oc.ca.gov**)

San Bernardino County, California (the country's largest county in land area) (**http://www.co.san-bernardino.ca.us**)

Shelby County, Tennessee (**http://www.co.shelby.tn.us**)

A mayor's office often can be reached through a city's home page. For example, Atlanta, Georgia's mayor can be found through that city's site (**http://www.ci .atlanta.ga.us**).

Every state also has a personnel office. See, for example, that for New York (**http://www.ric.goer.state.ny.us/employment/default.htm**)

Chapter 11

Communication Flows in Administration: The Fuzzing of Valucs

On February 7, 2003, there appeared on the website of the Center for Public Integrity an 86-page draft of the Justice Department's proposed sequel to the USA Patriot Act. It so radically subverts the constitutional rights of Americans and so appalled a member of John Ashcroft's staff that he or she had leaked it to Charles Lewis, head of the Committee for Public Integrity. That staff member became a whistle-blower. That very night, Charles Lewis revealed parts of the proposed law on Bill Moyer's PBS television program, *NOW*. Section 501 of the bill would strip American citizens of their citizenship for providing "material support" to a group designated by the administration as "terrorist," even if the individual did not know an organization was considered such and had legal activities to which the person was donating funds. Until this proposal, an American could only lose citizenship if he or she expressed clear intent to abandon it. But if Patriot II were enacted, the government need only "infer" your intent to be without a country. Section 303 allows the government to "collect, analyze, and maintain DNA samples" of "suspected terrorists." Until now, the FBI could only lawfully collect DNA identification records of people *convicted* of various federal crimes. And section 313 provides "an incentive for neighbors to spy on neighbor . . . by granting immunity to businesses that phone in false terrorism tips, even if their actions are taken with reckless disregard for the truth." And any "government whistle-blowers who reveal any information under this section commit a criminal offense even if their motivation was to protect the public from corporate wrongdoing or government neglect," according to the ACLU.

Three days after the draft bill was leaked by the whistle-blower on Ashcroft's staff, Senator Patrick Leahy of Vermont, ranking Democratic member of the Judiciary Committee, stated: "For months, and just as recently as last week, Justice Department officials have denied to members of the Judiciary Committee that they were drafting another antiterrorism package. . . . The early signals from the administration about its intentions for this bill are ominous." A secret government is, by its very nature, ominous. Perhaps that is why all 50 of the American states have some sort of "whistle-blower protection" laws on their books. In July 2002, for example, the state of New York expanded its whistle-blower legislation to protect health care providers from fear of retaliation for disclosing to supervisors or public agencies activities that constitute improper patient care or for refusing to participate in such activities. If they do face retaliation, they may seek relief in civil courts and cannot be required to pay their employer's attorney and court costs. Whistle-blower protection laws all have the same general objectives: to expose, deter, and curtail wrongdoing. Whistle-blower activity inherently reveals divisions in government over basic values.

Drawn from Nat Hentoff and Lisa Schiff
The patriot whistleblower, *Free Inquiry, 23*(3) (Summer 2003): 20;
Whistleblower protections expand in N.Y., *RN, 65*(7) (July 2002): 16.

Introduction

When implementing public policy, administrators will inevitably please some people and offend others. A major function of leadership in a public organization is to craft communications in ways that inform and please the most and offend the least. **Communication** is defined as the exchange of information and the transmission of meaning, and it is the very essence of organizations. Communication is best understood as a social process that significantly influences the functioning of any agency, and it is best viewed in relation to the social system in which it occurs and to the particular functions it performs in that system. The communication system of an organization is every bit as critical as its chain of command.[1]

Communication in agencies has five dimensions:

1. the size of the communication loop,
2. the nature of the communication circuit,
3. the openness of the communication circuit,

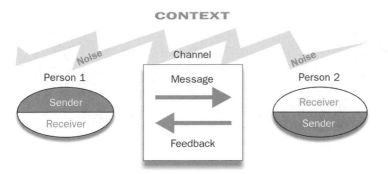

CONTEXT

FIGURE 11.1
A Typical Communication Model

Source: From Phillip Clampitt, *Communicating for managerial effectiveness*, p. 34. Copyright © 1991. Reprinted by permission of Sage Publications, Inc.

4. the efficiency of the circuit, and
5. the quality of fit between the circuit and its systemic function.[2]

Communication in Administration

Both public administrators and organizational theorists increasingly emphasize the critical role of communication. In recent decades, scholars of the communication process have noted that communication problems develop not only from information flows that are too slow, incomplete, or distorted (intentionally or not), but also from information that is too abundant, a problem referred to as *communications overload*. Sometimes staffs deal with governing boards or executives by intentionally "flooding" them with information. Too much information overwhelms board members or elected executives, who still must attempt to handle it all and grasp its import.[3]

Figure 11.1 presents a typical model of the communication process using a systems model framework. Although the model is simple, the communication process it depicts is not. The person who sends the message and the person who receives it must code and decode the information—somewhat complicated processes with plenty of opportunity for error, misinterpretation, and distortion.[4]

All information transfer goes through a **coding process**: Any system (a person, an organization) that sends or receives information uses a characteristic coding and decoding process that omits, selects, refines, elaborates, distorts, and transforms.[5]

Value Content in Communication

Values are often the subject matter of organizational communication. Many types of communication, in fact, involve selling an agency's value perspective to a particular audience. Managers may have to sell such a perspective to agency members to transform the organization's values, resolve value conflicts, or mitigate their effects within the agency.

Values enter the communication process implicitly through the coding–decoding processes. Values shape the language and imagery used in messages, sometimes but not always consciously so. Cartoon 11.1 demonstrates how value-charged language easily enters the message projected by government. It spoofs the message of current immigration policy by rewriting what the Statue of Liberty says to today's would-be immigrants.

" GIVE ME YOUR RICH, YOUR FAMOUS, YOUR NOBEL LAUREATES, YOUR RUSSIAN POETS AND POLISH EMISSARIES, YOUR RESPECTABLE WHITE ANTI-SOVIETS YEARNING TO BREATHE FREE...... "

An exploratory study of arguments in the jury decision-making process

Types of Communication

Two types of communication—formal and informal—play a vital role in organizations. Although communication is essential to any agency, it can become dysfunctional. Small groups play important roles in organizational communication flows, both formal and informal. The flow of communication may be upward, downward, horizontal, or diagonal or crisscrossed. This chapter describes the types of communication flow and the problems associated with each type.

Formal Communication

Formal communication refers to written communication messages that follow an organization's formal chains of command.[6] Its volume and content is influenced by the size of the agency and by the public character of government bureaucracy. Approximately two-thirds of a manager's communication time is spent on composing, sending, and processing vertical messages and just one-third on horizontal communication.[7] Managers tend to use more formal communication because the role of an agency's executive is to direct, coordinate, and control the activities of persons below them.

Formal communication is essential to any organization. It promotes the value of accountability. Effective use of formal communication reduces disparities and discrepancies in policy, procedures, rules, and regulations. When properly used, formal communication saves time and allows information to be more fully developed. Written communication enables the manager or supervisor to indicate more fully the ramifications of orders and directives sent through formal communication channels.

Formal communication has obvious disadvantages. First, the sheer volume of information is the most often discussed. Large organizations, especially if they are highly centralized and involve "tall" hierarchical structure, simply generate too much paperwork, which creates enormous costs in producing, processing, and storing formal communication. Second, precisely because it is formal, such communication is less humane. It is "objective" by design. Third, formal communication is also partly designed for self-protection—to cover one's backside by spreading responsibility. Fourth, while formal communication allows for accountability, it also can be used to avoid or reduce accountability if things seem to be going wrong. Written communication distributed through formal channels is often used to "spread the blame." And as we saw in the opening vignette to this chapter, written communication can be the stuff of a whistle-blower's leak.

Written formal communication takes the form of letters, memoranda, files or records, reports, and manuals that specify practices and procedures. A distinguishing characteristic of records and reports is that they specify the people who completed them and the occasions or occurrences of particular events or circumstances when they are expected to make reports and the information that is to be included in those reports. These operating rules of formal communication relieve individual agency members from having to continually decide what part of any information should be passed on to which members and in what format. Manuals, for example, communicate practices intended to have a relatively permanent application. They promote a common understanding among members of the agency's structures and policy. They emphasize such values as centralization, uniformity, and completeness.[8]

Formal communication makes certain actions, decisions, or policies "legal" within the framework of an agency's powers. The channels of formal communication coincide with and parallel the organization's formal authoritative structure.[9]

Table 11.1 illustrates the types of information that local government officials need and consult. It presents data as to how frequently local government officials reported needing certain types of information that were processed through formal communication channels.

How well lower-level or external audiences of formal communications accept the transmitted information depends in part on the credibility of the information sources. Table 11.2 summarizes factors that influence the sender's credibility and suggests techniques to enhance that credibility.

The sheer volume of paperwork from formal communication within the U.S. government has led to periodic attempts to reform and reduce such volume. The Paperwork Reduction Act of 1980, for example, charged the OMB with controlling the flow of paperwork. (More will be said of these periodic attempts to deal with information overload later.) Problems of communication within formal channels of government have long played a role in reform efforts, the latest of which was manifested in the reinventing government movement discussed in Chapters 5, 6, and 7.

Informal Communication

Informal communication refers to oral communication that flows inside and outside formal channels of communication and written communication that does not follow formal channels. It is more spontaneous and intrinsically more gratifying. Informal communication is frequently more informative than formal communication and usually transmitted more rapidly up, down, and across an organization. It is an essential component of the socialization network by which an organization develops, spreads, and maintains its organizational culture.

Every agency develops a system of informal communication, no matter how elaborate its system of formal communication. Informal communication may consist of information that flows along formal channels but is not formal—that is, not recorded, filed, or maintained—or that flows along informal channels. Because

TABLE 11.1

Types of Information Needed and Consulted by Local Officials (Minimum of 30%)

	Types of Information Needed Daily or Weekly	
	% Needing at Least Once a Week	% Needing Every Day
Directories of names, addresses, phone numbers	33	38
Legal information	41	24
Information on policies of city council or board of supervisors	36	22
Agency rules and regulations	33	24
Departmental budget or financial information	27	22
Information about new developments in field	21	11
Information on local agencies and organizations	25	7

	Types of Information Resources Consulted Daily or Weekly	
	% Needing at Least Once a Week	% Needing Every Day
Directories of names, addresses, phone numbers	33	38
Internal department records from own department (not library)	37	30
Personal collection of books, reports, files	23	40
Departmental library or information center	28	19
Consultation with knowledgeable colleague, expert, or outside consultant	31	12
Co-worker's collection of books, reports, files	32	5

Source: Adapted from Mark Levin, The information-seeking behavior of public officials, *American Review of Public Administration*, *21*(4) (1991): 278–279. Copyright © 1991. Reprinted by permission of Sage Publications, Inc.

that communication is not official, it can more readily be withdrawn, altered, adjusted, augmented, or even canceled. Informal communication often arises from a functional need to communicate when no formal channel exists. It is frequently horizontal in direction, filling gaps in the formal communication network and connecting peers rather than superiors to subordinates. When officials who communicate informally are of different or unequal rank, the informal nature of the communication downplays status differences.[10] All agencies develop informal communication flows along those lines.

Informal communication is greatly influenced by technological developments, such as e-mail, faxes, photocopies, telephone answering machines, and voice mail. The groupthink syndrome discussed earlier exemplifies a communication problem that more often occurs during crisis decision-making situations. As we have seen,

TABLE 11.2

Factors and Techniques for Credibility

Factor	Basis	Initial Credibility Stressed by	Credibility Increased by
Rank	Hierarchical power	Emphasizing title or rank	Associating oneself with someone of high rank (e.g., countersignature or introduction)
Goodwill	Personal relationship, track record	Referring to relationship or track record	Building goodwill by citing audience benefits
	Trustworthiness	Acknowledging conflict of interest; offering balanced evaluation	
Expertise	Knowledge, competence	Including a biography or résumé	Associating oneself with or quoting someone the audience considers expert
Image	Attractiveness, audience desires to emulate	Emphasizing attributes audience finds attractive	Building one's image by identifying with audience's benefits; using nonverbals and language audience considers dynamic
Shared values	Morality, standards	Establishing a common ground or similarities at the beginning of the communication	
		Tying the message to shared values	

Source: Mary Munter, *Guide to managerial communication* (5th ed.), p. 9. © 2000. Reprinted by permission of Pearson Education, Inc., Upper Saddle River, NJ.

groupthink refers to a situation in which decision makers seek to achieve concurrence among members in a small decision-making group and where such concurrence becomes more important than making calculated, carefully considered decisions. Groupthink is more likely to occur when the amount of useful information is so severely constrained that viable policy alternatives cannot be generated or when important questions fail to get asked. Box 11.1, "A Failure of Intelligence," illustrates groupthink behavior and how it can result in decision making that is flawed or marred by unintended consequences.

Informal communication links informal groups in an organization, and it fills a vacuum in the formal chain of command. It can often get around the "stovepiping" problem referred to earlier. It is so frequently used because it is more readily accessible. Informal communication is often referred to as the *grapevine*—all of the internal and nonsystematic channels of communication within an organization.[11]

The grapevine is used when the message is urgent or the information concerns friends and work associates. Physical proximity between sender and receiver also promotes the flow of information along the grapevine, although electronic links make distance less important to any grapevine system. The grapevine is used to spread rumors and is influenced by status seeking and maladjustment to the job. It also serves as an emotional outlet, as a filler in social conversation, or simply as a way for an individual to avoid suspense. Social friendships among individuals in an organization encourage "shop talk," and informal communication is often used to advance a member's personal aims. Large organizations also tend to

INFOTRAC
COLLEGE EDITION

Groupthink and the Gulf Crisis

Box 11.1

A Failure of Intelligence

America's intelligence system failed to see terrorists threats coming from al-Qaeda prior to 9/11/2001 that should have been evident. After 9/11, it saw terrorist threats coming from Iraq that did not exist. A system that fails to warn of real threats and warns of unreal ones is a broken system. The unanimous and bipartisan report coming from the Congressional commission investigating the intelligence mistakes leading up to 9/11 dealt harshly with both the CIA and the FBI. It found that better intelligence gathering might have prevented the attacks. And a unanimous and bipartisan Senate Intelligence Committee has discredited the CIA's prewar assessments that Iraq had banned chemical and biological weapons and was seeking nuclear arms. Such assessments, it found, "either overstated or were not supported by the underlying intelligence." The senators blamed a "series of failures" of intelligence that occurred because of "shoddy work," faulty management, outmoded procedures, groupthink, and a flawed culture."

The White House and Congress are now struggling with what to do about those failures and are sorting through several contradictory proposals. One proposal would create a cabinet-level intelligence "czar" with enhanced control over the sprawling $40 billion system for collecting and analyzing information about security threats. A second would do the opposite—removing the CIA director from any control over intelligence agencies, as a method to encourage more checks and balances. A third proposal would better insulate the director of central intelligence from "politics" by giving the position a fixed term, for example, of five or seven years. Still a fourth, and contradictory, one would make the director more politically accountable to both the President and Congress.

Such proposals seem to miss a core lesson from history. When U.S. foreign policy is based primarily on what our spy agencies say, it runs the risk of being disastrously wrong. Better intelligence is not a substitute for better policy. This is particularly the case when the threat is in the form of terrorism. Terrorism is a concept and a tactic. One simply cannot fight a war against a tactic like one can a nation-state. There is no finite number of terrorists in the world you can find and capture or destroy. At any given time, their number varies, depending on how many people are driven by anger and hate to join the ranks of terrorists. Smoking out, imprisoning, or killing terrorists based on information supplied by intelligence agencies cannot be the prime means of preventing future terrorist attacks. That means effective foreign policy to deal with the problem involves restarting the Middle East peace process. It requires shoring up the economies of the Middle East. It means strengthening the legitimacy of moderate Muslim leaders instead of encouraging extremism.

Equally flawed is the notion that "preemptive wars" against nations our intelligence agencies have identified as likely adversaries will offer much protection. Terrorists are not dependent on a few rogue nations. They recruit and train in unstable parts of the world with weak or nonexistent governments. They can and do move their bases and camps easily. That the United States suffers from a failure of intelligence is indisputable. But the calamitous state of our spy agencies is only one part of that failure and structural tinkering with spy agencies only a small part of any solution to that failure.

develop *cliques*—groups that build an informal networks of communication and use them to secure power.[12] In addition to transmitting information that has not been transmitted formally, the grapevine serves as a useful barometer of opinion within an agency. Administrators can use a grapevine to keep current on topics that are of interest to organizational members as well as their attitudes about such topics. An astute manager also can use the grapevine to spread useful information quickly.[13]

In general, the grapevine:

- is a significant part of any organizational communication system, both for quantity and quality of information;
- provides useful input to management;

- helps management understand employees' problems, attitudes, and information gaps;
- can significantly enhance management decisions;
- can significantly affect the quality of management's communication processes if management has the capacity to understand and relate to them;
- cannot be suppressed or directly controlled but can be influenced;
- generates both positive and negative influences on an organization;
- can provide useful insights even when the information it carries is known to be incorrect;
- generally carries more correct than incorrect information;
- typically carries an incomplete story;
- spreads information faster than formal communication;
- stimulates communication;
- is a forum for equal activity among men and women;
- finds significance in nonverbal communication as a way of interpreting verbal information;
- creates message centers in informal leaders; and
- is a normal response to group work.

Communication's Role in Organizations

Communication networks are simply essential. For an agency to function efficiently, information must flow from management levels to employees, and vice versa. Communication is only completed when the sender conveys *meaningful* messages with accurate information that cause the receiver to react in the manner intended by the sender. To be effective, the process of decision making depends on accurate facts and figures to inform any decision—which, in turn, requires accurate transmission of information up, down, and across the bureaucracy. It is relatively easy to design a communication network for an agency to handle information transmission and to say that it must be accurate, unbiased, complete, and properly transmitted—but making it so is difficult.

Communication Networks and Efficiency

The ever-growing specialization in organization, coupled with increasing interdependency, makes it increasingly vital that information flow efficiently up, down, and across. The **efficiency of communication** in an agency is measured by the number of communications that are successfully transmitted in a given network.[14] Upper-level management can promote such efficiency by emphasizing quality rather than quantity, by delegating administrative responsibility in a clearly defined manner, and by ensuring that the structure of the agency—including its chain of command and formal communication network—is clearly understood by all managers.[15]

Bottlenecks in the Flow   A common problem of communication in organizations is the development of a bottleneck, or a place where information gets stuck, slowed down, or distorted as it flows up or down the hierarchy. Bottlenecks are especially

CARTOON 11.2
Dilbert on project meetings
What often happens at meetings when supervisors or management replace line personnel when discussing organizational projects?

Source: DILBERT: © Scott Adams/Dist. by United Feature Syndicate, Inc. Reprinted with permission.

associated with upward communication. As noted, upward communication tends to be more formal—reports to superiors, for example. A bottleneck often develops from a basic problem of upward communication: the administration's hierarchical structure. Employees at lower levels are often reluctant to pass along information that may harm them or put them in a bad light with superiors, especially negative information. Information gets stale as it goes upward, and delays frequently involve disadvantages and inefficiencies. Information also often changes as it goes up, influenced by both conscious and unconscious distortions. There is, for example, a natural human tendency to soften or shade news that is perceived to be unwelcome. Distortion can be found in downward communication flows as well. Particularly in large organizations, employees tend to obey only those rules they believe in, and they can become quite adept at evading rules or bending them to suit their needs.[16] A problem of superior/subordinate communication is gently but insightfully spoofed in Cartoon 11.2. Which personnel are or are not involved in meetings can indeed be critically important and influence much more than an organization's communication flow.

Managers and supervisors need **operational feedback**—systematic information acquisition and analysis that is closely tied to the agency's ongoing functions. Such feedback is an integral part of those functions. In agencies, it is natural for supervisors to give orders and for subordinates to receive them. But upward communication goes against that natural grain or flow and limits feedback.[17]

Communications Overload   The sheer volume of information processed in large departments, moreover, can become a problem and lead to communication overload. To operate efficiently, departments must react to such overload in some way by:

- omitting some information to reduce volume,
- transmitting some erroneous information,
- developing a system of information queuing,
- filtering the information and restricting who receives both upward or downward communication,
- sending up approximations of information rather than complete or uncondensed data,
- using multiple channels to send information upward or downward, and
- sometimes simply escaping from the task of processing the information—which, of course, creates a bottleneck in the communication network.[18]

Dysfunctional Communication   Communication flows that develop too many problems become dysfunctional. The more problems that develop in the formal communication system, the more members rely on and use the informal network—the grapevine. Managers also can react to the spread of rumors by:

- increasing factual information and trying to make sure it is readily accessible,
- holding small group meetings to counter rumors,
- using bulletin boards (also known as "rumor boards"),
- training managers to recognize the reasons why rumors develop, and
- preventing idleness and monotony in work groups and among management.[19]

Among the best ways to prevent dysfunctional communication is simply the attitude that superiors project. When superiors are seen as open to bad news, it is less likely to become bottlenecked along the way. Employee trade unions are often effective measures to deal with rumors, because they provide a second channel of information that is more readily accepted as credible. Unions generally insist on formal measures to hear complaints. Supervisors also can actively encourage the use of suggestion boxes, establish investigatory units to get undistorted information, and use a method known as the *straight scoop,* by which the supervisor ignores the chain of command and reaches downward several layers into the organization to get information directly.[20]

Small Groups in Organizational Communication Channels

The number of communication tasks that administrators need to perform involve many that could be performed by others. Leaders can delegate drafting of communications, screening of incoming communication, and liaison with units and groups in large departments to staff members, who may themselves become key small groups in any organization.

Such small groups develop their own norms of behavior, codes of language, and transmissions of messages and both formal and informal means to enforce their norms. The power of small groups often exceeds that of formal authority. Informal rules or norms, for example, may ban "squealing." This may itself be a cause of information distortion and can contribute to dysfunctional communication. The formal organization, however, cannot exist without its informal counterparts.[21] The decentralization reforms advocated by the new public management and the reinventing government movements would tend to enhance informal information development in organizations.

Small groups, as primary forms of informal organization, develop when the members of an organization seek to satisfy needs that the formal organization ignores, thwarts, or simply devalues.[22] Small-group members most often communicate with one another orally and informally—person to person, face to face. Such information transfer is less susceptible to both upward and downward distortion.

Representatives of lobbying organizations often become involved in small groups that affect decision making in larger organizations. They do so precisely because the nature of small-group behavior enables them to exert greater influence in the decision-making process.

The Flows of Communication

Theories of management that focus on communication tend to emphasize the flow of communication, especially downward flow. As already noted, information may be communicated upward, downward, horizontally, or diagonally. Each directional flow is discussed briefly here.

Downward Communication

Downward communication concerns the flow from superior to subordinate. It follows the authority pattern of hierarchical positions. Management uses downward communication to direct, coordinate, and control. Typically, communication flowing downward involves one of five basic types:

1. specific job or task directives;
2. information about tasks (job rationale);
3. communication about procedures and practices—issuing or explaining policies, rules, regulations, procedures, and benefits;
4. feedback to subordinates about their job performance; and
5. indoctrination of goals—involving communication that is more ideological in character in which a sense of mission is given.

Downward communication often involves management articulating value perspectives and attempting to infuse lower levels of an agency with those values.[23] That is not always an easy task. If the downward communication is limited or somewhat unclear, then lower levels may ignore it or respond with minimal compliance. If they reject those values, then they may also resist and test out with specific behavior their own ideas and values rather than the policy that comes "down from on high."

Distortion enters the downward flow when managers who experience value resistance react rigidly, often resorting to secrecy, tighter controls, or outright manipulation of information. Agency members react to that with suspicion and distrust, filling information gaps with rumors and exhibiting cynicism or apathy or perhaps even leaking information to the outside media or other agencies.

Ineffective downward communication results from several reasons:

- lack of clearly defined objectives,
- lack of proper understanding among top-to-bottom supervisors about downward communication,
- failure to take sufficient time to ensure current communication techniques are effective,
- nonresponsiveness to holding meetings to clarify problems, and
- insufficient communication training.[24]

Several things can be done to improve downward communication:

1. specify an objective for communicating;
2. ensure that the content of the message possesses the qualities of accuracy, specificity, forcefulness, a receiver orientation, simplicity, and no hidden meanings; and

3. use the best communication techniques to get the message effectively to the receiver.[25]

Gordon Tullock's 1965 model of communication distortion suggests several antidistortion factors that can be built into an organization's communication system.[26] Tullock suggests that upper-level management use *redundancy*—that is, require duplication of reports that the manager suspects may be distorted. Competition and redundancy may be somewhat wasteful of overall agency resources, but they allow supervisors to verify the accuracy of the reports that flow upward. One method of duplication is to use sources of upward flow that are external to the agency. Another method involves creating overlapping areas of responsibility within a bureau, each of which reports upward on some overlapping aspect. Another duplication method is to create overlapping areas in different bureaus.

Another antidistortion device is for the information recipient to build in counter-biases. Managers themselves often previously served in an agency's lower levels and can remember the distortions they used when reporting information to superiors. They can use that knowledge to "adjust" reports from subordinates to take into account those biases. Superiors also might build into communication directives and required reports measures that are designed to reduce distortion by requiring that information in the reports do the following:

- shift from the future toward the present or past,
- shift away from qualitative and immeasurable factors and toward quantitative and measurable factors, and
- shift from quantitative factors that cannot be verified easily to those that can be.

A third way to deal with distortion is to eliminate the "middlemen" by reducing the levels or layers of hierarchy through which information flows. This approach requires either designing an organization that is flat or using various "bypass" devices.

Not all superiors are free, of course, to design and maintain a flat organization. The legislature or an elected chief executive usually designs the hierarchy. Officials in an agency, however, often may influence the span of control and have a degree of discretion as to how many reports are sent and to whom. Flatter hierarchies tend to function better when the agency is dealing with highly routinized activities that can be reported by objective indices.

Bypassing devices can be used for information flowing in various directions. Several used in the upward flow are:

1. the *straight scoop*, wherein high-level officials directly contact officials far below them in their own hierarchy, getting the information directly or transmitting complex orders directly to those who are responsible for carrying out those orders;

2. the *checkout*, in which supervisors test ideas by passing them downward informally before using formal channels to see how such information will be received by or affect the agency; and

3. *co-optation*, or higher-level officials giving lower-level officials a feeling of belonging to inner councils of a bureau, which increases the likelihood that co-opted members will accept, implement, and even sell decisions in which they feel invested.

FIGURE 11.2
Controlling the Controllers

1. Any federal regulatory agency, whether dependent or independent in structure, wishing to initiate a rule or regulation in its jurisdiction: MUST FIRST

2. Seek initial approval of the Office of Management and Budget (OMB): WHO IF APPROVES, THEN

3. Allows the agency to prepare a draft of the proposed regulation. The agency must then send the draft version to the OMB at least 60 days before its publication of the proposed rule or regulation in the *Federal Register.*

4. The agency receives feedback from the OMB as to the proposed rule or regulation. The OMB may approve, modify, or disapprove of the rule or regulation.

5. When OMB approves, the rule or regulation is then published in the *Federal Register.* Interested parties have a 30- to 60-day period for public notice and comment. After that period, the agency prepares final rule and an impact analysis. It must send these back to

6. OMB may again approve, modify, or disapprove this version of the proposed rule or regulation. If approved:

7. The rule or regulation is published in final rule form in the *Federal Register.* Regulation goes into effect in 30 days after publication of the final form. Rule or regulation is then published in the *Code of Federal Regulations.*

Figure 11.2 illustrates how information flows downward in the federal government's executive branch, where reports and regulatory rules, regulations, and procedures are screened by the Office of Management and Budget.

The use of downward communication to direct or set an organization's mission and influence its policies and procedures is illustrated in Figure 11.3, which presents a series of behaviors directed by a university president in an opening convocation of the school's faculty and staff. As leader of the university, the president articulated a vision of how he wanted and expected the university to function under his administration. It illustrates how leaders project their values downward through an organization in this case, a state university serving more than 14,000 students.

Upward Communication
Upward communication is from subordinates to superiors. It provides feedback to management, task coordination, and emotional and social support to the individual member.[27] Because of screening, filtering, and the interpretation of information

PHOTO 11.1
Albert Karnig, President of California State University–San Bernardino
Formal convocations are good events for organizational leaders to articulate their visions of mission, goals, and objectives. What communication problems, however, are associated with changing the values of an organization through such occasions? What are some of the values in Figure 11.3 that this president is trying to inspire in the faculty and staff of this university?

Source: Office of Public Relations, California State University– San Bernardino.

Principles—and the Behaviors That Mark Them

1. Integrity—consistently meaning what we say and saying what we mean.
2. Amicability—a forthcoming attitude that builds relationships, instead of unnecessary coolness and hostility.
3. Responsiveness—meeting the needs of those seeking assistance—respectfully; accurately, and, where possible, swiftly.
4. Caring and celebration—a place with concern for one another and frequent observance of successes.

Processes—and the Behaviors That Mark Them

5. Promote community—with myriad unit, division and university-wide activities, receptions and other events.
6. Advance collegiality, participation and consultation—wherever possible, involving the campus in the university's decisions and directions.
7. Engage and empower—with opportunities for participation that go beyond the merely symbolic.
8. Reflect campus diversity—by being thoughtful about its many aspects and ultimately serving as a model for other universities.

Policies—and the Behaviors That Mark Them

9. Concentrate on long-term (as well as short-term) objectives—rather than banging hard decisions onto someone else's court or shifting them onto someone else's future watch.
10. Have clear goals and outcomes in mind—instead of developing fuzzed-up and murky objectives in order to secure near-term support; the intent should be to leave the university a better place in the future.
11. Emphasize student, faculty and staff development—because students are the reason for the university's existence and faculty and staff are the reasons for its successes.
12. Decentralize decisions to levels accountable for outcomes—with both local decision making and the assumption of responsibility pivotal in meeting university goals.
13. Are faithfully and successfully executed—with equal attention and concern devoted to effective implementation at the end as to process issues at the beginning.

FIGURE 11.3
California State University— San Bernardino President Karnig's Behavioral, Process, and Policy Principles

Source: President's Convocation, California State University, San Bernardino, September 1999. With permission from Albert Karnig, CSUSB.

transmitted within an agency, there is a tendency for widespread problems in upward communication.

The common types of upward communication are:

- formal inquiries;
- reports by first-level supervisors;
- formal attitude surveys;
- grievance or complaint procedures and information;
- counseling;
- exit interviews;
- talks with union representatives;
- formal meetings;
- suggestions to improve processes, procedures, rules and regulations;
- the identification of problems emerging in the organization's environment;
- significant developments in work units;
- alerts to mistakes that downgrade operational efficiency; and
- inquiries about problems that lower-level employees do not know how to handle or for which no routine procedure has been established.

Distortions in upward communication reflect and are increased by the following:

1. employees' fears of expressing their true feelings to supervisors;
2. employees' feelings of estrangement from management—that it is remote and out of touch with employees' values and worries;
3. lack of rewards for good ideas;
4. lack of supervisory accessibility and responsiveness; and
5. feelings that higher-level management does not promptly act on problems.[28]

Such distortions involve delays, screening out of important information, changing information, and sending inaccurate data in reports.

Factors that seem to limit or minimize upward communication distortion are:

- subordinates' sense of or lack of trust in their superiors,
- subordinates' perceptions of their superiors' influence over their future, and
- subordinates' mobility aspirations.

Factors that tend to increase distortion in upward communication are:

- aspects of the authority structure of an organization, such as multiple levels of management to which reports must be sent,
- severe competition or strong rivalries among subordinates or between subunits,
- downward distortions of information, and
- a general climate of cynicism and distrust.[29]

In older and more stable departments, upper-level managers tend to know the types of distortions likely to occur and can use counterdistortion devices; these managers tend to use bypass devices less often than do managers in newer and more dynamic agencies. Two counterdistortion devices are the *end run*, a bypass designed to get around an immediate supervisor who refuses to communicate certain ideas up formal channels and thus creates a communications bottleneck; and the *speedup*, a bypass used to accomplish things quickly by avoiding slow-moving formal channels or forcing midlevel supervisors and managers to pass information upward within such a short period of time that they cannot condense and thereby distort information.[30]

When agency personnel distrust management or fundamentally disagree with the values that leadership is promoting, they sometimes use the communication device of *leaking* vital or critical information outside the agency, typically to news media or legislative or executive oversight staff agencies. The leaker is considered a whistle-blower. This communication ploy may bypass an immediate supervisor, who is often the source of the problem, but whistle-blowing is frequently costly and always somewhat risky for lower-level employees. Whistle-blowers are often considered snitches even by their peers and are sometimes ostracized by fellow employees. Upper-level supervisors may question the whistle-blower's loyalty in future dealings, even when he or she provides accurate information that corrects a problem.

Table 11.3 summarizes some typical methods of communication, both formal and informal, that affect both upward and downward communication.

EPA Inspector may not be subpoenaed in whistle-blower case

Horizontal Communication

Horizontal communication involves moving information among peers at the same level of an organization. It typically concerns reports about personnel, performance, problems, organizational practices and policies, and what needs to be done and how it can be done. It can move from one departmental subunit to another at the same or a comparable level.[31] It is sometimes known as *lateral* or *across-lines* communication. It generally involves the strongest of all flows of information. At an agency's lower levels, horizontal communication commonly exceeds vertical communication in volume by quite a lot. Units exchange horizontal communication both formally and informally to solve problems and coordinate workflow. Horizontal communication usually involves highly goal-oriented information. It typically relates to task coordination, problem solving, information sharing, and conflict resolution.[32] The pattern of horizontal communication reveals which people in an agency really work together closely. Formal communication that is horizontal is still usually inadequate, which is why grapevine channels develop.

Horizontal communication problems may weaken an agency's authority structure, contribute to communications overload, disrupt harmony by spreading rumors and other dysfunctional information, and promote or exacerbate the development of cliques and rivalries among subunits.[33]

Diagonal Information

One type of diagonal communication is called **crisscrossing information**, or information transmitted when a subordinate in one unit talks to a boss in another unit, and vice versa.[34] Cross-communication tends to be informal. It is useful to arrange staff meetings and small-group meetings and often reflects the physical arrangements of an organization. Different units that share the same building, for example, tend to communicate more often using cross-communication flows. Its usage is also promoted by in-service training programs, rotation of employees, and department-wide activities. Table 11.4 summarizes the types of distortions that take place within organizational

TABLE 11.3

Methods of Communication Matrix

	Informal	Formal
Oral	Personal contacts Interviewing and counseling Telecommunications Employee tours and orientation	Staff meetings Public address system Conferences Order and instructions
Written	Agency magazines and newsletters Bulletin boards Daily news digests	Agency policies Management newsletters Agency reports
Both oral and written	Face-to-face contacts between superior and subordinates where written information is exchanged	Agency meetings where reports and data are presented
Visual	E-mail Sound and action exhibits Closed-circuit television	Agency films and videos Slides, PowerPoint presentations Charts

Source: From Phillip Clampitt, *Communicating for managerial effectiveness*, p. 65. Copyright © 1991. Reprinted by permission of Sage Publications, Inc.

communication flows that are downward, upward, horizontal, or crisscrossing (diagonal) in nature.

Another major way distortion can be avoided is the use of messages whose meaning cannot be altered during transmission by using predesigned definitions or coding and easily quantified information. To be distortion-proof, messages must be transmitted without condensation or expansion from their original form. To avoid communication overload, only a limited amount of information can be transmitted

TABLE 11.4

Types of Distortion in Organizational Communication

Communication Level	Deliberate Distortion	Unintentional Distortion
Upward	Desire to look good Avoiding responsibility for failure Reluctance to give the boss bad news Bypassing levels	Subordinate's trust in superior Subordinate's aspiration needs Insecurity of employees Physical distance Formal organization structure
Downward	Inadequate feedback Uncomfortable with bad news	Managerial anxiety Multiple transmissions
Horizontal	Gossip and rumors Work specialization	Used as a substitute for downward and upward communication Overproliferation of horizontal communication
Diagonal	Bypassing levels	Communication gaps
All directions	Information ownership	Uncertainty absorption

Source: Jane Whitney Gibson and Richard M. Hodgetts, *Organizational communication: A managerial perspective* (2nd ed.), p. 269. © 1997. Reprinted by permission of Pearson Education, Inc., Upper Saddle River, NJ.

PHOTO 11.2
**President Bush Approves the Depart-
ment of Homeland Security Act**
*President Bush addresses media at the
signing of the Homeland Security Act, East
Room, November 25, 2002. What national
values engendered such strong political
support for the bill to establish the new
Department of Homeland Security? What
role did the national commission play?*

Source: White House Photo by Eric Draper, courtesy
of the White House Photo Office.

upward or downward in this manner. Developing distortion-proof messages tends
to be more often used when:

1. precise accuracy of information is extraordinarily important,
2. the agency has a tall hierarchy,
3. rapid transmission from the lowest to the highest level is vitally important, and
4. important decisions are subject to relatively precise quantification.[35]

The causes of a high volume in communication are:

- the total number of organizational members,
- the structure of the communications network,
- transmission rules as to when and to whom messages will be sent,
- the degree of interdependence of organizational subunits and activities,
- the rapidity of change in the agency's environment, and
- the type of search mechanisms that an agency uses to scan its environment.

Here are the relationships between message volume and agency efficiency: The
higher the volume of communication,

- the greater the delays in decision making in the organization;
- the poorer the coordination in decisions; and
- the more personnel and resources per unit of output are used in communicating
  information and orders.[36]

Figure 11.4 presents the organizational chart for the newly established Department of Homeland Security, which combined 22 agencies and 179,000 employees.
This huge merger of federal agencies was supposed to make the federal government,

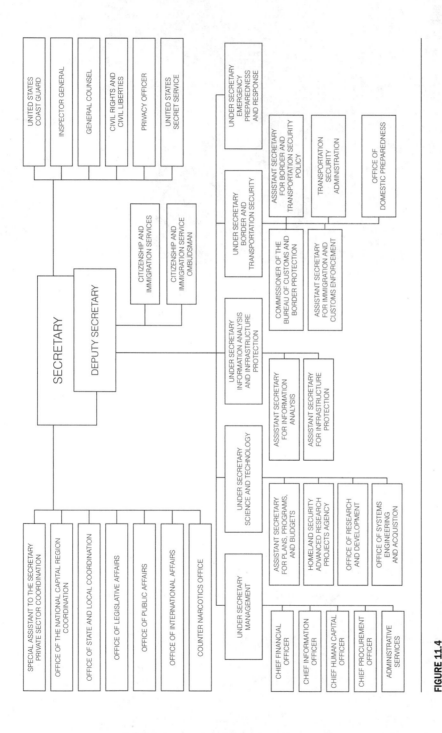

FIGURE 11.4

Organizational Chart, Department of Homeland Security

Source: *U.S. government manual, 2003, 234.*

in homeland defense matters at least, more responsive, more effective, and more efficient. It is certainly arguable whether that reorganization into a behemoth federal bureaucracy advances those values. Box 11.2, "Information Issues in Building a Bigger Bureaucracy," raises some information issues inherent in the bureaucratic haggling involved in attempting such a monumental organizational change.

Communication Technology

Communication technology greatly affects the flow and efficiency of communication in all directions. The Internet in particular has been an enormously important communication technology development that promotes horizontal and crisscrossing information flows. Box 11.3, "From Mandate to Compliance," looks at the issue of using information technology to enhance security by the U.S. Customs and Boarder Protection and by various "port-authority" governments.

The chapter closes with Reading 11.1, "The State of State Whistle-Blower Protection," which briefly overviews the legislative and judicial protections for whistle-blowers in all 50 states.

INFOTRAC
COLLEGE EDITION

Information and communication technologies and the network organization: critical analysis

Box 11.2

Information Issues in Building a Bigger Bureaucracy

From investigations after 9/11/2001 we are learning of the many disparate pieces of intelligence data that could have resulted in an earlier response by the government toward taking some action against several of the culprits involved. Mismanagement, a lack of coordination, cultural clashes among agencies, and stovepipe operations within agencies have been specified as problems involved in the failure to do so. The finger-pointing as to which agency or agencies were responsible for the inaction has given impetus to the need for change. That change requires greater coordination of our intelligence capabilities with the many agencies concerned with homeland protection. A more viable system, one in which the government would be more proactive in integrating and synthesizing those disparate pieces of intelligence, and thereby being more able to respond rapidly, has become the goal sought by policy analysts.

One of the first issues is integrating the intelligence gathering from foreign lands into repositories that can move selected information from classified and secret to lower-level classifications or open systems for use by homeland security and law enforcement agencies. Intelligence information is normally gathered and stored into highly classified, compartmentalized, and highly restricted federal government systems. Moving such information from its gathering perspective to targeted pieces of data that can be used by law enforcement authorities is a fair undertaking of declassifying and properly handling legal safeguards. And such movement from the gathering realm to the realm of protection of the homeland (which involves such agencies as Immigration and Naturalization, U.S. Customs, Bureau of Counselor Affairs, U.S. Coast Guard, U.S. Secret Service, FBI, and local law enforcement agencies, among others) necessitates a fundamental shift of operations from just collecting data to legal protections with regard to information and data analysis. Each of these systems

has highly compartmentalized methodologies for handling data, which accounts for the "stovepipes" issues mentioned earlier. Policy makers are devising processes and systems to arrange an operation to "scrub and share" classified information with appropriate levels.

Within the intelligence community, plans are under way for upgrading information technology that will provide the technical systems for interagency (or interorganizational) sharing of information and collaborative working arrangements. The Central Intelligence Agency (CIA) and the National Security Agency (NSA) are moving ahead with major technology renewal programs. In part, these focus on the modernization of information technology systems to improve intelligence analysis and to streamline processes and capabilities for collaboration and sharing that will permeate through intelligence agencies and into homeland security agencies. The Department of State is also working to establish greater cooperation and information-sharing processes among the multiple agencies involved with intelligence gathering, law enforcement, and homeland border protection.

The public administration literature is filled with past examples of large-scale change and government reorganization efforts that have started with the noblest of intentions, only to have become derailed. For example, the "tax modernization" at the Internal Revenue Service (IRS), which encompassed ongoing technology and organizational change activities all within one agency, nonetheless spanned the last 10 years. A series of reform efforts, including reengineering, quality management, centralizing organizational authority, and instituting the latest of information technology, through which the IRS struggled to demonstrate viable results finally produced the 2003 E-Z tax returns. It seems that incalculable efforts are needed for organizational changes in federal agencies. The meetings, the energy expended to coordinate, the multiple levels of working groups, the policy changes, and the various decision makers essential to effect change are all quite daunting. For large, complex organizations, managing change and innovation are related, and they are dependent upon the organization's ability to comprehend and decide how potential future technologies and organizational impacts would be affected.

While the noble intent of this latest massive federal government reorganization is to make America safer, evidence to date suggests there has been more talk (and increasing budgets) than effective action. It would appear that the federal government has been spending more energy on trying to make Americans feel safe by building up a bureaucratic organization for the future than actually making America a safer place to live now. To do the latter means transforming what we already have into effective, efficient organization, not creating another traditional federal bureaucracy. The management case against this type of reorganization includes the following issues:

- *Mission complexity*. The DHS is being tasked with protecting the nation's borders by monitoring nearly 5.7 million cargo containers and 600 million passengers on American aircraft annually as well as patrolling 95,000 miles of coastline and 430 major airports. It is also responsible for preparing for and preventing terrorist attacks, coordinating first responders at state and local levels for emergencies, and monitoring intelligence to protect against threats to the homeland.
- *Cultural incompatibility*. Mission complexity leads to major problems in trying to combine the cultures and technology (integrating different infrastructure platforms, software applications for e-mail, databases, networking, and security protocols), all the while maintaining good communication internally, between federal agencies and among first responders at the state and local levels, and coordinating employee relations. By adding complexities and creating another bureaucracy, the behemoth organization is more likely to become bogged down with red tape and waste. It is an approach that is more likely to contra-

dict or oppose a more responsive, effective and efficient agency.
- *Task obfuscation*. Making America a safer place to live by reducing the threat of terrorist attack is no easy task. The challenges of the merger, however, only make an already difficult task even harder. It appears that the DHS is making Americans feel safe, a much easier task, than really improving the quality of internal security. The feeling of security is accomplished by the budgetary strategy of increasing funding for security (included in budgets for 2003, 2004, and 2005). But contrary to popular belief, more funding does not necessarily mean more resources or even more money being spent in the field. Some agencies, such as the Federal Emergency Management Agency (FEMA), the Coast Guard, and the Secret Service, are simply being given more responsibilities with little or no money. And the mere creation of a larger bureaucracy is likely to involve greater levels of overhead and administrative costs.
- *Symbolic versus real performance results*. Creating the DHS engenders a false sense of safety. There is a perception that something is being done, that America is more secure. The DHS has done a job of making people feel safe by providing security through such things as increased airport security equipment, new airline regulations, and sending more troops abroad. But do these initiatives really make America safer? It would seem that the focus has been more on creating a bureaucracy than on making decisions that actually secure America. The ability to gauge the performance of the many agencies merged into the DHS will require comparable performance data that will not be available for years.

Homeland security requires an organization that is collaborative, quick acting, and efficient. These are hardly the qualities inherent in a huge federal bureaucracy.

Source: Based on Kenneth Mitchell, The other homeland security threat: Bureaucratic haggling, *The Public Manager*, *32* (1) (Spring 2003): 15–18; and Elishia Krauss, Building a bigger bureaucracy, *The Public Manager*, *32* (1) (Spring 2003): 57–58. Reprinted with permission of The Bureaucrat, Inc.

Box 11.3

From Mandate to Compliance

Developments such as globalization, the increasing development of the United States as an "information economy," rapid environmental change, and the reform movement in government toward a customer-service orientation feed the evolving view of information technology as "enabler of change." The new forms of information technology impact organizational restructuring and the adoption of new ways of working—the postbureaucratic network organization—wherein traditional functional and hierarchical boundaries are increasingly permeable. Government employees communicate directly with whomever is most relevant to the immediate task at hand. The new public management movement, for example, advocates "temporary project teams" to enhance the values of employee empowerment, innovation, and entrepreneurial enterprises. Such new organization exploits the knowledge of individuals, or "intellectual capital." Consultation via informal, lateral channels improves the individual's ability to keep up with rapid changes in techniques and with new knowledge to understand and implement innovations. Strong horizontal communication structures undercut the power of hierarchy and enhance division specialties with considerable autonomy.

The distance between a security mandate and security compliance can be vast. In response to pressures from the United States after the 9/11 attacks, the International Maritime Organization (IMO) compelled the world's port authorities to strengthen their security systems by July 1, 2004. Only 654 of the 6,114 ports subject to the international code were in compliance by that date. The U.S. Customs and Border protection directorate considers the physical security of the host country the biggest risk it faces.

Port security concerns exemplify broader homeland security interests. Measured worldwide, only 10 percent of the critical infrastructure has been able to achieve compliance with the mandate. In other words, 90 percent of the world's ports aren't cutting it. Much of the ports' infrastructure and the operational information technology systems suffer security shortfalls because security was not built in. Power plants, water systems, medical facilities, and ports are struggling to "patch up vulnerabilities." If worldwide ports are any indication, the idea of transforming an existing enterprise so that security is no longer an afterthought is still in its early stages. Headway is being made, however, by employing concepts

such as enterprise security architecture (ESA), which uses risk- and vulnerability-assessment techniques to guide investment management practice and other modern system architecture practices to turn security into an integral component of their operating systems that blend numerous business processes to model systems of evaluating, measuring, and accepting risk.

Other agencies, such as the Health and Human Services department, are also employing enterprise architecture (EA) to achieve authentication and accreditation compliance. EA is shaping specific frameworks issued by the Office of Management and Budget.

None of this is particularly easy, however, because agencies must chart their way across every "touch-point" in their computer information technology systems. Customs and Borders have recently launched the Container Security Initiative, the Customs Trade Partnership program, and US Visit, all of which upped the ante on the level of information sharing the United States now performs across its own disparate agencies and in foreign ports.

The journey from mandate to compliance is a long and expensive one. Risk management and compliance are costly, in part because data standards and data integration are lacking. This cost of integration and the lack of standards are the two biggest obstacles to affordable risk compliance efforts. The data issues particularly make compliance with the tough new mandates under the Patriot Act difficult for financial reporting mechanisms that ultimately must satisfy the General Accounting Office (Congress) and the Office of Management and Budget (White House). The expense of compliance, or the inability to implement it, creates a gap in the information-sharing abilities of agencies. The gap is traceable to data that are lacking critical attributes that follow from standardization, such as transactional and collateral detail, identity credentialing and entitlements, security protection, encryption, integrity validation, and digital signatures. As information sharing is increasingly mandated, more participants as stakeholders become involved in the agency's systems at the operational level. Data standardization then becomes an even more critical issue—one that is currently clearly lacking.

Source: Adapted from From mandate to compliance, *Washington Technology, Homeland Security: Bridging the Gap Advertising Supplement* (August 2004).

Reading 11.1

The State of State Whistle-Blower Protection

Policy makers' recognition of whistle-blower's potential effectiveness as a mechanism to expose wrongdoing has become increasingly widespread during the past two decades. The benefits and drawbacks of the Federal False Claims Act have received considerable attention. Many other initiatives aimed at encouraging whistle-blowing have been pursued by the states. Numerous courts have interpreted federal and state statutes. Whistle-blowers in many states have sought common-law-based redress under the public policy exception to the employment-at-will rule.

Whistle-blower–protection statutes have been enacted in each of the 50 states. All of these laws have the same objective: to expose, deter, and curtail wrongdoing. But such state laws vary considerably, and judicial interpretations of similar provisions are inconsistent from state to state.

The federal level has two primary models of whistle-blowing laws: those aimed at encouraging whistle-blowing through incentives and those aimed at protecting the whistle-blower from retaliation. Most federal and state statutes use the protection model and provide a cause of action for whistle-blowers who experience job-related retaliation because of their revelations.

In the 1980s, the focus of whistle-blower protection shifted from the federal level to the states. This was the result of two events: the passage of whistle-blower–protection statutes and the erosion of the employment-at-will doctrine through the adoption of the tort theory of firing in violation of public policy. While the first court to adopt this theory did so in a whistle-blowing case in 1959, it took another two decades before a significant number of state courts were willing to erode employer autonomy in order to protect the public good by protecting whistle-blowers.

The wrongful-firing theory holds that employers should not be able to use their power as employers to subvert public policy as established by the legislatures or the courts. Employees who are actually or constructively fired for refusing to violate a law, rule, or regulation, or who report a violation of such, can sue their employer in tort under this theory. Punitive damages are often awarded in these cases since the employer's actions are seen as being especially wrongful. While

most states have adopted this theory, courts are relatively conservative in what they recognize as protected whistle-blowing, and if the whistle-blower cannot point to a well-established law, rule, or regulation that is being violated, he or she is unlikely to be protected.

Each of the 50 states and the District of Columbia have enacted whistle-blower–protection statutes in some form. While all these laws contain antiretaliation provisions, they vary greatly in many other respects. Important points of divergence include the type of whistle-blower protected; the appropriate recipient of the report of wrongdoing; the subject of protected whistle-blowing; the motive of the whistle-blower; the quality of evidence of wrongdoing required; and the remedies provided to the employee suffering retaliation. Of these, the greatest divergence is among legislatively designated recipients. However, virtually all state statutes prohibit or discourage reporting to the media.

A review of the state laws suggests that most legislatures continue to embrace whistle-blower–antiretaliation measures as a mechanism for deterring and uncovering unlawful conduct, as summarized in Table 11.5. The growth in adoption and expansion of whistle-blower statutes has occurred despite the dearth of evidence as to their effectiveness in spurring whistle-blowing or actually preventing retaliation. The much more effective financial incentives model has not been widely adopted at the state level. Only two states, Illinois and Florida, offer significant rewards through a false-claims statute. Three other states—Oregon, South Carolina, and Wisconsin—make whistle-blowing rewards possible, but the dollar amounts at stake are so insignificant that they are unlikely to influence whistle-blowing activity. This seemingly anomalous legislative preference is likely the result of legislative ignorance of the research comparing the efficacy of these two approaches. It may also be indicative of legislative and societal discomfort with the notion of rewarding "tattletales." The table shows that 39 states offer general whistle-blower protection to public employees, but less than half offer the same protection to all workers. This reflects the prevailing view that society has a more significant interest and a greater stake in reports of misconduct in government agencies than in the private sector.

TABLE 11.5

Category	Subcategory	Number of States	States
Protection from retaliation		50 plus DC	
	General protection for all employees	23	AZ, CA, CT, HI, IL, KY, LA, ME, MA, MI, MN, MT, NE, NH, NJ, NY, ND, OH, OR, PA, SD, TN, VT
	General protection for public employees	39	AL, AK, AS, AR, CA, CO, CT, DE, FL, ID, IL, IN, IA, KS, KY, ME, MD, MA, MO, MT, NE, ND, NV, NH, NJ, NY, NC, OH, OK, OR, PA, RI, SC, SD, TX, VT, WA, WV, WI
Monetary rewards for reporting violations		3	AR, FL, IL

Some states provide recourse for workers in specific industries and government agencies, for example, among public employees: public school teachers, fire-fighters, state contract employees, peace officers, state university staff, civil service, municipal employees, public works contractors, transportation authority workers, department of corrections, public utility, and educational facility employees. Government program categories include OSHA, 29 states; health care workers, 33 states; civil rights, 32 states; minimum wage, 19 states; government assistance programs (CA, MS); child care/child welfare, 17 states; environment, 19 states.

Although whistle-blower protection is most often justified with reference to societal interests, state laws are more likely to cover retaliation for employee harms than for disclosures of conduct threatening to other groups or the public. As with most employee-protection statutes, the whistle-blower laws can be read expansively or narrowly. The language of most of the laws gives the courts several interpretive opportunities. Litigation has tended to focus on whether the substantive standards of the statute were met, whether the plaintiff must prove an actual violation of a law, rule, or regulation or merely have a reasonable belief that wrongdoing occurred, whether the plaintiff's claim has been preempted, whether a statutory claim can exist with a common law claim, and the availability of damages. In general, courts have adopted straightforward statutory interpretation approaches to determine where a mistaken, albeit reasonably held belief of wrongdoing has occurred will support application of state whistle-blowing–protection laws. Most of the reported decisions conclude that an actual violation of law or

regulation is not a prerequisite to recovery. In many jurisdictions, a fired whistle-blower who seeks redress may have one legal basis for his or her claim. Some causes of action, however, have been determined to be preempted by federal law. A number of state courts have permitted both common law and statutory claims based on a single fact pattern. Others have determined that certain claims may not be simultaneously pursued.

State laws that conflict with federal schemes are preempted under the Supremacy Clause. Given the sheer number of state (111) and federal (112) whistle-blower–protection provisions, it is not surprising that the preemptive effect of the latter upon the former have been examined in a number of decisions. In general, the Supreme Court recognizes three circumstances in which state law is preempted: (1) those in which federal law specifically articulates the boundaries of possible state action; (2) those the court may infer congressional intent to displace state law in a given context from a "scheme of federal regulation" so pervasive as to make reasonable the inference that Congress left no room for the states to supplement it; and (3) in fields in which the federal interest is so dominant that the federal system will be assumed to preclude enforcement of state laws on the same subject. State law that conflicts with federal law is preempted. Because employment regulation is generally viewed as within the states' traditional police powers, the courts are somewhat disinclined to view such laws as preempted.

Source: Elletta Callahan and Terry M. Dworkin, The state of state whistle-blower protection, *American Business Law Journal*, *38*(1) (Fall 2000): 99–111. Excerpt and Table 11.5 reprinted with permission of Blackwell Publishing.

Net Assignment

Using your school's website, investigate and describe at least five different categories of information the school makes available. What are the values your school promotes through its information to students? to outsiders? How does your school expect you will behave in reflecting those values?

Summary

Communication in the administration of public agencies can be formal or informal. Communication networks influence the flow of information through and around an agency's formal chains of command. Various factors promote or disrupt efficiency in communication. Bottlenecks develop and contribute to dysfunctional organizational behavior.

We can distinguish four flows of communication: downward, upward, horizontal, and diagonal. Each type of flow carries its own potential for distortion that supervisors must learn to counter.

Glossary of Key Terms

communication   The exchange of information and the transmission of meaning; the very essence of organization and a social process that influences the functioning of any organization; best viewed in relation to the social system in which it occurs and the particular function it performs in that system.

coding process   Any system that receives information has a characteristic coding process, a limited set of coding categories to which it assimilates the information received; results in omission, selection, refinement, elaboration, distortion, and transformation.

crisscrossing information   A subordinate in one unit talks to a boss in another unit, or vice versa.

downward communication   From superior to subordinate, following the authority pattern of hierarchical positions; used to direct, coordinate, and control.

efficiency of communication   Measured by the number of communications flowing in a given network.

formal communication   Written communication that follows the formal chain of command in an organization; influenced by the size of an organization and its public nature.

horizontal communication   Movement of information among peers at the same organizational level.

informal communication   Oral or written communication that does not follow formal channels.

operational feedback   Systematic information acquisition and analysis closely tied to the organization's ongoing functions and sometimes an integral part of those functions.

upward communication   Information that ascends the hierarchical levels of an organization and provides task coordination and emotional and social support to the individual; flows from subordinate to superior.

Review Questions

1. What factors tend to be more associated with the use of formal communication versus informal communication in organizations?

2. What promotes or decreases efficiency in organizational communication systems?

3. How do small groups in organizations affect communication flows? What can be done to lessen such problems?

4. Discuss the flows of communication. What factors influence the volume of each type of flow? What antidistortion measures can be used in upward and downward communication flows?

5. What types of communication problems discussed in this chapter are evident or are likely to develop within the new DHS? Do you think creating the new DHS will actually increase homeland security? What values, conflicting with those advocated by the new public management approach, seem to be more pronounced in the politics that led to the creation of the DHS? What evidence of groupthink behavior do you note in the rush to create the behemoth DHS?

Surfing the Net

Useful websites for the topics in this chapter include the following:

Annenberg Public Policy Center (**http://www.appcpenn.org**) (analyzes television coverage of politics)

Center for Media and Public Affairs (**http://www.cmpa.com**)

CNN/Time Magazine's All Politics (**http://www.cnn.com/ALLPOLITICS**)

CSPAN (**http://www.c-span.org**)

Federal Communications Commissions (**http://www.fcc.gov**)

FedWorld (**http://fedworld.gov**)

U.S. Department of Commerce (**http://www.doc.gov**) (includes a list of all federal agencies that have Web sites)

Federal Web Locator (**http://www.lib.auburn.edu/madd/docs/fedloc.html**)

National Association of State Information Resource Executives (**http: //www.nasire.org**)

A useful site for information about local government is the Local Government Institute (**http://www.lgi.org**).

New York's Center for Technology in Government (**http: //www.ctg.albany.edu**) reports on how local governments throughout New York are using technology effectively.

The Pew Research Center for People and the Press (**http://www.people-press.org**) reports on surveys of attitudes and the level of awareness that Americans have about government and politics.

A similarly useful site is the Public Interest Research Group (**http://www.pirg.org**).

The Ultimate Collection of News Links (**http://pppp.net/links/news**) provides links to more than 6,000 news sources, from newspapers to magazines to subject-specific weekly and monthly publications.

Another locator is Yahoo's news site (**http://www.yahoo.com/NEWS**). Use it to find radio, television, and other types of news sources.

Chapter 12

Financial Management: Taxing, Budgeting, and Spending

How do you stop a runaway elephant? If words could do it, particularly words from the Republican camp, there might just be a sliver of hope of reigning in what the *Wall Street Journal* describes as "the most profligate administration since the 1960s." Reaching back to his Navy days for a more colorful metaphor, Sen. John McCain says, "I've never known a sailor, drunken or sober, with the imagination this Congress has." The omnibus appropriations bill just approved, covering seven of the 13 spending bills Congress was supposed to complete months ago, is well and truly dubbed "a pork-laden monstrosity" (by Club for Growth, a political action committee). "Grotesquely stuffed with pork," echoes the *Washington Post*. The federal budget, declares the investment firm Goldman Sachs, is, quite simply, "out of control." And the beat goes on.

What we have here is nothing short of fiscal disaster. America has gone from a $280 billion surplus when George W. Bush was inaugurated to $500 billion annual deficits as far as the eye can see. And those deficits would be $100 billion higher if the government wasn't raiding the Social Security surpluses, now treated not as a lockbox but a candy jar. These numbers understate the scale of the spending binge because historically lower interest rates have sharply cut interest costs on the $3.9 trillion federal debt.

U.S. Comptroller David Walker, who heads the Government Accountability Office, stated (October 25, 2004): "Now federal spending is nearly 20 percent of gross domestic product, the economy's annual output, and many people think that is too big. In addition, the government collects 16.2 percent of GDP in taxes. The rest is red ink. . . .

In 2040, the deficit would be nearly 30 percent of GDP, according to his figures, which assume that President Bush's tax cuts are made permanent and spending rises at the same rate as the economy."

Guns, butter, and hubris, *U.S. News and World Report* (February 2, 2004): 60; and CBO official gives warning on federal deficit, Knight Ridder/Tribune News Service (October 25, 2004): 2352.

Introduction

Placing Monetary Values on Priorities

Clashing values are at the heart of most budgetary decision making. Political scientist Thomas Dye has described budgets as the "priorities of government with price tags attached."[1] **Priorities** are simply the values that government expresses in its expenditure and revenue decisions.

Financial management in public administration involves taxing, budgeting, spending, auditing, accounting, and evaluating functions. At all three levels of government, politics circumscribe the budget process and the various areas of expenditure. In addition, two approaches to budget making influence governmental appropriations and execution. Managers seek greater control over debt through budget reform measures, and government, in its fiscal and monetary policy making, attempts to help these managers "control" the overall economy through various economic control devices.

Values and Financial Planning

Financial management is inherently value laden. When government decides who and how to tax and what to spend its revenues on, it is setting its priorities. It promotes some values and deemphasizes or even avoids others.

The Role of the Budget Process

Financial management is central to administrative politics and the operations of governmental agencies and programs. **Budgeting** is the formal mechanism for obtaining, distributing, and monitoring the revenues used by administrative agencies. As such, it involves balancing the values of efficiency and effectiveness. The **budget process** not only includes government making decisions on spending needs and determining how to pay for them, but also and equally importantly controlling the bureaucracy and shaping government programs through the process of legislative appropriations and the elected executive's development of the budget.

Since the 1960s, the federal budget has increasingly been involved in an attempt to manage the nation's economy. Budget decisions are made and presented in terms of how they influence general economic growth as well as the specific economic interests and concerns of a given substantive policy area. Budgets not only are designed to address public policy problems, but also are intended to manage an economic sector (agriculture, manufacturing, housing, and so on), a region (for example, the Southeast, Appalachia, the Pacific Northwest), a state, or even the entire nation's economy. In this age of a global economy in which the major economic powers become increasingly tied through their economies, fiscal and monetary policy is even used to affect world economics, albeit to a much more limited extent. Budget processes thus are highly complex and can pursue a multiplicity of goals and preferences, even across many institutional boundaries.

The Functions of Financial Management

Generally speaking, governments rely on one or more of the following eight sources of revenue to finance their spending:

1. direct taxes (such as personal and corporate income taxes);
2. indirect taxes (such as sales and value-added taxes);
3. user fees for certain government customers;
4. grants from another level of government;
5. profits from government enterprises;
6. borrowing through public bonds and loans as well as from private lenders;
7. innovative finance techniques, such as public–private partnerships, franchises, and licensing to private-sector providers; and
8. earnings from savings or investments.[2]

The Taxing Function

Taxes, whether direct or indirect, are compulsory payments that create revenues for government to finance public programs and services. They are generally accepted as legitimate when levied by elected representatives most commonly serving on legislative bodies.

Tax policy determines who pays the bills of government. Several values are inherent in all tax policy making, including the following:

- the ability to bear the burden,
- the adequacy of revenue sources,
- the appropriateness of the revenue source to the expenditure category,
- the diversity of revenue sources,
- equity (treating like cases alike on the basis of prescribed rules),
- the fairness of the tax, and
- the simplicity of the tax process.

INFOTRAC
COLLEGE EDITION

The importance of involvement in the federal budget process

The Tax Burden

Decisions about the tax burden concern who does and does not pay. There are two basic types of taxes: progressive and regressive. A **progressive tax** is one in which individuals with higher incomes pay a larger percentage of those incomes in taxes than do people with lesser means. Income taxes are usually progressive. A **regressive tax** is one in which people with lower income pay a higher overall percentage of their income in taxes than do people with greater income. General sales taxes, for example, are regressive. A flat tax on income is likewise regressive in nature.

FIGURE 12.1
California Revenue Sources,
FY 2004–2005

Source: http://www.dof.ca.gov/HTML/
Budget04–05/BudgetSum04/Budget
_Summary2004–05; accessed 11/17/04.

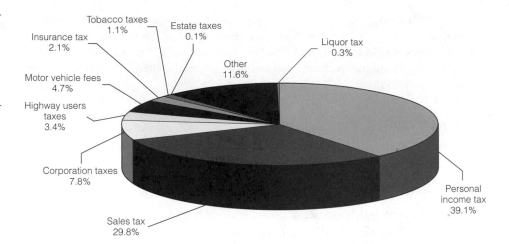

FIGURE 12.1
California Revenue Sources,
FY 2004–2005

Source: http://www.dof.ca.gov/HTML/
Budget04–05/BudgetSum04/Budget
_Summary2004–05; accessed 11/17/04.

A **tax expenditure** refers to the practice of giving favorable tax breaks (often called "loopholes") for certain kinds of spending by individuals, nonprofit organizations, and corporate enterprises. It is intended to promote specific types of social policies by manipulating or inducing behavior through such incentives.

Many budget experts view the tax expenditure budget as a useful tool in managing the size and scope of the federal government, but a growing contingent of conservative critics has raised questions about the concept. The term is attributed to Stanley S. Surrey, who, as Assistant Secretary of the U.S. Treasury for Tax Policy, instructed his staff to compile a list of preferences and concessions in the income tax that had the nature of expenditure programs. His goal was straightforward: to draw attention to these items in hopes of building momentum for tax reform, which would redirect the tax system toward its core function of raising revenues (Burman, 2003: 613).

The federal government relies heavily on personal income taxes and several insurance trust funds. Direct taxes—personal, corporate, capital gains, and so on—are enacted by the U.S. Congress. Tax decisions are made by the Ways and Means Committee in the House of Representatives and the Finance Committee in the Senate. State governments, through their respective state legislatures, typically depend on a greater variety of revenue sources. Figure 12.1, for example, illustrates the sources of revenues for the state of California, FY 2004–05.

Local governments rely primarily on the property tax, a far less flexible revenue source. Because property tax bills are paid in lump sums, they are less elastic. Property taxpayers have sometimes led "tax revolts" in which voters use initiative processes to impose strict limitations on property tax increases. Tax reform, however, does not always involve cutting or limiting taxes. It may mean developing a new tax revenue source—for example, from new technologies or new private-sector sources of wealth—or simply maximizing the inventiveness of fiscal experts. Taxes are perennially volatile policy issues, and policy proposals have been known to make or break a candidate's campaign.

Federal revenue sources have become less diverse, whereas state and local revenue systems have become increasingly diverse. The wide variety of taxing authorities can engender confusion as well as great disparities in the tax burdens borne at the state and local levels. The property tax assessed on one house, for example, may be many times that assessed on a nearly identical home in a different jurisdiction. States also vary considerably in the amounts of revenue they derive from income tax or sales tax sources.

Table 12.1 compares state governments in terms of their total revenues for fiscal year (FY) 2000.

Measured as a percentage of personal income, taxes in the United States are not particularly high. The U.S. tax burden, in fact, is lower than in many other major industrialized countries. Still, significant opposition to taxes arises mostly from the belief that governments are inefficient and even wasteful in their spending habits. Public surveys about the fairness of the tax burden reveal that people see local property taxes and federal income taxes as the least fair taxes. Asked about which level of government they get the least for their tax dollar, 49 percent of those surveyed said the federal government gave them the least; 18 percent said it was the local government, and 16 percent cited state government.[3]

The tax revolt movement of the 1970s and 1980s led to strong political pressures to control or manage overall spending levels. The tax-and-spend policies of the 1970s, in fact, were replaced in the 1980s by a trend to tax, spend, and borrow. Budgets focus not only on the central question of what government should do, but also on who should be involved in deciding that central question.[4] Spending decisions—concerning both amount and substantive policy areas on which to spend revenues—are central to the budget process.

The Budget-Making Function

A **budget** can be understood simply as a plan for projected income and expenditures. Budgets estimate future costs and plan how to use employees, supplies, and related resources to meet those costs. Budget decisions follow a set **budget cycle**: the routine steps in the budget process that involve the preparation, authorization, implementation, and auditing of the budget.

INFOTRAC
COLLEGE EDITION

State revenue cyclicality

Types of Budgets

Budgets can be usefully categorized on the basis of who makes them, their time frames, the amount of detailed information provided by the budget documents, and the overall approach to budget making used by the various government actors involved. Distinctions based on who makes the budget provide two fundamental types: the executive budget and the legislative budget.

In an **executive budget**, the budget document is prepared by the chief of the executive branch (the president, governor, mayor, and so on) and is submitted to the appropriate legislative body for review, modification, and adoption (that is, authorization and appropriation). Most governments in the United States use an executive budget.

In a **legislative budget**, the legislative body (state legislature, county board of supervisors, city council, and so on) prepares the budget document after individual departments submit their requests directly to the legislative body, usually to specific legislative committees (for example, a state agriculture department to the agriculture committee, a highway department to the transportation committee, and a fish and wildlife department to a natural resource committee). A total budget request is not known until all of the various committees have approved or modified their respective requests and then the respective bills are added up.

TABLE 12.1

Total State Revenues, 2000

State	State and Local Total ($ Million)	Total per Capita ($)	Per Capita Rank
Alabama	25,726	5,785	37
Alaska	10,525	16,787	1
Arizona	27,778	5,414	47
Arkansas	13,833	5,175	25
California	270,380	7,982	14
Colorado	29,603	6,883	43
Connecticut	25,828	7,583	5
Delaware	6,224	7,938	2
Florida	92,402	5,782	50
Georgia	49,310	6,024	45
Hawaii	8,488	7,004	6
Idaho	7,590	5,866	33
Illinois	80,695	6,498	40
Indiana	32,716	5,381	41
Iowa	17,220	5,885	29
Kansas	16,235	6,040	36
Kentucky	25,200	6,235	21
Louisiana	27,109	6,066	31
Maine	8,554	6,709	12
Maryland	33,949	6,410	27
Massachusetts	48,103	7,261	10
Michigan	70,112	7,005	15
Minnesota	38,785	7,885	11
Mississippi	16,672	5,860	28
Missouri	31,635	5,654	44
Montana	5,643	6,256	19
Nebraska	11,650	6,809	30
Nevada	11,885	5,948	48
New Hampshire	6,948	5,621	38
New Jersey	62,331	7,408	20

TABLE 12.1 *(continued)*

State	State and Local Total ($ Million)	Total per Capita ($)	Per Capita Rank
New Mexico	13,073	7,187	20
New York	188,907	9,955	7
North Carolina	50,542	6,279	23
North Dakota	4,495	7,002	8
Ohio	80,074	7,053	35
Oklahoma	18,760	5,436	39
Oregon	28,644	8,373	13
Pennsylvania	80,546	6,559	36
Rhode Island	7,427	7,087	17
South Carolina	23,467	5,849	32
South Dakota	4,227	5,666	42
Tennessee	33,625	5,910	46
Texas	120,666	5,787	49
Utah	14,954	6,697	24
Vermont	4,019	6,599	3
Virginia	44,175	6,240	34
Washington	46,372	7,868	22
West Virginia	10,760	5,951	18
Wisconsin	43,003	8,071	16
Wyoming	7,030	14,231	4
District of Columbia	6,383	11,159	—
United States	1,942,328	5,396	—

Source: *Statistical abstract of the United States, 2003*, Tables 448, 455; accessed online 11/17/04.

Economic analysts evaluate executive budgets as being the more efficient. Having budget authority centralized in an executive's office (along with a budget staff agency) enhances the chief executive's ability to control the executive branch bureaucracy. A legislative budget approach, on the other hand, emphasizes responsiveness at the expense of efficiency. It enhances the legislative branch's oversight powers with respect to executive branch departments.

Distinctions based on the time frame of the budget provide two types: the capital budget and the operating budget. The **capital budget** details plans for large-expenditure items (such as bridges, buildings, fire engines, and like infra- structural items). These are financed over extended periods of time (typically from 3 to 5 years for large-equipment purchases and 20 to 30 years for buildings). Decision makers for state capital budgets differ from those who make operating budgets and are often limited to the governor, state treasurer, and comptroller. Capital budgets also are often constrained by constitutional limitations on the overall level of state indebtedness. These limitations frequently require that voters approve bond issues to finance the projects in the capital budget.

An **operating budget**, or fiscal budget, concerns the annual expenditures for expendable items: salaries, wages, pensions, employee benefits, supplies, contracts for equipment repair and maintenance, new-equipment purchases for smaller-equipment items, utilities, and the like. Those who make operating budgets include the chief executive, a central budget staff (for example, the OMB at the federal level), cabinet-level department heads, economic advisory staff (for example, the Council of Economic Advisers to the president), and the legislature and its budget committees and budget staff agencies.

Budgets based on the amount of detailed information in the budget document provide two basic types: a line-item budget and a program (or performance) budget. A **line-item budget** classifies budget accounts to narrow, highly detailed objects of expenditure used by agencies, typically without reference to their ultimate purpose or the objective served by the expenditure. Line-item budgets emphasize the value of accountability and enhance the legislature's oversight of the executive branch by providing it with detailed information that can help it with later budget decisions— that is, allowing it to exercise its "power of the purse." A **performance** (or **program**) **budget** focuses on an agency's objectives and accomplishments. This type of budget increases management responsibility and accountability and emphasizes the agency's programs—as in the federal government's use of its Program Planning Budgeting System (PPBS) during the late 1960s. It is a tool for defining priorities and evaluating a department's or a program's accomplishments.

Gubernatorial use of the line-item veto for narrative deletion

The overall approach to the budget-making process distinguishes two types: the incremental budget and the zero-based budget. **Incremental budgeting** refers to a method of budget preparation and review that emphasizes small increases or decreases over existing budget allocations for current programs that all involved consider to be the budget base. Incremental budgeting responds to several pressures to increase or decrease spending. Pressures to increase costs arise from administrators who seek to appease employees and agency clientele groups. Pressures to decrease costs come from taxpayers and various review officials: superiors, budget bureau staffs, and legislators. When making cuts, legislators often find a sense of fulfillment and importance.[5]

Zero-based budgeting demands a justification for the entire budget. Capital budgets are typically executive budgets that are more often zero-based in approach and program budgets in detail. Operating budgets are usually executive budgets that are incremental in nature and line-item in detail. Most real-world budgets combine these basic types.

Budgeting is increasingly complicated by the intergovernmental transfer of funds. In other words, revenues move to a local department or agency from a federal department and decidedly affect the local agency's relations with other governmental agencies and funding sources at its own level. Intergovernmental funding induces activities in some areas that otherwise might not be pursued. Such expenditure policy by one level can dramatically affect another level, which is especially the case when national and state departments affect local economies by closing major government operations, bases, or installations. The national budget can be as important for its effects on the national economy as it is to the operation of government agencies that are funded by federal allocations.

The Auditing Function

The audit is the final phase of the budget process. Audits review an agency's operations with regard to financial transactions, determining whether financial resources were used in accordance with the law, efficiently, and toward producing the desired results. Traditionally, an audit refers to a financial report by an individual or organization to determine whether or not it accurately shows the agency's expenditures, deductions, or other allowances set by laws and budgetary regulations. The independent examination of the books—the agency's financial records—establishes whether the agency is complying with the law and accepted accounting practices. Audits compare what an agency has done to an objective standard of expected behavior.

Types of Audits

Audits—independent examinations—refer to more than just studying financial records. Several types are distinguished.[6] An *energy audit* looks at how well an agency uses or wastes its energy resources, and it generally seeks to promote conservation. A *social audit* assesses social issues in an organizational context. In terms of reason or purpose, governments use a *compliance audit* to assess whether it has financially complied with the law. The Office of Federal Contract Compliance Programs in the Department of Labor, for instance, audits agencies to ensure there is no discrimination by government contractors based on race, religion, color, sex, or national origin, as well as to assess that affirmative action programs are in place to employ veterans and handicapped workers.[7] A *performance audit* looks at the economy and efficiency of an agency and how well it has achieved its stated program results. When auditing for efficiency, the auditing agency compares the actions of the agency under examination with the program objectives assigned to it. Such audits focus on whether those objectives were correct goals to begin with, and they change auditors from bookkeepers or accountants to evaluators. Performance auditing is an inherently political activity dressed up in apolitical clothes.[8] In terms of *who* does the auditing, we can distinguish between an internal and an external audit.

INFOTRAC
COLLEGE EDITION

Doesn't add up

Auditing Agencies

Several governmental offices routinely perform the auditing function. Perhaps the most notable agency in the United States is the General Accounting Office (GAO), the federal agency responsible for auditing all other federal agencies. The GAO is headed by the comptroller general of the United States. The comptroller (the comparable position is often called controller in many states and localities) is appointed by the president, with the approval of the Senate, for a 15-year term. The GAO issues more than a thousand reports annually, and its officials often testify before congressional investigations and policy hearings. The office employs more than 4,000 accountants, lawyers, engineers, and policy analysts.

At the state level, most states have an auditing office that serves the legislature. The agency is headed by a state comptroller or controller. In 25 states, the auditor is a separately elected state official who makes up part of the plural executive.[9] In the other states, the controller is appointed by the legislature. A state controller is usually one of the major decision makers for a state's capital budget. For states with constitutional requirements for a balanced budget and constitutional limitations on the level of debt, the power of the controller's office is enhanced. Local governments often employ outside accounting agencies to audit their financial records, although large cities and counties typically have their own internal auditing agencies.

The Accounting Function

Accounting refers to the system of keeping financial records. Government practices and procedures for gathering and maintaining financial records are essential to effective management and auditing. For the federal government, in 1991 a combination of the primary agencies concerned with accounting established the Federal Accounting Standards Advisory Board. Its parent agencies—the GAO, the OMB, and the treasury department—receive recommendations from the advisory board for methods to be followed by all government departments and agencies. The resulting standards are jointly issued by the GAO and the OMB.[10]

Types of Accounting

Government often uses one or a mixture of two types of accounting: cash accounting and accrual accounting. *Cash accounting* seeks to control and track the transfer of cash funds appropriated by the legislature to the various departments and agencies. As governmental operations became more complex, government began to use *accrual accounting*, which involves more meaningful reporting, financial statements, and asset management. This system enables more accurate measures of income and expenditure and whether or not cash payments associated with earnings and debts have actually taken place. Accrual accounting lists debts owed when the debt becomes a legal obligation, which is often before any money is actually paid out. Using accrual accounting practices, for example, an agency would stipulate its level of indebtedness to include the amount or value of an approved building or the contract to purchase a large and expensive piece of equipment—or legally bind itself to pay out certain entitlement benefits to its employees—as soon as these amounts are officially encumbered instead of counting them as debts only after the funds are spent. The GAO requires agencies to capitalize all fixed assets and depreciate them over time. Liabilities that have been accrued, such as employees' annual sick leave, are accounted for, and accounts receivable (that is, money owed to the agency) must be identified. Most governments now use some form of modified accrual accounting that leaves room for politicians to emphasize liabilities and deemphasize debt.

Accounting Practices

In the traditional cash accounting approach, government often failed to identify fixed assets—holdings in land, buildings, and other assets. Under the broader approach of **asset management**, government plans for the maintenance of assets throughout their life cycles. This approach emphasizes the value of assets, examining their return on investment and establishing asset-disposal programs. Governments often maintain assets that are commercial enterprises—utilities, airlines, and railroads, for example. Governments also hold public assets with intrinsic value (for example, parks, public buildings, art and archive collections) as well as own and operate facilities that produce income (such as bridges and tunnels) that can continue to be money producers once the associated debt has been retired. When governments face fiscal crises, they may be pressured to reshuffle assets and perhaps dispose of or privatize assets that are deemed nonessential. In such privatization moves, local governments have sold cemeteries, waste water treatment plants, publicly owned utilities, airports, and so on.

The simple process of compiling a register or list of public assets allows them to be professionally valued. Inventories become the base for a government's balance sheet and enable better asset management. The divestiture, privatization, or contracting out of such assets may be advocated as ways to improve efficiency or simply to free funds that can be shifted to programs of higher priority. The registration of public assets enables the assessment of aggregate debt levels to be tied to the capability of the government to service (that is, pay) the assets. Alterations in asset portfolios (holdings) can be consciously related to liabilities. Accrual accounting practices emphasize asset and liability management within the agenda of public financial administration.

Accrual accounting standards and practices better enable *financial reporting*— written statements of an accountant's opinions or audit reports—after an audit. An independent accountant or auditor can assess the fairness of the financial statement, specify exceptions and qualifications, and offer other comments as to the limitation of the auditing procedures followed and to recommend changes in accounting methods from those used previously. These assessments and recommendations are often important functions of an evaluation.

Strategic asset management

The Evaluating Function

Program evaluation is the systematic examination of any activity undertaken by government to determine short- and long-range effects. Program evaluation is done by executives, legislatures, and both internal and external evaluation agencies. Evaluation often suggests changes in the goals that a program is designed to achieve. Change is what evaluation emphasizes and what government agencies typically abhor.[11] There are at least four reasons to do evaluations: postponement, ducking responsibility, public relations, and fulfilling grant requirements.

1. With postponement, decision makers often look for ways to delay decisions, and the evaluation report becomes a ploy for such a delay.

2. To duck responsibility, administrators may use evaluation to produce objective evidence that makes decisions for them; the trappings of research may be used to both legitimize and cloak desired decisions.

3. For public relations purposes, evaluation can be used by agencies for self-glorification. Highly favorable program evaluation by agencies (generally conducted internally) will be given the greatest visibility. Administrators need support to justify programs and projects in which they believe, and support for existing programs is often a primary motivation for evaluation.

4. To make sure an agency fulfills its grant requirements in an era of increasing intergovernmental financing of and involvement with programs, the granting agency may require an evaluation.[12]

FIGURE 12.2
Federal Budget Summary: 1980–2003
Source: *Statistical abstract of the United States,*
2003, Figure 9.1; accessed online 11/17/04.

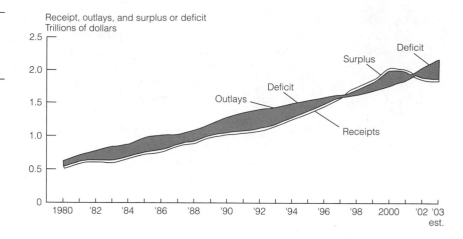

FIGURE 12.2
Federal Budget Summary: 1980–2003
Source: *Statistical abstract of the United States,*
2003, Figure 9.1; accessed online 11/17/04.

Congress established the GAO to conduct program evaluation, and Congress often legislates the office's role in assessment. Several governments—Hawaii, Michigan, and Wisconsin, for example—have created comparable staff agencies to conduct legislative program evaluation. Other states—New York, New Jersey, Illinois, and Virginia, for instance—have set up legislative commissions for that purpose. Colorado, the first state to enact a sunset law that fixed termination dates for government agencies and programs, requires formal evaluation and subsequent affirmative legislation for an agency or program to continue. Program evaluation by legislative fiat uses set specific periods—commonly, five years—to force evaluation and tighten legislative oversight.

Fiscal Policy Outcomes and Electoral Accountability in U.S. States

The Politics of the Budgetary Process

Budgets are inherently political documents. They are instruments for planning, to be sure, but they are also for coordination and control. They affect every aspect of administration and empower those who make them. Budget directors at all levels of government are among the most powerful nonelected officials in government. Especially during periods of scarce resources, the budget casts a long shadow over all administrative activity. The budget process in U.S. politics reflects competing ideologies, the role of the federal system in structuring government, and the influences of various decision-making models.

The budget process is lengthy, with small subunits estimating what they need for the coming year, oversight agencies reviewing and frequently cutting back such requests, and the elected executive sorting out conflicting and competing priorities. It is described in some detail in Reading 12.1 at the end of this chapter. The reading also highlights proposals being considered by the Congress, some more seriously than others, to reform the U.S. budget process.

Figure 12.2 compares federal receipts, outlays, and the surplus or deficits of the U.S. government budgets for fiscal years 1980–2003. The federal deficit reached a record $413 billion in FY 2004.

Sources of Revenue

The federal government's major sources of revenue are: the individual income tax, which provides roughly 40 percent; social insurance receipts, about 33 percent; borrowing, about 8 percent; corporate income tax, about 11 percent; excise taxes, about 4 percent; and other sources, about 4 percent. Perhaps the least familiar category is the excise tax. An **excise tax** is a tax or duty placed on the manufacture, sale, or consumption of a commodity within the country. Tobacco and liquor taxes are major sources of excise tax dollars. In the early history of the nation, excise taxes and import and export duties were primary sources of revenue for the national government. Now, however, nearly half of all federal revenue comes from personal and corporate income taxes. The national government began the graduated income tax on personal income in 1913, following the innovative use of that tax by Wisconsin in 1911.

The principal sources of revenue and their approximate percentages of total revenues to state and local governments are:

1. sales tax—30 percent;
2. fees, charges, and interest—28 percent;
3. property tax—25 percent;
4. federal grants—20 percent;
5. personal income tax   12 percent; and
6. corporate income tax—3 percent.

In 2000, state and local governments collected in excess of $1.942 trillion from all sources, an average of about $5,500 per person in the nation. As indicated in Table 12.1, state per capita numbers varied from $16,787 for Alaska to $5,175 for Arkansas. Of that total, $1.54 trillion is from general revenue sources, of which approximately 82 percent came from their own sources and about 18 percent from the federal government. The top 10 states in total taxes collected per capita are: Alaska, Delaware, Vermont, Wyoming, Connecticut, Hawaii, New York, North Dakota, New Mexico, and Massachusetts.

Approximately $5 of every $25 collected in state and local taxes comes from income taxes. Corporate income taxes generated slightly more than $1 of every $25 in state and local taxes collected. Sales taxes produced nearly $9 of every $25 in state and local tax revenue, making up about 36 percent of state and local tax collections.

States with low income taxes or significant numbers of tourists rely more heavily on sales taxes. Property taxes are the most disliked state and local tax, but they generate roughly 32 percent of all their tax revenues—approximately $8 of every $25 levied. Wide variations in property tax bases have generated wide disparities in local government finances and have made the property tax the most controversial in recent years.

Fees, charges, and interest increasingly serve as a source of state and local income other than taxes—approximately 30 percent of total own-source revenues (that is, revenues from fees, charges, and interest). These fees include charges by state universities, local government hospital charges, lotteries, sewer assessments, rents and royalties from state land, highway and bridge tolls, and airport landing fees.

Local governments have had to rely heavily on property taxes, but the unpopularity of this source of revenue has led many local governments to search for alternative means.

Box 12.1

Passing Down the Deficit

A study by the Center on Budget and Policy Priorities analyzes and quantifies the adverse impacts of federal policies on the fiscal crisis that states have been struggling with since 2001. The study, the first state-specific data on those impacts, finds a net loss relative to the size of state budgets ranging from 1.4 percent of the general fund budget in Alaska to a high of 13.3 percent in Florida. In 11 states, federal policies have imposed net costs averaging at least 10 percent of their general fund budgets. Seven of the largest states have had net costs resulting from federal policies exceeding $5 billion.

The states bearing the greatest relative cost of federal policies tend to be among the least affluent states in the country, as measured by per capita income and poverty rate. States that have a relatively heavy influence on federal funding for their budgets also are among those that have been the hardest hit. States that are most reliant on raising revenues through sales tax are another group that is bearing a high cost of federal policies.

Among the factors that have contributed to these monetary losses and to the fiscal distress of the states are: (1) changes in federal tax policy (because many states tie their own tax codes to the federal code); (2) federal preemption of state and local taxing authority; (3) the failure of the federal government to help states and localities collect taxes owed to them on catalogue and Internet sales; (4) mandates that require states to spend funds for particular purposes; and (5) federal policies that shift the cost of prescription drugs for the poorest elderly onto the states.

The Center study notes that ballooning federal deficits serve to constrain Washington's ability to assist states through such programs as the fiscal relief package that provided $20 billion to states in 2003.

Source: U.S. Newswire (May 6, 2004); accessed online 11/17/04.

The federal government's deficit level affects the states and, ultimately, local governments as well. Box 12.1 discusses how federal policies worsen the already-dire state fiscal crisis.

Areas of Expenditure

Each level of government differs likewise in its areas of greatest expenditure. Although overall government purchases of goods and services have risen sharply for state and local governments since 1996, they have actually declined slightly for the federal government during that same period. State governments spend more money on education than on any other policy area, followed closely by social services (basic welfare). Table 12.2 presents total state and local government spending by public policy area in fiscal year 2000. In that year, state and local governments combined spent $1.747 trillion, or roughly $5,354 per capita, to operate their schools and colleges, provide and maintain transportation, fund welfare, build and support hospitals and provide basic health services, enhance the physical infrastructure, enforce the law and preserve public safety, and maintain their natural resources and provide parks and recreation services.

Budget Theories and Practices

In many ways, budget documents are the most important manifestations of public policy because they record the outcomes of the political process: winners and losers of policy competition. They delineate government's total service effort. As political

TABLE 12.2

State and Local Spending by Area, FY 2000

Area	Total Spending (%)
Education	29.8
Public welfare	13.3
Health/hospitals	7.0
Highways	5.8
Police/fire protection	4.3
Corrections	2.7
Sewage	1.6
Solid waste	1.0
Parks/recreation	1.5
Interest on debt	3.9

Source: Computed from data from *Statistical abstract of the United States, 2003*, Table 447; accessed online 11/17/04.

documents, budgets allocate scarce resources among competing social and economic needs. As managerial documents, they specify the ways and means for providing for government services. By establishing the costs for various programs, they set up the criteria by which government programs are to be reviewed and evaluated.

Budgets have become the main instruments by which government attempts to manage economic growth and development. Budgets become accounting instruments by which officials are held accountable for what government does and does not manage to accomplish.

Figure 12.3 presents the formal budget process for California, depicting a fairly common process. The figure illustrates the complexity of budgeting, which, from start to finish, generally takes some 18 months.

At the national level, and for large and complex state economies such as California's, the budget becomes an instrument of macroeconomic policy. How best to do so is the subject of economic theory. Two major budget theories are discussed here: Keynesian and supply-side economics.

Keynesian Theory

Keynesian economic theory is founded on the work of the late British economist John Maynard Keynes, whose work in the mid-1930s called for using government's fiscal and monetary policy-making powers to manage a capitalistic economy that was then in the depths of depression. Keynes developed a school of thought that provides the framework for much of modern economic theory. Keynesian theory advocates a primary role for government in affecting such major trends as total national income, consumer savings and spending, large-scale capital investment, levels of employment and unemployment, the size of a nation's money supply, rates

FIGURE 12.3
The Formal Budget Process in California

Source: Department of Finance, cited in Ken DeBow and John C. Syer, *Power and politics in California* (Boston: Allyn & Bacon, 1997): 206.

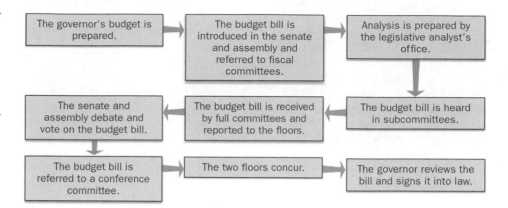

and levels of prices for goods and services, total levels of government expenditures, and the balance of payments between and among nations in the world economy. Keynesian theory justified deficit spending to stimulate a sluggish economy or increasing interest rates to cool off an overheated one.

Economists note that public financial management pursues the following four main goals of raising and spending public revenues: allocation, distribution, stabilization, and growth.

1. Through its allocation goals, government seeks to ensure that an appropriate level of spending reaches those sectors of the economy where it is most needed.

2. By using distribution goals, government seeks to ensure a balance in public funding among regions, classes of people, and the public and private sectors.

3. Through stabilization goals, government seeks to use public spending to stabilize the macroeconomy, as prescribed by Keynesian economic theory.

4. Through growth goals, government tries to use the power of its spending to spur economic growth and generate wealth.[13]

Supply-Side Economics

An alternative approach to Keynesian economic theory is commonly known as supply-side economics. It was popularized during the Reagan administration. Economist Arthur Laffer is perhaps most associated with this approach, although its underlying tenets have been around for hundreds of years and are reflected in Alexander Hamilton's positions in the *Federalist Papers* (No. 21). Supply-side economists emphasize lowering tax rates, especially that on capital gains, in order to encourage capital flow into the economy. Capital flow, in turn, is seen as "trickling down" by generating jobs, growth, and new tax revenues. George H. Bush, during the presidential campaign of 1980 and before he become the vice presidential nominee, had criticized Ronald Reagan's supply-side proposals as "voodoo economics." In fact, its implementation during the 1980s failed to generate the levels of growth and tax revenues necessary to fund increased defense spending, which had been one of Reagan's primary campaign pledges. Reagan's experiment with supply-side economics tripled the national debt by the end of his administration. The debt

Box 12.2

My Time with Supply-Side Economics

Supply-side economics is a major innovation in economics. It says that fiscal policy works by changing relative prices and shifting the aggregate supply curve, not by raising or lowering disposable income and shifting the aggregate demand curve. Supply-side economics reconciled micro- and macroeconomics by making relative-price analysis the basis for macroconclusions. The argument is straightforward: Relative prices govern people's decisions about how they allocate their income between consumption and saving and how they allocate their time between work and leisure. . . .

Supply-side economics presented a fundamental challenge to Keynesian demand management. Keynesian multiplier rankings, which showed government spending to be a more effective stimulus to the economy than tax-rate reduction, had turned demand management into a ramp for government spending programs. Powerful vested interests organized in support of this policy.

Keynesian economists objected to the fiscal emphasis on relative price effects. They claimed that people have targeted levels of income and wealth regardless of the cost of acquiring them. A tax cut would let them reach their target levels of income and wealth sooner, resulting in a reduction of work effort or labor supply. . . .

The claim that the elasticities of work and saving to tax rates were zero or negative possibly could be true for some individuals but not in the aggregate. Keynesians did not realize that in making this argument, they were aggregating a series of partial-equilibrium analyses while ignoring the general-equilibrium effect. If the aggregate response to a tax-rate reduction is less effort, total production would fall, and people would not be able to maintain their living standards. . . .

Supply-side economics came out of the policy process. It was the answer to the "malaise" of the Carter years, "stagflation," and the worsening "Phillips curve" tradeoffs between inflation and unemployment. Supply-side economists convinced policy makers, both Democrat and Republican, that "stagflation" resulted from a policy mix that pumped up demand with easy money while restricting output with high tax rates. . . .

The interest-rate approach to the cost of capital predates the income tax. Supply-side economics brought the insight that marginal tax rates enter directly into the cost of capital. . . . A reduction in marginal tax rates makes profitable investment opportunities that previously could not return a normal profit after meeting tax and depreciation charges.

This perspective provided a more promising policy for stimulating investment than the Keynesian idea of using monetary policy to drive market interest rates below the marginal return on plant and equipment. In a world of global capital markets, central banks cannot alter the real interest rate in financial markets independent of the technological, tax, and risk factors that determine the cost of capital. During the 1970s, such attempts in the United States resulted in higher nominal interest rates and a rise in inflation. . . .

Supply-side economics also added the insight that the total resources claimed by government (tax revenues plus borrowing) is an inadequate measure of the tax burden because it ignores the production that is lost owing to disincentives. . . .

As a policy, supply-side economics first won over Republicans in the House. Jack Kemp was the leader. Next, it won over important Democratic committee chairmen in the Senate, such as Joint Economic Committee chairman Lloyd Bentsen and Finance Committee chairman Russell Long. . . . By the time of Ronald Reagan's election as president, there was bipartisan support in Congress for a supply-side change in the policy mix. Inflation would be restrained with monetary policy, and output would be expanded by lowering the after-tax cost of labor and capital. . . .

The collapse in U.S. capital outflow is clearly the origin of the large trade deficit, which by definition is a mirror image of the capital surplus. Not until 1986, with the dollar falling and U.S. interest rates low, did the foreign capital flow increase significantly.

Source: This article is reprinted with permission of the publisher from *The Independent Review: A Journal of Political Economy* (Winter 2003, vol. VII, no. 3, pp. 393–398). Copyright © 2003, The Independent Institute, 100 Swan Way, Oakland, California 94621–1428 USA; info@independent.org; www.independent.org..

ultimately rose from slightly more than $909 billion in 1980 to a quadrupled level at more than $5.2 trillion by 1996.[14] Box 12.2, "My Time with Supply-Side Economics," summarizes this perspective.

The budget-making process reflects the fragmented nature of decision making in U.S. politics, especially the institutional conflicts between the executive and legislative branches, as well as among the three levels of government. Congress exhibits considerable differences and at times outright conflict in the manner in which its two houses perform their respective roles in revenue and spending decisions. Tax bills originate in the House and are handled by the Ways and Means Committee. The Senate's Finance Committee, however, reviews all tax bills. Appropriation bills are also treated separately by both chambers' respective appropriation committees. Furthermore, in 1974, Congress established independent budget committees in each chamber. These institutional fragmentation factors are exacerbated by political fragmentation—for example, when the two branches or the respective houses are controlled by opposing political parties. The complexity of the budget process affords many points of access to competing interest groups (thereby promoting the value of responsiveness). The system requires compromise as the ultimate basis for virtually all budgetary decisions.[15]

The budget covers a fiscal year rather than a calendar year. State and local governments typically run from July 1 to June 30. The federal fiscal year is from October 1 to September 30. The process is complicated by several stages. **Budget obligation** or authority concerns budget items that are separate from the actual outlay of funds (appropriations). Obligations or authorizations include orders placed, services to be rendered, and commitments (often called *entitlements*) that will require a future outlay of funds. *Outlays* are expenditures in a given fiscal year, whether or not the funds were actually obligated in that fiscal year. Budgets can be distinguished as involving five stages:

1. *preparation*, which is the purview of the executive branch;
2. *authorization*, which is largely a function of the legislative branch;
3. *appropriations*, which is also mostly a legislative function;
4. *execution*, which is carried out mostly by the executive branch; and
5. *audit* or evaluation, which is conducted by both branches but mostly independent of one another.

Budget Authorization and Appropriation

In the authorization stage, the legislative branch generally determines total spending levels—also known as *spending caps*—for each program. Decision making at this stage is mostly done by standing committees in each chamber of the legislature, permanent subject-matter committees that make recommendations to the full houses regarding those departments and agencies that fall under their respective jurisdictions. If authorization bills in the two houses fail to agree, then a bill is considered by a conference committee composed of key members of both chambers, who attempt to iron out differences between the versions passed by the two houses. On budget authorization matters, compromises on these differences are generally agreed to, and authorization bills are then forwarded to the chief executive for approval. State and local governments often draw up budgets without an authorization stage, reflecting less formalized budget processes and weaker standing committees.

Appropriations is a critical stage in the budget process. No appropriation is made without prior authorization. At state and local levels, the executive budget is commonly submitted as is to legislative committees directly for appropriations approval. Sometimes, authorization bills contain language that mandates a certain level of spending, a process known as **backdoor financing**. Sometimes, such practices are linked to **earmarked funding** or revenue sources (monies raised by a certain source that must be spent on a given policy area or service, such as gasoline taxes on highway construction or maintenance).

A trend of great importance to this stage of the process is the dramatic growth in **entitlement** programs. In these programs, prior legislation establishes eligibility standards, and the subsequent level of outlays is determined by the number of eligible individuals who then apply for such authorized benefits.[16] Medicare, Social Security, and various veterans benefits all exemplify entitlement programs at the national level. Often such benefit programs have **indexed costs**—that is, they increase as the cost of living goes up. Entitlements (and earmarked programs) reduce the authority and control of the legislative branch to manage the rate of growth in overall government spending. Increasing portions of the budget have become essentially fixed costs that are basically outside of the legislative branch's annual fiscal discretionary power. Bureaucracies, of course, favor such fixed funding sources. Legislators, and often chief executives and even high-level political appointed managers, are less enamored with such fixed revenue sources and subsequent spending outlays. One budget analyst has suggested that, in practice, nearly 95 percent of budgets are basically "uncontrollable" in any given fiscal year because such expenditures are legally mandated and the level of expenditures is actually determined by economic and demographic factors beyond the legislature's control—a problem evident at all three levels of government.[17] It is, moreover, a growing problem that reflects the increased power of interest groups relative to political parties in influencing public policy. Special- or vested-interest groups, as we have seen in earlier chapters, often work as coalition partners in creating "iron triangles" of policy making, and those policy actors favor the more secure and predictable funding levels that come through such fixed revenue sources. They can also be used to fund a benefit one group receives but whose cost is shifted to some other portion of society.

Budget Execution and Implementation

Budget execution or *implementation* involves the process of actually spending money authorized and appropriated by the legislative branch. Appropriated funds are apportioned from the treasury and typically cover a three-month period (a fiscal year quarter) for the various executive branch departments and agencies. Spending of appropriated funds is monitored by the agency's leadership (either civil servant executives or high-level political appointees), the OMB (or comparable state or local agency), standing legislative committees having specific agency oversight jurisdiction, and the GAO or similar auditing structures of the legislative branch.

Administrative agencies exercise considerable discretion in spending. Agency managers may transfer funds from one account to another and sometimes reprogram funds for use in different but related ways. Chief executives and high-level managers may defer spending from one quarter to another to build cash reserves or to slow down the effects of spending outlays on the economy. The deferral of spending has been a source of conflict between the two branches of government and is discussed

more fully later under budgetary reforms. Since 1974, the president's attempt to defer spending or proposed **recisions** (actual cancellations of appropriated spending) must be transmitted in a special message to Congress.

Budget Strategies

The complexity of the budget process and its typically incremental nature leads to various budget strategies that agency managers may employ in the process designed to protect their budget base during times of fiscal retrenchment, increase their base during periods of rising growth, and expand their base during periods of economic surplus.[18]

Such budgetary strategy games can backfire on agency managers. "Cutting the popular program," for example, is a strategy used to defend an agency's base. The manager intentionally makes the deepest cuts in the agency's most popular programs when the central budget office orders the agency to make cuts, under the assumption that such programs are so popular that the legislative branch will add funds to the agency's budget at the review and appropriations stages. The legislative branch, however, may surprise an agency head during a fiscal crisis and not add the money back to the agency's appropriations. Cartoon 12.1 makes light of this point. It shows a manager's use of a strategy that has apparently backfired.

Budgetary strategies reflect the natural conflict between the executive and legislative branches that are inherent in the structural arrangements of the budgetary process. That conflict has been a major source of various budget-reform measures.

Budget Reforms

The institutional battle between the president and Congress was epitomized by President Richard Nixon's conflicts with a Democratic Party–controlled Congress during much of the 1970s. In an effort to deal with rising inflation rates, Nixon sought to reduce spending by impounding funds after they had been authorized and appropriated by Congress. Congress reacted strongly in response to the perceived partisan nature of the Nixon impoundment that especially targeted President Lyndon Johnson's Great Society programs. Some members filed a suit with the U.S. Supreme Court against Nixon's impoundments. While Court proceedings dragged on, Congress reacted also early in 1974 by passing the Congressional Budget and Impoundment Control Act. It abolished earlier authorization for the president to withhold funds and limited the permissible reasons for deferring the spending of appropriated funds. Permission would be required from both chambers to sustain impoundment longer than 45 days, and either the president or the comptroller general would have to issue monthly reports on any such deferred spending.

The 1974 act established a budget committee to review annual budgets in their entirety. The House Budget Committee had partial overlapping membership with the House Ways and Means Committee, the better to ensure coordination of efforts. The act created the Congressional Budget Office (CBO) to assist Congress and its various committees in analyzing submitted budget proposals. Generally, the CBO has been more accurate than the OMB in such projections. The act enabled Congress to enact at least two concurrent budget resolutions each year (in the spring and fall). The spring resolution was to set targets for revenues, spending, and an annual surplus or deficit. The fall resolution was to finalize figures for each. The act established a new budgetary timetable that governed the process until subsequent enactment of the Gramm-Rudman-Hollings Act in 1985 (see later). Finally, the 1974 act banned new backdoor spending programs, although existing ones were not affected. Backdoor spending program costs continued to rise.[19]

Congressional Influence

Congressional and public reaction to the excesses and scandals of the Nixon administration strengthened congressional budgetary roles until the late 1970s. Political conditions in the Congress then made it less able to control spending. President Reagan took office with a self-declared mandate to cut domestic, nondefense spending. Liberal versus conservative splits in Congress enabled him to enact most of his "Reaganomic" programs. Recurring difficulties in making accurate projections (by both the OMB and the CBO) and the big increase in the national deficit increased tensions between the two branches. Congress increasingly failed to enact a budget on time and also increasingly used the **continuing resolution** to continue expenditures at the same level as in the preceding fiscal year, fueling demands for further budget reform.

In 1985, Congress enacted the Balanced Budget and Emergency Deficit Control Act, more commonly known as Gramm-Rudman-Hollings (GRH). It mandated a balanced budget by 1991, specifying reduced spending (pegged at $36 billion a year) starting in fiscal year 1986. If appropriations failed to achieve the deficit-reduction targets for any year, across-the-board cuts were to automatically kick in to eliminate the excess deficit. GRH exempted many safety-net programs, including Social Security, veterans' benefits, Medicaid, interest on the debt, family welfare programs (AFDC), Supplemental Security Income (SSI), food stamps, and child nutrition. These exemptions essentially removed roughly 75 percent of national spending from **sequestration** (cuts imposed by automatically holding back appropriated funds if the deficit targets were not met—in essence, congressional impoundment). This meant that the heaviest burden of sequestration fell on such programs as education, student loans, energy conservation, and defense.[20]

GHR increased the importance of the OMB and CBO in the budget process through their assessment of the anticipated revenues and the resulting necessity of spending cuts. The Supreme Court ruled, in 1986, however, that the role of the comptroller general in sequestration was an unconstitutional violation of the separation of powers clause.[21]

FIGURE 12.4
Change in the Federal Budget since April 2001
Cumulative change for 2001–2004.

Source: http://www.whitehouse.gov/omb/budget/fy2005/overview.html; accessed 11/17/04.

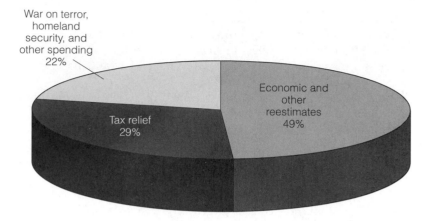

INFOTRAC
COLLEGE EDITION

Continued overall R&D growth forecast

Congress amended GRH in 1987 to overcome the court's objections by authorizing the OMB to make such cuts with the CBO's "advisory" recommendations. The 1987 amendments reduced the deficit targets and changed the deadline for achieving the balanced budget from 1991 to 1993. In 1990, Congress enacted the more successful Budget Enforcement Act, which again amended GRH to use "baseline budgets" rather than actual outlays. It gave increased powers to the president to enforce deficit-reduction targets. It pushed the sequestration process to FY 1995 (see Rubin, 2003).[22]

In 1993 Congress acted again, passing the Omnibus Budget Reconciliation Act, which extended GRH through 1998, set higher spending limits, and directed that governing increases in direct spending be offset by decreases in annual appropriations to a broader array of entitlement programs (thereby punching holes in the safety net).

The revival of the economy during President Bill Clinton's second term and the administration's ability to achieve projected budget surpluses reduced budget reform pressures—but not differences between Congress and the administration over budget priorities. At the beginning of the first administration of President George W. Bush, the debate between the two branches, including the new president, focused on what to do with a budget surplus.

Much of the credit for achieving a budget surplus came from dramatic decreases in welfare spending. These reductions reflect the improved state of the economy and subsequent reductions in welfare spending brought about by the Welfare Reform Act of 1996.[23]

The "what to do with the surplus" debate was short lived, however. A recession, the effects of extensive tax cuts, a series of corporate scandals that resulted in a crisis in investor confidence, the attacks of 9/11, and the subsequent war on terrorism rapidly increased defense and homeland security spending, and the wars in Afghanistan and Iraq combined to produce steep and rising budget deficits. That trend is depicted in Figure 12.2. Figure 12.4 presents the relatively largest of such policy factors affecting the changes in the federal budget between FY 2001 and FY 2004, from a budget surplus of several billion dollars to the record deficit of $413 billion in FY 2004.

Problems of Debt

Some people confuse the national deficit with the national debt, but they are two quite different things. A **deficit** is the amount of money a government spends in any given fiscal year above the amount it collects from all revenue sources for that same fiscal year. Annual federal deficits increased dramatically in the 1980s and early 1990s, quadrupling between 1980 and 1992 from less than $74 billion to more than $290 billion.[24]

Every state except Vermont and Wyoming and most local governments cannot deficit spend because they are constitutionally limited to enacting and working within a balanced budget.[25] Of course, one method to balance their budgets is to incur debt, which they did rather liberally during the 1980s.[26] Within the United States, quite literally tens of thousands of governments can issue bonds and incur debt.

The **debt** is the total amount of money owed by a government. It is, in short, the total of all the yearly deficits that have not been repaid, plus the accumulated interest.[27] The national debt is the total outstanding debt of the federal government. It rose from its historically lowest level of a mere $38,000 (yes, thousand) in 1835 to more than $1 trillion by 1981. It has increased exponentially since then. Whereas it took 156 years to accumulate that first $1 trillion, it took a mere five years more to double that amount and a decade to triple to $3 trillion. In the next half-decade, that amount doubled again, reaching nearly $6 trillion by 1996.[28]

Obviously, one problem associated with such a huge debt level is the cost of paying the interest on the debt, a cost that is eating up an increasing and, for many people, alarming portion of the fiscal budget, rising from 7 percent in FY 1969 to 14 percent in FY 1997 and approaching 20 percent in FY 2004.[29]

> Out of these figures comes an important reality: The performance of the private economy is critical to the condition of the national budget. This is, of course, true on the revenue side, because a robust economy generates more tax dollars at the same tax rates than a sluggish economy does. It is also true on the expenditure side, however, because, during a period of slow economic growth, tax collections decline and payments to individuals increase, thus putting more pressure on a government treasury already suffering from decreased revenues. The recession in the early 1980s made it more difficult to move toward a balanced budget; slow growth in the GNP during most of the years since then has not eased the situation.[30]

In a sense, of course, debt reflects the value of equity. "Debt is a way of matching costs with those who benefit from the borrowing, of seeing that future generations pay their fair share of the costs of roads or bridges we put into place now, of ensuring 'intergenerational equity.'"[31] This perspective reflects the view attributed to President Herbert Hoover, who reportedly said, "Blessed are the young, for they shall inherit the national debt."[32] Today, President Bush might well say, "Blessed are our grandchildren, for they shall inherit the national debt."

Attempts to control deficits and thereby reduce the debt led to **decremental budgeting**, or incremental budgeting's opposite. This means that legislators, chief executives, and their budget staffs cut funding in small steps, again while recognizing the need for a base and concentrating their attention on the effect of reductions in the range of 2 percent to 5 percent.

In incremental budgeting, policy specialists weigh in quite heavily, though they are less visible to the general public. Incremental budgeting is inherently distributive, reflecting historical trends. It is annual, repetitive, predictable, and essentially automatic. This approach to budgeting rewards stability in interest-group and bureaucratic coalitions. By contrast,

> [d]ecremental budgeting is chaotic and conflict laden. It may result in coercion, involve confrontation, and generate mistrust. It is clearly redistributive, breaks precedent, is multiyear, erratic, unpredictable, painful, can foster unstable coalitions, and requires active leadership for overcoming such obstacles.[33]

The effort to control the debt became a political rallying point by the early 1990s. A wave of concern over the debt, coupled with the Republicans' "Contract with America" to control spending, enabled them to capture a majority in both houses of Congress for only the third time in 62 years. They retained their control in 1996, largely on the basis of a platform that promised fiscal responsibility.[34]

The differing perspectives on the budget between the Clinton administration and Democrats on the one hand and Congress and Republicans on the other hand was dramatic. Instead of "intergenerational equity," the Republicans saw the huge debt burdening future generations unfairly and onerously. Newt Gingrich wrote, "If you have a child or grandchild born in 1995, that child can expect to pay $187,000 in extra taxes over his or her lifetime just to pay the interest on the debt. That comes to about $3,500 every year of the child's working life."[35]

Enactment of laws such as the Balanced Budget Act of 1990 seemed to do little, however, to reduce annual deficits and the debt. Cuts in spending deep enough to balance the budget when the economy is not growing vigorously take enormous political will and a fundamental shift in priorities. Leon Panetta, President Clinton's OMB director, noted: "You can build whatever kind of system you want, but the bottom line is still politics and guts."[36]

In addition to political will, of course, the ability to reduce deficits and control the debt requires accurate economic forecasting. The U.S. economy is so huge and complex that analyzing it and predicting its behavior is always problematic at best. Economic forecasters tend to reflect political needs and trends, often being overly optimistic when "rosy" predictions suit the administration or party in power. President George H. Bush and his advisers, for example, were reluctant to use the "R" word—*recession*—long after nonadministration economists and the media were characterizing the economy as being in recession.

Another aspect of the debt level that influences the political will to make difficult spending choices relates to the total size of the economy. As a percentage of the **gross national product (GNP)**, the level of debt in the United States is not especially high, especially when compared with such ratios in other modern industrialized nations. In FY 1996, for example, Britain, Canada, France, Germany, Greece, Italy, Japan, and Sweden all had greater national debts than the United States as measured by percentage of their respective GNPs. Where Greece, Sweden, and Italy's ratio of debt exceeded 10 percent of their GNPs and Japan's was more than 4 percent, the debt of the United States was less than 3 percent of its GNP in 1996.[37]

At least four future reforms have been suggested to establish a budget process that better deals with deficits and debts: (1) create a biennial budget, (2) establish a capital budget, (3) grant line-item veto powers to the president, and (4) enact a balanced budget constitutional amendment.[38] These proposed reforms are high-lighted in Reading 12.1 They are all budget processes used by some or many state governments.

Economic Policy

Fiscal Policy

The word *fiscal* comes from Old French and has its roots in the Latin words for "treasury" and "basket," which sum up the topic well.[39] **Fiscal policy** refers to government actions designed to stabilize the private economy. It includes taxation and tax-expenditure policy, levels of overall spending, and management of the level of debt.[40] The Council of Economic Advisers (CEA) and the OMB are the federal government's primary staff agencies for advising the president on fiscal policy making.

The most significant tool of fiscal policy is the use of taxes not only to raise revenue to run government programs, but also to influence the total volume of spending by private citizens and organizations (the overall *demand* of a nation's economy, which Keynesian economists see as the driving force of an economy, as discussed earlier in Box 12.2).

When properly timed (never an easy task), raising taxes can cool off inflationary spending by reducing the total amount of disposable personal income. Conversely, cutting taxes can spur a sluggish economy by encouraging consumer spending. Government spending, viewed as an investment, can generate considerable ripple effects on a state or local government's economy. The opening or closing of a large national government facility such as a military base can dramatically affect a local economy and, through a "multiplier effect," increase or decrease the money in circulation in an area three- and even fourfold.

When governments intentionally deficit spend by borrowing to spur the economy, it exacerbates problems of debt management. Most state and local governments are limited constitutionally to levels of indebtedness, which is typically linked to their total property tax base or a percentage of their tax revenues.

A somewhat less visible tool of fiscal policy is called *tax expenditure financing*, in which governments provide favorable tax breaks, or "loopholes," for certain kinds of spending by individuals, corporations, and organizations—both nonprofit and for-profit—to induce certain desired social goals or to encourage certain economic activity. Mortgage tax breaks of fairly small amounts can spur or cool off the housing construction industry, for example, and tax credits for education can dramatically affect how many students choose to go on to higher education. Investment by oil and natural gas companies is spurred by a tax-deferral policy that encourages them to find new sources of oil and gas. Tax expenditures have grown increasingly popular at all levels of government.

INFOTRAC
COLLEGE EDITION

Presidential rhetoric and economic leadership

Monetary Policy

Monetary policy concerns efforts to control the supply of money available to an economy. The principle institution at the national level to set monetary policy is the board of governors of the Federal Reserve System (commonly referred to as the Fed), which regulates the supply of money released into circulation. Constraining the money supply, like tax increases, is used to cool off inflation rates. Increasing the money in circulation, like a tax cut, will stimulate economic activity.

Another major tool of the Fed is to influence the rate of interest charged for the use of money. The Fed sets the amount of "reserve" cash or funds that lending institutions must maintain. This level can then be used to lower or raise the interest rate by determining the *prime rate*—the lending rate that banks provide to their most important borrowers. Like the ripple effect of spending, influencing the prime rate spurs new investment, housing construction, and the financing of home mortgages. Ultimately, the credit interest rate charged on all types of borrowing, from cars to computers to appliances, is affected. The Fed thereby influences overall credit management.

In a similar if somewhat less visible way, government loan programs can influence a wide range of domestic private-sector activity. Disaster relief loans, small business loans, and VA or FHA loans to buy a house or add a building to a business can all have noteworthy ripple effects on the economy. Generally, federal and state government loans are set at an interest rate that is lower than what is charged by private lenders. Even small changes in the cost of borrowing money will dramatically affect the decisions of millions of business executives, families, and individuals. Loan guarantees by state and local governments are used more often and are increasingly significant to broad segments of society.[41]

Privatization

Another method to deal with deficits, debt, and overall financial management issues is the increasingly popular approach of **privatization**. Rather simply, this means that a service previously provided by government is now produced by a nongovernmental organization. This approach is thought to promote efficiency by harnessing the competitive forces of the marketplace to inefficient workers, by encouraging better management than achievable through political organizations with all their conflicting pressures, and by placing the costs and benefits of managerial decisions directly on the decision makers by tying their rewards to the efficiency of their actions.[42] There is empirical evidence that private enterprises are more efficient than public ones, having greater productivity and producing utilities at less cost. Privatization, as we have already seen, is a particularly popular recommendation for reform of the reinventing government and the new public management reform movements. Critics argue, however, that fairness and effectiveness are more important values for a government service than efficiency.[43]

Privatization is especially popular at the local level, where many thousands of communities contract out for such services as trash removal, utility provision and billing, street lighting, ambulance services, jail and prison operations, golf course maintenance, firefighting services, and even street maintenance.[44]

Public choice theorists in particular argue the case that public officials, being self-interested, avoid risks and seek to promote their careers, resulting in the tendency to seek to enlarge their programs and increase their budgets. These theorists argue that bigger government is more inefficient and operates against the public interest in favor of the bureaucrat's own or the agency's interest. Explanations by public choice theorists fit well into the antigovernment attitudes that are engendered by periodic scandals such as Watergate and that coincided with the conservative political philosophy of the Reagan and senior and junior Bush administrations.[45] The approach dovetailed as well with the reinventing government approach promoted by Clinton and Gore.[46]

Privatization generally takes one of three common forms:[47]

1. the sale of government assets,

2. private financing of public facilities (toll roads or lanes, bridges, and so on), and

3. the private provision of an essentially public type of service (trash collection, education, fire or ambulance service, and the like).

Contracting out for services affords greater political flexibility. Debts can be paid off, the size of government can be reduced, and responsiveness can be enhanced by maneuvering around entrenched and cumbersome bureaucracies. Advocates emphasize that privatization allows for a greater ability to experiment with new delivery systems and the enhanced use of specialists and people of unusual talents without having to be concerned about affirmative action and veterans' status limitations of government civil service systems. Short-term savings can be realized via reduced pay scales and fringe benefits, and more long-term benefits by reducing pension costs. Political risk taking is easier when government actors are less visible and less directly associated with a policy being provided by a private contractor or through some innovative public–private partnership arrangement.[48]

Consider Reading 12.1, "The Congressional Budget Process and Some Proposed Reforms," which describes the current U.S. budget process in a brief historical perspective and then discusses a few of the major proposals actively before the Congress to reform, mostly in an incremental fashion, that budget process. The importance of a revived national (and now even global) economy to spur economic development is evident. Economic growth is a value budget decision makers pursue (at all levels of government, not just federal). It is linked to cycles of recession and prosperity.

Reading 12.1

The Congressional Budget Process and Some Proposed Reforms

The Budget Process Today

Before approval of the Congressional Budget and Impoundment Control Act in 1974, the budget Congress passed was the piecemeal culmination of legislation affecting discretionary appropriations, entitlements, and tax policy. Since then, the House and Senate budget committees—themselves creations of the 1974 law—have been charged with reporting a concurrent resolution that forms the "blueprint" for the budget. This budget resolution contains aggregate ceilings for discretionary and mandatory spending, as well as revenue targets, that authorizing and appropriations committees are required to meet. After the resolution is passed, committees are allocated funds which they can distribute at considerable discretion.

In most years, two subprocesses then unfold: reconciliation and appropriations. Reconciliation is designed to turn the resolution into a detailed and comprehensive law directing the termination, creation, and alteration of government programs, the manipulation of entitlements, and changes in tax law. Reconciliation bills do not need to be passed every year, and recently, they have not been. In 1998, Congress did not even pass a budget resolution—something that was ostensibly against the law—and the reconciliation bill of 1999—the Republican's big tax cut—was vetoed by the president.

Appropriations are made every year. In order for the government to operate, 13 appropriation bills—or at least a continuing resolution (CR)—must become law before the fiscal year ends on September 30. Once passed, the bills, proposed in line with the allocations from the resolution, release the discretionary funds spent by the federal government.

The post-1974 modifications to this process have been relatively minor. The Gramm-Rudman-Hollings law of 1985 did not achieve its primary goal of phasing out deficits, largely because ballooning entitlement programs were spared the fiscal scythe. The Budget Enforcement Act (BEA) of 1990, however, established caps for discretionary spending in three broad issue areas and the pay-as-you-go (PAYGO) restrictions, which mandated that any changes in taxes or entitlements must be offset to conform with the principle of deficit neutrality. Any violations of the caps or the PAYGO principle results in an Office of Management and Budget (OMB) sequester or across-the-board spending cut. The 1993 Omnibus Budget Reconciliation Act consolidated the caps within a single category and extended the principle to fiscal 1998, while the 1997 reconciliation legislation required Congress to observe the caps through fiscal 2002 in order to bring the unified budget into balance.

The current budget process is simultaneously centralized, coordinated, routinized, and very complex. Given other developments in congressional politics—especially those relating to the ideological homogenization and polarization of the parties—it is not surprising the process is characterized by tremendous partisanship and is controlled, especially in the House, by the majority leadership. Despite some initial and spectacular failures, however, the process put into place in 1974 finally fulfilled the major hope of its designers; it has produced a surplus, although short lived.

Some Reform Proposals

Interestingly, however, the reform to resolution-reconciliation that gets the most press these days would actually invigorate the procedure. This is the proposal to make the budget resolution a joint, instead of concurrent, resolution. The effect would be as dramatic as it is simple. A joint resolution, unlike the concurrent version, requires presentment to the president and would, consequently, become law.

The main argument for making the resolution a statutory vehicle is that doing so would force the president to play a formal role early in the budget process. Currently, presidents seem somewhat superficially involved in fiscal policy making. After presenting a budget on the first Monday in February, the president recedes into the background as members of Congress squabble over substantive policy. The president only reenters the arena in the fall, when reconciliation is on the floor or even in conference, to engage in a series of "summits" with leaders of the congressional majority. Providing for formal executive participation through a joint resolution would, as Leon Panetta has stated, avoid "eight months of posturing and one month of dealing." It would also force the president to submit a more realistic, defensible budget rather than a "wish list" and reference point for intramural congressional fighting.

As Roy Meyers of the University of Maryland has argued, an added benefit of preparing a joint budget resolution might be that the public would apportion blame for failure to reach interbranch agreement "equally and not primarily to the Congress" (1998: 4). If the public sees both branches at fault when the government shuts down or needed changes in fiscal policy are not forthcoming, then all participants might be more eager to strike agreement. . . .

A joint resolution could also bring a greater degree of incrementalism to the process. It would consecrate executive–legislative consensus on aggregates, and the final reconciliation bill would manifest agreement on details. . . . Finally, a joint resolution might dilute frustration among many in Congress that the final resolution is merely what congressional budget makers want the budget to look like—a process nearly as oligarchical as the making of the president's budget within the bureaucratic executive branch. During periods of divided government, a joint resolution would provide the congressional minority with the not-inconsequential role of carrying the president's water for him in the early phase of budget making. . . .

Biennial Budgets

If anything, members of Congress have looked at biennial budgeting—defined broadly as a two-year budget cycle—more closely than they have the joint resolution. As a general concept, the biennial budget currently enjoys considerable support in Washington. For example, important congressional leaders who support it are Speaker Dennis Hastert (R-IL) and Senate Budget Committee Chair Pete Domenici (R-NM). . . .

Several basic models for biennial budgeting exist and each has its advocates. The model that draws the most attention on the Hill is that described in Domenici's frequently cited Biennial Budgeting and Appropriations Act. If adopted, the process would reserve the first session of a Congress for resolution and appropriations. The second session—the election year—would be given over to authorization and oversight.

Arguments for the fundamental concept are numerous. Twenty-three states follow such a process and . . . biennial budgeting can bring greater stability to the planning processes of federal agencies and state governments. Now that federal departments and agencies are required by the Government Performance and Result Act to state and measure attainment of specific goals, knowing how much money they would have a year in advance would benefit them greatly.

In addition, having to pass budgets only once every two years would give Congress more time to legislate in other areas. Robert Art drew this conclusion in his 1989 study of the only true federal experiment with biennial budgeting undertaken by the Department of Defense in fiscal 1988 and 1989. A two-year cycle would also allow Congress to more fully perform its critical oversight function.

Another argument concerning Domenici's proposal was phrased succinctly by Representative Charles Bass (R-NH): "Elections and appropriations don't mix to make good government" (2000). The closer to the election a budget is passed, this position asserts, the more pork it contains. . . .

Inflexibility and spending increases [critics argue . . .] would be likely consequences. The current budget-making process requires legislators to take both short-term—appropriations—and long-term—reconciliation acts and multiyear authorizations—considerations. In contrast, two-year budgets would inevitably require self-correction before the biennium expires and forecasting the economy would likely become increasingly difficult. Supplemental appropriations bills would likely proliferate both in size and number. Augmented spending would also be encouraged as agencies padded their funding requests to hedge against potential problems in the later parts of the cycle.

Two-year budgets could also actually weaken oversight. Executive agencies seem to respond constructively to potential threats to their funding. Especially galling to some legislators is the fact that the biennial budgets "would increase the power of executive branch bureaucrats, giving them a longer leash and two years' worth of money to spend" (Moakley, 2000). . . . Finally, biennial budgets might only delay wrecks that would involve what Peter Sperry (2000) of the Heritage Foundation has called "bigger trains." . . .

Other Procedures That Undermine Appropriators

Perhaps even more alarming for appropriators has been the proclivity of members to suggest placing discretionary programs "off-budget." This entails creating funds in which revenues are collected for specific purposes and cannot be used for activities such as new spending in other areas, tax cuts, or debt reduction. . . . As supporters of such moves are quick to note, the types of public works pork over which appropriators salivate are often the subject of "off-budget" proposals.

The power of appropriators would be further limited if two other reforms are enacted. . . . The first is to get the federal government to emulate many states and create a "budget reserve account" (or, to use its sobriquet, a "rainy day" fund). Simply put, this requirement would set aside emergency funds within the budget resolution to be drawn from the fund when a statutorily defined "emergency" has been declared. Appropriators, who currently approve roughly two supplements a year, would play no role in identifying emergencies or deciding how rainy-day money would be spent.

The other reform concerns an automatic continuing resolution, or ACR. Passing CRs is necessary when appropriations bills do not become law by the beginning of the fiscal year. Affected departments and agencies are then funded by the stopgap measure. Proposed ACRs generally set funding levels at the previous year's amounts and can last from a month until indefinitely. They would impact appropriators because the end of the fiscal year deadline provides the appropriations committees with powerful leverage as they shape funding bills. With an automatic fallback in place, however, Congress would no longer need regular appropriations bills or a CR to avoid the now-dreaded government shutdown. . . .

[This list of major reform proposals] suggests the current process is sound . . . and implies that if change will occur, it will be incremental. . . . This is because the contemporary congressional budget process is appreciated by many people. . . . By bundling many policy changes into a single legislative vehicle, reconciliation allows leaders to concentrate their efforts and resources on a single, extremely public vote where the stakes for the parties are high. It also means that popular proposals are mixed in with unpalatable ones. Republican favorites are blended with Democratic pets. These characteristics make the task of forging majority coalitions in Congress and winning presidential support easier (Sinclair, 2000: 3–5).

Another attractive quality of the process is that resolution and reconciliation are governed by rules designed to facilitate the treatment of the budget on the floor of each chamber. This is especially important in the Senate. The 1974 act statutorily established rules for the budget resolution that prevent filibustering and enforced a germaneness requirement for floor amendments—unless 60 votes can be garnered for them, they must be waived.

Source: Andrew J. Taylor, The Congressional budget process in an era of surpluses, *PS: Political Science and Politics*, *33* (3) (September 2000): 575–581. © American Political Science Association. Reprinted with permission of Cambridge University Press.

Net Assignment

Using InfoTrac College Edition and Internet search engines, enter the key search word *privatization* to search for states or communities that are using this approach. Describe what you find, choose one example, and report the objective behind the use as well as pros and cons.

Summary

American values compete to influence governmental financial management. The primary functions of financial management focus on tax policy to determine who pays government's bills and on the complex process of budget making. Various types of budgets from various perspectives are executive and legislative, capital and operating, line-item and program, performance and zero-based.

Auditing and institutional auditors serve several functions. Government uses two types of accounting—cash and accrual—both of which rely on asset management and financial reporting. The evaluation function links program evaluation to budget implementation.

At the three levels of government, the politics of the budget process balances the major sources of revenue against the major areas of expenditure. Institutional conflicts between the legislative and executive branches develop in the appropriation and budget-execution stages. Two theories of budgeting—Keynesian and supply-side economics—rest on competing values.

Budget reforms derive from institutional motivations. Reforms link to debt, which has grown and increasingly affects all other aspects of the budgetary process and budget-making politics. Institutions responsible for fiscal and monetary policy attempt to provide tools that will control debt and manage the economy. Privatization, and the values it represents, has grown in political popularity as one way to cope with governmental debt.

Glossary of Key Terms

asset management   An approach to government planning for the maintenance of public assets throughout their life cycle that (1) views the assets in terms of their return on investment and (2) establishes asset-disposal programs.

backdoor financing   Legislation authorizing a certain level of spending for an agency that can include language ordering the agency to spend the amount of money for specific uses.

budget   Plan for projected income and expenditures; estimate of future costs and plan for the use of employees, supplies, and related resources.

budget cycle   Routine steps in the budget process involving the preparation, authorization, appropriation, implementation, and audit of the budget.

budgeting   The formal mechanism to obtain, distribute, and monitor the revenues used by governmental administrative agencies.

budget obligation   Budget item that is separate from the actual outlay of funds and requires the future expenditure of funds.

budget process   Governmental decisions on spending needs and how to pay for them.

capital budget   Plans for large expenditures (such as bridges, buildings, fire engines) usually financed over extended periods of time (5 to 30 years).

compliance audit   An examination of the financial records of a government or an agency to assess whether it has financially complied with the law.

continuing resolution   Authority Congress grants to agencies, in the absence of annual appropriation legislation, to continue spending funds based on the previous year's budget.

debt   Total amount of money owed by a government plus the accumulated interest owed on the total; accumulated unpaid yearly deficits plus interest.

decremental budgeting   The opposite of incremental budgeting; budget makers seek to cut spending by concentrating on small reductions rather than on any agency's program base.

deficit   The amount of money a government spends in a given fiscal year above what it collects from all revenue sources for that same period.

earmarked funding   Legal requirement that revenues from a given source be expended for a given function or purpose—such as gasoline taxes on highway construction or maintenance.

energy audit   An assessment of how well an agency uses or wastes its energy resources.

entitlement   Legal obligation created through legislation that requires the payment of benefits to any person or unit of government that meets eligibility requirements set in the law.

excise tax   Tax placed on the manufacture, sale, or consumption of various commodities.

executive budget   Budget document prepared by the chief of the executive branch and submitted to the legislature for review, modification, and adoption.

fiscal policy   Government actions designed to stabilize the private economy by manipulating taxing or spending policy and managing debt.

gross national product (GNP)   Total value (in constant dollars) of all goods and services produced by a nation in a given fiscal year.

incremental budgeting   Method of budget preparation and review stressing small increments in existing budget allocations for current programs (referred to as the *budget base*).

indexed costs   Policy or law ties awards or benefits to the cost of living; they go up automatically as the cost index increases.

legislative budget   A type of budget in which the legislative body (state legislature, county board of supervisors, or city council) prepares the budget document after departments submit their budget requests directly to the body (usually to a specific committee).

line-item budget   Classification of budget accounts to narrow, detailed objects of expenditure used by an agency, typically without reference to the ultimate purpose or objective served by the expenditure.

monetary policy   Efforts to control the supply of money available to an economy by regulating the supply of currency in circulation and manipulating (credit) interest rates.

operating budget   A budget, or plan of revenues and expenditures, that concerns the annual expenditures for such expendable items as salaries, wages, pensions, employee benefits, supplies, contracts for equipment repair and maintenance, new-equipment purchases, and utilities.

performance audit   An assessment of an agency's efficiency and how well it has achieved its stated program goals.

performance budget   Budget that focuses on an agency's objectives and accomplishments; used to increase management responsibility and accountability.

priorities   The values of government expressed in its expenditure and revenue decisions.

privatization   When a service previously provided by a government agency is now produced by a nongovernment organization (also often referred to as *contracting out*).

program budget   Budget focusing on an agency's programs, as in Planning Programming Budget System (PPBS); a tool for defining priorities and evaluating accomplishments.

progressive tax   Any tax in which people with higher incomes pay a larger percentage in taxes than do people of lesser means; generally, graduated income taxes are progressive.

recisions   The actual cancellations of appropriated funding.

regressive tax   Any tax in which people with lower incomes pay a higher overall percentage of their income in taxes than do people of greater income. Generally, sales taxes are regressive.

sequestration   Congressional mandates that defer spending of funds from one fiscal quarter to another to build cash reserves or to slow down the effects of spending on an economy.

social audit   An assessment of how well an agency copes with social issues in an organizational context.

tax expenditure   Practice of giving favorable tax breaks (loopholes) for certain kinds of spending by individuals as well as to nonprofit or for-profit organizations.

zero-based budgeting   Budget process that rejects incremental budgeting by demanding a justification of the entire budget (base and incremental increases).

Review Questions

1. How are competing values in budgetary decision making reflected in the two somewhat-competing functions of budgeting: (1) providing government with the resources needed to accomplish its program goals and (2) the need and desire to manage the private-sector economy?

2. Distinguish the five functions of public financial management, and identify which policy actors are more prominently involved in each function.

3. Compare and contrast the major sources of revenue for the federal government with those of the states, and likewise distinguish their varying areas of expenditure. Can you distinguish the competing values involved with the various types of tax revenue sources associated with these levels?

4. Compare the ideas and values stressed by both Keynesian and supply-side economic theories. How do those two approaches differ in the way they would likely advise using fiscal and monetary policy to manage the economy? to control debt levels?

5. What are some budgetary implications of high deficit spending? Why has this approach ebbed and flowed with the economic cycle? Who most benefits and who most loses as a result of the very high deficits?

Surfing the Net

The following websites are related to the topics and material found in this chapter.

Association of Government Accountants (**http://www.agacgfm.org**)

Center for Responsive Politics' opensecrets.org (**http://www.crp.org**)

Congressional Budget Office (**http://www.cbo.gov**)

Council for Urban Economic Development (**http://www.cued.org**)

Council of Development Finance Agencies (**http://www.history.rochester.edu/cdfa**)

Council of State Governments (**http://www.statesnews.org**)

Federal Reserve system (**http://woodrow.mpls.frb.fed.us/info/sys/collection.html**)

Federation of Tax Administrators (**http://www.taxadmin.org**)

Government Finance Officers Association (**http://www.gfoa.org**)

International City/County Management Association (**http://www.icma.org**)

National Association of State Budget Officers (**http://www.nasbo.org**)

National Association of Counties (**http://www.naco.org**)

National Association of Development Organizations (**http://www.nado.org**)

National Association of Local Government Auditors (**http://www.nalga.org**)

National Association of State Auditors, Comptrollers and Treasurers (**http://www.sso.org/nasact/nasact.htm**)

National League of Cities (**http://www.nlc.org**)

Office of Management and Budget (**http://www.whitehouse.gov/OMB**)

Urban Institute (**http://www.urban.org**)

U.S. Department of Commerce (**http://www.doc.gov**)

U.S. Department of the Treasury (**http://www.ustreas.gov**)

Chapter 13

Administrative Law and the Control of Public Agencies

A sweeping new ergonomics regulation issued in the last days of the Clinton administration will now have "no force or effect," following swift action by Congress and the Bush administration to rescind the rule. The National Association of Manufacturers (NAM) hailed the action as "a total victory over an unreasonable and oppressive regulation." Congress passed the resolution and President Bush signed it late last month.

In a statement about the rule, NAM underlined the point that "No organization will have to comply with it. No states will be required to adopt a similar rule, and no further legislation over the validity of the rule will be required."

Ergonomic regulation set aside,
Forest Products Journal, 51(6) (June 2001): 10.

Introduction

Law and Ethics as Sources of Public Values

The opening vignette illustrates the simple fact that central to all government is its exercise of *sovereignty*—the legal and accepted authority to control people living within a certain geographic area over which it enjoys jurisdiction—and the regulation of public and private behavior of both private individuals and organizations. Government regulations seek to change the way such individuals and organizations (particularly corporations) behave while they pursue their self-interest. Government may attempt, for example, to prevent them from harming others—for instance, their consumers, suppliers, competitors, distributors, or even society at large—and future generations by polluting the environment with long-lasting toxic chemicals. It often does this through **tort action**—that is, by a civil suit that seeks monetary compensation for damages or harm allegedly done to a plaintiff by a defendant. Government also has **rule-making authority**, or a quasi-legislative action that allows it to issue formal rules to cover a general class of activities.

How government goes about its administrative tasks is a central topic of this chapter. The complex relationships between administrative agencies and the courts, who oversee how such agencies may regulate private behavior, is vital to understanding how regulatory behavior is limited and held accountable. Many values are at issue in discussing administrative law and the relation of the courts to bureaucracy: conflict or harmony between levels of government or between agencies and private organizations; procedural fairness to those who are brought before administrative agencies; the substantive correctness of the rules and regulations government organizations promulgate; the success or failure of organizations in achieving their stated policy goals; the coordination of government activity versus contradiction or duplication of efforts; the consistency of rules with the policy agenda; and economy and efficiency versus effectiveness, to suggest but a few obvious ones.

Courts, Democratic Ideals, and Administrative Law

Courts, in particular, are concerned with how administrative agencies regulate private behavior as administrative philosophies and ideologies change. Ideological changes and managerial styles affect the central value conflict between democracy and bureaucracy. Governmental bureaucracy is concerned with productivity—with *how* things are done. Democratic ideology, however, is focused on values and ethics—with how things should or should not be done. Changing styles of administration, such as what has recently been called the "new public management," shift values, challenge old assumptions, and expose the operating values to analysis and comparison.[1] Regulatory reforms enacted during the 1980s and 1990s, for example, raise issues and questions about the ethics of using procedural restraints on bureaucratic regulatory agencies, such as the EPA and OSHA, to disrupt or impede the regulatory process and the effect of procedural controls on regulatory policy.[2]

Politics and administration, of course, cannot be separated. Politics is central to determining the values and approaches implemented by regulatory agencies. Styles of management influence the balance between administrative efficiency and democratic accountability. Controlling government officials—those elected or appointed or exercising public power through government contracts—necessitates bottom-up control if democratic accountability is to be maintained. As governments increasingly contract out for services, the judiciary is more challenged to maintain accountability when legal authority is transferred to private third parties. Critics have assessed the courts' inconsistent ability to do so as contributing to a loss of accountability.[3]

When governments contract out the management of prisons, for example, the transferal of authority raises issues about whether or not prison employees are liable to legal action and the extent to which legal defense against being sued is available to guards at privately run prisons managed by a corporation.[4]

Policy changes can likewise affect values and the relation of government to control of private behavior. Welfare reform policy enacted in the 1990s by both the federal and many state governments, for instance, uses the power and authority of government to provide moral direction to welfare agency clients.[5]

One other factor instrumental in shifting popular attitudes toward governmental regulatory behavior is changing technology. The development of the Internet, for example, raises many challenges for public managers. Tens of thousands of government agencies now have websites, and agency managers must grapple with and understand the new technology while minimizing or strictly controlling the sometimes-undesirable and even unethical consequences that the Internet offers for social and group life in public organizations.[6]

Accountability

The complexity of these issues partly reflects the many approaches to accountability and methods for achieving it. Scholars of public management, among others, have identified five types of accountability:

1. bureaucratic–hierarchical,
2. legal,
3. professional,
4. political, and
5. moral–ethical.

They further categorize 10 methods for achieving accountability that are particularly relevant to changes that arise from privatization and contracting out of public services:

1. auditing,
2. monitoring,
3. licensing,
4. court oversight,
5. contracts,
6. codes of ethics,
7. whistle-blowing,
8. registries,
9. outcome-based assessment, and
10. market forces.[7]

As society changes demographically, agency managers must make sure they hire and train employees who will reflect the social diversity that the agency and its

TABLE 13.1

Diversity Training Model

Core Values	Goals	Interventions	
		Processes	Activities
Inclusivity	Create a welcoming place	Integration into organization	Training in cultural awareness
	Develop a multiculturally competent staff	Relationship building	Outreach and retention
Challenging oppression	Formulate critical analysis and take action	Consciousness raising	Power shifts

Source: Cheryl Hyde, A model for diversity training in human service agencies, *Administration in Social Work, 22*(4) (1998): 23. Reprinted with permission of The Haworth Press, Inc.

programs both become part of and serve. Table 13.1 offers a model of agency diversity training, for instance, that suggests how agency managers might use the training function to shift staff attitudes and behaviors from core values to specific goals and then to the resulting processes and activities that are designed to match changes in diversity both in society and in the agency itself.

The Rise of Regulation

Regulation is a major activity at all levels of government. Government rules and regulations grow as society becomes more complex. They have four principal aims:

1. protect individuals from one another (buyers from sellers, employees from employers, tenants from landlords, lenders from borrowers, and the like);
2. protects groups of individuals from the actions of other groups;
3. alleviate human suffering by
   a. providing some sort of social aid such as Social Security benefits or aid to the disabled;
   b. relieving the needs of the elderly, the poor, and those who suffer from natural disasters such as floods;
   c. cleaning up human-created problems such as toxic waste spills; and
   d. providing relief for those who are unemployed; and
4. minimize corruption, dishonesty, and the abuse of power by government officials.

These assorted purposes and the resulting programs require rules and regulations to ensure that assistance is fairly and equitably distributed. Rules and regulations abound by the tens of thousands as a result.

Some federal regulatory agencies and some state regulatory agencies as well serve in policy-impacting roles other than just regulatory or self-regulatory policy. The Internal Revenue Service (IRS), for example, is involved in redistributive policy (where resources are intentionally drawn from one segment or sector of the public to finance benefits given to another sector). Similarly, an agency such as the Agricultural Research Service is a distributive agency (providing a good or service directly to the general public or to a given clientele group) that also serves as an economic and social regulatory agency. Virtually all regulatory agencies involved in the implementation of a regulatory policy observe the impact of those policies as outputs of government. As such, they play a role in responding to those outputs, often by initiating proposals to amend or modify policies. Likewise, their interpretive rules may initiate a new policy direction.

State and Local Regulation

Measured by the amounts of money spent, the number of employees managed, and the number and variety of activities regulated, one can easily say *most* regulation is conducted at the state and local levels. State governments collectively have hundreds of such agencies that supervise utility commissions, control intrastate rates and services of myriad businesses, and oversee banking by state-chartered banks, among other responsibilities. State governments also regulate the used-car industry through so called lemon laws that impose disclosure and warranties regulations on car dealers, and they implement minimum-wage and antidiscrimination laws. They affect the environment in many ways through environmental protection agencies and agricultural departments that promulgate regulations on how farmers may use pesticides. Many states also have recycling laws, bottle-deposit laws, and the like. State governments also regulate a myriad of health and safety laws that are aimed at protecting employees, consumers, and the general public. They use their licensing power to regulate occupational enterprises from nursing homes to restaurants to saloons to insurance companies and so on.

INFOTRAC
COLLEGE EDITION

Regulation and risk management

Most states, in fact, regulate most professions—attorneys, physicians, pharmacists, teachers, and zoologists—as well as many occupations and industries—barbers, cosmologists, and real estate agents, for example.[8] The regulation of professions and occupations, however, tends to be done through the use of *self-regulation*. In other words, the profession, occupation, or industry being regulated sets the standards that the state will enforce. In recent decades, regulation at the national level also has shifted toward self-regulation. Critics of this trend, however, decry its effects on environmental protection and pollution reduction. William Ruckelshaus, a former administrator of the Environmental Protection Agency (EPA) who rebuilt the agency's credibility and morale in the 1980s, was once asked his opinion of the "voluntary regulation" policy of his predecessor, Anne Gorsuch. "The only thing voluntary about voluntary regulation," Ruckelshaus said, "is if the EPA voluntarily chooses not to enforce the law."[9]

Collectively, local governments have the greatest number and variety of regulating agencies. They supervise health and safety policy enacted by higher-level governments. They attempt to control land use through zoning agencies. They try to control how honestly businesses conduct their affairs by regulating weights and measures. More than 800 occupations are regulated at the local level: funeral directors, chauffeurs, milk processors, plumbers, hearing aid dealers, and private investigators, to name a few.[10]

The Upward Expansion of Regulation

Regulations that began at the state and local levels gradually moved up to the national level when demands increased for national legislation that would better cope with increasingly large and powerful corporations whose influence grew beyond the capacities of local and state government to control.

National regulation began in the 1880s and emphasized economic regulation by either preventing certain kinds of business practices or requiring certain operating procedures. The late 1880s saw the development of the **independent regulatory** agency **(IRA)**, the first of them aimed at regulating interstate commerce. The granddaddy of all such agencies, the Interstate Commerce Commission (ICC), regulated the railroads. An IRA is charged with regulating some private economic activity and is structured to be more or less independent of both executive cabinet departments and the legislative branch. Such regulatory agencies typically are headed by plural executives (a board or commission) rather than a single administrator. Terms for membership on such boards are fixed and staggered, and members serve for lengths designed to prevent any single state or federal executive from being able to appoint a majority. The budgets of such agencies are typically financed by fees or charges imposed on the industry or sector being regulated, which helps to weaken the state or federal executive's and legislature's budgetary control of or influence over the agency. Gradually, regulation developed to include the **dependent regulatory agency (DRA)**, an agency charged with regulating economic activity but housed within an existing cabinet department.

My view from the doorstep of FCC change

Old-Style Economic Regulation   Old-style **economic regulation** controls an economic activity by focusing on market aspects of industrial behavior, such as rates, quality and quantity of service, and competitive practices within a particular industry or sector of the economy.[11] The first DRAs were old-style economic regulatory agencies housed within existing cabinet-level departments. Federal DRAs include the National Highway and Traffic Safety Administration (NHTSA) in the Department of Transportation, as well as the Food and Drug Administration (FDA) in the Department of Health and Human Services. At the state level, examples would be an alcohol and beverage control agency in a state department of commerce, a fish and game agency in a department of natural resources, a state water-resources control board in a department of environmental protection, and a motor vehicle administration in a state department of transportation.

Most old-style economic regulations are found in four policy areas: antitrust, financial institutions, transportation, and communications. The emphasis is on a specific industrial sector, and the standards and guidelines promulgated are limited to a sector or to one specific aspect of the business operation rather than to the economy as a whole. Regulations in this style use a "rifle" as opposed to a "shotgun" approach by targeting the specific activity being regulated. By the 1980s, federal economic regulatory agencies numbered more than two dozen entities that were established as both independent and dependent structures. Table 13.2 lists various federal economic regulatory agencies.

Social Regulation   After World War II, and especially during the 1970s, federal regulatory activity increasingly emphasized a new style. **Social regulation** is concerned with the nature and types of goods and services being produced in an economy. These regulatory agencies focus on the social effects of industrial- and other business-production processes. Public concern in the 1960s shifted to human threats to the environment (air pollution, acid rain, asbestos and other cancer-causing agents, toxic chemical and nuclear waste, and so on) and societal trends seen as damaging to the ecosystem itself. The decade of the 1970s witnessed an expansion in the number of agencies and the amount of federal resources as government shifted social regulation to new areas of health, environmental, and safety regulation.[12] Spending for job safety and working conditions more than doubled, and the staffs of these agencies increased by nearly 50 percent.[13]

TABLE 13.2

Examples of Federal Economic and Social Regulatory Agencies: From A to U

Economic Regulatory Agencies	Social Regulatory Agencies
Antitrust Division, Department of Justice	Agricultural Marketing Service
Atomic Energy Commission	Animal and Plant Health Inspection Service
Civil Aeronautics Board	Army Corps of Engineers
Commodity Futures Trading Commission	Bureau of Alcohol, Tobacco, and Firearms
Comptroller of the Treasury	Coast Guard
Economic Regulatory Commission	Consumer Product Safety Commission
Farm Credit Administration	Defense Nuclear Facilities Safety Board
Federal Aviation Commission	Economic Regulatory Commission
Federal Deposit Insurance Corporation	Employment Standards Administration
Federal Energy Regulatory Commission	Environmental Protection Agency
Federal Housing Finance Board	Equal Employment Opportunity Commission
Federal Maritime Commission	Federal Aviation Administration
Federal Power Commission	Federal Housing Finance Board
Federal Reserve Banks	Federal Mine Safety and Health
Federal Reserve System Board of Governors Review Commission	Fish and Wildlife Service
Federal Trade Commission	Food and Drug Administration
Internal Revenue Service, Department of the Treasury	Food Safety and Inspection Service
Interstate Commerce Commission	Immigration and Naturalization Service
National Credit Union Administration	Merit System Protection Board
National Labor Relations Board	National Labor Relations Board
National Mediation Board	National Transportation Safety Board
National Transportation Safety Board	Nuclear Regulatory Commission
Nuclear Regulatory Commission	Occupational Safety and Health
Patent and Trademark Office Administration	Office of Government Ethics
Postal Rate Commission	Office of Surface Mining Reclamation
Securities and Exchange Commission	Selective Service Commission
Tennessee Valley Authority and Enforcement	Small Business Administration
Trade and Development Agency	Thrift Deposit Protection Board
U.S. International Trade Commission	U.S. Commission on Civil Rights

Social regulation cuts across industrial sectors. It applies rules to all business, but with an emphasis on limited aspects of business activities: employment opportunities, environmental protection, and occupational safety. Social regulation seeks to eliminate undesirable by-products of production processes and protect consumers and the public from products deemed unsafe or unhealthy. Social regulation covers a wider spectrum of businesses and affects many more consumers than does old-style economic regulation. Table 13.2 also lists exemplary federal agencies involved in social regulation.

Subsidiary Regulation   A third approach to regulation has been labeled **subsidiary regulation**. It involves regulatory activities that accompany Social Security, Medicare and Medicaid, Temporary Assistance to Needy Families (TANF), food stamps, veterans' benefits, IRS regulatory concerns, and regulations associated with categorical grant programs. Subsidiary regulation involves both individual citizens and state and local governments as both recipients and participants in grant programs.[14]

This brief overview of the types of regulation makes it clear that a complex array of regulatory approaches results in regulatory policies that are diverse, value laden, and occasionally contradictory. As private businesses and organized labor became increasingly large and powerful, control of these societal forces and institutional arrangements required a counterbalancing by government that was correspondingly vast. As government regulatory powers and activities increased, so did the need for the courts to oversee and adjudicate the process, a status derived from the Constitution's prohibition on government from depriving any person of life, liberty, or property without due process of law. It is the peculiar role of the courts to assess how adequately government policy respects and upholds due process. As regulatory agencies increased their rule-making role and the adjudication of those rules, the courts became ever more involved in judicial review of those activities.

These external control institutions—the elected executive or other executive agencies, especially staff agencies such as the OMB, the legislature (Congress or state legislatures), and the judiciary—each play distinctive roles in how they influence bureaucratic behavior. The executive, for example, tends to control through budgetary influences (and the threat to cut them) and by appointment of high-level political appointees who have managerial or planning functions that direct or impact bureaucratic behavior. The legislatures tend to influence through agency structural design, through their approval or disapproval of budgets, through policy area jurisdictional assignments, including mandates, through the use of the legislative veto and legislative oversight, and through their evaluation and oversight of agencies. Of particular note is their use of staff agencies, such as the General Accounting Office or legislative auditing agencies, to oversee bureaucratic behavior. The judiciary influences bureaucratic behavior through case decisions or writs, which often set standards that reach beyond the agency involved in any particular case. All three institutional branches, of course, help set the predominant values that, in turn, affect what bureaucrats do or don't do.

Regulation and the Courts

Courts oversee the administrative regulatory system of agencies in several ways. Administrative law establishes that at least four requirements must obtain for due process to be upheld: (1) Adequate notice of the rules and regulations must be

INFOTRAC
COLLEGE EDITION

Seat at the table

given; (2) the reasons for the rules and regulations must be disclosed; (3) plaintiffs in the process must be provided a hearing (agency-based adjudication); and (4) plaintiffs must be given the right to further appeal (that is, to external adjudication by the courts).[15] The courts typically oversee administrative regulatory agencies through the appeal process. Individuals and especially corporations may file suits that seek court injunctions against agencies that require them to issue rules mandated by or implied in the statutes. At other times, the agency sues a company when it seeks to punish the company for noncompliance with agency rules or orders. Finally, suits may be filed that involve two or more corporations in dispute with one another in which court decisions affect agency rules and regulations as tangential aspects to the suit.

Issues that involve disputes over state or local regulatory policy are heard by state supreme courts (or various special courts of appeal, such as tax appeal courts, that are often set up for such jurisdictional matters). Issues that involve federal regulations are heard before (1) a federal circuit court of appeals, which hears cases directly on appeal from regulatory agencies; (2) federal district courts, where many actions are brought by or against various federal agencies; (3) various federal courts of special jurisdiction (court of claims, U.S. Court of Customs and Patent Appeals, U.S. Military Court of Appeals, and the U.S. Tax Court, for instance); and the United States Supreme Court, whose caseload is approximately 20 percent cases on appeals from or regarding administrative agencies.

Because court cases are time-consuming and expensive, organizations are increasingly using another route—arbitration—which may work to avoid court cases. Box 13.1 briefly discusses the role of arbitration as an option to court cases.

Which court a case is brought to is determined by the principle of *standing to sue*, which determines under what circumstances access to a given court is granted. Access to sue may be based on *class action suits*, which have been gaining in popularity since the 1970s. Class action suits are often brought by citizens to deter damages by corporations to their interest or to spur an agency to enforce statutes designed to protect the individual. Participants in class action suits need to demonstrate they have suffered some sort of monetary damage. Usually such suits involve only one or a few people, but occasionally they involve thousands (for example, recent suits against tobacco companies).

Indeed, a fairly recent trend worthy of note here is the use of class action suits brought by the attorney generals of a number of state governments. State attorneys general (SAGs) have taken the lead in recent years in regulatory enforcement because they are able to piggyback on the popular product liability movement, and they have been bringing suit against big national corporations (and even international ones), which are viewed as having deep pockets. Many of the SAGs are Democrats whose values support this approach. And it is good politics as well. These cases bring high visibility to a state attorney general who may be considering a run for the governorship of his or her state. Winning such a case brings name recognition. SAGs are building on their stunning success against the tobacco industry. A "superstar" of this approach is New York State's Attorney General Eliot Spitzer, who popularized the "regulation by litigation" approach (see Reading 13.1, "Trends in State Regulatory Power: Balancing Regulation and Deregulation," at the end of this chapter).

Another basis for access are suits brought by individuals and organizations (such as business corporations) acting as "private attorneys general." These involve matters

Box 13.1

Arbitration Can Slash Legal Costs

Litigation is incredibly expensive, and even victories can come at a high cost. That's why many organizations are writing arbitration agreements into their contracts with customers, employees, suppliers, distributors, and service providers. Arbitration lets organizations resolve disputes quickly, often in a few weeks or months. Shortening the process can greatly reduce the cost.

Taking a dispute to arbitration is like going to court, with all the usual legal protections. Parties to a dispute may appear at hearings, present evidence, or call and question each other's witnesses. The hearings take place in person, by phone, by mail—even by videoconference or over the Internet. To ensure that arbitrators handle cases and interpret the law correctly, all arbitration awards are reviewed by courts in a process called "confirmation."

[For an organization] to ensure that disputes go to arbitration instead of to court . . . it is critical to draft an arbitration agreement that is fair and will stand up to judicial scrutiny. If an arbitration agreement is unfair, the courts will throw it out. With that in mind, here are five tips toward drafting better agreements:

1. Keep It Friendly: If you want to maintain the relationship, pursue the least abrasive approach. In your contract language, you may want to include a dispute resolution process that starts with an agreement to negotiate in good faith for a period of time, followed by mediation, followed by binding arbitration if the parties cannot resolve the dispute. To avoid delays, be sure to specify a time frame for each procedure.

2. Specify What's Covered: If you want the arbitration agreement to govern all disputes arising between the contracting parties, state that clearly in the contract.

3. Invoke the Federal Arbitration Act: Different states have different laws governing arbitration. If you want to draft an agreement that can be used in several states, invoke the Federal Arbitration Act. It ensures that the arbitration agreement will be enforced uniformly in different state courts.

4. Avoid Unnecessary Travel: Courts reject agreements that force the weaker party to needlessly travel a long distance. So specify a location that is convenient for both parties.

5. Consider the Other Party's Costs: In some states, the law mandates that the financially stronger party cover some or all of the cost of arbitration. The courts see this as a way of maintaining a level playing field.

Source: Curtis Brown, Arbitration can slash legal costs, *Financial Executive*, *19*(9) (December 2003): 64.

based not on money damages but on efforts to compel an agency (or corporation) either to do something it is not doing that plaintiffs argue it should be doing (typically filed against a regulatory agency) or to cease doing something that affects a public-interest group—such as the environment, consumers, and so on. Here plaintiffs need to show that a *legal wrong* is involved in which the individual or group has suffered some wrong prohibited by law, common law, or the U.S. Constitution or the constitution of a particular state.

Social legislation, especially much of that passed in the 1970s, contained provisions that authorized people to sue administrators for taking unauthorized action or for failing to perform duties deemed nondiscretionary (i.e., mandated by law). Judges who are thought to be "judicial activists" will often find implied right to redress. During the 1960s and 1970s, for example, U.S. Supreme Court justices were often judicial activists and handed down decisions that were sweeping in their scope and that set precedents that affected the behavior of many governmental agencies and regulatory behavior at all levels of government. Some decisions,

PHOTO 13.1
New York State Attorney General Eliot Spitzer
How has the use of class action suits by the various state attorneys general affected judicial oversight of bureaucracies? Do you think the extensive punitive fines awarded in such suits serve as an effective deterrence to others?
Source: Courtesy of Mr. Spitzer.

such as *Roe* v. *Wade* (1973), became watershed cases that instigated many more cases by interpreting an implied right (in this case, of privacy) that subsequently affected not only the decriminalization of abortion, but also the health service system, the welfare system, and myriad governmental agencies and local, state, and federal programs.

The tort liability of government officials is another avenue of access to the courts for oversight of regulatory agencies. A tort action involves a civil suit that seeks monetary damages for harm done to a plaintiff by a defendant. Tort actions often concern product liability issues, working condition or occupational safety issues, exposure to harmful or health-impairing conditions, and so on. Although such suits are frequently directed against private corporations, the decisions often affect the rules and regulations of regulatory agencies.[16]

The Supreme Court may intervene to limit government action when the substantive or procedural fairness of administration actions are in question. For example, in *Morgan* v. *United States* (304 U.S. 1, 1938), the court ruled that an agency had to improve its hearing procedures. In *Goldberg* v. *Kelly* (397 U.S. 254, 1970), the court ruled that an AFDC recipient's right to a hearing depended on the extent to which the person might be expected to suffer a substantial loss. *Federal Crop Insurance Corporation* v. *Merrill* (332 U.S. 380, 1947) ruled that agency regulations had to be written.

INFOTRAC
COLLEGE EDITION

New Supreme Court rulings on liability claims and arbitration

PHOTO 13.2
Crash Test Dummies Save Lives
To what extent do social regulations try to "save us from ourselves"?
Source: AP/Wide World Photos.

Technology Issues

Sometimes new technologies confront the court and require it to rule on a wide variety of social issues. It ruled, for example, to balance a federal employee's right to privacy against the public's disclosure rights as stipulated in the Freedom of Information Act (FOIA) (1966)—as it did in *United States Department of Defense* v. *Federal Labor Relations Authority* (510 U.S. 487, 1994).[17] The rapid development of the Internet also has created myriad social problems that the court has been forced to examine. The Internet has allowed children access to hardcore pornography, and it has made depictions of child molestation, sado-masochism, and bestiality easily available. It also has spread information on weapons and bombs of various types that youngsters have used to attack their schools and peers. Internet chat rooms are used by pedophiles to make contact with potential victims.

Congress responded, using the FCC's authority over existing "dial-a-porn" laws and applying them to the Internet. It passed the Communications Decency Act (CDA) as part of its sweeping Telecommunications Act of 1996. The decency act was immediately challenged in federal court in a suit filed by the American Civil Liberties Union (ACLU), which alleged that the law infringed on freedom of speech, deeming material as indecent and forcing matter that was appropriate for adults down to the level of what was appropriate for children. In June 1997, the Supreme Court unanimously struck down the CDA as "government-imposed, content-based restriction in speech" and a "wholly unprecedented breadth of law" (*Reno* v. *ACLU*).[18] Box 13.2, "Telecommunication Reforms and Deregulation," addresses issues raised by the Telecommunications Act of 1996.

Box 13.2

Telecommunication Reforms and Deregulation

The Telecommunications Act of 1996 is very broad, and addresses emerging national issues such as universal service guarantees to all individuals; deregulation of local telephone and cable television service to promote competition; reforms to regulations that inhibit access to the "information super-highway"; and greater access to advanced technologies such as satellite communications.

The issues of satellite dish placement and telecommunications provider access to inside wiring have become two of the most important facing property management. The industry is most concerned that when attempting to guarantee universal access to advanced telecommunications products and services, Congress, the FCC, and individual states be aware of the potential problems and dangers caused by regulations

that prevent [multiple-family] building owners and managers from controlling access to private rights of way and to the outsides of their buildings. . . .

Owners should have the right to negotiate mutually acceptable terms and conditions for granting access to building space and the valuable tenant markets contained within. This position of choice applies to first-time installations as well as subsequent communication firms that service a given area or municipality. There should be no question of allowing the owner or manager to review the planned installation as a representative of the property's interest.

Source: Amanda Drukman, Telecommunication reforms and deregulation, *Journal of Property Management, 69* (4) (July/August 2004): 6.

Privacy versus the Public's Right to Know

Computer access to government records through the Freedom of Information Act raises issues about the public's right to information that the government has on individuals versus the privacy rights of federal employees. The court developed a judicial doctrine—the "core purpose test"—to guide its deliberation and rulings in trying to balance those conflicting rights and values. In 1996, Congress essentially overruled three decades of case law concerning the FOIA by allowing access to records for any reason, not just for "public purpose," and thereby enabling private individuals access to other people's information.[19] In 1998, Congress responded to setbacks from judicial reviews by proposing a bill (S. 981) entitled the "Regulatory Improvement Act of 1998." If ever enacted, it would limit the power of judicial review by courts when considering cost–benefit analysis and risk assessment, allowing only a judicial review of final rules by an agency.[20]

Courts are limited in their power over bureaucracies in several ways. They are structurally passive—that is, they can only act on cases brought to them. Not all questions or problems are *justiciable*, that is, subject to being settled in court. Administrative law often deals with a fusion of power rather than a separation of power. Courts must rely on administrative agencies to enforce their rules and to willingly comply with court decisions.

Court powers over administrative agencies come from the courts' powers of judicial review, from administrators' "anticipated reaction" (how administrators think courts are likely to act), from the moral suasion of the courts, and from their specific *writ* powers. These powers include the (1) *writ of mandamus* (an order to an official to perform a particular task), (2) *writ of prohibition* (an order that forbids a particular act), (3) *writ of quo warranto* (requiring an agency to set forth the legal authority for its actions), (4) *writ of injunction* (an order designed to prevent a threatened harm), and (5) *writ of habeas corpus* (an order to judicially determine why someone is held in custody or jail or prison).

Administrative Law and Regulatory Agencies

Administrative law is a fairly complex term for which there is no complete agreement about its meaning or usage. In the U.S. political system, administrative law, like constitutional law, is remarkably adaptive. It is a living and evolving body of law that is constantly being interpreted and revised by courts, executives, legislatures, and administrators. It provides a stable basis for the behavior of administrators in U.S. society.

For our purposes here, we define **administrative law** as those laws and regulations created by the activities of governmental agencies that make rules and adjudicate cases concerning private rights and obligations and the limits needed to control such agencies. Included in the body of laws (or rules and regulations) of administrative agencies that collectively make up administrative law are **interpretative rules**—those rules that specify an agency's views of the meaning of its regulations or of the statutes it administers. The meaning or language of an agency's interpretative rules is often at issue in legal challenges to an agency, and the meaning assigned by judges and courts may not always agree with those of the agency's administrators or adjudication judges.

Although administrative agencies enjoy wide discretion in developing the now-massive body of administrative law, their discretion has its limits. These limits may be imposed by the legislature when it establishes an agency or when it enacts amending laws regarding an agency's jurisdiction, as well as by the courts through their judicial review of agency actions and rulings.

A considerable array of controlling laws affect individual citizens. Figure 13.1 depicts the web of federal, state, and local controls over a typical citizen's life. Administrative law and procedures have become more standardized, particularly at the national level, since the enactment of the Administrative Procedures Act of 1946 (APA). Agencies must follow the general outline and procedures laid out in the statute. Newer emphases in administrative law focus on:

- increasing public participation in the administrative process,
- processes that involve informal and discretionary government regulatory activity,
- the evolving mission statement each administrative agency develops for itself, and
- the development of more effective oversight of those activities, especially by the legislature and the courts.

INFOTRAC
COLLEGE EDITION

An old judicial role for a new litigation era

Public participation is a trend that has emerged mostly since the 1960s and often through court insistence. Administrative processes in both formal and discretionary governmental activity seek to cover individuals who are institutionalized in public facilities, aliens, and the governance of educational institutions—emphasizing the broadening of rights in previously neglected areas. Legislative and court oversight expanded in focus, detail, and the methods used to evaluate agencies, and such oversight also promoted sweeping regulatory reform.[21]

The APA specifies that administrative rules must be published in the *Federal Register*, which allows interested individuals to comment before any rule or regulation published there becomes final. Interest groups especially follow the publication

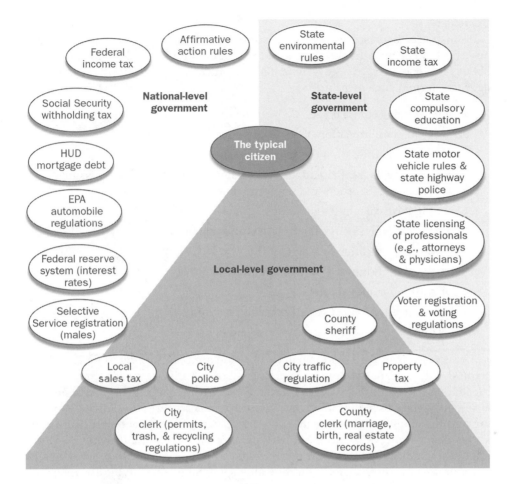

FIGURE 13.1
Pervasive Governmental Influences on a Citizen's Life

and become involved in the process if their interests are affected. They thus also become part of the oversight process. More will be said of their involvement and role in the next chapter.

The Limits of Administrative Law

Administrative law is restricted to agency actions that cover the rights of private parties. It excludes the legal relationships among government officers and departments or the different levels of government (matters covered in constitutional law). Administrative law concerns the quasi-legislative and quasi-judicial actions of administrative agencies. The administrators of such agencies are policy makers—but with a limited range of authority when making rules. Questions about the rights of individuals make administrative agency procedures courtlike or quasi-judicial. Administrative agencies with regulatory powers have administrative judges who make pertinent judgments in courtlike settings and activity. Administrative law applies legal principles that originate from constitutions, common law, statutory law, and regulatory law to the affected government agencies.[22]

INFOTRAC
COLLEGE EDITION

Understanding adjudication: origins, targets, and outcomes of ethics complaints

Discretion

Administrative agencies use both formal and informal activities. Their informal advice includes opinions about rules and regulations, and licensing or information about how one receives a governmental authorization or benefit. Administrative agencies' formal powers include:

1. investigating complaints;
2. ordering the elimination of certain practices;
3. setting standards;
4. prosecuting flagrant violations of laws and standards, including issuing cease-and-desist orders and imposing fines;
5. setting forth rules and regulations;
6. holding hearings before issuing rules and regulations;
7. holding adjudication hearings;
8. issuing, withholding, and revoking licenses;
9. providing for appeal procedures;
10. ordering temporary cessations of activities; and
11. seizing property and imposing fines and penalties.

Limitations over regulatory agency discretion are built into the rights and **procedural rule** safeguards designed into an administrative agency's organization, procedures, or practices as well as through judicial review. Other control devices also limit agency discretion. One such device is media scrutiny. Investigative reporting and the ability of media members to hold agencies up to public ridicule does serve as something of a check on agency abuse of power. Another device is the establishment of an **ombudsman,** or an official who is charged with processing and examining complaints against the bureaucracy. Ombudsmen typically report to state legislatures or Congress or to the office of a governor, county executive, or mayor. Citizen action groups such as Common Cause also can serve as informal watchdogs of administrative agencies. Still further limitations are built into sunshine and sunset laws.

INFOTRAC
COLLEGE EDITION

The ombudsman revisited: 30 years of Hawaiian experience

Regulatory Procedures and the Adjudication Process

Typically, an administrative agency with regulatory powers is established by statutory authority. The statute creates the agency, describes its primary mission or goals (often in quite broad and general terms), and lays out its jurisdictional responsibilities—and, in so doing, something of its limitations as well. The legislature at the same time might pass a general regulatory statute stating the broad outlines of the law; the agency then develops appropriate rules, regulations, standards, or guidelines it intends to use to implement or modify the law or to meet new situations. The agency then publishes advance notice of proposed rules (in the *Federal Register*, for example) for at least 30 days and normally longer (60–90 days, for instance). During this period, the agency may hold hearings or receive written comments from interested individuals and groups who are likely to be affected by the rules. The agency then publishes the final rule and codifies it into the agency's code of regulations (in the *Code of Federal Regulations*, for example).[23]

This final step can sometimes take years to complete. The process favors *organized* interest groups that have vested interest in the rules and regulations, the role of which will be discussed more fully in the next chapter. These groups are often viewed as *clientele groups* by the agency. "Public opinion" on the rule or topic is structured through this process—and tends not to reflect the sentiment of the average citizen, who rarely pays any attention to proposed rules. The public airing of proposed rules and regulations, however, means that the potential is always there for the public to become aroused and involved. Administrative officials are cognizant of that fact and sometimes act on the basis of anticipated reactions.

Adjudication of agency rules and regulations is conducted on a case-by-case basis. It roughly uses the procedural safeguards more or less typical of a court of law. Most cases are settled during informal hearings or proceedings. Adjudication of cases sometimes becomes highly formalized, as when class action suits are filed that involve millions of dollars or—in the cases of recent product liability rulings such as those involving tobacco, breast implants, and some pharmaceuticals—even billions of dollars. Formalized proceedings are used when a contested case has no precedent. Such formalized proceedings have rules about the government attorney involved, the use of evidence, testimony, and cross-examination of witnesses in the case. Some interest groups are represented by public counsel, akin to a public defender in a criminal suit, who speaks for the interest groups' perspective at the hearing.

The most common figure in an adjudication proceeding is the administrative law judge (ALJ), or hearing examiner, who acts for the agency in conducting the proceedings and hearing testimony before writing a preliminary finding or decision. This adjudicative step is designed to keep the case from going to court. Thousands of administrative judges at the federal and state levels work within myriad regulatory agencies. Their role is to prevent rules and regulations that are arbitrary or unfair or that do not conform to the law at issue. The judges' opinions do not constitute the final authority on the matter, because they can be appealed to an outside court, but their recommendations are routinely followed and become the final result in most cases.[24] When not accepted, however, they are appealed to the appropriate appellate court that has jurisdiction over the matter.

Recently, an appeals court overturned a California Department of Motor Vehicles antipollution regulation that imposed a "smog tax." A California Superior Court had earlier determined that the fee violated both federal and state commerce laws. The state had collected in excess of $455 million from the smog tax from new residents who registered their out-of-state vehicles. A $300 surcharge was imposed on vehicles not manufactured in accordance with California's emission control standards (which exceed federal standards and those of any other state). Despite the Superior Court's 1997 ruling that the fee violated state and federal commerce laws, the Department of Motor Vehicles continued to collect the fee. The federal appeals court also declared the fee unconstitutional, ruling that the state owed, with interest, a refund of $724 million. Although the court ordered refunds only to the parties who sued, Governor Gray Davis called for refunds to go to the more than 1 million people who paid the fee during the 1990s.[25]

The Expanding Role of Administrative Judges

Technological and economic developments also expand the need for administrative regulatory agencies. Challenges to rules and regulations more routinely happen when the matter and the rules govern something new for which there is no legal precedent.

The federal Balanced Budget Act of 1997 expanded the authority of the FCC to assign frequencies on the electromagnetic spectrum using a competitive bidding or auction process. The newness of the technology and the intense competition among firms trying to carve their niches in the growing telecommunications market have virtually guaranteed many challenges to this new process, each of which necessitates a hearing before an administrative law judge.[26]

The APA stipulates that an interested party has the right to petition an agency to issue, amend, or repeal a rule. The act also expanded the use of administrative law judges. The number of administrative law judges has grown significantly. Before 1978, they were known simply as *hearing officers*. Currently, more than 1,000 administrative judges work at the federal level, with more than 700 in the Social Security Administration alone.[27] Increases in the number of ALJs reflects American society's increasing propensity to use adjudication. Indeed, even one-time critics of the APA have contributed to their increasing numbers. The American Bar Association, for example, once a leading opponent of federal regulatory agencies, has become the APA's chief protector over the years.[28]

The Influence of Social Change

These data actually include another reason why use of federal administrative judges has expanded: As government benefits became *entitlements* and were politically viewed as sacred cows or untouchable safety nets, rulings that denied such benefits were increasingly challenged, which required more cases to be heard by administrative law judges.

Changes in immigration law regarding asylum, refugee status, the legalization of previously categorized illegal aliens, the effects of employer-sanction provisions of the Immigration Reform and Control Act of 1986, and the immigration restrictions in the 1996 immigration law and welfare reform law all combined to bring many more cases before Immigration and Naturalization Service (INS) administrative law judges. As the flow of immigrants (both legal and illegal) increased to more than 1 million per year during the 1990s, the expansion of hearings rose accordingly. These legal and social developments, like Social Security entitlements, has extended and expanded the use of administrative law judges to cope with the greater number of hearings.[29]

Changes in personnel policy—which reflect cultural shifts in gender roles, for instance—and executive orders and statutory enactments that affect and establish affirmative action programs also have generated their own rulings and subsequent challenges. Sexual harassment issues have similarly led to more hearings and conflict over rules and regulations on the matter as society grapples with what legally constitutes sexual harassment. The growing number of women in the workforce and their entry into and gradual rise in occupations to which they were previously excluded further increase the need for hearings. Administrative law judges, in fact, hear cases on a wide range of issues related to women in the workforce, including the following:

- sex discrimination (and, more recently, discrimination based on age and physical handicap);
- issues of employee hiring, compensation, and benefits;
- pay differences based on gender;

- management decisions about job assignments and transfers as well as promotions and discharges; and

- matters related to "other" job-assignment duties (often with considerations about pay and prestige).[30]

The Influence of Economic Changes

The highly competitive economic market generates ever greater numbers of rules and regulations and challenges to them. Issues and conflicts between large and small firms emerge as new companies enter various markets. Laws such as the Small Business Regulatory Enforcement Fairness Act of 1996 (SBREFA) often grant regulatory relief to small firms to encourage competition, even though these small firms are frequently responsible for a disproportionate number of social ills that provoke challenges: occupational injuries, racial and sexual discrimination, pollution of all kinds, lack of employee access to health care, and so on. SBREFA assumes the value that "small is good and big is bad." Administrative hearings and court challenges to that value assumption are a given.[31]

The trend toward **deregulation** that was so strongly promoted during the administrations of Ronald Reagan and George H. Bush resulted in many cutbacks to the regulatory approaches, rules, and regulations of the social regulation era of the 1970s. Deregulation not only "gets government off the backs of business," the goal of those who have pushed the conservative approach for the past 25 years, but also cuts back on the practical effects of such regulation—sometimes with clearly harmful social or environmental effects. These political trends raise challenges and increase the number and variety of agencies and cases that require hearings before administrative law judges.

Challenges to administrative rules and regulations before both administrative law judges and the courts partly depend on whether information is available to a challenger to bring an action against an agency. Such information may not always be freely available. We now examine the internal and external controls on regulatory agencies and the particular role played by the insider—the whistle-blower—who brings that information to the outside world.

External and Internal Controls

External control resides mostly with the legislative and judicial branches in their oversight capacities over all bureaucracies, regulatory and otherwise. At the national level, the APA requires that an order be issued only "after opportunity for an agency hearing," as do most laws that establish regulatory agencies. Federal hearings are presided over by an administrative law judge who has been appointed by the agency with approval of the Office of Personnel Management. The judge's tenure and pay are determined by the Office of Personnel Management and the Merit System Protection Board. Hearings before an administrative law judge include oral hearings, cross-examination of witnesses, and full recording of documentary evidence. After the ALJ's findings, his or her recommendations are first appealed to the agency's head and may then be appealed to an appropriate court. The legislature, besides its statutory power to create such agencies and stipulate their jurisdiction, controls agencies through its investigative powers.

FIGURE 13.2
A Model of Unethical Behavior

Source: Adapted from Daniel J. Bass, Kenneth Butterfield, and Bruce Skaggs, Relationships and unethical behavior: A social network perspective, *Academy of Management Review, 23* (1) (1998): 16. Copyright 1998 by Academy of Management. Reproduced with permission of Academy of Management.

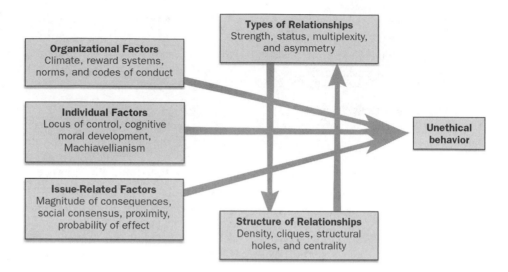

The most effective control of administrators' abuse of powers occurs when they develop *internal control*—that is, they internalize the norms and values that limit their power and sanction appropriate behavior. These are not easily developed in enough bureaucrats and thus are not pervasive in all agencies. Indeed, many forces contribute to corruption and unethical behavior.

Figure 13.2 offers a model of unethical behavior that shows the complexity of factors contributing to unethical behavior. Large-scale agencies with huge budgets and often-sweeping regulatory powers have many organizational factors that may lead to unethical behavior within an agency. Their decisions and budgets often involve enormous amounts of money that may tempt members to behave unethically (through influence peddling, bribery, and extortion). Internal reward systems intended to promote one value also may serve to promote unethical behavior. The Internal Revenue Service, for example, developed an elaborate set of points by which its accountants were evaluated for pay and promotion. These internal rewards were intended to encourage efficiency, but they induced agents involved in tax audits to recover taxes through intimidation, especially by abusing small taxpayers with audits. Police departments also typically develop codes of conduct ("Back up your partner," "Don't rat on a fellow officer," and so on) that can result in cover-ups of abuse and corruption.

Individual factors refers to the moral norms and values that develop within the individual bureaucrat. Police departments, for example, tend to recruit authoritarian personality types. Regulatory agencies may similarly attract Machiavellian schemers whose internal values justify manipulating rules and regulations in unethical ways because, for them, the end justifies the means.

Issue-related factors are also involved. Regulatory agencies may have individuals who view the issues like zealots. Their strong belief in the agency's mission or the correctness of the policy they implement—saving the environment, saving the world from terrorists, saving children from pedophiles and pornographers, and so on—may become so critically important that it seems to justify the use of unethical means. These factors are often affected by relationships the individual bureaucrat has with colleagues. Cliques may develop that promote unethical behavior among their members.

Critically important to internalized control is the value of **trust**—a psychological state of being willing to be vulnerable based on positive expectations of another's intentions or behavior. Different types of trust may be distinguished: fiduciary, mutual, social, character-based, process-based, institutional-based, deterrence-based, calculus-based, and rational-based.[32]

Ethical behavior is promoted when individuals accept and internalize the value of *integrity*—a loyalty to rational principles and values. Integrity promotes both honesty and conscientiousness, which are critically important values to a fair and just implementation of regulatory policy.[33]

The Role of the Whistle-Blower

One control aspect that spans the external/internal distinction is that of the **whistle-blower**, a public employee who informs on the acts of his or her own department or agency when such actions are seen as improper.[34] As we have seen already, the whistle-blower function can be encouraged by statutory incentives. Congress has awarded a whistle-blower bounty as a tool to support its investigations and to sanction its combat against fraud by government suppliers in the Whistle-Blower Protection Act (Public Law 101-12, April 1989). The bounty is a mechanism that essentially deputizes a firm's employees to monitor regulatory compliance.[35]

Statutes that protect whistle-blowers have encouraged the practice, as have the courts, which are highly protective of such employees. The 1989 law created an office of special counsel as a distinct agency whose role was to protect employees from recrimination for whistle-blowing and from other prohibited personnel practices. The special counsel can investigate any agency the office reasonably believes "violated any law, rule, or regulation . . . [for] gross mismanagement, a gross waste of funds, an abuse of authority, or a substantial and specific danger to public health or safety." Its second function is to protect the whistle-blowing employee who discloses such agency misconduct. The act puts the burden on the agency to counter the whistle-blower's allegations.[36]

Perhaps of equal value to whistle-blowing control over agencies has been the mass media. The trend toward investigative reporting, especially in print media, and recent developments in broadcast journalism, especially television, have increased public awareness and interest in media as control devices that rival formal governmental control mechanisms in influence. Media have had a long tradition of exposing government corruption, misdeeds, ineptitude, and abuse of power. News media encourage whistle-blowers by offering considerable publicity. Their attention can help protect the whistle-blower as much as any statutory protection. At the local level in particular newspapers, television, and radio stations act as informal ombudsmen, soliciting citizen complaints about the bureaucracy and then investigating those complaints.[37]

INFOTRAC
COLLEGE EDITION

The worst of both worlds

The Regulatory System and Competing Values

Democracy stresses both responsibility and accountability. A democratic government is one that is controlled. But as we have seen here, that involves balancing conflicting values. Bureaucratic administrators, of course, often chafe under such controls. They want to get things done. Citizens, on the other hand, often view governmental bureaucracies, especially those that are regulatory in nature, as slow, cumbersome, and meddlesome. Too much control will stifle action and can breed distrust and opposition. Too little control breeds governmental intrusion, arrogance, and the abuse of power.

Interest groups react to governmental regulation and protest when the values they cherish are threatened by the values imposed through government regulatory authority. Not only do outside interest groups protest when they feel their values are threatened, but also so do some within an agency if they feel the policy of their agency is wrong or is being ignored.

Indeed, voter-expressed dissatisfaction with the traditional model of government regulation fueled the "deregulation" political movement. In no small measure this reflected a reaction to federal mandates and federal regulatory rules that ignored market conditions. Statutory reform often needs to precede regulatory reform, and political support is increasing for both to be more carefully tailored to the specific market imperfections that government involvement is designed to correct. Old-style regulation often was viewed as impeding the market economy from adapting to new conditions. As one critic noted:

> Regulation has always been important to economic and social prosperity. But it often imposes unnecessary social costs, reducing competitiveness and economic growth. Over the past few years, the broader public has begun to demand improved government efficiency. . . . Congressional Republicans continue to push for key changes in regulatory procedures. These include increased use of cost/benefit analysis, compensation to property owners for the loss in value of private property due to regulation, risk analysis, peer review of agency scientific findings, and broader legal powers to challenge agency determinations in court." (Kennedy, 2001: 57)

On the other hand, bureaucratic institutions can and do utilize their considerable resources to influence real outcomes of regulatory policy. For example, political and bureaucratic institutions, resources, and regulatory actions shape insurance regulation in the American states. Solvency regulations at the state level are regulatory activity critical to both consumers and businesses with a de facto interest in ensuring that the insurance policies they hold are financially secure—a not-insignificant issue following, for instance, the series of four hurricanes that devastated so much of Florida in 2004. Political and bureaucratic institutions exert an important influence of firm solvency (Ruhil and Teske, 2003: 353).

This chapter closes with Reading 13.1, "Trends in State Regulatory Power: Balancing Regulation and Deregulation," which summarizes so many of the issues raised in this chapter and how the regulation/deregulation balance is being sought between national and state government regulations and within the states over which methods and approaches best achieve that balance. It notes the increasing use of the courts to settle conflicts and the increasing trend in successful regulatory actions undertaken by state attorney generals.

INFOTRAC
COLLEGE EDITION

Institutions, bureaucratic decisions, and policy outcomes

Reading 13.1

Trends in State Regulatory Power: Balancing Regulation and Deregulation

There are two distinct normative perspectives on state regulation. The negative one suggests that regulation largely is captured by the most powerful interests in the state, who easily dominate understaffed part-time legislatures and agencies. It also suggests that states collectively "race to the bottom" in a lowest common denominator attempt to attract business investment with loose regulatory policies, and that state regulation is an unnecessary additional barrier for American firms competing in a global economy that is influenced by the World Trade Organization and regulations from other national and international organizations. The positive perspective is that the states have improved their policy-making ability and institutions over time, that devolution has added strength, that the need to balance budgets has provided a level of discipline and accountability for state actors not seen at the federal level, and that states may now be the most trusted and capable partners in the American federal system.

In theory, state regulation can better match policies to the preferences of its citizens and businesses, it can serve the functions of experimental laboratories, and it has incentives to regulate in efficient ways. On the other hand, a single federal regulatory regime, rather than 50 different state policies, promotes consistency and stability for firms competing in national (and international) markets, it incorporates jurisdictional externalities, it employs greater analytic resources than individual states, and many political scientists still perceive national regulation to be less susceptible to extreme interest-group capture than state regulation.

Whether one views state regulation positively or negatively, there is no denying its importance. The states regulate up to 20 percent of the American economy. Though regulatory expenditures are generally less than 1 percent of state government budgets, regulation forces private actors to spend considerable monies, and about one-third of state agencies mainly address regulatory issues. Today, states retain their role as the only regulators of business activities like corporate chartering, insurance, workers compensation, and occupational licensing. States share some regulation with the federal government, usually along the historical intrastate/interstate division, as in telecommunications and electricity, and with a few areas of transportation. States implement specific federal regulations in areas like occupational safety and environmental regulation, where they sometimes have authority to go beyond federal standards, try different implementation approaches to meet these standards, or address problems not handled by federal legislation.

States have some overlapping jurisdictions with the federal government in discretionary enforcement areas like consumer and financial regulation. Research suggests that the states are engaged in a complicated relationship with federal regulators, often filling enforcement gaps, a trend we can label "de-enforcement," in a period also marked by both deregulation and devolution. Industry capture and regulatory "races-to-the-bottom" are legitimate concerns about state regulation, but some find that most areas of state regulation are characterized by contested environments in which institutional actors make independent policy choices. And some of these institutions are being reformed in important ways. . . .

While the devolving of power to the states is an important reality in welfare, transportation, health, and some education programs, in regulatory policy, devolution is not dominant. Instead, "economic regulation" of prices, market structure, and firm entry has been characterized by partial or complete federal deregulatory preemption of the states. At the same time, federal attempts to reduce "social regulation" of risk and information, and related "de-enforcement," have prompted state activities to fill that gap, which we might call "re-enforcement." . . .

In economic regulation, the federal government preempted state efforts to regulate transportation industry prices and entry, specifically and statutorily in airline deregulation in 1978, state railroad deregulation in 1980, state intercity busing deregulation in 1982, and, later, state trucking deregulation in 1994. While preempting the states, the federal government largely stopped its own economic regulation, even eliminating the Civil Aeronautics Board and the venerable Interstate Commerce Commission. . . . Most recently, as Congress relaxed the separations between different kinds of financial firms in the 1999 Financial Services Act, they set up a greater possible role for federal regulation over the insurance industry, the oldest and perhaps the most important industry regulated only by the states. While federal officials have not preempted state telecommunications and electricity regulation as much, with the 1996 Telecommunications Act and the 1992 Energy Act, Congress paved the way for further state deregulation and preempted some state regulations. Federal preemption has not gone any further in these two industries in part because local providers continue to face only limited competition.

While these federal deregulatory and preemptive actions decreased the power of states over many areas of economic regulation, they decreased the federal role just as much, or even more. . . . In response, many organized labor, environmental, and consumer groups resisted these attempts, and they often used the states as a form of venue shopping to achieve their goals. These regulatory activists have found some success in shaping policies in several states, including, but not limited to, California, New York, and Massachusetts.

Observers first noticed this balancing effect on regulatory federalism during the Reagan administration. In the 1990s, President Bill Clinton moderated the federal reduction in social regulatory enforcement, but the political power and explicit antiregulatory agenda of the 1994 Republican-controlled Congress continued to make regulatory activists wary of federal activities, so they pressed on with state efforts. For example, in health care, pro-regulatory groups pressured several states to adopt patients' bill of rights and prescription drug laws during the 1990s, when Congress would not pass these bills. After 2000, skepticism from pro-regulatory activists accelerated, maintaining their focus at the state level, especially as several powerful Bush regulatory appointees have publicly argued for reductions in social regulation.

Regulatory activists have mainly utilized two state-level venues to advance their policies—legislatures and state attorneys general (SAGs). For example, in the late 1980s, 20 state legislatures considered numerous bills to regulate nutrition labeling, action that was preempted by the passage of the 1990 federal Food Labeling Act, as food manufacturers feared facing 50 different standards. Environmental groups pressed 21 state legislatures to pass laws requiring plastic six-pack connectors to be biodegradable—business groups then pushed Congress to press the U.S. Environmental Protection Agency to develop uniform national biodegradable rules in 1993. In 2001, seven states adopted "do not call" laws against telemarketers, which proved so popular that Federal Trade Commission Chair Timothy Muris developed a national rule limiting telemarketing, an action he admitted would have been unlikely without the states moving first. In 2002, the California legislature passed a bill requiring steep reductions in greenhouse gases from automobiles, after rejection by Congress. It is an action that may force automobile manufacturers to comply with the new standards not only in California, but across the country, since it is not feasible to produce two product lines.

While legislative action is important, the expanded activities of SAGs now play the most critical role, particularly as the idea of "regulation by litigation" expands beyond areas like tobacco litigation. SAG activity is exemplified best by New York's Eliot Spitzer. Observers note: "his assault this year on the seamier habits of leading brokerage houses has vaulted him to another plane, a national figure with a higher profile than many governors and senators." . . .

Other recent examples include six SAGs challenging in court the Bush administration's proposal to relax environmental standards for upgrades of industrial facilities, 29 SAGs suing Bristol-Myers over the blocking of a generic drug alternative to BuSpar, and eight SAGs suing the U.S. Department of Energy over relaxation of appliance energy efficiency rules. SAGs do not always act in concert; although nine SAGs backed a U.S. Department of Justice antitrust settlement with Microsoft in 2002, nine others insisted on continuing the case. . . .

Business groups actively challenge state-level regulatory activities, in state legislatures, agency hearings, business-sponsored initiatives, and in court. Business groups are also now working hard to shape their own agendas in SAG elections by pouring millions of dollars into elections. This recruitment and funding of more business-oriented SAGs is paying dividends, as 10 of 15 SAGs elected in November 2002 were Republicans, compared to a previous 34–16 Democratic advantage. . . .

Thus, increasingly we see this cycle, where federal de-enforcement of social regulation prompts varying forms of state re-enforcement, which sometimes leads back to business pressure for new federal regulations. . . .

But whether the expanded state role leads to more activist regulatory policy, as presently seems to be the case, or not, state regulation does provide a degree of balance that may be useful in a nation that is often divided at near 50/50 percentages about such forms of government activity. The continued balance of regulation and deregulation and state versus federal authority will be important challenges for American policymakers.

Source: Paul Teske, Trends in state regulatory power: Balancing regulation and deregulation, *Spectrum*, *77*(3) (Summer 2004): 20–23.

Net Assignment

Enumerate and compare your state's laws on auto emissions and auto inspection with those of a neighboring state. How do they compare with federal guidelines on auto emissions?

Summary

Democratic ideals and administrative law can conflict as well as reinforce each other. Regulation has developed into three types: economic (old style), social, and subsidiary. Particular agencies exemplify how each type is emphasized.

Administrative law and the regulatory agencies have a complex relationship that balances the wide latitude or discretionary power of administrative agencies with attempts to limit or control them. Regulatory procedures and practices focus on the adjudication function. The role of judges in administrative law, their relationship with the courts that oversee the regulatory processes, and their place in the regulatory system have all expanded.

External and internal controls operate in administrative agencies and over their bureaucratic administrators, with whistle-blowers playing a role that effectively spans the external/internal distinction. Agencies internalize values and forces that foster unethical behavior, and these must be overcome by a countervalue system.

Glossary of Key Terms

administrative law   Law or regulation created or affected by the activities of governmental agencies that make rules and adjudicate cases concerning private rights and obligations and the limits necessary to control such agencies.

dependent regulatory agency (DRA)   Agency charged with regulating an economic activity but housed within an existing cabinet department.

deregulation   Policy or process of reducing the national government's overall regulatory presence.

economic regulation   Regulation of economic activities that focuses on market aspects of industrial behavior, such as rates, quality or quantity of service, and competitive practices in a particular industry or segment of the economy.

independent regulatory agency (IRA)   Agency charged with regulating some private economic activity and structured to be more or less independent of the executive branch departments or the legislative branch or both.

interpretative rules   An agency's views of the meaning of its regulations or the statutes it administers.

ombudsman   Official charged with processing and examining complaints against a bureaucracy.

procedural rule   Requirement for an agency's organization, procedure, or practice.

rule-making authority   Quasi-legislative ability to issue formal rules that cover a general class of activities and give specificity to a general legislative statute.

social regulation   Concerns the nature and types of goods and services and the social effects of industrial production processes.

subsidiary regulation   All regulatory action accompanying Social Security, Medicare, Medicaid, AFDC (now TANF), food stamps, veterans benefits, IRS regulations, and categorical grant program regulations; clientele are state and local governments.

tort action   Civil suit seeking monetary damages for harm allegedly done to a plaintiff by a defendant.

trust   Psychological state of being willing to be vulnerable based on positive expectations of another's intentions or behavior.

whistle-blower   Public employee who informs on the action of his or her own department or agency when such action is deemed by the individual to be improper, illegal, or unethical.

Review Questions

1. Can you distinguish between economic and social regulation and exemplify the types of laws that promote each type of regulation? Discuss agencies that implement each type.

2. Why has administrative law grown so dramatically since World War II? What are some of the values it seeks to implement?

3. How do courts oversee and control administrative regulatory agencies? In what ways are courts limited in their ability to do so?

4. Why have whistle-blowers increased in number, and how do trends in the media support or protect them?

5. Environmental agencies exist at both the federal and state levels. How and why do they tend to conflict with one another about how to protect clean air? How have they used the courts in that conflict over competing values?

Surfing the Net

The following websites are useful in exploring the material discussed in this chapter.

American Civil Liberties (**http://www.aclu.org**)

Center for Democracy and Technology (**http://www.cdt.org**)

State sites are useful. Try the following California sites.

California Environmental Protection Agency (**http://www.calepa.ca.gov**) and its Office of Environmental Health Hazard Assessment (similar to the federal OSHA) (**http://www.oehha.ca.gov/home.html**)

California Office of Administrative Law (**http://www.oal.ca.gov**)

The Council of State Governments (**http://www.csg.org**) site is highly useful one for accessing all of the various states and to find related sites (administrative law, environmental protection, etc.).

Federal Communications Commission (FCC) (**http://www.fcc.gov**)

Library of Congress judicial branch resources (**http://lcweb.loc.gov/global/ judiciary.html**) (access to U.S. codes, state statutes, federal regulations, judicial opinions on regulations, etc.)

Office of the (U.S.) Solicitor General (**http://www.usdoj.gov/osg**)

The Oyez Project (**http://oyez.at.nwu.edu**) is an excellent site for court case synopses, oral arguments, and the U.S. Supreme Court's database.

New York State Center for Technology in Government (**http://www.ctg.albany.edu**)

U.S. Social Security Administration (**http://www.ssa.gov**)

Chapter 14

Clientele Pressure and Government Policy: Interest Groups as Sources of Values

An advisory task force aims to recommend to the Alaska Department of Environmental Conservation (DEC) by October a plan for dealing with the state's

unique problems complying with the U.S. EPA's 15-ppm sulfur limit on ultralow-sulfur diesel (ULSD) in 2006. In turn, DEC must propose a compliance plan by next April. . . .

Highway diesel fuel is only 5 percent of the diesel market in Alaska, and even if mobile nonroad diesel demand is thrown into the equation, that only adds another 5 percent to the potential ULSD pool. . . .

The problem? That's not enough to justify a ULSD hydrotreating investment.

Heating oil, power generation, and jet fuel are the vast majority of middle distillate demand in Alaska. These are high-sulfur fuels. Thus, it's unlikely that upcoming EPA nonroad diesel rules now under discussion would have much impact this decade, and maybe won't affect Alaska's ULSD demand for many years afterward.

Given that no Alaska refiner today has any distillate hydrotreater, and thin demand prospects for ULSD, that means that the likeliest source of ULSD for Alaska would probably have to come from Canada or the "lower 48" U.S. states. . . . U.S. west coast "lower 48 states" refiners typically can avoid making arctic-grade diesel fuel, given the relatively mild climate along the Pacific coast. For these refiners, superior cold-flow, high-sulfur middle distillate doesn't wind up as diesel, but rather as jet fuel.

Another possibility: Refiners in Edmonton, Alberta (Canada), theoretically could ship arctic ULSD via pipeline to British Columbia, then transfer this special ULSD to barges for ultimate delivery to Alaska, starting in 2006. But this would involve a rather hefty logistics cost given the long distance from Edmonton to Alaska.

Jack Peckman
Alaska task force to push ULSD strategy by
October, *Diesel Fuel News*, *5*(16) (August 6, 2001): 8.

Introduction

Regulations in U.S. society are indeed ubiquitous. The interplay between the U.S. EPA and state agencies such as Alaska's DEC are common and illustrate the complexities involved in regulatory policy arising from the policy environment. Readers are typically shocked to discover that an ordinary hamburger in the United States has 41,000 regulations that govern its production and sale to the fast-food consumer! (See Box 14.2 for a discussion of that fact.) This chapter continues the discussion of regulatory politics, with a special emphasis on the role and effects of clientele interest groups.

Values imbue the entire administrative process, particularly regulatory agencies and administrative law. **Administrative responsibility** is a concept that incorporates such values as accountability, competence, fairness, and responsiveness. Chapter 13 discussed internal and external sources of those values and the conflict within administrations and agencies over them. This chapter examines the societal sources of those values and the special role that interest groups play in articulating values and influencing governmental administration in its pursuit of those values. The chapter once again looks at economic, social, and subsidiary regulation, this time with an eye to group connections.[1] The structures and procedures of agencies are addressed from the perspective of how clientele groups interact with agencies and with the types and stages of the administrative rule making.

An **administrative regulatory agency** combines legislative, executive, and judicial powers. **Clientele groups** are fervent and substantial constituencies of particular agencies. Clientele groups most often develop where program benefits are concentrated but where the costs are widely distributed.[2] We will examine clientele groups, their strategies for influencing the policy process, and how agencies may become captive to them. We also will discuss the involvement of clientele groups in administrative complaint and public hearing activities as well as in general lobbying efforts, and we will present the characteristics that make interest groups effective in influencing public policy and its implementation by administrative agencies.

In looking at current and future directions of regulation, we see how clientele groups benefit from being plugged into the regulatory process and what happens to those lesser or unorganized segments of society when they lack the clientele group relationships with key government agencies that most affect their lives.

Government interacts with interest groups in four specific ways, by:

1. supporting or aiding economic development,
2. serving as incubators of business through loans,
3. securing loan guarantees, and
4. providing tax incentives and similar policies that are designed to induce businesses to move into a jurisdictional area.

Regulatory politics has been evolving since the early 1980s toward an emphasis on deregulation, self- or voluntary regulation, and regulatory budgeting.

The chapter closes with Reading 14.1, "Structures Matter, but Leadership Matters More," which illustrates how a political leader can put together a regional coalition of vested interests to overcome a structural bias against them. It discusses a successful campaign mounted to defeat a new master plan for Los Angeles International Airport.

Societal Values and What Government Regulates

Economic Regulation

As detailed in Chapter 13, the first approach to regulation was economic. It focused on the rates charged, the quality or quantity of a good or service being produced and distributed, and the competitive practices of a given industry or segment of the economy. It typically established specific types of agency structures (independent boards or commissions). Competition within an industry promotes this approach. When businesses in an industry begin to lose out in their competition with other firms, they may react by requesting intervention by government to regulate or set standards. Economic regulation commonly emphasizes firm conduct; market structures (monopoly, oligarchy, or competitive); entry, exit, or merger trends; and the rate (price-setting) behavior of a particular industrial sector.

If one company achieves monopoly control of an industry—as it was recently alleged for Microsoft Corporation in the computer software industry—other firms or even groups in society may demand that regulators enforce antitrust policies and restore competition. Economic competition, fairness, and efficiency are thus key values to be emphasized by economic regulation. Full disclosure and accurate information to consumers from businesses are also common objectives of economic regulation. The amount of sway that interest groups enjoy in influencing economic regulatory policy depends in part on different intervener types. Business groups are the most involved—but they are not homogeneous, and their competition often drives the process.

Interest groups organized on the basis of economic issues have the greatest degree of interaction with government and regulatory policy. They often seek to develop clientele relationships with relevant agencies; the agencies, in turn, frequently seek such support as well. Economic interest groups who develop strong clientele relationships with relevant government agencies include:

- business and trade association groups, such as the National Association of Manufacturers, at the national level;
- a chamber of commerce chapter at the local level;

INFOTRAC
COLLEGE EDITION

Openness, inflation, and the Phillips curve: a puzzle

- organized labor groups, such as the AFL-CIO at the national level and a local electrical workers union at the local level; and

- professional associations, such as the American Bar Association and the American Medical Association, and their state and local chapters. The higher the level of government a group seeks to influence, the more financial resources are needed to effectively influence an agency's rule making.

Social Regulation

Social regulation, as we have seen, emphasizes consumer, health, and job-safety issues; the protection of the work environment; and energy policy and its effects on the general physical environment. Social regulation is business-wide, cutting across industries and economic sectors. It regulates a specialized aspect of business—such as environmental protection, occupational safety, and its employment policy—rather than overall business practices. Social regulation tends to use not only independent regulatory agencies but also dependent ones within existing federal, state, or local departments. Social and environmental interest groups such as Common Cause, Public Citizen, the Environmental Defense Fund, and Greenpeace interact with these agencies to influence social regulatory policy making and implementation.

Subsidiary Regulation

Subsidiary regulation involves regulatory actions of mostly standard or cabinet-level departments that administer entitlement programs such as Social Security, TANF, food stamps, and the like as well as intergovernmental grant programs. Clientele groups to subsidiary regulatory agencies are exemplified by advocacy organizations such as the American Civil Liberties Union (ACLU), Americans for Democratic Action (ADA), and state and local government lobbying organizations such as the National Association of Counties and the National League of Cities. Interest groups lobby government agencies of all types and at all levels. Clientele lobbyists develop especially close relations with their relevant agencies.

Government regulation has expanded greatly since the 1930s. Scholars have referred to this process as **regulatory ratchet**—the tendency of regulatory agencies to add more and more regulations to their list without eliminating those that become obsolete.[3]

The nearly exponential expansion of regulatory agencies and the number and ubiquitous nature of their rules and regulations contributed greatly toward the political movement to deregulate. This trend was most pronounced during the administrations of Presidents Reagan and George H. Bush. Table 14.1 lists major milestones of the federal deregulation trend since the late 1970s.

Regulatory Agencies and Clientele Groups

Interest groups may develop clientele relations with any type of governmental agency with which they regularly interact. The level of the governmental agency and its structural aspects determine the resources needed for a clientele relationship to develop. Regular (or cabinet-level) departments of the federal government tend to develop such relations with national and umbrella coalitions of interest groups whose membership are affected by departmental policies. Thus, the U.S. Department of Agriculture relates to national-level farm organizations, such as the American Farm

INFOTRAC
COLLEGE EDITION

The impact of political parties, interest groups, and social movement organizations on public policy

TABLE 14.1

Some Major Milestones in the Federal Deregulation Trend

Year	Law	Effects
1978	Airline Deregulation Act	Eliminated the Civil Aeronautics Board; gave airlines control over fares charged and routes flown.
1978	Natural Gas Policy Act	Decontrolled interstate natural gas prices but allowed states to control such prices within their boundaries.
1980	Depository Institutions and Monetary Control Act	Deregulated interest rates offered on deposits; also allowed savings and loans and banks to expand the services they offered.
1980	Motor Carriers Act	Reduced control of the Interstate Commerce Commission over interstate trucking rates and routes.
1980	Staggers Rail Act	Gave railroads more flexibility in setting rates and dropping unprofitable routes.
1982	Bus Regulatory Reform Act	Allowed intercity bus lines to operate without applying for federal licenses in most circumstances.
1984	Cable Communications Policy Act	Deregulated 90 percent of cable TV rates by the end of 1986.
1996	Telecommunications Act	Allowed phone companies to enter the cable business and other communications markets.
1997	Overturning of the Communications Decency Act	U.S. Supreme Court struck down the CDA and the FCC's ability to regulate the Internet.
1999	Financial Services Act	Reduced the separation of financial services between banks and savings and loan institutions.
2001	Ergonomics regulations set aside by the Bush administration	Rescinds the ergonomics rules established by the outgoing Clinton administration.

Question: Who favors deregulation? What values are promoted through deregulation?

Source: Adapted with permission from Sidlow and Henschen, *America at odds* (Belmont, CA: Wadsworth, 1998): 475; with updates by Michael LeMay.

Bureau Federation, the National Farmers Union, and the United Farm Workers. On the business side, the department develops relations with particular crop-based associations, such as the National Cotton Growers Association, the National Peanut Growers Association, and the American Dairy Producers Association.

Similarly, the Department of Commerce works regularly with national business coalitions, such as the United States Chamber of Commerce, the National Association of Manufacturers, and the like. The Department of Labor's clientele groups are national organizations of labor unions, such as the AFL-CIO, the Teamsters Union, and the American Federation of State, County, and Municipal Employees (AFSCME).

The Department of Education works closely with the National Education Association and the American Federation of Teachers. The Department of Energy's clientele groups are mostly national associations of energy producers.

Groups that routinely advocate civil rights policy, such as the ACLU and the National Association for the Advancement of Colored People (NAACP), develop clientele relations with the Department of Justice. The American Legion and the Veterans of Foreign Wars likewise work with the Department of Veterans Affairs. As we can see, each federal department has natural constituencies whose interests coincide with the department's policy jurisdiction. They typically share common values and find it mutually beneficial to establish clientele relations.

Agencies develop **strategies of support**—that is, routine methods they use to seek regular comment and feedback from clientele groups. Independent regulatory agencies also establish a method of **complaint handling**, or a formal and expeditious way of receiving and processing complaints to the agency that most often arise from vested interest groups. The Federal Elections Commission (FEC), for example, seeks comment and cooperation from the major political parties in overseeing national elections and in arranging for presidential candidate debates. Minor political parties, however, such as the Reform Party, seek to have equal status on the presidential debate stage with the two major parties and thus often complain about the rules and regulations established by the FEC and by state election commissions. Both the FEC and the state commissions organize and supervise elections and determine the dates and methods used in both primary and general elections.

Regulatory rules also affect the competition among interest groups in an industry and give all sides an incentive to organize to influence public policy in their favor. Some of these rules are embodied in federal agencies, such as the National Labor Relations Board (NLRB), which was established by the National Labor Relations Act of 1935 (better known as the Wagner Act) and which pits organized labor against industry.[4]

Box 14.1 presents arguments for the empowering of ethics agencies that have regulatory functions and advocates structural arrangements to better ensure that empowerment.

Captive Agencies

Independent regulatory agencies sometimes become clientele agencies when they are captured by the interest groups they were established to regulate. Companies competing in an industry, for example, may come to seek its regulation. An industry may view regulation as desirable and design it in a way that benefits the industry. When an agency is captured, for example, its regulations can effectively use governmental power and authority to keep would-be competitors out of the industry. Many analysts have viewed the Interstate Commerce Commission as the captive of the railroads.[5]

One analyst has suggested that regulatory bodies evolve through a predictable life cycle. At birth, they regulate the industry under their jurisdiction with rigor and on behalf of consumers, rate payers, or the general public. Once an agency has eliminated the worst of the abuses that gave rise to its establishment, it passes into a second stage. This stage often couples frustration over inadequate control of the industry with public apathy about the agency's concerns. As a result, in the second stage the agency compromises with the industry and begins to view the firms as part of its constituency.

In a final stage, the agency becomes protective of the status quo and therefore a captive of the industry, which typically gains effective control over the appointments to the regulatory commission and uses the agency's power to its benefit.[6]

At the state level, this pattern is especially used by professional associations with governing or licensing boards and commissions. State bar association members, for example, write the bar entrance exams that prospective attorneys must pass if they wish to practice law in a state. Each major profession has followed this pattern.

Box 14.1

Empowering Governmental Ethics Agencies

The modern era of governmental ethics law regulation began with the Watergate scandal of the early 1970s. What was distinctive about the new regulatory scheme was the creation of independent agencies to administer and enforce the law. Many of the Watergate transgressions (such as illegal corporate contributions) did not occur because of a lack of ethics laws, which had existed for decades, but because of a lack of their enforcement. Indeed, noted campaign finance scholar Herbert E. Alexander remarked that the problem with the governmental ethics program "has not been the law itself but the implementation of it." To solve this problem, many of the states and the federal government created independent ethics commissions to uphold good government statutes.

The importance of such agencies to the efficient administration of ethics rules cannot be exaggerated. There is a critical relationship between the effectiveness of any law and the police who enforce it. In order to guarantee the effectiveness of governmental ethics laws and to establish trust in the political process, ethics regulatory agencies need to be viable. These agencies are currently too small, too weak, and insufficiently independent.

Simply enacting new or strengthened ethics laws will prove meaningless unless the regulatory agencies charged with administering and enforcing these laws are empowered to do so. The effectiveness of an agency depends on its having the necessary autonomy, funding, and enforcement capability. Naturally, there are numerous ways to achieve these goals. Although there is probably no optimal approach to empowerment, a number of useful strategies have emerged over the past three decades.

An ethics agency should be established as an independent authority. It has to be insulated from any possibility or appearance of undue influence by other governmental officials. Therefore, the selection, compensation, supervision, and removal of employees should be under the exclusive control of the agency. An ethics agency also should have the authority to retain its own legal staff.

The method of appointing members to an ethics agency is crucial in determining the degree of autonomy. Of overriding importance to the effectiveness of the commission is the trustworthiness of those appointed to run it. Ideal choices for a commissioner would be: a university president, a retired judge, a prominent member of the clergy, a past leader of a public interest group, or a former governmental official. The best way to obtain such people is by giving the chief executive sole authority to appoint from a list provided by a distinguished nonpartisan advisory panel.

Other important elements in preserving an ethics agency's independence are: the length of the members' terms, the selection of officers, and a code of ethics. The term of each member should be longer than the term of the appointing authority, and members' terms should be staggered. A limit on service to no more than two consecutive terms prevents board members from becoming dependent on those who appoint them. A chairperson and vice-chairperson from opposite parties should be chosen by the appointing authority for fixed terms. An agency code of ethics should include a ban on participation in partisan events as well as a prohibition against making campaign contributions. Persons who are regulated by an agency should be ineligible for appointment to it for a number of years, and retiring members should be prohibited from representing regulated individuals or groups before the agency for a set period. In sum, bodies regulating governmental ethics should be bipartisan in their composition but nonpartisan and independent in their conduct.

Ethics agencies must be given enough funding to do their jobs. These guardians of open and honest government invariably are among the lowest-budgeted bodies at the state level. An effective ethics board should have enough resources to function well. One of the most important expenditures for bodies that are responsible for handling massive amounts of data is computerization. Although many agencies have been able to establish computerized disclosure systems over the past half-decade, some have not been given the funding to maintain and upgrade them properly.

Enforcement authority is critical to the effectiveness of an ethics commission. It must be vested with substantive investigatory and enforcement powers, including the ability to perform investigations, issue subpoenas, do random audits, write advisory opinions, serve complaints alleging civil violations, and refer evidence of criminal activity to appropriate prosecutorial authorities. A commission should be able to respond to outside complaints and generate investigations internally. Moreover, the ability to assess significant monetary fines is essential to enforcement of an ethics law.

Democracy is a fragile possession. It must be carefully maintained and protected. Empowering state ethics agencies is a crucial step in keeping the public trust and confidence that is essential to the preservation of our democratic institutions. The time for clear and decisive action is now.

Source: Frederick Hermann, Empowering governmental ethics agencies, *Spectrum*, 7(3) (Summer 2004): 33–34.

Revising regulations to lessen their economic impact on an industry is a common goal of clientele groups. The trucking industry provides a good example. The industry has managed to get discounts in highway user fees despite their doing the greater damage to roads. Nearly half of all states once had weight–distance taxes on trucks to better assess their fair share of the cost of road maintenance. Over the years, intense industry lobbying has eliminated the taxes in all but five states. The industry also pushes at both the state and the national level to allow truckers to use ever-bigger rigs. In Arkansas, however, where the industry managed to scuttle the weight–distance tax in 1991, resentment by the public boiled over, and the state highway commission considered reinstating the tax. When the tax issue came to a vote in 1999, however, the Arkansas Trucking Association lobbied heavily and was able to defeat it. Instead, the state imposed a three-cents-per-gallon gas tax on cars and a four-cents-per-gallon tax hike on diesel fuel for trucks.[7]

The Office of National Drug Control Policy provides another good example. It imposed antidrug ad legislation on the major networks, requiring the broadcast industry to match each governmentally purchased antidrug ad with a free one. Commercial time, however, has become increasingly lucrative, so the television industry convinced the drug office that, instead of free ads, the networks would embed antidrug messages or themes into regular program scripts, saving the entertainment industry an estimated $22 million in 1999. Even the Partnership for a Drug-Free America, which created the antidrug commercials, approved of the arrangement, considering such messages embedded into the story lines of popular programs such as *ER* as more effective ways to reach a teenage audience.[8]

Regulated industries may go even further and seek to have regulatory rules completely rescinded. In this way, during the Reagan administration, the airline industry was deregulated. Cartoon 14.1 pokes fun at the effects of this deregulation.

Types of Rules and Stages of Rule Making

Agency rules are of several types. They may be informal or "notice and comment" or "on the record." **Legislative rules**—or **substantive rules**—are authorized by statute and applied by well-established procedures with the full force and effect of law. **Interpretative rules** advise clients on how an agency interprets a statute or regulation. Essentially, they examine and refine the construction of legislative rules that a given agency is authorized to administer. **Procedural rules** govern an agency's internal practices. All regulating agencies set up such rules to govern their procedures.[9]

The Twelve Stages of Rule Making

George Berkley and John Rouse argue that agency rule making is better understood if it is perceived to be a sequence of activities—the 12 stages of rule making. Interest groups, particularly clientele-type groups, play an active though varying role in each stage.

Stage 1   In Stage 1, rule making begins when a legislative body (Congress, a state legislature, a county board of supervisors, or a city council) establishes the activity. If the rules are administrative, they must be validated by a statutory purpose. In this stage, interest groups lobby to support it, oppose it, or modify the general approach to such regulatory activity. In this stage, the legislative entity sometimes establishes the agency or its discretion or both. It typically lays down basic procedural requirements and may stipulate the number or frequency of rules to be produced. In short, it sets the general guidelines for the agency's more specific rule making.

Stage 2   Stage 2 deals with individual rule making. Statutes may be enacted to take effect on a certain date if an agency fails to issue an alternative regulation. When rules are not explicitly mandated, then internal and external sources for ideas about the rules become involved. If groups have established a clientele relationship with the agency, then it generally will reach out and seek their comment and feedback. Internal sources include political elective leaders, high-level career bureaucrats, industry advisory committees, office staffs, field staffs, government general counsel, and, of course, enforcement officials. External sources may be individuals in the general public; most often, they are organized interest groups with a vested interest in the subject area being regulated.

Stage 3   Stage 3 involves authorization to proceed with rule making. In this stage, the agency sets up a priority-setting and approval process. Priority setting determines how the agency will respond to external demands and how it will allocate its resources to rule making. Rule-making authorization ranges from the highly structured to the broadly permissive.

Stage 4   Stage 4 concerns planning the rule making. During this stage, the agency commonly reaches out and actively seeks public comment. Goals, legal requirements, technical and political information requirements, and who and how participation will occur are planned for at this stage. Securing resources and assigning staff are also handled in this stage, and clientele interest groups often strongly influence the plans.

Stage 5   In Stage 5, draft rules are developed. Information is collected and analyzed, and both internal and external consultation takes place about the rule's draft language and its preamble. Plans for implementing the rule dominate this stage. The agency actively seeks feedback from clientele groups about the rule's likely effects and whether the agency will need to collect and report additional information.

Stage 6   In Stage 6, the agency internally reviews the draft rule. Such internal review is both horizontal and vertical within the agency. Vertical reviews are by supervisors and senior officials. Horizontal reviews are across the agency and concentrate in those particular offices that the proposed rule will most affect. The proposed rule is reviewed for its consistency with the agency's broader programs.

Stage 7   Stage 7 is an external review of the draft rule. Outside staff agencies (the governor's budget office, the state's office of personnel, and so on), other agencies at that level or at some other level of government, and affected interest groups all participate. The legislative body and clientele interest groups in particular are consulted.

Stage 8   Stage 8 entails revisions and then the publication of the draft rule in an appropriate public outlet such as the *Federal Register*.

Stage 9   Stage 9 involves general public participation. The agency may conduct public hearings (at which clientele groups again have the opportunity to weigh in with their values) and then review and analyze general public reaction to the draft rule.

Stage 10   In Stage 10, depending on the reactions registered during Stage 9, action may be taken on the draft rule. The agency may promulgate the new rule as is, make minor revisions, or even abandon the rule-making effort.

Stage 11   Stage 11 concerns post-rule-making activity. If all went well, this stage may be quite inactive. If the rule making is flawed, however, lawsuits may result. Staff may be required to reinterpret vague provisions. Clientele groups impacted by the rule may file for reconsideration or amendment to the rule. Administrative agencies may issue technical corrections to the rule.

Stage 12   Stage 12 may develop when unanticipated consequences or simply political opposition is sufficient to require the process to begin again.[10]

Box 14.2 offers a view of the rule-making process at Stage 11. It describes the problems with regulating the fast-food industry: in this case, regulatory overkill. Although the rules are intended to protect the public from consuming unsafe food products, the regulatory system is clearly excessive. A regulation about the thickness of a pickle slice is the sort of excess that fanned the political fires of deregulation and lessened the regulatory roles of the federal, state, and local governments.

Box 14.2

Regulatory Overkill: Your Typical Fast-Food Burger

Would you believe 41,000 regulations govern the typical fast-food hamburger sandwich?

The status of regulation to the point of regulatory overkill is perhaps well exemplified by the tens of thousands of regulations that govern the production, distribution, and sale of food items as common as the typical fast-food burger.

The reader will likely be surprised to learn that the "Big Mac" type of all-American burger had, according to a 1980 study by the Colorado State University, about 41,000 regulations that governed it. These resulted from over 200 laws on the books of national, state, and local governments. They concerned all aspects of fast-food products and were promulgated by many federal and state agencies issuing regulatory rules to implement the 200 or so laws, and from approximately 111,000 court cases at all levels of government that set precedents governing the hamburger. These ranged from the United States Department of Agriculture, which regulates grazing practices for the cattle used for the hamburger meat, to state and federal inspection agencies overseeing the slaughterhouses and the methods used to process the meat for sale to supermarkets, restaurants, and fast-food outlets, to the FDA that regulates the processing and handling of the food products by wholesalers and suppliers to the fast-food chains, to local governments that inspect the restaurants for cleanliness.

Government regulates the pesticides used on the crops of wheat that make up the buns. Livestock are inspected to ensure they are free of diseases such as tuberculosis, whose bacteria can be passed on to humans. Even in 1980, such regulations added an average 10 cents per pound to the cost of the meat being used in the typical fast-food hamburger sandwich. Government regulations impacting the typical fast-food hamburger sandwich address the bun on which it is served (with regulations as to how many milligrams it has of iron and riboflavin) and the number of sesame seeds it has on the bun; limits as to how much pesticide (e.g., no more than five parts per million parts of fat or DDT) may be found in the meat; how fresh the lettuce used must be; how slow the catsup used on the hamburger sandwich must flow (that is, its thickness); how seasoned and what ingredients are used in the mayonnaise; how much fat, water, binders, or extenders are included in the meat patty; whether or not growth promoters were used raising the cattle; the thickness that the slice of pickle must be on the sandwich; a half-dozen meat inspections by federal agencies on the meat before and after its slaughter, deboning, grinding, and fabrication and packing into patties; how mature (ripeness) the tomato must be; and the milk and fat content of the slice of cheese used, how long the cheese was stored, and at what minimum temperatures.

Clientele Groups and Captive Agencies

Why does policy—administrative, regulatory, or otherwise—change in response to interest groups? Figure 14.1 presents a traditional view of policy as the result of group conflict. In this perspective, policy is seen as reaching an equilibrium (a balancing point) among competing factions of interest groups. The major actors—lobbyists for opposing faction groups, their legislative supporters, vested bureaucratic actors, and the like—are seen as acting interdependently while seeking to maximize their relative gains. They become involved in competitive bargaining and intrafactional bargaining in what is viewed as a zero-sum game: One faction's gains or losses are directly related to the losses or gains of another, competing faction or coalition of groups. Groups compete over fixed payoffs in the policy dispute. Policy is the result of the factional "weight" for or against specific policy proposals. "Public policy at any given point is the equilibrium reached in the group struggle."[11]

A policy changes as it moves from Point 1 to Point 2 as a competing faction brings its weight or pressure to bear on the policy process. Sometimes this happens when new groups join and add their strength and resources to the coalition of groups on one side of the issue. It also may reflect that given interest groups involved are

INFOTRAC
COLLEGE EDITION

**FEC looks into
regulating 527s**

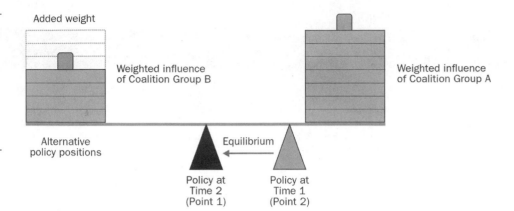

FIGURE 14.1
**A Traditional Group
Conflict View of Policy
as Equilibrium**

Source: Adapted from Thomas Dye,
Understanding public policy (8th ed.)
(Upper Saddle River, NJ: Prentice-Hall,
1995): 27; in Michael LeMay, *Anatomy
of a public policy* (New York: Praeger,
1994): 62.

growing and have more resources that they can and are willing to commit to the competition. As this example shows, as political weight is added to the side of Coalition Group B, policy shifts in its direction until a new balance or equilibrium point is achieved. Thus, for example, regulatory policy on energy-producing companies shifted in the 1970s and 1980s as various new environmental groups joined consumers to counterbalance the previously greater influence of energy producers. Public policy to promote conservation was enacted rather than inducing consumption by finding new energy supplies. Since the 2000 presidential election, it looks as if the balance is swinging back toward the energy producers.

The resources that groups may add to the political policy competition include money, membership (as both voters and campaign workers), inside connections, access to media or key governmental policy makers, knowledge of the political policy process, knowledge about the subject matter of the proposed policy, the organization's leadership, and so on. As these are increased for one coalition or decreased for another, the weight and balance point in the competition change.

This traditional perspective offers a somewhat static picture of the process—a sort of snapshot of an ongoing, moving picture (process). Figure 14.2 presents a somewhat more dynamic graphic presentation of group influence. In this perspective, public policy is seen as resolving group conflict through cooperation, that is, by constructive and mutually beneficial resolution rather than a simple win–loss solution or by splitting the differences between opposing factions of groups. This more cooperative resolution scenario for the solution to policy conflict assumes that two conditions are met:

1. the factions engaged in the policy debate are interdependent; that is, each faction can affect the other's prospects for policy change; and

2. the factions involved must have mixed motives.

This latter condition changes the nature of the conflict, in that groups may have conflict that is not predicated on a zero-sum notion. They may be able to view their competing interests as complementary as well as conflicting.[12]

This perspective sees policy not as a simple balancing point between opposing group factions, but as a resulting vector or path of direction of an ongoing policy that is the sum of all the contributions or influences involving the various factional actors. Imagine policy at any given time as a billiard ball being struck more or less

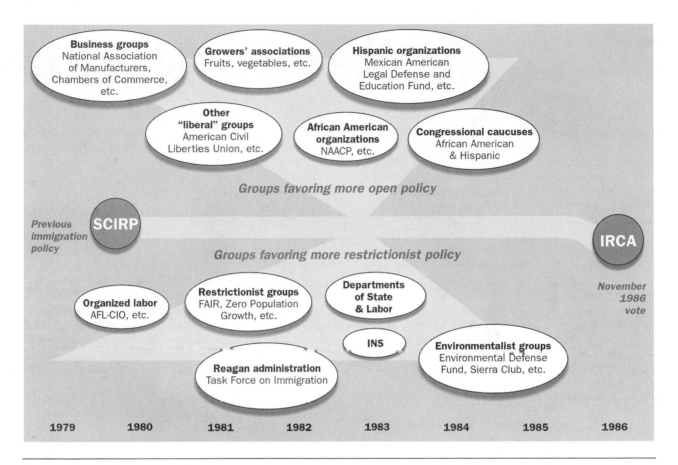

Groups favoring more open policy

Groups favoring more restrictionist policy

FIGURE 14.2

A Cooperative Resolution of Policy Conflict: The IRCA Case

Which federal agency regulates immigration policy? Who are its clientele groups?

Source: Adapted from Michael LeMay, *Anatomy of a public policy* (New York: Praeger, 1994): 64.

simultaneously by several other balls as it rolls along. It will move in the direction of the sum of the forces of all the striking balls. Figure 14.2, for example, labels the various interest group factions involved in changing U.S. immigration policy—and the resulting Immigration Reform and Control Act of 1986 (IRCA). This law increased the INS's regulatory powers in several ways: over illegal immigrants attempting to enter the country by increasing the resources allocated to the Border Patrol and by employer sanctions that enabled the INS to regulate businesses that hired undocumented aliens as workers.

In this more dynamic view, policy is seen as continuing along its previous path unless acted on and redirected—that is, policy has inertia. In this case, the new policy is more restrictionist, but it moves less in that direction (the vector representing the IRCA) than it would have if the policy competition had been won by those who favored even tighter restrictions. The forces that promoted the legalization side kept the vector closer to a more open immigration policy than would otherwise have been the case. This more dynamic view stresses both the timing and the weight of

Box 14.3

Leveling the Playing Field

The way in which our society defines a problem goes a long way toward shaping the solution. One poster child for ill-defined problems has to be campaign finance. For decades, political reformers have based their critiques and strategies on the idea that the problem with our electoral system is primarily one of corruption—the quid pro quo exchange of campaign contributions for access and preferential treatment on specific issues of public policy. It's a seductive story, and a prevalent one: from the Lincoln Bedroom guest list and "pardongate" scandals of the Clinton administration to the current administration's Enron and Halliburton ties, there's a constant stream of examples of how the system works to the direct benefit of those who "pay to play."

But by focusing on corruption we miss a larger and far more important point. The fundamental problem of money in politics is not access buying or influence peddling: It is that those with more money have more influence over election outcomes than those with less money. The rich don't just dominate the access game; rather they dominate the elections themselves, deciding who the political leaders are in the first place. . . .

What's more, viewing campaign finance reform through a quid pro quo lens can lead to reforms that actually hamstring efforts to allow nonwealthy people to build a modicum of political power. For example, the recent Bipartisan Campaign Reform Act restricted the largest soft money contributions raised by parties, but at the same time it increased the limits on hard money contributions made directly to candidates. Not all soft money donors were rich, however; members of labor unions, for example, were able to compile their thousands of small contributions into amounts large enough to gain working people some leverage in the political process, thus enhancing both the social justice movement and "small d" democracy. The reforms of 2002 meant that a nurse or schoolteacher could no longer pool her $5 of union dues with others' to give $100,000 to a political party. Instead, each union member is now free to make a $2,000 contribution to a candidate—as is every CEO. It is not hard to guess who is more likely to take advantage of the privilege.

It is difficult to overstate the importance of money in American politics. In the 2000 congressional election cycle, the candidate who raised the most money won 94 percent of the time. But this tells only part of the story, since candidates who are not successful fundraisers generally don't even get nominated in contested primaries. Candidates who raised the most money in party primaries won 90 percent of their races in the 2002 congressional election cycle.

But even this does not get at the root of the problem, since potential candidates who do not demonstrate the ability to raise large contributions—or are not able to finance their campaigns out of their own wealth—are rarely recruited and encouraged to run for office at an early stage by political parties. As a result, many would-be public servants abandon thoughts of elected office before the first vote is cast.

So if money is truly the currency of politics, where can a candidate go to get it? In short, the wealthy. In the 2002 congressional primaries, 90 percent of itemized donations to candidates were of $500 or more. Yet, only one-tenth of one percent of voting-age Americans make campaign contributions at that level. A 1997 survey found that, of individuals who gave $200 or more to candidates in the 1996 congressional elections, nearly 80 percent earned more than $100,000 per year—a level of income achieved by only 14 percent of American households. More than one-third of the contributors—and the vast majority of contributors who gave large amounts of money or contributed to many political candidates—made more than $250,000 per year, an income level achieved by less than 1.5 percent of households.

Not all of these wealthy people represent corporations or interests with a specific axe to grind in the public policy process—the "special interests" of fame and lore. Many simply want to have a say in our democracy, just as ordinary Americans do. There are two differences between "them" and the rest of the population. The wealthy have a very different set of economic concerns than ordinary Americans—concerns that are reflected in the candidates they choose to support. And they have the resources to make a substantial difference in whether their chosen candidate is elected to office. "We the people" increasingly don't. . . .

For when you come right down to it, the vast majority of Americans—those who don't earn at least six figures—are all in the same boat. Whether they be liberal or conservative, middle class or poor, they are equally disempowered and disenfranchised by the current system.

Source: Adapted from Douglas Phelps, Leveling the playing field, *National Civic Review*, 93 (2) (Summer 2004): 60–63. Reprinted with permission of John Wiley & Sons, Inc.

the pressure brought to bear in the policy process. Timing of influence can be critically important to the final outcome. Resolving policy conflict through cooperation means developing acceptable proposals that improve the situation of both sides or all factions vis-à-vis their competition. In this perspective, all of the factions perceive that they have won a little or lost less in the conflict than they would have without cooperating to achieve resolution. Each group sees some of its values enacted into policy.[13]

The Unorganized Lose Out

What both models depict is policy in general—and administrative rule-making policy in particular—responding to *organized interest* group influence. Poorly organized or simply unorganized groups cannot compete with those that have organized effectively and developed structured political power. Clientele groups develop built-in access and thereby influence the policy process to their benefit. If the general public has a position on a policy but holds it apathetically, then it cannot counter the influence of a coalition of groups with vested interests in the policy or its implementation. Unorganized citizens lose out consistently to well-organized groups that are intensely committed to their positions and willing to expend time, energy, and resources to promote their policy views.

Box 14.3 points out the problems of the poor, and poorly organized, members of society versus those who have wealth and are organized to exert their influence. It calls for the "leveling of the playing field" in political campaign finance.

Strategies of Support

Clientele agencies need and actively seek the support and cooperation of their clientele groups. They develop support in several ways. Clientele groups' members are selected and appointed to agency positions (staffs, advisory committees, and so on). Typically, a president appoints a business executive as secretary of commerce, a labor union leader as secretary of labor, an educator as secretary of education, and a medical doctor as director of the National Institutes of Health. Governors appoint developers to business promotional agencies, farmers to state agricultural agencies, trucking executives or perhaps someone from the state's chapter of AAA to the department of transportation. Mayors may appoint union leaders from the building trades industry to a local housing or zoning board, a savings-and-loan executive to a blue-ribbon commission to attract new industry to a city, and so on.

Advisory Positions and Task Forces

Clientele group members who serve on advisory committees to an agency help shape its rules and regulations. At the local level, for example, parents serve schools in advisory capacities. At the federal level, the departments of Health and Human Services (HHS) and Housing and Urban Development (HUD) might parcel out work to nonprofit organizations who develop into clientele support groups.

Agencies use their contract power to develop support by using contracts and grants to foster clientele support for the agency in the political and legislative arenas—to ward off budgetary cutbacks, for example, or to support the expansion of an agency's staff size, program responsibilities, and so on. The agency also receives valuable feedback and data from clientele groups.

Advisory committees and task forces are effective ways of soliciting information from clientele groups. They serve as a sort of weather vane by which the agency discerns ideological and emotional currents among coalitions of interest groups and as barometers to point out new ideas or approaches the agency is considering to use as well as to test reaction among select members of the clientele. Task forces may also serve as recruiting sources for future staff members and even high-level appointees to an agency. They also may even serve as lightning rods, deflecting criticism and complaints from an agency. On occasion, advisory committees and task forces may be used to help implement policy. Such groups, of course, attain some power within the agency in the process.[14] The INS, for example, when implementing IRCA, used various nonprofit immigration service agencies that it called *qualified designated entities*. They were to help bring in undocumented aliens to start the legalization process. They became internalized sources of change in INS policy, sometimes even challenging the central or regional INS field offices' interpretations of rules and regulations that were developed to implement the law.[15]

HUD uses tenant groups to help administer state housing projects. These groups have acquired the right to approve employee hiring. In some cities, tenant groups have even won the right to operate entire projects. The Bureau of Indian Affairs (BIA) has been gradually turning over more responsibility to tribal councils to run such programs as reservation schools and health clinics. The Clinton administration's task force on health care reform included several hundred people from all phases of the health care industry, although such groups could not ultimately reach consensus, and the administration's broad and sweeping reform plan had to be scaled back and approached piecemeal.[16]

Although such efforts most often develop support among clientele groups, they do not stifle all fears or demands. Agencies must develop an effective system of complaint handling to deal with clientele dissatisfaction. Such a system provides discontented clients a way to voice their grievances and perhaps have them redressed. When effectively integrated into an agency's program, complaint handling provides a wealth of valuable information. It may highlight problem areas that need to be reorganized, personnel who need to be better trained or shifted in their responsibilities, bottlenecks in agency procedures for handling matters, and internal control processes that must be modified for evaluating existing operations or implementing future ones. Agencies increasingly use ombudsmen to handle clientele complaints. The INS, for example, had regional ombudsmen to cut through the agency's chronic problems with red tape. The Department of Commerce has an ombudsman for business to aid and advise businesspeople in dealing with the department.[17]

INFOTRAC
COLLEGE EDITION

Citizen district councils in Detroit: the promise and limits of using planning advisory boards to promote citizen participation

Public Hearings

Public hearings are another strategy for developing clientele support. Many agencies include them as integral parts of their due process procedures. Public hearings are held before rule changes to help develop clientele support or diffuse antagonism. Public hearings help clear the air. They also afford the well-organized an excellent opportunity to lobby public opinion and pressure the agency. Public hearings, however, typically provide equal time to both proponents and opponents of proposed changes.

They are not without costs. Hearings can delay action, consume valuable time, and add to the expense of a program. Vociferous opponents may use hearings to block action. Media coverage tends to emphasize conflict and negativity if they exist at all, sometimes exaggerating the degree of opposition to a proposed rule or policy change. Broadcast media especially cover public hearings at all levels of government, and clientele interest groups use them to keep from being cut off or cut back from benefits they accept as entitlements.

Regulatory agencies struggle to achieve a balance between what the general public is demanding, often voiced at public hearings, and what industry clientele groups are willing to accept. Regulatory agency policy, moreover, can result in **cross-subsidies**, wherein surrogate market regulations create conditions with one set of customers (for example, long-distance telephone callers) paying prices intended to subsidize another set of customers (users of local telephone services). Such intraindustry conflict raises exceedingly difficult issues for an agency. Which competing clientele groups should it seek to satisfy? In some cases, these situations contribute to the deregulation movement and to the option of letting the marketplace itself resolve the conflict.

Holding public hearings gives clientele groups the opportunity to use crowd lobbying techniques. Organized interest groups rally their members to appear at or outside public hearings and thus marshal public opinion to their side of the issue. Crowd lobbying may influence news media and broader public opinion on an issue. Even when it fails to win over bureaucrats or legislators, it may be used by the group's leadership as a direct and often-powerful way to give members a sense of participation in the shaping of policy that will directly affect their day-to-day lives. It helps give members a sense of belonging to an important and effective group and imparts a sense of being an integral part of the policy-making process. Sometimes agencies use such occasions to garner public support for legislative changes or funding-level support for their programs or to protect important agency programs during times of deep budget cuts.

INFOTRAC
COLLEGE EDITION

Parenthood, partnership status, and pensions: cohort differences among women

New Public Management

Two trends in the administrative regulatory reform movement are likely to increase the power and role of clientele groups. **New public management (NPM)** is a general approach to regulation in stark contrast to the traditional managerial model. It is highly market oriented, advocates self-regulation, trusts those who are regulated, and believes that government should become partners with those it regulates.[18] Newer areas of regulation, such as waste management and reduction, increasingly use this approach. State governments especially rely on voluntary cooperation of industry to achieve hazardous waste reduction, and most of the involved companies do seem committed to reducing hazardous waste. Advocates argue that it is a more cost-effective way to approach regulation.[19] It gives greater power to interest groups in the entire regulatory process. One study of state governmental regulation of building safety found that the key to moving from mandatory to energetic building safety regulation is determined by the lower levels of opposition to strong building codes by interest groups.[20]

The cost efficiency of regulation is clearly an important value emphasized by both the new public management approach and regulatory budgeting. As one analyst notes, "A striking feature of regulatory budgeting is that it focuses solely on

costs rather than the benefits of regulation."[21] Regulatory budgeting involves assessing the costs of each proposed regulatory rule and weighing whether the new regulation is worth the additional costs. It is popular among clientele groups and continues the trend toward deregulation. It blurs the line between private and public funds. Although regulatory budgeting is widely popular among those who are regulated, critics argue it is inherently antiregulatory and being used to roll back positive gains in worker safety, the environment, and consumer protection laws and regulations developed largely since 1970.

In practice, the use of regulatory budgeting excludes indirect costs. If adopted widely, federal agencies would increasingly enact programs that impose large indirect costs on society but small direct benefits. Because there is no precise way to measure an optimum level of regulatory expenditure, the size of the regulatory

budget could easily be set too high or too low. Although regulatory budgeting acknowledges the costs of regulation, it does not require that government pay these costs through increased taxes or by deficit spending. Including regulatory budgeting in one fiscal year would leave regulators unable to respond to unanticipated health or safety risks that result from regulatory cutbacks justified by regulatory budgeting until the following fiscal year.[22]

What Makes a Clientele Group Effective?

To be effective supporters of administrative agencies, clientele interest groups need certain characteristics that are likely to make them more effective as supporters. Many characteristics may be useful. We now discuss four rather obvious factors of interest group clout.[23]

First, other things being equal, the *size of membership* in a group is a critical factor in its strength. Members can be transformed into voters or workers in an electoral campaign. Members contribute dues and make similar contributions to the group that may be used to finance a PAC that becomes the electioneering arm of the interest group. The larger the membership, the more financial resources the group can accumulate and devote to lobbying, campaign activities, or public relations campaigns to influence general public opinion.

A second obvious factor in clientele group strength is the group's *degree of dispersion*. An agency with a large clientele base that is concentrated in only one or two states will be less supported than an agency with roughly the same size of group membership spread over a broader geographic area. At the state level, a statewide dispersal is more effective than one concentrated in a given city or county.

The third critically important factor is the *degree of organization* of the group. Well-organized and cohesive groups such as the NRA and AARP can lobby far more effectively than poorly organized groups. Unorganized or poorly organized groups simply get left out of the policy process. They tend to have policy "done unto them" rather than getting policy done for their benefit. Organization includes the effectiveness of the clientele group's leadership in terms of marshaling and applying the organization's pressure.

The fourth and final factor is the *degree of ardor or intensity* clientele group members feel for their cause. The degree of devotion to the cause that a clientele group shows in supporting an agency is closely correlated with its degree of dependence on the agency. Intensely loyal clientele supporters are simply more willing to work harder or sacrifice more resources to support an agency than are members of a group that is only lukewarm in its commitment to the issue.

Box 14.4, "Energy Efficiency and a New Model for Public and Private Partnership," illustrates the case in Vermont, where a public/private partnership known as "Efficiency Vermont" was used to deal with the electric energy service industry. Cost–benefit tests agreed on by all were used by regulators to ensure the cost effectiveness of the program as compared to other alternatives.

The Current and Future Directions of Regulation

The new public management and regulatory budgeting trends increasingly emphasize self-regulation, privatization, and partnerships between business and government. They are well-established movements in government and public administration

INFOTRAC
COLLEGE EDITION

The state of government management and performance

INFOTRAC
COLLEGE EDITION

The new public management and substantive democracy

Box 14.4

Energy Efficiency and a New Model for Public and Private Partnerships

The best-intentioned initiatives are not always easy to implement in the realm of public policy. So it is with the delivery of energy efficiency programs. The dilemma is this: Traditional delivery mechanisms for energy efficiency programs—programs which save money for individual consumers—cut into the profits of the regulated utilities that historically have provided these services.

Electricity service is still a regulated monopoly in most states, and public utility regulators rely upon utility-directed delivery of energy efficiency to meet policy objectives. Regulated utilities provide energy efficiency as one service to customers in return for the privilege of holding a monopoly franchise. It is part of their obligation to serve and, in many states, their obligation to acquire their resources at the least possible cost. But make no mistake—utilities are also obliged to maximize returns for their shareholders. Selling energy improves the bottom line—reducing energy consumption is not always seen as a profit-maximizing strategy.

Let us examine the problem more closely. The primary mission of electric utility monopolies is to sell electricity to consumers. Consumers in most states are captive customers; retail choice for electric consumers is still not widespread and is not available in Vermont. Utilities build or contract to supply sufficient amounts of electricity so that consumers will have instantaneous power at the flick of a switch. This is no mean feat. Utilities must have sufficient power on hand to meet the maximum or peak electrical load within their service territory—day in and day out. A diverse portfolio of energy sources is put together by each utility to meet these needs. Vermont, like many other states, recognizes that if a utility's peak is reduced through energy efficiency measures, then fewer power supply assets will be needed in its resource portfolio. Energy efficiency reduces power both in on-peak hours and throughout the day. Thus, Vermont requires electric utilities to offer energy efficiency services as part of a balanced portfolio of power supply options. A cost–benefit test is employed by regulators to ensure that such programs are cost effective compared to the alternatives.

The process by which regulators determine whether a utility has an appropriate mix of power supply and energy efficiency resources is fraught with contention, largely due to the conflict noted above. Public utility commissions are quasi-judicial agencies, and decisions are generally made either through a rule-making or contested case proceeding. A lengthy and litigious courtroom proceeding is all too often the forum for resolving the sufficiency and appropriateness of energy efficiency programs. Costs of litigation are passed on to consumers—and program implementation must await final decisions, perhaps even higher-court appeals. Worst of all, Vermont has 22 electric utilities, and each one had to come before the regulators for review of these programs. The result was a patchwork of energy efficiency programs throughout the state.

In Vermont, it took a thoughtful group of policy makers and utility representatives to invent a public–private partnership that now provides Vermont electric consumers with the tools they need to reduce their electric usage and thus lower their energy bill. The new model is known as the Efficiency Utility. It is a statewide entity whose sole mission is the provision of energy efficiency services. Prior to the implementation of the model, utilities provided these services and rolled the costs of the programs into retail electric rates. Now most electric efficiency programs throughout the state are administered by a single statewide entity funded through a "systems benefit" charge on ratepayer bills. . . .

Efficiency Vermont was chosen to deliver these programs after a competitive bidding process. It operates under a performance-based contract in which specific benchmarks are set to measure the program's success. The performance indicators included in the contract are: (1) the level of energy savings achieved; (2) the level of total resource benefits achieved; and (3) program-specific measures.

The new model of delivering energy efficiency has surpassed expectations. Since early 2000, Efficiency Vermont has achieved 99,248 megawatt-hours of energy savings. This is enough to supply approximately 2 percent of Vermont's electricity needs. In 2002 alone, Efficiency Vermont invested $16.8 million to deliver energy efficiency to its customers and achieved 39,560 megawatt-hours of annual electric savings. . . .

Another aspect of the Efficiency Utility's success is the partnerships it has built with architects, builders, design professionals, trade associations, contractors, and retail vendors. Development of this infrastructure is expected to pay off in long-term benefits. The goal is to transform the market for energy efficiency within the state. . . .

The Vermont model can work in any state. It reduces the level of regulatory controversy, provides administrative efficiencies, and improves environmental integrity.

Source: Sandra Waldstein, Energy efficiency and a new model for public and private partnerships, *Spectrum, 76*(4) (Fall 2003): 9–11.

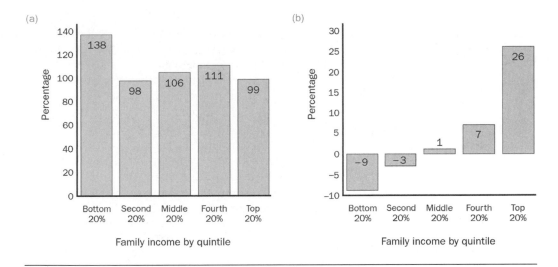

FIGURE 14.3

Two Views of Income Distribution

Distribution of the growth of U.S. family income by quintile: (a) 1950–1978; (b) 1979–1995

Source: Reprinted from the *Journal of Economic Issues* by special permission of the copyright holder, the Association for Evolutionary Economics.

generally and regulatory policy making more particularly. They emphasize such values as efficiency, treating recipients of government policy and agency programs as consumers, and more generally incorporating market and competition orientations into government policy. The business-like approach to management of public agencies seems to work better in some policy areas than others. Some governmental programs and services are less adaptable to this approach. Higher education (university) administrations are now attempting to transform the management of universities to the corporate model, but clashing values between administrators who support a business model and faculty and staff members who emphasize other values can cause serious tensions. As one critic of this trend notes, "Despite the efficiencies, improved quality in 'production' processes, and other benefits resulting from the adoption of management techniques in university administration, there can be serious costs."[24]

Such costs include greater line-staff conflict. The faculty values *centrality* of faculty participation in university governance, but a new management style emphasizes centrality of administration, at the direct expense of faculty participation. Critics note that decision making is less open and clearly less collegial, conditions that the faculty weighs more heavily than do efficiency-conscious administrators.

Deregulation and self-regulation also strain agency relations with an increasingly skeptical media. A more flexible policy regarding environmental pollution, for example, can lead to investigative reporters charging that an agency has failed "to catch and punish the cities and companies that pollute the state's waters."[25]

Well-organized and "plugged-in" clientele groups get policies that benefit them. The poorly organized in society simply get left out. Results of the trends discussed earlier can be seen in the two graphs in Figure 14.3. They show the distribution of the growth in U.S. family income by quintile (20 percent increment) for two periods: 1950–1978 and 1979–1995. During the first period, when social and subsidiary regulations increased dramatically, the growth in income was enjoyed by all five quintiles of the population in fairly even degrees. Indeed, the poorest quintile enjoyed the greatest percent growth in family income from 1950 to 1978. With the emergence of deregulation and new public management ever since the 1980s, the distribution of family income growth has been dramatically different. Where the growth in family income of the bottom two quintiles (that is, the lowest 40 percent of the population) *declined* by 9 percent and 3 percent, respectively, the growth among the top quintile *increased* by a substantial 26 percent. As the graphs clearly show, between 1979 and 1995, the rich got richer and the poor got poorer.

The public–private partnership approach, however, may introduce innovations in programs that help the poorer segments of society. Box 14.4 describes a public–private partnership, Efficiency Vermont, that improves efficiency and helps reduce and thus save costs to the consumer.

Government Support for Groups

New approaches by government policy do more than simply reduce regulation. Government also supports groups in many positive ways. Clientele agencies often provide their vested interest groups with benefits distributed to them but financed or paid for by general taxpayers. Loan guarantees, low-cost government loans, grants-in-aid, and contracts to specific groups favor those vested interest groups that are involved in the policy process at the expense of those that are left out because they are unorganized or poorly organized.

INFOTRAC
COLLEGE EDITION

The role of foundations in informing policy makers

Economic Development Support

Governments assist business groups especially in economic development. Enterprise zones with favored tax reductions or waivers for businesses that relocate to the zone are one example. Establishing so-called business incubators, wherein government invests in infrastructure and sometimes even builds the facilities to attract business to industrial parks, is another common approach, especially at the local level, where the competition to attract business and the resulting corporate tax revenues to local coffers is intense. Be it outright subsidies, creating a favorable regulatory environment, economic incentives, or reducing the costs of doing business by deregulation or voluntary or cooperative approach to regulation, state and local governments especially are vying with one another to be more business friendly. They support workforce development; assist in technology development and innovation, often incurring research-and-development costs; support business in getting favorable financing; improve infrastructure; and develop business-related amenities. The national-level government assists business by finding and expanding international markets. Governments at all levels provide free population information and data that are often critically important to businesses. Government regulatory policy is often important in "leveling the playing field" on which businesses compete in the private marketplace, especially in areas of new technologies.[26]

This chapter closes with Reading 14.1, "Structures Matter, but Leadership Matters More." It illustrates decision making regarding the master plan for development and expansion of Los Angeles International Airport (LAX). Intergovernmental relations between federal, state, and local agencies and their respective goals and guidelines further complicate this area of public policy. The reading exemplifies the influence of regional political coalitions and the conflicting values they pursue.

Reading 14.1

Structures Matter, but Leadership Matters More

Fragmentation of government authority frustrates collective action to address important challenges. In the face of critical issues too big for municipalities to handle on their own but too small to warrant state intervention, the all-too-common response is deadlock and drift: Affordable housing goes unbuilt, roadways become more congested, schools grow more overcrowded, critical infrastructure crumbles, and the ladder of social opportunity becomes harder to climb. Southern California, with nearly 200 municipalities, offers an extreme case. Power is widely diffused, among federal, state, and a web of local governments. Dispersal of authority also extends to private groups, and in many cases to residents capable of mobilizing against any number of collective objectives. As a University of Southern California report laments: "The region's governance structure does not appear capable of a creative and collaborative response to the changing realities of metropolitan Los Angeles."

The problems associated with regional fragmentation have spawned a cottage industry of proposals for structural reform. For example, a report by the Metropolitan Area Research Corporation urges southern California communities and their elected representatives to support measures that would shift authority from the municipal level to the regional level—pooling their sales-tax base, adopting a regional planning framework that supports smart growth, and making the Southern California Association of Governments (SCAG) a directly elected body with expanded authority over regional planning and transportation. The opposite impulse is also evident. The City of Los Angeles, America's second largest city, has given neighborhood councils and area planning commissions expanded authority, if only as a way to diffuse support for neighborhood secession. At the state level, the California Assembly speaker's Commission on Regionalism recommends a number of state policies that would create incentives for greater municipal cooperation, including reforming the post–Proposition 13 fiscal system, amending the California Constitution to prevent the state legislature from diverting locally levied revenues, and amending the state Constitution to encourage regional planning and finance compacts.

In our well-placed concern with the deficiencies affecting the formal structures of government, we should not lose sight of the informal practice of politics and the opportunities that already exist for greater regional cooperation. When it comes to governance in southern California, structures matter, but leadership matters more. Last year's defeat of a modernization plan for Los Angeles International Airport (LAX) is instructive. Once a municipally owned airstrip surrounded by bean fields, LAX is the linchpin of southern California's aviation system, accommodating three-quarters of the demand for air travel in the region. Designed to accommodate up to 40 million passengers a year, LAX struggles to handle 67 million passengers and 2.2 million tons of cargo annually. The LAX master plan, six years and $60 million to $100 million in the making, called for reconfiguring the airport's four existing runways and adding new access taxiways, ground traffic improvements, a new passenger terminal, expanded parking, and more efficient cargo facilities. Short of federalizing airport planning, it is difficult to imagine a structural reform that would have better positioned the master plan for adoption.

Los Angeles World Airports (LAWA), the City of Los Angeles department that owns and operates LAX and three other southern California airports, enjoyed the legal jurisdiction to complete the master plan. With approval of the mayor, city council, and airport commission, LAWA had the authority to finance the improvements. The master plan had the support of the airline industry and therefore the support of the Federal Aviation Administration (FAA), the federal agency that would need to sign off on the plan. Prominent local business interests with a material stake in the region's economic competitiveness approved of the plan, as did labor unions that looked forward to thousands of new construction jobs. As mayor, Richard Riordan championed the master plan, which had the support of the airport commission and (most likely) the majority of the city council. In sum, the formal structures of Los Angeles government indicated all-but-certain approval of the LAX master plan.

Nevertheless, Mike Gordon, mayor of the tiny City of El Segundo adjacent to LAX, was able to ground the master plan. In Gordon's own account, "The City of El Segundo and all the other cities in southern California have virtually no ability to impact LAX. . . . The City of Los Angeles controls the decision 100 percent: their master plan, their airport commission, their city council, and their mayor." To counter the overwhelming advantages bestowed on the master plan under the existing governmental structures, Gordon used direct, personal contacts and appeals to self-interest to assemble a regionwide coalition of city, county, and congressional officials capable of influencing those with direct decision-making authority over LAX. . . .

Given the diversity of opinion regarding the region's aviation infrastructure, Gordon was careful to tailor his anti-LAX message to appeal to specific local concerns. Gordon persuaded officials from Riverside and San Bernardino counties to join the coalition by arguing that worsening bottlenecks at LAX would force airlines to provide service at Inland Empire airports—and bring new jobs with them. Gordon capitalized on the concern of some city officials from eastern Los Angeles County that improvements at LAX would mean more flights and more airplane noise for their communities. Other officials from eastern Los Angeles County hope for more air service to Ontario Airport, which is for them more convenient by freeway than LAX. Gordon enlisted city officials in northern Orange County who sought to pressure airlines to serve Ontario Airport, thereby alleviating political pressure for expanded air service at John Wayne Airport. In short, through direct, personal contact, Gordon mobilized officials from communities indirectly affected by LAX by appealing to the specific interests of those communities. By this method, Gordon assembled a coalition that included officials representing communities across southern California, including most of the region's congressional delegation.

Gordon's coalition successfully orchestrated a SCAG vote challenging the air passenger capacity limits projected in the LAX master plan. Although the regional body has no direct ability to shape City of Los Angeles policy at LAX, the vote would have been a black mark had the plan gone before the FAA for its approvals. Covering all his bases, Gordon also persuaded 12 members of southern California's congressional delegation to put FAA officials on notice that they were expected to reject the master plan should the plan reach the agency. Representative Jerry Lewis from Redlands warned that he would question U.S. Transportation Secretary Norman Mineta about LAX when the department's budget reached the House Appropriations Committee.

Gordon also made LAX a high-profile issue in the 2001 Los Angeles mayoral election. A neighborhood group opposed to LAX expansion identified 11,000 high-propensity voters who claimed they would not vote for a candidate who supported airport expansion. In a crowded field, no candidate could afford to be on the wrong side of that issue, and all six major candidates were persuaded to sign a pledge that they would oppose the master plan if elected. The ultimate victor, James Hahn, was among the last candidates to do so. Hahn knew LAX needed to be modernized, but he also knew he needed African American voters to win the election. When prominent African American Congress member Maxine Waters threatened to pull her endorsement, Hahn's inkwell began to flow.

LAWA was wholly unprepared for what had transpired. Belatedly, airport department staff and consultants mounted a community outreach program to demonstrate to residents near LAX how the master plan would mitigate the negative impacts of the airport's operations. Call it arrogance, naiveté, or a vestige of the Progressive Era, but LAWA's political strategy focused all but entirely on winning approval of the Los Angeles city council. "That's really all you need," explained one LAWA executive late in the summer of 2000. "There is no question in my mind that if the vote were taken today about the LAX master plan, we would get eight votes."

Airport executives were keenly aware of the coalition amassing against the master plan, but they clearly underestimated the coalition's potential influence and their own ability to mount an effective counteroffensive to shape opinion among the regional elite. . . .

In the aftermath of the quadruple airplane hijackings in September 2001, LAWA planners were sent back to the drawing board to design a new master plan focused not on increasing the capacity of LAX but on improving airport security. In a stunning policy reversal, LAWA executive director Lydia Kennard announced two weeks after the attacks, "Clearly, the need for expansion has dissipated, if not evaporated. But we have an airport that's functionally obsolete from a security and safety standpoint."

Formal government structures gave the master plan every advantage, yet the plan was all but dead by the time the terrorist attacks made airport security the top priority for LAWA planners. Putting aside the advisability of Gordon's goal—LAX is in fact a critical economic engine for the region—his political strategy offers important lessons for leadership in a fragmented metropolis. In brief, the Gordon model of regional politics begins with the understanding that formal structures shape the parameters of an effective political strategy. Political strategies may seek to focus on direct decision makers, voters, and actors

with indirect influence. Enlisting the support of indirect decision makers is best accomplished through direct, specially tailored personal appeals. In the case of Gordon's geographically based coalition, appeals based on local issues proved effective. Other coalitions require appeals to other interests: ethnic groups, environmental concerns, homeowner groups, labor unions, economic sectors, and so forth. What is particularly remarkable about Gordon's efforts was that he was able to enlist coalition members without tangible benefits to offer in exchange—only a vision of possible benefits in a distant and uncertain future.

Source: Adapted from Structures matter, but leadership matters more, *National Civic Review*, 93 (1) (Spring 2004): 28–33. Reprinted with permission of John Wiley & Sons, Inc.

Net Assignment

Using InfoTrac and Internet search engines, find a local controversy about government regulation imposed on a business group by the city or the state. Describe the controversy, the conflicting values, the financial costs on either side, and how you believe the conflict should resolve.

Summary

Organized interest groups, termed *clientele groups*, operate as an external source of values and value conflict for administrative agencies. Various agency structures link to types of regulatory policy and feedback from clientele groups.

Regulatory processes goes through several stages as the agency develops the parameters of a given regulation—at each stage, clientele groups play a role. Some agencies can become captive to the very clientele groups they are supposed to manage or control through regulation.

Interest groups exercise two kinds of influence on public policy that can be conceptualized as models: (1) traditional policy as an equilibrium and (2) a more dynamic vector. Each model graphically portrays how interest groups influence public policy to their benefit. And each shows how much policy making—especially government rule-making processes—tend to favor the better organized groups in society. Unorganized groups get left out, while organized groups get rewarded. This policy results in the rich getting richer and the poor getting poorer.

Agencies develop—and occasionally curry—support among clientele groups in the ways they handle complaints and structure public hearings. In return, clientele groups use the most effective techniques to support their agencies.

Current trends in regulatory policy tend to support clientele groups, but the complex interactions of federal and state regulatory agencies and local courts complicate the regulatory process. Government administrators recognize that government–business partnerships carry a cost in value conflict.

Glossary of Key Terms

administrative regulatory agency   An agency with combined legislative, executive, and judicial powers.

administrative responsibility   A concept that incorporates the values of accountability, competence, fairness, and responsiveness.

clientele groups   Fervent and substantial constituencies of particular agencies, often where benefits are concentrated but costs widely distributed.

complaint handling   A formal and expeditious way of receiving and processing complaints.

cross-subsidies   Surrogate market regulations that create a condition in which one set of customers pays prices that are intended to subsidize another set of customers.

interpretative rules   Rules that advise clients on how an agency interprets a statute or regulation.

legislative rules   Also known as substantive rules, these rules are authorized by statute and applied by well-established procedure with the full force and effect of law.

new public management (NPM)   A general approach to regulation in stark contrast to the traditional managerial model; strongly market-oriented, promotes self-regulation, and trusts that the regulated and government can become partners.

procedural rules   Rules that govern an agency's internal practices.

regulatory ratchet   Tendency of regulatory agencies to add more and more regulations to their list without deleting those that become obsolete.

strategies of support   Methods used by government agencies to seek regular input from clientele groups.

substantive rules   *See* legislative rules.

Review Questions

1. Distinguish economic, social, and subsidiary regulation, and give two examples of agencies that implement each approach to regulatory policy. What clientele groups are associated with each exemplary agency?

2. Discuss how the stages of the rule-making process afford clientele groups opportunities to influence the process in their favor.

3. Discuss the resources or factors that make clientele groups more effective. What are some of the methods they use to transform those factors into influence over policy making?

4. Discuss the consequences, intended or unintended, of the new public management approach to regulatory policy making. What are some of the values that are central to this approach? What are its main policy implications?

5. Discuss the clashing values inherent in the controversy over a new master plan for Los Angeles International Airport, as discussed in Reading 14.1. What are examples of the values they espouse? How do these values clash with the general public's interest in airport safety or air traveler convenience?

Surfing the Net

Several federal agencies are good examples of clientele agencies. Listed here are their websites and those of the appropriate clientele groups.

U.S. Department of Agriculture (**http://www.usda.gov**)

American Farm Bureau Federation (**http://www.fb.com**)

National Farmer's Union (**http://www.nfu.org**)

United Farm Workers (**http://www.ufw.org**)

U.S. Department of Commerce (**http://www.doc.gov**)

U.S. Chamber of Commerce (**http://www.uschamber.org**)

U.S. Department of Education (**http://www.ed.gov**)

National Education Association (**http://www.nea.org**)

U.S. Department of Justice (**http://www.usdoj.gov**)

American Civil Liberties Union (**http://www.aclu.org**)

National Association for the Advancement of Colored People (NAACP) (**http://www.naacp.org**)

U.S. Department of Labor (**http://www.dol.gov**)

AFL-CIO (**http://www.aflcio.org/home.htm**)

U.S. Department of Health and Human Services (**http://www.dhhs.gov**)

U.S. Social Security Administration (**http://www.ssa.gov**)

AARP (**http://www.aarp.org**)

U.S. Department of Veterans Affairs (**http://www.va.gov**)

American Legion (**http://www.legion.org**)

U.S. Federal Elections Commission (**http://www.fec.gov**)

Democratic National Committee (**http://www.democrats.org**)

Republican National Committee (**http://www.rnc.org**)

Libertarian Party (**http://www.lp.org**)

Reform Party (**http://www.reformparty.org**)

American Conservative Union (**http://www.conservative.org**)

Americans for Democratic Action (**http://www.adaction.org**)

Some state and local government sites provide access to state and local regulating or providing agencies that also lobby clientele groups before upper-level government agencies and programs, especially those concerned with subsidiary policy. Those sites are the following:

Council of State Governments (**http://www.csg.org**)

International City–County Management Association (**http://www.icma.org**)

National Association of Counties (**http://www.naco.org**)

National League of Cities (**http://www.nlc.org**)

State and Local Government on the Net (**http://www.piperinfo.com/state/index.cfm**) is a useful site for a variety of issues.

Urban Institute (**http://www.urban.org/pubs/immig/immig.htm**)

Chapter Notes

Chapter 1

1. William H. Woodwell Jr. (1999), Government for sale, *The National Voter, 48*(2): 11–12.
2. Congressional Quarterly Press (1998), *State and local government sourcebook: 1998* (Washington, DC: Author): 14.
3. This entire section on phases or eras draws heavily from Nicholas Henry (1999), *Public administration and public affairs* (7th ed.) (Upper Saddle River, NJ: Prentice-Hall).

Chapter 2

1. David Easton (1953), *The political system* (New York: Knopf).
2. See Barbara Craig & David O'Brien (1993), *Abortion and American politics* (Chatham, NJ: Chatham House); and National Abortion Federation (1991), *Who will provide?* (Washington, DC: American Council for Obstetrics and Gynecology).
3. For a discussion of the moral values clashing in this policy debate, see C. Everett Koop, Why defend partial-birth abortions? *The New York Times* (September 26, 1996); The partial-birth debate in 1998, *The Humanist* (March–April 1998).
4. For a good review of the expansion and transformation of affirmative action programs, see Henry (1999), 314–315.
5. The Court ruled that while affirmative action plans were constitutional, they had to take race into account only by limited, carefully conceived plans to reduce the effects of specific prior discrimination (*Wygant* v. *Jackson Board of Education*, *Local 93 of the International Firefighters* v. *Cleveland*, and *Local 28 Sheetmetal Workers* v. *Equal Employment Opportunity Commission*). The Court further ruled that quota plans that diffused the burden of implementation over many people were acceptable but that race-conscious relief plans must be narrowly drawn to the specific problems they were designed to resolve (*United States* v. *Paradise*, 1987). The justices also ruled that Arabs, Jews, and other ethnic groups could no longer be counted as whites in group discrimination suits (*St. Francis* v. *Al-Khazraji*, 1987).

   In addition, the Court decided a series of cases that increased the burden of proof of discrimination, which made challenges easier to affirmative action. In *City of Richmond* v. *Croson* (1989), it ruled against set-aside programs for failing to show a compelling need or that the plan was "narrowly tailored" to solve a specific problem. In *Wards Cove Packing Company* v. *Antonio* (1989), it reversed the judicial doctrine of "disparate impact," which it defined as an employment practice that resulted in reducing the number of women or minorities, even if unintentional, in an organization or its higher-paying positions. The Court ruled that employers did not have the burden of demonstrating that discrimination had not occurred, shifting the burden to complainants to show intent to discriminate. The Court ruled that newly employed white firefighters could sue their department, challenging prior court rulings on past discrimination practices if the new firefighters had not been employed by the department at the time of the original suits (*Martin* v. *Wilks*, 1989). This ruling called into serious question the permanency of standing court orders to end employment discrimination.

6. See Kay Lawson (Ed.) (1981), *Political parties and linkage: A comparative perspective* (New Haven, CT: Yale University Press).

7. It ruled, for example, that firing a public employee on the basis of his or her political affiliation was impermissible (*Rutan v. Republican Party of Illinois*, 497 U.S. 62, 1990).

8. For a succinct discussion of third, or minor, parties, see Barbara Bardes et al. (1998), *American government and politics today: The essentials* (Belmont, CA: Wadsworth): 280.

9. See, for example, Edward Sidlow & Beth Henschen (1998), *America at odds* (Belmont, CA: Wadsworth): 212–215; *Congressional Quarterly Weekly Report* (June 13, 1992): 1729.

10. David Rosenbloom (1998), *Public administration: Understanding management, politics, and law in the public sector* (4th ed.) (New York: McGraw-Hill): 85.

11. Amtrak offering its passengers a guarantee, *Associated Press* (June 18, 1999).

12. Reclaiming brownfields, *Governing* (January 1998): 32.

13. Zachary A. Smith (1995), *The environmental policy paradox* (2nd ed.) (Englewood Cliffs, NJ: Prentice-Hall): 1.

14. Smith (1995), 3–4. See also Norman Vig & Michael Craft (Eds.) (1990), *Environmental policy in the 1990s* (Washington, DC: Congressional Quarterly Press).

15. Vig & Craft (1990), 13–18.

16. Frederick Crupp (1986), The third stage of environmentalists, *Environmental Defense Fund Newsletter, 17:* 4.

17. Smith (1995), 223. See also Riley E. Dunlap (1987), Public opinion on the environment in the Reagan era, *Environment, 29:* 15.

18. See also Abigail Thernstrom (1987), *Whose votes count? Affirmative action in American voting rights* (Cambridge, MA: Harvard University Press).

Chapter 3

1. See, for instance, Thomas McCollough (1991), *The moral imagination and public life* (Chatham, NJ: Chatham House).

2. Steve Ott (1989), *The organizational culture* (Pacific Grove, CA: Brooks/Cole).

3. Irving Janis (1972), *Victims of groupthink* (Boston: Houghton-Mifflin).

4. Graham Allison (1971), *Essence of decision* (Boston: Little, Brown).

5. These are summarized from Douglas Yates (1982), *Bureaucratic democracy* (Cambridge, MA: Harvard University Press).

6. Michael LeMay (1994), *Anatomy of a public policy* (New York: Praeger).

7. Lee Bohman & Terrence Deal (1991), *Reframing organizations: Artistry, choice, and leadership* (San Francisco: Jossey-Bass).

8. Anthony Downs (1957), *An economic theory of democracy* (New York: Harper & Row): 96–98.

9. Anthony Downs (1967), *Inside bureaucracy* (Boston: Little, Brown): 24–25, 96–98.

10. Downs (1967), 238.

11. Guy Peters (1989), *The politics of bureaucracy* (3rd ed.) (New York: Longman): 184–185.

12. This discussion is drawn from Downs (1967), 239–240.

13. Downs (1967), 242–244.

14. See, for example, George Gordon & Michael Milakovich (1998), *Public administration in America* (6th ed.) (New York: St. Martin's Press): 50–73.

15. See Hugh Helco (1978), Issue networks and the executive establishment, in Anthony King (Ed.), *The new American political system* (Washington, DC: American Enterprise Institute for Public Policy Research).

16. See, for instance, the classical principles in Frederick Taylor (1911), *The principles of scientific management* (New York: Norton) (republished 1967); or Max Weber's principles discussed in Julien Freund (1969), *The sociology of Max Weber* (New York: Vintage Books): 1420–1480; or Luther Gulick & Leon Urwick (1937), *Papers on the science of administration* (New York: Institute of Public Administration).

17. In Rosenbloom (1998), 194.
18. See Gordon & Milakovich (1998), 63.

Chapter 4

1. See Gordon & Milakovich (1998), 79–111; Advisory Commission on Intergovernmental Relations (1988), *Significant features of fiscal federalism, 1988* (Vols. I, II) (Washington, DC: U.S. Government Printing Office); Deil S. Wright (1988), *Understanding intergovernmental relations* (3rd ed.) (Pacific Grove, CA: Brooks/Cole).
2. See Benjamin Ginsberg, Theodore Lowi, & Margaret Weir (1999), *We, the people* (2nd ed.) (New York: Norton): 134.
3. Gordon & Milakovich (1998), 88.
4. See Martha Derthick (1987), American federalism: Madison's middle ground in the 1980s. *Public Administration Review, 47*; Paul Peterson (1995), *The price of federalism* (Washington, DC: Brookings Institution); Thomas R. Swartz & John E. Peck (Eds.) (1990), *The changing face of fiscal federalism* (Armonk, NY: M. E. Sharpe).
5. Timothy Conlan & David R. Blau (1992), Federal mandates: The record of reform and future prospects, *Intergovernmental Perspectives, 18:* 7–11; Linda Wager (1993), A declaration of war: Local governments are tired of picking up the tab for state programs, *State Government News, 36:* 18–22.
6. Bipartisan Commission on Entitlements and Tax Reform (1994), *Interim report to the president* (Washington, DC: U.S. Government Printing): 11.
7. Alan Ehrenhalt (1995), Mandates from above, *Governing* (September); Swartz & Peck (1990).
8. Jay Shafritz & E. W. Russell (1998), *Introducing public administration* (New York: Longman): 164.
9. Shafritz & Russell (1998), 155–156.
10. Ken DeBow & John Syer (1997), *Power and politics in California* (Boston: Allyn & Bacon): 246.

Chapter 5

1. See Shafritz & Russell (1998), 201–203.
2. Shafritz & Russell (1998), 203–204.
3. This discussion relies on that by Shafritz & Russell (1998), 204–208, which summarizes Adam Smith's views and contributions to classical organization theory.
4. F. Taylor (1911). See also the succinct discussion of Taylorism in Gordon & Milakovich (1998), *Public administration in America* (New York: St. Martin's Press): 120–122.
5. F. Taylor (1911), 25.
6. Gordon & Milakovich (1998), 121. See also the discussion of Taylor's contributions in Shafritz & Russell (1998), 209–211.
7. Shafritz & Russell (1998), 209–210.
8. Shafritz & Russell (1998), 212.
9. See the succinct summary of Weber's theory in Gordon & Milakovich (1998), 118–120; or in George Berkley & John Rouse (1997), *The craft of public administration* (7th ed.) (Madison, WI: Brown & Benchmark): 103–106.
10. Berkley & Rouse (1997), 104.
11. This summary is drawn from the following sources: Gordon & Milakovich (1998), 118; J. M. Pfiffner & F. P. Sherwood (1960), *Administrative organization* (Englewood Cliffs, NJ: Prentice-Hall): 56–57; Shafritz & Russell (1998), 218; Berkley & Rouse (1997), 107; and James W. Fesler & Donald F. Kettl (1996), *The politics of the administrative process* (2nd ed.) (Chatham, NJ: Chatham House): 51–53. For a more complete reading on Weber's work, see Freund (1969).
12. This assessment is from Gordon & Milakovich (1998), 120. A similar conclusion is reached by Pfiffner & Sherwood (1960), 102.

13. See Fesler & Kettl (1996), 52; Talcott Parsons (1956), Suggestions for a sociological approach to the theory of organizations, *Administrative Science Quarterly, 1*: 64.

14. Gordon & Milakovich (1998), 122–123; Leonard D. White (1954), *Introduction to the study of public administration* (originally published 1926) (Upper Saddle River, NJ: Prentice-Hall).

15. This discussion draws from Berkley & Rouse (1997), 113–114. See also Shafritz & Russell (1998), 257–263.

16. Berkley & Rouse (1997), 114.

17. Berkley & Rouse (1997), 114. See their discussion of Chester Bernard (pp. 109–110). See also the discussion of Bernard in Gordon & Milakovich (1998), 125–126.

18. For excellent summaries of their work and its impact on the human relations movement, see Shafritz & Russell (1998), 257–263; Berkley & Rouse (1997), 108–109; and Gordon & Milakovich (1998), 124–125. This discussion was drawn from those sources and Fesler & Kettl (1996), 57–59.

19. F. J. Roethisberger & William Dickson (1946), *Management and the worker* (Cambridge, MA: Harvard University Press): 102.

20. Roethisberger & Dickson (1946), 522.

21. Berkley & Rouse (1997), 109; Pfiffner & Sherwood (1960), 102.

22. Abraham Maslow (1943), A theory of human motivation, *Psychological Review, 50:* 370–396. See the succinct discussion of Maslow's ideas and effect within the human relations movement in Shafritz & Russell (1998), 258–259; Berkley & Rouse (1997), 114; and Gordon & Milakovich (1998), 129.

23. Gordon & Milakovich (1998), 128.

24. New York: McGraw-Hill; summarized in Shafritz & Russell (1998), 261–263.

25. Chris Argyris (1957), *Personality and organization* (New York: McGraw-Hill). See also his later (1990) work, *Integrating the individual and the organization* (New Brunswick, NJ: Transaction).

26. Rensis Likert (1967), *The human organization: Its management and value* (New York: McGraw-Hill). For a brief but solid summary of the work, see Berkley & Rouse (1997), 115, from which this discussion was drawn.

27. Berkley & Rouse (1997), 115.

28. Gordon & Milakovich (1998), 126–127.

29. Robert Blauner (1964), *Alienation and freedom* (Chicago: University of Chicago Press).

30. Berkley & Rouse (1997), 110–111; and Shafritz & Russell (1998), 219–222.

31. This assertion, articulated by Shafritz & Russell (1998), 221, is widely accepted.

32. As discussed in Berkley & Rouse (1997), 111.

33. See *Administrative behavior* (1997) (4th ed.) (New York: Free Press).

34. Shafritz & Russell (1998), 221.

35. Shafritz & Russell (1998), 221.

36. Dwight Waldo (1948), *The administrative state* (New York: Ronald Press). See also his 1948 article Development of a theory of democratic administration, *American Political Science Review, 46:* 501–503, and his 1980 book, *The enterprise of public administration* (Novato, CA: Chandler & Sharp).

37. Shafritz & Russell (1998), 265.

38. Catheryn Seckler-Hudson (1955), *Organization and management* (Washington, DC: American University Press). Seckler-Hudson was then dean of the School of Public Administration at American University and the author of influential works on public-sector planning, budgeting, and organization. See Shafritz & Russell (1998), 196.

39. Jay Shafritz & J. Steven Ott (Eds.) (1996), *Classics of organization theory* (4th ed.) (Belmont, CA: Wadsworth).

40. Norbert Weiner (1948), *Cybernetics* (Cambridge: MIT Press). This discussion is taken from Shafritz & Ott (1996), 255; and Shafritz & Russell (1998), 224–225.

41. James Thompson (1967), *Organizations in action* (New York: McGraw-Hill), and summarized in Shafritz & Ott (1996), 287–301.
42. David Easton (1965), *A framework for political analysis* (Chicago: University of Chicago Press) (reprinted in 1979). In *The political system: An inquiry into the state of political science* (New York: Alfred A. Knopf, 1953), Easton popularized the concept of politics as a system.
43. Daniel Katz & Robert Kahn (1978), *The social psychology of organizations* (2nd ed.) (New York: Wiley). A good summary is found in Shafritz & Ott (1996), 274–286.
44. This discussion is taken from Gordon & Milakovich (1998), 134.
45. William Ouchi (1982), *Theory Z* (New York: Avon Books). Clyde McKee (1983), *An analysis of Theory Z: How it is used in Japan's public sector,* Paper presented at annual meeting of the American Political Science Association, Chicago, September. Gordon & Milakovich (1998), 135–136.
46. Peter Senge (1994), *The fifth discipline* (New York: Doubleday).
47. Gordon & Milakovich (1998), 137.
48. Robert Dilworth (1996), Institutionalizing learning organizations in the public sector. *Public Productivity and Management Review, 19:* 407–421.

Chapter 6

1. Charles E. Lindblom (1959), The science of muddling through. *Public Administration Review, 19:* 79 88.
2. Fesler & Kettl (1996), 217.
3. Anthony Downs (1957), *An economic theory of democracy* (New York: Harper & Row): 4.
4. Downs (1957), 5.
5. Downs (1957), 4–5.
6. Fesler & Kettl (1996), 221–222. See also Rosenbloom (1998), 328–333.
7. Downs (1957), 4. See the summary of his description in Gordon & Milakovich (1998), 166–167.
8. Lindblom (1959), 81.
9. Lindblom (1959), 81; Downs (1967); Aaron Wildavsky (1984), *The new politics of the budgetary process* (Boston: Little, Brown); and an excellent summary of the critiques of the model in Gordon & Milakovich (1998), 167–168, and in Rosenbloom (1998), 333–335.
10. Gordon & Milakovich (1998), 167.
11. See the discussion and assessment of PPBS in Fesler & Kettl (1996), 222–224.
12. See all of the Charles Lindblom citations in the bibliography. His ideas and overall approach are summarized well in Fesler & Kettl (1996), 227–232; and in Gordon & Milakovich (1998), 168–171. See also Phillip Cooper et al. (1998), *Public administration for the twenty-first century* (Fort Worth, TX: Harcourt Brace): 166.
13. Amitai Etzioni (1986), Mixed scanning revisited. *Public Administration Review, 46:* 8–14.
14. Rosenbloom (1998), 338–341.
15. Gordon & Milakovich (1998), 168–169.
16. Allison (1971). See also the discussion in Fesler & Kettl (1996), 228–230, from which this summary was drawn.
17. Allison (1971), 6.
18. Fesler & Kettl (1996), 230.
19. Fesler & Kettl (1996), 230. See also Michael Cohen, James March, & Johan Olsen (1972), A garbage-can model of organizational choice. *Administrative Science Quarterly, 17:* 1–25.
20. See Gordon & Milakovich (1998), 190, and their assessment of the garbage-can model.
21. Yehezkel Dror (1964), Muddling through—"Science" or "inertia?" *Public Administration Review, 24:* 153–157.

22. Gordon & Milakovich (1998), 170.

23. Amitai Etzioni (1967), Mixed scanning: A "third" approach to decision making. *Public Administration Review, 27:* 385–392.

24. Etzioni (1967), 389–390.

25. This discussion draws from Fesler & Kettl (1996), 232–236.

26. Fesler & Kettl (1996), 236. See especially Grant McConnell (1966), *Private power and American democracy* (New York: Knopf); and Robert Yin & Douglas Yates (1975), *Street-level governments* (Lexington, MA: Lexington Books).

27. Fesler & Kettl (1996), 237. For a view of policy as the end result of conflict among competing groups assuming both pluralist democracy and better or more rational policies, see E. E. Schattschneider (1960), *The semi-sovereign people* (New York: Holt, Rinehart & Winston).

28. Downs (1957; 1967); James Buchanan & Gordon Tullock (1962), *The calculus of consent* (Ann Arbor: University of Michigan Press); and Gordon Tullock (1965), *The politics of bureaucracy* (Washington, DC: Public Affairs Press). See also the summary discussion of the model in Fesler & Kettl (1996), 237–241.

29. Stuart Butler (1985), *Privatizing federal spending* (New York: Universe Books).

30. This discussion draws on Gordon & Milakovich (1998), 175–180.

31. Gordon & Milakovich (1998), 242–247. See also, Irving Janis & Leon Mann (1977), *Decision making* (New York: Free Press).

32. Gordon Tullock (1965), *The politics of bureaucracy* (Washington, DC: Public Affairs Press); Downs (1967).

33. In Gordon & Milakovich (1998), 245.

Chapter 7

1. See the discussion of managerialism in Christopher Pollitt (1993), *Managerialism and the public services* (2nd ed.) (Cambridge, MA: Blackwell Business), 1–27.

2. Michael Hammer & James Champy (1993), *Reengineering the corporation* (New York: HarperCollins). See the discussion of this approach in Shafritz & Russell (1998), 287–289, from which this discussion was drawn.

3. David Osborne & Ted Gaebler (1992), *Reinventing government* (Reading, MA: Addison-Wesley).

4. Peter Drucker (1954), *The practice of management* (New York: Harper).

5. Chris Argyris (1957); Argyris (1962), *Interpersonal confidence and organizational effectiveness* (Homewood, IL: Dorsey Press); and Argyris (1990), *Integrating the individual and the organization* (New Brunswick, NJ: Transaction). See also the discussion of OD in Shafritz & Russell (1998), 240–244; or Henry (1999), 459–460.

6. Russell L. Ackoff & Patrick Rivett (1963), *A manager's guide to operations research* (New York: Wiley); C. P. Snow (1961), *Science and government* (Cambridge, MA: Harvard University Press); and C. West Churchman (1968), *The systems approach* (New York: Dell).

7. See the succinct but thorough discussion of PERT and CPM in Henry (1999), 166–169, from which this discussion was drawn.

8. See W. Edwards Deming (1986), *Out of crisis* (Cambridge: MIT Press), and (1993), *The new economics* (Cambridge: MIT Press). See also Albert Hyde (1992), Implications of total quality management for the public sector, *Public Productivity and Management Review, 16:* 23–76; E. E. Lawler, S. A. Mohranan, & G. E. Ledford Jr. (1992), *Employee involvement in total quality management* (San Francisco: Jossey-Bass); J. D. Orsburn et al. (1990), *Self-directed work teams: The new American challenge* (Homewood, IL: Business One Irwin); R. T. Pascale & A. G. Athos (1981), *The art of Japanese management* (New York: Simon & Schuster); and John Bowman (1989), Quality circles: Promises, problems, and prospects in Florida, *Public Personnel Management, 18:* 375–403.

9. Deming (1986, 1993), Hyde (1992), Orsburn et al. (1990), Pascale & Athos (1981), and Bowman (1989). For a discussion of TQM application at the state level, see Jonathan Walters (1994), TQM: Surviving the cynics, *Governing* (September): 40–45; Ronald C. Nyhan & Herbert A. Marlowe Jr. (1995), Performance measurement in the public sector: Challenges and opportunities, *Public Productivity and Management Review, 18:* 333–348; and Robert S. Kravchuk & Robert Leighton (1993), Implementing TQM in the states, *Public Productivity and Management Review, 17:* 74–75.

10. Shafritz & Russell (1998), 292–294.

11. Shafritz & Russell (1998), 294.

12. David Osborne & Ted Graebler (1992), *Reinventing government* (Reading, MA: Addison-Wesley).

13. This discussion draws from Shafritz & Russell (1998), 297–302.

14. Shafritz & Russell (1998), 302–306.

15. J. M. Juran (1992), *Juran on quality by design* (New York: Free Press); Juran (1988), *Juran's quality control handbook* (4th ed.) (New York: McGraw-Hill); and Juran (1988), *Juran on leadership for quality* (New York: McGraw-Hill).

16. See Shafritz & Russell (1998), 310.

17. Marc Holzer (1995), Productivity and quality management, in Jack Rabin et al. (Eds.), *Handbook of public administration and labor relations* (New York: Dekker). See also Marc Holzer (1992), *Public productivity handbook* (New York: Dekker).

18. See, for example, Albert Hyde (1992), Implications of total quality management for the public sector, *Public Productivity and Management Review, 16:* 23–76, or Albert Hyde (1992), The proverbs of total quality management: Recharting the path to quality improvement in the public sector, *Public Productivity and Management Review, 16*(1): 25–37; Donald Rosenhoover & Harold Kuhn Jr. (1996), Total quality management and the public sector, *Public Administration Quarterly, 19:* 435–455; and Robert Kravchuk & Robert Leighton (1993), Implementing TQM in the states, *Public Productivity and Management Review, 17:* 74–75.

19. For city-level uses, see Evan Berman & Jonathan West (1995), Municipal commitment to TQM: A survey of recent progress, *Public Administration Review, 55:* 57–66.

20. See Jonathan West, Evan Berman, & Michael Milakovich (1993), Implementing TQM in local government: A leadership challenge, *Public Productivity and Management Review, 17:* 179–187; Jonathan Walters (1995), Quality by any other name, *Governing, 8*(12): 5; Jonathan Walters (1992), The cult of total quality, *Governing, 15*(8): 40; and Kim Hill & Kenneth Mladenka (1992), *Democratic governance in American states and cities* (Pacific Grove, CA: Brooks/Cole).

21. Gordon & Milakovich (1998), 375. See also Michael Milakovich (1991), Total quality management in the public sector, *National Productivity Review, 10:* 195–215; and Evan Berman, Michael Milakovich, & Jonathan West (1994), Implementing TQM in the states, *Spectrum, 67:* 6–13.

22. Shafritz & Russell (1998), 327.

23. Shafritz & Russell (1998), 336–343.

24. Shafritz & Russell (1998), 343.

25. Shafritz & Russell (1998), 344–352.

Chapter 8

1. Fesler & Kettl (1996), 368.

2. Fesler & Kettl (1996), 377.

3. Lisabeth Schorr (1998), *Common purpose* (New York: Anchor Books).

4. Frank J. Thompson (Ed.) (1990), *Classics of public personnel policy* (2nd ed.) (Oak Park, IL: Moore): 123.

5. Aaron Wildavsky, as cited in Rosenbloom (1998), 398.
6. Rosenbloom (1998), 398.
7. This model's description is derived from Allison (1971).
8. Rosenbloom (1998), 399.
9. Gary Bryner (1998), *Politics and public morality: The great American welfare reform debate* (New York: Norton).
10. Thomas Dye (1999), *Politics in America* (3rd ed.) (Upper Saddle River, NJ: Prentice-Hall): 633.
11. *Governing, 13*(5) (special issue): 26–36.
12. Jay Shafritz & E. W. Russell (1999), *Introducing public administration* (2nd ed.) (New York: Longman): 499.
13. Carol Weiss (1972), *Evaluation research* (Englewood Cliffs, NJ: Prentice-Hall).
14. Shafritz & Russell (1998), 502.

Chapter 9

1. N. Joseph Cayer (1986), *Public personnel administration in the United States* (2nd ed.) (New York: St. Martin's Press): 1.
2. See, for example, the formulation of Gordon & Milakovich (1998), 255–257. A simpler typology of three phases is suggested by Rosenbloom (1998), 207–219. For a solid history of the federal civil service, see Paul P. Van Riper (1958), *History of the United States civil service* (Evanston, IL: Row, Peterson, 1958).
3. Gordon & Milakovich (1998), 259–260.
4. Report of the Congressional Joint Commission on Reclassification of Salaries, 1920, as cited in Shafritz & Russell (1998), 406.
5. Carolyn Ban & Patricia Ingraham (1988), Retaining quality federal employees: Life after PACE, *Public Administration Review, 48:* 708–718; and Gordon & Milakovich (1998), 263–264.
6. Gordon & Milakovich (1998), 266.
7. N. Joseph Cayer (1980), *Managing human resources* (New York: St. Martin's Press); Richard Kearney (1992), *Labor relations in the public sector* (2nd ed.) (New York: Dekker).
8. This summary was taken from Gordon & Milakovich (1998), 276.
9. Shafritz & Russell (1998), 407.
10. For example, see Richard Beatty & Craig Schneier (1981), *Personnel administration* (Reading, MA: Addison-Wesley, 1981), 52–53.
11. Shafritz & Russell (1998), 410.
12. See the discussion in Henry (1999), 301; Gordon & Milakovich (1998), 277–278; or Shafritz & Russell (1998), 439–446.
13. Richard Kearney (1984), *Labor relations in the public sector* (New York: Dekker); and Rosenbloom (1998), 264–265.
14. This summary is drawn from Rosenbloom (1998), 267–268; Shafritz & Russell (1998), 422–23, 432; and the several court cases cited in notes 16–18.
15. See Executive Order 10988, *Federal Register, 27*(17) (January 1962): 551; and the Wagner Act, 1935.
16. *Abood* v. *Detroit Board of Education*, 430 U.S. 209 (1977).
17. *Chicago Teachers Union* v. *Hudson*, 475 U.S. 292 (1986).
18. *City of Madison Joint School District No. 8* v. *Wisconsin Employment Relations Commission*, 429 U.S. 167 (1976); *Civil Service Commission* v. *National Association of Letter Carriers*, 413 U.S. 548 (1973). The Hatch Act prohibited employees from taking an active part in the political management of partisan electoral campaigns. It was revised in 1993 at the urging of federal employee unions, who argued that it was too restrictive. Most employees now can engage in various campaign activities, including giving speeches, holding an office in a political organization, stuffing envelopes, making phone calls, and distributing

campaign literature. The main restrictions were retained and concern the solicitation of money for political purposes. The 1993 revision does not apply to the Senior Executive Service, law judges, and several agencies related to defense and intelligence as well as to others, such as election commissions, that could be compromised by public displays of partisanship.

19. Christy Harris (1996), Workers get more say in contracting out, *Federal Times, 29:* 5.
20. See Nicholas Henry (1999), 282–283; Gordon & Milakovich (1998), 255; Shafritz & Russell (1998), 415–418.
21. Shafritz & Russell (1998), 418; Henry (1999), 288; O. Glenn Stahls (1983), *Public personnel management* (8th ed.) (New York: Harper & Row): 43.
22. Shafritz & Russell (1998), 422; Henry (1999), 294–295; Larry Lane (1994), Public-sector performance management, *Review of Public Personnel Administration, 14:* 27; Gordon & Milakovich (1998), 273–274, 280–281.
23. Gordon & Milakovich (1998), 283.
24. This discussion draws from Henry (1999), 319–334.
25. Two major Supreme Court cases addressed the bona fide occupational qualification issue: *Rosenfeld* v. *Southern Pacific Company* (1968), which overturned a California law concerning limitations on how much weight women could lift; and *Weeks* v. *Southern Bell and Telegraph* (1969), which held that state protective labor laws could not be used to deny women jobs or promotions and that the burden of proof regarding the fairness of bona fide occupational disqualification lay with employers, not employees.
26. Henry (1999), 320–321.
27. See the succinct summary in Shafritz & Russell (1998), 423–424.
28. This entire discussion is drawn from Henry (1999), 300–304.
29. Henry (1999), 297–299.

Chapter 10

1. John Harrigan (1998), *Politics and policy in states and communities* (6th ed.) (New York: Harper & Row): 249–252; and David Lawrence (1999), *California: The politics of diversity* (Belmont, CA: Wadsworth): 157–158.
2. David Barber (1992), *The presidential character* (4th ed.) (Upper Saddle River, NJ: Prentice-Hall).
3. See the discussion in Jay Shafritz & W. E. Russell (1998), *Introducing public administration* (New York: Longman): 372–374.
4. Talcott Parsons (1960), *Structure and process in modern societies* (New York: Free Press). See the discussion of Parson's work in Gordon & Milakovich (1998), 226–228.
5. David Lawrence (1999), *California: The politics of diversity*. Belmont, CA: Wadsworth, 1999: 51.
6. Robert Tannenbaum & Warren Schmidt (1973), How to choose a leadership pattern, *Harvard Business Review,* 164–167.
7. Leading beyond the borders: Mayor Jim Rout, *Governing* (January 2000): 45.
8. See, for example, the list in Berkley & Rouse (1997), 207–212; Edwin Locke (1991), *The essence of leadership* (New York: Lexington Books): 23–24; and those in Shafritz & Russell (1998), 363–364.
9. See Laurence Peter (1969), *The Peter principle* (New York: William Morrow).
10. Katz & Kahn (1978); David Lilenthal (1967), *Management: A humanist art* (New York: Columbia University Press): 67. This discussion draws from Berkley & Rouse (1997), 207–210.
11. Daniel Katz & Robert Kahn (1966), *The social psychology of organizations* (New York: Wiley): 318 Berkley & Rouse (1997), 211.
12. Douglas McGregor (1966), *Leadership and motivation* (Cambridge: MIT Press): 47–48, 73–74.

13. See the source of the concepts of transactional and transformational leadership in Robert Tannenbaum & Warren Schmidt (1973), How to choose a leadership pattern, *Harvard Business Review*, 162–175; and James G. Hunt et al. (Eds.) (1988), *Emerging leadership vistas* (Lexington, MA: Heath); and the summary discussion in Shafritz & Russell (1998), 364–365.

14. Hunt et al. (1988); and Downs (1967), 5–23.

15. Hunt et al. (1988). See also Al Gore (1993), *From red tape to results: Creating a government that works better and costs less* (Washington, DC: National Performance Review); and David Osborne & Ted Gaebler (1992), *Reinventing government* (Reading, MA: Addison-Wesley).

16. This section draws on the discussion of leadership styles in Gordon & Milakovich (1998), 231–238.

17. Dorwin Cartwright & Alvin Zander (Eds.) (1968), *Group dynamics: Research and theory* (3rd ed.) (New York: Harper & Row).

18. Douglas McGregor (1985), *The human side of enterprise* (New York: McGraw-Hill): 47–48.

19. Jonathan Walters (1999), Vision of revival, *Governing*, 12(11): 24.

20. This section draws heavily from the discussion in Shafritz & Russell (1998), 376–388.

Chapter 11

1. See Katz & Kahn (1966), especially Chapter 14 (pp. 427–473), for a thorough discussion of the complex role of communication in organizations.

2. Katz & Kahn (1966), 472.

3. Berkley & Rouse (1997), 237. See also Everett Rogers & Rekha Agarwala-Rogers, *Communication in organizations* (New York: Free Press, 1976): 90–95.

4. Leo Thayer (1986), *Communication and communication systems in organization, management and interpersonal relations* (Lanham, MD: University Press of America): 123.

5. Katz & Kahn (1966), 433.

6. Berkley & Rouse (1997), 238.

7. Katz & Kahn (1966), 448.

8. Herbert Simon (1976), *Administrative behavior* (New York: Free Press): 159–160.

9. Downs (1967), 113.

10. Downs (1967), 113. See also Berkley & Rouse (1997), 246–248.

11. Ted McLaughlin (1964), *Communication* (Columbus, OH: Charles E. Merrill): 269–281.

12. Simon (1966), 161.

13. Phillip Lewis (1980), *Organizational communication* (Columbus, OH: Grid): 70–71.

14. Katz & Kahn (1966), 436.

15. McLaughlin (1964), 278–280.

16. Berkley & Rouse (1997), 249–255.

17. Katz & Kahn (1966), 455; Berkley & Rouse (1997), 256.

18. J. G. Miller (1969), Information, input, overload, and psychopathology, *American Journal of Psychiatry, 116:* 695–704. See also the discussion in Katz & Kahn (1966), 451.

19. McLaughlin (1964), 278–280.

20. Simon (1966), 163–169.

21. Peter Blau (1955), *Bureaucracy in modern society* (Chicago: University of Chicago Press): 152. See also the point made in Berkley & Rouse (1997), 249–252.

22. Chris Argyris (1957), *Personality and organization* (New York: Harper & Row).

23. Katz & Kahn (1966), 440. See also Lewis (1980), 61–62; and Berkley & Rouse (1997), 260.

24. Lewis (1980), 62–63; Berkley & Rouse (1997), 260.

25. Lewis (1980), 63.

26. Gordon Tullock (1965), *The politics of bureaucracy* (Washington, DC: Public Affairs Press): 137–141. See also an excellent summary of Tullock's views with additional insights offered by Downs (1967), including his summary.

27. Katz & Kahn (1966), 444–445.
28. Lewis (1980), 64–65.
29. Lewis (1980), 65.
30. Downs (1967), 125.
31. Katz & Kahn (1966), 446–448.
32. Lewis (1980), 67.
33. Simon (1966), 161.
34. Katz & Kahn (1966), 448. See also Berkley & Rouse (1997), 260–261.
35. Downs (1967), 126–127.
36. Downs (1967), 130–131.

Chapter 12

1. Thomas Dye (1997), *Politics in states and communities* (9th ed.) (Upper Saddle River, NJ: Prentice-Hall): 516.
2. This summary is taken from Jay M. Shafritz & E. W. Russell (1998), *Introducing public administration* (New York: Longman): 515–516.
3. U.S. Advisory Commission on Intergovernmental Relations (1992), *Changing public attitudes on government and taxes, 1992* (Washington, DC: Author).
4. Aaron Wildavsky (1992b), Political implications of budget reform: A retrospective, *Public Administration Review, 52:* 595.
5. Thomas Anton (1967), Role and symbols in the determination of state expenditures, *Midwest Journal of Public Administration, 11*(1): 29. For a succinct discussion of state budgeting since the 1970s, see Berkley & Rouse (1997), 303–304.
6. Shafritz & Russell (1998), 554–562.
7. Shafritz & Russell (1998), 556.
8. Shafritz & Russell (1998), 558.
9. Council of State Governments (1998), *The book of the states, 1998–1999* (Lexington, KY: Author): 33.
10. Shafritz & Russell (1998), 563. This section draws from their discussion on pp. 563–568.
11. Aaron Wildavsky (1972), The self-evaluating organization, *Public Administration Review, 32*(5).
12. See Shafritz & Russell (1998), 569–570.
13. Richard M. Musgrave & Peggy B. Musgrave (1984), *Public finance in theory and practice* (4th ed.) (New York: McGraw-Hill). Keynes's most famous work, *The general theory of employment, interest, and money,* was first published in 1936 (New York: Harcourt Brace Jovanovich; reprinted in 1964).
14. Henry (1999), 256. See also Paul Craig Roberts (1984), *The supply-side revolution* (Cambridge, MA: Harvard University Press), for a positive perspective; for a critical insider's view, see David Stockman (1986), *The triumph of politics* (New York: Harper & Row). See also Gordon & Milakovich (1998), 333; and Shafritz & Russell (1998), 501–502.
15. See Gordon & Milakovich (1998), 319–320; see also Fesler & Kettl (1996), 257–258.
16. Aaron Wildavsky (1992b), *The new politics of the budgetary process* (2nd ed.) (New York: HarperCollins): Chapter 7.
17. See, for example, Allen Schick (1983b), Politics through law: Congressional limitations on executive discretion. In Anthony King (Ed.), *Both ends of the avenue* (Washington, DC: American Enterprise Institute for Public Policy Research): 154–184; or Schick's (1980) *Congress and money: Budgeting, spending, and taxing* (Washington, DC: Urban Institute, 1980) or (1983a) Incremental budgeting in a decremental age, *Policy Sciences, 16:* 1–25. Similar arguments or points are made by Henry (1999), 255–256, and Fesler & Kettl (1996), 256–258.
18. See Wildavsky (1992a) and Henry (1999), 268–270.

19. This section summarizes the description of the act in Gordon & Milakovich (1998), 324–325, and Henry (1999), 271–272.
20. Donald Axelrod (1995), *Budgeting for modern government* (New York: St. Martin's Press): 201–209. See also the summary of GRH in Henry (1999), 272–273; and Berkley & Rouse (1997), 296–297; or Fesler & Kettl (1996), 269–272.
21. *Bowsher v. Synar* (106 S. Ct. 3181, 92 L Ed, 2nd, 583).
22. Gordon & Milakovich (1998), 329–330, or Henry (1999), 273–274.
23. For an excellent summary of the Personal Responsibility and Work Opportunity Reconciliation Act of 1996, see *1996 Congressional Quarterly Almanac*, Vol. 52 (Washington, DC: Congressional Quarterly, 1997): 6-17–6-18.
24. Henry (1999), 256.
25. National Association of State Budget Officers (1992), *State balanced budget requirements: Provisions and practices* (Washington, DC: Author).
26. Penelope Lemov (1992), The decade of red ink, *Governing*, 22–26.
27. Shafritz & Russell (1998), 524.
28. Shafritz & Russell (1998), 524. See also Henry (1999), 256.
29. Gordon & Milakovich (1998), 333.
30. Shafritz & Russell (1998), 524.
31. Berkley & Rouse (1997), 298.
32. Shafritz & Russell (1998), 524.
33. Berkley & Rouse (1997), 298.
34. Henry (1999), 256. See also Newt Gingrich (1995), *To renew America* (New York: HarperCollins).
35. Cited in Shafritz & Russell (1998), 524.
36. Cited in Berkley & Rouse (1997), 297.
37. Shafritz & Russell (1998), 525.
38. Fesler & Kettl (1996), 273–275.
39. Fesler & Kettl (1996), 434. See also Gordon & Milakovich (1998), 307.
40. Gordon & Milakovich (1998), 303–306.
41. Gordon & Milakovich (1998), 306–307.
42. E. S. Savas (1982), *Privatizing the public sector* (Chatham, NJ: Chatham House): 89.
43. Berkley & Rouse (1997), 318–320.
44. Gordon & Milakovich (1998), 348.
45. Fesler & Kettl (1996), 238–240.
46. Al Gore (1993), *From red tape to results* (Washington, DC: U.S. Government Printing Office).
47. Shafritz & Russell (1998), 126.
48. Henry (1999), 374.

Chapter 13

1. Montgomery Van Wart & Evan Berman (1999), Contemporary public sector values: Narrower scope, tougher standards, and new rules of the game, *Public Productivity and Management Review, 22*(3): 326–347.
2. James Anderson (1998), The struggle to reform regulatory procedures, 1978–1998, *Policy Studies Journal, 26*(3): 482–498.
3. Rita Mae Kelly (1998), An inclusive democratic polity, representative bureaucracy, and the new public management, *Public Administration Review, 58*(3): 201–208; and Robert Gilmour & Laura Jensen (1998), Reinventing government accountability: Public functions, privatization, and the meaning of "state action," *Public Administration Review, 58*(3): 247–258.

4. The "qualified immunity issue" was dealt with in a 5–4 U.S. Supreme Court decision; see Heidi Koenig (1998), *Richardson* v. *McKnight*—What does the future hold for nongovernmental employees? *Public Administration Review, 58*(1): 8–9.

5. Robert Stoker & Laura Wilson (1998), Verifying compliance: Social regulation and welfare reform, *Public Administration Review, 58*(5): 395–405.

6. Donald Menzel (1998), www.ethics.gov: Issues and challenges facing public managers, *Public Administration Review, 58*(5): 445–452.

7. See, for example, Lisa A. Kicke & J. Steven Ott (1999), Public agency accountability in human services contracting, *Public Administration and Management Review, 22*(4): 502–516.

8. See Fesler & Kettl (1996), 345–346; Richard Andrews (1998), Environmental regulation and business self-regulation, *Policy Sciences, 31*(3): 177–197; Jeffrey Cohen (1992), *The politics of telecommunication regulation: The states and divestiture of AT&T* (Armonk, NY: Sharpe); Patty D. Renfrow & David A. Houston (1987), A comparative analysis of rule-making provisions in state administrative procedures acts, *Policy Studies Review, 6:* 657–665; Evan Rinquist (1993), *Environmental protection at the state level: Politics and progress in controlling pollution* (Armonk, NY: M. E. Sharpe); Kenneth Warren (1997), *Administrative law in the American system* (3rd ed.) (Upper Saddle River, NJ: Prentice- Hall); and William T. Gormley Jr. (1998), Regulating enforcement styles, *Political Research Quarterly, 51*(2): 363–383.

9. Cited in Andrews (1998), 177.

10. Fesler & Kettl (1996), 345–346; and James B. Wade, Anand Swaminathan, & Michael Scott Saxon (1998), Normative and resource flow consequences of local regulation in the American brewing industry, 1845–1918, *Administrative Science Quarterly, 43*(4): 905–935.

11. Warren (1997).

12. Warren (1997). See also Melinda Warren & Kenneth Chilton (1989), *The regulatory legacy of the Reagan revolution* (St. Louis: Center for the Study of Business); Melinda Warren & Barry Jones (1995), *Reinventing the regulatory system: No downsizing in administration plan* (St. Louis: Center for the Study of Business); Gordon & Milakovich (1998), 392–394; and Berkley & Rouse (1997), 347–348.

13. Berkley & Rouse (1997), 398, 403–404.

14. Berkley & Rouse (1997), 405.

15. Berkley & Rouse (1997), 353–354.

16. Fesler & Kettl (1996), 354–358.

17. See Gordon & Milakovich (1998), 417–418; and James T. O'Reilly (1998), Expanding the purpose of federal records access: New private entitlement or new threat to privacy? *Administrative Law Journal, 50*(1): 371–389.

18. David Lawrence (1999), *America: The politics of diversity* (Belmont, CA: Wadsworth): 345–346.

19. Mark H. Grunewald (1998), E-FOIA and the "Mother of All Complaints": Information delivery and delay reduction, *Administrative Law Review, 50*(2): 345–369; O'Reilly (1998), 371–389.

20. Daniel Cohen (1998), S981, The Regulatory Improvement Act of 1998: The most recent attempt to develop a solution in search of a problem, *Administrative Law Journal, 50*(4): 699–721.

21. This section draws from Berkley & Rouse (1997), 347–348.

22. Berkley & Rouse (1997), 351.

23. Office of the Federal Register (1980), *The Federal Register: What it is and how to use it* (Washington, DC: U.S. Government Printing Office): 91.

24. A. Lee Fritschler & James M. Hoefler (1996), *Smoking and politics: Policymaking and the federal bureaucracy* (5th ed.) (Upper Saddle River, NJ: Prentice-Hall): 138–139.

25. Ellen Purlman (1999), Appeals court nixes California's smog-impact tax, *Governing* (December): 49.

26. Kathleen O'Brien, Ham Buchanan, & Julia Buchanan (1998), From one end of the spectrum to the other: The FCC's auction authority under the Balanced Budget Act of 1997, *Administrative Law Review, 50*(4): 771–772.

27. Jeffrey Lubbers (1998), The ABA section of administrative law and regulatory practice: From objector to protector of the APA, *Administrative Law Review, 50*(1): 157–171.

28. *U.S. Code of Federal Regulations:* 3105, 5372, 7521.

29. See, for example, Mark Hatfield (2000), INS reorganization: Separating the cops from the judges, in Lydio F. Tomasi (Ed.) (2000), *In defense of the alien* (New York: Center for Migration Studies); David Martin (2000), Expedited removal, detention and due process, in Tomasi (2000); and Robert Bach (2000), Immigration law enforcement in the United States, in Tomasi (2000).

30. Paul G. Greenlaw, John Kohl, & Robert Lee Jr. (1998), Title VII sex discrimination in the public sector in the 1990s: The courts' view, *Public Personnel Management, 27*(2): 249–268.

31. Richard J. Pierce Jr. (1998), Small is not beautiful: The case against special regulatory treatment of small firms, *Administrative Law Review, 50*(3): 537–578.

32. Thomas Becker (1998), Integrity in organizations: Beyond honesty and conscientiousness, *Academy of Management Review, 21*(1): 154–161.

33. Ralph Nader, Peter Petkas, & Kate Blackwell (Eds.) (1972), *Whistle-blowing* (New York: Bantam Books). See also George Berkley (1969), *The democratic policeman* (Boston: Beacon Press): 159–160.

34. William E. Kovacic (1998), Law, economics, and the reinvention of public administration: Using rational agreements to reduce the costs of procurement regulation and other forms of government intervention in the economy, *Administrative Law Review, 50*(1): 141–156.

35. General Accounting Office (1993), *Whistle-blower protection: Reasons for whistle-blower dissatisfaction need to be explored* (GGD-94–21) (Washington, DC: U.S. Government Printing Office); U.S. Merit Systems Protection Board (1993), *Whistle-blowing in the federal government: An update* (Washington, DC: U.S. Government Printing Office).

36. Berkley & Rouse (1997), 370–371.

37. Fesler & Kettl (1996), 375–377.

Chapter 14

1. This section is drawn from Berkley & Rouse (1997), 401–405.

2. Rosenbloom (1998), 417.

3. Eugene Bardock & Robert Kagan (1982), *Going by the book: The problems of regulatory unreasonableness* (Philadelphia: Temple University Press): Chapter 7.

4. Rosenbloom (1998), 417.

5. McConnell (1966); and Marver Bernstein (1955), *Regulating business by independent regulatory commission* (Princeton, NJ: Princeton University Press).

6. McConnell (1966), Chapter 8; and Rosenbloom (1998), 415–416.

7. Big rigs and beat-up roads, *Governing, 12*(10): 28–30.

8. Deal lets government influence TV scripts, *AP News Wire* (January 17, 2000).

9. Stanley Reigel & P. John Owen (1982), *Administrative law* (Ann Arbor, MI: Ann Arbor Science): 39–59; Berkley & Rouse (1997), 412–413; and Cornelius Kerwin (1994), *Rulemaking* (Washington, DC: Congressional Quarterly Press): 84.

10. This discussion is drawn from Berkley & Rouse (1997), 412–414.

11. Thomas Dye (1992), *Understanding public policy* (7th ed.) (Englewood Cliffs, NJ: Prentice-Hall): 27.

12. Paul Quirk (1989), The cooperative resolution of policy conflict, *American Political Science Review, 83*(3): 905–906.

13. LeMay (1994), 63–65.

14. Berkley & Rouse (1997), 385–388.

15. LeMay (1994), 81–109.
16. Berkley & Rouse (1997), 388.
17. Berkley & Rouse (1997), 388–390.
18. Rosenbloom (1998), 20–27.
19. David Folz & Jean H. Peretz (1997), Evaluating state hazardous waste reduction policy, *State and Local Government Review, 29*(3): 134–146.
20. Peter J. May (1997), State regulatory roles: Choices in the regulation of building safety, *State and Local Government Review, 29*(2): 70–80.
21. Samuel Hughes (1998), Regulatory budgeting, *Policy Sciences, 31*(4): 247–278; R. T. Meyers (1998), Regulatory budgeting: A bad idea whose time has come? *Policy Sciences, 31*(4): 371–384.
22. Meyers (1998), 274–276. See also Andrews (1998), Environmental regulation and business self-regulation, *Policy Sciences, 31*(3), 177–197; and Gormley (1998), 363–383.
23. Berkley & Rouse (1997), 385–386.
24. William Waugh Jr. (1998), Conflicting values and cultures: The management threat to university governance, *Policy Studies Review, 15*(4): 72.
25. Trust and the press, *Governing, 13*(2) (2003): 78.
26. David Elkins, Richard Bingham, & William Bowen (1996), Patterns of state economic development policy: Programmatically rich and programmatically lean policy patterns, *State and Local Government Review, 128*(3): 158–172; Deborah Markley & Kevin McNamara (1996), Local economic and state fiscal impacts of business incubators, *State and Local Government Review, 28*(1): 17–27.

Suggested Readings

Chapter 1

Adams, Guy, & Danny Balfour. (2004). *Unmasking administrative evil*. Armonk, NY: Sharpe.

Box, Richard. (2004). *Critical social theory in public administration*. Armonk, NY: Sharpe.

Box, Richard. (2004). *Public administration and society*. Armonk, NY: Sharpe.

Downs, Anthony. (1967). *Inside bureaucracy*. Boston: Little, Brown.

Frederickson, H. George, & Kevin B. Smith. (2003). *Public administration: A primer*. Boulder, CO: Westview.

Golembiewski, Robert T. (1996). The future of public administration: End of a short stay in the sun? Or a new day a-dawning? *Public Administration Review, 56:* 139–148.

Goodnow, Frank J. (1900). *Politics and administration*. New York: Macmillan.

Goodsell, Charles T. (2004). *The case for bureaucracy*. Washington, DC: Congressional Quarterly Press.

Gulick, Luther, & Lyndall Urwick (Eds.). (1937). *Papers on the science of administration*. New York: Institute of Public Administration.

Hess, Stephen, & James Pfiffner. (2002). *Organizing the presidency*. Washington, DC: Brookings Institution.

Hult, Karen, & Charles E. Walcott. (2004). *Empowering the white house*. Lawrence: University of Kansas Press.

Lipsky, Michael. (1980). *Street-level bureaucracy: Dilemmas of the individual in public service*. New York: Russell Sage Foundation.

Patterson, Bradley H. (2000). *The White House staff: Inside the West Wing and beyond*. Washington, DC: Brookings Institution.

Raadschelders, Jos. C. N. (2003). *Government: A public administration perspective*. Armonk, NY: Sharpe.

Shafritz, Jay M., & Albert C. Hyde. (1997). *Classics of public administration* (4th ed.). New York: Harcourt Brace.

Taylor, Frederick. (1911). *The principles of scientific management*. New York: Harper. (Reprinted by Norton, 1967.)

Waldo, Dwight. (1948). *The administrative state: A study of the political theory of American public administration*. New York: Ronald Press.

Waldo, Dwight. (1968). Public administration. In Marian D. Irish (Ed.), *Political science: Advance of the discipline*. Englewood Cliffs, NJ: Prentice-Hall.

Weber, Max. (1964). In A. M. Henderson & Talcott Parsons (Trans. & Ed.), *Theory of social and economic organization*. New York: Oxford University Press.

White, Leonard. (1948). *The Federalists: A study in administrative history, 1789–1801*. New York: Free Press.

Chapter 2

Berry, Jeffrey. (1989). *The interest group society* (2nd ed.). Glenview, IL: Scott, Foresman.

Brewster, Lawrence, & Michael Brown. (1998). *The public agenda: Issues in American politics* (4th ed.). New York: St. Martin's Press.

Cochran, Clarke E., et al. (1999). *American public policy: An introduction* (6th ed.). New York: St. Martin's Press.

Commoner, Barry. (1971). *The closing circle*. New York: Knopf.

Conway, M. M. (2002). *Political participation in the United States*. Washington, DC: Congressional Quarterly Press.

Durant, Robert F., Daniel Fiorino, & Rosemary O'Leary (Eds.). (2004). *Environmental governance reconsidered*. Cambridge, MA: MIT Press.

Easton, David. (1953). *The political system*. New York: Knopf.

Edwards, David V., & Alessandra Lippuci. (1998). *Practicing American politics*. New York: Worth.

Guerrero, Andrea. (2002). *Silence at Boalt Hall: The dismantling of affirmative action*. Berkeley: University of California Press.

Hill, K. A., & J. E. Hughes. (1998). *Cyberpolitics: Citizen activism in the age of the Internet*. Lanham, MD: Rowman & Littlefield.

Hill, Michael, & Peter L. Hupe. (2002). *Implementing public policy*. Thousand Oaks, CA: Sage.

Hrebener, Robert, & Ruth Scott. (1990). *Interest group politics in America* (2nd ed.). Englewood Cliffs, NJ: Prentice-Hall.

Latham, Earl. (1952). *The group basis of politics*. Ithaca, NY: Cornell University Press.

Lawson, Kay (Ed.). (1981). *Political parties and linkage: A comparative perspective*. New Haven, CT: Yale University Press.

Rice, Mitchell F. (Ed.). (2004). *Diversity and public administration*. Armonk, NY: Sharpe.

Rourke, Francis E. (1969). *Bureaucracy, politics, and public policy*. Boston: Little, Brown.

Salisbury, Robert, et al. (1992). Triangles, networks, and hollow cores: The complex geometry of Washington interest representation. In Mark Petracca (Ed.), *The politics of interests*. Boulder, CO: Westview.

Thobaken, Robert G., Donna M. Schlagheck, & Charles Funderburk. (1995). *Issues in American political life* (2nd ed.). Englewood Cliffs, NJ: Prentice-Hall.

Truman, David B. (1951). *The governmental process*. New York: Knopf.

Vig, Norman J., & Michael Kraft (Eds.). (1990). *Environmental policy in the 1990s*. Washington, DC: Congressional Quarterly Press.

Chapter 3

Allison, Graham. (1971). *The essence of decision*. Boston: Little, Brown.

Bendor, Jonathan, et al. (1987). Stacking the deck: Bureaucratic mission and policy design. *American Political Science Review, 81*(3): 873–896.

Carroll, James D. (1975). Service, knowledge and choice: The future as post-industrial administration. *Public Administration Review, 35:* 578.

Cooper, Phillip, et al. (1998). *Public administration for the twenty-first century* (pp. 252–259). Fort Worth: Harcourt Brace.

Douglas, Mary. (1986). *How institutions think*. Syracuse, NY: Syracuse University Press.

Downs, Anthony. (1967). *Inside bureaucracy*. Boston: Little, Brown.

Gore, Albert. (1993). *From red tape to results: Creating a government that works better and costs less*. Report of the National Performance Review. Washington, DC: U.S. Government Printing Office.

Gulick, Luther, & Lyndall Urwick (Eds.). (1937). *Papers on the science of administration*. New York: Institute of Public Administration.

Howitt, Arnold M., & Robyn Pangi (Eds.). (2003). *Countering terrorism*. Cambridge, MA: MIT Press.

Janis, Irving L. (1972). *Victims of groupthink*. Boston: Houghton Mifflin.

Kaufman, Herbert. (1969). Administrative decentralization and political power. *Public Administration Review, 29:* 3–15.

Kowert, Paul A. (2002). *Groupthink or deadlock: When do leaders learn from their advisors?* Albany: State University of New York Press.

LeMay, Michael. (1994). *Anatomy of a public policy* (pp. 71–79). New York: Praeger.

Osborne, David, & Ted Gaebler. (1992). *Reinventing government*. Reading, MA: Addison-Wesley.

Ott, J. Steven. (1989). *The organizational culture*. Pacific Grove, CA: Brooks/Cole.

Porter, David O., & Eugene A. Olson. (1976). Some critical issues in government centralization and decentralization. *Public Administration Review, 36*(1): 72–84.

Schein, Elgar H. (1985). *Organizational culture and leadership*. San Francisco: Jossey-Bass.

Simon, Herbert A. (1946). The proverbs of administration. *Public Administration Review, 6:* 53–67.

Trice, Harrison M., & Janice M. Beyer. (1993). *The cultures of work organizations*. Englewood Cliffs, NJ: Prentice-Hall.

Chapter 4

Anton, Thomas. (1989). *American federalism and public policy: How the system works*. Philadelphia: Temple University Press.

Elazar, Daniel. (1984). *American federalism: A view from the states* (3rd ed.). New York: Harper & Row.

Handler, Joel, & Yaheskel Hasenfeld. (1997). *We the poor people: Work, poverty and welfare*. New Haven, CT: Yale University Press.

Jones, Benjamin J., & Deborah Reuter. (1992). Interstate compacts and agreements. In *The book of the states, 1991–1992*. Lexington, KY: Council of State Governments.

Kettl, Donald F. (1987). *The regulation of American federalism*. Baltimore: Johns Hopkins University Press.

Nathan, Richard P., & Thomas L. Gais. (2000). *Implementing the Personal Responsibility Act of 1996: A first look*. New York: Rockefeller Institute Press.

Osborne, David, & Ted Gaebler. (1992). *Reinventing government*. Reading, MA: Addison-Wesley.

Ostrom, Vincent. (1991). *The meaning of American federalism: Constituting a self-governing society*. San Francisco: ICS Press.

O'Toole, Laurence J. (Ed.). (1993). *American intergovernmental relations: Foundations, perspectives, and issues* (2nd ed.). Washington, DC: Congressional Quarterly Press.

Peterson, Paul. (1995). *The price of federalism*. Washington, DC: Brookings Institution.

Rivlin, Alice. (1992). *Reviving the American dream*. Washington, DC: Brookings Institution.

Sjoquist, David S. (Ed.). (2003). *State and local finances under pressure*. Northampton, MA: Edward Elgar.

Thomas, Craig W. (2003). *Bureaucratic landscapes: Interagency cooperation and the preservation of biodiversity*. Cambridge, MA: MIT Press.

U.S. Advisory Commission on Intergovernmental Relations. (1972). *Multistate regionalism*. Washington, DC: U.S. Government Printing Office.

U.S. Advisory Commission on Intergovernmental Relations. (1988). *Significant features of fiscal federalism, 1988* (Vols. 1–2). Washington, DC: U.S. Government Printing Office.

Wager, Linda. (1993). A declaration of war: Local governments are tired of picking up the tab for state programs. *State Government News, 36:* 18–22.

Walker, David. (1995). *The rebirth of federalism*. Chatham, NJ: Chatham House.

Wright, Deil S. (1990). Federalism, intergovernmental relations, and intergovernmental management: Historical reflections and conceptual comparisons. *Public Administration Review, 60*(5): 168–178.

Zimmerman, Joseph. (1992). *Contemporary American federalism*. New York: Praeger.

Zimmerman, Joseph. (2002). *Interstate cooperation: Compacts and administrative agreements*. Westport, CT: Praeger.

Chapter 5

Argyris, Chris. (1957). *Personality and organization*. New York: McGraw-Hill.

Arnold, Peri. (1986). *Making the managerial presidency*. Princeton, NJ: Princeton University Press.

Barzelay, Michael. (1992). *Breaking through bureaucracy: A new vision for managing government*. Berkeley: University of California Press.

Barzelay, Michael. (2000). *The new public management: Improving research and policy dialogue*. Berkeley: University of California Press.

Bernard, Chester. (1938). *The functions of the executive*. Cambridge, MA: Harvard University Press.

Boston, Jonathan, et al. (1996). *Public management: The New Zealand model*. Auckland: Oxford University Press.

Drucker, Peter F. (1950). *The new society: The anatomy of the industrial order*. New York: Harper.

Easton, David. (1979). *A framework for political analysis* (2nd ed.). Chicago: University of Chicago Press.

Follett, Mary Parker. (1924). *Creative experience*. New York: Longmans, Green.

Frederickson, H. George. (1997). *The spirit of public administration*. San Francisco: Jossey-Bass.

Gerth, H. H., & C. Wright Mills (Trans. & Ed.). (1946). *From Max Weber: Essays in sociology*. New York: Oxford University Press.

Golembiewski, Robert T. (1985). *Humanizing public organizations*. Mt. Airy, MD: Lomond Publications.

Goodsell, Charles T. (1994). *The case for bureaucracy* (3rd ed.). Chatham, NJ: Chatham House.

Gore, Albert. (1993). *The Gore report on reinventing government.* New York: Times Books.

Gormley, William J. (1989). *Taming the bureaucracy.* Princeton, NJ: Princeton University Press.

Gulick, Luther, & Lyndall Urwick (Eds.). (1937). *Papers on the science of administration.* New York: Institute of Public Administration.

Kaplan, H. Roy, & Curt Tausky. (1977). Humanism in organizations: A critical appraisal. *Public Administration Review, 37:* 171–180.

Katz, Daniel, & Robert L. Kahn. (1978). *The social psychology of organizations* (2nd ed.). New York: Wiley.

Kettl, Donald, & J. Dilulio Jr. (Eds.). (1995). *Appraising government reform.* Washington, DC: Brookings Institution.

Likert, Rensis. (1967). *The human organization: Its management and values.* New York: McGraw-Hill.

Lindblom, Charles. (1965). *The intelligence of democracy: Decision making through mutual adjustment.* New York: Free Press.

March, James G., & Herbert A. Simon. (1958). *Organizations.* New York: Wiley.

Maslow, Abraham. (1954). *Motivation and personality.* New York: Harper & Brothers.

Mayo, Elton. (1933). *The human problems of an industrial civilization.* New York: Macmillan.

McGregor, Douglas. (1960). *The human side of enterprise.* New York: McGraw-Hill.

McKee, Clyde. (1983). *An analysis of Theory Z: How it is used in Japan's public sector.* Paper presented at the American Political Science Association Meeting, Chicago, September.

Moe, Ronald C. (2003). *Administrative renewal.* Lanham, MD: University Press of America.

Osborne, David, & Ted Gaebler. (1992). *Reinventing government.* Reading, MA: Addison-Wesley.

Osborne, David, & Peter Plastrik. (1997). *Banishing bureaucracy: The five strategies for reinventing government.* New York: Addison-Wesley.

Ouchi, William G. (1982). *Theory Z: How American business can meet the Japanese challenge.* New York: Avon Books.

Parsons, Talcott. (1956). Suggestions for a sociological approach to the theory of organizations. *Administrative Science Quarterly, 1:* 64.

Seckler-Hudson, Catheryn. (1955). *Organization and management: Theory and practice.* Washington, DC: American University Press.

Senge, Peter M. (1994). *The fifth discipline: The art and practice of the learning organization.* New York: Doubleday.

Simon, Herbert A. (1946). The proverbs of administration. *Public Administration Review, 6:* 53–67.

Simon, Herbert A. (1997). *Administrative behavior: A study in decision-making processes in administrative organizations* (4th ed.). New York: Free Press.

Stillman, Richard. (2003). *The American bureaucracy: The core of modern government.* Belmont, CA: Wadsworth.

Taylor, Frederick W. (1911). *The principles of scientific management.* New York: Harper. (Reprinted by Norton, 1967.)

Waldo, Dwight. (1948). *The administrative state: A study of the political theory of American public administration.* New York: Ronald Press.

Waldo, Dwight. (1952). Developing a theory of democratic administration. *American Political Science Review, 44.*

Weber, Max. (1946). In H. H. Gerth & C. Wright Mills (Trans. & Ed.), *From Max Weber: Essays in sociology.* New York: Oxford University Press.

Weiner, Norbert. (1948). *Cybernetics.* Cambridge, MA: MIT Press.

Chapter 6

Allison, Graham. (1971). *The essence of decision.* Boston: Little, Brown.

Butler, Stuart. (1985). *Privatizing federal spending.* New York: Universe Books.

Cohen, M. D., & J. P. Olsen. (1972). A garbage-can model of organizational choice. *Administrative Science Quarterly, 17:* 1–25.

DeHoog, Ruth Hoogland. (1984). *Contracting out for human services.* Albany: State University of New York Press.

Dror, Yeheskel. (1964). Muddling through—"science" or "inertia" in "government decision making." *Public Administration Review, 24:* 153–157.

Etzioni, Amitai. (1967). Mixed-scanning: A "third" approach to decision-making. *Public Administration Review, 27:* 385–392.

Etzioni, Amitai. (1986). Mixed scanning revisited. *Public Administration Review, 46:* 8–14.

Farber, Daniel, & Philip Frickey. (1991). *Law and public choice: A critical introduction.* Chicago: University of Chicago Press.

Frederickson, H. George, & Jocelyn Johnston (Eds.). (1999). *Public management reform and innovation.* College Station: University of Alabama Press.

Garnett, James. (1980). *Reorganizing state government: The executive branch.* Boulder, CO: Westview.

Janis, Irving L. (1972). *Victims of groupthink.* Boston: Houghton Mifflin.

Janis, Irving L., & Leon Mann. (1977). *Decision making.* New York: Free Press.

King, Cheryl, & Lisa Zanetti (Eds.). (2004). *Transformational public service: Portraits of theory in practice.* Armonk, NY: Sharpe.

Lindblom, Charles E. (1959). The science of muddling through. *Public Administration Review, 19:* 79–88.

Lindblom, Charles E. (1979). Still muddling, not yet through. *Public Administration Review, 39:* 517–526.

Lindblom, Charles E. (1980). *The policy-making process* (2nd ed.). Englewood Cliffs, NJ: Prentice-Hall.

March, James G. (1994). *A primer on decision making: How decisions happen.* New York: Free Press.

March, James G., & Johan Olsen. (1995). *Democratic governance.* New York: Free Press.

McChesney, Fred, & William Shugart II (Eds.). (1995). *The causes and consequences of anti-trust: The public choice perspective.* Chicago: University of Chicago Press.

Miles, Rufus E. (1978). The origin and meaning of Miles' law. *Public Administration Review, 38:* 399–403.

Murray, Michael. (1986). *Decisions: A comparative critique.* Marshfield, MA: Pittman.

Ostrom, Elinor, Roger Parks, & Gordon Whitaker. (1978). *Patterns in metropolitan policing.* Cambridge, MA: Ballinger.

Pfeffer, J., & H. Leblebici. (1976). The effect of uncertainty on the use of social influence in organizational decision making. *Administrative Science Quarterly, 21:* 227–245.

Pfeffer, J., & G. R. Salancik. (1974). Organizational decision making as a political process: The case of a university budget. *Administrative Science Quarterly, 19:* 135–151.

Savas, E. S. (1987). *Privatization: The key to better government.* Chatham, NJ: Chatham House.

Simon, Herbert A. (1959). Theories of decision making in economics and behavioral sciences. *American Economic Review, 49:* 253–283.

Simon, Herbert A. (1979). Rational decision making in a business organization. *American Economic Review, 69:* 493–513.

Smith, Gilbert, & David May. (1980). The artificial debate between rationalist and incrementalist models of decision making. *Policy and Politics, 8:* 147–161.

Wachtel, T. (1992). *The electronic congress: A blueprint for participatory democracy.* Pipersville, PA: Piper's Press.

Wildavsky, Aaron. (1992). *The new politics of the budgetary process* (2nd ed.). New York: Harper-Collins.

Yin, Robert, & Douglas Yates. (1975). *Street-level governments.* Lexington, MA: Lexington Books.

Zey, Maury (Ed.). (1992). *Decision making: Alternatives to rational choice models.* Newbury Park, CA: Sage.

Chapter 7

Argyris, Chris. (1957). *Personality and organization.* New York: McGraw-Hill.

Bryson, John M. (1995). *Strategic planning for public and nonprofit organizations* (2nd ed.). San Francisco: Jossey-Bass.

Deming, W. Edwards. (1986). *Out of crisis.* Cambridge, MA: MIT Press.

Drucker, Peter. (1954). *The practice of management.* New York: Harper.

Halachmi, Arie, & Geert Bouchaert (Eds.). (1995). *Public productivity through quality and strategic management*. Amsterdam: IOS Press.

Hammer, Michael, & James Champy. (1993). *Reengineering the corporation*. New York: HarperCollins.

Hyde, Albert C. (1992). Implications of total quality management for the public sector. *Public Productivity and Management Review, 16:* 23–76.

Juran, J. M. (1992). *Juran on quality by design*. New York: Free Press.

Nutt, Paul C., & Robert Backoff. (1992). *Strategic management of public and third sector organizations*. San Francisco: Jossey-Bass.

Osborne, David, & Ted Gaebler. (1992). *Reinventing government*. Reading, MA: Addison-Wesley.

Pollitt, Christopher. (1993). *Managerialism and the public services* (2nd ed.). Cambridge, MA: Blackwell Business.

Rainey, Hal G. (1996). *Understanding and managing public organizations* (2nd ed.). San Francisco: Jossey-Bass.

Russell, Gregory, & Robert Waste. (1998). The limits of reinventing government. *American Review of Public Administration, 28*(4): 325–346.

Sarbaugh-Thompson, Marjorie. (1998). Change from below: Integrating bottom-up entrepreneurship into a program development framework. *American Review of Public Administration, 28*(1): 3–25.

Snow, C. P. (1961). *Science and government*. Cambridge, MA: Harvard University Press.

Walters, Jonathan. (1992). The cult of total quality. *Governing, 5:* 38–42.

Chapter 8

Allison, Graham. (1971). *The essence of decision*. Boston: Little, Brown.

Bryner, Gary. (1998). *Politics and public morality: The great American welfare reform debate*. New York: Norton.

Farmer, Brian R. (2003). *American domestic policy*. Lanham, MD: University Press of America.

Fesler, James, & Donald Kettl. (1996). *The politics of the administrative process* (2nd ed.). Chatham, NJ: Chatham House.

Gore, Albert. (1993). *From red tape to results: Creating a government that works better and costs less*. Report of the National Performance Review. Washington, DC: U.S. Government Printing Office.

Greiner, John M., et al. (1981). *Productivity and motivation: A review of state and local government initiatives*. Washington, DC: Urban Institute Press.

Henry, Nicholas. (1999). *Public administration and public affairs* (7th ed., pp. 346–368). Upper Saddle River, NJ: Prentice-Hall.

Hyde, Albert C., & Jay M. Shafritz (Eds.). (1979). *Program evaluation in the public sector*. New York: Praeger.

McNabb, David E. (2002). *Research methods in public administration and nonprofit management*. Armonk, NY: Sharpe.

Mosher, Frederick C. (1979). *The GAO: The quest for accountability in American government*. Boulder, CO: Westview.

National Performance Review. (1995). *Reinventing roundtable 2*. Washington, DC: U.S. Government Printing Office.

Rivlin, Alice. (1971). *Systematic thinking for social action*. Washington, DC: Brookings Institution.

Rosenbloom, David H. (1998). *Public administration: Understanding management, politics, and the law in the public sector* (4th ed., pp. 361–403). New York: McGraw-Hill.

Russell, E. W., & G. Macmillan. (1994). *Managing community assets in local government*. Melbourne: Montech.

Schorr, Lisbeth B. (1998). *Common purpose: Strengthening families and neighborhoods to rebuild America*. New York: Anchor Books.

U.S. Office of Management and Budget. (1994). *Primer on performance measurement*. Washington, DC: U.S. Government Printing Office.

Weiss, Carol. (1997). *Evaluation: Methods for studying programs and policies*. Englewood Cliffs, NJ: Prentice-Hall.

Wholey, Joseph S. (1983). *Evaluation and effective public management*. Boston: Little, Brown.

Wholey, Joseph S., Harry Hatry, & Kathryne E. Newcomer (Eds.). (1994). *Handbook of practical program evaluation*. San Francisco: Jossey-Bass.

Chapter 9

Ban, Carolyn, & Norma M. Riccucci (Eds.). (1997). *Public personnel management* (2nd ed.). New York: Longman.

Cayer, N. Joseph. (1986). *Public personnel administration in the United States* (2nd ed.). New York: St. Martin's Press.

Condrey, Stephen (Ed.). (1998). *Handbook of human resources management*. San Francisco: Jossey-Bass.

Conway, Margaret, Gertrude Steuernagel, & David Ahern. (1997). *Women and political participation*. Washington, DC: Congressional Quarterly Press.

Dresang, Dennis L. (1991). *Public personnel management and public policy* (2nd ed.). Boston: Little, Brown.

Felbinger, Charles R., & Wendy Haynes (Eds.). (2004). *Outstanding women in public administration*. Armonk, NY: Sharpe.

Freedman, Ann. (1993). *Patronage: An American tradition*. Chicago: Nelson-Hall.

Gore, Albert. (1993). *From red tape to results: Creating a government that works better and costs less*. Report of the National Performance Review. Washington, DC: U.S. Government Printing Office.

Hays, Steven W., & Richard C. Kearney (Eds.). (1995). *Public personnel administration: Problems and prospects* (3rd ed.). Englewood Cliffs, NJ: Prentice-Hall.

Huddleston, Mark, & William Boyer. (1996). *The higher civil service in the United States: Quest for reform*. Pittsburgh: University of Pittsburgh Press.

Ingraham, Patricia, & Carolyn Bans (Eds.). (1984). *Legislating bureaucratic change: The civil service reform act of 1978*. Albany: State University of New York Press.

Ingraham, Patricia, & Barbara Romzek (Eds.). (1994). *Rethinking public personnel systems*. San Francisco: Jossey-Bass.

Ingraham, Patricia, & David Rosenbloom (Eds.). (1992). *The promise and paradox of civil service reform*. Pittsburgh: University of Pittsburgh Press.

Jones, Lawrence, & Fred Thompson. (1999). *Public management: Institutional renewal for the 21st century*. Sanford, CT: JAI Press.

Kearney, Richard C. (1992). *Labor relations in the public sector* (2nd ed.). New York: Dekker.

Kettl, Donald F. (1994). *Reinventing government? Appraising the National Performance Review*. Washington, DC: Brookings Institution.

Lane, Larry M. (1994). Public sector performance management. *Review of Public Personnel Administration, 14*: 27.

Perry, James, & Ann Marie Thomson. (2004). *Civil service: What difference does it make?* Armonk, NY: Sharpe.

Peters, Guy, & Jon Pierre (Eds.). (2003). *Handbook of public administration*. Thousand Oaks, CA: Sage.

Rabin, Jack, et al. (Eds.). (1994). *Handbook of public sector labor relations*. New York: Dekker.

Seldon, Sally C. (1997). *The promise of representative bureaucracy: Diversity and responsiveness in a government agency*. Armonk, NY: Sharpe.

Shafritz, Jay, et al. (1992). *Personnel management in government* (4th ed.). New York: Dekker.

Sterett, Susan M. (2003). *Public pensions: Gender and civil service in the states, 1850–1937*. Ithaca, NY: Cornell University Press.

Stivers, Camilla. (2002). *Gender images in public administration* (2nd ed.). Thousand Oaks, CA: Sage.

Thompson, Frank J. (Ed.). (1990). *Classics of public personnel policy* (2nd ed.). Oak Park, IL: Moore.

Tompkins, Jonathan. (1995). *Human resource management in government*. New York: HarperCollins.

U.S. Merit Systems Protection Board. (1998). *The changing federal workplace: Employee perspectives*. Washington, DC: U.S. Government Printing Office.

Chapter 10

Bardach, Eugene. (1998). *Managerial craftsmanship*. Washington, DC: Brookings Institution.

Bass, B. M. (1985). *Leadership and performance beyond expectations*. New York: Free Press.

Bass, B. M., & B. J. Avolio. (1994). *Improving organizational effectiveness through transformational leadership.* Thousand Oaks, CA: Sage.

Bass, B. M., & B. J. Avolio. (1997). *Full range of leadership.* Palo Alto, CA: Mind Garden.

Bennis, W. G., & B. Nanus. (1982). *Leaders: The strategies for taking charge.* New York: Harper & Row.

Borins, Sandford. (1998). *Innovating with integrity: How local heroes are transforming American government.* Washington, DC: Georgetown University Press.

Commission on Public Service Task Force Reports (Volker Commission). (1990). *Leadership for America: Rebuilding the public service.* Lexington, MA: Lexington Books.

Conner, Daryl R. (1998). *Leading at the edge of chaos: How to create a nimble organization.* New York: Wiley.

De Leon, Linda, & Robert Denhardt. (2000). The political theory of reinvention. *Public Administration Review, 60*(2): 89–97.

Doig, Jameson W., & Ervin C. Hargrove (Eds.). (1987). *Leadership and innovation: A biographical perspective on entrepreneurs in government.* Baltimore: Johns Hopkins University Press.

Drucker, Peter. (1967). *The effective executive.* New York: Harper & Row.

Edwards, George C., III, & Stephen J. Wayne. (1994). *Presidential leadership: Politics and policymaking* (3rd ed.). New York: St. Martin's Press.

Ellis, Richard, & Aaron Wildavsky. (1989). *Dilemmas of presidential leadership: From Washington through Lincoln.* New Brunswick, NJ: Transaction.

Fielder, Fred E. (1967). *A theory of leadership effectiveness.* New York: McGraw-Hill.

Fielder, Fred E., M. M. Chemers, & L. Mahar. (1976). *Improving leadership effectiveness: The leader match concept.* New York: Wiley.

Gellia, Zui D. (2001). Social work perceptions of transformational and transactional leadership in health care. *Social Work Research, 25*(1): 17–31.

Greenstein, Fred I. (2000). *The presidential difference: Leadership style from FDR to Clinton.* New York: Free Press.

Hunt, James G., et al. (Eds.). (1988). *Emerging leadership vistas.* Lexington, MA: Heath.

Johnson, Craig E. (2004). *Meeting the ethical challenges of leadership.* Thousand Oaks, CA: Sage.

Joiner, Charles W. (1987). *Leadership for change.* Cambridge, MA: Ballinger.

Kayyem, Juliette, & Robyn Pangi (Eds.). (2003). *The first to arrive: The state and local response to terrorism.* Cambridge, MA: MIT Press.

Kernell, Samuel. (1997). *Going public: New strategies of presidential leadership* (3rd ed.). Washington, DC: Congressional Quarterly Press.

Levin, Martin, & Mary Sanger. (1994). *Making government work: How entrepreneurial executives turn bright ideas into real results.* San Francisco: Jossey-Bass.

Locke, Edwin. (1991). *The essence of leadership.* Lexington, MA: Lexington Books.

McGregor, Douglas. (1966). *Leadership and motivation.* Cambridge, MA: MIT Press.

McGregor, Douglas. (1985). *The theory of human enterprise.* New York: McGraw-Hill.

National Academy of Public Administration. (1985). *Leadership in jeopardy: The fraying of the presidential appointment system.* Washington, DC: Author.

Neustadt, Richard. (1991). *Presidential power and the modern presidents.* New York: Free Press.

Pfiffner, James P. (Ed.). (1991). *The managerial presidency.* Pacific Grove, CA: Brooks/Cole.

Radin, Beryl A. (2002). *The accountable juggler: The art of leadership in a federal agency.* Washington, DC: Congressional Quarterly Press.

Riccucci, Norma M. (1995). *Unsung heroes: Federal execucrats making a difference.* Washington, DC: Georgetown University Press.

Rogers, Everett M. (1995). *Diffusion of innovations* (4th ed.). New York: Free Press.

Rosenthal, Alan. (1990). *Governors and legislatures: Contending powers.* Washington, DC: Congressional Quarterly Press.

Sims, Ronald, & Scott A. Quartro (Eds.). (2004). *Leadership: Succeeding in private, public, and not-for-profit sectors.* Armonk, NY: Sharpe.

Stogdill, Ralph M. (1974). *Handbook of leadership: A study of theory and research.* New York: Free Press.

Svara, J. H. (1990). *Official leadership in the city: Patterns of conflict and cooperation.* New York: Oxford University Press.

Tannenbaum, Robert J., & Warren H. Schmidt. (1973). How to choose a leadership pattern. *Harvard Business Review, 51:* 162–175.

Terry, Larry D. (1995). *Leadership in public bureaucracies.* Thousand Oaks, CA: Sage.

Van Wart, Montgomery. (2005). *Dynamics of leadership in public service: Theory and practice.* Armonk, NY: Sharpe.

Wildavsky, Aaron. (1991). *The beleaguered presidency.* New Brunswick, NJ: Transaction.

Wills, Garry. (1994). What makes a good leader? *Atlantic Monthly, 273*(4): 63–80.

Chapter 11

Argyris, Chris. (1957). *Personality and organization.* New York: McGraw-Hill.

Bowen, James, & Zi-Lei Qiu. (1992). Satisficing when buying information. *Organizational Behavior and Human Decision Processes, 51*(1): 471–481.

Clampitt, Phillip G. (1991). *Communicating for managerial effectiveness.* Newbury Park, CA: Sage.

Downs, Anthony. (1967). *Inside bureaucracy.* Boston: Little, Brown.

Drucker, Peter. (1967). *The effective executive.* New York: Harper & Row.

Feldman, Martha S., & James G. March. (1981). Information in organizations as signal and symbol. *Administrative Science Quarterly, 26:* 171–186.

Ferguson, Sherry Deveraux, & Stewart Ferguson. (1988). *Organizational communication* (2nd ed.). New Brunswick, NJ: Transaction.

Gibson, Jane W., & Richard M. Hodgetts. (1991). *Organizational communication: A managerial perspective* (2nd ed.). New York: HarperCollins.

Katz, Daniel, & Robert L. Kahn. (1978). *The social psychology of organizations* (2nd ed.). New York: Wiley.

Kaufman, Herbert. (1973). *Administrative feedback: Monitoring subordinates behavior.* Washington, DC: Brookings Institution.

Klauss, Rudi. (1982). *Interpersonal communications in organizations.* New York: Academic Press.

Levin, Marc A. (1991). The information-seeking behavior of local government officials. *American Review of Public Administration, 21:* 271–286.

Lewis, Phillip V. (1980). *Organizational communication: The essence of effective management* (2nd ed.). Columbus, OH: Grid Publishing.

Lilenthal, David. E. (1967). *Management: A humanist art.* New York: Columbia University Press.

McGregor, Douglas. (1966). *Leadership and motivation.* Cambridge, MA: MIT Press.

McLaughlin, Ted J. (1964). *Communication.* Columbus, OH: Merrill.

Moonman, Eric. (1970). *Communication in an expanding organization.* London: Tavistock.

Munter, Mary. (1997). *Guide to managerial communication.* Upper Saddle River, NJ: Prentice-Hall.

Parkinson, C. Northcote, & Nigel Rowe. (1978). *Communicate: Parkinson's formula for business survival.* Englewood Cliffs, NJ: Prentice-Hall.

Putman, Linda, & Michael Paconowsky. (1983). *Communication and organization.* Beverly Hills, CA: Sage.

Rogers, Everett, & Rekha Agarwala-Rogers. (1976). *Communication in organizations* (pp. 90–95). New York: Free Press.

Schneider, Arnold, William C. Donagly, & Pamela J. Newman. (1975). *Organizational communication.* New York: McGraw-Hill.

Scott, William P. (1986). *The selling of communication.* New York: Nichols.

Simon, Herbert A. (1997). *Administrative behavior: A study in decision-making processes in administrative organizations* (4th ed.). New York: Free Press.

Thayer, Leo O. (1986). *Communication and communication systems in organization, management, and interpersonal relations.* Lanham, MD: University Press of America.

Vardaman, George T. (1968). *Managerial control through communication.* New York: Wiley.

Weinshall, Theodore D. (1979). *Managerial communication: Concepts, approaches, and techniques.* New York: Academic Press.

Chapter 12

Axelrod, Donald. (1995). *Budgeting for modern government* (2nd ed.). New York: St. Martin's Press.

Bureau of the Census. (1996). *Budget of the United States, fiscal year 1997.* Washington, DC: U.S. Government Printing Office.

Bureau of the Census. (1997). *Budget of the United States, 1997: Historical tables*. Washington, DC: U.S. Government Printing Office.

Bureau of the Census. (2003). *Statistical abstract of the United States, 2002*. Washington, DC: U.S. Government Printing Office.

Calleo, David. (1992). *The bankrupting of America: How the federal budget is impoverishing the nation*. New York: William Morrow.

Congressional Budget Office. (1994). *The economics and budget outlook, fiscal years 1995–1999*. Washington, DC: U.S. Government Printing Office.

Council of State Governments. (1998). *The book of the states, 1998–1999*. Lexington, KY: Council of State Governments.

Frederickson, H. George. (1995). Misdiagnosing the Orange County scandal. *Governing, 4:* 9.

General Accounting Office. (1987). *Budget issues: Current status and recent trends of state biennial and annual budgeting*. Washington, DC: U.S. Government Printing Office.

General Accounting Office. (1993). *Balanced budget requirements: State experiences and implications for the federal government* (AFMD-93-58). Washington, DC: U.S. Government Printing Office.

Gingrich, Newt. (1995). *To renew America*. New York: HarperCollins.

Gore, Albert. (1993). *From red tape to results: Creating a government that works better and costs less*. Report of the National Performance Review. Washington, DC: U.S. Government Printing Office.

Gosling, James J. (1997). *Budgeting politics in American government* (2nd ed.). New York: Garland Press.

Governing. (1998). *State and local sourcebook, 1998* (supplement).

Heilbroner, Robert, & Peter Bernstein. (1989). *The debt and the deficit: False alarms, real possibilities*. New York: Norton.

Hyde, Albert. (1992). *Government budgeting: Theory, process, politics* (2nd ed.). Pacific Grove, CA: Brooks/Cole.

Kelly, Janet M., & William Rwinbark. (2003). *Performance budgeting for state and local government*. Armonk, NY: Sharpe.

Kettl, Donald. (1992). *Deficit politics: Public budgeting in institutional and historical context*. New York: Macmillan.

Keynes, John M. (1964). *The general theory of employment, interest, and money*. New York: Harcourt Brace Jovanovich.

Lemov, Penelope. (1992). The decade of red ink. *Governing, 5*(11): 22–26.

Lynch, Thomas D. (1995). *Public budgeting in America* (4th ed.). Englewood Cliffs, NJ: Prentice-Hall.

Mikesell, John L. (1995). *Fiscal administration* (4th ed.). Pacific Grove, CA: Brooks/Cole.

Miranda, Rowan. (1994). Privatization and the budget maximizing bureaucrat. *Public Productivity and Management Review, 17*(4): 17–34.

National Association of Budget Officers. (1992). State balanced budget requirements: Provisions and practices. Washington, DC: Author.

Pyhrr, Peter A. (1977). The zero-base approach to government budgeting. *Public Administration Review, 37*(1): 1–8.

Raimondo, Henry J. (1993). State budgeting in the nineties. In *The state of the states* (pp. 31–49). Washington, DC: Congressional Quarterly Press.

Rauch, Jonathan. (1986). Biennial budgeting taking root. *National Journal, 27:* 2318–2319.

Roberts, Paul C. (1984). *The supply-side revolution*. Cambridge, MA: Harvard University Press.

Rubin, Irene. (2003). *Balancing the federal budget*. Washington, DC: Congressional Quarterly Press.

Savas, E. S. (1982). *Privatizing the public sector*. Chatham, NJ: Chatham House.

Schick, Allen. (1983). Incremental budgeting in a decremental age. *Policy Sciences, 16*(1): 1–26.

Schick, Allen. (1995). *The federal budget: Politics, policy, process*. Washington, DC: Brookings Institution.

Sinclair, Barbara. (1997). *Unorthodox lawmaking: New legislative processes in the U.S. Congress*. Washington, DC: Congressional Quarterly Press.

Stockman, David. (1986). *The triumph of politics*. New York: Harper & Row.

U.S. Advisory Commission on Intergovernmental Relations. (1992). *Changing public attitudes on government and taxes, 1992*. Washington, DC: U.S. Government Printing Office.

Wildavsky, Aaron. (1992). *The new politics of the budgetary process* (2nd ed.). New York: HarperCollins.

Wildavsky, Aaron. (1992). Political implications of budget reform: A retrospective. *Public Administration Review, 52:* 594–603.

Chapter 13

Alford, C. Fred. (2002). *Whistleblowers: Broken lives and organizational power*. Ithaca, NY: Cornell University Press.

Anderson, James E. (1998). The struggle to reform regulatory procedures, 1978–1998. *Policy Studies Journal, 26*(3): 482–498.

Andrews, Richard N. L. (1998). Environmental regulation and business self-regulation. *Policy Sciences, 31*(3): 177–197.

Bardoch, Eugene, & Robert Kagan. (1982). *Going by the book: The problem of regulatory unreasonableness*. Philadelphia: Temple University Press.

Brass, Daniel J., Kenneth Butterfield, & Bruce Skaggs. (1998). Relationships and unethical behavior: A social network perspective. *Academy of Management Review, 23*(1): 14–31.

Cann, Steven J. (2001). *Administrative law*. Thousand Oaks, CA: Sage.

Carter, Lief, & Christine Harrington. (1991). *Administrative law and politics*. New York: HarperCollins.

Cohen, Jeffrey E. (1992). *The politics of telecommunication regulation: The states and divestiture of AT&T*. Armonk, NY: Sharpe.

Cooper, Phillip J. (1985). Conflict or constructive tension: The changing relationship of judges and administrators. *Public Administration Review, 45*(6): 651–660.

Derthick, Martha, & Paul Quirk. (1985). *The politics of deregulation*. Washington, DC: Brookings Institution.

Dicke, Lisa A., & J. Steven Ott. (1999). Public agency accountability in human services contracting. *Public Productivity and Management Review, 22*(4): 502–516.

Dobel, J. Patrick. (1998). Judging the private lives of public officials. *Administration and Society, 30*(2): 115–142.

Gilmour, Robert S., & Laura S. Jensen. (1998). Reinventing government accountability: Public functions, privatization, and the meaning of "state action." *Public Administration Review, 58*(3): 247–258.

Gormley, William, & Steven J. Balla. (2003). *Bureaucracy and democracy: Accountability and performance*. Washington, DC: Congressional Quarterly Press.

Gormley, William T., Jr. (1998). Regulatory enforcement styles. *Political Research Quarterly, 51*(2): 363–383.

Greenlaw, Paul S., John Kohl, & Robert Lee Jr. (1998). Title VII sex discrimination in the public sector in the 1990s: The courts' view. *Public Personnel Management, 27*(2): 249–268.

Grunewald, Mark H. (1998). E-FOIA and the mother of all complaints: Information delivery and delay reduction. *Administrative Law Review, 50*(2): 345–369.

Ham, Kathleen O'Brien, & Julia C. Buchanan. (1998). From one end of the spectrum to the other: The FCC's auction authority under the Balanced Budget Act of 1997. *Administrative Law Review, 50*(4): 771–789.

Kelly, Rita M. (1998). An inclusive democratic polity, representative bureaucracies, and the new public management. *Public Administration Review, 58*(3): 201–208.

Landy, Mark K., Marc J. Roberts, & Stephen R. Thomas. (1994). *The Environmental Protection Agency: From Nixon to Clinton*. New York: Oxford University Press.

Lubbers, Jeffrey S. (1998). The ABA section of administrative law and regulatory practice—from objector to protector of the APA. *Administrative Law Review, 50*(1): 157–171.

Mashaw, Jerry L., & Richard A. Merrill. (1992). *Administrative law*. St. Paul, MN: West.

Meier, Kenneth J. (2000). *Politics and bureaucracy: Policymaking in the 4th branch of government*. Orlando, FL: Harcourt.

Melnick, R. Shep. (1983). *Regulation and the courts: The case of the Clean Air Act*. Washington, DC: Brookings Institution.

Menzel, Donald C. (1998). www.ethics.gov: Issues and challenges facing public managers. *Public Administration Review, 58*(5): 445–452.

Nader, Ralph, Peter Petkas, & Kate Blackwell (Eds.). (1972). *Whistleblowing*. New York: Bantam.

O'Reilly, James T. (1998). Expanding the purpose of federal records access: New private entitlement or new threat to privacy? *Administrative Law Review, 50*(2): 371–389.

Pierce, Richard T., Jr. (1998). Small is not beautiful: The case against special regulatory treatment of small firms. *Administrative Law Review, 50*(3): 537–578.

Posner, Barry Z., & Warren H. Schmidt. (1996). The values of business and federal government executives: More different than alike. *Public Personnel Management, 25*(3): 277–290.

Reagan, Michael D. (1987). *Regulation: The politics of policy.* Boston: Little, Brown.

Renfrow, Patty D., & David J. Houston. (1987). A comparative analysis of rulemaking provisions in state administrative procedures acts. *Policy Studies Review, 6:* 657–665.

Rinquist, Evan J. (1993). *Environmental protection at the state level: Politics and progress in controlling pollution.* Armonk, NY: Sharpe.

Rosenbloom, David, & Rosemary O'Leary. (1997). *Public administration and law* (2nd ed.). New York: Dekker.

Rosenbloom, David H., & Richard D. Schwartz (Eds.). (1994). *Handbook of regulation and administrative law.* New York: Dekker.

Shapiro, Martin. (1988). *Who guards the guardians? Judicial control of administration.* Athens: University of Georgia Press.

Simeone, Joseph J. (1992). The function, flexibility, and future of United States judges of the executive department. *Administrative Law Review, 44*(1): 159–188.

Skowronek, Stephen. (1982). *Building a new American state: The expansion of national administrative capacities, 1877–1920.* New York: Cambridge University Press.

Stoker, Robert P., & Laura Wilson. (1998). Verifying compliance: Social regulation and welfare reform. *Public Administration Review, 58*(5): 395–405.

Thomas, Craig W. (1998). Maintaining and restoring trust in government agencies and their employees. *Administration and Society, 30*(2): 166–193.

Tolchin, Susan, & Martin Tolchin. (1983). *Dismantling America: The rush to deregulate.* Boston: Houghton Mifflin.

Van Wart, Montgomery, & Evan Berman. (1999). Contemporary public sector productivity values: Narrower scope, tougher standards, and the new rules of the game. *Public Productivity and Management Review, 22*(3): 326–347.

Warren, Kenneth F. (1997). *Administrative law in the American system* (3rd ed.). Upper Saddle River, NJ: Prentice-Hall.

Warren, Melinda, & Kenneth Chilton. (1989). *The regulatory legacy of the Reagan revolution.* St. Louis: Center for the Study of Business.

Warren, Melinda, & Barry Jones. (1995). *Reinventing the regulatory system: No downsizing in administration plan.* St. Louis: Center for the Study of Business.

Woll, Peter. (1972). Administrative law in the 1970s. *Public Administration Review, 32*(5): 557–564.

Chapter 14

Administrative Procedure Act (PL 404, 60 Stat. 237, 1946, 5 U.S.C.A. 551).

Bardach, Eugene, & Robert Kagan. (1982). *Going by the book: The problems of regulatory unreasonableness.* Philadelphia: Temple University Press.

Berkley, George, & John Rouse. (1997). *The craft of public administration* (7th ed., pp. 383–431). Madison, WI: Brown & Benchmark.

Bryner, Gary. (1987). *Bureaucratic discretion: Law and policy in federal regulatory agencies.* New York: Pergamon Press.

Carter, Lief H. (1983). *Administrative law and politics: Cases and comments.* Boston: Little, Brown.

Douglas, Arnold R. (1998). The politics of reforming Social Security. *Political Science Quarterly, 113*(2): 213–240.

Eisner, Marc. (1993). *Regulatory politics in transition.* Baltimore: Johns Hopkins University Press.

Elkins, David R., Richard D. Bingham, & William M. Bowen. (1996). Patterns in state economic development policy: Programmatically rich and programmatically lean policy patterns. *State and Local Government Review, 25*(3): 158–172.

Folz, David H., & Jean H. Peretz. (1997). Evaluating state hazardous waste reduction policy. *State and Local Government Review, 29*(3): 134–146.

Friedman, Barry. (1995). *Regulation in the Reagan-Bush era*. Pittsburgh: University of Pittsburgh Press.

Gerston, Larry, Cynthia Fraleigh, & Robert Schwab. (1988). *The deregulated society*. Pacific Grove, CA: Brooks/Cole.

Gormley, William T., Jr. (1998). Regulatory enforcement styles. *Political Research Quarterly, 51*(2): 363–383.

Heffron, Florence, & Neil McFeeley. (1983). *The administrative regulatory process*. New York: Longman.

Hughes, Samuel. (1998). Regulatory budgeting. *Policy Sciences, 31*(4): 247–278.

Kearney, Richard C. (1999). Judicial performance evaluation in the states. *Public Administration Quarterly, 22*(4): 468–489.

Kelly, Rita Mae. (1998). An inclusive democratic polity, representative bureaucracies, and the new public management. *Public Administration Review, 58*(3): 201–208.

Kerwin, Cornelius. (1994). *Rulemaking*. Washington, DC: Congressional Quarterly Press.

Kovacic, William E. (1998). Law, economics, and the reinvention of public administration: Using rational agreements to reduce the cost of procurement regulation and other forms of government intervention in the economy. *Administrative Law Review, 50*(1): 141–156.

LeMay, Michael. (1994). *Anatomy of a public policy*. New York: Praeger.

Markley, Deborah M., & Kevin T. McNamara. (1996). Local economic and state fiscal impacts of business incubators. *State and Local Government Review, 28*(1): 17–27.

May, Peter J. (1997). State regulatory roles: Choices in the regulation of building safety. *State and Local Government Review, 29*(2): 70–80.

Meyers, R. T. (1998). Regulatory budgeting: A bad idea whose time has come? *Policy Sciences, 31*(4): 371–384.

O'Reilly, James T. *Administrative rule making: Structuring, opposing, and defending federal agency regulations*. New York: McGraw-Hill.

Quirk, Paul. (1989). The cooperative resolution of policy conflict. *American Political Science Review, 83*(3): 905–921.

Tramontozzi, Paul N., & Kenneth Chilton. (1987). *U.S. regulatory agencies under Reagan, 1980–1988*. St. Louis: Center for the Study of Business.

Walter, John. (1998). Can a safety net subsidy be contained? *Economic Quarterly, 84*(1): 1–20.

Waugh, William L., Jr. (1998). Conflicting values and cultures: The managerial threat to university governance. *Policy Studies Review, 15*(4): 61–73.

West, William F. (1985). *Administrative rule making: Politics and processes*. Westport, CT: Greenwood Press.

Wholey, Douglas R., & Susan M. Sanchez. (1991). The effects of regulatory tools on organizational populations. *Academy of Management Review, 16*(4): 743–767.

Bibliography

Aberbach, Joel D., Robert D. Putnam, & Bert A. Rockman. (1981). *Bureaucrats and politicians in Western democracies*. Cambridge, MA: Harvard University Press.

Ackoff, Russell, & Patrick Rivett. (1963). *A manager's guide to operations research*. New York: Wiley.

Adams, Guy B., & Danny L. Balfour. (2004). *Unmasking administrative evil*. Armonk, NY: Sharpe.

Administrative Procedures Act (PL 404, 60 Stat. 237, 1946, 5 U.S.C.A. 551).

Advisory Commission on Intergovernmental Relations. (1988). *Significant features of fiscal federalism, 1988*. Washington, DC: U.S. Government Printing Office.

Alford, C. Fred. (2002). *Whistleblowers*. Ithaca, NY: Cornell University Press.

Allison, Graham. (1971). *The essence of decision*. Boston: Little, Brown.

Allison, Graham T., Jr. (1994). Public and private management: Are they fundamentally alike in all unimportant respects? In Frederick Lane (Ed.), *Current issues in public administration* (5th ed.). New York: St. Martin's Press.

American Lawyer Media L.P. (2002). Spoils for the vanquished. *New Jersey Law Journal, 167*(1): 22.

American Prospect. (2003). Screening on the cheap. *The American Prospect, 14*(2): 6.

Anderson, James E. (1998). The struggle to reform regulatory procedures, 1978–1998. *Policy Studies Journal, 26*(3): 482–498.

Andrews, Richard N. L. (1998). Environmental regulation and business self-regulation. *Policy Sciences, 31*(3): 177–197.

Anton, Thomas. (1967). Roles and symbols in the determination of state expenditures. *Midwest Journal of Political Science, 11*(1): 27–43.

Anton, Thomas. (1989). *American federalism and public policy: How the system works*. Philadelphia: Temple University Press.

AP News Wire (2000, January 17). Deal lets government influence tv scripts.

Appleby, Paul. (1945). *Big democracy*. New York: Knopf.

Argyris, Chris. (1957). *Personality and organization*. New York: McGraw-Hill.

Argyris, Chris. (1962). *Interpersonal confidence and organizational effectiveness*. Homewood, IL: Dorsey Press.

Argyris, Chris. (1990). *Integrating the individual and the organization*. New Brunswick, NJ: Transaction.

Arnold, Peri. (1986). *Making the managerial presidency*. Princeton, NJ: Princeton University Press.

Axelrod, Donald. (1995). *Budgeting for modern government* (2nd ed.). New York: St. Martin's Press.

Bach, Robert. (2000). Immigration law enforcement in the United States. In Lydio F. Tomasi (Ed.), *In defense of the alien*. New York: Center for Migration Studies.

Bajjaly, Stephen T. (1998). Strategic information systems planning for the public sector. *American Review of Public Administration, 28*(1): 75–85.

Balk, Walter. (1996). *Managerial reform and professional empowerment in the public sector*. New York: Quorum Books.

Ban, Carolyn, & Patricia Ingraham. (1988). Retaining quality federal employees: Life after PACE. *Public Administration Review, 48*: 708–718.

Ban, Carolyn, & Norma M. Riccucci (Eds.). (1997). *Public personnel management* (2nd ed.). New York: Longman.

Barber, David. (1992). *The presidential character* (4th ed.). Upper Saddle River, NJ: Prentice-Hall.

Bardach, Eugene. (1998). *Managerial craftsmanship*. Washington, DC: Brookings Institution.

Bardach, Eugene, & Robert Kagan. (1982). *Going by the book: The problems of regulatory unreasonableness*. Philadelphia: Temple University Press.

Bardes, Barbara, Mack Shelly II, & Steffen W. Schmidt. (1998). *American government and politics today: The essentials*. Belmont, CA: Wadsworth.

Barzelay, Michael. (1992). *Breaking through bureaucracy: A new vision for managing in government*. Berkeley: University of California Press.

Barzelay, Michael. (2000). *The new public management*. Berkeley: University of California Press.

Bass, B. M. (1985). *Leadership and performance beyond expectations*. New York: Free Press.

Bass, B. M., & B. J. Avolio. (1994). *Improving organizational effectiveness through transformational leadership*. Thousand Oaks, CA: Sage.

Bass, B. M., & B. J. Avolio. (1997). *Full range of leadership*. Palo Alto, CA: Mind Garden.

Bass, Charles. (2000). U.S. Congress, House Committee on Rules. *Biennial budgeting: A tool for improving government fiscal management and oversight*. http://www.house.gov/rules/rules-trans09.htm. 106th Congress, 2nd Session. Accessed March 30.

Bass, Daniel J., Kenneth Butterfield, & Bruce Skaggs. (1998). Relationships and unethical behavior: A social network perspective. *Academy of Management Review, 23*(1): 16.

Beatty, Richard W., & Craig E. Schneier. (1981). *Personnel administration: An experiential skillbuilding approach* (2nd ed.). Reading, MA: Addison-Wesley.

Becker, Thomas E. (1998). Integrity in organizations: Beyond honesty and conscientiousness. *Academy of Management Review, 23*(1): 154–161.

Behn, Robert. (1995). Linking goals to change. Paper presented at the Third National Public Management Research Conference, Lawrence, Kansas, October 5–7.

Behn, Robert. (1998). What right do public managers have to lead? *Public Administration Review, 58*(3): 209–224.

Bendor, Jonathan, et al. (1987). Stacking the deck: Bureaucratic mission and policy design. *American Political Science Review, 81*(3): 873–896.

Bennis, W. G., & B. Nanus. (1982). *Leaders: The strategy for taking charge*. New York: Harper & Row.

Bentley, Arthur F. (1908). *The process of government*. Cambridge, MA: Belknap Press.

Berkley, George. (1969). *The democratic policeman*. Boston: Beacon Press.

Berkley, George, & Douglas Fox. (1978). *80,000 governments*. Boston: Allyn & Bacon.

Berkley, George, & John Rouse. (1997). *The craft of public administration* (7th ed.). Madison, WI: Brown & Benchmark.

Berman, Evan, & Jonathan West. (1995). Municipal commitment to TQM: A survey of recent progress. *Public Administration Review, 55*: 57–66.

Berman, Evan, Michael Milakovich, & Jonathan West. (1994). Implementing TQM in the states. *Spectrum, 67*: 6–13.

Berman, Larry (Ed.). (1990). *Looking back on the Reagan presidency*. Baltimore: Johns Hopkins University Press.

Bernard, Chester. (1938). *The functions of the executive*. Cambridge, MA: Harvard University Press.

Bernstein, Marver. (1955). *Regulating business by independent regulatory commission*. Princeton, NJ: Princeton University Press.

Berry, F. S., R. Chackerian, & B. Wechsler. (1999). Reinventing state government in Florida. In H. George Frederickson & Jocelyn Johnston (Eds.), *Public management reform and innovation: Research theory and application*. College Station: University of Alabama Press.

Berry, Jeffrey. (1989). *The interest group society* (2nd ed.). Glenview, IL: Scott, Foresman.

Best, James J. (1981). Presidential cabinet appointments: 1953–1976. *Presidential Studies Quarterly, 11*: 62–66.

Bipartisan Commission on Entitlements and Tax Reform. (1994). *Interim report to the president*. Washington, DC: U.S. Government Printing Office.

Blau, Peter. (1955). *Bureaucracy in modern society*. Chicago: University of Chicago Press.

Blau, Peter M., & Marshall W. Meyer. (1994). Why study bureaucracy? In Frederick S. Lane (Ed.), *Current issues in public administration* (5th ed.). New York: St. Martin's Press.

Blauner, Robert. (1964). *Alienation and freedom*. Chicago: University of Chicago Press.

Bohman, Lee G., & Terrence E. Deal. (1991). *Reframing organization: Artistry, choice, and leadership*. San Francisco: Jossey-Bass.

Borins, Sandford. (1998). *Innovating with integrity*. Washington, DC: Georgetown University Press.

Borins, Sanford. (2000). Loose cannons and rule breakers, or enterprising leaders? Some evidence about innovative managers. *Public Administration Review, 60*(6): 496.

Boston, Jonathan. (1994). Purchasing policy advice: The limits of contracting out. *Governance, 7:* 1–30.

Boston, Jonathan, John Martin, June Pallot, & Pat Walsh. (1996). *Public management: The New Zealand model*. Auckland: Oxford University Press.

Bowen, James, & Zi-Lei Qiu. (1992). Satisficing when buying information. *Organizational Behavior and Human Decision Processes, 51*(1): 471–481.

Bowman, Ann O' M. (2002). American federalism on the horizon. *Publius, 32*(2): 3–24.

Bowman, John. (1989). Quality circles: Promises, problems and prospects in Florida. *Public Personnel Management, 18:* 375–403.

Box, Richard C. (2004a). *Critical social theory in public administration*. Armonk, NY: Sharpe.

Box, Richard C. (2004b). *Public administration and society*. Armonk, NY: Sharpe.

Boyne, George A. (1998). The determinants of variations in local service contracting: Garbage in, garbage out? *Urban Affairs Review, 34*(1): 150–164.

Bradley, Michael. (1973). Decision-making for environmental resources management. *Journal of Environmental Management, 1:* 289–302.

Brass, Daniel J., Kenneth Butterfield, & Bruce Skaggs. (1998). Relationships and unethical behavior: A social network perspective. *Academy of Management Review, 23*(1): 14–31.

Brewster, Lawrence, & Michael Brown. (1998). *The public agenda: Issues in American politics* (4th ed.). New York: St. Martin's Press.

Brown, Curtis. (2003). Arbitration can slash legal costs. *Financial Executive, 19*(9): 64.

Brown, M. M., & J. L. Brudney. (2003). Learning organizations in the public sector? *Public Administration Review, 63*(1): 30–43.

Brownlow Committee Report. (1937). *President's committee on administrative management*. Washington, DC: U.S. Government Printing Office.

Brudney, Jeffrey, & Deil S. Wright. (2002). Revisiting administrative reform in the American states: The status of reinventing government during the 1990s. *Public Administration Review, 62*(3): 353–362.

Brudney, Jeffrey L., F. Ted Herbert, & Deil S. Wright. (2000). From organizational values to organizational roles: Examining representative bureaucracy in state administration. *Journal of Public Administration Research and Theory, 10*(3): 491–508.

Brumback, Gary B. (1996). Getting the right people ethically. *Public Personnel Management, 25*(3): 267–276.

Bryner, Gary. (1987). *Bureaucratic discretion: Law and policy in federal regulatory agencies*. New York: Pergamon Press.

Bryner, Gary. (1998). *Politics and public morality: The great American welfare reform debate*. New York: Norton.

Bryson, John M. (1995). *Strategic planning for public and nonprofit organizations* (2nd ed.). San Francisco: Jossey-Bass.

Buchanan, James, & Gordon Tullock. (1962). *The calculus of consent*. Ann Arbor: University of Michigan Press.

Buchholz, Rogene. (1988). *Public policy issues for management*. Englewood Cliffs, NJ: Prentice-Hall.

Bureau of the Census. (1996). *Budget of the United States, fiscal year 1997*. Washington, DC: U.S. Government Printing Office.

Bureau of the Census. (1997). *Budget of the United States, 1997: Historical tables*. Washington, DC: U.S. Government Printing Office.

Bureau of the Census. (2003). *Statistical abstract of the United States, 2002*. Washington, DC: U.S. Government Printing Office.

Bureau of the Census. (2004). *Statistical abstract of the United States, 2003*. Washington, DC: U.S. Government Printing Office.

Burman, Leonard E. (2003). Is the tax expenditure concept still relevant? *National Tax Journal, 56*(3): 613–628.

Butler, Stuart. (1985). *Privatizing federal spending*. New York: Universe Books.

California Department of General Services. (2004). *The executive branch of California directory*. Sacramento, CA: Author.

Calista, Donald. (2002). A critique of "reinventing government" in America: Measuring and explaining administrative reform. *Public Administration Review, 62*(3): 347–353.

Callahan, Elleta S., & Terry M. Dworkin. (2000). The state of state whistleblower protection. *American Business Law Journal, 38*(1): 99–111.

Calleo, David. (1992). *The bankrupting of America: How the federal budget is impoverishing the nation*. New York: William Morrow.

Cann, Steven J. (2001). *Administrative law*. Thousand Oaks, CA: Sage.

Carroll, James D. (1975). Service, knowledge and choice: The future as post-industrial administration. *Public Administration Review, 35*: 578.

Carroll, James D. (1995). The rhetoric of reform and political reality in the National Performance Review. *Public Administration Review, 55*(3): 302–312.

Carter, Lief, & Christine Harrington. (1991). *Administrative law and politics*. New York: HarperCollins.

Cartwright, Dorwin, & Alvin Zander (Eds.). (1968). *Group dynamics: Research and theory* (3rd ed.). New York: Harper & Row.

Cayer, N. Joseph. (1980). *Managing human resources*. New York: St. Martin's Press.

Cayer, N. Joseph. (1986). *Public personnel administration in the United States* (2nd ed.). New York: St. Martin's Press.

Chackerian, Richard. (1996). State government reorganization: 1900–1995. *Journal of Public Administration Research and Theory, 6*(1): 25–47.

Chackerian, Richard, & Paul Mavima. (2001). Comprehensive administrative reform implementation: Moving beyond single issue implementation research. *Journal of Public Administration Research and Theory, 11*(3): 353–365.

Chandler, Timothy, & Timothy A. Judge. (1998). Management chief negotiators, bargaining strategies, and the likelihood of impasse in public sector collective bargaining. *American Review of Public Administration, 28*(2): 146–165.

Chang, Lawrence. (1992). The view from Washington and the view from nowhere: Cuban Missile Crisis historiography and the epistemology of decision making. In James A. Nathan (Ed.), *The Cuban Missile Crisis revisited* (pp. 131–160). New York: St. Martin's Press.

Chang, Lisa E. (2004). *Grutter v. Bollinger et al.*: Affirmative action lessons for the private employer. *Employee Relations Law Journal, 30*(3): 3–16.

Chi, Keon S., Kelly Arnold, & Heather Perkins. (2003). Privatization in state government: Trends and issues. *Spectrum, 76*(4): 12.

Choi, Young B. (1993). *Paradigms and conventions: Uncertainty, decision-making, and entrepreneurship*. Ann Arbor: University of Michigan Press.

Churchman, C. West. (1968). *The systems approach*. New York: Dell.

Clampitt, Phillip G. (1991). *Communicating for managerial effectiveness*. Newbury Park, CA: Sage.

Clark, Harold W., & Marian Laymann. (2004). Recruitment: Tools, tips and practical applications. *Corrections Today, 66*(5): 80.

Coates, Breena. (2004). E-entrepreneurship in a disadvantaged community: Project E-Net in California. *International Journal on E-Learning, 3*(3): 25–32.

Cochran, Clarke E., et al. (1999). *American public policy: An introduction* (6th ed.). New York: St. Martin's Press.

Coe, Barbara A. (1997). How structural conflicts stymie reinvention. *Public Administration Review, 57*(2): 168–173.

Cohen, Daniel. (1998). S981, The Regulatory Improvement Act of 1998: The most recent attempt to develop a solution in search of a problem. *Administrative Law Journal, 50*(4): 699–721.

Cohen, Jeffrey E. (1992). *The politics of telecommunication regulation: The states and divestiture of AT&T*. Armonk, NY: Sharpe.

Cohen, Michael D., & James G. March. (1974). *Leadership and ambiguity: The American college president*. New York: Carnegie Foundation for the Advancement of Teaching.

Cohen, Michael D., James G. March, & J. P. Olsen. (1972). A garbage-can model of organizational choice. *Administrative Science Quarterly, 17*(1): 1–25.

Commission on Public Service Task Force Reports (Volker Commission). (1990). *Leadership for America: Rebuilding the public service*. Lexington, MA: Lexington Books.

Commoner, Barry. (1971). *The closing circle*. New York: Knopf.

Conant, James. (1993). Executive branch reorganization in the states: 1965–1991. In *The book of the states, 1992–1993* (pp. 64–74). Lexington, KY: Council of State Governments.

Conant, James. (1986). Reorganization and the bottom line. *Public Administration Review, 46:* 48–56.

Condrey, Stephen (Ed.). (1998). *Handbook of human resources management*. San Francisco: Jossey-Bass.

Congressional Budget Office. (1994). *The economics and budget outlook, fiscal years 1995–1999*. Washington, DC: U.S. Government Printing Office.

Congressional Quarterly Press. (1997). *1996 Congressional Quarterly almanac* (Vol. 52, pp. 6-17–6-18). Washington, DC: Author.

Congressional Quarterly Press. (1998). *State and local government sourcebook: 1998*. Washington, DC: Author.

Congressional Quarterly Press. (1999). *Federal regulatory directory* (5th ed.). Washington, DC: Author.

Conlan, Timothy J., & David R. Blau. (1992). Federal mandates: The record of reform and future prospects. *Intergovernmental Perspective, 18:* 7–11.

Conner, Daryl R. (1998). *Leading at the edge of chaos*. New York: Wiley.

Conway, M. M. (2002). *Political participation in the United States*. Washington, DC: Congressional Quarterly Press.

Conway, M. Margaret, Gertrude Steuernagel, & David Ahern. (1997). *Women and political participation*. Washington, DC: Congressional Quarterly Press.

Cooper, Phillip J. (1985). Conflict or constructive tension: The changing relationship of judges and administrators. *Public Administration Review, 45*(6): 651–660.

Cooper, Phillip J. (1988). *Public law and public administration* (2nd ed.). Palo Alto, CA: Mayfield.

Cooper, Phillip J., et al. (1998). *Public administration for the twenty-first century*. Fort Worth: Harcourt Brace.

Council of State Governments. (1998). *The book of the states, 1998–1999*. Lexington, KY: Author.

Craig, Barbara Hinkson, & David O'Brien. (1993). *Abortion and American politics*. Chatham, NJ: Chatham House.

Craig, John. (2002). Performance-based budgeting in a performance-based budget-cutting environment. *The Public Manager, 31*(3): 57–60.

Crupp, Frederick. (1986). The third stage of environmentalism. *Environmental Defense Fund Newsletter, 17*(3): 4.

Dahl, Robert. (1947). Science of public administration: Three problems. *Public Administration Review, 7*(11): 1–11.

Dakin, Susan. (2003). Challenging old models of knowledge and learning. *Environments, 31*(1): 93.

Deal lets government influence tv scripts, (2000), *AP News Wire*, January 17, 2000.

DeBow, Ken, & John C. Syer. (1997). *Power and politics in California*. Boston: Allyn & Bacon.

DeHoog, Ruth Hoogland. (1984). *Contracting out for human services*. Albany: State University of New York Press.

DeHoog, Ruth Hoogland, David Lowery, & William Lyons. (1990). Citizen satisfaction with local governance, *Journal of Politics, 52*(1): 807–837.

DeLeon, Linda, & Robert B. Dunhardt. (2000). The political theory of reinvention. *Public Administration Review, 60*(2): 89–97.

Deming, W. Edwards. (1986). *Out of crisis*. Cambridge, MA: MIT Press.

Deming, W. Edwards. (1993). *The new economics*. Cambridge, MA: MIT Press.

Denhardt, Robert B., & Janet V. Denhardt. (2000). The new public service: Serving rather than steering. *Public Administration Review, 60*(6): 549–559.

Derrancs, Charles. (2002). Bush invokes rare provision. *Black Issues in Higher Education, 19*(3 & 5): 10 & 8.

Derthick, Martha. (1987). America's federalism: Madison's middle ground in the 1980s. *Public Administration Review, 47:* 125–153.

Derthick, Martha, & Paul Quirk. (1985). *The politics of deregulation.* Washington, DC: Brookings Institution.

Dicke, Lisa A., & J. Steven Ott. (1999). Public agency accountability in human services contracting. *Public Productivity and Management Review, 22*(4): 502–516.

Dillon, John F. (1911). *Commentaries on the law of municipal corporations* (5th ed.). Boston: Little, Brown.

Dilulio, John J., Jr., Gerald Garvey, & Donald Kettl. (1993). *Improving government performance: An owner's manual.* Washington, DC: Brookings Institution.

Dilworth, Robert. (1996). Institutionalizing learning organizations in the public sector. *Public Productivity and Management Review, 19:* 407–421.

Dobel, J. Patrick. (1998). Judging the private lives of public officials. *Administration and Society, 30*(2): 115–142.

Dobel, J. Patrick. (2001). Paradigms, traditions, and keeping the faith. *Public Administration Review, 61*(2): 166–176.

Dodsen, Marvin E., & Thomas Garrett. (2004). Inefficient education spending in public school districts. *Contemporary Economic Policy, 22*(2): 270–281.

Doig, Jameson W., & Ervin C. Hargrove (Eds.). (1987). *Leadership and innovation: A biographical perspective on entrepreneurs in government.* Baltimore: Johns Hopkins University Press.

Dolan, Julie. (2002). The budget-minimizing bureaucrat? Empirical evidence from the Senior Executive Service. *Public Administration Review, 62*(1): 42–51.

Douglas, Arnold R. (1998). The politics of reforming Social Security. *Political Science Quarterly, 113*(2): 213–240.

Douglas, Mary. (1986). *How institutions think.* Syracuse, NY: Syracuse University Press.

Downs, Anthony. (1957). *An economic theory of democracy.* New York: Harper & Row.

Downs, Anthony. (1967). *Inside bureaucracy.* Boston: Little, Brown.

Dresang, Dennis L. (1991). *Public personnel management and public policy* (2nd ed.). Boston: Little, Brown.

Dror, Yeheskel. (1964). Muddling through—"science" or "inertia" in "government decision making." *Public Administration Review, 24:* 153–157.

Drucker, Peter F. (1950). *The new society: The anatomy of the industrial order.* New York: Harper.

Drucker, Peter F. (1954). *The practice of management.* New York: Harper.

Drucker, Peter F. (1967). *The effective executive.* New York: Harper & Row.

Drucker, Peter F. (1988). The coming of the new organization. *Harvard Business Review, 66*(1): 4553–4558.

Drucker, Peter F. (1995). Really reinventing government. *Atlantic Monthly, 275:* 57.

Drukman, Amanda. (2004). Telecommunication reforms and deregulation. *Journal of Property Management, 69*(4): 6.

Dunlap, Riley E. (1987). Public opinion in the environment of the Reagan era. *Environment, 29:* 6–11.

Durant, Robert F., Daniel J. Fiorino, & Rosemary O'Leary (Eds.). (2004). *Environmental governance reconsidered.* Cambridge, MA: MIT Press.

Dye, Thomas. (1983). *Who's running America?* (6th ed.). Upper Saddle River, NJ: Prentice-Hall.

Dye, Thomas. (1992). *Understanding public policy* (7th ed.). Englewood Cliffs, NJ: Prentice-Hall.

Dye, Thomas. (1995). *Understanding public policy* (8th ed.). Upper Saddle River, NJ: Prentice-Hall.

Dye, Thomas. (1997). *Politics in states and communities* (9th ed.). Upper Saddle River, NJ: Prentice-Hall.

Dye, Thomas. (1999). *Politics in America* (3rd ed.). Upper Saddle River, NJ: Prentice-Hall.

Easton, David. (1953). *The political system.* New York: Knopf.

Easton, David. (1979). *A framework for political analysis* (2nd ed.). Chicago: University of Chicago Press.

Economist, The. (1998, February 21). Valley of the damned: Water policy, pp. 26–29.

Edwards, David V., & Alessandra Lippuci. (1998). *Practicing American politics.* New York: Worth.

Edwards, George C. (1986). The two presidencies: A reevaluation. *American Politics Quarterly,* *14*(3): 247–263.

Edwards, George C., & Stephen J. Wayne. (1994). *Presidential leadership: Politics and policymaking* (3rd ed.). New York: St. Martin's Press.

Edwards, George C., Martin Wattenberg, & Robert Lineberry. (1998). *Government in America* (8th ed.). New York: Longman.

Ehrenhalt, Alan. (1995). Mandates from above. *Governing, 9:* 38.

Eisner, Marc. (1993). *Regulatory politics in transition.* Baltimore: Johns Hopkins University Press.

Elazar, Daniel. (1962). *The American partnership: Intergovernmental cooperation in the 19th-century United States.* Chicago: University of Chicago Press.

Elazar, Daniel. (1984). *American federalism: A view from the states* (3rd ed.). New York: Harper & Row.

Elkins, David R., Richard D. Bingham, & William M. Bowen. (1996). Patterns in state economic development policy: Programmatically rich and programmatically lean policy patterns. *State and Local Government Review, 25*(3): 158–172.

Ellis, Richard, & Aaron Wildavsky. (1989). *Dilemmas of presidential leadership: From Washington through Lincoln.* New Brunswick, NJ: Transaction.

Etzioni, Amitai. (1967). Mixed-scanning: A "third" approach to decision-making. *Public Administration Review, 27:* 385–392.

Etzioni, Amitai. (1986). Mixed scanning revisited. *Public Administration Review, 46:* 8–14.

Farber, Daniel A., & Philip P. Frickey. (1991). *Law and public choice: A critical introduction.* Chicago: University of Chicago Press.

Farmer, Brian R. (2003). *American domestic policy.* Lanham, MD: University of America Press.

Farmer, David J. (2005). *To kill the king: Post-traditional democratic governance and bureaucracy.* Armonk, NY: Sharpe.

Feldbinger, Claire R., & Wendy A. Haynes (Eds.). (2004). *Outstanding women in public administration.* Armonk, NY: Sharpe.

Feldman, Martha S., & James G. March. (1981). Information in organizations as signal and symbol. *Administrative Science Quarterly, 26:* 171–186.

Ferguson, Sherry Deveraux, & Stewart Ferguson. (1988). *Organizational communication* (2nd ed.). New Brunswick, NJ: Transaction.

Ferris, James, & Elizabeth Graddy. (1991). Production costs, transaction costs, and local government contractor choice. *Economics Inquiry, 29:* 431–554.

Fesler, James, & Donald Kettl. (1996). *The politics of the administrative process* (2nd ed.). Chatham, NJ: Chatham House.

Fiedler, Fred. (1967). *A theory of leadership.* New York: McGraw-Hill.

Fiedler, Fred, M. M. Cherners, & L. Mahar. (1976). *Improving leadership effectiveness: The leader match concept.* New York: Wiley.

Fiegenbaum, Armand V. (1983). *Total quality control.* New York: McGraw-Hill.

Follett, Mary Parker. (1918). *The new state group organization—the solution to popular government.* New York: Longmans, Green.

Follett, Mary Parker. (1924). *Creative experience.* New York: Longmans, Green.

Folz, David H., & Jean H. Peretz. (1997). Evaluating state hazardous waste reduction policy. *State and Local Government Review, 29*(3): 134–146.

Forest Products Journal. Ergonomic regulation set aside. *Forest Products Journal, 51*(6): 10.

Frederickson, H. George. (1996). Comparing the reinventing government movement with the new public administration. *Public Administration Review, 56*(3): 263–270.

Frederickson, H. George. (1997). *The spirit of public administration.* San Francisco: Jossey-Bass.

Frederickson, H. George, & Jocelyn Johnston (Eds.). (1999). *Public management reform and innovation: Research, theory and application.* College Station: University of Alabama Press.

Frederickson, H. George, & Kevin B. Smith. (2003). *Public administration: A primer.* Boulder, CO: Westview.

Freedman, Ann. (1993). *Patronage: An American tradition.* Chicago: Nelson-Hall.

Freund, Julien. (1969). *The sociology of Max Weber.* New York: Vintage Books.

Friedman, Barry. (1995). *Regulation in the Reagan–Bush era*. Pittsburgh: University of Pittsburgh Press.

Fritschler, A. Lee, & James M. Hoefler. (1996). *Smoking and politics: Policymaking and the federal bureaucracy* (5th ed.). Upper Saddle River, NJ: Prentice-Hall.

Fukuhara, Rackham S. (1977). Productivity improvement in cities. In *The municipal yearbook, 1977* (pp. 193–200). Washington, DC: ICMA.

Gallagher, Mary. (2002). Judge upholds Hatch Act prohibition. *New Jersey Law Journal, 169*(12): 7.

Garnett, James. (1980). *Reorganizing state government: The executive branch*. Boulder, CO: Westview.

Gellis, Zui D. (2001). Social work perceptions of transformational and transactional leadership in health care. *Social Work Research, 25*(1): 17–31.

General Accounting Office. (1987). *Budget issues: Current status and recent trends of state biennial and annual budgeting*. Washington, DC: U.S. Government Printing Office.

General Accounting Office. (1992). *Organizational culture: Techniques companies use to perpetuate or change beliefs and values*. Washington, DC: U.S. Government Printing Office.

General Accounting Office. (1993). *Balanced budget requirements: State experiences and implications for the federal government* (AFMD-93-58). Washington, DC: U.S. Government Printing Office.

General Accounting Office. (1993). *Whistle-blower protection: Lessons for whistle-blower dissatisfaction need to be explored* (GGD-94-21). Washington, DC: U.S. Government Printing Office.

General Accounting Office. (1997). *The Government Performance and Results Act: 1997 governmentwide implementation will be uneven* (GAO/GGD-97-109). Washington, DC: U.S. Government Printing Office.

General Accounting Office. (2002). *Homeland security: Information sharing activities face continued management challenges* (GAO-02-1122T). Washington, DC: U.S. Government Printing Office.

Gerston, Larry, Cynthia Fraleigh, & Robert Schwab. (1988). *The deregulated society*. Pacific Grove, CA: Brooks/Cole.

Gerth, H. H., & C. Wright Mills (Trans. & Ed.). (1946). *From Max Weber: Essays in sociology*. New York: Oxford University Press.

Gerwin, D. (1969). A process model of budgeting in a public school system. *Management Science, 15:* 338–361.

Gibson, Jane W., & Richard M. Hodgetts. (1991). *Organizational communication: A managerial perspective* (2nd ed.). New York: HarperCollins.

Gilmour, Robert S., & Laura S. Jensen. (1998). Reinventing government accountability: Public functions, privatization, and the meaning of "state action." *Public Administration Review, 58*(3): 247–258.

Gingrich, Newt. (1995). *To renew America*. New York: HarperCollins.

Ginsberg, Benjamin, Theodore Lowi, & Margaret Weir. (1999). *We the people* (2nd ed.). New York: Norton.

Golembiewski, Robert T. (1985). *Humanizing public organizations*. Mt. Airy, MD: Lomond Publications.

Golembiewski, Robert T. (1996). The future of public administration: End of a short stay in the sun? Or a new day a-dawning? *Public Administration Review, 56:* 139–148.

Gomby, D. S., P. L. Culross, & R. E. Behrman. (1999). Home visiting: Recent program evaluation, analysis and recommendations. *The Future of Children, 9:* 4–27.

Goodnow, Frank J. (1900). *Politics and administration*. New York: Macmillan.

Goodsell, Charles T. (1992). Reinvent government or rediscover it? *Public Administration Review, 53*(1): 85–87.

Goodsell, Charles T. (1994). *The case for bureaucracy* (3rd ed.). Chatham, NJ: Chatham House.

Goold, Scott. (2003). USA: The battle of the bars. *Tobacco Control, 12*(3): 6–8.

Gordon, George J., & Michael Milakovich. (1998). *Public administration in America* (6th ed.). New York: St. Martin's Press.

Gore, Albert. (1993). *From red tape to results: Creating a government that works better and costs less*. Report of the National Performance Review. Washington, DC: U.S. Government Printing Office.

Gore, Albert. (1993). *The Gore report on reinventing government*. New York: Times Books.

Gore, William E., & J. W. Dyson. (1964). *The making of decisions*. New York: Free Press.

Gormley, William T., Jr. (1993). Counter-bureaucracies in theory and practice. Paper presented at the Annual Meeting of the American Political Science Association, Washington, DC, December.

Gormley, William E., & Steven J. Balla. (2003). *Bureaucracy and democracy: Accountability and performance*. Washington, DC: Congressional Quarterly Press.

Gormley, William J. (1989). *Taming the bureaucracy: Muscles, prayers and other strategies*. Princeton, NJ: Princeton University Press.

Gormley, William T., Jr. (1998). Regulatory enforcement styles. *Political Research Quarterly, 51*(2): 363–383.

Gosling, James J. (1997). *Budgeting politics in American government* (2nd ed.). New York: Garland Press.

Governing. (1998, January). Reclaiming brownfields, *Governing*, 32.

Governing. (1998). *State and local sourcebook, 1998* (supplement).

Governing. (2000). Big rigs and beat up roads. *Governing, 12*(10): 28–30.

Governing. (2000, January). Leading beyond the borders: Mayor Jim Rout. *Governing*, 45.

Governing. (2002). *State and local sourcebook, 2001* (supplement).

Governing. (2003). Trust and the press. *Governing, 13*(2): 78.

Government Manual, 2003. Washington, DC: U.S. Government Printing Office.

Government Computer News. (2004). From mandate to compliance. *Government Computer News, 23*: 25.

Greenlaw, Paul S., John Kohl, & Robert Lee Jr. (1998). Title VII sex discrimination in the public sector in the 1990s: The courts' view. *Public Personnel Management, 27*(2): 249–268.

Greenstein, Fred I. (2000). *The presidential difference: Leadership style from FDR to Clinton*. New York: Free Press.

Greiner, John M., et al. (1981). *Productivity and motivation: A review of state and local government initiatives*. Washington, DC: Urban Institute Press.

Grodzins, Morton. (1966). *The American system: A new view of government in the United States*. Chicago: Rand McNally.

Grunewald, Mark H. (1998). E-FOIA and the mother of all complaints: Information delivery and delay reduction. *Administrative Law Review, 50*(2): 345–369.

Guerrero, Andrea. (2002). *Silence at Boalt Hall: The dismantling of affirmative action*. Berkeley: University of California Press.

Gulick, Luther. (1933). Notes on a theory of organization. *Bulletin of the International Management Institute*. New York: International Management Institute.

Gulick, Luther, & Lyndall Urwick (Eds.). (1937). *Papers on the science of administration*. New York: Institute of Public Administration.

Halachmi, Arie, & Geert Bouchaert (Eds.). (1995). *Public productivity through quality and strategic management*. Amsterdam: IOS Press.

Halberstam, David. (1969). *The best and the brightest*. New York: Random House.

Hammer, Michael, & James Champy. (1993). *Reengineering the corporation*. New York: HarperCollins.

Handler, Joel, & Jeheskel Hasenfeld. (1997). *We the poor people: Work, poverty and welfare*. New Haven, CT: Yale University Press.

Hardee, Nicole, & Betty Silver. (2002). Measuring and managing human capital intelligence. *The Public Manager, 31*(4): 33–36.

Harrigan, John. (1998). *Politics and policy in states and communities* (6th ed.). New York: Harper & Row.

Harris, Christy. (1996). Workers get more say in contracting out. *Federal Times, 29*: 5.

Harris, Richard A., & Sidney M. Mukis. (1993). *The politics of regulatory change: A tale of two agencies*. Washington, DC: Congressional Quarterly Press.

Hatfield, Mark. (2000). INS reorganization: Separating the cops from the judges. In Lydio F. Tomasi (Ed.), *In defense of the alien* (p. 23). New York: Center for Migration Studies.

Hays, Steven W., & Richard C. Kearney (Eds.). (1995). *Public personnel administration: Problems and prospects* (3rd ed.). Englewood Cliffs, NJ: Prentice-Hall.

Haystead, John. (2003). More noble than others. *Pharmaceutical Technology, 2*: 130.

Hefetz, Amic, & Mildred Warner. (2004). Privatization and its reverse: Explaining the dynamics of the government contracting process. *Journal of Public Administration Research and Theory, 14*(2): 171–191.

Heffron, Florence, & Neil McFeeley. (1983). *The administrative regulatory process.* New York: Longman.

Heilbroner, Robert, & Peter Bernstein. (1989). *The debt and the deficit: False alarms, real possibilities.* New York: Norton.

Helco, Hugh. (1978). Issue networks and the executive establishment. In Anthony King (Ed.), *The new American political system.* Washington, DC: American Enterprise Institute.

Henry, Nicholas. (1999). *Public administration and public affairs* (7th ed.). Upper Saddle River, NJ: Prentice-Hall.

Hentoff, Nat. (2003). The patriot whistleblower. *Free Inquiry, 23*(3): 20−21.

Hermann, Frederick. (2004). Empowering governmental ethics agencies. *Spectrum, 7*(3): 33−34.

Hess, Stephen, & James P. Pfiffner. (2002). *Organizing the presidency.* Washington, DC: Brookings Institution.

Hill, Kim, & Kenneth Mladenka. (1992). *Democratic governance in American states and cities.* Pacific Grove, CA: Brooks/Cole.

Hill, K. A., & J. E. Hughes. (1998). *Cyberpolitics: Citizen activism in the age of the Internet.* Lanham, MD: Rowman & Littlefield.

Hill, Michael, & Peter L. Hispe. (2002). *Implementing public policy.* Thousand Oaks, CA: Sage.

Holden, E. W., & A. M. Brannan (Eds.). (2002). Evaluating systems of care: The comprehensive community mental health service for children and their families program. *Children's Services: Social Policy Research and Practice, 5:* 1−74.

Holzer, Marc. (1992). *Public productivity handbook.* New York: Dekker.

Holzer, Marc. (1995). Productivity and quality management. In Jack Rabin, Thomas Vocino, W. Bartley Hildreth, & Gerald J. Miller (Eds.), *Handbook of public personnel administration and labor relations.* New York: Dekker.

Hood, Christopher. (1991). A public management for all seasons? *Public Administration Review, 69*(1): 3−19.

Hood, Christopher. (2001). Risk regulation under pressure: Problem solving or blame shifting? *Administration and Society, 33*(1): 21−53.

Hood, Christopher, & Gray Peters. (2004). The middle-aging of new public management: Into the age of paradox? *Journal of Public Administration Research and Theory, 14*(3): 267−283.

Howell, William G. (2000). *Power without persuasion: A theory of presidential action.* Princeton, NJ: Princeton University Press.

Howitt, Arnold M., & Robyn L. Pangi (Eds.). (2003). *Countering terrorism.* Cambridge, MA: MIT Press.

Hrebener, Robert, & Ruth Scott. (1990). *Interest group politics in America* (2nd ed.). Englewood Cliffs, NJ: Prentice-Hall.

Huddleston, Mark W., & William Boyer. (1996). *The higher civil services in the United States: Quest for reform.* Pittsburgh: University of Pittsburgh Press.

Hughes, Owen. (1994). *Public management and administration.* London: Macmillan.

Hughes, Samuel. (1998). Regulatory budgeting. *Policy Sciences, 31*(4): 247−278.

Hult, Karen M., & Charles E. Walcott. (2004). *Empowering the White House: Governance under Nixon, Ford, and Carter.* Lawrence: University of Kansas Press.

Hunt, James G., et al. (Eds.). (1988). *Emerging leadership vistas.* Lexington, MA: Heath.

Hyde, Albert C. (1992). Implications of total quality management for the public sector. *Public Productivity and Management Review, 16:* 23−76.

Hyde, Albert C. (1992). *Government budgeting: Theory, process, politics* (2nd ed.). Pacific Grove, CA: Brooks/Cole.

Hyde, Albert C. (1992c). The proverbs of total quality management: Recharting the path to quality improvement in the public sector. *Public Productivity and Management Review, 16*(1): 25−37.

Hyde, Albert C., & Jay M. Shafritz (Eds.). (1979). *Program evaluation in the public sector.* New York: Praeger.

Hyde, Cheryl. (1998). A model for diversity training in human service agencies. *Administration in Social Work, 22*(4): 19−33.

Imbroscio, David L., Thad Williamson, & Gar Alperovitz. (2003). Local policy responses to globalization: Place-based ownership models of economic enterprises, *Policy Studies Journal, 31*(1): 31.

Ingraham, Patricia W., & Barbara Romzek (Eds.). (1994). *Rethinking public personnel systems*. San Francisco: Jossey-Bass.

Ingraham, Patricia W., & Carolyn Bans (Eds.). (1984). *Legislating bureaucratic change: The civil service reform act of 1978*. Albany: State University of New York Press.

Ingraham, Patricia W., & David H. Rosenbloom (Eds.). (1992). *The promise and the paradox of civil service reform*. Pittsburgh: University of Pittsburgh Press.

Janis, Irving L. (1972). *Victims of groupthink*. Boston: Houghton Mifflin.

Janis, Irving L. (1982). *Victims of groupthink* (2nd ed.). Boston: Houghton Mifflin.

Janis, Irving L., & Leon Mann. (1977). *Decision making*. New York: Free Press.

Jewitt, Aubrey. (2001). Workers compensation reform in Florida: Why did innovative return to work programs fail? *Policy Studies Review, 18*(3): 189–248.

Johnson, Craig E. (2004). *Meeting the ethical challenges of leadership*. Thousand Oaks, CA: Sage.

Johnson, William A., Jr. (1999). Visions of revival. *Governing, 11*: 24.

Joiner, Charles W. (1987). *Leadership for change*. Cambridge, MA: Ballinger.

Jones, Benjamin J., & Deborah Reuter. (1992). Interstate compacts and agreements. In *The book of the states, 1991–1992*. Lexington, KY: Council of State Governments.

Jones, Charles O. (1988). *The trusteeship presidency: Jimmy Carter and the U.S. Congress*. Baton Rouge: Louisiana State University Press.

Jones, Lawrence, & Fred Thompson. (1999). *Public management: Institutional renewal for the 21st century*. Stanford, CT: JAI Press.

Juran, J. M. (1988a). *Juran's quality control handbook* (4th ed.). New York: McGraw-Hill.

Juran, J. M. (1988b). *Juran on leadership for quality*. New York: McGraw-Hill.

Juran, J. M. (1992). *Juran on quality by design*. New York: Free Press.

Kaplan, H. Roy, & Curt Tausky. (1977). Humanism in organizations: A critical appraisal. *Public Administration Review, 37*: 171–180.

Karunaratne, Garvin. (2004). *The administrative bungling that hijacked the 2000 U.S. presidential election*. Lanham, MD: University Press of America.

Katz, Daniel, & Robert Kahn. (1966). *The social psychology of organizations*. New York: Wiley.

Katz, Daniel, & Robert L. Kahn. (1978). *The social psychology of organizations* (2nd ed.). New York: Wiley.

Katzenbach, J. R., & D. K. Smith. (1993). *The wisdom of teams: Creating the high performance organization*. Boston: Harvard Business School Press.

Kaufman, Herbert. (1956). Emerging conflicts in the doctrines of public administration. *American Political Science Review, 50*: 1057–1073.

Kaufman, Herbert. (1969). Administrative decentralization and political power. *Public Administration Review, 29*: 3–15.

Kaufman, Herbert. (1973). *Administrative feedback: Monitoring subordinates' behavior*. Washington, DC: Brookings Institution.

Kayyem, Juliette. (2003). The homeland security muddle. *The American Prospect, 14*(10): 46–48.

Kayyem, Juliette N., & Robyn L. Pangi (Eds.). (2003). *First to arrive: The state and local response to terrorism*. Cambridge, MA: MIT Press.

Kearney, Richard C. (1984). *Labor relations in the public sector*. New York: Dekker.

Kearney, Richard C. (1992). *Labor relations in the public sector* (2nd ed.). New York: Dekker.

Kearney, Richard C. (1999). Judicial performance evaluation in the states. *Public Administration Quarterly, 22*(4): 468–489.

Kellough, J. Edward. (1998). The reinventing government movement: A review and critique. *Public Administration Quarterly, 22*(1): 6–20.

Kelly, Janet M., & William C. Rwenbark. (2003). *Performance budgeting for state and local government*. Armonk, NY: Sharpe.

Kelly, Rita Mae. (1998). An inclusive democratic polity, representative bureaucracies, and the new public management. *Public Administration Review, 58*(3): 201–208.

Kennedy, Joseph V. (2001). A better way to regulate. *Policy Review, 109:* 57–65.

Kernell, Samuel. (1997). *Going public: New strategies of presidential leadership* (3rd ed.). Washington, DC: Congressional Quarterly Press.

Kerwin, Cornelius. (1994). *Rulemaking.* Washington, DC: Congressional Quarterly Press.

Kettl, Donald F. (1987). *The regulation of American federalism.* Baltimore: Johns Hopkins University Press.

Kettl, Donald F. (1992). *Deficit politics: Public budgeting in institutional and historical context.* New York: Macmillan.

Kettl, Donald F. (1993). Improving government performance: An owner's manual. Washington, DC: Brookings Institution.

Kettl, Donald F. (1994). *Reinventing government? Appraising the National Performance Review.* Washington, DC: Brookings Institution.

Kettl, Donald F. (2000). Public administration at the millennium. *Journal of Public Administration Research and Theory, 10*(1): 7–34.

Kettl, Donald F., & J. Dilulio Jr. (Eds.). (1995). *Appraising government reform.* Washington, DC: Brookings Institution.

Kettl, Donald, Patricia W. Ingraham, Ronald Sanders, & Constance Horner. (1996). *Civil service reform.* Washington, DC: Brookings Institution.

Keynes, John M. (1964). *The general theory of employment, interest, and money.* New York: Harcourt Brace Jovanovich.

Kicke, Lisa A., & J. Steven Ott. (1999). Public agency accountability in human services contracting. *Public Administration and Management Review, 22*(4): 502–516.

Kincaid, John. (2001). The state of U.S. federalism, 2000–2001. *Publius, 31*(3): 1–71.

Kincaid, John. (2003). The crisis in fiscal federalism. *Spectrum, 76*(3): 5–10.

King, Cheryl, & Lisa Zanetti (Eds.). (2004). *Transformational public service: Portraits of theory in practice.* Armonk, NY: Sharpe.

Kingdon, John W. (1984). *Agendas, alternatives, and public policy.* Boston: Pearson Education.

Klauss, Rudi. (1982). *Interpersonal communications in organizations.* New York: Academic Press.

Knott, Jack H. (1998). A return to spoils: The wrong solution for the right problem. *Administration and Society, 29*(6): 660–670.

Koenig, Heidi. (1998). *Richardson v. McKnight*—what does the future hold for nongovernmental employees? *Public Administration Review, 58*(1): 8–9.

Kolbert, Elizabeth. (1998, February 9). Schools face tough choices about repairs. *New York Times,* p. B-1.

Koop, C. Everett. (1996, September 26). Why defend partial abortions? *New York Times,* p. A-1.

Koop, C. Everett. (1998, March/April). The partial birth debate in 1998. *The Humanist.*

Kovacic, William E. (1998). Law, economics, and the reinvention of public administration: Using rational agreements to reduce the cost of procurement regulation and other forms of government intervention in the economy. *Administrative Law Review, 50*(1): 141–156.

Kowert, Paul A. (2002). *Groupthink or deadlock: When do leaders learn from their advisors?* Albany: State University of New York Press.

Krauss, Elishia. (2003). Building a bigger bureaucracy. *The Public Manager, 32*(2): 57–58.

Kravchuck, Robert S., & Robert Leighton. (1993). Implementing TQM in the states. *Public Productivity and Management Review, 17:* 74–75.

Lammers, William, & Michael A. Genovese. (2000). *The presidency and domestic policy: Comparing leadership styles from FDR to Clinton.* Washington, DC: Congressional Quarterly Press.

Landy, Mark K., Marc J. Roberts, & Stephen R. Thomas. (1994). *The environmental protection agency: From Nixon to Clinton.* New York: Oxford University Press.

Lane, Frederick. (1994). *Current issues in public administration* (5th ed.). New York: St. Martin's Press.

Lane, Larry M. (1994). Public sector performance management. *Review of Public Personnel Administration, 14:* 27.

Lathan, Earl. (1952). *The group basis of politics.* Ithaca, NY: Cornell University Press.

Lavigna, Robert T. (1996). Innovation in recruiting and hiring: Attracting the best and the brightest to Wisconsin state government. *Public Personnel Management, 25*(4): 423–432.

Lawler, E. E., S. A. Mohranan, & G. E. Ledford Jr. (1992). *Employee involvement in total quality management*. San Francisco: Jossey-Bass.

Lawrence, David. (1999). *America: The politics of diversity*. Belmont, CA: Wadsworth.

Lawrence, David. (1999). *California: The politics of diversity*. Belmont, CA: Wadsworth.

Lawson, Kay (Ed.). (1981). *Political parties and linkage: A comparative perspective*. New Haven, CT: Yale University Press.

LeMay, Michael. (1987). *From open door to dutch door*. New York: Praeger.

LeMay, Michael. (1994). *Anatomy of a public policy*. New York: Praeger.

Lemov, Penelope. (1992). The decade of red ink. *Governing, 5*(11): 22–26.

Lens, Vicki. (2002). TANF: What went wrong and what to do next. *Social Work, 47*(3): 279–291.

Lerner, Allan W. (1976). *The politics of decision making: Strategy, cooperation, and conflict*. Beverly Hills, CA: Sage.

Levin, Marc A. (1991). The information-seeking behavior of local government officials. *American Review of Public Administration, 21:* 271–286.

Levin, Martin A., & Mary Bryner Sanger. (1994). *Making government work: How entrepreneurial executives turn bright ideas into real results*. San Francisco: Jossey-Bass.

Levy, Harold. (1995). Report of the commission on school facilities and maintenance reform. New York State.

Lewis, Gregory B. (1994). Women, occupations and federal agencies: Occupation mix and interagency differences in sexual inequality in federal white-collar employment. *Public Administration Review, 54*(3): 271–276.

Lewis, Phillip V. (1980). *Organizational communication: The essence of effective management* (2nd ed.). Columbus, OH: Grid Publishing.

Likert, Rensis. (1961). *New patterns of management*. New York: McGraw-Hill.

Likert, Rensis. (1967). *The human organization: Its management and values*. New York: McGraw-Hill.

Lilenthal, David E. (1967). *Management: A humanist art*. New York: Columbia University Press.

Lindblom, Charles E. (1959). The science of muddling through. *Public Administration Review, 19:* 79–88.

Lindblom, Charles E. (1965). *The intelligence of democracy: Decision making through mutual adjustment*. New York: Free Press.

Lindblom, Charles E. (1979). Still muddling, not yet through. *Public Administration Review, 39:* 517–526.

Lindblom, Charles E. (1980). *The policy-making process* (2nd ed.). Englewood Cliffs, NJ: Prentice-Hall.

Lipsky, Michael. (1980). *Street-level bureaucracy: Dilemmas of the individual in public service*. New York: Russell Sage Foundation.

Locke, Edwin. (1991). *The essence of leadership*. Lexington, MA: Lexington Books.

Lowery, David. (1998). Consumer sovereignty and quasi-market failure. *Journal of Public Administration Research and Theory, 8:* 137–172.

Lowery, David. (1999). Answering the public choice challenge: A neoprogressive research agenda. *Governance, 12*(1): 29–56.

Lowery, David. (2000). The presidency, the bureaucracy, and reinvention: A gentle plea for chaos. *Presidential Studies Quarterly, 30*(1): 79–93.

Lowery, David, & William Lyons. (1989). The impact of jurisdictional boundaries: An individual-level test of the Tiebout model. *Journal of Politics, 51:* 73–97.

Lubbers, Jeffrey S. (1998). The ABA section of administrative law and regulatory practice—from objector to protector of the APA. *Administrative Law Review, 50*(1): 157–171.

Lynch, Thomas D. (1995). *Public budgeting in America* (4th ed.). Englewood Cliffs, NJ: Prentice-Hall.

Lynn, Lawrence E., Jr. (2001). The myth of the bureaucratic paradigm: What traditional public administration really stood for. *Public Administration Review, 61*(2): 144–171.

Lyons, William E., & David Lowery. (1989). Governmental fragmentation vs. consolidation: Five public choice myths about creating informed, involved, and happy citizens. *Public Administration Review, 49:* 533–543.

Madison, James. (1788, February 6). The Federalist No. 51. *The Independent Journal*. New York.

Malakoff, David, & Martin Enserick. (2003). Researchers await government response to self-regulation plea. *Science, 302*(5644): 368–370.

Maor, Moshe. (1999). The paradox of managerialism. *Public Administration Review, 59*(1): 5–18.

Maranto, Robert. (1998). Thinking the unthinkable: A case for spoils in the federal bureaucracy. *Administration and Society, 29*(6): 628–642.

March, James G. (1989). *Decisions and organizations.* Oxford: Blackwell.

March, James G. (1994). *A primer on decision making: How decisions happen.* New York: Free Press.

March, James G., & Johan P. Olsen (Eds.). (1976). *Ambiguity and choice in organizations.* Bergen, Norway: Universitetsforlaget.

March, James G., & Johan P. Olsen. (1995). *Democratic governance.* New York: Free Press.

March, James G., & Herbert A. Simon. (1958). *Organizations.* New York: Wiley.

Markle Foundation Task Force on National Security in the Information Age. (2002). Protecting America's freedom in the information age. Available online at http://www.markletaskforce.org

Markley, Deborah M., & Kevin T. McNamara. (1996). Local economic and state fiscal impacts of business incubators. *State and Local Government Review, 28*(1): 17–27.

Marks, Mara A. (2004). Structures matter, but leadership matters more. *National Civic Review, 93*(1): 28–39.

Martin, David. (2000). Expedited removal, detention and due process. In Lydio F. Tomasi (Ed.), *In defense of the alien.* New York: Center for Migration Studies.

Marx, Fritz Morstein. (1946). *Elements of public administration.* Englewood Cliffs, NJ: Prentice-Hall.

Maslaw, Jerry L., & Richard A. Merrill. (1992). *Administrative law.* St. Paul, MN: West.

Maslow, Abraham. (1943). A theory of human motivation. *Psychological Review, 50*(4): 370–396.

Maslow, Abraham. (1954). *Motivation and personality.* New York: Harper & Brothers.

Maslow, Abraham. (1970). *Motivation and personality* (2nd ed.). New York: Harper & Brothers.

Mathis, William. (2004). No Child Left Behind Act: What will it cost the states? *Spectrum, 77*(2): 8–12.

Matland, R. E. (1995). Synthesizing the implementation literature: The ambiguity–conflict model of policy implementation. *Journal of Public Administration Research and Theory, 5:* 145–175.

May, Peter J. (1997). State regulatory roles: Choices in the regulation of building safety. *State and Local Government Review, 29*(2): 70–80.

Mayer, Kenneth, & Kevin Price. (2002). Unlimited presidential power. *Presidential Studies Quarterly, 32*(2): 367–387.

Mayo, Elton. (1933). *The human problems of an industrial civilization.* New York: Macmillan.

McChesney, Fred S., & William F. Shugart II (Eds.). (1995). *The causes and consequences of antitrust: The public choice perspective.* Chicago: University of Chicago Press.

McCollough, Thomas E. (1991). *The moral imagination and public life.* Chatham, NJ: Chatham House.

McConnell, Grant. (1966). *Private power and American democracy.* New York: Knopf.

McCullough, David. (1992). *Truman.* New York: Simon & Schuster.

McGregor, Douglas. (1960). *The human side of enterprise.* New York: McGraw-Hill.

McGregor, Douglas. (1966). *Leadership and motivation.* Cambridge, MA: MIT Press.

McGregor, Douglas. (1985). *The theory of human enterprise.* New York: McGraw-Hill.

McGregor, Douglas (1985). *The human side of enterprise.* New York: McGraw-Hill.

McKay, Ruth-Burnice. (2001). Groupthink in municipal infrastructure planning. *Environments, 29*(2): 1–20.

McKee, Clyde. (1983). *An analysis of Theory Z: How it is used in Japan's public sector.* Paper presented at the American Political Science Association Meeting, Chicago, September.

McLaughlin, Ted J. (1964). *Communication.* Columbus, OH: Merrill.

McNabb, David E. (2002). *Research methods in public administration and nonprofit management.* Armonk, NY: Sharpe.

Meier, Kenneth J. (1985). *Regulation: Politics, bureaucracy, and economics.* New York: St. Martin's Press.

Meier, Kenneth J. (1993). *Politics and the bureaucracy.* Pacific Grove, CA: Brooks/Cole.

Meier, Kenneth J. (1993). Representative bureaucracy: A theoretical and empirical exposition. *Research in Public Administration, 2*(1): 1–35.

Meier, Kenneth J. (2000). *Politics and bureaucracy: Policymaking in the 4th branch of government.* Orlando, FL: Harcourt.

Melkers, Julia, & Katherine Willoughby. (1998). The state of the states: Performance-based budget requirements in 47 of 50. *Public Administration Review, 58*(1): 66–73.

Melnick, R. Shep. (1983). *Regulation and the courts: The case of the Clean Air Act.* Washington, DC: Brookings Institution.

Menzel, Donald C. (1998). www.ethics.gov: Issues and challenges facing public managers. *Public Administration Review, 58*(5): 445–452.

Merewitz, Leonard, & Stephen H. Sosnick. (1971). *The budget's new clothes: A critique of planning–programming–budgeting and benefit–cost analysis.* Chicago: Markham.

Merton, Robert. (1936). The unanticipated consequences of purposive social action. *American Sociological Review, 1*(6): 894–904.

Meyers, R. T. (1998). Regulatory budgeting: A bad idea whose time has come? *Policy Sciences, 31*(4): 371–384.

Mikesell, John L. (1995). *Fiscal administration* (4th ed.). Pacific Grove, CA: Brooks/Cole.

Milakovich, Michael. (1991). Total quality management in the public sector. *National Productivity Review, 10:* 195–215.

Miles, Rufus E. (1978). The origin and meaning of Miles' law. *Public Administration Review, 38:* 399–403.

Miller, Cheryl. (1998). Banishing bureaucracy: The five strategies for reinventing government. *Political Science Quarterly, 111*(1): 168–169.

Miller, Hugh T., & James Simmons. (1998). The irony of privatization. *Administration and Society, 30*(5): 513–532.

Miller, J. G. (1969). Information, input, overload, and psychopathology. *American Journal of Psychiatry, 116:* 695–704.

Mitchell, Kenneth. (2003). The other homeland security threat: Bureaucratic haggling. *The Public Manager, 32*(1): 15–18.

Mitchell-Weaver, Clyde, David Miller, & Ronald Deal Jr. (2000, May). Multilevel governance and metropolitan regionalism in the U.S.A. *Urban Studies,* 851–861.

Moakley, John J. (2000). U.S. Congress, House Committee on Rules. *Biennial budgeting: A tool for improving government fiscal management and oversight.* http://www.house.gov/rules/rules-trans09.htm. 106th Congress, 2nd Session. Accessed: March 30.

Moe, Ronald C. (1994). The reinventing government exercise: Misinterpreting the problem, misjudging the consequences. *Public Administration Review, 54*(2): 111–122.

Moe, Ronald C. (2000). Government reinvention revisited. *The Public Manager, 29*(3): 37–42.

Moe, Ronald C. (2003). *Administrative renewal.* Lanham, MD: University Press of America.

Moe, Terry. (1982). Regulating performance and presidential administration. *American Journal of Political Science, 26:* 197–224.

Moe, Terry. (1993). The British battle for choice. In K. L. Billingsley (Ed.), *Voices on choice.* San Francisco: Pacific Research Institute.

Moe, Terry, & William Howell. (1999). A theory of unilateral action. *Presidential Studies Quarterly, 29*(4): 850–871.

Moonman, Eric. (1970). *Communication in an expanding organization.* London: Tavistock.

Morgan, Douglas, Kelly Bacon, Ron Bunch, Charles Cameron, & Robert Deis. (1996). What middle-managers do in local government: Stewardship of the public trust and the limits of reinventing government. *Public Administration Review, 56*(4): 359–366.

Morgan, Gareth (Ed.). (1983). *Beyond method: Strategies for social research.* Beverly Hills, CA: Sage.

Morgan, Gareth. (1986). *Images of organization.* Beverly Hills, CA: Sage.

Moore, W. E., & M. M. Tumin. (1949). Some social functions of ignorance. *American Sociological Review, 14:* 787–795.

Mosher, Frederick C. (1979). *The GAO: The quest for accountability in American government.* Boulder, CO: Westview.

Mulder, Eldon. (2002). Performance-based budgeting in Alaska. *Spectrum, 2:* 14.

Munter, Mary. (1982, 1997). *Guide to managerial communication.* Upper Saddle River, NJ: Prentice-Hall.

Murray, Michael. (1986). *Decisions: A comparative critique.* Marshfield, MA: Pittman.

Musgrave, Richard R., & Peggy B. Musgrave. (1984). *Public finance in theory and practice* (4th ed.). New York: McGraw-Hill.

Nachmias, David. (1979). *Public policy evaluation.* New York: St. Martin's Press.

Nader, Ralph, Peter Petkas, & Kate Blackwell (Eds.). (1972). *Whistleblowing.* New York: Bantam.

Nalbandian, John. (2001). The manager as political leader. *National Civic Review, 90*(1): 63–68.

Nathan, Richard P. (1975). *The plot that failed: Nixon and the administrative presidency.* New York: Wiley.

Nathan, Richard. (1983). *The administrative presidency.* New York: Wiley.

Nathan, Richard P. (1995). Reinventing government: What does it mean? *Public Administration Review, 55*(2): 213–215.

Nathan, Richard P., & Thomas L. Gais. (2000). *Implementing the Personal Responsibility Act of 1996: A first look.* Albany, NY: Rockefeller Institute Press.

National Abortion Federation. (1991). *Who will provide?* Washington, DC: National Abortion Federation, American Council for Obstetrics and Gynecology.

National Academy of Public Administration. (1985). *Leadership in jeopardy: The fraying of the presidential appointment system.* Washington, DC: Author.

National Association of Budget Officers. (1992). *State balanced budget requirements: Provisions and practices.* Washington, DC: Author.

National Commission on Public Service and Task Force Reports (Volcker Commission). (1990). *Leadership for America: Rebuilding the public service.* Lexington, MA: Lexington Books.

National Conference of State Legislatures. (2004, March). States get stuck with $29 billion bill. *Mandate Monitor.*

National Performance Review. (1995). *Reinventing roundtable 2.* Washington, DC: U.S. Government Printing Office.

Neikirk, William. (2004, October). CBO official gives warning on federal deficit. Knight Ridder/Tribune News Service, 2352.

Neustadt, Richard. (1991). *Presidential power and the modern presidents.* New York: Free Press.

Nicholson-Crotty, Sean. (2004). The politics and administration of privatization: Contracting out for corrections management in the U.S. *Policy Studies Journal, 32*(1): 41–58.

Niskanen, William. (1971). *Bureaucracy and representative government.* Chicago: Aldine.

Nowland-Foreman, Garth. (1998). Purchase of service contracting, voluntary organizations, and civil society. *American Behavioral Scientist, 42*(1): 108–114.

Nutt, Paul C., & Robert Backoff. (1992). *Strategic management of public and third sector organizations.* San Francisco: Jossey-Bass.

Nyhan, Ronald C., & Herbert A. Marlowe Jr. (1995). Performance measurement in the public sector: Challenges and opportunities, *Public Productivity and Management Review, 18:* 333–348.

O'Brien, Kathleen, Ham Buchanan, & Julia C. Buchanan. (1998). From one end of the spectrum to the other: The FCC's auction authority under the Balanced Budget Act of 1997. *Administrative Law Review, 50*(4): 771–789.

Office of the Federal Register. (1980). *The Federal Register: What it is and how to use it.* Washington, DC: U.S. Government Printing Office.

Oldfield, Duane M., & Aaron Wildavsky. (1989). Reconsidering the two presidencies. *Society, 26*(5): 54–59.

O'Neill, Hugh M., Richard W. Pouder, & Ann K. Buchholtz. (1998). Patterns in the diffusion of strategies across organizations. *Academy of Management Review, 23*(1): 98–114.

Opitz, Wolfgang, Connie Nelson, & David Osborne. (2004). Results-based budgeting: Making ends meet in Washington state. *Spectrum, 77*(1): 27–32.

O'Reilly, James T. (1998). Expanding the purpose of federal records access: New private entitlement or new threat to privacy? *Administrative Law Review, 50*(2): 371–389.

Orsburn, J. D., et al. (1990). *Self-directed work teams: The New American challenge.* Homewood, IL: Business One Irwin.

Osborne, David, & Ted Gaebler. (1992). *Reinventing government*. Reading, MA: Addison-Wesley.

Osborne, David, & Peter Plastrik. (1997). *Banishing bureaucracy: The five strategies for reinventing government*. New York: Addison-Wesley.

Ostrom, Elinor, & Vincent Ostrom. (1971). Public choice: A different approach to the study of public administration. *Public Administration Review, 31:* 203–216.

Ostrom, Elinor, Roger B. Parks, & Gordon P. Whitaker. (1978). *Patterns in metropolitan policing*. Cambridge, MA: Ballinger.

Ostrom, Vincent. (1991). *The meaning of American federalism: Constituting a self-governing society*. San Francisco: ICS Press.

O'Toole, Laurence J. (Ed.). (1993). *American intergovernmental relations: Foundations, perspectives, and issues* (2nd ed.). Washington, DC: Congressional Quarterly Press.

Ott, J. Steven. (1989). *The organizational culture*. Pacific Grove, CA: Brooks/Cole.

Ouchi, William G. (1982). *Theory Z: How American business can meet the Japanese challenge*. New York: Avon Books.

Overman, E. Sam, & Donna T. Lorraine. (1994). Information for control: Another management proverb? *Public Administration Review, 54*(2): 193–195.

Palley, Elizabeth. (2003). The role of the courts in the development and implementation of the IDEA. *Social Services Review, 77*(4): 605–620.

Parkinson, C. Northcote, & Nigel Rowe. (1978). *Communicate: Parkinson's formula for business survival*. Englewood Cliffs, NJ: Prentice-Hall.

Parsons, Talcott. (1956). Suggestions for a sociological approach to the theory of organizations. *Administrative Science Quarterly, 1.* 64.

Parsons, Talcott. (1960). *Structure and process in modern societies*. New York: Free Press.

Pascale, R. T., & A. G. Athos. (1981). *The art of Japanese management*. New York: Simon & Schuster.

Patterson, Bradley H. (2000). *The White House staff: Inside the West Wing and beyond*. Washington, DC: Brookings Institution.

Patterson, Bradley H., & James P. Pfiffner. (2001). The White House Office of Presidential Personnel. *Presidential Studies Quarterly, 31*(3): 415–438.

Paul, Diedre Glenn. (2004). The train has left. *Journal of Adolescent and Adult Literacy, 47*(8): 648–657.

Peckman, Jack. (2001). Alaska task force to push ULSD strategy by October. *Diesel Fuel News, 5*(16): 8.

Percy, Stephen L., Brett Hawkins, & Peter Meier. (1995). Revisiting Tiebout: Moving rationales and interjurisdictional relocation. *Publius, 25:* 1–17.

Perl, Anthony, & James A. Dunn Jr. (1997). Reinventing Amtrak: The politics of survival. *Journal of Policy Analysis and Management, 16*(4): 598–614.

Perry, James L., & Ann Marie Thomson. (2004). *Civil Service: What difference does it make?* Armonk, NY: Sharpe.

Perse, Elizabeth, & Douglas Ferguson. (2000). The benefits and costs of web surfing. *Communication Quarterly, 48*(4): 343–360.

Peter, Laurence J. (1969). *The Peter principle*. New York: William Morrow.

Peters, B. Guy. (1989). *The politics of bureaucracy* (3rd ed.). New York: Longman.

Peters, B. Guy. (1996). *The future of governing: Four emerging models*. Lawrence: University of Kansas Press.

Peters, B. Guy, & Jon Pierre (Eds.). (2003). *Handbook of public administration*. Thousand Oaks, CA: Sage.

Peterson, Carla. (2002). Reflections on the challenges of program evaluation. *Topics in Early Childhood Education: Special Education, 2:* 82–86.

Peterson, Janice. (2000). Welfare reform and inequality: The TANF and UI programs. *Journal of Economic Issues, 34*(2): 517–526.

Peterson, Janice. (2002). The TANF reauthorization debate. *Journal of Economic Issues, 36*(2): 431–440.

Peterson, Paul. (1995). *The price of federalism*. Washington, DC: Brookings Institution.

Pfeffer, Jeffrey. (1981). *Power in organizations*. Marshfield, MA: Pittman.

Pfeffer, Jeffrey. (1985). Organizations and organization theory. In Gardner Lindsey & Elliot Aronson (Eds.), *Handbook of social psychology*. New York: Random House.

Pfeffer, Jeffrey. (1992). *Managing with power: Politics and influence in organization.* Boston: Harvard Business School Press.

Pfeffer, Jeffrey, & H. Leblebici. (1976). The effect of uncertainty on the use of social influence in organizational decision making. *Administrative Science Quarterly, 21:* 227–245.

Pfeffer, Jeffrey, & G. R. Salancik. (1974). Organizational decision making as a political process: The case of a university budget. *Administrative Science Quarterly, 19:* 135–151.

Pfiffner, James P. (Ed.). (1991). *The managerial presidency.* Pacific Grove, CA: Brooks/Cole.

Pfiffner, John M., & Frank P. Sherwood. (1960). *Administrative organization.* Englewood Cliffs, NJ: Prentice-Hall.

Phelps, Douglas. (2004). Leveling the playing field. *National Civic Review, 93*(2): 60–64.

Pierce, Richard T., Jr. (1998). Small is not beautiful: The case against special regulatory treatment of small firms. *Administrative Law Review, 50*(3): 537–578.

Platt, Tony, & Cecilia O'Leary. (2003). Patriot acts. *Social Justice, 30*(1): 5–22.

Poister, Theodore H., & Robert P. McGowan. (1984). The use of management tools in municipal government: A national survey. *Public Administration Review, 44:* 218.

Poister, Theodore H., & Gregory Streib. (1989). Management tools in municipal government: Trends over the past decade. *Public Administration Review, 49:* 240–248.

Poister, Theodore H., & Gregory Streib. (1994). Municipal management tools from 1976 to 1993: An overview and update. *Public Productivity and Management Review, 18:* 115–125.

Pollitt, Christopher. (1993). *Managerialism and the public services* (2nd ed.). Cambridge, MA: Blackwell Business.

Porter, David O., & Eugene A. Olson. (1976). Some critical issues in government centralization and decentralization. *Public Administration Review, 36*(1): 72–84.

Posner, Barry Z., & Warren H. Schmidt. (1996). The values of business and federal government executives: More different than alike. *Public Personnel Management, 25*(3): 277–290.

Presthus, Robert. (1962). *The organization society.* New York: Knopf.

Purlman, Ellen. (1999, December). Appeals court nixes California's smog-impact tax. *Governing,* 49.

Putnam, Linda, & Michael Paconowsky. (1983). *Communication and organizations.* Beverly Hills, CA: Sage.

Pyhrr, Peter A. (1977). The zero-base approach to government budgeting. *Public Administration Review, 37*(1): 1–8.

Quinn, James B., Henry Mintzbert, & Robert M. James (Eds.). (1992). *The strategy process.* Englewood Cliffs, NJ: Prentice-Hall.

Quirk, Paul. (1989). The cooperative resolution of policy conflict. *American Political Science Review, 83*(3): 905–921.

Raadschelders, Jos C. N. (2003). *Government: A public administration perspective.* Armonk, NY: Sharpe.

Rabin, Jack, et al. (Eds.). (1994). *Handbook of public sector labor relations.* New York: Dekker.

Radin, Beryl A. (2002). *The accountable juggler: The art of leadership in a federal agency.* Washington, DC: Congressional Quarterly Press.

Raimondo, Henry J. (1993). State budgeting in the nineties. In *The state of the states* (pp. 31–49). Washington, DC: Congressional Quarterly Press.

Rainey, Hal G. (1996). *Understanding and managing public organizations* (2nd ed.). San Francisco: Jossey-Bass.

Rauch, Jonathan. (1986). Biennial budgeting taking root. *National Journal, 27:* 2318–2319.

Reagan, Michael. (1972). *The new federalism.* New York: Oxford University Press.

Reagan, Michael. (1987). *Regulation: The politics of policy.* Boston: Little, Brown.

Reedy, George. (1970). *The twilight of the presidency.* New York: World.

Reich, Robert. (2004). A failure of intelligence. *The American Prospect, 15*(8): 72.

Reigel, Stanley A., & P. John Owen. (1982). *Administrative law: The law of government agencies.* Ann Arbor, MI: Ann Arbor Science.

Reissman, Leonard. (1949). The study of race conceptions in bureaucracy. *Social Forces, 27:* 305–310.

Remsen, Ken. (2003, July 25). No cow left behind. *Burlington Free Press.*

Renfrow, Patty D., & David J. Houston. (1987). A comparative analysis of rulemaking provisions in state administrative procedures acts. *Policy Studies Review, 6:* 657–665.

Riccucci, Norma M. (1995). *Unsung heroes: Federal execucrats making a difference*. Washington, DC: Georgetown University Press.

Riccucci, Norma M. (2001). The old public management versus the new public management: When does public administration fit in? *Public Administration Review, 61*(2): 172–175.

Rice, Mitchell F. (Ed.). (2004). *Diversity and public administration*. Armonk, NY: Sharpe.

Ridzi, Frank. (2004). Making TANF work: Organizational restructuring, staff buy-in, and performance monitoring in local implementation. *Journal of Sociology and Social Welfare, 31*(2): 27–49.

Rinquist, Evan J. (1993). *Environmental protection at the state level: Politics and progress in controlling pollution*. Armonk, NY: Sharpe.

Ripley, Randall, & Grace Franklin. (1986). *Policy implementation and bureaucracy* (2nd ed.). Chicago: Dorsey Press.

Ripley, Randall, & Grace Franklin. (1991). *Congress, the bureaucracy, and public policy* (5th ed.). Pacific Grove, CA: Brooks/Cole.

Rivlin, Alice. (1971). *Systematic thinking for social action*. Washington, DC: Brookings Institution.

Rivlin, Alice. (1992). *Reviving the American dream*. Washington, DC: Brookings Institution.

Robert, Richard, & Michael Sanara (Eds.). (1987). *Steering the elephant: How Washington works*. New York: Universe Books.

Roberts, Paul C. (1984). *The supply-side revolution*. Cambridge, MA: Harvard University Press.

Roberts, Paul C. (2003). My time with supply-side economics. *Independent Review, 7*(3): 393–398.

Rochman, Bert A. (1984). *The leadership question: The presidency and the American system*. New York: Praeger.

Roethisberger, F. J., & William Dickson. (1946). *Management and the worker*. Cambridge, MA: Harvard University Press.

Rogers, Everett M. (1995). *Diffusion of innovations* (4th ed.). New York: Free Press.

Rogers, Everett, & Rekha Agarwala-Rogers. (1976). *Communication in organizations*. New York: Free Press.

Roots, Roger. (2003). Terrorized into absurdity: The creation of the transportation security administration. *Independent Review, 7*(4): 503–518.

Rosenblatt, Abram, & Michelle W. Woodbridge. (2003). Deconstructing research on systems of care for youth with EBD: Frameworks for policy research. *Journal of Emotional and Behavioral Disorders, 11*(1): 27–38.

Rosenbloom, David, & Rosemary O'Leary. (1997). *Public administration and law* (2nd ed.). New York: Dekker.

Rosenbloom, David H. (1994). Fuzzy law for the high court. *Public Administration Review, 54*(6): 503–506.

Rosenbloom, David H. (2001). History lessons for reinventors. *Public Administration Review, 61*(2): 161–162.

Rosenbloom, David H. (1998). *Public administration: Understanding management, politics, and the law in the public sector* (4th ed.). New York: McGraw-Hill.

Rosenbloom, David H., & Richard D. Schwartz (Eds.). (1994). *Handbook of regulation and administrative law*. New York: Dekker.

Rosenbloom, David H., Deborah D. Goldman, & Patricia A. Ingraham. (1994). *Contemporary public administration*. New York: McGraw-Hill.

Rosenhoover, Donald, & Harold Kuhn Jr. (1996). Total quality management and the public sector. *Public Administration Quarterly, 19:* 435–455.

Rosenthal, Alan. (1990). *Governors and legislatures: Contending powers*. Washington, DC: Congressional Quarterly Press.

Ross, Hana, & Frank J. Chaloupka. (2004). The effects of public policies and prices on youth smoking. *Southern Economic Journal, 70*(4): 796–816.

Rourke, Francis E. (1969). *Bureaucracy, politics, and public policy*. Boston: Little, Brown.

Rourke, Francis E. (1984). *Bureaucracy, politics, and public policy* (3rd ed.). Boston: Little, Brown.

Rousseau, Denise M., et al. (1998). Not so different after all: A cross-discipline view of trust. *Academy of Management Review, 23*(3): 393–404.

Rubin, Irene S. (2003). *Balancing the federal budget*. Washington, DC: Congressional Quarterly Press.

Ruhil, Anirudh V. S., & Paul Teske. (2003). Institutions, bureaucratic decisions, and policy outcomes: State insurance solvency regulation. *Policy Studies Journal, 31*(3): 353–373.

Russell, E. W., & G. Macmillan. (1994). *Managing community assets in local government*. Melbourne: Montech.

Russell, Gregory, & Robert Waste. (1998). The limits of reinventing government. *American Review of Public Administration, 28*(4): 325–346.

Salisbury, Robert H. (1969). An exchange theory of interest groups. *Midwest Journal of Political Science, 13:* 1–32.

Salisbury, Robert, et al. (1992). Triangles, networks, and hollow cores: The complex geometry of Washington interest representation. In Mark Petracca (Ed.), *The politics of interests*. Boulder, CO: Westview.

Sarbaugh-Thompson, Marjorie. (1998). Change from below: Integrating bottom-up entrepreneurship into a program development framework. *American Review of Public Administration, 28*(1): 3–25.

Savas, E. S. (1982). *Privatizing the public sector*. Chatham, NJ: Chatham House.

Savas, E. S. (1987). *Privatization: The key to better government*. Chatham, NJ: Chatham House.

Sayre, Wallace S. (1958). Premises of public administration: Past and emerging. *Public Administration Review, 18*(2): 102–105.

Schattschneider, E. E. (1960). *The semi-sovereign people*. New York: Holt, Rinehart & Winston.

Schein, Elgar H. (1985). *Organizational culture and leadership*. San Francisco: Jossey-Bass.

Schick, Allen. (1973). A death in the bureaucracy: The demise of the federal PPB. *Public Administration Review, 33:* 146–156.

Schick, Allen. (1978). The road from ZBB. *Public Administration Review, 38*(2): 177–180.

Schick, Allen. (1980). *Congress and money: Budgeting, spending, and taxing*. Washington, DC: Urban Institute Press.

Schick, Allen. (1983a). Incremental budgeting in a decremental age. *Policy Sciences, 16*(1): 1–26.

Schick, Allen. (1983b). Politics through law: Congressional limitations on executive discretion. In Anthony King (Ed.), *Both ends of the avenue*. Washington, DC: American Enterprise Institute.

Schick, Allen. (1990). *The capacity to budget*. Washington, DC: Urban Institute Press.

Schick, Allen. (1995). *The federal budget: Politics, policy, process*. Washington, DC: Brookings Institution.

Schiff, Lisa. (2002). Whistleblower protections expand in N.Y. *RN, 65*(7): 16.

Schneider, Arnold, William C. Donagly, & Pamela J. Newman. (1975). *Organizational communication*. New York: McGraw-Hill.

Schorr, Lisbeth B. (1998). *Common purpose: Strengthening families and neighborhoods to rebuild America*. New York: Anchor Books.

Schwartz, Bernard. (1976). *Administrative law*. Boston: Little, Brown.

Schwenk, C. R. (1990). Conflict in organizational decision-making: An exploratory study of its effects in for-profit and not-for-profit organizations. *Management Science, 36:* 436–448.

Scott, William P. (1986). *The selling of communication*. New York: Nichols.

Seckler-Hudson, Catheryn. (1955). *Organization and management: Theory and practice*. Washington, DC: American University Press.

Segal, Lydia. (2002). Roadblocks in reforming corrupt agencies. *Public Administration Review, 62*(4): 445–446.

Selden, Sally C. (1997). *The promise of representative bureaucracy: Diversity and responsiveness in a government agency*. Armonk, NY: Sharpe.

Selznick, Philip. (1948). Foundations of the theory of organization. *American Sociological Review, 12:* 25–35.

Senge, Peter M. (1994). *The fifth discipline: The art and practice of the learning organization*. New York: Doubleday.

Shafritz, Jay, & Albert C. Hyde. (1997). *Classics in public administration* (4th ed.). New York: Harcourt Brace.

Shafritz, Jay, & J. Steven Ott. (1996). *The classics of organizational theory* (4th ed.). Belmont, CA: Wadsworth.

Shafritz, Jay, & E. W. Russell. (1998). *Introducing public administration.* New York: Longman.

Shafritz, Jay, et al. (1992). *Personnel management in government* (4th ed.). New York: Dekker.

Shapiro, Martin. (1988). *Who guards the guardians? Judicial control of administration.* Athens: University of Georgia Press.

Sidlow, Edward, & Beth Henschen. (1998). *America at odds.* Belmont, CA: Wadsworth.

Simeone, Joseph J. (1992). The function, flexibility, and future of United States judges of the executive department. *Administrative Law Review, 44*(1): 159–188.

Simon, Herbert A. (1946). The proverbs of administration. *Public Administration Review, 6:* 53–67.

Simon, Herbert A. (1947). *Administrative behavior.* New York: Simon & Schuster.

Simon, Herbert A. (1955). A behavioral model of rational choice. *Quarterly Journal of Economics, 69:* 99–118.

Simon, Herbert A. (1959). Theories of decision making in economics and behavioral sciences. *American Economic Review, 49:* 253–283.

Simon, Herbert A. (1965). Administrative decision-making. *Public Administration Review, 25:* 31–37.

Simon, Herbert A. (1967). Motivational and emotional controls of cognition. *Psychological Review, 74*(1): 29–39.

Simon, Herbert A. (1976). *Administrative behavior.* New York: Free Press.

Simon, Herbert A. (1979). Rational decision making in a business organization. *American Economic Review, 69:* 493–513.

Simon, Herbert A. (1997). *Administrative behavior: A study in decision-making processes in administrative organizations* (4th ed.). New York: Free Press.

Sims, Ronald, & Scott A. Quartro (Eds.). (2004). *Leadership: Succeeding in private, public, and not-for-profit sectors.* Armonk, NY: Sharpe.

Sinclair, Barbara. (1997). *Unorthodox lawmaking: New legislative processes in the U.S. Congress.* Washington, DC: Congressional Quarterly Press.

Sinclair, Barbara. (2000). *Unorthodox lawmaking: Budget bills, and comprehensive policymaking in the 1990s.* Paper presented at the Presidential and Congressional Budgets: Priorities in Conflict Conference, Washington, DC.

Sjoquist, David S. (Ed.). (2003). *State and local finances under pressure.* Northampton, MA: Edward Elgar.

Skowronek, Stephen. (1982). *Building a new American state: The expansion of national administrative capacities, 1877–1920.* New York: Cambridge University Press.

Smith, Gilbert, & David May. (1980). The artificial debate between rationalist and incrementalist models of decision making. *Policy and Politics, 8:* 147–161.

Smith, Zachary A. (1995). *The environmental policy paradox* (2nd ed.). Englewood Cliffs, NJ: Prentice-Hall.

Sneider, Daniel. (2004). The groupthink failure: A centralized bureaucracy won't improve intelligence. *San Jose Mercury News,* September 10. Accessed at: www.mercurynews.com, Article CJ122097605.

Snow, C. P. (1961). *Science and government.* Cambridge, MA: Harvard University Press.

Sperry, Peter. (2000, March 30). Interview with author.

Stahls, O. Glenn. (1983). *Public personnel management* (8th ed.). New York: Harper & Row.

Sterett, Susan M. (2003). *Public pensions: Gender and civil service in the states, 1850–1937.* Ithaca, NY: Cornell University Press.

Stickrath, Thomas J., & Richard L. Sheppard Jr. (2004). Wanted: The best and the brightest—innovative approaches to selection and hiring. *Corrections Today, 66*(5): 64–71.

Stillman, Richard. (1974). *The rise of the city manager.* Albuquerque: University of New Mexico Press.

Stillman, Richard. (2003). *The American bureaucracy: The care of modern government* (3rd ed.). Belmont, CA: Wadsworth.

Stivers, Camilla. (2002). *Gender images in public administration* (2nd ed.). Thousand Oaks, CA: Sage.

Stockman, David. (1986). *The triumph of politics.* New York: Harper & Row.

Stogdill, Ralph M. (1974). *Handbook of leadership: A study of theory and research.* New York: Free Press.

Stoker, Robert P., & Laura Wilson. (1998). Verifying compliance: Social regulation and welfare reform. *Public Administration Review, 58*(5): 395–405.

Strauss, Peter L., Todd Rakoff, & W. A. Gelhorn. (1995). *Gelhorn and Byse's administrative law: Cases and comments.* Westbury, NY: Foundation Press.

Svara, James H. (1990). *Official leadership in the city: Patterns of conflict and cooperation.* New York: Oxford University Press.

Svara, James H. (2001). The myth of the dichotomy: Complementarity of politics and administration in the past and future of public administration. *Public Administration Review, 61*(2): 176–186.

Svara, James H. (2003). Effective mayoral leadership in council–manager cities: Reassessing the facilitative model. *National Civic Review, 92*(2): 157–173.

Swan, Wallace. (1983). Decision making. In Thomas D. Lynch (Ed.), *Organization theory and management.* New York: Dekker.

Swartz, Thomas R., & John E. Peck (Eds.). (1990). *The changing face of fiscal federalism.* Armonk, NY: Sharpe.

Swiss, James E. (1992a). Adapting TQM to government. *Public Administration Review, 52:* 356–362.

Swiss, James E. (1992b). *Public management systems: Monitoring and managing government performance.* Englewood Cliffs, NJ: Prentice-Hall.

Sylvia, Ronald, Kathleen Sylvia, & Elizabeth Gunn. (1997). *Program planning and evaluation for the public manager.* Prospect Heights, IL: Waveland Press.

Tannenbaum, Mark. (2003). Organization values and leadership. *The Public Manager, 32*(2): 19–21.

Tannenbaum, Robert J., & Warren H. Schmidt. (1973). How to choose a leadership pattern. *Harvard Business Review, 51:* 162–175.

Taylor, Andrew J. (2000). The congressional budget process in an era of surplus. *P.S. Political Science and Politics, 33*(3): 575–581.

Taylor, Frederick. (1911). *The principles of scientific management.* New York: Harper. (Reprinted by Norton, 1967.)

Terry, Larry D. (1995). *Leadership in public bureaucracies.* Thousand Oaks, CA: Sage.

Terry, Larry D. (1998). Administrative leadership, neo-managerialism, and the public management movement. *Public Administration Review, 58*(3): 194–200.

Teske, Paul. (2003). Trends in state regulatory power: Balancing regulation and deregulation. *Spectrum, 77*(3): 20–23.

Thayer, Leo O. (1986). *Communication and communication systems in organization, management, and interpersonal relations.* Lanham, MD: University Press of America.

Thernstrom, Abigail M. (1987). *Whose votes count? Affirmative action and minority voting rights.* Cambridge, MA: Harvard University Press.

Thobaken, Robert G., Donna M. Schlagheck, & Charles Funderburk. (1995). *Issues in American political life* (2nd ed.). Englewood Cliffs, NJ: Prentice-Hall.

Thomas, Craig W. (1998). Maintaining and restoring trust in government agencies and their employees. *Administration and Society, 30*(2): 166–193.

Thomas, Craig W. (2003). *Bureaucratic landscapes: Interagency cooperation and the preservation of biodiversity.* Cambridge, MA: MIT Press.

Thompson, Frank J. (Ed.). (1990). *Classics of public personnel policy* (2nd ed.). Oak Park, IL: Moore.

Thompson, James D. (1967). *Organization in action.* New York: McGraw-Hill.

Tiebout, Charles M. (1956). A pure theory of local expenditures. *Journal of Political Economy, 44:* 416–424.

Tolchin, Susan, & Martin Tolchin. (1983). *Dismantling America: The rush to deregulate.* Boston: Houghton Mifflin.

Tompkins, Jonathan. (1995). *Human resource management in government.* New York: HarperCollins.

Toutant, Charles. (2002). Camden to pay $1.1 million to settle suits of passed over in-house lawyers. *New Jersey Law Journal, 169*(6): 7.

Tramontozzi, Paul N., & Kenneth Chilton. (1987). *U.S. regulatory agencies under Reagan, 1980–1988.* St. Louis: Center for the Study of Business.

Trattner, John H. (1988). *The prime book: The 100 toughest management and policy making jobs in Washington*. Lanham, MD: Madison Books.

Trice, Harrison M., & Janice M. Beyer. (1993). *The cultures of work organizations*. Englewood Cliffs, NJ: Prentice-Hall.

Truman, David B. (1951). *The governmental process*. New York: Knopf.

Tullock, Gordon. (1965). *The politics of bureaucracy*. Washington, DC: Public Affairs Press.

U.S. Advisory Commission on Intergovernmental Relations. (1972). *Multistate regionalism*. Washington, DC: U.S. Government Printing Office.

U.S. Advisory Commission on Intergovernmental Relations. (1988). *Significant features of fiscal federalism, 1988* (Vols. 1–2). Washington, DC: U.S. Government Printing Office.

U.S. Advisory Commission on Intergovernmental Relations. (1992). *Changing public attitudes on government and taxes, 1992*. Washington, DC: U.S. Government Printing Office.

U.S. Merit Systems Protection Board. (1989). *Ten years after the CSRA: A ten year retrospective of the MSPM, 1978–1988*. Washington, DC: U.S. Government Printing Office.

U.S. Merit Systems Protection Board. (1993). *Whistle-blowing in the federal government: An update*. Washington, DC: U.S. Government Printing Office.

U.S. Merit Systems Protection Board. (1998). *The changing federal workplace: Employee perspective*. Washington, DC: U.S. Government Printing Office.

U.S. Newswire. (2004, May 6). Passing down the deficit. Accessed online November 17, 2004.

U.S. Office of Management and Budget. (1994). *Primer on performance measurement*. Washington, DC: U.S. Government Printing Office.

U.S. Office of Personnel Management. (1995). *The status of the senior executive service: 1994*. Washington, DC: Office of Personnel Management.

Van Riper, Paul. (1958). *History of United States civil service*. Evanston, IL: Row, Peterson.

Van Wart, Montgomery, & Evan Berman. (1999). Contemporary public sector productivity values: Narrower scope, tougher standards, and the new rules of the game. *Public Productivity and Management Review, 22*(3): 326–347.

Van Wart, Montgomery, & Evan Berman. (2005). *Dynamics of leadership in public service: Theory and practice*. Armonk, NY: Sharpe.

Vardaman, George T. (1968). *Managerial control through communication*. New York: Wiley.

Vig, Norman J., & Michael Kraft (Eds.). (1990). *Environmental policy in the 1990s*. Washington, DC: Congressional Quarterly Press.

Vogel, David. (1986). *National styles of regulation: Environmental policy in Great Britain and the United States*. Ithaca, NY: Cornell University Press.

Wachtel, T. (1992). *The electronic congress: A blueprint for participatory democracy*. Pipersville, PA: Piper's Press.

Wade, James B., Anand Swaminathan, & Michael Scott Saxon. (1998). Normative and resource flow consequences of local regulation in the American brewing industry, 1845–1918. *Administrative Science Quarterly, 43*(4): 905–935.

Wager, Linda. (1993). A declaration of war: Local governments are tired of picking up the tab for state programs. *State Government News, 36:* 18–22.

Waldo, Dwight. (1948). *The administrative state: A study of the political theory of American public administration*. New York: Ronald Press.

Waldo, Dwight. (1948). Development of a theory of democratic administration. *American Public Administration Review, 46:* 501–503.

Waldo, Dwight. (1968). Public administration. In Marian D. Irish (Ed.), *Political science: Advance of the discipline*. Englewood Cliffs, NJ: Prentice-Hall.

Waldo, Dwight. (1978). Organization theory: Revisiting the elephant. *Public Administration Review,* 589–597.

Waldo, Dwight. (1980). *The enterprise of public administration*. Novato, CA: Chandler & Sharp.

Waldstein, Sandra. (2003). Energy efficiency and a new model for public and private partnerships. *Spectrum, 76*(4): 9–11.

Walker, David. (1995). *The rebirth of federalism*. Chatham, NJ: Chatham House.

Walter, John. (1998). Can a safety net subsidy be contained? *Economic Quarterly, 84*(1): 1–20.

Walters, Jonathan. (1992). The cult of total quality. *Governing, 5:* 38–42.

Walters, Jonathan. (1994). TQM: Surviving the cynics. *Governing, 7:* 40–45.

Walters, Jonathan. (1995). Quality by any other name. *Governing, 8*(12): 5.

Walters, Jonathan. (1999). Vision of revival. *Governing, 12*(11): 24.

Ward, Colin. (2004). The new managerialism, *Town and Country Planning,* 73(2): 44.

Warren, Kenneth F. (1997). *Administrative law in the American system* (3rd ed.). Upper Saddle River, NJ: Prentice-Hall.

Warren, Melinda, & Kenneth Chilton. (1989). *The regulatory legacy of the Reagan revolution.* St. Louis: Center for the Study of Business.

Warren, Melinda, & Barry Jones. (1995). *Reinventing the regulatory system: No downsizing in administration plan.* St. Louis: Center for the Study of Business.

Waterman, Richard W. (1989). *Presidential influence and the administrative state.* Knoxville: University of Tennessee Press.

Waugh, William L., Jr. (1998). Conflicting values and cultures: The managerial threat to university governance. *Policy Studies Review, 15*(4): 61–73.

Weber, Max. (1946). *From Max Weber: Essays in sociology* (H. H. Gerth & C. Wright Mills, Trans. & Ed.). New York: Oxford University Press.

Weber, Max. (1964). *Theory of social and economic organization* (A. M. Henderson & Talcott Parsons, Trans. & Ed.). New York: Oxford University Press.

Wechsler, Barton. (1994). Reinventing Florida's civil service system: The failure of reform? *Review of Public Personnel Administration, 14:* 64–76.

Weil, Alan, & Kenneth Finegold. (2002). Welfare reform: TANF reauthorization. *Spectrum, 75*(2): 24–26.

Weiner, Norbert. (1948). *Cybernetics.* Cambridge, MA: MIT Press.

Weingast, Barry, & Mark Moran. (1983). Bureaucratic discretion or congressional control? Regulatory policymaking by the Federal Trade Commission, *Journal of Political Economy, 91*(5): 765–800.

Weinshall, Theodore D. (1979). *Managerial communication: Concepts, approaches, and techniques.* New York: Academic Press.

Weiss, Carol. (1972). *Evaluation research.* Englewood Cliffs, NJ: Prentice-Hall.

Weiss, Carol. (1997). *Evaluation: Methods for studying programs and policies.* Englewood Cliffs, NJ: Prentice-Hall.

Weissberg, Robert. (2003). Technology evolution and citizen activism: The net and the rebirth of limited government. *Policy Studies Journal, 31*(3): 385–396.

Welch, Susan, John Gruhl, John Comer, Susan M. Rigdon, & Michael Steinman. (1999). *American government* (7th ed.). Belmont, CA: Wadsworth.

West, Edie. (2004). Back to basics. *MedSurg Nursing, 13*(5): 346–347.

West, Jonathan, Evan Berman, & Michael Milakovich. (1993). Implementing TQM in local government: A leadership challenge. *Public Productivity and Management Review, 17:* 179–187.

West, William, & Robert Durant. (2000). Merit, management, and neutral competence. *Public Administration Review, 60*(2): 111–121.

White, Lawrence J. (1981). *Reforming regulation: Process and problems.* Englewood Cliffs, NJ: Prentice-Hall.

White, Leonard. (1926). *Introduction to the study of public administration.* New York: Macmillan.

White, Leonard. (1948). *The Federalists: A study in administrative history, 1789–1801.* New York: Free Press.

Wholey, Joseph S. (1983). *Evaluation and effective public management.* Boston: Little, Brown.

Wholey, Joseph S., Harry Hatry, & Kathryne E. Newcomer (Eds.). (1994). *Handbook of practical program evaluation.* San Francisco: Jossey-Bass.

Wildavsky, Aaron. (1984). *The new politics of the budgetary process.* Boston: Little, Brown.

Wildavsky, Aaron. (1991). *The beleaguered presidency.* New Brunswick, NJ: Transaction.

Wildavsky, Aaron. (1992a). *The new politics of the budgetary process* (2nd ed.). New York: HarperCollins.

Wildavsky, Aaron. (1992b). Political implications of budget reform: A retrospective. *Public Administration Review, 52:* 594–603.

Williams, Daniel W. (2000). Reinventing the proverbs of government. *Public Administration Review, 60*(6): 522–534.

Williams, Lois, & Lawrence E. Leak. (1996). School privatization's first big test: EAI in Baltimore. *Educational Leadership, 54*(2): 56–60.

Willoughby, William. (1927). *Principles of public administration.* Washington, DC: Brookings Institution.

Wills, Garry. (1981). *Explaining America: The Federalist.* Garden City, NY: Doubleday.

Wills, Garry. (1994). What makes a good leader? *Atlantic Monthly, 273*(4): 63–80.

Wilson, David. (1986). *Top decisions.* San Francisco: Jossey-Bass.

Wilson, James Q. (Ed.). (1980). *The politics of regulation.* New York: Basic Books.

Wilson, Woodrow. (1887). The study of administration. *Political Science Quarterly, 11*(2): 197–222.

Winograd, Morley. (1998). Getting results Americans care about. *The Public Manager, 27*(3): 17–18.

Woll, Peter. (1972). Administrative law in the 1970s. *Public Administration Review, 32*(5): 557–564.

Woodwell, William H., Jr. (1999). Government for sale. *The National Voter, 48*(2): 11–12.

Wright, Deil S. (1988). *Understanding intergovernmental relations* (3rd ed.). Pacific Grove, CA: Brooks/Cole.

Wright, Deil S. (1990). Federalism, intergovernmental relations, and intergovernmental management: Historical reflections and conceptual comparisons. *Public Administration Review, 50.*

Yankelovich, Daniel. (1994). How changes in the economy are reshaping American values. In Henry T Aron, Thomas Mann, & Timothy Taylor (Eds.), *Values and public policy* (pp. 23–24). Washington, DC: Brookings Institution.

Yanow, Dvora. (2003). *Constructing "race" and "ethnicity" in America: Category-making in public policy and administration.* Armonk, NY: Sharpe.

Yates, Douglas. (1982). *Bureaucratic democracy: The search for democracy and efficiency in American government.* Cambridge, MA: Harvard University Press.

Yin, Robert, & Douglas Yates. (1975). *Street-level governments.* Lexington, MA: Lexington Books.

Zey, Maury (Ed.). (1992). *Decision making: Alternatives to rational choice models.* Newbury Park, CA: Sage.

Zimmerman, Joseph. (1992). *Contemporary American federalism.* New York: Praeger.

Zimmerman, Joseph (2002). *Interstate cooperation: Compacts and administrative agreements.* Westport, CT: Praeger.

Zuckerman, Mortimer. (2004, February 2). Guns, butter, and hubris. *U.S. News and World Report,* p. 60.

Index